The Fear of Crime

The International Library of Criminology, Criminal Justice and Penology
Series Editors: Gerald Mars and David Nelken

Titles in the Series:

The Fear of Crime

Edited by

Jason Ditton

University of Sheffield

and

Stephen Farrall

Keele University

DARTMOUTH

Aldershot • Burlington USA • Singapore • Sydney

Published by
Dartmouth Publishing Company Limited
Ashgate Publishing Limited
Gower House
Croft Road
Aldershot
Hants GU11 3HR
England

Ashgate Publishing Company
131 Main Street
Burlington
Vermont 05401-5600
USA

Ashgate website: http://www.ashgate.com

British Library Cataloguing in Publication Data
The fear of crime. – (The international library of
    criminology, criminal justice and penology)
    1. Fear of crime – United States 2. Fear of crime – United
    States – History 3. Victims of crimes surveys – United
    States – Evaluation 4. Crime – United States – Public
    opinion – History
    I. Ditton, Jason II. Farrall, Stephen
    364.9'73

Library of Congress Cataloging-in-Publication Data
The fear of crime / edited by Jason Ditton and Stephen Farrall.
        p. cm. – (The international library of criminology, criminal justice & penology)
    Includes bibliographical references.
    ISBN 1-84014-063-1
        1. Fear of crime. 2. Victims of crimes. 3. Victims of crimes surveys. I. Ditton, Jason.
    II. Farrall, Stephen. III. Series.

    HV6250.25 .F43 2000
    362.88—dc21   00-029980

ISBN 1 84014 063 1

Printed and bound by Athenaeum Press, Ltd.,
Gateshead, Tyne & Wear.

Contents

PART IV   THE METHODS OF SURVEYING

PART V   THEORETICAL MODELS OF EXPLANATION

Acknowledgements

The editors and publishers wish to thank the following for permission to use copyright material.

A B Academic Publishers for the essays: Richard Block (1993), 'A Cross-National Comparison of Victims of Crime: Victim Surveys of Twelve Countries', *International Review of Victimology*, **2**, pp. 183–207. Copyright © 1993 A B Academic Publishers; Martin Killias (1990), 'New Methodological Perspectives for Victimization Surveys: The Potentials of Computer-Assisted Telephone Surveys and Some Related Innovations', *International Review of Victimology*, **1**, pp. 153–67. Copyright © 1990 A B Academic Publishers; Jason Ditton, Jon Bannister, Elizabeth Gilchrist and Stephen Farrall (1999), 'Afraid or Angry? Recalibrating the "Fear" of Crime', *International Review of Victimology*, **6**, pp. 83–99. Copyright © 1999 A B Academic Publishers.

American Psychological Association for the essay: Anthony N. Doob and Glenn E. Macdonald (1979), 'Television Viewing and Fear of Victimization: Is the Relationship Causal?', *Journal of Personality and Social Psychology*, **37**, pp. 170–79. Copyright © 1979 American Psychological Association. Reprinted with permission.

The American Scholar for the essay: Frank F. Furstenberg jr (1971), 'Public Reaction to Crime in the Streets', *The American Scholar*, **40**, pp. 601–10. Reprinted from *The American Scholar*, Volume 40, Number 4, Autumn 1971. Copyright © 1971 Phi Beta Kappa Society.

Blackwell Publishers for the essay: Patricia Allatt (1984), 'Fear of Crime: The Effect of Improved Residential Security on a Difficult To Let Estate', *Howard Journal*, **23**, pp. 170–82.

Canadian Periodical for Community Studies for the essay: Vincent F. Sacco and William Glackman (1987), 'Vulnerability, Locus of Control, and Worry About Crime', *Canadian Journal of Community Mental Health*, **6**, pp. 99–111.

Heldref Publications for the essays: James W. Croake and Dennis E. Hinkle (1976), 'Methodological Problems in the Study of Fears', *Journal of Psychology*, **93**, pp. 197–202. Copyright © 1976 Heldref Publications; Adri van der Wurff, Leendert van Staalduinen and Peter Stringer (1989), 'Fear of Crime in Residential Environments: Testing a Social Psychological Model', *Journal of Social Psychology*, **129**, pp. 141–60. Copyright © 1989 Heldref Publications. Reprinted with permission of the Helen Dwight Reid Educational Foundation. Published by Heldref Publications, 1319 Eighteenth St, NW, Washington, DC 20036-1802.

Law and Society Association for the essay: Mary Holland Baker, Barbara C. Nienstedt, Ronald S. Everett and Richard McCleary (1983), 'The Impact of a Crime Wave: Perceptions, Fear, and Confidence in the Police', *Law and Society Review*, **17**, pp. 319–35. Reprinted by permission of the Law and Society Association.

Series Preface

The International Library of Criminology, Criminal Justice and Penology, represents an important publishing initiative to bring together the most significant journal essays in contemporary criminology, criminal justice and penology. The series makes available to researchers, teachers and students an extensive range of essays which are indispensable for obtaining an overview of the latest theories and findings in this fast changing subject.

This series consists of volumes dealing with criminological schools and theories as well as with approaches to particular areas of crime, criminal justice and penology. Each volume is edited by a recognised authority who has selected twenty or so of the best journal articles in the field of their special competence and provided an informative introduction giving a summary of the field and the relevance of the articles chosen. The original pagination is retained for ease of reference.

The difficulties of keeping on top of the steadily growing literature in criminology are complicated by the many disciplines from which its theories and findings are drawn (sociology, law, sociology of law, psychology, psychiatry, philosophy and economics are the most obvious). The development of new specialisms with their own journals (policing, victimology, mediation) as well as the debates between rival schools of thought (feminist criminology, left realism, critical criminology, abolitionism etc.) make necessary overviews that offer syntheses of the state of the art. These problems are addressed by the INTERNATIONAL LIBRARY in making available for research and teaching the key essays from specialist journals.

GERALD MARS
Professor in Applied Anthropology, Universities of North London
and Northumbria

DAVID NELKEN
Distinguished Research Professor, Cardiff Law Schoool,
University of Wales, Cardiff

Introduction

An Overview of the Field

The fear of crime is a creature of the last 30 years of the twentieth century. Its birth was, perhaps surprisingly, partly serendipitous, partly Machiavellian. It was serendipitous, in that it was essentially the by-product of attempts in the late 1960s in America to improve crime-counting. However, disillusionment with the ability of the national Uniform Crime Reports to provide an accurate measure of the amount of crime in America was only one of many reasons which led to the establishment of a Commission on Law Enforcement and Administration of Justice by President Johnson in July 1965. As part of its inquiry, the Commission organized three crime surveys (Biderman *et al.*, 1967; Ennis, 1967; Reiss, 1967).[1] Their main goal was to count unrecorded victimization, but all three also included novel questions relating to the degree of public alarm about crime in general. The main report of the Commission later commented:

> A chief reason that this Commission was organized was that there is widespread public anxiety about crime. In one sense, this entire report is an effort to focus that anxiety on the central problems of crime and criminal justice. A necessary part of that effort has been to study as carefully as possible the anxiety itself. The Commission has tried to find out precisely what aspects of crime Americans are anxious about, whether their anxiety is a realistic response to actual danger, how anxiety affects the daily life of Americans, what actions against crime by the criminal justice system and the government as a whole might best allay public anxiety. (President's Commission, 1967, p. 49)

Where had this anxiety come from? Here, things become distinctly murky, if not downright Machiavellian. Lewis and Salem comment on the background rather coyly:

> By the late 1960s, the soaring crime rate and the ghetto riots turned the attention of policymakers away from the criminal and towards the victim. The so-called backlash, reflected in public anger at the infusion of funds into the Black community and at the concern with the rights of the criminal rather than those of the victim, led to an interest in alternative approaches to the crime prevention problem that would give primary consideration to the behaviour of those who are threatened by criminal activity. (Lewis and Salem, 1986, p. 3)

Fair enough. But in digging deeper, and in particular in Richard Harris's remarkable – but little read – book (Harris, 1969), what we now rather blandly refer to as the fear of crime began life as the fear of blacks. Harris's account could be dismissed were it not for the fact that his book contains a highly favourable Introduction by Nicholas deB. Katzenbach, previously chairman of the Commission on Law Enforcement and the Administration of Justice. The book is of great interest, not least as, apart from the title, the fear of crime is only mentioned on one page within it. Instead, it chronicles the extraordinary American senatorial shenanigans which preceded the passage of the Omnibus Crime Control and Safe Streets Act on 6 June 1968 – a bill that Harris (ibid.: 14) refers to as 'a piece of demagoguery devised out of malevolence and enacted in hysteria'. Without going into too much detail, suffice it to say that the Act, sponsored by Senator McClellan, was designed to reassert the rights of the white and powerful over the new rights of the poor and black, which had then recently been imposed by *Mallory* v. *United States* (1957), *Gideon* v. *Wainwright* (1963), *Escobedo* v. *Illinois* (1964) and *Miranda* v. *Arizona* (1966).[2]

The *Mallory* decision effectively prevented the police from obtaining confessions, whether valid or not, by the pressure of holding suspects *incommunicado* and questioning them intensively and at inordinate length. *Gideon* stipulated that if a defendant in a criminal case could not afford a lawyer, the state had to provide one. *Escobedo* established that when a police investigation switched from the exploratory to the accusatory, a suspect had to be allowed to consult a lawyer. And *Miranda* held that a suspect in custody must be warned prior to any questioning that he or she has the right to remain silent.

So, 'public alarm' about crime emerged, via the manipulation of the Nixonian silent majority, from right-wing white concern about the extension of rights to the poor and the black. Indeed, in our first selection (Chapter 1) – one of the very first academic essays on the subject – Frank Furstenberg comments, 'fear of crime is the symptom of the silent majority's lashing back' (p. 3). In an admirably clear statement, Furstenberg elucidates the findings from the Presidential Commission, and presents some of the paradoxes that have become the staple diet of fear of crime research: that anxiety about crime is not always commensurate with the risk of victimization (with fear, ironically, being the most intense among inner-city low-income blacks); and that those least in danger are the most afraid. Curiously, at this point, age and gender could be dismissed as having 'no sizeable or consistent effect' on fear of crime (p. 9).

Chapter 1 illustrates where fear of crime first appeared as an academic problem, and retains some of its history: the silent majority 'lashing back', and fear of crime described as 'at least in part an expression of resentment of changing social conditions, especially efforts to eliminate racial injustice' (p. 8). In Chapter 2, Richard Block shows just how far we have come since then. A model of international comparative sophistication, Block's essay illustrates the huge methodological and colonial strides that have been taken since the late 1960s and also, but covertly, how the fear of crime has gradually been transformed from being a *reason* for conducting criminological enquiry into being the *object* of that enquiry, and from being a national concern about crime into a local fear of victimization. In sum, gradually over that 30-year period, general – if bigoted – societal concern about crime has been transmuted into a personal problem of individual vulnerability.

The Causes of Vulnerability

Over that period, gender has emerged as probably the biggest single demographic factor related positively to fear of crime. Chapter 3, an essay by Carol Brooks Gardner, is only one of many possible candidates, but was chosen as it was published originally more or less at the high point of dominance of the fear of crime literature by feminist issues. Since then, women's fear of crime has been described as stemming from heightened social and physical and social vulnerability (Skogan and Maxfield, 1981), from fear of rape (Warr, 1985), from general fear of men (Stanko, 1997), from fear for their families (Mesch and Fishman, 1998), or from irrationality (Hanmer and Saunders, 1984). Those wishing to catch up on gender-related enquiry published since then should consult Rachel Pain's exceptional contributions (Pain, 1995a, 1995b, 1997a, 1997b).

Chapter 4, by Jo Goodey, acts both as part of the explanation of women's fears and as a bridge between the concern with gender and the concern with the perhaps second most significant other variable – age. Goodey's respondents are children: with their experiences being the crucible within which the stereotypes of fearless males and fearful females are forged. But it is the elderly, rather than the young, that are most commonly associated with crime fearfulness, and the apparent paradox that this presents (the elderly are least likely to be victims of the types of crime they allegedly fear) has led many to overstate the effect of age on fear of crime.

Chapter 5, by Randy LaGrange and Kenneth Ferraro, reassesses the impact of age on fear of crime and concludes that the effect of age is not only overestimated, but also misplaced. The elderly, they claim, are no more afraid of crime than anybody else when it is measured concretely, but they are somewhat more fearful of, or more anxious about, crime when it is expressed as a general, 'formless' fear. Typically, older people adopt lifestyles that protect themselves from risk (Tulloch, *et al.*, 1999). Because of LaGrange and Ferraro's pioneering work, it is now becoming more fashionable to challenge, rather than celebrate the relationship between age and the fear of crime: a trend epitomized, perhaps, by Werner Greve's work (Greve, 1998).

In Chapter 6, Gertrude Moeller tackles one of the most curiously understated and yet most paradoxical correlates of fear of crime: race. Although, as we have shown, fear of crime began life as a polite code for fear of black people, the first crime surveys consistently found that black people were more anxious about crime than were whites (see, for example, Biderman *et al.*, 1967, p. 127). After the early studies, Liska *et al.* (1982) found that racial segregation was related directly to low levels of white crime fear, and Stinchcombe *et al.* (1980) that white crime fear was related to both proximity to black people and to racial prejudice. Later reviews of the field, particularly by Skogan (1995), have reassessed these contributions, and conclude that blacks are more likely to be fearful and that there are probably good reasons for this (in America, anyway, they are more likely to be victimized, and more likely to live in neighbour-hoods where serious crime is more frequent). Further, among whites, residential proximity to black people is related to their fear of crime, and racial prejudice and fear of crime are related in ways independent of the proximity of whites to black people.

In a perhaps surprising piece of work, Oscar Newman and Karen Franck (Chapter 7), show that residential building size can also affect residents' fear of crime levels far more significantly than it affects their risk of crime. As they put it, 'the larger the building, the higher the level of residents' fear'.

Chapter 8, by Wesley Skogan reviews what was once seen to be the key to understanding crime fear: prior crime victimization. Although the paradox is frequently asserted (that is, those most likely to be victimized are the most fearful, and vice versa), and prior victimization a highly commonsensical positive correlate, much research has been surprisingly inconclusive about the issue. Some (for example, Ratcliffe and McCullagh, 1998) feel that the problem lies with the identification and measurement of prior victimization (particularly repeat victimization) and others, such as Hope (1995) that temporal and spatial conditions are crucial but rarely taken into account. Skogan, in what is a clear and authoritative essay, shows that prior victimization affects fear-related attitudes and behaviour in clear and consistent ways, although the effects on different groups are themselves consistently different.

From its birth in the 1960s, however, general levels of crime fear have always been putatively associated with coverage of crime in the mass media. Indeed, the 1967 President's Commission commented:

> Past research on the mass media's connection with crime has concentrated primarily on depictions and accounts of violence in the mass media as possible causes of delinquency and crime. Little attention has thus far been given to what may be a far more direct and costly effect – the creation of distorted perceptions of the risk of crime and exaggerated fears of victimization. (President's Commission, 1967, p. 52)

Part III of this volume looks at the body of research which picked up this particular gauntlet.

The Sources of Information on Victimization

The first essay in Part III, by Mary Holland Baker, Barbara Nienstedt, Ronald Everett and Richard McCleary (Chapter 9), investigates the effects on the local population of a crime wave that affected Phoenix, Arizona during 1980. Curiously, those whom the fear of crime literature would predict to be the most affected (women and the elderly) were the least so; and those that would be predicted to be least affected (well-educated whites) were the most affected. As usual, then, even in early reports, commonsense expectations that there would be a single, dominant, or even non-contradictory effect on fear of crime from an expected source – here, the media – fails to stand up on first examination.

Indeed, attempts thereafter to relate people's crime fear to media portrayal of crime have met with even less success than the attempts to correlate it convincingly with the alleged demographic causes of vulnerability dealt with in Part II. Take, for example, the work, successively, of George Gerbner and Larry Gross (Chapter 10) and of Anthony Doob and Glenn Macdonald (Chapter 11). Gerbner and Gross established, fairly convincingly, that people generalize from the information that they get from watching television and, specifically, that those who watch a lot of television are more likely to feel that they might become involved in some kind of violence during a given week that do those who watch relatively little television. Doob and Macdonald attempted to replicate these crucial findings in a substantial survey conducted in Toronto. Overall, they found roughly the same picture as did Gerbner and Gross. However, when they controlled for the different levels of crime in the four sub-areas of the city in which they conducted their research, the picture changed dramatically. They conclude that when the actual incidence of crime is taken into account, there is no relationship between television viewing and the fear of being a crime victim.

In Chapter 12, Linda Heath and John Petraitis compound the confusion. They build on the earlier contradictory findings, and test the proposition that, although television viewing might not affect people's perceptions of crime in their immediate environment, it might affect their beliefs about more distant settings. In two separate studies, both reported in the same essay, they show convincingly that this is the case: that is, that television viewing does not compete with people's perceptions of their own locale, but greatly affects their views of far-away places.

Others claim that reading newspapers must have more influence because of the near mono-poly that newspapers have on reporting crime news, and because it has been shown repeatedly that newspaper reporting of crime news is highly selective and distorted, often sensationally over-reporting crimes involving sex and/or violence (Ditton and Duffy, 1983). In Chapter 13, Allen Liska and William Baccaglini produce the results of comparing the levels of crime, of reported fear of crime, and levels of newspaper reporting of crime in 26 American cities. The resulting pattern was complex: although clearest for homicide (which amounted to 0.2 per cent of crimes, but 29.9 per cent of crime stories) which increased people's levels of fear if they were local homicides (but only if they were reported in the first part of the newspaper), but, curiously, reduced fear if they were reports of homicides committed elsewhere.

The final essay in Part III reproduces Paul Williams and Julie Dickinson's more recent research into the relationship between newspaper reading and the fear of crime. They found a significant positive relationship between levels of fear and the type of newspaper read, which was seemingly independent of relevant demographic factors. Further, those who read newspapers which typically oversensationalized crime news were more fearful than those who read newspapers that did not.

Research so far has only scratched the probable surface of the relationship between the fear of crime and media portrayals of it. Unhappily, an area which, speculatively, has the greatest likelihood of advancing our understanding of the fear of crime has been significantly under-researched.

The Methods of Surveying

That the survey has been the methodology for investigating the fear of crime to the exclusion of virtually all others is the legacy of the historical period when such research was started (during the heyday of survey research). That it has remained in such a dominant position is symptomatic of the conservatism inherent within this body of research (in which old questions are endlessly recycled). However, despite this inbuilt trait (which can surely only lead to a view of crime fears which is distorted to say the least), numerous authors have questioned the appropriateness of the survey tool as the basis for this body of research. In Chapter 15, Kenneth Ferraro and Randy LaGrange – in one of the truly great essays on the subject – take issue with the main measure of fear of crime: 'how safe do you or would you feel being out alone in your neighbourhood at night?'. They criticize it (rightly in our opinion) for failing to mention the word 'crime', for relying upon a vague geographical reference, for asking people about something they may do very rarely and for mixing the hypothetical with the real. In addition, we would add that the use of the word 'how' at the start of the question is leading in the extreme. After reading this essay it is hard to fathom *why* researchers have continued to employ this question so readily or *how* they have justified such conservatism.

That Ferraro and LaGrange's essay was not published until 1987 should not be taken as evidence that the problems with measuring fear (be it of crime, wasps or mothers-in-law) were not known until then. In a 1976 essay still as relevant to survey researchers today, James Croake and Dennis Hinkle (Chapter 16) note that 'the longer the list [of fears], the greater the number of fears'. This is a somewhat trite point but one which survey researchers would appear to have overlooked. We are reminded of our undergraduate sociology classes (respectively 20 years apart) when Herbert Gans's dictum that surveys can only report what people say they do and feel and not what a researcher has seen they say, do and feel was drummed into us *ad nauseam*.

Leaving aside the issue of whether surveys offer the best source for gathering data about fear, let us turn now to consider (all too briefly) some of the more recent attempts to improve upon surveys as they are employed in the study of the fear of crime. Martin Killias, in Chapter 17, discusses the improvements made to the Swiss Crime Survey by the introduction of computer-assisted telephone interviewing. In Chapter 18, Anne Schneider provides a very good summary of some of the main problems with survey research into victimization – important to research on fear, as victimization has been cited as being a major mediating factor in fear levels. Other summaries of the problems of fear of crime methodologies (and suggestions for how to overcome these) can be found in Farrall *et al.* (1997), Bilsky (1993) and Fattah (1993).

Theoretical Models of Explanation

It should be said from the outset that attempts to explain the fear of crime have met with a limited level of success (see, for example, Ralph Taylor and Margaret Hale's work in Chapter 19). Chris Hale in his gargantuan review of the fear of crime literature (Hale, 1996), suggests that there are four broad dimensions to the theoretical attempts to explain the fear of crime: vulnerability, victimization experiences, the environment and, lastly, psychological factors. Our review here will devote greatest attention to the last of these – partly because the development of a reasonably robust social psychological model of the fear of crime is one of the most recent developments in this field, and partly because it suggests a new avenue for others to pursue.

Unlike many of the theoretical models of the fear of crime which have relied on socio-demographic variables to account for variations in fear levels, Adri Van der Wurff, Leendert Van Staalduinen and Peter Stringer employ a social psychological model in their essay which is here reproduced as Chapter 20. Their model is a carefully reasoned assessment of the processes by which fear may become realized in people's everyday lives. It should be noted that their model employs some of the logic derived from sociodemographic models of fear (vulnerability, stranger danger, concerns about unsupervised youths and the location of potential assaults are all to be found in their discussion of their model). Whilst their social psychological model does perform well, and outperforms the sociodemographic model against which they test it, as Hale (1996) notes, the sociodemographic model was missing some key variables. When Farrall *et al.* (2000) tested the same social psychological model using data collected in Scotland, and which employed a more complete sociodemographic model, the results were not as impressive (although still very good). The work of Van der Wurff and his colleagues is broadly supported by the replications undertaken by Farrall and his colleagues and, taken together, they suggest a useful avenue for future research on the fear of crime.

The other essays collected in Part V represent some of the key theoretical dimensions in explaining the fear of crime. Vincent Sacco and William Glackman, in Chapter 21, build a model in which vulnerability is conceptualized along physical, social and psychological dimensions. Ralph Taylor and Margaret Hale, in Chapter 19, propose and test three different models to account for variations in the fear of crime. Whilst all the models fitted the data, the percentage of worry accounted for was low (no more than 12 per cent). Ralph Taylor, Stephen Gottfredson and Sidney Brower (Chapter 22) employ concepts developed from the work on defensible space and local social ties to account for variations in fear levels amongst residents in housing blocks in America.

Policies to Reduce Fear

Despite differences in opinions over what provokes fear, which variables best explain its dispersion in society and which groups in society are most affected by fear, most academics and policy-makers can agree over one thing: *that something should be done about it*. In Part VI we turn our attention to the policies and programmes which have been initiated to combat fear of crime. In so doing, we discover something else that (almost) everyone agrees about: *that nothing can be done about it*.

Patricia Allatt, in Chapter 23, reports a study which attempted to alleviate rates of burglary and rates of fear about burglary. Allatt's data come from a classic control group-experimental group design. The project attempted to alleviate burglaries and fears about burglaries by increasing rates of household and flat security. However, it is not clear that the project was actually completed as envisaged, in that not all the households had been secured by the end of the fieldwork phase. The evaluation suggests that whilst rates of burglary did not decline, rates of fear did decline. Trevor Bennet's essay (Chapter 24) concludes that whilst the number of police patrols were increased, they did not appear to reduce levels of fear of crime. He concludes that the features of urban life which influence fear of crime cannot be influenced by the police. In Chapter 25, Jeffrey Henig and Michael Maxfield review a number of the possible explanations of fear and suggest possible programmes which could counteract fear. In one of the pioneering investigations of community crime prevention, Dan Lewis and Greta Salem, in Chapter 26, explore the theoretical foundations for reducing crime by changing the behaviour of potential victims. Finally, in Chapter 27, Gwyneth Nair, Jason Ditton and Samuel Phillips report their evaluation of a programme designed to reduce fear by making massive improvements to both domestic dwellings and to the external environment. In the words of the authors the project 'failed' – that is, fear was not reduced.

The Future?

Although there has been a great deal of research into fear of crime – Hale (1996) refers to the presence of over 200 reports, and a recent online search dredged up 837 entries – surprisingly little can be said conclusively about the fear of crime. Why so much labour has yielded so little is something of a mystery, but it may well be that researchers have been looking, at least partly, in the wrong direction. As a pointer to alternative approaches, the final chapter, Chapter 28, reports some of the findings that have emerged from the most extensive research project ever conducted into the 'fear' of crime in Britain. Here, Jason Ditton, Jon Bannister, Elizabeth Gilchrist and Stephen Farrall discovered that fear was not, in fact, the main reaction to either the possibility or actuality of criminal victimization – the main reaction was anger. Perhaps after 30 years or so, the initial public 'alarm' about crime has distilled into public anger over political inability to actually do much about crime?

Notes

1. See Sparks (1981) and Lewis and Salem (1986) for reflective commentary on these three surveys.
2. Richard Harris (1969), *The Fear of Crime*, New York: Praeger, pp. 22–3.

References

Biderman, A.D., Johnson, L.A., McIntyre, J. and Weir, A.W. (1967), 'Report on a pilot study in the District of Columbia on Victimization and Attitudes toward Law Enforcement', *President's Commission on Law Enforcement & Administration of Justice*, Field Surveys I, Washington DC: US Government Printing Office.

Bilsky, W. (1993), 'Blanks and Open Questions in Survey Research in Fear of Crime', in Bilsky, W., Pfeiffer, C. and Wetzels, P. (eds), *Fear Of Crime and Criminal Victimisation*, Stuttgart: Ferdinand Enke Verlag.

Ditton, J. and Duffy, J. (1983), 'Bias in the Newspaper Reporting of Crime News', *British Journal of Criminology*, **23**, pp. 159–65.

Ennis, P. (1967), 'Criminal Victimisation in the United States: A Report of a National Study', *President's Commission on Law Enforcement & Administration of Justice*, Field Surveys II, Washington DC: US Government Printing Office.

Farrall, S., Bannister, J., Ditton, J. and Gilchrist, E. (1997), 'Questioning the Measurement of the "Fear of Crime": Findings from a Major Methodological Study', *British Journal of Criminology*, **37**, pp. 658–79.

Farrall, S., Bannister, J., Ditton, J. and Gilchrist, E. (2000), 'Social Psychology and the Fear of Crime: Re-examining a Speculative Model', *British Journal of Criminology*, **40** (3), pp. 399–413.

Fattah, E. (1993), 'Research on Fear of Crime: Some Common Conceptual and Measurement Problems', in Bilsky, W., Pfeiffer, C. and Wetzels, P. (eds), *Fear of Crime and Criminal Victimisation*, Stuttgart: Ferdinand Enke Verlag, pp. 45–70.

Greve, W. (1998), 'Fear of Crime among the Elderly: Foresight not Fright', *International Review of Victimology*, **5**, pp. 277–309.

Hale, C. (1996), 'Fear of Crime: A Review of the Literature', *International Review of Victimology*, **4**, pp. 79–150.

Hanmer, J. and Saunders, S. (1984), *Well Founded Fear*, London: Hutchinson.

Harris, R. (1969), *The Fear of Crime*, New York: Praeger.

Hope, T. (1995), 'The Flux of Victimisation', *British Journal of Criminology*, **35** (3), pp. 327–42.

Lewis, D.A. and Salem, G. (1986), *Fear of Crime: Incivility and the Production of a Social Problem*, New Brunswick: Transaction Books.

Liska, A., Lawrence, J. and Sanchirico, A. (1982), 'Fear of Crime as a Social Fact', *Social Forces*, **60**, pp. 760–70.

Mesch, G. and Fishman, G. (1998), 'Fear of Crime and Individual Crime Protective Actions in Israel', *International Review of Victimology*, **5**, pp. 311–30.

Pain, R. (1995a), 'Elderly Women and Fear of Violent Crime: The Least Likely Victims?', *British Journal of Criminology*, **35** (4), pp. 584–98.

Pain, R. (1995b), 'Local Contexts and the Fear of Crime: Elderly People in North East England', *Northern Economic Review*, **24**, pp. 96–111.

Pain, R. (1997a) '"Old Age" and Ageism in Urban Research: The Case of Fear of Crime', *International Journal of Urban and Regional Research*, **21** (1), pp. 117–28.

Pain, R. (1997b), 'Whither Women's Fear? Perceptions of Sexual Violence in Public and Private Space', *International Review of Victimology*, **4**, pp. 297–312.

President's Commission (1967), *The Challenge of Crime in a Free Society*, Washington DC: US Government Printing Office.

Reiss, A. (1967), 'Studies in Crime and Law Enforcement in Major Metropolitan Areas', *President's*

Commission on Law Enforcement & Administration of Justice, Field Surveys III, Washington DC: US Government Printing Office.

Ratcliffe, J. and McCullagh, M. (1998), 'Identifying Repeat Victimisation with GIS', *British Journal of Criminology*, **38** (4), pp. 651–62.

Skogan, W.G. (1995), 'Crime and the Racial Fears of White Americans', *Annals of the American Academy of Political and Social Science*, **539**, pp. 59–71.

Skogan, W.G. and Maxfield, M.G. (1981), *Coping with Crime: Individual and Neighbourhood Reactions*, London: Sage.

Sparks, R.F. (1981), 'Surveys of Victimisation – An Optimistic Assessment', in Tonry, M. and Morris, N. (eds), *Crime and Justice: An Annual Review of Research*, Vol. 3, Chicago: University of Chicago Press, pp. 1–60.

Stanko, E. (1997), 'Safety Talk: Conceptualising Women's Risk Assessment as a "technology of the soul"', *Theoretical Criminology*, **1** (4), pp. 479–99.

Stinchcombe, A.L., Adams, R., Heimer, C.A., Scheppere, K.L., Smith, T.W. and Taylor, D.G. (1980), *Crime and Punishment – Changing Attitudes in America*, San Francisco: Jossey-Bass.

Tulloch, J., Lupton, D., Blood, W., Tulloch, M., Jennett, C. and Enders, M. (1999), *Fear of Crime*, Canberra: Attorney-General's Department.

Warr, M. (1985), 'Fear of Rape among Urban Women', *Social Problems*, **32**, pp. 238–50.

Part I
An Overview of the Field

[1]

Public Reaction to Crime in the Streets

FRANK F. FURSTENBERG, JR.

SOMETIME DURING THE 1960s—it is not easy to pin-point just when—crime emerged as a predominant public issue. By the end of the decade, some polls revealed that the public ranked crime as the most serious problem facing our society—above the Vietnam war, race relations, and inflation. Certainly there have been other times in our history when this issue has aroused great anxiety, and this is hardly the first time that politicians have exploited America's chronic apprehension that the moral order is breaking down. Nevertheless, at least in its magnitude, the current reaction to crime is unprecedented.

Two different explanations have been advanced to account for the sharp rise in public concern. Some critics have argued that the wave of anxiety is largely an irrational reaction to the rapid social change that has taken place during the past decade. According to this interpretation, fear of crime is a reverberation from racial and economic conflict that has surfaced over the past ten years. Behind the concern about crime is resentment of social change and resistance to further alterations in the status quo. In the vernacular of the mass media, fear of crime is the symptom of the silent majority's lashing back.

Not everyone has accepted this explanation. Some commentators are convinced that the public's reaction to crime is largely justified. They note that the rate of crime, according to official statistics, has been steadily increasing over the past ten years. Moreover, people are especially frightened by crimes of violence

○ FRANK F. FURSTENBERG, JR., assistant professor of sociology at the University of Pennsylvania, specializes in family studies, deviant behavior, and evaluational research. He is conducting research on methods of evaluating police performance and is concluding a study of the consequences of unplanned parenthood among teen-agers.

committed by strangers, and the public has been told that this type of crime in particular has become much more frequent. Consequently, some would insist that there is every reason for people to be more afraid of crime these days.

Existing data offer some support for each of these explanations. Until two years ago, the surveys conducted by the President's Commission on Crime in 1966 provided the best and virtually the only source of information on public reaction to crime.* Although undertaken primarily to measure the amount of victimization in the population, these studies also included questions on public attitudes toward crime, some of which dealt specifically with the subject of fear. The results revealed that fear was most intense among residents of ghetto areas, especially low-income blacks. At the same time, they showed that anxiety about crime was not always commensurate with the risk of victimization. Many people who had little reason to be afraid of criminal attack worried a great deal about crime. In their summary, the commissioners observed that factors other than victimization might be contributing to an "exaggerated level of fear" in the population.

In January of 1969 *Life* magazine commissioned the Louis Harris Organization to conduct a special survey of public reaction to crime in Baltimore. In addition to repeating relevant items from the Crime Commission studies, Harris asked a number of questions deliberately designed to measure the level of fear in the population. A preliminary analysis of the data was presented in *Life*. In all important respects, the findings supported the results of the Crime Commission. The Harris analysis, however, even more than the previous studies, stressed the inflated level of fear in Baltimore. To quote the account that appeared in *Life*, "many people's fear of crime is exaggerated, and—proportionate to the amount of crime in their area—the people *least* in danger are *most* afraid." Despite this dramatic conclusion, the Harris study also confirmed the finding of the Crime Commission that residents of high crime areas are most afraid of victimization. Thus, some of their results make fear seem a reasonable response to in-

* The Commission's major findings are summarized in a single volume, *The Challenge of Crime in a Free Society* (Avon Books, 1968).

PUBLIC REACTION TO CRIME IN THE STREETS

tolerable living conditions, and other data suggest that it is often irrational and unwarranted.

What seems like a paradox, however, may be only the consequence of conceptual confusion. Both the Crime Commission and Harris use *fear* of victimization and *concern* about crime interchangeably. When one examines the indicators they employed, it becomes immediately evident that the two concepts are not at all equivalent. Fear of crime is usually measured by a person's perception of his own chances of victimization, and concern by his estimate of the seriousness of the crime situation in this country. An individual may be troubled by the problem of crime, but not be in the least afraid of being personally victimized. For example, the Harris data showed that eighty-nine percent of the respondents believed that crime had increased over the past year in the United States, and eighty percent thought it had risen in Baltimore, whereas only thirty-nine percent felt that it had gone up in their neighborhoods. It is easy to see how crime might be regarded as a serious danger to society but not a personal threat. Sources and consequences of anxiety about crime may thus turn out to be quite different for different segments of the public. In effect, then, both explanations referred to earlier may be correct. To explore this possibility, I have reexamined part of the data collected by Harris in Baltimore.

A total of 1,545 people were interviewed in the Baltimore survey. The sample was stratified to give equal representation to residents living in high, medium and low crime areas. These areas were classified on the basis of police statistics that divided the city into nine sectors. The high crime area consisted of the three sectors with the highest rates of crime; the medium and low areas were similarly defined, providing a crude estimate of the objective risk of victimization for each respondent in the sample. As might be anticipated, most residents of high crime areas were low-income blacks, and those in low crime areas, mainly middle-class whites.

Early in the interview, respondents were provided with a card listing ten domestic problems and asked to select the "single most serious problem" that they "would like to see the government do something about." In the middle of the list was the problem of "crime and lawlessness." This item was ranked "most serious" by more respondents—almost a third of the entire sample—than any other on the list. Although the remaining two-thirds of the sample were not necessarily unconcerned about the problem of crime, the highly concerned, as we shall see, show more in common than just anxiety about crime.

Later in the interview, respondents were shown a second card, this one listing various types of crimes, and asked to estimate the possibility of each actually happening to them. Their estimates varied enormously; many respondents felt entirely safe, and others, totally insecure. The responses on each of the items were combined into a single index of fear, based on the individual's perception of vulnerability to eight different crimes.*

TABLE ONE

A. The Relationship Between Fear of Crime and Concern About Crime[1]

Fear of Crime Index	Crime Most Serious Problem	Crime Not Most Serious Problem
Low Fear (0–1)	20%	21%
(2–3)	14	10
(4–5)	11	9
(6–7)	8	10
(8–9)	11	10
(10–11)	6	6
(12–13)	7	7
High Fear (14+)	23	26
	(446)	(1,055)

X^2 = 8.582, 7 d.f., N.S.

[1] "Don't Know" and "No Answers" excluded from calculations in all tables.

B. The Relationship Between Concern About Crime and Risk of Victimization

Concern About Crime	High Crime Area	Medium Crime Area	Low Crime Area
Crime Not Most Serious Problem	74%	71%	66%
Crime Most Serious Problem	26	29	34
	(515)	(501)	(492)

X^2 = 7.468, 2 d.f., p < .05

* Six items on the list were excluded from the index either because they did not apply to all of the respondents (for example, rape) or because they were unrelated to others on the list (for example, unfair arrest). The eight items that remained were highly interrelated with gammas of .6 or above.

PUBLIC REACTION TO CRIME IN THE STREETS

As suspected, the two reactions to crime turn out to be completely unrelated to each other. Those most concerned about the problem of crime are no more or less afraid of victimization than anyone else. (TABLE ONE) That concern about crime does not emanate from a personal sense of danger becomes even more evident when the relationship of concern to the objective risk of victimization is examined. As risk of victimization decreases, concern about crime goes up. People in low crime areas are significantly *more* concerned about the problem of crime than those in high crime areas. (TABLE ONE) It should be noted that this finding does not mean that people in high crime areas are unconcerned about the problem of crime but rather that their priorities go elsewhere—to education, jobs and discrimination.

TABLE TWO

A. The Relationship Between Concern About Crime and Index of Commitment to Existing Social Order

	Low Commitment	Medium Commitment	High Commitment
Concern About Crime			
Crime Not Most Serious Problem	81%	72%	60%
Crime Is Most Serious Problem	19	28	40
	(453)	(518)	(537)

$X^2 = 53.585$, 2 d.f., p $<$ .001

B. The Relationship Between Concern About Crime and Attitudes About Racial Change

	Strongly Approve of Racial Change	Mildly Approve of Racial Change	Inconsistent Views	Mildly Disapprove of Racial Change	Strongly Disapprove of Racial Change
Concern About Crime					
Crime Not Most Serious Problem	87%	70%	72%	64%	58%
Crime Is Most Serious Problem	13	30	28	36	42
	(91)	(112)	(95)	(176)	(232)

$X^2 = 26.177$, 4 d.f., p $<$ .001

If concern is not a response to personal danger, does it in fact arise from resistance to and resentment of social change? Although the Harris study was not explicitly designed to answer this question, the survey did include a battery of items that measured the respondent's commitment to the existing social order and, implicitly, his opposition to changing social conditions.* Relating an index of these items to the measure of concern, one sees that discontent with changing social conditions is associated with high apprehension about the crime situation. Those respondents most disturbed by social change and those least disturbed show sizeable differences in their views of the crime problem. More than forty percent of those most threatened by change rank crime as the number one problem compared to nineteen percent of the respondents most committed to change. (TABLE TWO)†

The area of social change that aroused the greatest opposition was racial integration. Apparently resentment toward efforts to improve the situation of blacks sparked much of the opposition to change in general. Nearly a third of the whites‡ felt that Negroes had been demanding more than they were ready for, and believed that their attempts to gain equality should be slowed down. Another third held one or the other of these views, and only one-fifth rejected both statements. Concern about crime was highest among whites most antagonistic to racial reform (forty-two percent) and lowest among the strong supporters of racial equality (thirteen percent). Thus, our findings generally support the view that concern about crime is at least in part an expression of resentment of changing social conditions, especially efforts to eliminate racial injustice.

Do these same sentiments of discontent also produce a feeling

---

* In general, the items in this index measure respondents' beliefs about why lawlessness occurs and specifically whether they regard it as a response to rapid social change. For example, respondents were asked whether they agreed or disagreed with such statements as: 1) Law and order has broken down in the country because we have gotten away from the old moral values; 2) When some people have so much and others have so little, there is bound to be a lot of crime; and 3) Until there is justice for minorities, we cannot really expect law and order to improve in the country.

† Since whites are both more committed to the existing social conditions and more concerned about crime than are blacks, it is important to check the possibility that the relationship between these two factors is spurious; for example, that it might be only the result of their common association with the racial status of the respondents. The statistical association between concern about crime and opposition to change, however, persist within both racial groups, although it is stronger among whites than among blacks.

‡ Black respondents were not asked their opinion on these questions, presumably because their views were obvious.

PUBLIC REACTION TO CRIME IN THE STREETS

of personal vulnerability to crime? *A priori,* there is reason to suspect that they do not. After all, blacks are most afraid of crime and also less committed to maintaining the status quo. Within the entire population, there is an *inverse* relationship between the index of commitment to the existing social order and fear of crime; however, when this association is examined separately in each racial group it disappears altogether. Looking at our measure of resistance to changing racial relations, we do find that fear is slightly higher among the most prejudiced, but the relationship is not large enough to reach statistical significance. It seems then that political opinions have little to do with personal fear of crime.

TABLE THREE

A. The Relationship of Fear of Crime and Risk of Victimization

	High Crime Area	Medium Crime Area	Low Crime Area
Fear of Crime Index			
Low (0–4)	21%	39%	54%
Medium (5–11)	33	31	27
High (12+)	47	30	19
	(528)	(510)	(500)

$X^2 = 140.921$, 4 d.f., p < .001

B. The Relationship of Fear of Crime to Estimate of Neighborhood Safety[1]

	Less Safe Than Most	About Average	More Safe Than Most
Fear of Crime Index			
Low (0–4)	13%	30%	57%
Medium (5–11)	32	35	24.
High (12+)	55	35	20

$X^2 = 183.534$, 4 d.f., p < .001

[1] Based on an index of the respondent's estimate of the likelihood that various crimes occur in his neighborhood, compared to most other areas.

To a very great extent, people take their cues from their neighborhoods of how afraid to be. Within the neighborhood, the level of fear is fairly homogeneous. For example, the age and sex of the respondent had no sizeable or consistent effect on his fear of crime. Very few people living in high crime areas—less than twenty percent—were unafraid of victimization (that is, among the lowest

THE AMERICAN SCHOLAR

third on the fear index) and nearly half were extremely fearful. In the areas with low rates of crime, the figures were almost exactly reversed. (TABLE THREE) If a more precise measure of the objective risk of victimization had been available—for example, the rates of crime in the precinct or even in the district in which the respondent lived—we might expect to find an even higher association.

These results suggest that people generally have a fairly accurate notion of the amount of crime in their neighborhoods. This conclusion was further borne out when the probability of victimization, measured by police statistics, was related to the respondent's perception of the crime risk in his neighborhood. Most people in high crime areas thought that their neighborhoods were generally more dangerous than other parts of the city, and people in low crime areas correctly perceived the relative security of their neighborhoods. Even more than the official crime statistics, these informal evaluations seem to provide a basis for people's estimate of how afraid to be. (TABLE THREE)

It is beyond the scope of this analysis to go into how residents develop their impressions of the amount of crime in their neighborhoods. There is no reason, however, to believe that this process is either very subtle or obscure. People listen to police sirens, talk to their neighbors, and read the morning newspaper. From the Harris data, it is clear that firsthand knowledge of events in the neighborhood is especially important. Fear of crime was significantly higher among persons who were personally acquainted with a recent victim of a serious crime than among those who were not, and this association would have been even greater had the responses been restricted to friends living in the neighborhood.

Just as people learn how afraid to be from features of the neighborhood, their fear in turn affects the social landscape in which they live. An extraordinary number of precautions are taken by residents of high crime areas to reduce their chances of victimization. Many of these actions—such as avoiding strangers or not going out at night—provide cues to others that the neighborhood is hazardous. There is, then, a continuous escalation of fear in these localities as each person in the area confirms the suspicions of others that it is a dangerous place to live.

PUBLIC REACTION TO CRIME IN THE STREETS

It is not easy to see what, short of reducing crime, might be done to dissipate the climate of fear in these high crime areas. Although residents may be extremely fearful, a case can be made that the anxiety they feel is not excessive. According to the Harris data, more than one out of every ten respondents living in high crime areas had been the victim of a violent crime in the year preceding the survey. Efforts to convince these residents that their fear is excessive would be disingenuous, not to say a waste of time.

Nevertheless, some measures could be adopted that might lessen the anxiety felt by those vulnerable to victimization. For example, ordinances could be written requiring landlords to equip their buildings with adequate lights and locks, as tenants often cannot afford to install these simple protective devices. Safe zones, difficult though they might be to establish, could be designated within high-risk regions; in these areas people could congregate safely after dark. Funds might be made available to hire members of the community to patrol and supervise recreational locations. Special transportation—in the form of either mini-buses or maxi-cabs—might be provided to bring residents to these areas or to shopping districts, which in many neighborhoods now are off limits after dark. Finally, there should be government-subsidized victim insurance to cover the costs of personal injury or loss of property resulting from a crime. Financial compensation is the least society can offer when it is unable to provide reasonable protection to residents of high crime areas. Even if such measures did not greatly diminish fear of crime, they would at least offset some of its most detrimental social and economic effects.

If it is difficult to devise strategies for decreasing the amount of fear, it is harder still to think of ways of reducing the public concern about crime. As frustration mounts among those most troubled by crime, so do demands for political action. Predictably, those most concerned would like to see more authority granted local police and a curtailment of civil liberties. The symptoms of frustration, however, go beyond the articulation of reactionary political opinions. Although the citizens most concerned about crime generally live in the safer areas of the city, they are much more likely to possess firearms than those who did not rank crime as the major problem facing our society. About a fourth of those highly concerned have weapons, and most declare a willingness to use them should the occasion arise. Among these respondents, no doubt there are some, too, who are prepared to use the slightest provocation as a means of expressing their discontent with the current condition of American society.

In the meantime, little is being done to allay the concern of these citizens. By and large, conservative politicians have been prepared to applaud or exploit it; liberals, willing to denounce or dismiss it. Few political leaders have undertaken the difficult task of educating and reassuring the public that crime is not the necessary by-product of social change. Indeed, as the Crime Commission noted five years ago, the absence of social change, rather than its presence, is the more likely explanation for the high prevalence of crime in our society. Until this message is accepted by the public, it may be difficult to dispel the pressure for political repression and violent confrontation.

[2]

International Review of Victimology, 1993, Vol. 2 pp. 183–207
0269-7580/93 $10

A CROSS-NATIONAL COMPARISON OF VICTIMS OF CRIME: VICTIM SURVEYS OF TWELVE COUNTRIES[1]

RICHARD BLOCK[2]

Loyola University of Chicago, Lake Shore Campus, 6525 North Sheridan, Road, Chicago, Illinois 60626, USA

ABSTRACT

Comparison of national crime surveys must be made very cautiously because of differences in sampling. methodology and content. In this report methodological differences between the United States'National Crime Survey and victimization surveys of other countries are examined and survey estimates of victimization are adjusted. It is found that U.S. rates of assault/threat, robbery, and burglary are not extraordinarily higher than those of other eleven other countries or regions. However, U.S. levels of gun use are much higher and U.S. levels of both gun and non-gun lethal violence (using Killias, 1990) far exceed those of other industrialized societies.

INTRODUCTION

The United States is a pioneer in surveying a random population sample to derive a measure of victimization that is independent of police reports. In order to derive a measure of crime that is independent of the citizen's decision to notify the police. the Department of Justice introduced the National Crime Survey (NCS) in 1972. Each quarter, a random sample of U.S. households is surveyed about victimization in the previous six months. The NCS is one of the largest and longest continuing social surveys ever undertaken. For 1987, the year analyzed in this report, 46,000 households, including 93,000 individuals over the age of 12, took part in the survey.

Many countries have followed the U.S. lead, using methodologies and questions that are derived from the NCS model. Each survey asks a random sample of the population whether they have been a victim of crime over a specified time period. Victimization questions have been especially similar in these surveys because of the common need in all of them to convert legal concepts into everyday ideas of criminal acts. Surveys of crime have been completed in many countries and several, the Netherlands, England/Wales, Israel, and Hong Kong have fielded a series of surveys. In early 1989. the International Crime Survey (ICS), was completed in 14 countries of Europe, North America and Australia. A second survey of thirty five countries, (not including the United States) was completed in 1991. The completion of these international projects clearly demonstrates the widespread acceptance of the validity of such research (van Dijk, Mayhew and Killias, 1990).

184

This article attempts to use national surveys for cross national comparison of assaults and threats, robbery, and burglary. Using national victimization surveys rather than ICS, important methodological and sampling differences that limit comparisons are delineated and the fruitfulness of making these cross national comparisons is assessed. The analysis reported here is not based upon published reports. The director of each country's victim survey was asked to supply a questionnaire, information on methodology, and resulting publications. Most countries complied with these requests. After reviewing each country's questionnaire, an identical letter was sent to each project's research coordinator requesting methodological information and a specific set of tables. For most surveys, special computer analysis was necessary. In some cases, this was completed in the U.S. either at Loyola or at the Criminal Justice Archives of ICPSR at the University of Michigan. In other cases, it was completed in the survey country.

A METHODOLOGICAL COMPARISON OF THE NCS AND OTHER NATIONAL VICTIM SURVEYS

The key to any comparison of national victimization surveys is correction for methodological and fielding differences. The research presented here is based upon surveys of twelve countries or regions: Canada, England/Wales, the Federal Republic of Germany (Baden/Wurtenberg), Finland, Hong Kong, Hungary (Barayana), Israel, the Netherlands, Scotland, Sweden, Switzerland, and the United States.

Victimization questions are very similar among the studies. However, fielding and sampling techniques are not. Appendix A presents a methodological summary of each of the surveys used in this report. As can be seen in the appendix, fielding techniques encompass most of the methodologies of survey research, varying from mailed questionnaires, to telephone interviews, with or without computer assistance (CATI) and personal interviews. However, the fielding technique used does not appear to greatly affect the level of victimization. Sample size varies from 2,500 to the nearly 50,000 panels of the NCS, with correspondingly large differences in confidence intervals and error estimates. Response rates vary from 60 to near 100 per cent. Killias has hypothesized that a low response rate will be associated with a high crime rate; only those respondents will agree to participate who have something to report (Killias, 1987). However, the 1989 ICS did not confirm his hypothesis (van Dijk, Mayhew and Killias, 1990). The response rates and samples in these national surveys are on average considerably higher than in the recently completed international crime survey (78.6% vs. 41.3%).

In most countries, respondents are asked about crimes in the last year; however, the NCS panel survey covers only those crimes occurring in the last six months. Some other surveys ask first about all victimizations that ever occurred to the respondent or occurred in the last five years and then narrow the recall period to the last year. The U.S. and Hong Kong surveys interview every member of the household and derive independent reports of victimization. The Israeli survey interviews a single member as a reporter not only for the household but for every member of the household. This sampling method probably results in under reporting of victimizations of family members who were not respondents. The other surveys interview a single respondent in each household. That respondent represents himself or herself for personal crimes and the household for crimes such as burglary or auto theft.

Each of these methodological differences affects the level at which victimizations are reported. Methodological differences may increase or decrease the relative level of victimization across surveys.

In preparation for the National Crime Survey two important methodological problems were recognized and corrected. These corrections are the central problem in comparison of the NCS and other victim surveys (Biderman and Lynch, 1981).

External Telescoping

This may be defined as the incorporation of victimizations occurring outside a time period into a time period. The longer the recall period the less the chance of external telescoping. If respondents are asked about crimes occurring in their life time external telescoping is impossible. If respondents are asked about crimes occurring in the last month, the likelihood of external telescoping is very high. All surveys except the NCS are bounded only by the respondent's memory. Most surveys question respondents in January about occurrences in the last year. The NCS is a quarterly survey occurring throughout the year. Most external telescoping will occur at the earliest point of the recall period. Respondents will bring incidents that occurred before the time period into it. In addition crimes occurring after the reference period may also be brought into it. For example, respondents may include post New Year crimes as crimes occurring in the previous year.

The bounding technique used in the NCS is designed to eliminate external telescoping. An address is included in the NCS panel for seven cycles (3.5 years). The panel's first survey sets a bound for the second survey, but is not included in the calculation of victimization rates. Analysis of the NCS first time panel addresses (unbounded survey), and the second administration addresses indicate that external telescoping is a very substantial problem (Turner, 1984: Cantor, 1989). Comparisons of unbounded to bounded surveys result in unbounded rates for specific crime rates that are fifty to sixty percent higher than bounded rates. The bounding technique of the NCS successfully reduces external telescoping. However, it also reduces the level of victimization in the U.S. in comparison to other countries that do not use this technique.

Recency Bias (Memory Decay and Internal Telescoping)

A problem of all retrospective surveys is that more distant events tend to be forgotten. Recalled events will tend to cluster toward those most recent in time. More contemporary crimes are easily remembered, but those occurring even a few months earlier are often forgotten. The greater the length of a recall period, the greater the problem of recency bias. As a result the longer the span of recall of a victimization survey, the greater the recency bias (or memory decay). As Bushery (1981) has shown in the United States, more crimes will be reported in a three month recall than in a six month recall, and more in a six month recall than a one year recall period. If Bushery's findings are correct for other surveys, then memory decay should be greater in these surveys than in the NCS.

Internal telescoping may also lead to the bunching of recalled events to the more recent points in the recall period. Thus, November's crimes may be moved in memory to December. The methodology of the NCS is no better able to handle internal telescoping than the other victimization surveys. If only respondents interviewed in January for the NCS are considered, then victimizations tend to bunch in December, just as in the other surveys. However, because the NCS is administered each quarter during the year, internal telescoping is distributed evenly throughout rather than disproportionately near the end of the year. In all surveys, the net effect of internal telescoping for a year's estimate is zero. Surveys other than the NCS typically sample respondents in January. Thus, December of the previous year is the most recent month. Unfortunately, December is typically a high month for victimization of both property crimes and violence. It is impossible to separate recency bias in these surveys from internal telescoping and crime seasonality. Due to memory decay and internal telescoping, the most recent month is that with the highest victimization level. However, due to seasonality, the real level of victimization may also be high in December.

External telescoping and recency bias have opposite effects. A shorter time period reduces recency bias but increases external telescoping. The NCS solution to these problems is to create a panel of addresses, an absolute bound to reduce telescoping[3], and a compromise recall period of six months. An address is maintained in the interview panel for three and a half years. The first interview is used only for bounding. Interviews two through seven are referenced on the preceding interview for crimes occurring in the last six months.[4] While this technique rigorously addresses the known problems of retrospective surveys, it is extremely expensive and represents a long term commitment that no other country has been willing to finance.[5]

Figures 1 and 2 are schematic models of telescoping, recency bias and memory decay over a year's survey for the United States National Crime Survey (Figure 1) and for national surveys that use a one year recall bounded in the respondent's memory (Figure 2). Column One represents a real victimization level. Columns two, three and four represent the effect of recency bias/memory decay, internal and external telescoping. Column five represents the survey estimate of victimization. While external telescoping, internal telescoping, and memory decay are depicted separately in these models, it is not possible to measure them independently.

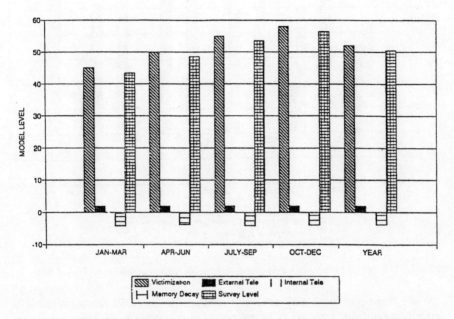

FIGURE 1.   Schematic Model of Methodology Effects for the US National Crime Survey

The National Crime Survey model (Figure One) suggests small. constant levels of external telescoping and recency bias, and no internal telescoping. External telescoping is limited by the NCS technique of bounding each survey by a previous survey. Recency bias is limited by a six month period of recall and by surveying respondents throughout the year. A respondent who was victimized in December may be questioned about the crime in a survey administered in January through May. The NCS methodology is designed to correct for external telescoping, recency bias and memory decay. Therefore, survey levels are close to a real but unmeasured victimization level.

In other surveys (Figure 2), high levels of external telescoping result from the lack of a fixed bound. However, their higher level of memory decay results from a longer recall period. Internal telescoping tends to move an incident closer to the date of survey administration. The relationship between real levels and survey levels vary over the year. Survey levels are on the average considerably higher than the real but unmeasured level of victimization.

188

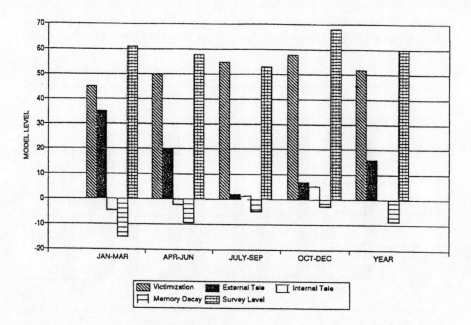

FIGURE 2.   Schematic Model of Methodology Effects for Surveys Outside the United States

While these problems may exist in victimization surveys administered at a single point in time, they are only important in comparison to surveys, such as the NCS, that use a different methodology. As estimated in the following section, comparison of these models suggests an upward adjustment to the NCS is necessary for comparison to other national surveys.

ADJUSTING FOR BOUNDING AND RECENCY BIAS/MEMORY DECAY

The NCS solutions to these two methodological problems of telescoping and recency bias/memory decay have prevented direct comparisons between it and other victim surveys. The US design is a panel survey of addresses. Each address is interviewed seven times about crimes occurring in the last six months. The first interview at the address serves as a bounding interview. It only delineates the time span of the re-interviews and is not included in calculation of crime rates. The other victim surveys interview respondents only once about crimes occurring in the last year. There is no formal bounding survey. For bounding purposes these surveys either occur soon after the New Year or are bounded only by the respondent's memory.

Because surveys of other countries ask respondents about the past year and the NCS asks about the last six months, recency bias/memory decay is likely to be substantially greater in the other surveys than in the NCS. This will result in a serious under counting of crimes relative to the United States. On the other hand, as has been previously shown, there is a very substantial fall off in estimated victimization from the bounding survey to the first re-interview of the NCS (Biderman and Cantor, 1984). For comparative purposes, the first NCS interview is methodologically most similar to the other surveys of this project than the second and later follow ups.

Table 1 is an attempt to derive multipliers for the effect of the NCS bounding technique. For this table, separate unweighted rates were calculated for bounded and unbounded surveys and a ratio of the bounded/unbounded was calculated using the NCS/VRS survey of 1983.[6] For less serious crimes, assault/threat with no injury and illegal entry where nothing is stolen, unbounded rates are more than double bounded rates.[7]

TABLE 1

The Effect of Bounding on the United States National Crime Survey (VRS)[8]

	Unweighted Data Age 16+		
	UNBOUND RATE	BOUND RATE	UNBOUND/BOUND bound multi
Assault/threat	24.92	12.40	2.01
with injury	3.08	2.05	1.50
no injury	21.84	10.35	2.11
Burglary	26.20	17.70	1.48
stolen	21.73	15.30	1.42
no stol	5.42	2.40	2.26
Number of cases	persons	households	
bounded	18214	9081	
unbounded	4831	2510	

Tables 2 and 3 demonstrate possible corrections for differential recency bias for assault/threats and burglary. As can be seen in the tables, especially for assault/threat, the U.S. bounded/six month recall fielding technique, combined with the administration of interviews throughout the year, results in a substantially smoother distribution of crimes over the year than in four surveys that ask the respondent to recall crimes over a year with a less precise bound.[9] In the four non-U.S. surveys, the percentage of crimes reported as occurring in the most recent six months is very substantially greater than in the earlier six months. For example, while in the NCS 47% of all assaults and threats are reported to occur in the first six months of the year, Table 2 shows that in England 30%, in Scotland

190

TABLE 2

The Derivation of Bounding and Memory Decay Estimates and a Correction Factor for Assault/Threat

	Percent Distribution of Assaults over Quarters of Year				
	U.S.	Eng.	Scot.	Neth.	H.K.
Jan–Mar	20.80	12.90	18.50	10.94	18.0
Apr–Jun	25.70	17.10	12.40	22.40	21.6
Jul–Sept	26.20	26.90	34.30	31.25	18.7
Oct–Dec	27.80	43.10	34.70	35.42	41.7
Jul–Dec/Jan–Jun = Decay					
	1.16	2.33	2.23	2.00	1.53

Avg Assault Decay other than US *2.02*

Ratio Assault Decay in Other/US = 1.74

Therefore, must multiply rate in first six months by 1.74 to derive a comparable rate to U.S. Approx Multiplier over the year *1.37*

U.S. Bound effect Assault: the Ratio of Bounded to Unbounded Assault Rates (Table One) *2.01*

Ratio US Bound Multiplier/Avg Memory Decay Multiplier = 1.47

TABLE 3

The Derivation of Bounding and Recency BiasMemory Decay and a Correction Factor for Burglary

	Percent Distribution of Burglaries over Quarters of Year				
	U.S.	Eng.	Scot.	Neth.	H.K.
Jan–Mar	21.10	24.60	30.80	16.99	19.30
Apr–Jun	25.10	18.80	11.90	25.49	26.70
Jul–Sept	27.00	28.50	25.30	24.84	26.00
Oct–Dec	26.80	28.10	32.00	31.37	28.00
Jul–Dec/Jan–Jun = Decay					
	1.16	1.30	1.34	1.32	1.17

Avg Burg Decay other than US *1.29*

Ratio Burglary Decay in Other/US = 1.10

Therefore, must multiply rate in first six months by 1.10 to derive a comparable rate to U.S. Approx Multiplier over the year *1.05*

U.S. Bound Affect Burglary (From Table One) *1.48*

Ratio US Bound Multiplier/Avg Memory Decay Multiplier = 1.48

31%, in the Netherlands 33%, and in Hong Kong 40% are reported between January and June.

As Table 3 illustrates, variation in burglary across seasons of the year is less systematic than for assaults (memory decay is less). Respondents are both less likely to forget or telescope burglary than assault. For burglary (1.29) the average ratio of the last six months of the year in comparison to the first six months is less than for assault. Both the memory decay correction and the bounding correction (Table 1) are smaller.

If the difference in percentage between the NCS and the other surveys is totally a result of differential recency bias/memory decay, than the other surveys would tend to understate crime rates relative to the U.S. for the January to June period. The average ratio of other country/U.S. assault decay is 1.74. That is, the ratio of assaults in the July–December six months to the January to June six-months in four countries compared to the United States is 1.74. This is a multiplier for other countries relative to the U.S. rates for the earlier six months. Averaged over a year, this memory decay/recency bias multiplier would be 1.37.

An estimate of the combined effects of bounding which relatively decreases U.S. crime rates and memory decay which relatively increases U.S. crime rates in comparison to any other countries is given by the ratio of the bounding correction/memory decay correction. Thus, NCS crime rates for assault should be multiplied by an estimated 1.47 to derive rates that are methodologically similar to those of four other surveys. Similarly, the burglary ratio is 1.41. Therefore, NCS crime rates for burglary should be multiplied by an estimated 1.41 to derive rates that are methodologically similar to those of the four other surveys.[10] These ratios – 1.47 for assault and 1.41 for burglary – are applied to the NCS as adjustment factors in Figures 3 and 4.

ASSAULTS AND THREATS, ROBBERY, AND BURGLARY

Table 4 presents a summary of the coverage of each of these crimes as used in this report. For those countries that ask separately about robbery, the questions are very consistent. For assault and burglary, as the crime moves from more serious to less serious, the consistency of inclusion declines. Particularly significant differences are in the inclusion or exclusion of attempted crimes and in the inclusion of threats and robberies as assaults.

Several countries exclude attempted burglaries or burglaries where nothing is stolen. In the Netherlands, Sweden, and Israel, robbery is included as another form of assault. Hong Kong includes only serious assaults. Switzerland excludes assaults by persons living in the household. Perhaps the most consistent comparisons would include only attacks (either armed or unarmed) and completed burglaries of primary residences. However, for this report a wider range of crimes are included in each category.

192

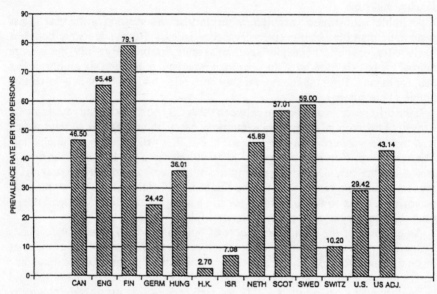

FIGURE 3.   Assault/Threat Prevalence
            Comparative Victim Survey Estimates

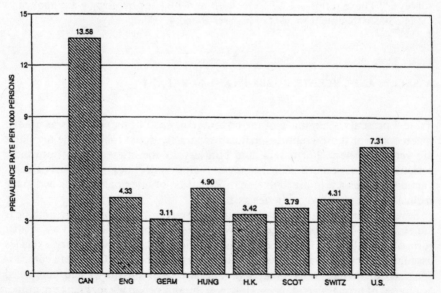

FIGURE 4.   Robbery Prevalence
            Comparative Victim Survey Estimates

TABLE 4

Summary Comparison of Attacks & Threats

	Attacks		Includes		Threats	
Country	Armed	Unarmed	Robbery	Rob Inj	Armed	Unarmed
Canada	Y	Y	N	N	Y	Y
England/Wales	Y	Y	N	N	Y	Y
Germany (Baden/Wurt)	Y	Y	N	Y	N	N
Finland	Y	Y	Y	Y	Y	Y
Hong Kong	Y	Y	N	N	Y	Y
Hungary (Barayana)	Y	Y	N	Y	N	N
Israel	Y	Y	Y	Y	Y	Y
Netherlands	Y	Y	Y	Y	N	N
Scotland	Y	Y	N	N	Y	Y
Sweden	Y	Y	Y	Y	Y	Y
Switzerland	Y	Y	N	N	Y	Y
United States	Y	Y	N	N	Y	Y

Summary Comparison of Robbery

	Force		Threat	
Country	Comp	Attempt	Comp	Attempt
Canada	Y	Y	Y	Y
England/Wales	Y	Y	Y	Y
Germany (Baden/Wurt)	Y	Y	Y	Y
Hong Kong	Y	Y	Y	Y
Hungary (Barayana)	Y	Y	Y	Y
Scotland	Y	Y	Y	Y
Switzerland	Y	Y	Y	Y
United States	Y	Y	Y	Y

Summary Comparison of Burglary

	House		Garage		Other	
Country	Comp	Attmpt	Comp	Attmpt	Comp	Attmpt
Canada	Y	Y	Y	Y	N	N
England/Wales	Y	Y	Y	Y	Y	Y
Germany (Baden/Wurt)	Y	Y	Y	Y	Y	Y
Hong Kong	Y	Y	Y	Y	N	N
Hungary (Barayana)	Y	Y	Y	Y	Y	Y
Israel	Y	Y	N	N	N	N
Netherlands	Y	N	Y	N	N	N
Scotland	Y	Y	Y	Y	Y	Y
Sweden	Y	N	Y	N	Y	N
Switzerland	Y	Y	Y	Y	Y	Y
United States	Y	Y	Y	Y	Y	N

194

For consistency, younger respondents (<15) were eliminated from the United States survey and comparisons are of prevalence per 1.000 individuals or households rather than incidence. In other words, the question asked is how many respondents per 1,000 were victims of at least one assault or threat in the reporting period and not how many assaults were committed per 1,000 respondents in the reporting year.[11] Because prevalence rather than incidence is counted, all surveys use the same rule for counting serial offenses (repeated victimizations against the same person and of the same crime type) – they are counted as one victimization.[12]

A PRELIMINARY COMPARISON OF RESULTS

Figures 3 and 4 represent a preliminary comparison of prevalence rates of victimization for assault, threat and robbery. Both unadjusted and adjusted U.S. rates are presented. U.S. rates are adjusted for the effects of bounding and telescoping.

Assault, Threat and Robbery

Rates of violent crime vary substantially across countries (Figure 3). The rate of assault, threat, and robbery prevalence estimate in Finland (79.1) is 29 times higher than that in Hong Kong (2.70). However, the low rates in Hong

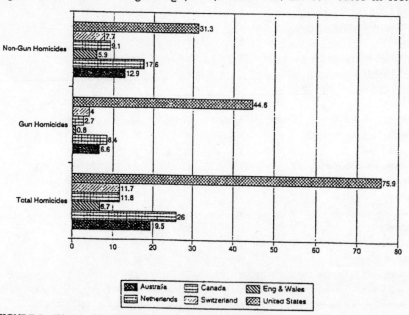

FIGURE 5. Weapon Use in Homicide: Six Nation Comparison
Average Annual Homicides Per Million 1983–1989. Source, Killias (1990)

Kong, Israel, and Switzerland probably result from differences in question or method. The survey of Hong Kong only includes serious assault; however, serious threats are included. The survey of Switzerland excludes assaults by household members, and the survey of Israel probably underestimates personal crime because a household respondent is asked to recall crimes against other members of the family.

Previous research has shown rates of violence in England and Scotland to be higher than in the U.S. Dutch assault rates have increased over time and were in 1986 very similar to those of other Northern European countries and to the U.S. and Canada. Finnish and Swedish rates are taken from a survey that concentrates heavily on violent crime. Dutch, Swedish, and Finnish assault rates include robberies and, therefore, slightly overstate a rate comparable to the U.S. and the other surveys. With the exception of the German survey, fielding and question differences may account for some of the difference between surveys in violence prevalence rates.

Demographically, U.S. assault and threat per 1,000 respondents are, as Table 5 shows, very similar to the average of the other surveys. U.S. rates for males (51.26) and females (31.21) are quite similar to those for other countries (47.68 and 25.18). The decline in assault and threat rates from the youngest respondents to the oldest respondents is equally dramatic. Assault and threat rates for respondents over age 60 are similar in the U.S. and the average of other surveys. While injury is less common in assault and threat in the U.S. survey (28.12%) than the average of the other surveys (47.60%), weapons are more commonly present in the U.S. assault (29.27%) than the average of the other surveys that asked the question (19.74%). Guns represented 15.9% of weapons used in assault in the three surveys that explicitly asked about the presence of firearms. In the U.S. survey, a gun was present 40.90% of weapon assaults. Thus, not only were weapons more likely to be present in U.S. assaults than in other countries, but guns were more likely to be present in victimizations with a weapon.

TABLE 5

U.S. Assaults and Threats Compared to the Average of Other Surveys

Prevalence Rates per 1000	United States	Other Survey Average
Male	51.26	47.68 (8)*
Female	31.21	25.18 (8)
Under 20	144.92	116.80 (7)
Over 60	10.07	10.46 (6)
Percent of Incidents		
Injury	28.12	47.60 (6)
Weapon	29.27	19.4 (4)
Gun or Weapon	40.90	15.91 (3)

* Number of Countries with Information Available

196

Robbery

In all countries investigated, rates of robbery (Figure 4) are far lower than those of assault or burglary. The Canadian rate is highest (13.58). However, the United States prevalence rate of robbery (7.31 per 1,000) is probably higher than that of the other countries that explicitly asked about robbery (avg. 4.01 per 1,000). Question coverage is nearly identical in the surveys. While it was not possible to adjust for recency bias and bounding, the adjustment is not likely to be large because of the seriousness of the crime. Serious crimes are both less likely to decay or to be effected by bounding. U.S. robbery rates for both males (8.75) and females (6.09) are higher than the average of the other countries (5.56 and 4.77). The fall off in risk of robbery with age is very similar in the U.S. and the average of other countries (Table 6).

TABLE 6

U.S. Robberies Compared to the Average of Other Surveys

Prevalence Rates per 1000	United States	Other Survey Average
Male	8.75	5.56 (5)*
Female	6.09	4.77 (5)
Under 20	13.66	15.29 (5)
Over 60	2.92	1.77 (5)
Percent of Incidents		
Injury	37.44	43.73 (4)
Weapon	46.26	32.87 (4)
Gun or Weapon	39.04	15.30 (3)

* Number of Countries with Information Available

The robbery pattern of injury and weapon use is similar to that in assault. While the rate of injury to U.S. robbery victims is not exceptionally high, the rate of weapon use (46.26%) and especially the rate of gun use (18.06%) is much higher than the average of the other countries that asked the question (32.87% weapon use, 2.56% gun use). Thirty-nine percent of all weapons used in robbery in the U.S. were guns compared to 15.30% of all weapons used in three other countries.

The relatively small differences in violence between the United States and other industrialized societies in these survey comparisons contradicts common sense. Common sense, however, may be derived from studies of lethal violence, a crime that is never included in victim surveys. As reported by Killias (1990), using police reports (Figure 5), U.S. rates of homicide far exceed those of other countries. Of the six nations studied, the average U.S. homicide rate from 1983–1986 was three times as high as Canada's and eleven times that of England and Wales. Attributing this solely to the availability of guns is incorrect. While the U.S. gun homicide rate far exceeds that of the other countries, the U.S. non-gun homicide rate is greater than the total homicide rate of any of the other five countries. Combining the current research and that of the ICS with Killias' work on homicide, it appears that the U.S. reputation for criminal violence is primarily derived from lethal violence and that these high levels of lethal violence include both gun and non-gun inflicted deaths.

Burglary

United States' burglary prevalence rates are among the highest in the survey (Figure 6); however, several countries have nearly equivalent rates. Of countries with lower rates, some cover fewer types of crime (eg. the Netherlands), others (eg. Switzerland) may cover more crime types. How might variation between countries be explained? Perhaps there is cultural variation in opportunities and guardianship. While many U.S. burglaries occur during the day in unguarded homes, in other countries, where women are less likely to be paid workers, homes are more likely to be guarded. Similarly, while second homes are included in several surveys, it is likely that fewer Hungarians own a second home than do Swedes.

The distribution of burglary risk is somewhat different in the United States and the other countries surveyed. In all countries, the risk of burglary is greatest in the most urbanized areas (Figure 7). However, in the United States, the relationship between urbanization and burglary risk is weaker than in other countries. Suburban (59.84) areas and areas outside urban areas (SMSAs) (63.99) have about the same rate of burglary. In other countries, especially England and Scotland, burglary risk is very strongly related to living in the city centre.

NOTIFICATION OF THE POLICE

Victimization surveys count both those crimes of which the police are aware and those that they are not. Therefore, most surveys ask the respondent whether or not they notified the police. The likelihood of notification of the police may be affected both by legal and cultural differences, the availability of other helping institutions, trust in the police, the definition of what is police business, and by crime seriousness. For example, a small legal change, the introduction of registration cards, resulted in a dramatic increase in the likelihood of police notification of pick-pocketing in Hong Kong. In some countries, violence occurring at home is not considered to be police business (indeed, it was excluded from the Swiss survey). In general, the probability of the police finding out about more serious crimes is greater than less serious crime. The probability of police notification of assaults is lower than robberies. Therefore, they are analyzed separately.

Table 7 includes all incidents reported in the survey. The police are more likely to learn about an assault in Hong Kong (49.19%) than in other surveys. However, the Hong Kong survey reports only on serious assaults. Of the other surveys, the

198

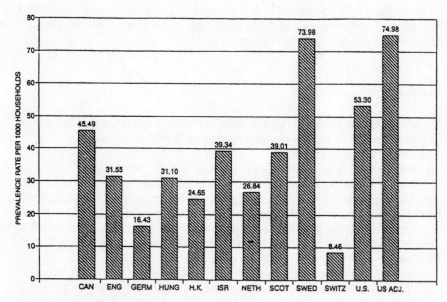

FIGURE 6.   Burglary Prevalence
            Comparative Victim Survey Estimates

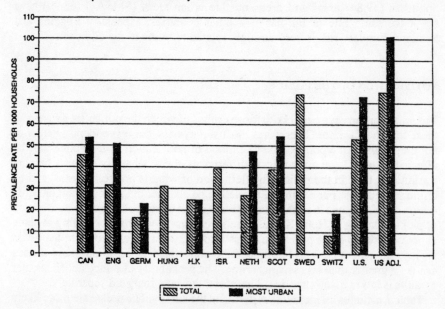

FIGURE 7.   Burglary Prevalence & Urbanization
            Comparative Victim Survey Estimates

TABLE 7

Notification of the Police

Contry	Assault	Robbery	Burglary
Canada	30.04	31.91	70.45
England/Wales	36.16	44.44	62.89
Germany	30.36	43.85	52.50
Hungary	18.18	33.33	61.25
Hong Kong	49.19	43.95	32.65
Israel	32.00	N.A.	52.50
Netherlands	33.94	N.A.	89.11
Scotland	36.05	66.67	56.71
Switzerland	30.34	84.15	82.76
Average	32.95	49.97	62.13
United States	44.64	56.61	51.31

Hungarian survey (18.18%) reports an exceptionally low rate of notification. The police are more likely to be notified about violence in the United States (44.64%) than the average of the other surveys (32.9%). The higher rate of notification in the U.S. survey may result from the greater prevalence of weapons in U.S. violence than in other countries.

Notification of robbery varies from 31.91% in Canada to 84.15% in Switzerland. The U.S. rate of robbery notification was 56.6% in comparison to an average of 50.5% for other countries. However, the number of robberies against residents of countries other than the U.S. in their native country is very small and statistical variation has a large component of error. Only burglaries where the criminal entered a home are included in the Dutch survey; therefore, it is not surprising that police notification is higher in the Netherlands (89.11%) than other countries. The rate of police notification in the U.S. (51.31%), is slightly below that for the average of other countries which include both completions and attempts (63.71%). Variation in notification may result from differences in insurance coverage or the proportion of attempts and completions. Some of these differences could be analyzed using the available surveys.

SUMMARY

Although all victim surveys have the same origin – the National Crime Survey of the United States – and ask similar questions, comparisons between surveys are difficult and must be made with extreme caution. Comparison of the United

200

States' NCS and other national victim surveys is especially difficult. Among the differences that make comparison difficult are the following.

Methodological Differences

Sample size

These varied from 2,500 to more than 60,000. Estimates made from smaller samples have much greater confidence intervals and standard errors for rate and percentage estimates than larger samples. An advantage of the International Crime Survey is that sample sizes are approximately the same; however, all are small.

Period of recall

The NCS asks about victimization in the last six months. Most other surveys ask for victimizations in the last year. This results in recency bias or memory decay that tends to over estimate U.S. victimization rates in contrast to those of other countries.

Bounding method

The NCS has an absolute bound, each address being included in a panel for three and one-half years. Victimizations are bounded by the most recent previous survey. Other surveys are bounded only in the respondent's mind and sometimes by the New Year. The less precise bounding of the other surveys tends to result in external telescoping that over-estimates victimization rates in other countries in comparison to the U.S.

Sampling Frame

Who is to be excluded and included, while not a major topic of this report, may affect rates of victimization. The NCS includes residents of institutions such as dormitories, has both English and Spanish versions, and includes both citizens and non-citizens. All of these groups are excluded from some of the surveys. They may have higher levels of victimization than persons included in the sampling frame. For this project, only respondents aged 15 or 16 and older are included.

Question Differences

Coverage

This concerns both the range of crimes that are included and those acts that are excluded. While in general questions appear similar, significant differences exist between countries. For example, among possible inclusions or exclusions in burglary are attempted break-ins, commercial crime, crimes in garages and other out-buildings, crimes in second homes, and successful break-ins during which nothing was stolen.

Language and Translation

The cultural meaning of the same act may vary from country to country. U.S. common usage does not differentiate between robbery and burglary. The NCS is careful to include victimizations which result from screening questions other than the one intended, but other surveys are not (Dodge, 1985). English and Scottish surveys, on the other hand, using a very complex set of coder decisions, are very careful in defining specific crime categories.

CONCLUDING REMARKS

Any comparison of United States' victimization rates based upon the National Crime Survey and the national crime surveys of other countries must be made very cautiously; however, U.S. robbery rates are probably higher than most other countries. Household burglary rates are high, but so are those of several other countries. U.S. prevalence rates of assault and threat are relatively low in comparison to countries that have similar coverage. However, both for assault and robbery, U.S. levels of weapon use, especially of guns, is much higher than that of the few other countries that asked the question. Based on Killias, United States' rates of lethal violence far exceed those of other countries. The U.S. rate of either gun or non-gun lethal violence exceeds the total rate of lethal violence for the other countries studied.

It is possible to control for some methodological, language and questionnaire differences in national victim surveys. In this report, bounding and recall, age of respondent, and the handling of series victims were taken into account. It is also possible to control for or at least be aware of differences in coverage.

Having worked through many comparative problems, I have concluded that comparison of national surveys other than the NCS may be possible if great caution is taken to insure similarity of coverage and fielding techniques. However, comparison of the United States NCS and that of other countries requires too many assumptions and adjustments. While it is possible to make these

202

adjustments, the resultant comparisons may be believable only in a very wide range. The best comparison of victimization experience is between identical surveys with identical methodologies. These surveys have twice been success-fully completed, however, the relatively small number of respondents to each survey and the differential response rates of the surveys limit comparison.

APPENDIX A

Methodological Summary of the Surveys Used for this Analysis

Country: Canada
Survey Title: General Social Survey
Administration History 1 Cycle
Year Used 1987
People Interviewed 9870
Households Interviewed 9870
Response Rate 83%
Fielding Techniques cati
Period Covered 1 year
Bounding Technique Jan/Feb interviews

Country: England/Wales
Survey Title: British Crime Survey
Administration History 1981, 1983, 1987, 1990
Year Used 1987
People Interviewed 5146
Households Interviewed 5146
Response Rate 74%
Fielding Techniques in house interview
Period Covered 1 year
Bounding Technique Jan/Feb interview

Country: Federal Republic of Germany (BADEN/WURTENBERG)
Survey Title: Comparative German-American-Hungarian Vict. Survey
Administration History once
Year Used 1981
People Interviewed 2252
Households Interviewed 2252
Response Rate 64%
Fielding Techniques mailed
Period Covered one year
Bounding Technique from date of interview

Country: Finland
Survey: Title Safety of Finnish Life
Administrative History 1980, 1988
People Interviewed 14,000
Households Interviewed Not Applicable
Response Rate 87%
Fielding Technique
Period Covered one year
Bounding Technique from date of interview

Country: Hong Kong
Survey Title: Crime and its Victims in Hong Kong 1989
Administration History 1978, 1981, 1986, 1989, 1991
Year Used 1986
People Interviewed 55437
Households Interviewed 17819
Response Rate 99%
Fielding Techniques house to house
Period Covered 1 year
Bounding Technique early January inter.

Country: Hungary (BARAYANA)
Survey Title: Concealed Victimization in Barayana (Hungary)
Administration History Once
Year Used 1981
People Interviewed 2446
Households Interviewed 2446
Response Rate 73%
Fielding Techniques mailed
Period Covered 1 year from int date
Bounding Technique from date of survey

Country: Israel
Survey Title: Victimization of Households in Israel
Administration History 1979, 1981, 1987
Year Used 1987
People Interviewed 5964 Non-Jewish households excluded
Households Interviewed 5964 Representing 20496 individuals
Response Rate unknown
Fielding Techniques in house interview
Period Covered 1 year
Bounding Technique from date of interview

204

County: The Netherlands
Survey Title: Victims of Crime
Administration History Annual/Bi-annual since 1975
Year Used 1986
People Interviewed 9502
Households Interviewed 9502
Response Rate 63%
Fielding Techniques in house interview
Period Covered 1 year
Bounding Technique given in Jan/Feb

Country: Scotland
Survey Title: Scottish Crime Survey
Administration History 1981, 1988
Year Used 1981
People Interviewed 5031
Households Interviewed 4255
Response Rate 81%
Fielding Techniques in house interview
Period Covered 1 year
Bounding Technique Jan/Feb interview

Country: Sweden
Survey Title: Annual Survey of Living Conditions
Administration History Yearly since 1975
Year Used 1988
People Interviewed 11841
Households Interviewed 11841
Response Rate 83%
Fielding Techniques In house interview
Period Covered 1 year
Bounding Technique one year from interview

Country: Switzerland
Survey Title:
Administration History 1984 Fr. 1986 Ger/It
Year Used 1984 French/1986 Ger/It
People Interviewed 6500
Households Interveiwed 6500
Response Rate 65%
Fielding Techniques CATI
Period Covered 1 year/life/6 years
Bounding Technique Jan interview

Country: United States
Survey Title: National Crime Survey (NCS)
Administration History Continuous from 1973
Year Used 1987
People Interviewed 97600
Households Interviewed 48400
Response Rate 93%
Fielding Techniques in pers/tele/cati
Period Covered 6 months
Bounding Technique since last panel

NOTES

1. This project is funded under Bureau of Justice Statistics Contract OJP-89-M-014. The project reflects the author's analysis not that of the Bureau of Justice Statistics or that of the many agencies and individuals who supplied information for the comparison.
2. A project involving studies of so many countries would not be possible without the help of many collaborators. I would like to thank the following, my co-workers for this comparison.
   Data Coordinators and Researchers:
   Canada, Roger Boe; England/Wales, Patricia Mayhew and Wesley Skogan; Germany, Harald Arnold; Hong Kong, K.S. Lau; Hungary, Lazlo Korinek; Israel, Giore Rahav; The Netherlands, Marianne Junger; Scotland, Douglas Payne; Sweden, Joachim Vogel and Lars Hall; Finland, Kauko Aaroma; Switzerland, Martin Killias; The United States (ICPSR), Spencer Pricenash and Victoria Schneider.
   Translators:
   Venezuela, Jesus Gonzalez; France and Switzerland, Michelle Pagnol; Hungary, Lia Hoffman-Irwin.
   Assistance at Loyola:
   Gayle Hoopaw, Jing Xhang, David Gabrovich.
   Finally, thanks go to Wesley Skogan for his continued support and to Carol Kalish of BJS for suggesting that I undertake the project.
3. The difference between a bounded and unbounded household is not absolute. A household is considered bounded if the address is bounded. However, over three and a half years, occupants of many addresses change. The surveys of new residents are considered to be bounded although they in fact are not as clearly indicated by the much higher levels of victimization reported by these respondents in their first interview. See Roman and Sliwa (1980) and Cantor (1989).
4. An additional advantage of the NCS panel interview methodology is a smoother distribution of crimes throughout the year in comparison to countries where a survey is asked only during a limited time period. Recency bias is greatest for the last month. If that month can occur in any quarter of the year, the monthly distribution will be smoother than if all questionnaires were administered during the same two or three weeks.
5. *Panel bias*: The reduction in reported crimes with each re-interview was an unexpected problem created by the NCS technique. Either behavioural changes or conditioning to the survey results in the number of crimes reported declining with each re-interview.
6. Included as unbounded surveys were those new to the panel and those old addresses with a new household.
7. While calculated somewhat differently, these are very similar to Murphy and Cowan (1976).

8. These estimates are based on the surveys administered in February 1985 covering the previous six months. All addresses not included in the survey before and all households not surveyed before are considered to be unbounded.
9. The surveys used for this analysis are the 1981 England/Wales and Scottish surveys, NCS/VRS survey, and the Dutch survey of 1984.
10. No correction was possible for robbery because of the few number of occurrences of this crime outside the United States.
11. Prevalence rates were not available for Hong Kong for this preliminary report.
12. Because of the treatment of series crimes, estimates presented here will differ from those of published reports.

BIBLIOGRAPHY

Biderman, A.D. and Cantor, D. (1984). A Longitudinal Analysis of Bounding, Respondent Conditioning, and Mobility as Sources of Panel Bias in the National Crime Survey. *Proceedings of the Section on Survey Research Methods* pp. 708–713, *American Statistical Association*.

Biderman, A.D. and Lynch, J.P. (1981). Recency bias in data in self-reported victimization. *Proceedings of the Social Statistics Section* pp. 31–40, *American Statistical Association*.

Bureau of Justice Statistics (1988). *Criminal Victimization in the United States, 1987.* Department of Justice; Washington D.C., 15.

Bushery, J.M. (1981). Recall bias for different reference periods in the National Crime Survey. *Proceedings of the Section on Survey Research Methods* pp. 238–243. *American Statistical Association.*

Cantor, David. (1989). Substantive implications of longitudinal design features: the National Crime Survey as a case study. In *Panel Surveys* (D. Kasprzyk et. al. eds.) pp. 25–51. John Wiley & Sons: New York.

Cantor, David (1985). Operational and Substantive Differences in Changing the NCS Reference Period. Proceedings of the Social Statistics Section pp. 128–137. American Statistical Association.

Dodge, Richard W. (1985). *Response to Screening Questions in the National Crime Survey.* U.S. Department of Justice. Bureau of Justice, Statistics Technical Report.

Killias, Martin (1987). New methodological perspectives for victimization surveys: lessons from Switzerland, National Crime Survey. The American Society of Criminology 39th Annual Meeting, Montreal, Quebec, Canada; November 1987.

Killias, Martin (1990). Gun ownership and violent crime: the Swiss experience in international perspective. *Security Journal,* 1, 1169–174.

LaVange, Lisa M. and Folsom, Ralph E. (1985). Regression Estimates of National Crime Survey Operations Effects: Adjustment for Non-Sampling Bias p. 109–114. Proceedings of the Social Statistics Section. American Statistical Association.

Murphy, Linda R. and Cowan, Charles D. (1984). Effects of bounding on telescoping in the National Crime Survey. *The National Crime Survey: Working Papers, Volume II: Methodological Studies.* Dept. of Justice. Bureau of Statistics, Washington D.C.

Roman, A.M. and Sliwa, G.A. (1982). *Final Report on the Study Examining the Increased Use of Telephone Interviewing in the National Crime Survey*) (Memorandum dated August 9, 1982). U.S. Bureau of Census; Washington, DC.

Saphire, Diane Griffin (1984). Estimation of Victimization Prevalence Using Data From The National Crime Survey. Springer-Verlag; New York.

Turner, Anthony G. (1984). The effect of memory bias on the design of the National Crime Survey. *The National Crime Survey: Working Papers, Volume II: Methodological Studies.*

van Dijk, Jan J.M., Mayhew, Pat and Killias, Martin (1989). First Findings from the 1989 Multinational Victimization Survey. Annual Meeting of the Society of Criminology, Reno, Nevada, November 1989.

207

van Dijk, Jan J.M., Mayhew, Pat, and Killias, Martin (1990). Experiences of Crime Across the World: Key Findings of the 1989 International Crime Survey. *Kluwer Law and Taxation Publishers; Deventer, The Netherlands.*

Part II
The Causes of Vulnerability

[3]

Safe Conduct: Women, Crime, and Self in Public Places*

CAROL BROOKS GARDNER, *Indiana University*

In this essay, I paint a portrait of women in public places and their concerns with crime prevention, based on a survey of the literature and in-depth interviews with women. I argue that there is a situationally appropriate self that crime-prevention advice literature suggests women adopt and that women attempt to adopt. This situated self, however, is sometimes constrained by the general character of public places and by the particular character of the belief system that women have and that the literature recommends with regard to crime prevention. In particular, I view normative beliefs about crime prevention as a "rhetoric" that involves negative contingencies for the woman's situated self in public, including frequent reliance on others, self-profanation, and lengthy or consuming preparations.

Being born a woman is my awful tragedy . . . . Yes, my consuming desire to mingle with road crews, sailors and soldiers, barroom regulars—-to be part of a scene, anonymous, listening, recording—all is spoiled by the fact that I am a girl, a female always in danger of assault and battery. My consuming interest in men and their lives is often misconstructed as a desire to seduce them, or as an invitation to intimacy. Yes, God, I want to talk to everybody I can as deeply as I can. I want to be able to sleep in an open field, to travel west, to walk freely at night.

> Sylvia Plath, *The Journals of Sylvia Plath, 1950-1962,*
> written at the age of nineteen

Women have different experiences in public places than do men, particularly when they appear alone. Belying the U.S. middle-class ideal of an egalitarian etiquette for public places (Goffman 1963, 1971), analysis of actual conduct shows that public places are dotted with contacts that evince judgments of status and discrimination no less finely tuned and expressive than those evinced in private regions (Gardner 1980, 1983, 1988). Although many social categories receive treatment in public places demonstrably different from the expected norms of middle-class etiquette (people with disabilities, children, gay people, and ethnic minorities are among these), the situation of women in public is striking. Women may have made considerable progress in occupation, education, and home life; yet in public places they are regularly subject to inferior treatment by men in the form, for instance, of catcalls, evaluative "compliments," and verbal contacts that subtly go astray when gender, not the business at hand, becomes a topic (Gardner 1980, 1983, 1988, 1989).

Besides these routine ways that women can experience public places differently from men, there is the more dramatic case of crime in public. Researchers remark that, though men experience crime in higher numbers, women report greater fear of crime (Balkin 1979; Brown, Flanagan, McLeod 1984; Clemente and Kleiman 1977; Dubow 1979; Riger and Gordon 1981). The place of gender-role expectations in this difference is crucial (Hindelang, Gottfredson, and Garofalo 1978; Janoff-Bulman and Frieze 1987; Maxfield 1984). In public, fear of rape is a cardinal fear for women (Riger and Gordon 1981), since public places are the sites for

* Research for this paper was supported by the President's Council of Indiana University, whom I thank. I also thank William Gronfein, the late Erving Goffman, and two anonymous reviewers for comments on previous versions of this paper. Versions of the study were presented at the 1987 International Symposium on Victimology in San Francisco and at the 1987 annual Sociologists for Women in Society meetings. Finally, I thank all of my interviewees for their help. Correspondence to: Gardner, Department of Sociology, Indiana University, Indianapolis, IN 46202.

most stranger rape (Ledray 1986). Women are never sure which of a man's activities are precursors to rape or other crime, and commonly class together any public harassment with public harassment preceding rape or other crimes (Grahame 1985; Kelly 1987). Popular advice and folk wisdom also can influence women's conduct in public, the way they are perceived, or the way they perceive themselves (Heath 1984; Brunvand 1981; Wachs 1988). Women's alleged responsibility for their own victimization has led them to define part of their task as "becoming streetwise," "taking necessary precautions," and "preventing crime" (S. Edwards 1987; Radford 1987).[1]

In this paper, I discuss the character of advice to women with regard to crime prevention in public and the character of women's beliefs about crime-preventive behavior. My goal is conjecture about women's situation. In addition to my own experience, I use two types of empirical materials to illustrate this essay: first, a review of the popular literature about crime prevention for women written in the last twenty years; and second, a set of 25 in-depth interviews with women about crime in public. I argue that the nature of both advice and experience is importantly related to possibilities for communication in public places in U.S. culture generally. For women, both advice and experience combine to affect the particular incarnation of the self appropriate to the situation of being in public places—a socially situated self, as Goffman defines it (1963:112).

This situated self appropriate to public places is supported, in addition to other elements, by various sets of strategies of presentation and impression management that may be thought of as rhetorics (Ball 1967). A rhetoric, sociologically speaking, is a "vocabulary of limited purpose," whose set of symbols communicates a particular set of meanings directed and arranged to present a specific impression. These vocabularies are visual and verbal, and they may appeal to other senses as well (Ball 1967:296). Such a rhetoric serves to legitimize and neutralize what otherwise might be seen as deviant (Ball 1967). In particular, women who wish to prevent crime in public are encouraged to take up a typical rhetoric that imputes limited competence. Correspondingly, the situated self they are encouraged to present is characterized by this rhetoric, which connotes ineptness rather than skill, apprehension rather than ability, a self debased rather than revered. My goal is not to judge the advice literature or my informants' activities as wise or unwise, but to contemplate the type of self that they can foster in women and suggest how the activities of that self can be played out given the general character of public places.

I begin by discussing the empirical materials I use here, then specify some pertinent general features of communication in public places, features I later suggest are at variance with the advice rhetoric aimed at helping prevent crime. Next, I discuss three elements of the rhetoric of limited competence offered to crime-conscious women in public. Finally, I describe how rhetorical strategies contribute to the situated selves women and men present in public and help to sustain the informal social control of public places.

Empirical Materials

The empirical materials I use to illustrate this essay come from two sources: a survey of popular literature directed toward women about crime prevention, and interviews with 25 women residents of Santa Fe, New Mexico in 1987.

I read all articles listed in *Reader's Guide to Periodical Literature* for the period 1970-1989 involving self-defense, crime prevention, women and crime, and women and rape and as-

---

1. Interestingly, there is also a contrary set of advice telling women in search of dates or husbands to turn casual contacts in public into grist for their mill, suggesting that they can recognize desirable men as well as men they need fear (Gallatin 1987; O'Connor and Silverman 1989; Sommerfield 1986).

sault. Under similar headings and titles, I also read all books listed in *Books in Print* for the period 1965-1989, extending the period to gain more authors and perspectives.

This literature, perhaps partly the congealing of a folklore already in place, itself reveals gender stereotypes even in its broad dimensions. For example, there continue to be many books and articles directed to women in the name of street crime prevention. There is no complementary male-directed literature: when crime-prevention books for men are written, they are on self-defense skills. Some advice books for women are simply directed to the men who, it is assumed, will be their teachers (Tegner, 1965:201-16).

Though there is also a general, non-gender-specific literature on crime prevention and self-defense, the subset of literature directed at women stands apart in the extremity of measures advised. The asymmetry may be sound: perhaps any street harassment is more traumatic for women, who express more fear of crime in the first place; there is certainly no equal for men of women's generalized fear of rape.

Of course, I can claim no causal relationship here between these particular articles and the feelings and actions of informants with whom I spoke. Instead, I use the literature as a body of normative beliefs about women, crime, and conduct in public places. It represents what is available for, not necessarily what is taken up by, women in the culture. It is a remarkably consistent body of beliefs at that. It is also one that, in general, my informants said they knew.

The women I interviewed were from Santa Fe, New Mexico, a small but cosmopolitan city of some 52,000 residents. The interviewees were all middle-class. I interviewed these 25 women as part of a larger project studying gender behavior in public places that involved, ultimately, interviews with nearly one hundred women. I approached these 25 informants in various public places in the city, often as a tag-end to a casual conversation, greeting, or service encounter, and asked them if they would be willing to be interviewed. No woman refused, but the resulting pool is, of course, a convenience sample rather than one systematically representative of the women of the city, much less of U.S. women as a whole. Had I used a sample of poor minority women living in high-crime areas, for example, I would probably have culled a more explicit shared set of folk wisdom in response to sure, not likely, crimes, and a more extreme set of responses in terms of weaponry. Certainly, too, such a sample would have had more direct experience as crime victims. They might also have expressed a set of strategies for dealing with crime similar to those of their male counterparts.

The interviews were freeform and in depth, concentrating on public places as possible sites for crime. I asked informants about their perceptions of crime in public places in the city; their experience with crime, with near-crime, and with events they did not think of as crime but were nevertheless distasteful. I asked about their understandings of what to do in case of street crime and whether they ever had put these beliefs into practice. I also asked about their sources of information.

Interviews lasted from one to 3 1/2 hours; the average interview was about two hours. Twenty of the 25 women had Anglo surnames, and five had Hispanic surnames. For the most part, these were young women: 16 were between 20 and 35, seven were between 36 and 45; only two were over 60. Twelve were married or living with a man. Six had had formal self-defense training, either in a women's self-defense class or through classes in martial arts; two others had attempted to train themselves in self-defense through books or videos; all but one identified themselves as purposive readers of literature on women and self-defense in, for example, newspapers and women's magazines. Three women identified themselves as victims of crime: one was a rape survivor; two others had experienced home robberies.

The Self and Communication in Public Places

As an arena for face-to-face interaction, communication between strangers in public places exhibits some general characteristics that are distinct from communication between acquaintances in public and from much communication in private places. This constellation of characteristics shapes possibilities for interaction that do and can occur, not only for women interested in preventing crime but for all other citizens as well.

In what follows, I briefly sketch the communication characteristics most relevant to the situation of the woman and crime prevention in public places. This communication influences what Goffman has spoken of as the situated self appropriate to public places. With *situated self*, Goffman implies a self as something constituted according to the social situation of the moment, rather than as any stable, trans-situational possession. A self is, in effect, loaned to its putative owner and defined in part by the social control requirements of particular situations (Goffman 1961:149-52). In problematic social situations, the relevant self develops strategies for coping that can be expresseed as rhetorics. Yet these rhetorics will be modified by the nature of communication possible or thought proper to social situations. Thus, any rhetoric involving crime prevention will be modified by the character of communication possible and thought proper in a particular setting.

Communication Characteristics

Communicative acts between individuals in public are heavily *appearance dependent*. That is, they rely on appraisal of the physical look, manner, nonverbal communication, and dress of the other—what Goffman has referred to as an appreciation of "body idiom" (Goffman 1963:33-34). It is understood that, all other things being equal, the citizen will attempt to give the best possible appearance in public.[2] Public places function as front regions (Goffman 1973:107-23), where performances are expected to be cut and polished, where impressions of proper decorum are expressed by adhering to more formal standards of dress, permissible sound levels, and prescribed activities and attitudes. In this way, an etiquette manual will tell a woman that the way she looks in public signifies "the way she wants to be seen by the world" (Geng 1971:76-77), and all citizens will be advised to restrict conspicuous activities such as kissing and smoking (Vanderbilt 1972:246-47, 316-18).

With only appearance to rely on, however, inescapable stereotypy results, as, for example, when a Korean-American in a black neighborhood is the object of catcalls that recapitulate stereotypes of Asian Americans (Navarro 1990), or a black who enters a Korean-American business experiences behavior reflecting stereotypes of blacks (Sims 1990). Or a citizen sometimes feels strangers fix reliably on blatant symbols of a status peripheral to the "real" self, as when a woman using an electric wheelchair says strangers bypass usual greetings to offer remarks on her chair (Gardner 1990).

Clearly, appearance dependence favors those whose appearance connotes statuses held in high regard; with regard to crime, it favors those taken stereotypically to be no easy victims or who can manipulate appearance to suggest strength or imperviousness to assault. Using traditional stereotypes, women will be seen by strangers as less capable of retaliation than men. As aspiring criminals will have to depend on judgments of appearance to select prospective victims, so those who seek to escape victimization must depend on assessment of strangers' appearance and manipulation of their own in order to avoid crime. One way to cope with crime in public therefore will be to develop an array of behavioral strategies that are also appearance dependent; alternatively, people will curtail others' visual access in order to prevent being judged a suitable target. The latter tack is taken in a small way by donning sun-

---

2. This is true barring some general fear for theft of valuable goods. To hide one's assets becomes, then, a general rule of conduct whose prudence overwhelms the temptation toward conspicuous display.

glasses that foil, among other things, a criminal judging one fearful and therefore an easy mark; similarly, a car may be used as a visual shell to both stymie appraisal of one's vulnerability and provide a physical baffle to intrusion.

Implicitly, then, in public the visual channel is preferred as an avenue of communication. A corollary of this appearance dependence is that silence is normative and speech between strangers is routinized and brief, and, aside from certain heavily scripted greetings or comments on the weather, is to be stimulated only by unusual circumstances. If talk is limited, routine, and warranted, then the citizen who fears crime will have no ordinary way to ascertain who is, and who is not, a potential foe—nor will seeming and actual foes have clear ways in which to make their identities less ambiguous.

Communication in public between strangers is also typically *transitory*; i.e., it is relatively fleeting compared to communication between acquaintances or communication in private places. It is also typically *episodic*: Face-to-face communication between strangers is interspersed with vacuum periods where contact is neither made nor attempted. Both these characteristics influence those fleeting contacts that are made, which therefore appear in relief and can become highly charged with meaning. Such brief, disjointed events will be all the person interested in preventing crime will have to judge the situation by; similarly they will be all the aspiring criminal will have to select a suitable target. Transitory and episodic communication can also favor purposeful strategies that cannot be sustained for long, as when a crime-fearing woman manages momentarily to adopt a no-nonsense expression.

Communication in public places also involves what Goffman (1963:20-21) refers to as *multiple social realities*. This phrase reflects the capacity of this one larger setting to host other, overlapping behavior settings—that is, a variety of individuals with highly differentiated motives, needs, wants, and agendas, as well as individuals from a great variety of social categories. Therefore, it is impossible to predict whether or not the given flow on a city street is likely to include someone with criminal intent. If one espouses a crime-preventive attitude or engages in crime-preventive strategies, it is hard to predict when this attitude or these strategies should be curtailed or suspended. At the same time, one's contact with even an innocuous-seeming stranger is necessarily history-less, so that suspicion can bleed onto even those one has no reason to fear.

Beliefs about Public Places

Coupled with these characteristics of communication in public places are certain normative ideas about what everyday life in public places is or should be like. First, much face-to-face communication between strangers is felt to be *insignificant*. In general, public places are transitways to other regions, not loci of interest in themselves; laws against loitering, lolling, and vagrancy exist in part to insure that public places remain waystations, not goals. Our feeling that events in public places are insignificant coexists with an obligation to present an appearance typically more formal than can be presented in the "relaxed" settings of private places. Second, these communications are believed to be *egalitarian* in character, expressive of the effective ceasefire that exists between strangers even of varying classes, racial groups, and genders. Much of our etiquette of public places is based on this second notion. It argues that we suspend personal interests, tastes, and involvements in order to effect a courtesy and openness owed to all (Benton 1956:15, 96-114; Martin 1982:99-100, 250-52, 280-81; Post 1969:91-96).

Likewise, we feel that public places are not—nor, rightly, should they be—owned by any single group, and that, aside from certain strongly territorial neighborhoods, no one individual or group has rights of control over strangers; these feelings mean that we are all, in a sense, trespassers when in public. However, they also mean that the personal space of ill-meaning others will abut our own, and that we have as little apparent right to prepare a defense as they have to prepare an offense.[3] Because of these general yet seldom explicated beliefs, we may have vague dissatisfaction with canons of advice that involve extensive ma-nipulation of events or appearances in public places—as crime prevention advice can seem to do.

We can also come to feel that individuals who attribute deep meaning to the small in-terchanges of face-to-face communication there make too much of what is, after all, trifling.[4] At the same time, these general features of communication in public places and our general feelings about the nature of public places importantly color the informal social control that is exerted there, making it necessarily random, brief, and directed to all—as impersonal, in fact, as public courtesy and goodwill are expected to be.

These same characteristics of and our feelings about communication in public places color the strategies that can be and are advised to those who would avoid crime. I will suggest that any crime-preventive rhetoric, however, will be somewhat at odds with other constitu-ents of the general situated self we believe is appropriate to public places.

Safety, Public Places, and the Rhetoric of Limited Competence

Prescriptions to women in public places as to how to achieve safety are framed in terms of a rhetoric of limited competence, that is, a series of presentational strategies that project dependency and lack of skill. Further, this rhetoric of limited competence is by nature ambig-uous (Zimmerman 1981:52): at the same time that it intends to communicate women's ability to deal with urban crime, it also communicates dependency and lack of skill.

The strategies that make up this rhetoric, part of the wisdom of the young urban woman in particular, about prudent behavior when on streets and even near home often ostensibly offer women ways to avoid harm. Yet they also advise women to adopt behavior that results in a profaned self, that is, a self that has unworthy qualities. This is much at odds with the understanding that one's public appearance should be one's best appearance. Thus, the situ-ated self appropriate to public places when a woman believes she is "preventing crime" can come to seem to her ridiculous, and the presentation process can seem impractical as well.

The Apparent Escort

One key precaution for public behavior counsels the woman alone in public simply not to be alone or, at least, not to seem alone. There are several levels at and degrees to which this injunction can be observed, ranging from what is thought of as simple prudence (such as reluctance or refusal to go out at night unless accompanied), to common customs of deception (such as wearing a wedding ring when one is unmarried to ward off unwanted men), to more wide-ranging methods (such as pretending one has a roommate to confer safety when one does not). I discuss how first the advice literature, then my informants, explained these strategies.

The advice literature often recommends engineering an escort by, for instance, having "a male fellow employee escort you to your car and see you safely started—you might even drive

---

3. Beliefs about insignificance and egalitarianism are fostered by some of the social scientific work on public places. Such work emphasizes the civility present there and treats breaches of civility as deviant. For example, Goffman emphasizes such quintessentially egalitarian rites as civil inattention, whereby individuals signal by means of a mutual glance, then a dropping of that glance, that due respect has been awarded and no harm is intended (1963:83-85). At the same time he relegates the flagrant disrespect some social categories receive in public to the deviant case of "exposed" positions (1963:125-28).

4. Of course, all I have said about the character of communication in public places with regard to women and crime may be as well said of the character of communication with regard to men in public places. An intriguing ques-tion for a future study, then, is the problem not of why women fear crime in public places but of why men do not.

him back to the office" (Barthol 1979:102), or even managing to be near a male by, for example, standing near the occupied ticket or toll booth in a subway station or near a police officer (Field 1980:112); walking close to a group of people walking, if they look safe and are not all males (Barthol 1979:99); never being embarrassed to ask a friend to accompany one home (Wegman 1978:57). Formal "ride switchboards" and "escort services" for women alone at night achieve the same goals (Rockwood and Thom 1979:82).

The women I interviewed often said they should effect a male escort, since attackers will presumably shy away from this strengthened front. This strategy is one that even non-crime-conscious women say they choose for the ease it confers when in public. Women sometimes engineer accompaniment, even planning in advance. A lawyer in her fifties said she kept up a friendship with a neighbor woman of whom she was not too fond in order to have someone "to go to the movies with, to have a drink with, or just to keep me company when I take out the garbage." A grade school teacher in her thirties who lived alone with her two small children once had been followed home, robbed, and nearly raped. She had a well-worked-out network of female and male acquaintances—one who could be counted on to take in a play with her, another who walked her to the store, a third whose car was at her beck and call—that she reciprocally "paid back"—though not in kind—by pet-sitting or baking cakes or breads. A graduate student in her twenties who lived with a boyfriend, with a less well-organized network of escorts, commented that at some times she felt these were "unfortunately instrumental friendships," but appreciated also that she had little choice.

If a woman were to undertake some measures of impression management the advice literature recommends, she would appear to be self-plus-companion, or woman near a person who could be enlisted as companion if need be. The woman who stands near a convenient police officer seems to be protected, yet is not truly accompanied, of course; she mimics co-presence. In yet other cases, however, the crime-advice literature suggests a woman imply a companion, i.e., give the impression of being accompanied (and presumably protected) by displaying, not a man who is or seems a companion, but evidence of a man, for example, by telling a woman to place a man's hat or pipe on the seat of her parked car to indicate she "might be accompanied on her return" (Berman 1980:247).

A few women said they employed some of these strategies, though they also expressed some discomfort or awkwardness at discussing them. A married college professor in her thirties, whose three grown sons provide her with useful artifacts for these misleading signals of male co-presence or availability, referred to them laughingly as "male spoor." She added that she felt odd at using them. A homemaker in her fifties related that, having read such a recommendation, she borrowed her brother's spare hat and gloves; she was surprised to discover that they allayed her fears, and she found herself anxious when they were accidentally removed from her car during cleaning: she had converted the items of clothing into talismans of safety. She was now embarrassed at her emotional investment in them. Other informants used a variety of expressions—"weird," "odd," "funny," "dishonest," and the like—to describe discomfort with these practices.

Women sometimes effectively create a companion male by enacting the role themselves. These strategies, by the way, are not a part of the advice literature. Interestingly, these women spoke of the measures, not as uncomfortably unusual, but as practically utilitarian. Though it might formally express a less competent or independent self, then, the rhetoric that women use need not always be experienced as such. In effect, a woman who enacted the role of a protector becomes self *and* companion, emphasizing that, as her "real" female self, she is powerless when in public. In this spirit, some five informants said they wore slacks, especially dark slacks or jeans, flat shoes, and jacket or coat styles they felt were homologous with men's styles.

Women's primary rationale was not explicitly to "sham" male gender but to wear clothes that were "practical" for purposes of escaping notice, evading criminals, or practicing self-defense. One said that her purpose was not so much to seem male as not to seem female. A single mother in her thirties who often worked late as a hotel clerk said she always effected this style of dress, and cited its effect in public as a selling point: she "dressed like a man" and felt strangers were more likely to respect her if they felt it possible that she was a man. An art gallery owner in her thirties added that she tied her long hair at the nape of her neck in order to look less "feminine." A 24-year-old secretary who lived with her boyfriend and their toddler effectively withdrew signs of female gender rather than substituting male: she tried to leave no trace in her car "that it's a woman's car—no women's magazines, no clothes, none of my baby's toys or clothes." When using these strategies, informants did not express discomfort, perhaps because they were direct actions rather than deceptive use of symbols or attachment to them.

There are more traditional practices that indicate that a woman is protected by a man when she is in fact alone. Usually, these do not involve the woman in misrepresenting gender. She is not to suggest she is something she is not—i.e., a man—nor is she to destroy evidence that she is a woman. Instead, she should indicate, either truthfully or not, by use of verbal invocation or significant symbols that she has access to a man who could protect her if need be. The advice literature recommends practices such as suggesting a woman walk in the middle of the street at night and, if approached, "look up at one of the windows or down the block and yell, 'Hey, Tom, I thought we were going to meet on Elm Avenue,'" for a criminal will not be "sure if Tom is real or not" (Ingber 1987:140). Even when there is no special danger, companionship is not to be discarded lightly: a woman, when at the movies, is sometimes told to go with the companion who "decides to venture into the lobby to buy popcorn," since "It might turn out to be fun, and it's certainly safer" (Burg 1979:144). Speaking to or of an illusory male for effect is termed "the Invisible Man Routine" (Burg 1979:147-148). Some measures are to be played out with no audience at all, as when a woman is advised when in a hotel to leave the television playing softly while she is out and the do-not-disturb sign on the door (Burg 1979:147-48).

In this way, women informants said they sometimes purposefully mentioned a boyfriend or husband during a service encounter or public conversation with a male stranger, thereby also preventing pickups. Thus, a secretary in her twenties took care to mention her ex-husband, whom she could continue to invoke if she disliked or feared the man with whom she spoke, but of whom she would rapidly dispose verbally if she chose to encourage acquaintance. Women also perceived modest deceptions as allowable, such as wearing a wedding ring though unwed. One woman claimed the advantage of this method was its expressiveness to all men: it required no strategic insertion into a conversation otherwise about plumbing, the weather, or pizza delivery, only that she display her hand. A woman might claim both existence and availability, for example, by reporting, when talking on the phone, not only that she had a husband but that he was home.[5]

Informants said that such minor deceptions were suitable as routine precautions. In situations more directly menacing, a woman might take more active measures, as when the public realm threatened to encroach on the private. If she is home and a man claiming to be a repairperson knocks, a woman alone sometimes attempts to signal that a man is with her. She sometimes also attempts to signal that her home is occupied by a man while she is still on the street, involving tacks that occasionally make her feel "more than normally foolish," as reported a lawyer in her fifties who nevertheless says she does just such things. In the same way, a nurse in her thirties, who once believed a man was following her home, yelled up to her window, "Chet, honey, I'll get the door," and was chagrined to hear her dog Chet dutifully

---

5. Sometimes women understand the various threads of advice to be in conflict. Thus, an unmarried secretary in her thirties decided to wear a wedding ring in order to suggest an absent protector; on the other hand, she feared the ring was also a lure for thieves, and compromised by wearing it only during daytime. She felt that theft was not likely in the daytime, but being followed home would be.

bark in response. An unmarried partner in a law firm, a woman in her forties, habitually yelled, "I'll get it, honey," when her bell rang; once she had to explain to her conservative parents at the door that there was no honey after all.

Two young women, a cosmetology student and a secretary both in their twenties, noted that when they answered the phone at home they often took care to modulate their voices to a lower pitch; a criminal caller trying to discover a woman was home alone would thereby be misled. After the first turn at talk assured them a familiar caller, they resumed normal pitch. These examples were recounted with some embarrassment, because it was possible that they would be noticed and mocked by friends or relatives—as both had been.

Accompanied, a woman can feel obliged as a student of safety precautions to make her accompaniment as obvious as possible as often as possible. Evidence of solitude can become uncomfortable for her, based in part on actual experience when accompaniment is ambiguous. A homemaker in her thirties noted that when she and her husband were standing some three feet apart in a theater lobby and not engaged in conversation, a strange man stepped up to her, took her arm familiarly, and attempted to walk her away: "What he was going to do I don't know. Then my husband grabbed him by the collar and [the strange man] grinned very charmingly and walked away."

If women believe that they cannot experience public places unaccompanied, then it is also true that some women come to count men less as individuals than as protectors, functioning either well or poorly, a conception congruent with traditional ideas of gentlemanly behavior (see Hanmer and Saunders 1983). When effective, men are sometimes thought of as saviors; when ineffective, as failed gallants. In this vein, an unmarried graduate student said humorously that she thinks of her escorts on dates more as St. Bernards than as human beings; male escorts, especially at night, are the price paid for a life in public, says a department store clerk in her twenties who does not enjoy dating but wants to get out of the house. A third woman, a gay nurse in her thirties, takes a gay male friend when she goes to bars in a certain part of town for the safety she will then have; an irony is that she is the superior defender by martial arts training. Thus, the situated self that women are constrained to present can come to affect their judgment of effectiveness of a companion's performance.

I have said that purposeful attempts to suggest a man exists where none does imply that the situated self of the woman in public is weak. Some women went beyond the door, so to speak, and said they fantasied protective accompaniment at home, sometimes somewhat elaborately. In this way, a woman who worked as a hotel clerk admitted ruefully her conversations with her nonexistent companion began outside the door of her house, but continued after she entered and while she systematically checked for unwanted criminal companions room by room, the conversation with the imaginary male interlocutor giving her heart. A single mother, she tried to mute them before her children, however, since she felt to act so was "a little odd." Another woman, a graduate student, said her initial words to her imaginary male roommate blended into talking to herself. A nurse reported that her briefly fabricated companion had had a name, habits in dress, and a preferred basketball team, all coincidentally her tastes also; her own actions reflected these tastes when, for instance, she picked out a tie of the sort that he would prefer and hung it deceptively on the bedroom door or left a Celtics game (not games involving other teams) blasting masculinely on the television when she had to go out at night.

Women sometimes say that, though they perform some of these measures, they feel they should apologize for them: they are "crazy" things to do, they make a woman feel "a little bizarre." This ritual accompaniment emphasizes to her that her "true" or "real" self provides insufficient protection for her own safety. She must create a tissue of a man, which can be suggested by the merest hints and evidences.

Caught up in these charades, however, other women report no discomfort. They speak humorously of their shadow mates, implying that they are not threats to a real self but strange rites required by the culture and not to be taken seriously. Perhaps a woman gains some sense of control over the situation of crime prevention if she can, in effect, design her own protector down to his tie. (On the benefical and liberating aspects of imaginary others, see Caughey 1984.)

It is not enough to note that, if women feel they have to engineer or mimic the presence of a man or suggest that they themselves are men, this is a sad commentary on modern urban life. Also important is the character of the situated self of public places that–according to some informants–such strategies create. Alone in public, women occasionally report that they still think of how safe they would feel or how much easier things in general would be, were they accompanied or were they male. Thus, a woman's time in public can be altered in ways unfamiliar to male citizens, in fact with strategies unfamiliar to most males. It is difficult to think of a situation where a man shams female accompaniment or female gender to ensure his safety, or where others advise him to do so.[6]

Profaning the Self in the Name of Safety

While behaving in a crime-conscious manner, women can come to feel constrained to present themselves in a way that belies their knowledge of proper female gender role behav‑ ior and proper public behavior in general, presenting an appearance whose worth they con‑ sciously denigrate rather than inflate. For the sake of preventing crime, women are advised to manipulate their dress and behavior in a number of ways that restrict apparel choices and emotional expressions, and require them to present something less than what otherwise would be considered their best possible appearance.

Minor strategies involve dress and manner; more major strategies are suggestions in the advice literature that, to deter crime, a woman should inform a man that she has some im‑ perceptible—but loathsome—characteristic or disease or should enact a psychological or phys‑ ically repulsive condition. Informants were aware of this range of crime-prevention wisdom, though by and large they put into practice only that involving appearance.

In general, the literature tells women in public to "dress with discretion so as not to stimulate interest" (*Good Housekeeping Magazine* 1972:193), or that "a woman is more likely to invite attack on the street if she is wearing tight, 'sexy' clothes. If you are heading for a party in a décolleté costume or an extra-brief skirt, it's best to ride up to the entrance rather than walk" (Hair and Baker 1970:94). Implicitly these cautions respond to the appearance depen‑ dence of communication in public. Whereas a woman wearing alluring clothing in a private context can use other communicative elements to assure others that she is not truly or only the sexually interested person she seems, the same woman in public lacks other communica‑ tive tools to mute the message clothing offers.[7]

Almost every woman I interviewed offered information about appearance, saying she tried to avoid "provocative" clothing that "invited" attacks from males, as well as an "invit‑ ing" manner. Most informants said they felt they should not behave in an over-friendly man‑ ner or in any way that suggests an over-friendly manner; that is, they should not employ a "sexy" walk or thrust their breasts out.

Some informants noted the drawbacks of dress and attitude manipulation: to succeed in

---

6. More familiar are admonishments to men to practice self-defense measures with an eye to attackers they might meet, a concern more elaborately advised for women, however. Women are also advised to invent another shadow presence, that of the imagined harasser or attacker; in this way, crime-preventive advice collaborates by exhorting a woman actively and extensively to role-play assaults with the criminal.

7. To be sure, all citizens will have reason to look out for crime, and all are cautioned, in some locales and circum‑ stances, to conceal assets in the name of crime prevention—as are all citizens on vacation in unfamiliar parts (Gieseking 1980) and as, increasingly, city-dwelling children are (Hechinger 1984). But concealing monetary assets—appropriately understood as not integral to the self—is different from concealing physical assets, for bodily features are highly associ‑ ated with the individual's "real" self.

making themselves unnoteworthy in public required an adjustment of appearance not worth
the sacrifice. Certainly it violated expectations of other citizens in public as to appropriate
female attire if a woman attempted to dress herself to look plain as a pie plate—all the more if
she managed to be mistaken for a man. A grade school teacher, a warm and exuberant
person, strongly felt that restrictions on one's manner were even more insidious: dressing
differently was a surface measure, she thought, but damping her good humor undermined
what was hers "naturally."

As well as manipulating dress and manner, women sometimes are told to avoid crime by
making themselves too repulsive a target for approach. That the criminal will probably then
turn to another woman as a target is apparently not to be a concern. In the literature, women
are counseled to adopt "non-aggressive—but disgusting—behavior" (Wilson 1977:151); to
claim "to be pregnant or epileptic or the carrier of a venereal disease" (Duckett 1982:68) or to
have "herpes or even AIDS" (Kaye 1985:74); to "pretend to have an epileptic seizure, or faint-
ing spell" (Berman 1980:247); to "faint or go limp; urinate, drool or even throw up" (Schraub
1979:153); to "quack like a duck" (Scribner 1988:69) or make sounds like a cow and flap her
arms like an airplane (Pickering 198:129). She is told not to be afraid to "make a scene [or] do
anything to attract attention to yourself. That's exactly what you want" (Field 1980:120),
though attracting attention to herself is not among the woman's desiderata in public places
according to traditional norms (Benton 1956:8), nor is behaving "sexually aggressively"
(Scribner 1988:69). She should "Act insane; eat grass, jump around, etc." (Krupp 1978:152);
she should "Sing out loud. . . . Make a fool of yourself" (Kaye 1985:74). Some of this advice
also is intended to disgust the potential criminal,[8] as when women are advised to tell rapists
that they have venereal disease (Schraub 1979:153), even carrying an old penicillin bottle to
bolster claims (Pickering 1983:121).

Informants reported knowing about, though very rarely putting into practice, this tack of
purposefully inspiring disgust. Only one woman said she tried these more extreme tactics, a
homemaker in her forties who effectively "gargled" and made noises at a man following her,
but felt so foolish she was not sure her efforts were worthwhile. All such profanation requires
a woman to present, not the more stringent definition of public comportment usually required of citizens, but a floridly flawed self. Here, the self is profaned because the actions are
of such a nature as to make her seem out of role in public, silly because overcautious or
simply unfathomable.

Thus, informants reported that they would feel ridiculous or humiliated if they were to
practice crime prevention by stimulating disgust. For example, a lawyer in her thirties mused
on the possibility of telling an assailant she had AIDS or venereal disease and then having to
further convincingly hypothesize how she came by these "repulsive" diseases. Because of
these feelings, she concluded she could never pull off this strategy.

But some women said they had contemplated being purposefully repulsive when they
felt threatened. Thinking the matter over at the time, they knew themselves to be too poor
deceivers to do so, whether because of inexperience or from overwhelming fear. Thus, a
homemaker in her thirties, once confronted with a suspect man, decided to pretend to have
an epileptic seizure, shortly thereafter remembering that she had no idea what such a seizure
looked like. A nurse, who had been raped, offered that, "If anybody goes after me again, this
[type of advice] won't help me. I'll be so scared I won't be able to spell AIDS, much less
convince someone I've got it."

Such advice would indeed seem strange if offered to a man threatened with street violence. It is now a commonplace that an attractively dressed woman does not "cause" a man
to rape her anymore than a well-dressed man causes a man to rob him. It is not so commonly
noted that we do not advise men to fake insanity or to sham morally impugning disease with

---

8. Tacitly, the advice also assumes certain social categories and states—the epileptic, the mentally disabled, the
pregnant, the menstruating—are worthy of disgust.

the alacrity that women are so advised. Of course, claims of sexually transmitted disease are aptly claimed when one fears sexual crimes like rape, not apt when one fears robbery.

The profanation of a woman's situated self in public places, then, results from beliefs she should either deliberately act ridiculous, inappropriately, or simply mute her personal attractions in hopes either of discomfiting her attacker or escaping his attention. At all levels, these strategies are at odds with the understandings that public places are regions where the individual presents a careful and "best" demeanor and look.

Anticipated Peril

A third type of distance from the normal citizens' situated self in public places is supplied by the advice to women and by their perception that they should take some measures of crime prevention in advance of actually appearing in public. Certain practices, in turn, bespeak an orientation to an action before that action is necessary. Evident precautions and planning contradict our general cultural feeling that events in public places are too trifling to warrant special thought and that an egalitarian civility prevails. Yet, tacitly appreciating the many social realities that public places contain and the impossibility of judging strangers with only transitory, episodic, and silent communications, women are also advised to extend their crime-consciousness back, before the actual moment of danger, in order to foil criminals. In effect, women are counseled to anticipate peril; some informants said they do just this, sometimes with awkward results.

The advice literature suggests there are some practices and some attitudes the woman should follow to prepare herself for the worst that might happen; moreover, she is to keep this advice in mind at all times: "Don't let down. Ever!" (Kaye 1985:74). Besides this general mental vigilance, there are preparations a woman can take to ward off or lessen the likelihood that she will become involved in danger, extending even to practices such as carrying a house key in her hand far in advance of when it will actually be needed (Schraub 1979:169), or positioning herself when she enters an elevator "near the control panel so you can hit the alarm button and as many floor buttons as possible if necessary" in case she is attacked (Krupp 1978:152).

Women are advised to take up many precautions in advance, sometimes far in advance, of trouble: a woman is told to carry her money in her bra (Barthol 1979:111), to hold her police whistle between her teeth as she walks home (Barthol 1979:111), to use her personal alarm "*before* a confrontation takes place, even if you're not sure you're in danger" (*Glamour Magazine* 1980:63). When a stranger enters an elevator she is on, she should pretend she has forgotten something and exit (*Today's Health Magazine* 1973); when on the street, she is told to scream or use her whistle "as soon as you *think* someone might be stalking you" (Berman 1980:247). Other citizens are certain to be puzzled, if not astounded, by such actions, as when a woman is told, if she thinks she is being followed, to run up and say "to a dependable soul: 'Hey Charlie, what's happening?' " (Krupp 1978:142).

Sometimes she must plan considerably ahead, as when she is told to choose her home with an eye to security (Wheeler 1982:69) or to get acquainted with her neighbors with a view toward enlisting them in case of danger (Bertram 1975:83). Such advice amounts to an honorable, not to say prudent, ulterior motive for making friends in the city.

Other long-range advice suggests that she make a list of dangerous public situations experienced by her and her friends and/or portrayed in local newspaper accounts for the last six months (Monkerud and Heiny 1980:14), that she mentally review crime-prevention techniques several times a day (Pickering 1983:7), that she make a calendar of self-defense practice times and a list of dangerous neighborhood features (Griffith 1978:165-69, 174-75). Preparations must continue inside her home, where she can practice "knowing how to scream," but into a pillow pressed over her face (Barthol 1979:25). Or a woman can practice screams driving with the windows rolled up: "anyone watching thinks you are singing!" (Barthol 1979:25).

Many manipulations of appearance involve consideration far beyond the immediate situation of danger, as when the advice literature tells a woman to choose her clothes with regard to their running and escape potential (Burg 1979:121) or for their noiselessness. She should not, for example, wear shoes with "tap-tap" heels that will alert "everyone within a couple of blocks . . . that a female target approacheth!" (Barthol 1979:100-01).

With an eye to anticipating crime, informants reported following a number of strategies of both small and long duration. For example, a homemaker in her twenties said that, before she left the house, she always put her credit cards and large bills in her three-year-old's toy purse, reasoning that even if she were robbed her small daughter would not be; a nurse in her thirties transferred cash to a bra and a purse alarm to her pocket, judging the effect in the mirror to make sure there were no telling bulges. A lawyer in her thirties said she gave herself a "crime check" in a full-length mirror each time she left her house, noting dress and presentation that might "invite" crime and, for each outfit, any handbag both match the outfit but not be "snatchable."

Some preparations were long-term and came to infect other ordinary, pleasurable parts of informants' lives. A 20-year-old homemaker regretted that she could no longer grow long nails, since she needed to be ready to fight an attacker if need be. A graduate student in her twenties with the opposite beliefs about nails regretted a need to grow long nails to serve as weapons for self-defense, for they did not jibe with the professorial image to which she aspired. A cosmetology student felt that it took her "six times as long to find a house" because of her crime-preventive standards. A law partner in her forties enjoyed buying clothes when a teen but said the pleasure was now spoiled since she scrutinized potential purchases "with an eye to, 'will this provoke some depraved maniacal sadist to attack me?' "

Women sometimes took anticipatory walks through the street, mentally mapping common routes with an eye to potential help in case of danger. Compared to other citizens, they were overinvested in the act of public passage, commonly considered insignificant, warranting no practice runs, and as a result spontaneous. Evocatively, however, a married lawyer in her thirties described steps in thinking through a route or assessing an area and concluded, "I never go any place for the first time—I've been there already in my head." Plainly, there is the danger that erecting false events such as these will be inimical to the experiential integrity of the act itself, making it always a rehearsed one.

The woman who observes necessary strategies for anticipating peril when in public places is certain, sooner or later, to be vigilant when there is no cause. Given the extremity of the recommendations, this is likely to happen in some form or other many times daily. Sometimes, of course, she will not know circumspection is unneeded. Informants occasionally alluded to a low-grade guilt over their "paranoia" toward other citizens, who were seen in retrospect to have meant, or at least to have done, no harm to them. Sometimes they had been revealed to have had suspicions where none was warranted, as a secretary in her thirties was mocked by a man on the street for transparently carrying her keys "defensively," or the cosmetologist who stepped aside well in advance to avoid a man she feared, who then said to her, "You idiot."

When women anticipated peril from men they first took to be strangers, then turned out to know, they often reported feeling particularly "stupid." But one informant, a junior professor in her thirties, had a different attitude. After she nearly Mace'd her department chair, they both laughed, "then he started kidding me about what a paranoid I was, and that's where the laughter stopped. I apologize to no one for insuring that I stay alive."

In sum, measures advised by the rhetoric of limited competence sometimes respond to and sometimes contradict general features of communication in public places. Women informants reported taking pains to avoid crime when in public. Yet because they are fearful of crime and because the character of public places makes it impossible reliably to judge the many strangers one encounters, save by appearance, women need rely on what are necessarily quickly and clearly transmitted messages or on preparation that takes place outside of the region. Measures will likely be taken where unwarranted, so that a contingency of this rhetoric remains that either a stranger or an acquaintance can innocently rebuke the woman for strategies not immediately useful. The true culprit, of course, is not so much the advice she receives or the folk beliefs she bears, but the environing fear of crime.

Discussion

The significance of this rhetoric can be seen in terms of (1) its contribution to the situated self women present in public, including the possibility that crime consciousness will overwhelm the woman's other concerns in public places; (2) its relationship to an informal social control in public places; (3) its effect on the complementary situated self men must demonstrate in public.

In some ways, there is less discrepancy than might be suspected between the general situated self due public places and the rhetoric of crime prevention that is a part of it. In general, the situated self of public places subjects women to other imputations of limited competence and supplies them with a self regularly profaned, especially when they are youthful, by street remarks, by differential and commonly poorer treatment in shops and restaurants, by varying expectations of what items of information about the self a woman is obliged to disclose (Gardner 1980, 1983, 1988, 1989).

To some extent, the message of the rhetoric of limited competence is consistent with other experiences of the situated self of public places. Insofar as it is consistent, it emphasizes other negative experiences. At the same time, it makes more unlikely that women can achieve the egalitarian courtesy and trust that is, within limits, normative for public places in middle-class society. This carries an unpleasant connotation for women's place in society, suggesting that social control of women in public places both exists and is diffusely available for any man in public places. Indeed, it is exercised by men whether they intend it or not.

Part of women's status in public, then, is expressed by a heightened concern with crime, quite in contrast to the concerns reported by and advised for men. An examination of what I have called the rhetoric of limited competence shows how this is possible.

First, there is a great deal of anticipatory preparation, both mental and material, counseled for the woman who is going out. This vigilance, she often believes (and popular literature assures her), must typically be undertaken in a careful yet undetectable manner, conveying a masked strength that is appropriate also to her gender role. Added to the tasks of public presentation all citizens, she faces another: remaining intently aware of the many possible dangers of public life. The logical extension of circumspection that is the fate of the over-alert game-player has been dealt with at length by Erving Goffman under the topic of "Where the Action Is" (see Goffman 1967:149-270).

Thus, women who attempt to be crime conscious, and simultaneously who are attempting to give the appearance of attractive and casual self-contained noninvolvement in public, understandably find it a strain simultaneously to prime themselves to run, scream, enter the nearest building, stand in a carefully considered "safe" spot, walk in the middle of the street with dignity, and refuse apparently innocent (and perhaps actually innocent) requests for aid, matches, and information. A woman can experience public places primarily as an exercise in self-defense, spoiling other possible gains.

Beyond admonishing women to take up a possibly burdensome menu of activities, the rhetoric of limited competence reinforces other negative informal social control women experience in public. As Radford (1987:43) suggests, a woman not seen to be controlled by one specific man in public can at will be controlled by any man. This informal control results in a wide scope of beliefs and actions by women, in response to the similarly wide band of behavior by men in public places that one writer has referred to as a "continuum of sexual violence" (Kelly 1987).

The experience of various types of negative control in public yields a situated self bounded in a neatly symbolic way by geography and site, as well as by circumstance and concern. Thus, beliefs about crime prevention could operate to keep women at home, where they are seen to be physically safer and less concerned with strategies of caution—and where, traditionally, they have belonged. And this social control exists outside public places, extending itself to poison major life decisions such as choosing a home as well as possibly occupying some part of her time in private with worry or with strategizing.

A further effect of crime-prevention beliefs is the portrait they paint of men. The felt obligation to behave in a crime-conscious manner can undermine, subtly or not so subtly, women's trust in the majority of quite innocent men whom women observe or with whom they come into contact in public places. Likewise, men conscious of women's fears in public will in part understand women's actions there according to how they find themselves reflected in women's behavior toward them.

In consequence, men sometimes may decide to go out of their way to appear innocent by, for example, conspicuously smiling and tipping a hat to a woman they pass in a run-down area or by ending any small piece of legitimate contact such as helping a woman open a door or manage a package with functional brevity and businesslike manner—all to communicate, in effect, that, though other males are suspected of harm they themselves are not and, furthermore, that they are sensitive enough to take the woman's point of view into consideration (Mehlman 1987). In this way, a man with no intention to fondle women in the subway reports placing his hands on a conspicuous subway pole to broadcast his innocence (Goffman 1971:38).

Other men who realize women's fears may exploit them short of the point of actual crime. Thus, most informants said they suspected any public approach by a man of having the nefarious as well as the innocent potential; all the more so can they suspect approaches, such as catcalls or pinches, that breach middle-class etiquette or enact conduct usually disapproved, such as following a woman for a block or two. It is important to appreciate that women's fear of crime in public places does not spoil public places for women alone, but that it also spoils, in some larger sense, men for women and women for men and public places for everyone.

Finally, although my analysis is one that treats all of these measures of crime prevention from the point of view of their possible effects on the situated self a woman presents in public places, my analysis is not meant to suggest, of course, that there are alternate strategies possible that would leave women in public places both safe and evidently self-possessed. Indeed, the concern of many of the women I interviewed—as well presumably as many of the women who read the popular literature on crime prevention—is to avoid the chance of rape or murder at the hands of unknown men who will assault them in public or follow them from public places to their homes. To analyze the character of the situated selves that these women believe and are told they must present in public in order to prevent crime is by no means to denigrate those beliefs and that advice: it is merely to note that along with those beliefs and advice comes what women themselves have sometimes noted to be sadly necessary measures.

References

Balkin, Steven
   1979   "Victimization rate, safety, and fear of crime." Social Problems 26:343-58.
Ball, Donald
   1965   "Sarcasm as sociation: the rhetoric of interaction." Canadian Review of Sociology and
            Anthropology 2:190-98.
   1967   "An abortion clinic ethnography." Social Problems 14:293-301.
Barthol, Robert
   1979   Protect Yourself. Englewood Cliffs, N.J.: Prentice-Hall.
Benton, Frances
   1956   Complete Etiquette. New York: Random House.
Berman, Clifford
   1980   "Crime. how not to be a victim." Good Housekeeping Magazine, September, 247.
Bertram, Camille M.
   1975   "Protection: how, when, where, and what to do." Harper's Bazaar Magazine, March, 83,
            131.
Benton, Frances
   1956   Complete Etiquette. New York: Random House.
Brown, Edward J., Timothy Flanagan, and Maureen McLeod (eds.)
   1984   Sourcebook of Criminal Justice Statistics—1983. Washington, D.C.: U.S. Government
            Printing Office.
Brunvand, Jan Harold
   1981   The Vanishing Hitchhiker: American Urban Legends and Their Meanings. New York:
            Norton.
Burg, Kathleen Keefe
   1979   The Womanly Art of Self-Defense. New York: A & W Visual Library.
Caughey, John L.
   1984   Imaginary Social Worlds. Lincoln, Neb.: University of Nebraska Press
Clemente, Frank, and Michael B. Kleiman
   1977   "Fear of crime in the United States: a multivariate analysis." Social Forces 56:519-31.
Dubow, Fred
   1979   Reactions to Crime: A Critical Review of the Literature. Washington, D.C.: U.S.
            Government Printing Office.
Duckett, Joy
   1982   "Rape prevention." Essence Magazine, September, 68.
Edmiston, Susan
   1973   "Up from cowardice." Redbook Magazine, August, 60-61, 162-63, 165.
Edwards, Audrey
   1982   "How three quick-thinking women escaped danger." Essence Magazine, September, 72.
Edwards, Susan
   1987   " 'Provoking her own demise'." In Women, Violence and Social Control, ed. Jalna
            Hanmer and Mary Maynard, 152-68. Atlantic Highlands, N.J.: Humanities.
Field, Jill Nevel
   1980   "Playing it safe: at home, on the street, in your car, on the bus or subway."
            Mademoiselle Magazine, September, 112, 120.
Gallatin, Dr. Martin
   1987   How to Be Married One Year from Today: Lover Shopping for Men and Women. New
            York: Shapolsky Publishers.
Gardner, Carol Brooks
   1980   "Passing by." Sociological Inquiry, 50:328-56.
   1983   "Aspects of gender behavior in public places in a small southwestern city." Unpublished
            Ph.D. dissertation, University of Pennsylvania.
   1988   "Access information: private lies and public peril." Social Problems 35:384-97.
   1989   Analyzing Gender in Public Places: Re-thinking Goffman's Vision of Everyday Life.
            American Sociologist 20:42-56.

1990   "Kinship claims and competence claims: people with disabilities in public places." Paper
        to be given at American Sociological Association annual meeting, Washington, D.C.
Geng, Veronica
1971   "Scorn not the street compliment!" In Cosmopolitan's New Etiquette Guide, ed. Helen
        Gurley Brown, 75-79. North Hollywood, Calif.: Wilshire Book Company.
Gieseking, Hal
1980   "Special report: summer criminals." Travel/Holiday Magazine, June, 77-78.
Glamour Magazine
1980   "Should you carry a personal alarm?" March, 63.
Goffman, Erving
1961   Asylums. Chicago: Aldine.
1963   Behavior in Public Places. Glencoe, Ill.: Free Press.
1967   "Where the action is." In Interaction Ritual, 149-270. Garden City, N.Y.: Doubleday.
1971   Relations in Public. New York: Basic Books.
1973   Presentation of Self in Everyday Life Woodstock, N.Y.: Overlook Press.
Good Housekeeping Magazine
1972   "Street-safety precautions every woman should follow," October, 193.
Grahame, Kamini Maraj
1985   "Sexual harassment." In No Safe Place, ed. Connie Guberman and Margie Wolfe, 111-30.
        Toronto: Women's Press.
Griffith, Liddon R.
1978   Mugging: You Can Protect Yourself. Englewood Cliffs, N.J.: Prentice-Hall.
Hair, Robert A., and Samm Sinclair Baker
1970   How to Protect Yourself Today. New York: Stein and Day.
Hanmer, Jalna, and Sheila Saunders
1983   "Blowing the cover of the protective male: a community study of violence to women."
        In The Public and the Private, ed. Eva Gamarnikow, Meg Stacey, Linda Imray, Audrey
        Middleton, Jalna Hanmer, Sheila Saunders, Patricia Allatt, Claire Ungerson, Ann
        Murcott, Marilyn Porter, Janet Finch, Peter Rushton, Hilary Graham, Laura McKee, and
        Margaret O'Brien. London: Heinemann.
Heath, Linda
1984   "Impact of newspaper crime reports on fear of crime: multimethodological
        investigation." Journal of Personality and Social Psychology 47:263-76.
Hechinger, Grace
1984   How to Raise a Street-Smart Child. New York: Facts on File.
Hindelang, Michael J., Michael R. Gottfredson, and James Garofalo
1978   The Victims of Personal Crime. Cambridge, Mass.: Ballinger.
Ingber, Dina
1987   "Staying safe: the smart woman's guide to self-defense." McCall's Magazine, March,138,
        140, 142.
Janoff-Bulman, Ronnie, and Irene Hanson Frieze
1987   "The role of gender in reactions to criminal victimization." In Gender and Stress, ed.
        Rosalind C. Barnett, Lois Biener, and Grace K. Baruch, 159-84. New York: Free Press.
Kaye, Elizabeth
1985   "Preventing robbery and rape." Harper's Bazaar Magazine, April, 72, 74.
Kelly, Liz
1987   "The continuum of sexual violence." In Women, Violence, and Social Control, ed. Jalna
        Hanmer and Mary Maynard, 46-60. Atlantic Highlands, N.J.: Humanities.
Krupp, Charla
1978   "Solving your problem: 84 ways to feel safer." Mademoiselle Magazine, October, 142-43,
        146, 152.
Ledray, Linda E.
1986   Recovering from Rape. New York: Holt.
Martin, Judith
1982   Miss Manners' Guide to Excruciatingly Correct Behavior. New York: Atheneum.

328   GARDNER

Maxfield, Michael G.
    1984   The limits of vulnerability in explaining fear of crime: a comparative neighbornood
            analysis." Research in Crime and Delinquency 21:233-50.
Mehlman, Peter
    1987   "Male guilt." Glamour, April, 332.
Monkerud, Donald, and Mary Heiny
    1980   Self-Defense for Women. Dubuque, Ia.: William C. Brown.
Navarro, Mireya
    1990   "For busy storeowner, nearby protests have raised fear of misunderstanding." The New
            York Times, May 17.
O'Connor, Dr. Margaret, and Dr. Jane Silverman
    1989   Finding Love: Creative Strategies for Finding Your Ideal Mate New York: Crown.
Pickering, Michael C. V.
    1983   A Manual for Women's Self-Defense. North Palm Beach, Fla.: The Athletic Institute.
Post, Elizabeth L.
    1969   Emily Post's Etiquette. New York: Funk & Wagnalls.
Radford, Jill
    1987   "Policing male violence—policing women." In Women, Violence, and Social Control, ec
            Jalna Hanmer and Mary Maynard, 30-45. Atlantic Highlands, N.J.: Humanities.
Riger, Stephanie, and Margaret T. Gordon
    1981   The fear of rape: a study in social control." Journal of Social Issues 37:71-92.
Rockwood, Marcia, and Mary Thom
    1979   "Making your block, office, parking lot, community rape-proof." Ms. Magazine, March,
            79-82.
Schraub, Susan
    1979   "Bazaar's anti-rape handbook." Harper's Bazaar Magazine, March, 152-53, 169.
Scribner, Marilyn
    1988   Free to Fight Back. Wheaton, Ill.: Harold Shaw.
Sims, Calvin
    1990   "Black shoppers call Korean merchants hostile and unfair." The New York Times, May
            17.
Sommerfield, Diana
    1986   Single, Straight Men: 106 Guaranteed Places to Find Them. New York: St. Martin's.
Tegner, Bruce
    1965   Bruce Tegner's Complete Book of Self-Defense. New York: Bantam.
Today's Health Magazine
    1973   "What a scream can do for you " June, 29-33, 64.
Vanderbilt, Amy
    1972   Amy Vanderbilt's Etiquette. Garden City, N.Y.: Doubleday.
Wachs, Eleanor
    1988   Crime-Victim Stories. Bloomington, Ind.: Indiana University Press.
Wegman, James
    1978   "How to be safe on the streets." Glamour, September, 57.
Wheeler, Elizabeth
    1982   "Protecting yourself." Essence Magazine, September, 69.
Wilson, Julie
    1977   "How to protect yourself." Harper's Bazaar Magazine, March, 93, 151.
Zimmerman, Mary K.
    1981   "The abortion clinic." In Social Psychology through Symbolic Interaction, ed. Gregory P
            Stone and Harvey A. Farberman, 43-52. New York: Wiley.

[4]

BRIT. J. CRIMINOL. VOL. 37 NO. 3 SUMMER 1997

BOYS DON'T CRY

Masculinities, Fear of Crime and Fearlessness

Jo Goodey*

The gendered stereotypes of 'fearless male/fearful female' are not supported by the reality of complex and multiple identities and the shifting meanings of fear and fearlessness which are brought to and evolve from these identities. Referring to evidence from the author's own research, childhood and adolescence are put forward as crucial stages in identity development where one can begin to unpack the processes by which gendered meanings of fear and fearlessness become 'fixed'. This paper argues that the image of the 'fearless' male, from childhood onwards, is not a helpful one. The benefits to the male sex from taking on a 'fearless' persona, alongside its negative social implications, are discussed with reference to hegemonic masculinity. Class and race are put forward as significant variables in the development of hegemonic masculinity's emotionally inarticulate persona and racism is highlighted as one of the ugliest expressions of exaggerated masculinity. The above is placed and developed within the theoretical context of the 'hegemonic masculine biography'.

The central concern of this paper is boys' emotional illiteracy which damages them as individuals, as a group and as part of society. It triggers a form of masculine bravado or fearlessness which can, in turn, display itself as reactive aggression against the self (the denial of one's own vulnerability) and others in the display of verbally and physically aggressive acts. Working with theoretical and everyday developments of adolescent masculinity formation can begin to highlight this field of study as an important arena for investigation. This is particularly the case for criminology, which is centrally concerned with the aftermath of taking on a negative masculine identity; that is, criminology focuses on exaggerated masculinities in the form of anti-social and criminal activities by adolescent and adult males.

Criminology's focus on the negative outcomes of exaggerated masculinities (street crime, white-collar crime, racism etc.) needs to be developed theoretically beyond an examination of these outcomes. Research should look into the processes and events surrounding the individual male's transition into the potentially criminal and 'fearless' persona. While various theories from anomie, subcultural studies and psychoanalysis have offered explanations for criminal and anti-social behaviour, the processes by which boys can become criminal men demand contextualization within what it is to become and be male in its various guises; that is, in the context of the individual's class, race, age and sexuality (to name but a few). Examination of 'growing up male' through research on childhood, adolescence and masculinities can present criminology with a solid base from which well-established and reworked 'facts' (e.g. most crime is committed by males) can be readdressed and reinterpreted. This paper attempts to

*Centre for Criminal Justice Studies, University of Leeds.

JO GOODEY

connect these elements, which are often regarded as disparate elements, to present a discussion on 'masculinities, fear of crime and fearlessness'.

Focusing on a few key writers, the paper will present a theoretical appraisal of the most useful roads to understanding the development of apparent male fearlessness in adolescence; the proviso being that boys can and do experience crime and danger as anything on a continuum from fearful to fearless. This continuum of experience stems from everyday social interactions which, in turn, are shaped by internal meanings which the individual attaches to these events; meanings which are not only to be interpreted on the level of what we say and do, but must be understood alongside what is left unsaid and the wider discourse of power relations. Hegemonic masculinity (Connell 1987), as a dominant reading of the dynamics of male power relations, will form the foundation of the paper in the context of multiple masculine identities.

A central focus of the paper is the author's research on the socialization of adolescents' gendered fear of crime. Though inadvertent, since the research was primarily concerned with the development of girls' fear, it serves to highlight the neglected arena of boys' fear, which is progressively downplayed as normative adult identities are adopted (Goodey 1996). In recognition of this, the paper will incorporate a few findings on boys' fear and fearlessness from the author's research which have sparked this current interest.[1] The findings will be discussed in the context of theoretical developments stemming from hegemonic masculinity to the author's own (tentative) adaptation of these theoretical insights in the form of the 'hegemonic masculine biography' (see below). Finally, the paper will suggest avenues for future research which should set forward more concrete responses to some of the ideas forwarded here.

Towards the 'Hegemonic Masculine Biography' as Theoretical Framework

The process by which boys learn to adopt the 'fearless façade' of exaggerated masculinity needs contextualizing within what I will refer to here as the 'hegemonic masculine biography'. This term needs explanation within the context of definitions of masculinity/femininity and the theory of hegemonic masculinity. A basic understanding of these theoretical ideas will present a framework from which the author's findings can be more usefully read.

What it is to be 'a man' or become 'a man' is something which is often reduced to that which is not female or feminine. One can turn to definitions which present quintessential differences between what it is to be male and female and offer a standard by which the individual can be judged as appropriately masculine or feminine. Those of us who are able to meet the criteria of the 'norm' are few and far between. The problem with attempts to define what it is to be 'male' is that definitions are not always useful or helpful while they tend to fall into the trap of essentialism; that is, understanding of 'maleness' often assumes the existence of inner distinctive qualities that are *not* feminine, without the articulation of what these qualities are beyond mere outward appearances. For example, the popular understanding of 'maleness' is *still* constricted within the idea that 'boys don't cry' (Sparks 1996) without any real

[1] This paper was developed from earlier papers presented at the 1995 British Criminology Conference (Loughborough) and the 1995 American Society of Criminology Conference (Boston).

BOYS DON'T CRY

interpretation of this stereotype and its accuracy. Normative definitions present limited social constructions of masculinity which cannot cope with the reality of a multiplicity of masculinities and the influence of an individual's personality on what it is to be male.

For the purposes of this paper, masculinity, as experienced by the individual, is best understood as being anywhere on a continuum from what is traditionally perceived as feminine or masculine. The fearful or fearless experience of crime and danger while, by definition, at different ends of a continuum of fear, can no longer be viewed as gendered experience. In turn, each individual's many experiences of fear and fearlessness shift back and forth along the fear continuum according to meta discourses in the lifecourse such as ageing and parenthood which are part of the individual's personal biography. In other words, the old man re-enters the 'fearful' stage of early childhood (Pain 1995) and the man as father can become acutely conscious of his child's vulnerability and his own vulnerability within the social construct of his role as male 'protector' (Valentine 1997). Similarly, the individual's fear level is influenced by his circumstantial feelings of vulnerability which are affected by a range of factors such as being alone or in a group (safety in numbers; Anderson *et al.* 1994) or whether it is dark or light outside (fear of the dark alleyway: Painter 1991). On top of these diverse and shifting influences upon the individual's experiences of fear are the relatively 'fixed' categories of sex, race, class and sexuality.

Opening up the diversity of individual experiences across the hour, the day and the lifecourse (Hockey and James 1993) is extremely useful when attempting to understand what the differential 'masculine' experience of fear and fearlessness is. However, interpreting what it is to become a 'fearless' man at the level of the individual fails to come to terms with the underlying social structures which inform the individual experience. Presented in normative or essentialist terms, ideas on gender and masculinity are removed from the complexity of relations acting between, within and upon these categories. An understanding of patriarchy can enlighten interpretation of gendered experience and oppression, but, as Connell states (1995: 76), 'To understand gender, then, we must constantly go beyond gender.' In other words, masculinity cannot be viewed only in opposition to femininity, but must be understood also in relation to other signifiers of oppression; namely class, race, age and sexuality.

Hegemonic masculinity presents just such a hierarchy of oppression in reference to how western, white, middle-class, heterosexual and 'thirty-something' masculinity is placed at the top of this hierarchy of privileged masculinities. In a somewhat idealistic reading (reminiscent of subcultural studies: Hall and Jefferson 1976) working-class masculinity, ethnic minority masculinity and homosexuality are viewed as marginalized or subordinated by hegemonic masculinity in relation to the dominant masculinity. And, while few men practice at the top of a hegemonic masculine pile, the majority of men reap the benefits of this system in relation to the overall subordination of women. As feminism (Dobash and Dobash 1979; Kelly 1988) has taught us, the action of some men, as rapists and wife-beaters, has kept the majority of women 'in their place' for fear of becoming the victim of male aggression. Similarly, hegemonic masculinity has kept the majority of men 'in their place' for fear of the repercussions that might ensue from having been defined as 'feminine'. Hegemonic masculinity teaches boys to be careful about expressing feelings of vulnerability (i.e. to whom and when; that is, if they feel able to or indeed are aware of such feelings in the first place).

JO GOODEY

In presenting a hierarchy of masculinities, hegemonic masculinity is in danger of being interpreted as a bounded catalogue of masculinities which fit neatly on top of one another. The beauty of social groups is that they defy any such categorization. One cannot think in terms of '*the* working class' or '*the* Afro-Caribbean' in the case of British society. Rather, one should be thinking of the interplay of masculinities with their intra-class and intra-ethnic variations which generate complex identities. Nowhere is this complexity of categorization more readily illustrated than in studies of school students. Mac an Ghaill's (1994) school research illustrates this point superbly as he refers to the diverse range of feelings and experiences of boys from similar socio-economic and ethnic backgrounds. Using multi-layered and shifting categories of masculinities can push understanding beyond the essentialist assumptions of what it is to be 'a man' and, in doing so, one can begin to unpack masculine experiences of fear. While the author's own research findings are limited to white, working-class adolescents in one place and at one time, the hierarchical posturings within this group emerge as complex and diverse and, therefore, ripe for assessment in the context of hegemonic masculinity theory.

When adopting hegemonic masculinity as a useful theoretical base from which research findings on masculinities can be interpreted, other theories must also be acknowledged as providing potential sources for understanding the processes by which boys *become* men. Elements of sex role theory and psychoanalysis can be very useful in providing a diverse range of understandings on what it is to become male or female. However, it is the underlying theme of children's unproblematic transition into their appropriate gender roles as presented by sex role theory (Parsons and Bales 1956) and classical psychoanalysis, which has been critiqued for its concern with construction of the gender archetype. These theories' concerns with the processes of conforming to one's gender have largely been surmounted by critical analysis of gender 'identity' construction which more usefully recognizes the complex and frequently difficult transition the child has towards expected adult norms.[2]

While sex role theory and (particularly) psychoanalysis can also be criticized for their neglect of the influence of social power structures on the individual, so hegemonic masculinity can be accused of presenting a monolithic interpretation of power relations (Horrocks 1994). Perhaps the most useful approach to be undertaken in any study of masculinities, fear of crime and fearlessness, is one which combines elements of the most 'useful' of these theories (such as Adler's (1927) 'masculine protest'—see footnote 2), while remaining conscious of the negative aspects of each. However, I would support the underlying incorporation of hegemonic masculinity theory into the above theories, as it presents a critique of current masculinity in relation to questions of social justice. In comparison, and as a reaction to its distortion of much of the feminist and social

---

[2] While largely rejecting sex role theory as a useful tool, Connell (1995) pays particular attention to Adler's psychoanalytic (1927) work on the 'masculine protest'. Adler saw this 'protest' as active in both normal and neurotic mental life as an over-compensation for the childhood experience of powerlessness; a protest displayed in aggression. Protest masculinity is most usefully interpreted, in the context of this paper, with reference to Connell's (1995: 111) comments on the powerlessness of working class males, ethnic minority males and, most significantly here, youth: 'the growing boy puts together a tense, freaky façade, making a claim to power where there are no real resources for power.' The radical psychoanalysis of Adler is also useful because it brings the social, in the form of gendered powerlessness, into an understanding of the individual's resultant protest.

BOYS DON'T CRY

justice debate, I am hesitant to take the 'men's movement' on board in any constructive discussion of masculinities.[3]

In consideration of what it is to *be* 'male' within the power dynamics of hegemonic masculinity, theoretical interpretation has to turn to what it is to *become* male. The 'hegemonic masculine biography', as an idea, posits the period of late childhood/early adolescence as crucial towards an understanding of fear/fearlessness development. The 'hegemonic masculine biography' demands detailed insight into the individual's experiences and everyday interactions with regard to their stated, understated or unstated meanings as stages for the enactment or expression of potential fear scenarios. The biography would speak for the individual but would be positioned in the wider context of lifecourse concerns and the demands of hegemonic masculinity. Internal and external meanings of the fear/fearlessness continuum could be encapsulated in the detail of the focused biography with the recognition that the individual is influenced by social structures which, in turn, are shaped by the individual. As a research tool, the biography could go some way towards an integrative examination of public, private and internal influences upon masculine identity development (the possibility for incorporating insights from the traditionally unhappy bedfellows of social science research and psychoanalysis is an agenda which the 'hegemonic masculine biography' could examine).

'Biography' is primarily useful because it accommodates lifecourse changes. While the ideal biography would follow an individual's development throughout their life, the biography as a social science research tool is not (normally) afforded this luxury. Researchers must usually be content with brief glimpses into boys' lives over a few weeks/months; this can also be combined with insights into boys' brief life histories (to date). The diverse masculine biography is effectively constructed with the cross-referencing of findings from boys of different age, class and race as they progress through the significant years of adolescence. There is no one collective masculine biography to speak of but, rather, a series of biographies. What research can look for are shared experiences of fear and fearlessness which can begin to divulge the meaning of what it is to become a 'fearless' male during the period of late childhood/early adolescence. Biography also describes the diverse experiences and meanings of masculine fear/fearlessness within micro (through to) macro arenas of change; that is, from the individual's daily encounters to the fluid meanings assigned these encounters in social history.

In other words, the young adolescent male may avoid confrontation with a rowdy group of his peers by crossing the road; this (micro) action will be assigned meaning in the context of the boy's own personal biography of risk avoidance and fear assessment,

---

[3] In reference to the 'men's movement', one can briefly refer to Horrocks's (1994: 91) book *Masculinity in Crisis*, in which he discusses exaggerated masculinity or 'hypermasculinity'. Horrocks rightly states that while men and women display elements of masculinity and femininity, 'men are constantly vigilant and repressive towards their own femininity'. However, Horrocks then goes on to bemoan the number of men who have not expressed their feminine side through writing and art, but he fails to mention that if asked to name famous writers/artists (etc.) most of us would name men. What Horrocks appears to be displaying is a limited interpretation of the pervasive power of hegemonic masculinity. Referring earlier in the paper to boys' 'emotional damage' one cannot deny the power behind emotional silence. Displaying aggression and an absence of fear and vulnerability can work to boys' and men's benefit; it does not automatically put them into the category of victim. However, enthusiasts of the 'men in crisis' movement seem conveniently to categorize men as 'victims' in the face of well-worn feminist debate while claiming, at the same time, that they do not intend to upstage women's position as 'the oppressed'.

JO GOODEY

while the group can consciously and subconsciously interpret his action in relation to
the influence their own masculine status and action has as a group and as individuals
who make up the group. Important to this interpretation of events is the relevance of
the following (among other things): whether those involved in such an encounter
already have a shared biography of experience (i.e. whether they are strangers or
acquaintances); the significance this encounter and the accumulation of ones like it will
hold over time for the individual, the group and the individuals who make up the group;
and the (macro) impact such experiences will have on the biographies of people who
experience such events second hand (i.e. witnesses, friends). The multiple and complex
layers of interpretation one can place on such events, with regard to their significance
in relation to the development of individual 'hegemonic masculine biographies' under
the shared umbrella of hegemonic masculinity, are too numerous to speculate upon
here. In-depth interpretation of individual experiences necessitates 'real' life examples
which the current study does not possess. At this stage of developing the theoretical
relevance of the 'hegemonic masculine biography' to fear and fearlessness, one can only
acknowledge that the meanings attached to boys' experiences and emotions are both
relationally hierarchical and shifting with time.

Translating the above into a practical assessment of hegemonic masculinity's
ascendance into adolescent 'fearlessness' is a difficult task. Mac an Ghaill's work on
masculinities, sexuality and schooling notes the fluidity of masculine/feminine
meanings as reflections of individual and institutional discourses. 'There was a certain
contextual fluidity in the construction of ascribed meanings that mediated the
institutional signifiers of what it means to be masculine or feminine within the school
and across other sites' (1994: 93). One could add that the shifting status of masculine
meanings is something which the white, privileged boy can afford; for example, he can
support the black footballer and, occasionally, he can feign the effeminacy of the
homosexual for the sake of peer group amusement. Similarly, the black or Asian boy
can adopt the norms of the dominant, white culture, *but* he tends only to practise his
racial and ethnic diversity if it is currently favoured by the dominant culture's normative
masculinity; e.g. black rap music. To step outside the realms of acceptable masculinity
is to endanger oneself as an atypical male. However, the extent to which the individual
boy is constrained to adopt his appropriate masculinity (and the extent to which his
brand of masculinity proves useful to him with regard to other males and females) is
open to discussion.

With this theoretical framework in mind, the paper can turn to some findings from
the author's research which begin to highlight the extent and complexity of young male
fear and fearlessness during childhood and early adolescence.

Boys' Fear of Crime and Fearlessness—Inserting the 'Hegemonic Masculine Biography'

My own work on children's gendered fear of public place crime, while focusing on girls,
provides a wealth of empirical research on the subject of boys' fear and fearlessness.
The research took place in a north of England school on an edge-of-town state housing
scheme and incorporated the use of focused single sex discussion sessions and a
questionnaire survey of 663 children. The school has a homogeneous population of
white, working class 11 to 16-year-olds, whose area, while not having the worst

BOYS DON'T CRY

reputation in the city, does possess a 'bad name'. However, the school and the estate were not selected on the basis of a reputation or a crime rate, but were chosen because the school was accessible and the local population presented a sample base from which to examine the variable 'gender', free from class or ethnic variance. While the absence of class and ethnic variation in the fear 'equation' can be readily critiqued (see below), one can use the research findings as a base from which to develop future empirical and theoretical research initiatives on the subject of childhood fear, gender and masculinities in relation to multiple class/race experiences.

Turning to a version of the classic victimization survey question: 'Have you been worried or has something made you feel "on edge" when outside?', the research questionnaire revealed (unsurprisingly in light of research findings from numerous victim surveys such as the British Crime Survey, the Islington Crime Survey, the Edinburgh Crime Survey, the US National Crime Survey and *specifically* surveys on children by Anderson *et al.* 1994 and Hartless *et al.* 1994) that more girls (72 per cent) than boys (46 per cent)[4] were worried when outside in public places. The interesting point here is not the obvious finding that more girls revealed fear than boys, but that boys *revealed* fear at all. With a breakdown of the results by age, one is able to see that at age 11 *more* boys (72 per cent) were worried outside than girls (57 per cent). However, from age 12, girls' fear outstripped boys' and, for both sexes, fear declined with age.

Taking statistical findings at face value is a dangerous research exercise and, with respect to the above findings, can obscure what respondents really think and do. A researcher's attention can easily be drawn to the unimportant as a reflection of what was not asked in the questions rather than what was. Consequently, the above can simply reveal the obvious *or* it can make us ask why boys' fear is higher than girls' fear at age 11 and, that being the case, why boys' fear dramatically tails off, in comparison with girls' fear, through adolescence. Again, these may seem like obvious responses to the above, but the central question, 'Why aren't boys and young men more afraid of crime?', needs asking; particularly when one considers their high risk of becoming a victim of assault.

Reflecting on this question and turning to extracts from discussions held with boys, evidence can be drawn from the research which begins to piece together the multiple and complex influences upon boys' expression of fear and fearlessness as a reflection of their gender, age, ethnicity and class. The degree to which this process is shaped by the respondents' collective upbringing in a white, working class, northern community is open to discussion. The 'collective' biography of hegemonic masculinity *can* be viewed as a meta-narrative for explaining gendered structures of power (much like patriarchy) which, in turn, *can* be broken down into its component parts (class, race, age, sexuality etc.) for a more focused reading of group experiences of what it is to be male and to become male in a certain place at a certain time. However, the 'hegemonic masculine biography' is a more useful tool when attempting to explain and make connections between discourses of masculine power and powerlessness in relation to *individual experience over time*. The following quotes offer a glimpse of what it is to become 'a man' for each member of this particular group of boys:

---

[4] The research employed the chi-square test and looked for statistical significance at the 95 per cent confidence level and above. The statistics cited in this paper were occurring at the 99.9 per cent confidence level and were, therefore, highly significant.

JO GOODEY

Do you think there's any age when you will feel less scared or worried?
Late teens.
When I'm adult.
14 . . .
What I mean is like physically when I'm an adult.
[Boys aged 12–13]

When do you think you might feel safer?
[asked after a discussion on intra-male aggression and bullying]
I'd say 17 'cos I think if someone's just like left school they know they wanna think they're a man.
[Boy aged 15–16]

These quotes reveal the 'hegemonic masculine biography' as boys perceive it; or, at least, in terms of what boys will articulate to the researcher during an interview session. It is a biography in which becoming an adult means becoming less fearful or, rather, showing less fear (note the use of the word '*think*' in the second quote). This process is clearly defined in terms of age, which can either denote the physical transition to adulthood and increased strength or the social transition into the non-childlike state of school-leaver. What is interesting here is the relative 'sameness' of the response themes by the younger and older boys. However, what this actually 'says' is somewhat harder to interpret, beyond the collective meanings attached by society and adolescent boys to attaining adulthood, that is (among other things) age and strength.

Each boy gives a separate response to the questions posed, with the age and signifier with which one becomes a man variously defined. With each different response the boys are working out their own particular experience and relationship to becoming 'a man' (their own particular hegemonic masculine biography), in relation to the responses of the rest of the group, which are often modified on hearing what someone else has to say. This dialogue is a necessary tool for learning and adaptation to 'adulthood', but cannot be simplistically viewed as a constraining process by which boys must be beholden to their peers; rather the process can also be seen as a right of passage which is enthusiastically undertaken. As the following discussion quote illustrates, boys are very aware of the demands on their masculinity in relation to girls and the uptake of a certain machismo. However, even in the discussion's transcribed form, one is able to decipher the enthusiasm with which these boys concede to their 'fate' (Willis 1977) of 'becoming male'.

I think they're [girls] right.
[in respect of being told that the girls accuse them of affecting a macho image]
You've got to give the woman some self-assurance haven't you? I mean, if somebody's walking behind you, you don't go 'Oh!—there's somebody coming!' You don't run off do you. You gotta stand there. You try and create an image.
Stand your ground.
[Boys aged 15–16]

The anonymity of the questionnaire was frequently able to reveal the pervasiveness of boys' fear beyond the constraints of peer group discussions (above), where the need for a show of masculine bravado frequently emerged. In contrast to the requirement to become 'a man' (age 17) and with the needs (real or imagined) of girls to consider, the questionnaire found that roughly three-quarters of girls *and* boys could admit that

BOYS DON'T CRY

'drunks' and 'druggies' worried them when out and about, while 48 per cent of boys and 28 per cent of girls specified 'older boys' as a similar category for concern. However, the startling three-quarters figure for 'drunks' and 'druggies' needs contextualizing by the recognition that these groups pose the atypical threat or 'folk devil' as a source of fear. It is hardly surprising that so many respondents, both girls and boys, felt able to declare their fear of the 'bogeyman'. What is more interesting, when comparing the dialogue of masculine bravado in the majority of discussion sessions with the findings of the questionnaire, is the fact that boys declared a greater fear of 'older boys' than did girls through the medium of the questionnaire and that this fear remained skewed in favour of boys' greater fear levels at all ages. However, as with all the questionnaire's categories of people, 'things' and occasions to be afraid, the numbers expressing fear, anxiety or concern declined for *both sexes* with age. The fact that both girls and boys experience an overall decline in levels of fear with increased age could be posited as a form of shared biographical journey as one enters adulthood. While the evidence here indicates that this decline is most definitely a gendered experience, the degree to which this apparent 'fearlessness' is shaped by the respondents' class and race can only be guessed at in relation to the experiences of other groups (for example; white, middle class adolescents or Afro-Caribbean, working class adolescents).

In consideration of the questionnaire's findings on boys' high levels of fear of 'older boys', one has to contextualize the adolescent male, particularly when hanging around in a group in public places, as frequently construed in the popular imagination as a milder form of 'folk devil' than the street drunk or druggie. To be labelled 'folk devil' the adolescent male usually has to be noted as causing an affray, while the drunk or druggie just has to 'be'. For boys to admit to feelings of fear towards an 'ordinary' group (that is, other boys) would seem to indicate the damaging extent of intra-male adolescent threat posed by older boy to younger boy. Perhaps what the above does reveal is the pervasiveness of bullying among boys in adolescence, with older boys (the oldest being young men) employing their superior strength. In an attempt to relate hegemonic masculine theory to the research findings, one can only speculate that what seems to be on display here is the lived reality of hegemonic masculinity which is operating at an intra-sex and intra-class level; the determinates of hegemony being age and strength among this group of boys who share a class, race and community background. At the individual level, the number of confrontational and aggressive encounters a boy has while growing up will shape his own experience and understanding of crime and fear in the context of his own personal 'hegemonic masculine biography'.

If any category of male is to be placed at the bottom of hegemonic masculinity's hierarchy, it is the boy. One could argue that the 'western child' comes above the 'developing world man' in the world's social order (although the man still has the advantage of superior strength—the weapon similarly threatened and used against women in the patriarchal order); however, in relation to the current research, this is not a central consideration. What has to be considered is the relative position of white, working class boys vis-à-vis the rest of white dominated society. While these boys do not suffer the marginalization of ethnic minority boys, they are on the lowest rung in terms of their class. Becoming men will advantage these boys, to some extent, over their youthful selves, but this has to be put in the context of the economic and social position they find themselves in now and will find themselves in in the foreseeable future. 'What future?' is the opportune question here, as it encapsulates the world of the

JO GOODEY

unemployment queue and life on a 'dead-end' estate for the majority of the boys in this research (Campbell 1993: youth in the 1990s, and particularly working class male youth, is relatively undervalued or redundant in economic and consumerist terms when compared with the 'golden age' of youth in the 1960s). The adolescent males in my research had yet to (if at all) attain the status of 'valued masculinity'. With this in mind, the dominant expression of male fearlessness which these boys tended to adopt for potentially threatening situations or people (*except* 'older boys') can be interpreted (once again) on a number of levels.

At its extreme, 'fearlessness' can be expressed as physical aggression among working-class boys in their attempt to assert their masculinity. In comparison, middle-class boys, while also having to take on the masculine criteria of fearlessness, are able to and tend to project their masculine hegemony through different channels, such as academic success, and, therefore, are able to avoid the arena of physical aggression to which working-class boys can be reduced (Willis 1977). 'Crimes in the street' also pose an opening for the expression of working-class masculinity (Jefferson 1994), as a reflection of having to prove one's fearlessness as a man ('crime of the suites' being a middle-class privilege: Box 1983); however, one can argue that property crime (in general) primarily occurs because of economic necessity. Commenting on class constraints upon masculinity development, Messerschmidt (1994: 82) states: 'Young men situationally accomplish public forms of masculinity in response to their socially structured circumstances; indeed, varieties of youth crime serve as a suitable resource for doing masculinity when other resources are unavailable.' When Messerschmidt comments on 'socially structured circumstances', it must be remembered that the individual's experience of 'becoming male' within this framework is not (necessarily) a constricting and negative process.

The personal and group damage which results in having to become 'a man' or 'doing masculinity' when limited alternatives are available has a significant social impact in terms of crime and anti-social behaviour. But, 'opposition masculinities' as Messerschmidt (1993) calls the above, or 'protest masculinity' against 'the feminine', as discussed by Adler (1927), have their advantages in informing and shaping the boys' place in relation to other subordinated masculinities, girls and women. Being seen to be 'fearless' (not admitting that you are scared when you find yourself walking home followed by a group of 'lads') is *not* a negative undertaking in terms of hegemonic masculinity. Sattel (1992) argues that male inexpressiveness is of no cultural value on its own but is essential to the assumption of male power. Emotional inarticulateness, Sattel suggests, is not simply the product of biology or socialization, but is the intentional manipulation of situations where threats to the male position occur. In other words, adolescent boys can actively decide not to offer their feelings of fear and vulnerability to each other (and their mothers, girlfriends etc.), in order to retain some semblance of control and power in relation to others. The fearlessness displayed by the boys in my research can be viewed as their necessary tool against being labelled a 'girl', a 'sissy', or a 'poof'.[5]

---

[5] The development of a fearless bravado can also mean the very real or imagined role of 'protector' (one can only speculate without evidence from those who are supposedly protected) regarding the individual male's girlfriend, sister or Mum; however, old-fashioned male chivalry has to be placed in its patriarchal frame.

BOYS DON'T CRY

Girls' feminine identity comes to identify them as the potential victims of crimes which are perceived as specific to them (sexual assault and rape), while boys learn to adopt a sense of fearlessness or machismo (alongside their growing physical strength) in the development of their masculine identity. It is not necessarily the case that fear in certain places regarding certain people's potential actions does reduce with age, rather it could be the case that the individual simply accepts and essentially 'hides' fear. Boys' fear is effectively internalized with age, as a form of coping strategy against the rigorous onset of the hegemonic masculine demands of adulthood.

One can postulate that a sense of vulnerability and (hence) fear is heightened during early adolescence as physical strength, particularly for boys, is not available yet. Also, one might add, adolescents have not accumulated the practical coping strategies against fear and danger which (some) adults are afforded; for example, the luxury of travelling by car instead of walking. By age 15–16 the adolescents in my research, with particular regard to their socio-economic background (white and working class), are young adults who have gained a degree of self-assurance which, it can be suggested, is reflected in their declining levels of fear. However, while their fear has declined this does not equate with their vulnerability to and risk of victimization.

Older boys from the research (however) *did* occasionally let their fears be known during discussion sessions, though admitting any sense of vulnerability is most often accomplished as a form of joking banter within all male groups. In comparison, girls' revelations of feeling afraid are not (in general) couched in easy to swallow terms for the rest of the group. However, having said this, I do not want to reduce the research findings to a polarized depiction of gendered behaviour, with girls as 'the fearful' and boys as 'the fearless'. As the following quote illustrates, girls can have their own form of aggressive reaction to crime and fear of crime which (here) is legitimated in this particular girl's biography of having lived on the research's (notorious) estate for the duration of her life; a fact which can hold true for the majority of the research's interviewees.

Crime does not worry me! I don't care about who breaks the law and who doesn't. It doesn't bother me one little bit. I suppose I have got used to it by now as I have lived on [the estate] 15 years.
[Girl aged 15]

In comparison, the following quotes from boys aged 15 and 16 appear to both confirm and confront the 'fearless' stereotype of the late adolescent male.

I wouldn't go round there [estate with a bad reputation in the city] 'cos of drugs and that.
It's too bad [above estate]. It's like people walk round just start on you for now't. Say like you're walking past someone, they'll say like 'You come here, did you just call me a name?' Something like that.
[Boys aged 15–16]

I'd go anywhere [on their estate]. I'd go through all of them [places on map] though I don't like 'em.
I'd go all over the place.
I'd go anywhere.
[Boys aged 15–16]

This confirmation and confrontation of 'fearlessness' is accomplished within the frame (as with the girl above) of legitimation "*cos of drugs and that*' and the peer group banter of storytelling '*say you're like walking past someone*'. It is the 'tough' language (at least to

JO GOODEY

the boys' ears) of the second quote which more readily suggests that any admittance of fear is a complex process of negotiation for late adolescent boys in a peer group setting. Only the phrase *'though I don't like 'em'* alerts the reader to the suggestion that these boys are living and playing up to the part of becoming or, in their particular cases, practically being an adult male in the context of white, working-class masculinity aged 15 and 16.

In the above extracts hegemonic masculinity reduces to the 'pecking order' or the internal hierarchy of the discussion group. That is, dominant characters who do not readily admit feelings of fear tend to dictate the form of the group discussion. Boys admit to and yet do not admit to feelings of vulnerability which they rapidly cover up behind them or which are swallowed up by the collective group ethos of exaggerated masculinity. It would appear that the individual's 'hegemonic masculine biography' is only briefly glimpsed in the course of the group discussion, through storytelling and general banter which legitimates the individual's particular experiences. The collective group biography and the exaggerated masculine biography of white, working-class masculinity tend to subsume individual difference in the setting of these discussion groups (one could add that displays of exaggerated masculinity are particularly important for older boys when faced with a young, female researcher; after all, hegemonic masculinity does not allow for full-blown displays of vulnerability in front of girls and women). Having recognized that individuality is partially subsumed to a form of exaggerated masculinity, one has to return to the acknowledgement (see earlier paragraphs and footnote 2) that masculinity, while limiting and somewhat compulsory, is also socially advantageous.

Returning to the questionnaire and examining responses to a hypothetical crime report in the local newspaper—'Crime Wave Sweeps Estate'—one might hope to see an insight into male feelings of concern or vulnerability away from the setting of the group discussion. However, when stating how they would respond to the headline, 17 per cent of boys (and 4 per cent of girls) said they wouldn't care. While boys' fear for their own safety was much lower than girls' fear for their own safety by age 15–16 (36 per cent of boys and 62 per cent of girls), this should not detract from the knowledge that a significant number of older boys *were* fearful. Further evidence of the extent and character of boys' fear/fearlessness can be found in the responses to the questionnaire question, 'Why would you not like to visit the place you have chosen?' (this attempted to decipher reasons for not visiting locally known (at least to young people) 'no go' places). Boys specified the following as their 'top three' reasons for not wishing to go to a specified place: 'It's too far away', 'Might get attacked' and 'Prefer to stay at home' (in comparison, girls' reasons were: 'Might get attacked', 'It's dark on the way there' and 'It's too far away'). The responses 'It's too far away' and 'Prefer to stay at home' could indicate, on one level, apathy, laziness and a non-committal disregard for the place in question, but, on another level, they could also indicate a diversionary response which allows a person to stay away from certain places and potentially threatening situations. Similarly, the response 'It's dark on the way there', does not necessarily indicate that people are afraid of the dark. Fear of the dark is one of the earliest fears we can possess, but its meaning is debatable. People tend to say 'I'm afraid of the dark' when it could be what, or rather who, could be in the dark that arouses fear; in turn, this level of analysis has to be acknowledged as limited.

BOYS DON'T CRY

If anything, the above illustrates the difficult and dangerous process of interpreting people's responses as given.[6] However, in reference to the response 'Might get attacked' one can be assured (to some degree) that this is indicative of people's fear, inasmuch as this is all they are able and willing to reveal within the confines of a structured questionnaire. The only thing one is unable to judge is the extent and nature of the assault they are referring to. When examining the gender and age breakdown to this response one is able to perceive the familiar reduction in girls' and boys' fear with age (a pattern to emerge throughout my research) with boys' fear remaining consistently lower than that of girls'; at age 11 55 per cent of boys and 68 per cent of girls specified fear of attack which reduced to 21 per cent of boys and 48 per cent of girls age 16.

Although boys' expression of fear (except for fear of 'older boys') does not tend to exceed girls' expression of fear *at all ages*, one cannot ignore the very high levels of fear revealed by younger boys. Aware of their position in the hegemonic masculine order, particularly with regard to their strength, younger boys do not (as yet) feel as constrained by the need to talk like 'a man' as their older counterparts do. The following quotes illustrate the nature of younger boys' fear towards potential dangers and crime in and around the estate where they live:

This area is generally OK. But it really scares you if you find a syringe on the ground where you're playing. Another thing where we don't like going are the underpasses because sometimes gangs of kids hang round there smoking [*sic*].
[Boy aged 12, back of questionnaire]

Near where I live I often get scared when I look across the main road to the dike [large drainage channel running through estate] and see older boys there because in the last few months there has been people at the dike with air rifles shooting at the buses and the drivers [*sic*].
[Boy aged 12, back of questionnaire]

That's when it gets scary though. When you're by yourself.
I mean you know these things won't happen [assault] all the time. You know it's not going to happen every time you walk past someone, but it's a possibility i'n it. It's always there in your mind.
[Boys aged 12–13]

As with the older boys, their personal experiences of crime and fear are placed in their individual biographies of having found things ('*syringes*'), seen things ('*older boys*') or imagined things ('*in your mind*') which have scared them. In turn, all these 'things' are well-established signifiers of threat which both boys and girls must learn to negotiate (often with great difficulty) within their socially assigned gender roles as they grow older.

It is the point at which boys no longer feel able to express their vulnerability and fear that is of most interest when examining the development of hegemonic masculine identity in relation to criminology. This 'point' or process of boys' masculine identification, however, is extremely difficult to identify in both real and theoretical terms as it is dynamic and, as yet, not widely researched. The abstraction and the contextualization of the individual's 'hegemonic masculine biography' within the wider theoretical framework of hegemonic masculinity is a difficult task. This is particularly

[6] It should also alert us to the problem of trying to decipher the multiplicity of individual meaning behind the confines of the collective questionnaire response.

JO GOODEY

the case in relation to the above research findings which have been extracted from a research undertaking whose remit was to discover the processes by which heightened gendered fear of crime evolves in *girls*. Ideally, documentation and theorization on what it is boys actually 'do, say and say about what they do' in relation to crime, fear of crime and fearlessness, needs to be placed within a dedicated research framework. The question of how and how completely masculinity constrains boys' expression of fear and their behaviour is one which can only be partially responded to by the above research findings.

Recent and Future Research on Male Fear of Crime and Fearlessness

Recent research on crime and masculinities *has* approached the subject of male fear in relation to *men's* victimization (Stanko 1990; Stanko and Hobdell 1993; Newburn and Stanko 1995), but this interest is relatively 'new' and has to battle against the mainstream criminological interest in men and adolescent boys (primarily) as delinquents and offenders and the mainstream victimological interest in women and children (primarily) as victims. Newburn and Stanko (1995) present a solid critique of victimology's failure to incorporate work on men's victimization and hence, one can propose, victimology's neglect of male fear (for exceptions see Shapland *et al.* 1985; Maguire and Corbett 1987; King 1992). Newburn and Stanko (1995) suggest that male victimization is largely under-researched because of the belief that men are unwilling to admit to their vulnerability and, in respect of this, research on male fear continues to be sidelined. Similarly, when men *do* reveal experiences of victimization and fear, these are often supplanted by attention to women's experiences. One can readily understand the research focus on women in light of their heightened and pervasive experience of victimization and fear. However, to ignore the male experience is to deny an insight into male vulnerability and, correspondingly, excludes an innovative appraisal of men as 'aggressors'. The two, victim and offender, fearful and fearless, are not mutually exclusive; the one informs the other. Rather than focus on adulthood, research should look at that period which is central to the formation of the individual's social and sexual identity; childhood and, specifically, adolescence. This will turn the concerns of mainstream criminology on their heads with the introduction of two bases for the theoretical development of research on fear of crime: first, research on male fear and, secondly, research on the construction of male 'fearlessness' through the development of normative masculinity in childhood.

It is not enough to advocate the incorporation of childhood studies into research on masculinities, victimization and fear of crime without the contextualization of research in terms of race and class. Future research on developmental male 'fearlessness' *particularly* needs to address the question of race, masculinity and racism as one of the most oppressive and damaging forms of hegemonic masculinity. An argument can be made that racism is a form of masculinity. As Newburn and Stanko (1994: 164) say: 'The small literature which addresses racist violence often neglects to articulate how being male is part of the way racist violence works.'[7] The extremes of intra-male

---

[7] The 'small literature' on race and masculinity or race and racism also tends to concentrate its efforts on Afro-Caribbean/African-American experience; hence, my specific reference to these ethnic groups in this part of the paper. More, as yet, needs to be said on other male experiences from different races (Asian, Chinese etc.).

BOYS DON'T CRY

powerplays can be expressed by those near the bottom of the male hierarchy in ugly displays of violent racism (and homophobia) against those at the very bottom. Hewitt's (1986) research on adolescents and young men in two multi-racial, working-class, London communities notes that racism is far more prevalent among boys than girls (the research concentrated on boys *because* they formed what Hewitt perceived as the problem) and suggests that unfamiliarity between races breeds racial prejudice. Building on Hewitt's ideas, I would concur that alongside the familiarity or 'contact hypothesis' (Hewitt 1986: 1) there is also the absence of male racist powerplay among white boys in communities where they are significantly outnumbered by black youth. The logistics of trying to assert *your* brand of masculinity when you are an ethnic minority (either white or black) is a dangerous game.

The history of ethnic minority oppression and racism, particularly against Afro-Caribbeans and African-Americans, can lead the male members of these groups to adopt an exaggerated form of emotional inexpressiveness (which, stylistically, can be very expressive) in their attempt to assert their masculinity from below. This emotional inexpressiveness can match or surpass that displayed by white, working-class boys and men. Majors and Billson (1992) and Taylor Gibbs and Merighi (1994) describe and discuss what they respectively call the 'compulsive masculine alternative/cool pose' and the 'pseudo masculine/exaggerated masculine' among black, male youth. The cultures of masculinity these writers variously detail can be described as adopting a form of defensive or coping strategy to counter their feelings of marginality and the overt and covert racism which others display towards them. The pressures not to show vulnerability and fear, I would speculate, are learnt by ethnic minority boys from a young age. My speculation is supported by Walker *et al.*'s (1988) research on ethnic minority males and the criminal justice system which found that 30 per cent of black, 33 per cent of Asian and 36 per cent of white boys aged 10–16 'worried about bullying or teasing' (1988: 125) and 94 per cent of black, 78 per cent of Asian and 72 per cent of white males aged 16–20 felt 'very or fairly safe' when walking alone in their area after dark (1988: 116). As Majors and Billson state: 'Presenting to the world an emotionless, fearless, and aloof front counters the low sense of inner control, lack of inner strength, absence of stability, damaged pride, shattered confidence and fragile social competence that come from living on the edge of society' (1992: 8).

Research on the institutionalization of hegemonic masculinity *in childhood* must be prepared to address the question of racism (and homophobia) against the background of wider class and (of course) female-centred oppression. Connell (1995: 238–9) suggests the development of a multicultural/gender-inclusive curriculum in schools to invert the hegemonic dominance of the old curriculum. Mac an Ghaill (1994) suggests similar initiatives and emphasizes the need to incorporate white youth in anti-racist programmes (Cohen 1986). Through initial reference to white boys' own experiences of conflict and danger, school programmes can begin to develop an understanding of what it is to be white and male, from which point understanding of different races, their experiences and racism can be integrated. Alternatively, school programmes can approach issues from the perspective of bullied and oppressed minorities so that hegemonic masculinity is immediately confronted and challenged. The London-based charity 'Kidscape' currently produces a wide range of leaflets, videos and books for schools on the subject of bullying and racism: such initiatives are ripe for including specific work on racism and what it is to become 'a man'. White youth needs to be

JO GOODEY

informed of its own potential for a positive identity beyond the rhetoric of New Right extremes. Ethnic minority youth (and girls) needs positive feedback that its own ways of doing and thinking are valued.

If anything, the above suggestions can be readily accused of two things; idealistic ambition and harmful essentialism—the latter because of the suggestion that the complexity of masculinity can be reduced to the dichotomy of 'bad white masculinity' versus 'other masculinities'. One cannot deny the racism of Asian on white or black on white but, I would argue, this has to be understood with regard to the history of race and racism and the adoption of negative hegemonic masculine standards (such as aggression) as the reactive actions of oppressed minorities. To combat racism between boys, school programmes should focus on masculinity's shared meanings of vulnerability beyond the brutality of verbal and physical aggression towards those who are different and who do not fit normative expectations. Fundamentally, the myth of normative masculinity needs to be shattered so that boys, as both the future actors and potential victims of the masculine ideal, can rest with the knowledge that 'boys can and do cry'. Here the 'hegemonic masculine biography' becomes a practical tool for relating shared experiences of fear and vulnerability in the face of other men's aggression and crime.

Concluding Comments

The central question asked by Mac an Ghaill's book (1994) *The Making of Men*, is how does the fragile male identity come to be represented as a stable, unitary category with fixed meanings. This 'stable' identity has traditionally fallen into western society's stereotype of the strong, rational and sometimes aggressive man. Male aggression forms a pillar of criminological investigation and the 'problem' identified by this paper in relation to the socially constructed idea that male aggression also means that 'boys don't cry' or, at least, they shouldn't be seen to. As a teacher from Mac an Ghaill's research (1994: 38) says: 'the tough boys develop their own macho script of cynicism to hide their feelings and so you end up with another generation of emotionally disabled men.' Connecting the formation of male identity around the image of the 'strong, silent type' of popular imagery (Sparks 1996) and everyday interaction, and problematizing this in relation to emotional disablement or damage, research can begin to unpack the gendered and multiple meanings of identity as they relate to crime, fear and fearlessness in the context of the individual and group experience of the 'hegemonic masculine biography'.

In his interviews with boys, Mac an Ghaill's (1994) research found two themes repeatedly referred to: first, that there was no safe space in which boys felt they could talk about their feelings of vulnerability and, secondly, boys suffered from the absence of an emotional language for expression of such feelings. Herein lies the problem of the hegemonic masculine ideal. Progress will truly have been achieved when boys can relate the courage demanded by 'turning the other cheek' in situations where aggression, or at least its appearance, are normally demanded of them. Boys become tomorrow's adults and for this reason, if no other, they should become the centre of future attempts to restructure the hegemonic masculine ideal. Horrocks (1994: 14) criticises Connell's challenge in *Gender and Power* (1987: 278–9) that every society could

BOYS DON'T CRY

'abolish' patriarchy, sexism and sexual oppression. In response to this I would suggest that, although Connell may appear somewhat idealistic, at least his challenge is one worth taking up if crime and aggression are to be contested at their roots as the problems of hegemonic masculinity.

One can combine *the best* of theoretical insights into masculinity (such as that offered by Mac an Ghaill 1994; Messerschmidt 1993; Connell 1995) with one of Connell's concluding statements from his book *Masculinities*, in which he says (1995: 243) 'I think a fresh politics of masculinity will develop in new arenas: for instance, the politics of the curriculum, work around AIDS/HIV and anti-racist politics.' Taking two of Connell's 'for instances', the school curriculum and racism, this paper has provided some pointers, through its research findings and theoretical development, towards these 'new arenas' in the hope that Connell's statement (1995: 238) that 'there is surprisingly little discussion of the role of education in the transformation of masculinity' can soon be challenged within the theoretical framework of the 'hegemonic masculine biography'.

REFERENCES

ADLER, A. (1927 [1992]), *Understanding Human Nature*. Oxford: One World.

ANDERSON, S., KINSEY, R., LOADER, I. and SMITH, C (1994), *Cautionary Tales: A Study of Young People and Crime in Edinburgh*. Aldershot: Avebury.

BOX, S. (1983), *Power, Crime and Mystification*. London: Tavistock.

CAMPBELL, B. (1993), *Goliath: Britain's Dangerous Places*. London: Methuen.

COHEN, P. (1986), *Anti-Racist Cultural Studies*. Curriculum Development Project in Schools and Community Education, June.

CONNELL, R. (1987), *Gender and Power*. London: Polity Press.

—— (1995), *Masculinities*. London: Polity Press.

DOBASH, R. E. and DOBASH, R. P. (1979), *Violence Against Wives: A Case Against Patriarchy*. New York: Free Press.

GOODEY, J. (1996) 'Adolescence and the Socialisation of Gendered Fear', in D. Milovanovic and M. Schwartz, eds., *Race, Gender and Class in Criminology*, 267–91. USA: Garland.

HALL, S. and JEFFERSON, T., eds. (1976 [1991]), *Resistance Through Rituals*. Hammersmith: Harper and Collins.

HARTLESS, J., DITTON, J., NAIR, G. and PHILLIPS, S. (1994), *More Sinned against than Sinning: A Study of Young Teenagers' Experience of Crime in Edinburgh*. Glasgow: Criminology Research Unit, Glasgow University.

HOCKEY, J. and JAMES, A. (1993), *Growing Up and Growing Old*. London: Sage.

HORROCKS, R. (1994), *Masculinity in Crisis*. New York: St. Martin's Press.

HEWITT, R. (1986), *White Talk Black Talk*. Cambridge: Cambridge University Press.

JEFFERSON, T. (1994), 'Crime, Criminology, Masculinity and Young Men', in A. Coote, ed., *Families, Children and Crime*, 72–84. London: Institute for Public Policy Research.

KELLY, L. (1988), *Surviving Sexual Violence*. Oxford: Polity.

KING, M. B. (1992), 'Male Sexual Assault in the Community', in G. Mezey and M. B. King, eds., *Male Victims of Sexual Assault*. Oxford: Oxford University Press.

MAC AN GHAILL, M. (1994), *The Making of Men*. Buckingham: Open University Press.

MAGUIRE, M. and CORBETT, C. (1987), *The Effects of Crime and the Work of Victim Support Schemes*. Aldershot: Gower.

JO GOODEY

MAJORS, R. and BILLSON, J. M. (1992), *Cool Pose*. New York: Lexington Books.

MESSERSCHMIDT, J. W. (1993), *Masculinities and Crime*. Lanham, MD: Rowman and Littlefield.

—— (1994), 'Schooling, Masculinities and Youth Crime by White Boys', in T. Newburn and E. A. Stanko, eds., *Just Boys Doing Business?*, 81–99. London: Routledge.

NEWBURN, T. and STANKO, E. A. (1995), 'When Men are Victims: The Failure of Victimology', in T. Newburn and E. A. Stanko, eds., *Just Boys Doing Business?*, 153–65. London: Routledge.

PAIN, R. (1995), 'Elderly Women and Fear of Violent Crime: The Least Likely Victims?', *British Journal of Criminology*, 35/4: 584–98.

PAINTER, K. (1991), *An Evaluation of Public Lighting as a Crime Prevention Strategy with Special Focus on Women and Elderly People*. Manchester: Faculty of Economic and Social Studies, The University of Manchester.

PARSONS, T. and BALES, R. F. (1956), *Family, Socialization and Interaction Process*. London: Routledge and Kegan Paul.

SATTEL, J. W. (1992), 'The Inexpressive Male: Tragedy or Sexual Politics?' in M. S. Kimmel and M. A. Messner, eds., *Men's Lives*, 350–58. New York: Macmillan.

SHAPLAND, J., WILMORE, J. and DUFF, P. (1985), *Victims in the Criminal Justice System*. Aldershot: Gower.

SPARKS, R. (1996), 'Masculinity and Heroism in the Hollywood "Blockbuster": The Culture Industry and Contemporary Images of Crime and Law Enforcement', *British Journal of Criminology* (special issue), 36/3: 348–60.

STANKO, E. A. (1990), *Everyday Violence*. London: Pandora.

STANKO, E. A. and HOBDELL, K. (1993), 'Assault on Men: Masculinity and Male Victimization', *British Journal of Criminology*, 33/3: 400–15.

TAYLOR GIBBS, J. and MERIGHI, J. R. (1994), 'Young Black Males: Marginality, Masculinity and Criminality', in T. Newburn and E. A. Stanko, eds., *Just Boys Doing Business?*, 64–80. London: Routledge.

VALENTINE, G. (1997), 'My Son's a Bit Dizzy. My Wife's a Bit Soft. Gender, Children and Cultures of Parenting', *Journal of Gender, Place and Culture*, 4/1: 37–62.

WALKER, M., JEFFERSON, T. and SENEVIRATNE, M. (1988), *Ethnic Minorities, Young People and the Criminal Justice System*. ESRC Project No. E06250023.

WILLIS, P. (1977), *Learning to Labour*. Aldershot: Saxon House.

[5]

The Elderly's
Fear of Crime

A Critical Examination of the Research

RANDY L. LaGRANGE
University of North Carolina at Wilmington

KENNETH F. FERRARO
Northern Illinois University

Research on fear of crime reveals that the pervasiveness and intensity of fear in the United States is substantially higher among the elderly than younger persons. The relationship between age and fear of crime is seemingly paradoxical because the elderly tend to be least often victimized. This article critically assesses much of the research on fear of crime among the elderly. Our analysis shows that (1) several of the standard fear of crime measures are poorly operationalized and (2) estimates of the extent of fear of crime are highly dependent on the type and quality of operationalization. We conclude that the amount of fear experienced in the everyday lives of most older persons has been overstated. Implications for policy and suggestions for further research are offered.

A dominant theme in the research literature and public opinion polls is that victimization fear among the elderly is pervasive and intense, and is considerably greater than the amount of fear experienced by younger persons. Some authors proclaim that frightened older persons isolate themselves from the outside

AUTHORS' NOTE: This article was originally presented at the Southern Sociological Society Meetings, April 9-12, 1986, New Orleans, Louisiana. We appreciate the comments of Virginia Kroncke, Cely LaGrange, and Eleanor Maxwell on earlier drafts. Please direct correspondence to Randy L. LaGrange, Department of Sociology, University of North Carolina at Wilmington, Wilmington, NC 28403.

RESEARCH ON AGING, Vol. 9 No. 3, September 1987 372-391
© 1987 Sage Publications, Inc.

world, live a life of self-imposed confinement, and are "captives" in their own homes (Schooler, 1970; Lawton and Kleban, 1971; Braungart, Hoyer, and Braungart, 1979). The level of fear among older persons is further dramatized by sensationalized stories reported in the popular media (e.g., "Fortress on 78th Street," 1971; "The Elderly," 1976).

Unfortunately, fear of crime lacks appropriate conceptual and measurement clarity in the literature (Furstenberg, 1971; Garofalo and Laub, 1978; DuBow, McCabe, and Kaplan, 1979; Yin, 1980). Furstenberg (1971) first demonstrated this in a reanalysis of survey data from Baltimore. The Baltimore study unexpectedly revealed that residents of low crime neighborhoods were *more* fearful of crime than residents of high crime neighborhoods. In attempting to make sense of this finding, Furstenberg distinguished between crime "concern" (a public issue) and crime "risk" (a judgment of personal safety) and found that while low crime area residents express a greater concern for crime as a community problem, high crime area residents do indeed perceive a greater personal risk of victimization. Despite Furstenberg's early effort, measurement problems have not been rigorously examined in much of the literature on fear of crime. DuBow and his associates (1979, p. 1) express their dismay over the level of sophistication in measuring fear of crime, maintaining that "there is a serious lack of both consistency and specificity in the reports." Garofalo and Laub (1978, p. 246) more strongly contend that "what has been measured in research as the 'fear of crime' is simply not fear of crime." Rather than serving as a useful indicator of the quality of community life, fear of crime has been measured in so many ways that it has marginal research value as a concept for rigorous scientific research and may misdirect policy initiatives intended to help older community residents.

The main proposition of this article is that fear of crime is not as serious a problem in the everyday lives of the elderly as the literature generally portrays. Conceptualization and measurement problems have hindered the development of appropriate fear of crime indicators. These problems, coupled with the volume of research on fear of crime among the elderly, underscore the need to examine this research critically. Here we attempt to demonstrate the shortcomings of several standard measures of fear of crime and to show that published research findings are often contradictory because of the particular indicators used to measure fear of crime. Our review is not exhaustive, but it is representative of the fear of crime literature and covers the nucleus of the relevant research. Although we concentrate on the literature assessing the amount of fear among the elderly, the principal arguments of the article are applicable across the age continuum.

Our assessment proceeds from a discussion of the general problem of fear of crime in American society to its manifestation in the everyday lives of individuals and, finally, to an examination of the variability of fear of crime based on the type of crime. The article concludes with implications for policy and suggestions for future fear of crime research.

The Problem of Fear of Crime

The 1974 Louis Harris poll (published in 1975) is commonly cited as "proof" of the fear of crime crisis among the elderly. Harris made the startling discovery that 23% of persons 65 and over from a national probability sample rated fear of crime as their most serious personal problem. This compared to 21% who mentioned poor health, 15% mentioning lack of money, and 10% who rated lack of appropriate medical care as their most serious problem. The wide dissemination of these results has made the fear of crime problem among the elderly well recognized by professionals and the public alike.

The major implication drawn from the Harris poll that fear of crime is an *age* issue is limited in several ways. For instance, it appears that income plays a far greater role in determining the seriousness of problems for older persons. Among the poorest elderly sampled by Harris (income under $3000), fear of crime is perceived as the third most serious personal problem (31%), falling slightly behind poor health (36%), and not having enough money (32%). Clearly, the elderly poor experience difficulty in coping with a host of life's problems. Yet this is true of low income persons of all ages. The Harris poll reveals that the proportion of low income individuals aged 18 to 54 who perceive fear of crime to be a very serious personal problem is *slightly higher* (27%) than the proportion of young elderly (55-64) and elderly (65 and over) *in the same income category* who perceive fear of crime as a very serious problem (24% in each age group).

In contrast to this major finding of the Harris poll that fear of crime is a substantial problem among the elderly, Yin (1982) arrives at a very different conclusion concerning the prevalence of fear of crime. Yin's random survey of over 1200 elderly persons living in the St. Paul, Minnesota, area reveals that only 1% mention fear of crime as a serious personal problem compared to, for example, 25% who mention poor health. While minor differences between Harris' national survey and Yin's local survey are expected due to sampling, Yin maintains that the clear contradiction in fear of crime estimates is due primarily to measurement differences; whereas the Harris survey utilized closed-ended questions to assess the severity of problems, Yin used an open-ended format. In other words, the Harris method may have overly sensitized respondents to the crime issue and amplified their true level of fear. Yin suggests that open-ended questions are more desirable because they avoid this amplification problem by relying on the respondent's frame of reference rather than the researcher's.

A comparison of the 1974 Harris poll and a 1982 Gallup poll further illustrates the problem of assessing the prevalence of fear of crime among the elderly when different measures are used. In the Gallup national probability sample of over 1500 adults, crime is rated as the most serious social problem by less than 5% of the respondents *in all age categories*. By comparison with other domestic problems such as unemployment, inflation, and the general economy, concern over the crime problem seems minimal. However, closer inspection of the Harris and Gallup polls suggests that the varying estimates in crime perceptions again are the result of measurement differences. Whereas the Harris poll asked respondents to identify those problems that were "very serious for them personally," the Gallup poll asked respondents what they thought was the "most serious problem facing the country today." The Harris and Gallup measures differ not only on the level of reference applied—personal versus general—but they also tap two distinct crime perceptions: fear of crime versus concern about crime (Furstenberg, 1971). Therefore, it is not surprising that these different measures result in quite different assessments of the problem.

This is not to argue that fear of crime is not a salient concern among the American public. Quite to the contrary, two decades of public opinion polling show considerable agreement that the crime issue continues to rank high as a social problem that Americans want "something done about." The data from two Harris surveys show that Americans became more likely to consider fear of crime a very serious problem *for older people* between 1974 and 1981 (Harris, 1981). In 1974, 50% of the public under 65 and 51% of the public over 65 considered fear of crime a very serious problem for older people. By 1981 these percentages rose to 74% for the public under 65 and 58% for the public over 65. Americans, especially younger Americans, think that elderly people are afraid of crime; and over one half of the elderly people think that *other* elderly are afraid of crime. However, when the elderly themselves are asked about their fear of crime, only about one-quarter report such fear—and these estimates are based on the Harris indicators that Yin (1982) criticizes as inflating the prevalence estimates of fear of crime. We contend that the portrait of fear drawn by surveys of the public is largely contingent on the measurement process, and many estimates of the prevalence of fear may be overstated.[1]

Fear of Crime in Everyday Life

Few researchers have clearly defined the fear of crime concept.[2] This is all too often manifested in its operationalization. The question utilized in the National Crime Survey (NCS) is commonplace and serves as a useful example: "How safe do you feel or would you feel being out alone in your neighborhood at night?" Several problems concerning this item's validity may be raised (Garofalo, 1979, p. 82). For instance, the word *crime,* or a specific act or acts that would constitute crime, is not included in the question itself (safe or unsafe from what?); the term *neighborhood* is not geographically defined; and the phrase "do you feel or would you feel" is methodologically inappropriate because it is double-barreled. It is one thing to ask an individual how safe they *do feel* being out alone in their neighborhood at night if this is a situation they regularly experience. It is something quite different to ask how safe they *would feel* if they seldom or never are alone in their neighborhood at night. In other words, this single fear of crime indicator, which is intended to be relevant to all respondents, in actuality becomes two distinct (though related) questions for different subsamples of respondents. For one subsample, the question has concrete meaning based on actual experience (the "do feel" group); for the other subsample, the question is more hypothetical and abstract and somewhat removed from everyday experiences (the "would feel" group).[3] In Skogan and Maxfield's (1981) comprehensive study of consequences of crime in Chicago, Philadelphia, and San Francisco, they too utilized the standard NCS question as their major measure of fear of crime. The authors justify the question wording by stating that: "The phrase 'or would you feel' was added to forestall replies along the lines of, 'But I never go out.' We did not want to confuse the issue of fear with that of behavior, which is quite distinct" (1981, p. 58). Skogan and Maxfield are correct that fear and behavior are distinct issues, but we fail to see how the wording of the question resolves more confusion than it creates. Instead, two specific questions directed at individuals who do and who do not go out alone at night would increase the precision of the fear of crime measure as well as the clarity of the responses.

Another problem with the NCS item seldom mentioned is that it is perhaps more of an assessment of one's *safety* than a measure of one's *fear.* That is, the question is phrased "How safe do you feel . . . ?" and not "How afraid (scared, frightened, fearful, etc.) do you feel . . .?" We emphasize that fear of crime (an emotional state) and assessments of safety are distinct crime perceptions. Moreover, it has been demonstrated that these separate crime perceptions are not necessarily highly correlated (Warr and Stafford, 1983). For example, young black, urban males generally are aware that they are high-risk targets for crime, and may well respond that they do not feel particularly safe alone on the streets at night. But this does not imply they experience emotional fear. The point is that although safety and fear are somewhat different crime perceptions and are separable at the theoretical and empirical levels, they are rarely distinguished in the literature (DuBow, McCabe, and Kaplan, 1979). While the concept "fear" of crime is often interchanged with terms such as *worry, anxiety,* or *concern* about crime in the general literature (Skogan and Maxfield, 1981), this does not dismiss responsibility for maintaining some level of theoretical purity and operational consistency in empirical research.

Consider a related question used in the General Social Survey: "Is there any area right around here—that is, within a mile—where you would be afraid to walk alone at night?" This question is the most frequently used measure of fear of crime reported in the literature (Ferraro and LaGrange, 1987). Note that the word *afraid* is used in the question, thereby delving more directly into the emotional aspect of fear. However, the question seems excessively foreboding. Is it any wonder that research demonstrates the seriousness of the fear of crime problem, especially among women, the urban, and the elderly, when they are asked if there is *any place within a mile where they would be afraid to walk alone at night?* This applies especially to many urban dwellers where crime rates fluctuate so dramatically within a mile radius that walking alone on the streets at night may entail substantial risk. An inner-city resident who maintains that they would not be afraid to walk the streets alone at night may be exaggerating his or her bravado, or simply exhibiting poor judgment of the real risks involved.

Jeffords's (1983) study demonstrates the need to develop fear of crime indicators that are relevant to the everyday experiences of individuals. After analyzing nearly 3000 mailed questionnaires from a probability sample of Texas residents, Jeffords reports that while the relationships between age and fear of (1) walking within *one mile* of one's home alone at night and (2) walking within *one block* of one's home alone at night are significant and positive (older respondents being more fearful), the relationship between age and fear of *being in one's home* alone at night is statistically significant and negative (see also Lawton et al., 1976; Davis and Brody, 1979; Clarke and Lewis, 1982). Because most individuals tend to be inside during the nighttime hours rather than out walking the streets alone, and this is especially true for older persons (Cook, Fremming, and Tyler, 1981), the "at home" measure of fear of crime appears to be more relevant to everyday experiences. Additionally, Jeffords (1983, p. 104) observes that although the elderly may leave their homes at night less often than younger persons, and actually may experience greater fear of crime when on the streets of large cities alone at night, "this does not necessarily mean that they have more overall anxiety or fear concerning crime." If particularly dangerous situations are seldom part of the everyday lives of the elderly—or any age group for that matter—there is little justification in using this type of scenario to measure their fear of crime.

A recent Gallup (1983) poll further documents the critical importance of developing fear of crime measures with meaningful content validity.[4] Table 1 shows the percentage of respondents from a national probability sample who report being fearful when two different questions are asked: (1) Is there any area right around here—that is, within a mile—where you would be afraid to walk alone *at night*?; and (2) Is there any area within a mile of here where you would be afraid to walk alone *during the day*? There are three points of interest in Table 1. First, the positive linear relationship between age and fear of crime commonly reported in the literature is not apparent. When the "walking alone at night" measure is used, a curvilinear (J-shaped) relationship is observed. The positive age and fear of crime relationship occurs only if one considers respondents 30 or older. Second, the relationship between age and fear of walking alone "during the daytime" is virtually eliminated. Third, and most important, the proportion of respondents identified as fearful by the standard nighttime item is from three to four times greater than the proportion of fearful respondents identified by the daytime item. The most straightforward conclusion to be drawn from the daytime measure is that fear of crime is not problematic for any age group because anywhere from 85% to 88% of the respondents report not being afraid. Although the daytime question is not a particularly good measure of fear of crime—as it is subject to many of the same criticisms leveled against the nighttime measure—it is more relevant to the everyday lives of individuals and especially to older adults who reduce their nighttime excursions appreciably.[5]

Fear of Crime by Crime Type

Fear of crime is not evenly distributed across different types of crime. The type of crime has a profound effect on the pervasiveness and intensity of reported fears. Crimes against the person, high-risk crimes, and crimes that result in substantial monetary loss generally evoke more fear than property crimes, low-risk crimes, or crimes that result in minimal monetary loss. However, there are exceptions. For example, what may be an inconsequential amount of money stolen from a wealthy individual could well be a tragic loss to someone poor. In this situation, one would expect the fear reactions to the thefts to be varied because of the differential impact of the loss rather than simply the amount of loss.[6]

Nonetheless, some crimes are inherently more fear-provoking than others. Encountering a knife-wielding mugger face-to-face rouses an intensity of fear that having a radio stolen from an unoccuppied car simply does not. Garofalo (1981, p. 840) makes a similar point: "Certainly, it seems reasonable to assume that the internal state of a person who remembers, at three a.m., that his ten-speed bicycle has been left outside unlocked is different than the internal state of a person who finds himself alone on a dark

TABLE 1

Percentage of Respondents Reporting Fear of Crime to Two
Different Gallup Poll (1983) Measures by Age (N = 1500)

Age	Fear of Crime	
	Walk at Night [a]	Walk at Day [b]
Less than 30	45	12
30-49	39	12
50-64	47	15
65 and over	54	14

SOURCE: Table adapted from Tables 2.5 and 2.6 in the *Sourcebook of Criminal Justice Statistics—1983* (U.S. Department of Justice, 1984, pp. 197, 199).
a. "Is there any area right around here—that is, within a mile—where you would be afraid to walk alone at night?"
b. "How about during the daytime? Is there any area within a mile of here where you would be afraid to walk alone during the daytime?"

city side-street at three a.m." It may seem that Garofalo is simply stating the obvious, yet few studies on fear of crime make distinctions among crime types. The distinction among "reactions" to different crimes may be well documented, but relatively few studies make distinctions of "fears" to different crimes. Ferraro and LaGrange's (1987) review of 46 studies on fear of crime reveals only 15 investigations that even minimally attempt to distinguish fear by crime types, and the majority of these crime-specific measures are of questionable quality. Instead of measuring fear reactions to specific crimes—such as robbery, burglary, property destruction, car theft, consumer fraud, and so on—the tendency is to use a single omnibus measure of fear of crime with an "implicit" referent to serious street crime. We suggest that this practice is partly responsible for the high levels of fear commonly reported in the literature. (As will be discussed later, the more diffuse and vague the measure of "fear of crime," the more likely that elderly respondents will score high on it.)

Sundeen and Mathieu (1976) were among the first to document that different crime referents lead to different assessments of the amount of fear. In their investigation, elderly residents living in retirement communities in California expressed greater fear of consumer fraud than predatory crime, and inner-city and suburban elderly were most fearful of robbery and car theft. Brodyaga et al. (1975), Wolf (1977), Warr and Stafford (1983), and Warr (1984) also have suggested the importance of specifying offense type when measuring fear.

Data from a 1982 *ABC News* poll, partially reproduced in Table 2, are particularly revealing on this issue. In this representative sample of over 2400 U.S. adults, respondents report whether they personally worry about being the victim of seven different crime situations: having their car or property vandalized, having their home burglarized, being robbed on the street, being injured by a robber on the streets, being injured by a burglar in their home, being raped (women only), and being murdered. These questions are meaningful for two reasons. First, they are acceptable examples of how to measure fear of crime as they directly assess the emotional aspect of perceiving crime (i.e., fear) and not the perception of one's risk.[7] Second, the seven situations allow one to test for varying fear reactions to different crimes.

The most striking finding from these data is that only two of the seven crime situations elicit a notable linear relationship between age and fear of crime, and this relationship is in a *negative* direction; that is, the percentage of respondents who worry about having their car or property vandalized and the percentage of women who worry about being raped decreases with increasing age. The remaining relationships are less evident. (Notice that the percentage differences for the other five items never exceed nine, while the percentage differences for vandalism and rape are 21 and 31, respectively.) Recognizing that the remaining relationships are modest, it is also apparent that the youngest age group has the most fear of home burglary and murder. Weak curvilinear relationships—again J-shaped—are manifest for the items dealing with robbery and injury from robbery or burglary (columns 3, 4, and 5 in Table 2).

The 1980 *Figgie Report on Fear of Crime* (Research and Forecasts, Inc., 1980) provides additional insight into the effect of crime type on fears. In this study, two dissimilar measures of fear of crime were used: (1) a "concrete" fear index was created from six *specific* questions that measure how often respondents worry

TABLE 2

Percentage of Respondents Who Worry About Being a Victim of Crime by Age (N = 2400)

	Car or property Vandalized	Home Burglarized	Robbed on Street	Injured by Robber	Injured by Burglar	Being Raped a	Being Murdered
18–24	59	50	31	30	33	65	28
25–29	45	44	30	26	29	54	21
30–49	42	44	28	27	28	44	20
50–64	44	47	33	31	32	37	19
65 and over	38	43	36	33	35	34	22

SOURCE: Data from 1982 *ABC News* Poll, adapted from Table 2.7 in the *Sourcebook of Criminal Justice Statistics—1983* (U.S. Department of Justice, 1984, p. 200).
NOTE: The question—"First, how much do you worry about . . . ? Do you worry a great deal, a good amount, not very much, or not at all?" (Percentage who worry "a great deal" or "a good amount.")
a. Question only asked of women.

about being a victim of murder, sexual assault, mugging, knifing, beating, or armed robbery; and (2) a "formless" fear index was created from six *nonspecific* questions measuring one's general sense of safety in the home, neighborhood, and the community. Table 3 reproduces the findings relevant to the age of respondents.

It is apparent from these data that the relationship between age and fear of crime is highly dependent on the operationalization of fear of crime. When persons are asked about their victimization fears of specific, identifiable criminal offenses, the elderly report being substantially *less* fearful than younger respondents; when the level of formless, nonspecific fear is assessed, the elderly report being slightly *more* fearful. Again, it is this latter type of fear measure that is most common in the research literature.

The *Figgie Report* findings point to a more general problem in the research literature of failing to distinguish fear from anxiety. Hinkle's (1976, p. 197) survey of the methodological problems in the study of fear concludes that "many studies that report fears may actually have investigated anxiety, and many reporting the results of anxiety studies may have been researching fears." Specifically, fear is an internal disturbance produced by an objectively harmful external condition (for example, the act of being robbed), while anxiety is an internal disturbance produced by an objectively harmless external condition (Sarnoff and Zimbardo, 1961). (Phobias are an extreme form of anxiety.) Extending this reasoning to the two fear of crime measures used in the *Figgie Report*, the "concrete" index comes closest to measuring actual fear while the "formless" index measures anxiety. Hence, the findings suggest that the elderly may experience greater anxiety about crime than younger persons, but less fear.

Discussion

Considerable debate exists over what is referred to as the victimization-fear paradox (Lindquist and Duke, 1982). That is, the level of fear among older persons is thought to be alarmingly

TABLE 3

Percentage of Respondents (by age) with Concrete
and Formless Fears of Criminal Victimization (N = 1000)

| | Level of Concrete Fear | | Level of Formless Fear | |
Age	High	Moderate to Low	High	Moderate to Low
18-29	49	51	36	64
30-39	46	54	30	70
40-49	34	66	34	66
50-59	40	60	41	59
60 and over	33	67	43	57

SOURCE: Data from the 1980 *Figgie Report on Fear of Crime: America Afraid*, adapted from Table 2.9 in the *Sourcebook of Criminal Justice Statistics—1983* (U.S. Department of Justice, 1984, p. 203). NOTE: The *concrete fear* index is a Guttman scale measuring how often a person worries about being a victim of murder, sexual assault, mugging, knifing, beating, or armed robbery. The *formless fear* index is a Guttman scale measuring the frequency of nonspecific worry about one's feelings of safety in the home, neighborhood, and larger community.

high given their relatively low victimization rates. Crime statistics reveal that younger persons (particularly older teenagers and young adults) are several times more likely to be victimized overall (U.S. Department of Justice, 1984), yet some research shows that older persons tend to experience greater fear (DuBow, McCabe, and Kaplan, 1979). Fueling this controversy are discussions of the "rationality" of older persons' fear (Jaycox, 1978) and statements implying that the only thing the elderly have to fear is fear (Lindquist and Duke, 1982, p. 118). Regardless of the rationality/irrationality issue, the literature generally indicates that fear of crime is a harsh reality for the elderly. As Clemente and Kleiman (1976, p. 208) maintain: "Simply put, fear among the elderly is real and pervasive. It matters little whether this fear is out of proportion to the objective probability of being victimized."

Contrary to this general body of literature, several published studies and the careful examination of three surveys with crime items reveal that, as a group, the elderly are no more fearful of crime than other age groups. Furthermore, when fear of crime is measured from specific types of crime rather than from a single indicator, it is often the younger persons who report being most fearful. This finding supports Yin's (1982, p. 240) thesis that "fear of crime is a less severe problem for the elderly than previous reports suggest," and offers a partial explanation of the victimization-fear paradox. The standard fear of crime measures criticized throughout this article as being too general, too hypothetically abstract, and too foreboding to have much relevance to everyday life (e.g., "Is there any area right around here—that is, within a mile—where you would be afraid to walk alone at night?") form the empirical foundation of the fear of crime research. Clearly such global and nonspecific fear of crime indicators mask genuine differences in victimization fears across the age range. This has the effect of exaggerating fear of crime among the elderly and perhaps even underestimating the level of fear among younger respondents.

This is not to argue that fear of crime is evenly distributed among the elderly, nor that some older persons experience no more overall fear than younger persons. Certainly some frightened elderly individuals do live a life of self-imposed confinement, and are "captives" in their own homes (Braungart, Hoyer, and Braungart, 1979). However, the same is true of the effect of fear on some younger persons. This is precisely where our efforts to alleviate the crime problems—and/or the problem of fear—should be concentrated.

Serious street crime may not be as important in generating fear as mundane, everyday events and situations that signify a lack of community order and control. As Wilson and Kelling (1985, p. 221) observe, "We tend to overlook or forget another source of fear—the fear of being bothered by disorderly people. Not violent people, nor, necessarily, criminals, but disreputable or obstreperous or unpredictable people: panhandlers, drunks, addicts, rowdy teenagers, prostitutes, loiterers, the mentally disturbed." The prospect of confronting a rowdy teenager or panhandler oftentimes is as traumatic as actually confronting a mugger. Wilson and Kelling maintain that "indeed, to a defenseless person, the two kinds of situations may be indistinguishable" (1985, p. 222). And the elderly are not alone in associating

community disorderliness with fear. The police could do much to
reduce the fear of being in public places simply by more
aggressively regulating "disorderly" behavior.

Even if the elderly are no more fearful as a group than younger
persons, the consequences of criminal victimization for the aged
often are more traumatic because of reduced financial status,
declining physical health, and a greater sense of vulnerability
(Wiltz, 1982). The elderly also are more likely to be victims of
certain types of crime, such as personal larceny, consumer fraud,
and con games, because they are considered relatively easy
targets. Yet to argue that the typical older American is wrought
with fear is to generalize from the exception. Until researchers
recognize the critical importance of developing appropriate fear
of crime indicators, and use them in their work, our understanding
of victimization fears will be limited, and meaningful policy
decisions impeded.

As mentioned earlier, most Americans—especially those under
65—consider fear of crime a very serious problem for the elderly.
However, careful examination of this issue indicates that the
elderly are no more afraid of crime when it is concretely
measured, but are somewhat more fearful—or anxious—of crime
when measured as formless fear. It may be that the public
reification of "old people are afraid of crime" is, in part,
responsible for the slightly higher levels of formless fear among
the elderly. It also appears that considerable empirical literature
on this subject has become part of the accepted body of
knowledge about fear of crime not because of a rigorous concern
for measurement procedures, but because the findings "make
sense" with public opinion. We recommend that future research
be conducted so that the concept of fear of crime is validly
measured and meaningful to the everyday lives of individuals.

NOTES

1. A potentially confounding factor impeding a proper interpretation of these survey
results is the change in public opinion over time. Assuming that the salience of fear of
crime as a social issue in part reflects the level of crime and media attention devoted to the

problem, the substantial increase in crime rates that occurred throughout the 1970s until the early 1980s would lead one to anticipate a heightened concern among the public in the Yin and Gallup polls compared to the earlier Harris survey. However, it appears that the public's perception of the crime problem has considerable stability over time. A comparison of the identical measure used by Harris in a 1974 national survey and a 1981 national survey shows only a 2% increase over time among the elderly respondents who feel that fear of crime is a very serious problem for them personally (23% versus 25%, respectively). The public's concern about crime as measured in the Gallup polls also shows a minimal percentage increase over the same years (from 3% in 1974 to 5% in 1981). Thus it seems that measurement difference is the principal factor contributing to the discrepancy among various opinion surveys on "fear of crime."

2. The striking absence of definitions of fear of crime is partly responsible for the conceptual confusion. Yin's (1980) review of the literature found only one: "the amount of anxiety and concern that persons have of becoming a victim" (Sundeen and Mathieu, 1976, p. 55). More often than not, fear of crime is "implicitly" defined by the measurement procedure itself, meaning that fear of crime becomes whatever the measure measures. This practice is difficult to justify methodologically and is all the more problematic considering that fear of crime is typically the major variable under study.

3. One may argue that the reason why these individuals do not go out alone at night is *because* they are fearful, yet the available evidence suggests that the great majority of persons of all ages do not limit their nighttime activities as a result of fear of crime (Cook, Fremming, and Tyler, 1981).

4. Although our focus is upon the quality of item content, there is equal cause for concern over other aspects of the measurement process. For example, there is a strong tendency to utilize single-item indicators of fear of crime when the desirability of multiple-item indices to measure complex theoretical constructs is well documented (Bohrnstedt and Borgatta, 1981). When multiple-item indices of fear of crime are used, reliability estimates are seldom reported, and evidence of the measure's validity is rare. (We note only in passing that Skogan and Maxfield [1981] are an exception because they attempt to demonstrate the *discriminant* validity of the NCS question. A more important issue that is not addressed, however, is whether the NCS measure exhibits *construct* validity—that is, whether it measures "fear of crime" or something else.) The question of overall methodological adequacy (e.g., sample size and design, analytical strategy, measurement of other variables) is of considerable importance as well, though not addressed in this work. We mention simply that the preponderance of the research appears to be methodologically sound on these other concerns.

5. We recognize that certain limitations confront the use of these secondary data. Therefore, we do not wish to overstate our conclusions. For instance, because we were unable to recapture the marginal frequencies of the original data in Table 1, we cannot state positively whether the observed relationship for the "nighttime" measure is more than chance association, nor whether the apparent nonrelationship for the "daytime" measure is statistically nonsignificant. (Given the large number of cases reported in Table 1, statistical significance would not be difficult to achieve.) While the analysis of percentage differences lacks the precision necessary to offer definitive conclusions, the general point is clear: fear of crime among the elderly may be exaggerated. The major advantage in using these secondary data is that they are from national probability samples and are unlikely to reflect idiosyncratic variation in crime perceptions of particular geographic regions or social categories.

6. Cook and her associates (1978) used two indicators of the economic consequences of crime that were designed to measure the differential impact of loss: the "absolute" amount (i.e., total dollar amount) and the "relative" amount (total dollar amount as a *percentage* of monthly income). They explain that "the loss of $50 to a person whose monthly income is $1000 is a less severe consequence of crime than the loss of $50 to a person whose monthly income is $400. It is only by using relative measures that the full impact of crime on the elderly can be assessed" (1978, p. 340).

7. For another useful example of how to measure fear of crime, consult the work of Warr (1984).

REFERENCES

Bohrnstedt, George W. and Edgar F. Borgatta. 1981. *Social Measurement: Current Issues*. Newbury Park, CA: Sage.

Braungart, Margaret M., William J. Hoyer, and Richard G. Braungart. 1979. "Fear of Crime and the Elderly." In *Police and the Elderly*, edited by A. P. Goldstein and William J. Hoyer. New York: Pergamon.

Brodyaga, Lisa, Margaret Gates, Susan Singer, Marna Tucker, and Richardson White. 1975. *Rape and Its Victims: A Report for Cities, Health Facilities, and Criminal Justice Agencies*. Washington, DC: Government Printing Office.

Clarke, Alan H. and Margaret Lewis. 1981. "Fear of Crime Among the Elderly." *British Journal of Criminology* 22:49-62.

Clemente, Frank and Michael B. Kleiman. 1976. "Fear of Crime Among the Aged." *Gerontologist* 16(3):207-210.

Cook, Thomas D., James Fremming, and Tom R. Tyler. 1981. "Criminal Victimization of the Elderly: Validating the Policy Assumptions." Pp. 223-251 in *Progress in Applied Social Psychology*, Vol. 1, edited by G. M. Stephenson and J. M. Davis. New York: John Wiley.

Cook, Fay Lomax, Wesley G. Skogan, Thomas D. Cook, and George E. Antunes. 1978. "Criminal Victimization of the Elderly: The Physical and Economic Consequences." *Gerontologist* 18(4):338-349.

Davis, Linda J. and Elaine M. Brody. 1979. *Rape and Older Women*. U.S. Department of Health, Education, and Welfare. Washington, DC: Government Printing Office.

DuBow, Frederic, Edward McCabe, and Gail Kaplan. 1979. *Reactions to Crime: A Critical Review of the Literature*. Washington, DC: National Institute of Law Enforcement and Criminal Justice.

"The Elderly: Prisoners of Fear." 1976. *Time* 108(November 29): 21-22.

Ferraro, Kenneth F. and Randy L. LaGrange. 1987. "The Measurement of Fear of Crime." *Sociological Inquiry* 57:70-101.

"Fortress on 78th Street." 1971. *Life* (November 19): 26-36.

Furstenberg, Frank F., Jr. 1971. "Public Reaction to Crime in the Street." *American Scholar* 40(4):601-610.

Gallup, George H. 1982. *The Gallup Report*. No. 206 (November). Princeton, NJ: Gallup Poll.

390   RESEARCH ON AGING

———1983. *The Gallup Report*. No. 210 (March). Princeton, NJ: Gallup Poll.

Garofalo, James. 1979. "Victimization and the Fear of Crime." *Journal of Research on Crime and Delinquency* 16:80-97.

———1982. "Fear of Crime as a Problem for the Elderly." *Social Problems* 30:240-245.

Garofalo, James and John Laub. 1978. "The Fear of Crime: Broadening Our Perspective." *Victimology* 3:242-253.

Harris, Louis. 1975. *The Myth and Reality of Aging in America.* Washington, DC: The National Council on Aging.

———1981. *Aging in the Eighties: America in Transition.* Washington, DC: National Council on Aging.

Hinkle, D. E. 1976. "Methodological Problems in the Study of Fears." *Journal of Psychology* 93:197-202.

Jaycox, Victoria. 1978. "The Elderly's Fear of Crime: Rational or Irrational." *Victimology* 3(3-4):329-334.

Jeffords, Clifford R. 1983. "The Situational Relationship Between Age and the Fear of Crime." *International Journal of Aging and Human Development* 17:103-111.

Lalli, Michael and Leonard Savitz. 1976. "Fear of Crime in the School Enterprise and Its Consequences." *Education and Urban Society* 8:401-416.

Lawton, M. Powell and M. Kleban. 1971. "The Aged Resident of the Inner City." *Gerontologist* 11:277-283.

Lawton, M. Powell, L. Nahemow, Sylvia Yaffe, and S. Feldman. 1976. "Psychological Aspects of Crime and Fear of Crime." In *Crime and the Elderly: Challenge and Response*, edited by Jack Goldsmith and Sharon S. Goldsmith. Lexington, MA: D. C. Heath.

Lindquist, John H. and Janice M. Duke. 1982. "The Elderly Victim at Risk: Explaining the Fear-Victimization Paradox." *Criminology* 20:115-126.

Research and Forecasts, Inc. 1980. *The Figgie Report on Fear of Crime: America Afraid.* Willoughby, OH: Figgie International, Inc.

Sarnoff, Irving and Philip G. Zimbardo. 1961. "Anxiety, Fear, and Social Affiliation." *Journal of Abnormal and Social Psychology* 62:356-363.

Schooler, C. 1970. "The Effect of Environment on Morale." *Gerontologist* 10:194-198.

Skogan, Wesley G. and Michael G. Maxfield. 1981. *Coping with Crime.* Newbury Park, CA: Sage.

Sundeen, Richard A. and James T. Mathieu. 1976. "The Urban Elderly: Environments of Fear." In *Crime and the Elderly: Challenge and Response*, edited by Jack Goldsmith and Sharon S. Goldsmith. Lexington, MA: Lexington Books.

U.S. Department of Justice. 1984. *Sourcebook of Criminal Justice Statistics—1983.* Bureau of Justice Statistics. Washington, DC: Government Printing Office.

Warr, Mark. 1984. "Fear of Victimization: Why Are Women and the Elderly More Afraid?" *Social Science Quarterly* 65:681-702.

Warr, Mark and Mark Stafford. 1983. "Fear of Victimization: A Look at the Proximate Causes." *Social Forces* 61:1033-1043.

Wilson, James Q. and George L. Kelling. 1985. "Broken Windows: The Police and Neighborhood Safety." Pp. 220-228 in *The Ambivalent Force*, edited by Abraham S. Blumberg and Elaine Niederhoffer. New York: Holt, Rinehart & Winston.

Wiltz, C. J. 1982. "Fear of Crime, Criminal Victimization and Elderly Blacks." *Phylon* 43:283-294.

Wolf, Robert. 1977. "An Aid to Designing Prevention Programs." *Police Chief* 44:27-29.

Yin, Peter. 1980. "Fear of Crime Among the Elderly: Some Issues and Suggestions."
     Social Problems 27:492-504.
——1981. "The Fear of Crime: Causes and Consequences." *Journal of Criminal Law
     and Criminology* 72:839-857.

*Randy L. LaGrange, Ph.D., is Assistant Professor of Sociology and Criminal
Justice at the University of North Carolina at Wilmington. His major interests
center on adolescent misconduct and police-related issues, with current research
interests in the fear of crime and social control in the community.*

*Kenneth F. Ferraro, Ph.D., is Assistant Professor of Sociology and Research
Associate, Center for Governmental Studies at Northern Illinois University,
DeKalb, IL 60115. His primary research interests include social gerontology and
medical sociology. Current research projects focus on public policy issues to
older related adults: fear of crime, labor force participation, and medical care
utilization.*

[6]

RESEARCH NOTES

Fear of Criminal Victimization: The Effect of Neighborhood Racial Composition

Gertrude L. Moeller, *Mississippi State University*

This analysis extends previous research on fear of crime by focusing on neighborhood racial composition as a salient predictor of fear of criminal victimization. Although its main effect was not strongly associated with fear, a multiplicative interaction term for neighborhood racial composition by race (WRAC) suggests that whites living in mostly black neighborhoods are the most fearful. Only sex and size of community were stronger predictors of fear. A parsimonious model including the variables sex, age, community size, and the interaction term WRAC is found to explain twenty-six percent of the variance in fear for personal safety on neighborhood streets at night.

Introduction

For the past two decades, researchers have reported high levels of fear of criminal victimization (e.g., Boggs 1971; Erskine 1974; Clemente and Kleiman 1977; Garofalo 1979; Braungart, Braungart and Hoyer 1980; Brooks 1981; Lee 1982; Stafford and Galle 1984). Fear of crime is itself a form of indirect victimization, resulting in psychological discomfort (McIntrye 1967; Conklin 1971; Brooks 1981), reduced opportunities for free movement, recreation, and sociability (Conklin 1971; Garofalo 1979), and diminished faith in the stability of the social order (Brooks 1981).

One commentary found in this literature is that fear is frequently far out of proportion with the objective probability of victimization, especially for women and the elderly (Clemente and Kleiman 1977; Garafalo 1979; Braungart et al. 1980; Liska, Lawrence and Sanchirico 1982). Media sensationalism and biased reporting are often cited as causes of disproportionate fear of crimes of personal violence, even among individuals who have a low probability of victimization (Clemente and Kleiman 1977; Braungart et al.

Sociological Inquiry, Vol. 59, No. 2, May 1989
©1989 by the University of Texas Press, P.O. Box 7819, Austin, TX 78713

210   GERTRUDE L. MOELLER

COMMUNITY SIZE. With the exception of Braungart et al. (1980) most studies report that community size is strongly associated with fear of walking alone at night (e.g., Wolfgang and Ferracuti 1967; Boggs 1971; Erskine 1974; Ollenburger 1981). Unlike the sex variable, community size is positively related to fear of crime and to actual crime rates (Wolfgang and Ferracuti 1967). Crime rates are considerably higher for urban areas, and urban dwellers expressed significantly more concern for their safety than did rural residents (Conklin 1971); for example there is a strong association between city size and fear of walking alone at night (Clemente and Kleiman 1977). Lee (1982), using a single-item measure of fear of crime similar to that in the Braungart et al. study, found that the urban elderly are significantly more likely to express fear than their rural counterparts.

AGE. There is no consensus on the effects of age on fear of crime. Studies which report a substantial effect of age upon fear of crime (Garofalo 1979; Ollenburger 1981) are contradicted by those which find little evidence of age differences in fear rates (Clemente and Kleiman 1977; Braungart et al. 1980). Lebowitz (1975) suggests that since the majority of the elderly are women, age may interact with sex, reducing its utility as a predictor. A recent critical review on fear of crime suggests that lack of a uniform indicator for fear of crime may account for these contradictory findings (Ferraro and LaGrange 1987).

RACE. Some support for the use of race as a predictor of fear of crime is found in the literature. According to Feagin (1970) and Biderman (Biderman, Johnson, McIntyre, and Weir 1976), in the seventies blacks expressed more anxiety about crime than did whites, and blacks also felt a greater need to arm themselves in defense of their homes. Two additional studies suggest that victimization and fear of crime are positively related to race (Gubrium 1974), and that middle-aged and elderly black persons report more fear than their white counterparts (Braungart et al. 1980). Brooks (1981) later argued that because blacks are more likely to be involved in crime than are whites, and because interracial crime is rare, blacks are eight times more likely to become victims of crime.

INCOME AND EDUCATION. As with race, the literature includes a few studies which link socioeconomic status to fear of crime. Gubrium (1974) reports an inverse relationship between income and victimization, while Erskine (1974) notes that the poor, the least educated, and blacks are most likely to report fear for personal safety in their neighborhood streets. Clemente and Kleiman's (1977) findings support Erskine, although the effect of education is weak.

NEIGHBORHOOD RACIAL COMPOSITION. Despite its theoretical promise, only one study has included a measure of racial composition of community as an independent variable predicting fear. Liska et al. (1982), citing Lizotte and Bordua (1980), suggest that the presence of nonwhites creates perceptions of increased risk of victimization among both white and nonwhite residents of a community. Their research findings support the hypotheses that percent nonwhite population positively affects fear for both whites and nonwhites and that segregation decreases fear for whites while increasing fear for nonwhites. However, the city represents the unit of measurement for segregation and percent nonwhite population, resulting in only 26 observations on these variables. Their analysis aggregates data so that two residents of a single city have the same score for segregation, even if one lives in an all-black or all-white neighborhood while the other lives in a racially mixed neighborhood. This necessitates making comparisons between populations of cities rather than between individual respondents, so that variability in fear within cities cannot be analyzed. This limitation can be overcome by using respondents' self-reports of proximity to opposite race residents.

Problem Statement

During the past twenty years, sex and community size have been identified as strong predictors of fear, and the aged have often been cited as more fearful. Yet contradictory empirical findings for community size and age have been cited above, and the research on race, income, and education is inconclusive. The final variable, neighborhood racial composition, holds promise as a correlate of fear but has received little research attention. This study examines the utility of each of these seven variables as predictors of fear of crime with particular attention to estimating the effect of individual perceptions of neighborhood racial composition on feelings of fear for personal safety on one's neighborhood streets at night and determines how well the set of variables explains variance in fear of crime. Finally, a comparison of the individual contribution of each variable allows the construction of a more efficient model for explaining variance in fear of crime.

Methodology

The data were collected by the Survey Research Laboratory at the University of Illinois during the Spring of 1981. A probability sample of adult heads of household in the state of Illinois was generated by random digit dialing in the Chicago SMSA and by systematic sampling from directories elsewhere in the state. A structured interview questionnaire was administered to 764 respondents by telephone.

The independent variables include sex, size of community, age, race, education, income, and neighborhood racial composition. Each respondent

212   GERTRUDE L. MOELLER

was asked to identify his community as a: (1) big city, (2) medium city, (3) suburb, (4) small town, or (5) rural area. Education was coded into eighteen categories on a scale of highest grade or year of school completed. Family income was coded into twelve categories on an ascending scale, in thousands of dollars. Neighborhood racial composition was coded as (1) all white, (2) mostly white, (3) about half and half, (4) mostly black, and (5) all black according to respondent evaluation. To test for interaction between respondent's sex and the effects of community size, family income, and race, three multiplicative interaction variables are included in the model (SEXSIZE, SEXFINC, and SEXWHT). Two additional interaction variables are used to test for interaction between neighborhood racial composition and community size (RSIZE) and neighborhood racial composition and race (WRAC).

The dependent variable, fear of criminal victimization, was coded as a dichotomous response to the question, ''is there any area right around where you live—that is, within a mile—where you would be afraid to walk alone at night?'' Lee (1982) objects to this question because it addresses fear of personal attack outside the home rather than pervasive anxiety about crime, while Ferraro and LaGrange (1987) note that it does not specify the object of fear. However, this item represents one of the most frequently used indicators of fear of crime (Clemente and Kleiman 1977; Ferraro and LaGrange 1987), facilitating comparison of findings from different populations. Also, because people fear crimes of personal violence, and because the streets are a high-risk environment for criminal attack, questions pertaining to fear of one's neighborhood streets address a basic component of fear of victimization (Erskine 1974; Hindelang, Gottfredson, and Garofalo 1978; Stafford and Galle 1984).

Largely ignored in a vast research literature is neighborhood racial composition. To determine whether neighborhood racial composition is a salient predictor of fear of crime, racial composition is included in a multivariate model for predicting fear of crime, and the results for this and the remaining independent variables are then compared with the findings previously reported. Finally, stepwise multiple regression is used to select a parsimonious model for predicting fear of personal safety on one's neighborhood streets at night.

Results

The mean, standard deviation, and number of cases for each variable in the analysis are shown in Table 1. Comparison with the 1980 Census data for the state of Illinois (U.S. Bureau of the Census 1980) suggests that women and older persons may be overrepresented in the sample. However, the sample proportion reporting fear (forty-two percent) is comparable with the 1981 national rate (forty-five percent) reported in *The Sourcebook of Criminal Justice Statistics–1982* (Flanagan and McLeod 1983). The sample is sixty percent female, with an average age of 44.9 years. The mean family income was $25,000, and the average number of years of school completed was 13.0. Eighty-three percent of the respondents were white, and there is a tendency for respondents to report living in mostly white neighborhoods.

Table 1

Mean and Standard Deviation for Independent and Dependent Variables, and Zero-Order Pearson Correlation Coefficients for All Variables with Fear of Walking Alone at Night

Variable (Term)	Mean	Standard Deviation	Correlation Coefficients
FEAR[a]	.42	.49	1.000
SEX[b]	1.60	.50	.329
FINC	25.20	15.00	– .167
RCOMP	2.10	1.40	.310
SIZE	2.80	1.42	– .373
RACE[c]	.83	.37	– .166
AGE	44.90	16.29	.085
EDUC	13.00	2.84	– .088
SEXFINC	12.70	15.74	.175
SEXSIZE	1.50	1.69	.083
SEXWHT	.46	.49	.195
RSIZE	4.90	3.66	.015
WRAC	1.50	1.40	.139

[a]No = 0; Yes = 1
[b]Male = 1; Female = 2
[c]Nonwhite = 0; White = 1

Correlation coefficients for all variables with fear suggest that sex, racial composition of neighborhood (RCOMP), and community size (SIZE) are strongly associated with fear for safety on one's neighborhood streets at night. Correlations are positive for SEX (.329) and RCOMP (.310), indicating that women and residents of mostly black neighborhoods are

214   GERTRUDE L. MOELLER

most likely to express fear. Community size is inversely related to fear (– .373), indicating that urban residents are most likely to express fear for safety on neighborhood streets (rural areas score highest on SIZE). Correlations are low for other variables in the model (i.e. income, education, age, and race). (SEXSIZE, SEXFINC, and SEXWHT are not highly correlated with fear, suggesting that the effects of community size, family income, and race on the dependent variable are not altered by the sex of the respondent.)

Although no excessively high intercorrelations were found between most of the independent variables, there is a moderately high negative relationship (– .495) between community size (SIZE) and racial composition of neighborhood (RCOMP). To determine whether higher fear rates in black neighborhoods are due to their urban location, a multiplicative interaction term, RSIZE. was created, the results of which are shown in Table 1. The low correlation with fear of crime (.015) indicates that RCQMP and SIZE are not confounded.

Racial composition of neighborhood is also highly correlated with race (– .569) revealing a tendency for whites to live in racially segregated neighborhoods. A multiplicative interaction term for neighborhood racial composition by race, WRAC, was created. Its correlation with fear of crime (.139) is not particularly high. However, to further test the possibility that whites and nonwhites react differently to residential desegregation, WRAC was included in the stepwise regression model.

Cross-classifications of fear of walking alone at night in one's neighborhood streets by each independent variable are presented in Table 2, with data for age, education, and income collapsed. Similar to previous survey findings, women and nonwhites more often report fear than do men and whites. The fear rate is also shown to increase with community size (SIZE) and to decrease with level of education. There is a tendency for reports of fear to increase with age; although fear is greatest among the oldest age group (fifty-six percent), the lowest proportion (thirty-four percent) is found in the 35–49 age group.

As expected, individuals in the highest income categories have the lowest fear rate (both are thirty percent). Fear among persons in the three middle categories show a gradual decline as income increases (forty-eight percent, forty-four percent, forty-three percent respectively). However, the highest rate of fear (sixty-two percent) is in the $6,000 to $10,000 category rather than in the lowest category ($6,000 or less). Overall, there is a trend of decreasing reports of fear with increasing income.

Of the multiplicative interaction terms discussed above, only RCOMP and WRAC were included in the stepwise regression reported in Table 3. From the information shown in the third column of this table (F Sig.), it is

Table 2
Percentage Distribution on Fear of Walking Alone at Night Within
One Mile of Home for Sample and Relevant Subsamples, 1981[a]

Category	N	Percent Afraid	Category	N	Percent Afraid
Sample	724	42	Income:		
			6,000 or less	36	48
Sex:			6,000–10,000	79	62
Males	319	23	10,000–15,000	94	48
Females	405	56	15,000–20,000	61	44
			20,000–30,000	180	43
Race:			30,000–40,000	104	30
White	602	38	40,000 plus	109	30
Nonwhite	120	60			
			Community Size:		
Age:			Big City	221	66
19–34	240	40	Medium City	80	57
35–49	197	34	Suburb	166	31
50–64	170	43	Small Town	167	24
65 plus	97	57	Rural Area	90	19
Education:					
< HS	122	56			
HS	270	38			
> HS	340	37			

[a]Item nonresponse results in an N of less than 764 for each variable.

clear that repondent's race alters the effect of neighborhood racial composition
on fear of crime. Examination of standardized and unstandardized regression
coefficients (B and Beta) and significance levels for RACE and RCOMP
(neighborhood racial composition) reveal that although the fear rate is higher
for nonwhites than for whites, and higher for residents of mostly black neighborhoods than for residents of mostly white neighborhoods, neither of these
effects is strong enough to explain much of the variance in the dependent
variable. On the other hand, the standardized regression coefficient (.006)

216   GERTRUDE L. MOELLER

Table 3
Unstandardized Regression Coefficient, Standardized Regression Coefficient,
F Significance, R Square, and R Square Change for the Full and
Reduced Models[a]

Variable	B	Beta	F Sig.	R^2	R^2 Change
SEX	.277 (.297)	.283 (.304)	.000 (.000)	.108	.108
WRAC	.002 (.016)	.006 (.047)	.021 (.001)	.129	.021
AGE	9.020E-05 (9.020E-05)	.003 (.003)	.024 (.010)	.135	.006
SIZE	− .036 (− .004)	− .104 (− .012)	.000 (.000)	.261	.125
FINC	− 9.800E-05	− .003	.077	.269	.008
EDUC	− 3.450E-04	− .002	.761	.269	.000
RCOMP	2.800E-03	.008	.798	.277	.007
RACE	.164	.124	.237	.279	.002

[a]Figures for the reduced model are reported in parentheses.

and significance level (.021) for WRAC indicate that although both white
and nonwhite residents living in all-black or mostly black neighborhoods are
more likely to report fear of crime, the effect is especially acute for whites.
Thus, we can identify white respondents living in racially mixed neighborhoods as those most likely to report fear of crime.

    Sex, size of community and age are also significant predictors of fear.
Sex has the strongest effect on fear, with a standardized regression coefficient
of .283 (Table 3, Beta) and an R^2 change of .108 (Table 3, R^2 Change).
The standardized regression coefficient for SIZE is − .104 (R^2 change =

.125). Age has the weakest effect, with a standardized regression coefficient of only .024 (R^2 change = .006).

It is appropriate at this point to return to three concerns expressed earlier in this paper. First, is racial composition of neighborhood a predictor of fear of criminal victimization? The findings indicate that when respondent's race is taken into account, the effect of self-reports of racial composition of neighborhood upon fear of walking alone at night on one's neighborhood streets is significant (P < .05). The magnitiude of this effect (.021) is surpassed only by that of sex and community size, the two variables most frequently associated with fear of criminal victimization in the literature. This observation is relevant to another concern, namely, the performance of independent variables identified in other studies. Of these, sex, size of community, and age are significant (P < .05). As expected, women and urban residents are most likely to report fear of walking alone at night. The elderly are also more likely to report fear, but this effect is weak. Although the three remaining variables make no significant contribution to the model, the sign of their regression coefficients are in the same direction as the relationships most often reported in the literature; i.e. fear decreases with increasing education and family income, and nonwhites are more likely to report fear than whites.

A third concern is the possibility of constructing a more parsimonious model for predicting fear of criminal victimization. Half the variables in Table 3 (FINC, EDUC, RCOMP, and RACE) combine to contribute only .017 in R^2 change to the total explanatory power of the model. This is less than that for any single remaining variable with the exception of AGE. Constructing a reduced model including only those variables which are statistically significant allows more efficient prediction of fear of criminal victimization, given the independent variables examined in this research. This model accounts for twenty-six percent of the variance explained, and each independent variable is statistically significant at the .01 level.

Discussion

While the research results are generally in agreement with those of previous studies, data in the tables refines and, in one case, contradicts conclusions drawn by other researchers, particularly for the variables SEX, RACE, RCOMP, and WRAC. Data for the remaining four variables, EDUC, FINC, SIZE, and AGE, inspire fewer comments. For example, this research provides little elaboration of the effects of income and education on fear of crime, except to suggest that these factors are probably not especially useful as predictors of fear.

SIZE appears to be the strongest predictor of fear. This is a particularly unusual finding since some researchers (e.g. Braungart et al.) have found that community size is not highly associated with fear of crime and since many studies have identified sex as the single strongest predictor of fear of crime (e.g. Erskine 1974; Clement and Kleiman 1977; Garofalo 1979; Braungart et al. 1980; Stafford and Galle 1984). There are several possible explanations for this finding. First, the discrepancy may result from the vast differences in methodologies used across studies. For example, the community size indicator used in this study relies on respondent evaluations of community size. A more objectively applied universal scaling system based on United States Census data might yield different results. Some non-random factor(s) may predispose fearful respondents to overestimate community size, thereby exaggerating the relationship between SIZE and FEAR. It is also possible that with the passage of time between the various studies in which the variable is addressed, changes have occurred in the relative strength of sex and community size as predictors of fear of crime.

AGE does not appear to be a strong predictor of fear. Perhaps, as Lebowitz (1975) suggested, the fact that most elderly persons reporting tend to be female causes AGE to interact with SEX. Since both women and the elderly were overrepresented in the sample, SEX, entered prior to AGE in the regression equation, could have had a suppressing effect.

Comparison of SEX with previous studies is especially noteworthy. For 1973–74, Clemente and Kleiman (1977) reported a difference in fear of 39 percentage points between women and men. In this study, women were much more likely to report fear of crime than men, but the percentage difference is only 33. This difference is accounted for by a reduction in the fear rate among women. Previous researchers have suggested that high fear among women results from irrationality—factors of personality, socialization, and media influence—rather than the objective probability of being victimized. The low fear rate for women in Illinois supports this view, since the *Uniform Crime Reports* for 1973–1981 show no significant decrease in victimization rates for forcible rape in the Chicago SMSA (U. S. Department of Justice 1973–74; 1975; 1976–77; 1978–19; 1980–81). Thus the lower fear rate among Illinois women in 1981 probably does not result from a decrease in victimization rates for women in the previous seven years. An alternative explanation is that changes in the status of women over the last decade (e.g. their evolving political, economic, and familial roles, as well as self-perceptions of competence and independence), have reduced women's fear of personal victimization.

Another possible explanation for the findings reported is that past reports of fear of crime among women were influenced and inflated by a perception of the desirable "femininity" of a positive response. The expression of fear suggests attributes such as vulnerability, delicacy, helplessness, and dependence. Thus, while women may once have been encouraged to report fear, changing roles may create a growing reluctance to express fear without clear cause.

If these explanations have merit, then partial support is provided to reaffirm a previous contention that high fear rates among women are "irrational," produced by factors other than objective risk of victimization. Although Stafford and Galle (1984) demonstrate that when exposed to risky environments, women are in fact more likely to be victimized than men, the notion of a social-psychological component to fear should not be discounted.

Race as a predictor of fear of crime has not yet been firmly established. The findings reported here show a low negative correlation of RACE with FEAR, which supports earlier contentions that nonwhites are more fearful of crime. However, when RACE was entered into the regression equation, the path coefficient indicates that whites are more likely to report fear of crime when all other variables are controlled for. This finding suggests that the higher fear of nonwhites is probably a result of factors other than race, such as concentration in urban areas. Respondent's perception of neighborhood racial composition (RCOMP) provides an additional means for estimating the effect of race in producing fear of crime.

Neither RACE nor RCOMP are strong predictors of fear of crime. However, when the two variables are combined with WRAC, race becomes an important factor in predicting fear of crime. WRAC is a strong predictor of FEAR. Whites living in mostly black neighborhoods are more likely to report fear of crime. Although race does not significantly influence fearfulness, the interactive perceptions of whites and nonwhites tend to lead to this outcome. Policy makers will have little success in reducing fear to levels more commensurate with likelihood of victimization and will find their efforts to end discriminatory residential segregation through racial integration of neighborhoods constantly endangered by grassroots opposition, until the race relations component of fear of crime is addressed directly.

In conclusion, these findings tend to support previous research, including the contention that a social-psychological component to fear of crime exists, especially among women. However, factors such as income and education are probably not useful in predicting fear and could be excluded without significantly reducing the utility of explanatory models. To support the social goal of residential desegregation, future analyses of fear should strive to include measures of race and neighborhood racial composition, and policy makers should note the need to directly address the role of race relations in producing high fear of crime which may undercut efforts at residential integration.

220   GERTRUDE L. MOELLER

REFERENCES

Biderman, Albert D., Louise A. Johnson, Jennie McIntyre, and Adrienne W. Weir. 1976.
    "Report on a Pilot Study in the District of Columbia on Victimization and Attitudes
    Toward Law Enforcement." Washington, D. C.: U. S. Government Printing Office.

Boggs, Sarah L. 1971. "Formal and Informal Crime Control: An Exploratory Study of Urban,
    Suburban, and Rural Orientations." *Sociological Quarterly* 12:319–327.

Braungart, Margaret, Richard G. Braungart, and William J. Hoyer. 1980. "Age, Sex and
    Social Factors in Fear of Crime." *Sociological Focus* 13:55–65.

Brooks, James. 1981. "The Fear of Crime in the United States." In *Perspectives on Crime Victims*,
    edited by Burt Gallaway and Joe Hudson. St. Louis, MO: C. V. Mosby Co.

Clemente, Frank, and Michael B. Kleiman. 1977. "Fear of Crime in the United States: A Multi-
    variate Analysis." *Social Forces* 56:519–531.

Conklin, John E. 1971. "Dimensions of Community Response to the Crime Problem." *Social
    Problems* 18:373–385.

Erskine, Hazel. 1974. "The Polls: Fear of Crime and Violence." *Public Opinion Quarterly* 38:
    131–145.

Feagin, Joseph R. 1970. "Home-Defense and the Police: Black and White Perspectives."
    American Behavioral Scientist 13:797–814.

Ferraro, Kenneth F., and Randy LaGrange. 1987. "The Measurement of Fear of Crime."
    Sociological Inquiry 57:70–110.

Flanagan, Timothy J., and Maureen McLeod. 1983. *Sourcebook of Criminal Justice Statistics–1982*,
    edited by Timothy J. Flanagan and Maureen McLeod. U. S. Department of Justice,
    Bureau of Justice Statistics. Washington, D. C.: U. S. Government Printing Office.

Garofalo, James. 1979. "Victimization and the Fear of Crime." *Journal of Research on Crime and
    Delinquency* 16:80–97.

Gubrium, Jaber F. 1974. "Victimization in Old Age." *Crime and Delinquency* 20:245–250.

Hindelang, Michael J., Michael R. Gottfredson, and James Garofalo. 1978. *Victims of Personal
    Crime: An Empirical Foundation for a Theory of Personal Victimization*. Cambridge, MA: Ballinger.

Lebowitz, Barry D. 1975. "Age and Fearfulness: Personal and Situational Factors." *Journal
    of Gerontology* 30:696–700.

Lee, Gary R. 1982. "Residential Location and Fear of Crime Among the Elderly." *Rural
    Sociology* 47:655–669.

Liska, Allen E., Joseph J. Lawrence, and Andrew Sanchirico. 1982. "Fear of Crime as a Social
    Fact." *Social Forces* 60:760–770.

Lizotte, Alan J., and David Bordua. 1980. "Firearms Ownership for Sport and Protection."
    American Sociological Review 45:299–343.

McIntyre, J. 1967. "Public Attitudes Toward Crime and Law Enforcement." *The Annals*
    374:34–46.

Ollenburger, Jane C. 1981. "Criminal Victimization and Fear of Crime." *Research on Aging*
    3:101–118.

Stafford, Mark C., and Omer R. Galle. 1984. "Victimization Rates, Exposure to Risk, and
    Fear of Crime." *Criminology* 22:173–185.

United States Bureau of the Census. 1980. *Census of Population Illinois: Characteristics of Population*.
    Washington, D. C.: U. S. Government Printing Office.

United States Department of Justice. 1973–1974. *Uniform Crime Reports for the United States*.
    Federal Bureau of Investigation. Washington, D. C.: U. S. Government Printing Office.

————. 1975. *Uniform Crime Reports for the United States*. Federal Bureau of Investigation. Wash-
    ington, D. C.: U. S. Government Printing Office, p. 69.

————. 1976–1977. *Uniform Crime Reports for the United States*. Federal Bureau of Investigation. Washington, D. C.: U. S. Government Printing Office, pp. 57.

————. 1978–1979. *Uniform Crime Reports for the United States*. Federal Bureau of Investigation. Washington, D. C.: U. S. Government Printing Office, pp. 62, 64.

————. 1980–1981. *Uniform Crime Reports for the United States*. Federal Bureau of Investigation. Washington, D. C.: U. S. Government Printing Office, pp. 64, 346.

Wolfgang, Marvin E., and Franco Ferracuti. 1967. *The Subculture of Violence*. Beverly Hills, CA: Sage.

[7]

The Effects of Building Size on Personal Crime and Fear of Crime

Oscar Newman
Institute for Community Design Analysis
Karen A. Franck
New Jersey School of Architecture
New Jersey Institute of Technology

The research that formed the basis of Newman's book *Defensible Space* demonstrated that building height is one of the leading predictors of robbery rate in low-income public housing projects. Research reported in this article was undertaken to extend the scope and detail of the earlier work and, most importantly, to examine the causal mechanisms underlying the relationship of physical design to crime and fear of crime. The study sites in this new research are moderate-income, federally-assisted housing developments and low-income public housing projects. The major source of data is a household survey of residents. The findings provide important empirical support for the postulates of defensible space theory by showing that building size affects personal crime and fear of crime through residents' control and use of the space outside their apartments. Building size has a large total effect on residents' fear of crime, but despite its important indirect effects on personal crime, the total effect of building size on personal crime is not as strong as expected. Possible reasons for this unexpected finding are used to suggest refinements to defensible space theory.

Defensible space theory posits that the physical design of residential settings has a strong influence on both the occurrence of crime and residents' fear of crime (Newman, 1972; 1973a; 1976).

This paper is based on the final report of a study of crime and instability supported by the Law Enforcement Assistance Administration, U.S. Department of Justice, Grant 76-NI-99-0036-S-2. An earlier version of this paper was presented at the Annual Meetings of the American Sociological Association in Toronto, August, 1981. The authors are grateful to Ralph Taylor and anonymous reviewers for their suggestions.

POPULATION AND ENVIRONMENT

Previous defensible space research has demonstrated that in low-income public housing projects in New York City a physical design feature, building height, ranked among the three most important predictors of robbery rate (Newman, 1973b). The other two leading predictors were the percentage of the population receiving welfare and the percentage of families with a female head of household.

The defensible space explanation for this link between physical design and crime is that certain design features of residential environments encourage people to extend their sphere of influence beyond the immediate confines of their individual dwelling units to adjacent areas. This extension of the home inhibits criminal activity and encourages a sense of safety. While this explanation was implicit in previous defensible space research, the specific mediating factors believed to account for the relationship between design and crime were not actually measured. The study described here was undertaken to redress this situation, to determine if the theoretical explanation for the relationship between design and crime could be empirically supported. To meet this objective, a theoretical causal model was developed in which a series of intervening variables are posited as the links between the physical and social characteristics of housing developments and the incidence of personal crime (robbery and assault), the intensity of residents' fear of crime, and the level of community instability (see Figure 1).

Each independent variable in the model is expected to affect each intervening and each dependent variable, and each intervening variable is expected to affect every variable that follows it in the causal sequence. For the purpose of graphic clarity all the independent variables have been grouped together and their individual effects are shown as single lines running from the entire group of independent variables.

Residents' use and control of space outside their apartments are included as intervening variables because they are the best indicators of how much residents have extended their sphere of influence over areas adjacent to their apartments. We expect that the larger the building, the less frequently residents will use the space outside their apartments and the less control they will have over the space. Low use and low control will, in turn, lead to a high incidence of personal crime and to a high level of fear. Rent collection and social interaction among residents are included because they constitute possible additional links between physical design and crime or fear of crime. Rent collection, which refers to man-

OSCAR NEWMAN AND KAREN A. FRANCK

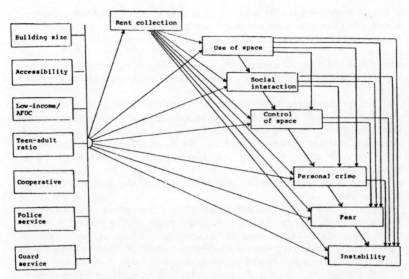

FIGURE 1. Theoretical Causal Model of the Key Factors Affecting Personal Crime, Fear and Instability.

agement's success in collecting rent, is a measure of management effectiveness. We expect that the larger the building, the less effective management will be and, in turn, the higher the crime and the fear of crime. Similarly, building size is expected to have a negative impact on the amount of social interaction among residents which, in turn, will have negative effects on crime and fear. (Throughout this paper the terms "positive" and "negative" refer exclusively to the signs of coefficients, not to good or bad consequences.) In addition to these indirect effects, building size is expected to have positive direct effects on crime and fear.

METHOD

The sites for this research consist of federally-assisted, moderate-income housing developments in Newark, San Francisco, and St. Louis and low-income, public housing projects in San Francisco. The sites are composed of row house, walk-up, and high-rise buildings. Those developments composed of two building types were broken down into two sites according to building type, bringing the total number of sites in the study

POPULATION AND ENVIRONMENT

to 63: 11 high-rise sites, 34 walk-up sites, and 18 row house sites. On the whole, the sites are small, ranging from 32 to 772 units with the average size being 169. The proportion of single-parent families on welfare ranges from zero in several moderate-income sites to 63% in one public housing site; the average for all sites is 23%. The majority of households in all the sites are families with children and most of the residents in these sites are black.

The primary source of data is a household survey of a stratified probability sample of 2,655 male and female adult residents. Supplementary information was obtained from housing records, site plans, site visits, and interviews with managers of the developments. Data gathered from these sources were used to derive variables and values on these variables that reflected the characteristics of sites. This is because the unit of analysis in this research is the housing site and not the individual household.

With only a few exceptions (accessibility, teen-adult ratio, cooperative ownership, and personal crime rate), most of the variables in the study are composites, formed as the unweighted sum of the individual items, which had been z-scored. The measurement of all the independent variables in the causal model is summarized in Table 1.

Building size, which is the only independent variable being considered in this paper, is measured with an index that combines two physical design characteristics of sites: (1) building type and (2) the number of apartment units that share a building entry and common circulation area. Buildings were classified into four types: row houses; regular walk-up buildings; gallerias, which are walk-ups with an open, single-loaded corridor; and high-rises. Values for the building type variable ranged from 1 for row houses to 4 for high-rises. In row houses the apartment entrance is the same as the building entrance, therefore, row houses are rated as having only one apartment unit per building entry. In regular walk-up buildings the number of apartment units sharing a building entry ranges from 2 to 19 with a mean of 7. For gallerias and regular walk-up buildings with an outdoor stairway, the number of apartments sharing the stairway is used to measure the number of units per entry and common circulation area. The range of units per entry in gallerias is from 4 to 116 with a mean of 25. In high-rises the number of units per entry ranges from 32 to 425 with a mean of 183. When the number of units per entry differed between buildings in the same site, the average value for those buildings was used. The two variables, building type and number of units per entry, were standardized and then combined to form a single variable.

Table 2 summarizes the measurement of the intervening and dependent variables. Personal crime includes robberies and assaults that occurred within the development during the 12 months preceding the household survey. The procedure for figuring the rate of personal crime was to divide the total number of such experiences, as reported in the

OSCAR NEWMAN AND KAREN A. FRANCK

Table 1

All Independent Variables in Causal Model

Variable Name	Description	Source
Building size	Index: Units per entry and building type	Site visits & site plans
Accessibility	Rating of vulnerability of buildings and apartments to intrusion by outsiders	Site visits
Low-income/AFDC	Index: Mean household income of residents and percent of one-parent welfare families	Household survey
Teen-adult ratio	Ratio of total number of teenagers (10-20 year olds) to number of adults	Household survey
Cooperative	Cooperative ownership by residents	Manager interview
Police service	Index: Frequency and type of police patrols	Police interview
Security guard service	Index: Presence and quality of security guard service	Manager interview & household survey

household survey, by the number of residents in that site and to multiply that figure by 1,000. It should be noted that in these sites personal crime is a fairly infrequent event. In 20 sites, or almost one-third of the cases, no one reported experiencing an assault or a robbery within the development during the preceding 12 months. The average rate per 1,000 residents is 44.44 and the standard deviation is 43.22. Given such low frequencies, the results regarding personal crime should be viewed with some caution.

Fear of crime is measured with an index of eight items that refer to various aspects of fear: perceived safety of certain areas, estimated likelihood of being burglarized, fear of being robbed or attacked, comparison of crime in the development to crime in the surrounding area, and estimate of the change in crime.

Since considerable attention will be addressed to the intervening variable control of space, the content of the items used to measure this construct is worth describing:

208

POPULATION AND ENVIRONMENT

Table 2
Intervening and Dependent Variables

Variable Name	Description	Source
Rent collection	Index: Management firmness and success in rent collection	Manager interview
Use of space	Index: Frequency of residents' use of space outside the apartments	Household survey
Social interaction	Index: Nature and frequency of social interaction and sense of belonging among residents	Household survey
Control of space	Index: Perceived likelihood that residents will intervene in criminal or suspicious situations	Household survey
Personal crime rate	Robberies and assaults per 1,000 residents	Household survey
Fear	Index: Residents' fear of crime	Household survey

L1. Estimated likelihood of intervention by resident in act of graffiti-painting by 13-year-old boys,
(Five-point scale from "Very unlikely" to "Very likely");
L2. Estimated likelihood that boys will stop painting graffiti,
(Five-point scale from "Very unlikely" to "Very likely");
L3. Estimated likelihood that resident would call police or management if boys do not stop,
(Five-point scale from "Very unlikely" to "Very likely");
L7. Type of intervention by resident when sees two suspicious-looking men outside building,
(Responses coded into 4 categories from "no intervention" to "direct intervention");
L8. Likelihood of help by resident in attack on person outside building,
(Five-point scale from "Very unlikely" to "Very likely").

After a value on each variable for each site had been derived, coefficients for total, direct, and indirect effects in the study's model were estimated. Since the model is recursive and the errors are assumed to be uncorrelated, ordinary least squares regression was used to estimate the coefficients (Hanushek & Jackson, 1977).

Both statistical significance and relative magnitude were used to judge the importance of effects. An alpha level of .15 was used to judge the significance of total and direct effects.[1] Since there are no techniques available within path analysis for testing the significance of indirect effects, their importance is best judged by their relative magnitude. In order to be interpreted at all, the coefficient for an individual indirect

OSCAR NEWMAN AND KAREN A. FRANCK

effect had to be larger than .05. A criterion of relative size also was used to evaluate direct, total, and total indirect effects. In order to do this, the following standards were adopted: large effects are greater than or equal to .30; moderate effects are between .15 and .29 in size; and small effects are from .06 through .14. Any effects that are equal to or smaller than .05 are considered to be virtually zero.

FINDINGS

Table 3 presents the breakdown of the relationships between building size and personal crime and between building size and residents' fear of crime. The total effect, listed in the first row of the table, represents the total causal impact of building size on personal crime or on fear of crime. It is the sum of the direct and total indirect effects (Alwin & Hauser, 1975) and reflects the extent of change in crime or fear produced by a change in building size, regardless of the mechanisms by which the change in crime or fear is produced. The direct effect, listed in the second row, is the effect that is *not* transmitted by any intervening variables included in the model. The total indirect effect, listed in the third row, is the sum of all the effects of building size on crime, or on fear of crime, that *are* transmitted by the intervening variables, in all possible combinations. The total indirect effect is the sum of all the individual indirect effects. The noncausal component of the relationship is the unanalyzed portion of the total association and is computed by subtracting the total effect from the zero-order correlation. The total association, listed in the last row, is the zero-order correlation. The zero-order correlations between all variables in the model are listed in Table 4.

When the effects of building size were computed, the effects of all other independent variables in the model were held constant, namely the effects of: accessibility of buildings to unwanted intrusion; the proportion of low-income and one-parent, welfare families; the ratio of teenagers to adults; whether the development is cooperatively owned by the residents; the quality of security guard service; and the quality of police service.

The total effect of building size on personal crime rate is positive, as predicted, but small (.11). And yet the total indirect effect of building size on personal crime, which is also positive, is not small: it is .23, which by the standards adopted in this study is a moderate-sized effect. This sizable total indirect effect is offset by a smaller direct effect that is negative ($-.12$).

POPULATION AND ENVIRONMENT

Although building size does not have a powerful total effect on the rate of personal crime, it does have a large and significant positive effect on residents' fear of crime (.41). This effect is both direct (.23) and indirect (.19). Clearly, the larger the building, the higher the level of residents' fear. Further analysis indicates that high-rise sites show significantly higher levels of fear among residents than either walk-up or row house sites, but there is no difference in the levels of fear between the latter two building types (Newman & Franck, 1980).

Figure 2 is a path diagram showing the direct and indirect effects of building size on personal crime and on fear of crime. In order to be included in the diagram, a direct path had to be either statistically significant ($p < .15$) or part of an indirect path (with a coefficient larger than .05) from building size to personal crime or to fear of crime. The residual effects on personal crime and fear of crime also are shown in Figure 2. The standard error for each path coefficient is written in parentheses below each path.

Building size has direct effects in the predicted direction on rent collection (-.19), use of space (-.51), social interaction (-.31), and fear of crime (.22). All of these direct effects are significant

Table 3

Effects of Building Size on Personal Crime

and Fear of Crime

Effects of Building Size	Personal Crime	Fear of Crime
Total effect	.11	.41[a]
Direct effect	-.12	.23[d]
Total indirect effect	.23	.18
Non-causal component	-.16	-.06
Total association	-.05	.35

[a]$p < .01$; [b]$p < .05$; [c]$p < .10$; [d]$p < .15$

211

OSCAR NEWMAN AND KAREN A. FRANCK

Table 4

Correlation Matrix
of All Independent, Intervening, and Dependent Variables
(Lower triangle: correlation coefficients)
(Upper triangle: N of cases for correlation)

	Building size	Accessibility	Low-income/AFDC	Teen-adult ratio	Cooperative	Police service	Guard service	Rent collection	Use of space	Social interaction	Control of space	Personal crime rate	Fear
Building size	1.00	63	63	63	63	57	54	51	63	63	63	63	63
Accessibility	-.13	1.00	63	63	63	57	54	51	63	63	63	63	63
Low-income/AFDC	.02	.49	1.00	63	63	57	54	51	63	63	63	63	63
Teen-adult ratio	-.18	.26	.46	1.00	63	57	54	51	63	63	63	63	63
Cooperative	-.17	-.27	-.30	-.11	1.00	57	54	51	63	63	63	63	63
Police service	-.23	-.07	-.09	-.28	.01	1.00	49	47	57	57	57	57	57
Guard service	.18	-.29	-.12	-.07	.09	-.39	1.00	47	54	54	54	54	54
Rent collection	-.14	-.28	-.70	-.32	.07	-.01	.01	1.00	51	51	51	51	51
Use of space	-.56	-.12	-.25	.21	.27	.08	.06	.13	1.00	63	63	63	63
Social interaction	-.29	-.33	-.21	.24	.39	-.34	-.24	.02	.45	1.00	63	63	63
Control of space	-.22	-.45	-.71	-.32	.32	-.16	.18	.50	.29	.49	1.00	63	63
Personal crime rate	-.05	.02	.24	.16	.18	.27	-.06	-.48	0	.12	-.32	1.00	63
Fear	.35	.36	.69	.37	-.26	-.11	.14	-.51	-.43	-.27	-.71	.26	1.00
Instability	.37	.40	.58	.25	-.39	-.11	.14	-.54	-.31	-.44	-.61	.06	.50

POPULATION AND ENVIRONMENT

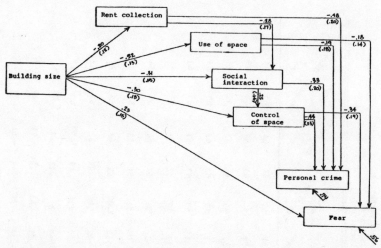

FIGURE 2. Major Effects of Building Size on Personal Crime and Fear of Crime.

($p < .15$). Figure 2 allows us to trace out the important individual indirect effects of building size on crime and fear. Building size has four major indirect effects on personal crime through rent collection (.10), use of space (.10), control of space (.13), and social interaction (-.10). The first three of these effects are in the predicted direction, that is, positive: the larger the building, the higher the personal crime rate. The fourth indirect effect, however, is in the opposite direction: building size has the expected negative effect on social interaction among residents, but social interaction has an unexpected positive effect on personal crime, thus creating the negative indirect effect. There are at least two explanations for this unexpected finding. If we interpret the effect strictly in terms of this study's causal model, we would conclude that the more residents interact with each other in a housing environment, the more likely they are to victimize each other. Based on prevailing theories about community, this seems unlikely. Another explanation is that incidents of person to person crime in a housing development bring people together to solve the crime problem, and in this way they come to know each other better and to interact more frequently. In designing the causal model for the study, we assumed that the direction of causal influence was primarily from social interaction to personal crime rate and not vice versa. The positive ef-

OSCAR NEWMAN AND KAREN A. FRANCK

fect that we found suggests that this may have been a mistaken assumption. The relationship could be one of reciprocal causation, where each affects the other but where the effect of personal crime on social interaction outweighs the reverse effect. A nonrecursive model would be required to simulate such a relationship.

Figure 2 also shows that the total indirect effect of building size on fear of crime is primarily transmitted through two intervening variables: residents' use of space (.10) and residents' control of space (.12). We can conclude that residents in large buildings are more afraid of crime than residents in small buildings for two reasons. First, because the areas outdoors are used less frequently in large buildings, and lower use results in higher fear. Second, because residents have less control over these areas in large buildings, and lack of control also leads to fear. Of course, building size also has a significant direct effect on fear. This means that regardless of how frequently outdoor areas are used or how much control residents have over the areas, residents in large buildings will be more afraid than residents in small buildings.

DISCUSSION

This discussion covers the indirect effects of building size on crime and fear of crime and a comparison of the present results concerning the total effect of building size on personal crime with those from the initial defensible space research.

Indirect Effects of Building Size

Defensible space theory posits that residents' control of space outside their apartments is a major link between the physical design of the housing environment and crime, and between design and fear of crime: the larger the building, the less control residents are able to exert and, in turn, the greater the crime and the fear of crime. The results from this study confirm this tenet: building size has indirect effects on both personal crime and fear of crime through control of space. This is the first time these relationships have been measured and therefore the first time the postulate has received empirical support.

Another tenet of defensible space theory that has not been previously studied concerns the importance of residents' use of space outside their homes as an additional link between design

214

POPULATION AND ENVIRONMENT

and crime or fear of crime. The postulate is much the same as for control: the larger the building, the less frequently residents will use the spaces outside their apartments, and in turn, the greater the crime and fear of crime. The present study provides empirical support for this postulate as well: residents' use of space transmits effects from building size both to personal crime and to fear of crime in the expected manner. Thus, a second explanation for the deleterious effects of large buildings is the inability of residents in them to make use of the spaces outside their apartments.

Both use of space and control of space reflect the degree to which residents have extended the realm of their own homes beyond the interior of their apartment units to encompass adjacent areas. Newman (1972; 1973) and others, including Rainwater (1966), Yancey (1971), and Cooper (1970; 1972), have long suggested that the degree to which such an extension of the home environment occurs is a function of the design of that environment, particularly of the number of apartments that share the adjacent areas, measured by building size in the present study. Prior to the present study, the evidence for such an effect was meager or largely impressionistic. The findings from this study help to document this expected relationship between the design of the environment outside the apartment unit and the degree to which residents extend the realm of use and control beyond the confines of their own apartments. Moreover, this study indicates that such an extension of the home can work to inhibit both the occurrence of crime and the fear of crime.

As it turns out, the level of social interaction among residents also functions as a link between design and crime, but not in the expected way. The larger the building, the lower the level of social interaction and, in turn, the lower the rate of personal crime. Social interaction can be viewed as another way in which residents extend or enlarge their homes beyond the immediate confines of their individual apartment units but, unlike use of space or control of space, it involves relationships among residents. The negative effect on personal crime suggests that this form of extension of the home is not as advantageous as the other forms and that relationships among residents may be problematic. It is also possible, as suggested earlier, that the model has incorrectly specified the relationship between personal crime and social interaction.

The final intervening variable to be considered with respect to the indirect effects of building size is rent collection, which is used in this research as a measure of management's ability to provide

215

OSCAR NEWMAN AND KAREN A. FRANCK

services. Rent collection also mediates an effect from building size to personal crime: the larger the building, the less able management is to provide services and, in turn, the higher the rate of personal crime. Thus building size not only affects actions and attitudes on the part of residents, it also affects management's ability to perform its duties and that affects the occurrence of crime.

Comparison with Earlier Findings

The present study and the study conducted in New York City that formed the basis of *Defensible Space* (Newman, 1972; 1973) are very different in terms of objectives, research design, sites, and measures. At the same time, however, the two studies are closely linked in terms of theory since the rationale and theoretical framework for the present study were drawn largely from the earlier work. Therefore, it seems reasonable to compare the two sets of results concerning the effects of building design on crime rate as long as the differences in method between the two studies are also kept in mind.

The original defensible space study was conducted in only one city and all the sites were low-income public housing projects under the management of a single housing authority. The present study was conducted in three different cities and the sites consist of both low-income public housing projects and federally-assisted, moderate-income developments. The public housing projects in this study are all managed by a single housing authority, but the moderate-income developments are managed by many different management companies or by managers selected by the sponsoring board of the development. The source of crime data in the earlier study was New York City Housing Authority Police records whereas the source of crime data in the present study is a victimization survey conducted with residents at each study site.

The most important hypothesis that the two studies share is that building size and crime rate are expected to be positively related: regardless of the variables used to measure the constructs, the larger the building, the higher the crime rate. In the earlier work building size was measured by building height, and in this study building size is measured by an index of the number of units per entry and building type. The two measures are comparable in that each is an indicator of building size.

In the earlier work crime rate was measured by various types of crime, each figured as a rate per 1,000 residents. In this study also personal crime is measured as a rate per 1,000 residents. The

216

POPULATION AND ENVIRONMENT

type of crime measured in the earlier work that is most similar in content to personal crime as measured in the present study is robbery rate. For the 53 cases in the original defensible space study on which correlations were based, the correlation between building height and robbery rate was .36 ($p < .01$).[2] In the present study the correlation between building size and personal crime rate is -.05. These two zero-order correlations are significantly different from each other ($p < .05$).

A test of the difference between the partial correlations[3] from the two studies indicates that although there is a substantial difference in the magnitude of the correlations (.27 in the earlier work and .07 in the present study), the difference is not statistically significant. The combination of the large difference in magnitude and the low power we have for detecting a significant difference presents a somewhat ambiguous picture.[4] On balance, we consider the results of the two studies to be, in effect, different. We therefore conclude that building size had a stronger impact on crime in the earlier study than it had in the present research.

There are many possible explanations for this difference in results. It could be a consequence of the differences in method described earlier. There are, however, two additional differences between the two studies that are more plausible explanations and that suggest possible refinements to defensible space theory. The first concerns the distributions of building size in the two studies and the second concerns the distributions of project size.

Size of buildings. Of the 53 cases used in the regression analysis for the original defensible space study, only two were row house sites, only one was a walk-up site, and the remaining 50 were high-rise buildings ranging from 6 stories to 21. In the present study 18 of the total of 63 sites are row houses, 34 are walk-up sites, and only 11 are composed of high-rise buildings, ranging in height from 5 to 28 stories. Thus, in the earlier work the overwhelming majority of the sites (94%) were high-rises of different heights, whereas in the present study row houses and walk-ups form a very large portion of the total number of sites (83%).

The precision of the estimated mean crime rate for sites with a particular building size is a function of the number of sites with buildings of that size: the greater the number of sites, the more precise the estimate is. Thus, the estimated crime rates in the earlier study were most reliable for the high-rises and least reliable for the row house and walk-up sites. The exact opposite is true of the present study: the estimates for the high-rise sites are the least reliable

217

OSCAR NEWMAN AND KAREN A. FRANCK

and the estimates for the row house and walk-up sites are the most reliable. The most accurate comparison in the first study was among high-rises of various heights whereas the most accurate comparison in the present study is between row houses and walk-ups.

Analysis of the mean crime rates for different categories of building size (Newman & Franck, 1980) shows that in the earlier research there was a steady increase in robbery rate from high-rises that are between 5 and 8 stories in height to those that are between 9 and 15 stories in height to those that are 16 and higher, and the steepest increase-was between the latter two categories. The means for these categories were based on sample sizes of 25, 11, and 14, respectively. In the present study the greatest number of cases are in the categories of row house (N=18) and walk-up (N=34), and the difference in mean personal crime rate between these two groups is very small. Thus, the building size effect on robbery rate that was demonstrated in the original defensible space study may have been primarily due to differences among high-rises of different heights, and the absence of any building size effect on personal crime rate in the present study may be due to the lack of any difference in crime rate between walk-ups and row houses.

Size of sites. Whereas building size refers to the type and height of buildings, size of site refers to the total number of dwelling units in all the buildings making up the site. In the earlier study only three of the sites (6%) were smaller than 300 units in size and 23 sites (43%) were larger than 1,000 units. In the present study 55 sites (87%) are smaller than 300 units, only one site is larger than 600 units, and no site is larger than 1,000 units. The mean site size in the earlier study was 962.83; in the present study it is 168.75. On the average, the sites in the earlier study were almost six times larger.

It may be that the effect of building size on robbery rate that was found in the original defensible space study was due to the relatively large size of all the 53 sites that were analyzed whereas the absence of such an effect in the present study may be due to the relatively small size of the sites. This explanation suggests that there is an interaction effect between building size and size of site on personal crime such that building size has an effect on personal crime (or robbery) *only* in large sites. The possibility that there is such an interaction effect is indicated by results from the original defensible space study (Newman, 1972, p. 28). Newman (1972, p.

218

POPULATION AND ENVIRONMENT

28) reports results showing that overall crime rate was higher in sites composed of buildings higher than six stories than in sites composed of buildings six stories and lower, regardless of the size of the site. However, the difference in crime rate between the two categories of building height was considerably greater for sites that are larger than 1,000 units than for sites that are 1,000 units or smaller. Thus building size, as measured by these two categories of building height, had a greater effect on crime rate in large sites than in smaller ones.

Together, the two possible explanations for the differences in results suggest a more qualified set of conclusions from both studies. The earlier work indicated that building size had a positive effect on robbery rate. However, because of the characteristics of the sites studied, the effect that was demonstrated may be peculiar to high-rise buildings of different heights, to sites that are larger than 300 units, or to high-rise buildings that *also* form sites larger than 300 units. The present study suggests that building size has very little effect on personal crime rate. But because of the characteristics of this sample, the small effect may be peculiar to comparisons between row houses and walk-ups, to sites that are smaller than 300 units, or to row houses and walk-ups that *also* form small sites. Although all of these possibilities are in the realm of speculation, they are nonetheless plausible and indicate directions for future research concerning the main effects and the interaction effects of building size and size of site on crime rate.

CONCLUSION

Findings from the present study indicate that building size has only a small total effect on personal crime rate, whereas findings from earlier research (Newman, 1972; 1973a) indicated that building size has a powerful effect on robbery rate. This difference in findings suggests to us that a strong relationship between building size and crime may be limited to high-rise buildings of different heights, to large housing developments, or to high-rise buildings that also form large developments. What we may be seeing is a threshold effect whereby building size and crime are related only when building size or project size reaches a crucial level (Gillis, 1979).

Despite its small total effect on personal crime, building size has important indirect effects on personal crime, and on fear of crime, that are mediated by residents' use and control of the

OSCAR NEWMAN AND KAREN A. FRANCK

spaces outside their apartments, suggesting that use and control also may have accounted for the strong relationship between building height and robbery rate found in the earlier study. The present study extends the earlier research in other ways as well. It shows that as building size increases, rent collection, use of space, social interaction, and control of space all decrease, and fear of crime increases. Thus, regardless of the social characteristics of residents or the nature of police and security guard services, building size has a consistent effect on the nature of life in federally-assisted housing developments: the larger the building, the more problematic life is.

REFERENCE NOTES

1. The decision to use an alpha level of .15 was based on a careful evaluation of the potential consequences of making Type I and Type II errors of inference. Setting the probability of Type I error at .15 allowed us, with a sample size of 63 and small to moderate degrees of relationship, to control the Type II error rate at .2 to .3. In this way we tried to balance the relative costs that would be incurred by making the two different kinds of errors of inference. Using a lower and more conventional alpha level would have made the power of our tests of significance exceedingly low, thereby making it difficult to detect any significant relationships. For a more detailed presentation of this rationale please see Newman and Franck (1980), Appendix E.
2. The correlations and regression results for total robbery rate (robberies occurring in all locations in the project) do not appear in *Defensible Space*. The source of these results is the *Final Report* from the Project for Security Design in Urban Residential Areas to the National Institute for Law Enforcement and Criminal Justice (Newman, 1973b). The regression and correlation results that do appear in the appendix of *Defensible Space* are based on the same 53 sites that were used in the analysis of robbery rate.
3. The independent variables that were partialled out in the earlier study were: the percent of residents receiving welfare, the total number of apartment units in the site, the percent of female-headed households, the percent of residents over 60 years old, mean family size, per capita income, visibility of the lobby, visibility of the elevator from outside the primary entry door, felony rate of the precinct, percent of windows facing the street, rating of height of project compared to height of buildings in surrounding area, rating of number of other housing projects in the vicinity. The independent variables partialled out in the present study are listed in Table 1.
4. Low power in this case results from the relatively large number of variables and the relatively small number of sites in both studies. Given the power we have, in order to be statistically significant at the .05 level, the difference between the two partial correlations would have to be at least .41.

REFERENCES

Alwin, D.F., & Hauser, R. The decomposition of effects in path analysis. *American Sociological Review*, 1975, *40*, 37-47.

Cooper, C. *Residents' attitude toward the environment at St. Francis Square, San Francisco*. Working Paper No. 126. Berkeley: Institute of Urban and Regional Development, 1970.

220

POPULATION AND ENVIRONMENT

Cooper, C., Day, N., & Levine, B. *Resident dissatisfaction in multi-family housing.* Working Paper No. 160. Berkeley: Institute of Urban and Regional Planning, 1972.

Gillis, A. R. Household density and human crowding. *Journal of Population,* 1979, *2,* 104-117.

Hanushek, E.A., & Jackson, J.E. *Statistical methods for social scientists.* New York: Academic Press, 1977.

Newman, O. *Defensible Space.* New York: Macmillan, 1972.

Newman, O. *Architectural design for crime prevention.* Washington, D.C.: Law Enforcement Assistance Administration, National Institute of Law Enforcement and Criminal Justice, 1973 (a).

Newman, O. *Final report: Project for security design in urban residential areas.* Washington, D.C.: Law Enforcement Assistance Administration, National Institute of Law Envorcement and Criminal Justice, 1973(b).

Newman, O. *Design guidelines for creating defensible space.* Washington, D.C.: Law Enforcement Assistance Administration, National Institute of Law Enforcement and Criminal Justice, 1976.

Newman, O., & Franck, K.A. *Factors Influencing Crime and Instability in Urban Housing Developments.* Washington, D.C.: Law Enforcement Assistance Administration, National Institute of Law Enforcement and Criminal Justice, 1980.

Rainwater, L. Fear and house as haven in the lower class. *Journal of American Institute of Planners,* 1966, *32,* 23-30.

Yancey, W.L. Architecture, interaction, and social control. In J. Helmer and N.A. Eddington (Eds.), *Urbanman.* New York: The Free Press, 1973.

[8]

Collection of the data described here was supported by Grant No. 83-IJ-CX-0003 from the National Institute of Justice, US Department of Justice, to the Police Foundation, Washington, D.C. Points of view or opinions stated in this report do not necessarily represent the official position of the U.S. Department of Justice or the Police Foundation. The data are available from the Criminal Justice Data Archive at the University of Michigan.

The Impact of Victimization on Fear

Wesley G. Skogan

This report examines the relationship between criminal victimization and fear of crime. Past research has been surprisingly inconclusive about this issue, and some people's fears have been branded "irrational" because the two did not appear to be tightly linked. However, the data analyzed here indicate that victimization affects both fear-related attitudes and behavior in a clear and consistent manner. This report also suggests that the impact of victimization is relatively uniform. Some research has indicated that certain groups are especially affected by crime, a claim that might be used to justify special treatment for selected victims and has been used to support demands for special "treatment" of selected offenders. However, the strong effects of victimization registered in these data were not differentially distributed across subgroups. In sum, most people do learn from their experiences, although other kinds of learning are rational as well.

This report examines the relationship between criminal victimization and fear of crime. The link between the two may seem obvious, but there are several reasons for looking more deeply into their connection.

First, there are so many anomalies in the distribution of fear that it appears at first glance the two are only weakly related. For some groups in the population crime and fear "go together" in consistent ways; city dwellers and the poor, for example, are both more fearful and more likely to be victimized. However, high levels of fear also are reported by some who generally enjoy lower levels of victimization, including women and the elderly. Early studies found other incongruities—for

WESLEY G. SKOGAN: Professor of Political Science and Urban Affairs, Northwestern University.

CRIME & DELINQUENCY, Vol. 33 No. 1, January 1987 135-154
© 1987 Sage Publications, Inc.

example, that area burglary rates were not related to how worried residents were about being burglarized (Waller and Okihiro, 1978). Finally, sheer *levels* of the two seemingly do not match: survey measures of fear suggest that many more people are fearful than are victimized, even in large cities. It is easy to conclude that victimization cannot explain most people's fears, and that fear of crime is to some extent "irrational."

Second, surprisingly little is known about the general impact of victimization, or about its differential impact upon victims. Most research has focused on particular crimes or categories of victims. It has told us important things about the concerns of burglary victims (Waller and Okihiro, 1978), the stages of recovery among rape victims (Burgess and Holmstrom, 1974), and the impact of homicide on the members of victim's families (Bard and Connolly, 1983). However, the exclusion of nonvictims from much of this research has left unanswered the question of how greatly victims differ from comparable nonvictim populations as a result of their experience, and its focus on specific crimes and victims has not facilitated a comparative analysis of either the impact of different kinds of victimization or the impact of victimization on different kinds of people.

This article addresses these issues. It first examines the relationship between fear of crime (broadly defined, including some measures of behavior) and people's victimization experiences. Then it examines whether the impact of crime is general, or differentially linked to such factors as the isolation and vulnerability of victims and to the resources they have at their disposal to deal with their plight.

These are lively topics. As noted above, past research is surprisingly undefinitive about the impact of victimization. In the political arena, uncertainty about the "rationality" of fear of crime has contributed to the demise of at least one policy issue, that of crime against the elderly (Cook and Skogan, 1984). The "differential impact" hypothesis is a legislative question as well. There has been a debate in several states over the recognition of special classes of victims, whose victimizers would be meted out special punishment. While there are many philosophical and political grounds for considering such action, one justification for doing so has been claims about the special consequences of victimization for vulnerable groups.

AN OVERVIEW OF PAST RESEARCH

Interest in the apparent "irrationality" of high levels of fear was fueled by the weak correspondence of many survey measures of fear of crime to people's self-reported victimization experiences. In a review of the literature, Rifai (1982, p. 193) concluded "there has been no convincing evidence that criminal victimization produces greater fear of crime than does the lack of being victimized." DuBow, McCabe, and Kaplan (1979) reached the same conclusion. For the population as a whole the correlation between the two is weak, and even appears to be negative (victims reporting lower levels of fear) for some categories of personal crime. Indicators of levels of fear of personal victimization also are simply much higher than the amount of serious personal crime, another mismatch that clouds the issue. Some argue that "fear of crime" is often irrational because many people do not appear to *do* much about it—there seems to be only a slim behavioral component to the attitude. This view is represented by the common belief (probably wrong—see Karmen, 1980) that most stolen cars have keys in them, and that burglary is easy because many people are not cautious enough (Bureau of Justice Statistics, 1985, p. 5). One of the anomalies of the research literature is that:

> attempts to record behavior change following victimization as a measure of impact have generally been frustrated since there usually is little measurable change that is reflected in what could be termed crime preventive or victimization preventive behavior [Rifai, 1982, p. 193].

A number of explanations have been advanced for the apparent mismatch between victimization and fear. Perhaps the most controversial has been the argument that the two are not strongly linked because most crime is trivial in its consequences, and *isn't* fear-provoking. As Reiss (1982) noted in his article "How Serious is 'Serious Crime,'" few assaults measured in the National Crime Survey (NCS) lead to an injury, most rape and robbery is described as unsuccessful, many burglaries are only "attempted," and the vast bulk of stolen property is of little value. Rifai (1982, p. 199) concludes, "a number of case studies of burglaries and thefts have suggested in fact that most of those types of victimizations were of little consequence in the daily lives of their victims." Sparks, Genn, and Dodd (1977) even speculated that victimization by robbery and assault *reduces* fear. They explained a negative correlation between the two by hypothesizing that people may "fear the worst" before they have any direct experience with crime; but when they do, and survive relatively unscathed, their anxiety may be alleviated. Finally, the British Crime Survey includes questions that ask victims about the effects of their experience: In the 1983 survey, half reported suffering no practical problems, and two-thirds no emotional upset (Mayhew, 1984).

Victimization and fear may also appear to be loosely related for the opposite reason, because they are *strongly* connected. It seems likely the relationship between the two is partly reciprocal. If victimization leads to fear-related behaviors, it may reduce victims' *exposure to risk* and thus lower their chance of victimization in the future. This cannot be true for everyone in the population, for there is a statistical tendency for victims as a whole to be revictimized at a rate higher than chance would predict (at least some are "victim prone"). However, researchers have used the exposure-to-risk hypothesis to explain the low rates of victimization among such high-fear groups as women (Riger, 1981) and the elderly (Cook and Skogan, 1984). A strong, reciprocal relationship between victimization and fear over time would lead survey data gathered at one "slice" of time to suggest the two are unrelated.

The mismatch between levels of victimization and fear, and apparent anomalies in their social distribution, has also stimulated research on "other" causes of fear of crime. They are numerous, and it is apparent that reports of "fear of crime" are diffuse attitudes that are sensitive to a number of aspects of daily life (Garofalo and Laub, 1979). Survey reports of fear are related to such factors as perceptions of neighborhood deterioration, vandalism, "uncivil" behavior by youths, public drinking, and other disorderly conduct (Taylor and Hale, 1985). They are correlated with perceptions of "moral decline" and anxiety about strangers (Rifai, 1982), and among whites fear is tied to concern about neighborhood racial change (Taub, Taylor, and Dunham, 1984). Both attitudinal studies (Riger, 1978) and the demographic correlates of fear (Baumer, 1978) suggest that potential physical vulnerability to victimizers stimulates fear. Participation in rumor networks also stimulates fear, in a kind of "vicarious victimization," especially when the stories that circulate concern victims from the recipient's area (Skogan and Maxfield, 1981).

The list of researchers' "other" causes of fear is long and growing. Its significance here is to demonstrate that victimization and fear co-occur in a world of interrelated individual, experiential, and neighborhood phenomena. Direct, recent, personal experience with crime clearly is only one determinant of fear. To highlight the unique contribution of such victimization experiences one must somehow control for those "other factors." In the white-mouse world of experiments this is fairly simple, but it is unlikely that many people would appreciate a randomized opportunity to be robbed, so these studies must involve statistical analysis of some complexity.

Previous correlational studies have been limited by the availability of suitable data. Measures of experience with crime require adequate victimization survey techniques (see Sparks, 1981). Many surveys are too small to uncover enough victims of personal crime for useful analysis; studies with a methodologically sound (brief) "recall period" for measuring victimization typically uncover very few, usually about 6%, of those interviewed for violent crime. Generally, the more conventionally serious an incident is, the less frequently it occurs. To overcome these problems, Skogan and Maxfield (1981) analyzed the Census Bureau's large city victimization surveys, tabulating the relationship between victimization experiences and fear. However, those data still reflected the complex social distribution of the two—for example, victims of weapon crimes reported lower levels of fear than did nonvictims, for they were overwhelmingly young males. Skogan and Maxfield used multivariate statistical techniques to control for a number of demographic factors confounding the victimization-fear relationship, and ultimately demonstrated a weak, but positive, correlation between the two. However, they could only control for what was available—a few simple demographic factors—and other, unmeasured variables possibly would have been more effective.

The data used in this research can go further in clarifying the victimization-fear nexus. It is drawn from a large *panel* study interviewing people at two widely separated points in time. The panel design of the survey enables one to control directly for levels of fear and reports of behavior measured *before* victimization which then struck some respondents between the first and second interview.

Findings from this data might shed some light on yet another issue clouding the victimization-fear relationship. It may be that some consequences of victimization are subject to fairly rapid *decay*, and the passage of time between experience and interview in this study misses such effects. Several studies suggest that most of the effects of victimization on most victims disappear in a relatively short time.

Friedman et al.'s (1982) four-month follow-up interviews suggested that most problems that victims had rated as "serious" were resolved during the ensuing period. Maguire (1984, p. 21) concludes that "the consensus of opinion seems to be that most emotional effects 'wear off' within a few weeks or months, victims recovering more or less spontaneously or with moral support from family or friends." A pattern of decay would be consistent with a reading of "no effect" in our second wave of panel interviews, although this would still leave the "earlier effect" hypothesis unproved. On the other hand, there is also plenty of evidence that the impact of victimization can persist for a considerable period, which is one reason to control for pre-Wave 1 victimization in this study. For example, in reinterviews, Shapland (1984) found the effects of personal victimization enduring—and even increasing—for at least two years after the incident. Similar, long-term effects have been reported by Burgess and Holmstrom (1974) and others. A pattern of *persistence* of effects should be detectable in the panel design for this study (The apparent persistence of the effects of victimization revealed by some studies raises the interesting question, "When does someone *cease* being a victim, and return to 'nonvictim' status?"; this unfortunately cannot be answered here.)

The second issue of concern here is that of the *differential* impact of victimization. Whatever the effect of victimization, is it a general one? Are some kinds of victims more severely effected, and might claims of special status for particular classes of victims be justified by the special consequences of victimization for them?

In research terms the issue is, "Are there measurable factors which magnify or ameliorate the impact of crime, so that some people are more or less effected than are others?" This is a practical question as well. As Maguire (1984, p. 18) notes,

> it is important for service agencies (particularly agencies which, like Victim Support Scheme, select those they will visit from large numbers referred by the police) to have some indication of the social characteristics of victims who may be most in need.

He reports it has been found "with some regularity" that various groups are more vulnerable to the emotional effects of victimization, but concludes that such differential effects are not large enough to justify focusing on some groups to the exclusion of others. "Most service agencies should not give special priority to any one group but should be open to victims of all ages, both sexes and all social classes" (p. 19). Bard and Sangrey (1979) also hypothesize that prior characteristics that victims bring to their experience influence their reactions to being victimized. With respect to fear of crime, research on such factors can be summarized in the form of four hypotheses to be tested.

Isolation. Surveys indicate that socially isolated people are more fearful (Kennedy and Silverman, 1984-1985; Silverman and Kennedy, 1985), and research on victims suggests that networks of "supporters" play an important role in alleviating people's fears and making victims "whole" again (Friedman et al., 1982; Yin, 1980). Social isolates, those with few friendly neighbors, may have no one to share their concerns with. Victims have a strong need for such support (Coates, Wortman, and Abbey, 1979). Fear may be magnified among victims who live alone. Single adults and others who live alone may be more fearful because they do not have anyone to take care of them. The isolation-fear relationship is particularly strong for women (Silverman and Kennedy, 1985) and the elderly (Lebowitz, 1975). Maguire (1980) reports that female burglary victims separated from their husbands are especially likely to experience acute stress as a result.

Three indicators of isolation were used to test the "isolation" hypothesis: whether or not respondents lived alone, the number of neighbors they knew personally, and the length of time they had lived in the neighborhood.

Resources. Some victims have greater capacity for coping with the consequences of that experience. Property damage and financial loss from crime can place an enduring burden on victims. This is particularly true for the poor, who are least likely to have insurance (Skogan and Maxfield, 1981). Friedman et al., (1982) found that poor and less educated victims reported more practical "coping" problems than did others, and higher levels of fear. In the case of rape, there is evidence that poor (and black and elderly) victims react more strongly to their experience (Atkeson et al., 1982; Sales, Baum, and Shore, 1984). Victims with more knowledge and experience, and facility in dealing with public and private bureaucracies, may more readily find support and assistance if they need it. Finally, although renters often report higher rates of victimization and fear than do home owners, the latter have more control over their property and a long-term commitment to it that facilitates crime-prevention efforts (Lavrakas, 1981; Skogan and Maxfield, 1981).

142   **CRIME & DELINQUENCY / JANUARY 1986**

Three indicators of the resources available to our respondents were used to test the hypothesis: family income, home ownership, and education.

Vulnerability. Research on fear indicates that women and the elderly feel particularly vulnerable to crime and its consequences, and there is some evidence that the impact of victimization is magnified for those groups. In their study of residential burglary, Waller and Okihiro (1978) asked victims "what they felt" when they learned of their plight. Women, but very rarely men, volunteered that they felt fearful. Bourque et al. (1978) measured reactions by crime victims on seven-symptom scale, and found that women were more affected than were men.

There is similar evidence regarding the elderly. Garofalo (1977) examined survey data on the relationship between victimization and fear, and found that almost all attitudinal differences between victims and nonvictims in the general sample were due to the impact of victimization on the elderly; for other age groups those differences were virtually nonexistent. Friedman et al. (1982) found the highest fear levels among female and elderly victims, but because this is also true of the general population, the absence of nonvictims in their study makes this finding difficult to interpret. Both Knudten et al. (1977) and Friedman et al. found elderly victims reported essentially the same number of practical problems as did victims in younger age categories.

This differential impact of victimization may be attributable to the relative vulnerability of women and the elderly. They feel open to attack, relatively powerless to resist, and fear exposure to traumatic physical consequences if they are attacked. Large surveys in both the U.S. (Antunes et al., 1977) and Canada (Ministry of the Solicitor General, 1983) reveal that, when injured, elderly crime victims are more likely to need extensive medical treatment. Perhaps because of perceived vulnerability, both groups usually report they frequently restrict their activities to limit their exposure to risk of victimization. Sheppele and Bart (1983) found that among women who did so, and were victimized anyway, the consequences of the experience were magnified.

Previous Experience. Finally, it may be that the impact of victimization is dependent upon people's attitudes beforehand. Several researchers have speculated that victimization may have more serious consequences for those who *already were more fearful*. Presumably the experience reinforces their perceptions of an "unjust world" and emphasizes their personal vulnerability (Kahn, 1984; Sheppele and Bart, 1983; Friedman et al., 1982). On the other hand, as noted above, Sparks et al. (1977) and others take the opposite view, based upon survey findings regarding the banality of most victimization experiences. As Yin (1980, p. 497) puts it, "any victimization experience that does not create serious harm . . . might actually aid the victim in forming a more realistic assessment of the nature of crime, thereby reducing fear of crime." As we have seen, by many measures this could be true of most criminal encounters.

In this analysis, the impact of past experiences and victim's attitudinal "predispositions" are captured by first-wave measures of fear. The hypothesis that victims who initially are more fearful subsequently are more affected by crime is one concerning statistical interaction between those early measures and interwave victimization.

THE DATA

Data to assess the impact of victimization on fear was gathered in personal interviews with 1,738 residents of seven selected neighborhoods in Newark, New Jersey, and Houston, Texas. The neighborhoods were relatively high-crime areas featuring a mixture of single-family homes and rental apartments. Respondents in Newark were virtually all black, while in Houston blacks, whites, and Hispanics were represented in all of the areas. Households were randomly selected from lists of all residential addresses in each neighborhood; individual respondents were then chosen at random from among household residents 19 years of age and older. The data are available from the Criminal Justice Data Archive at the University of Michigan.

A unique aspect of the data is that it includes two interviews with each respondent, spaced one year apart. The "panel" feature of the data helps solve several substantive and methodological problems.

As indicated above, one issue is that there are multiple, confounding determinants of both fear of crime and related behavior. As in past research, it is possible to develop measures of some of these sources of fear and control for them statistically. However, there are many of them, some may be inadvertently left out of the analysis, others may be poorly measured, and some are doubtlessly unknown. Another difficulty in untangling the unique impact of a particular victimization experience on fear is that people may have had other experiences with crime in the past. It is necessary to distinguish one crime from another. Finally, there are a number of well-known methodological problems in measuring victimization. Victims may have difficulty in recalling incidents, especially if they were less consequential. This could artifactually increase the observed correlation between measures of victimization and fear. As this research relies on the accurate assessment of recent victimization experiences, it was necessary to develop a data collection method that was as accurate as possible.

A useful (if inevitably only partial) solution to the "confounding" problem was to interview respondents twice. The first interview established "baseline" information on fear, crime-related behaviors, and past victimization experiences for each individual. Then, a second wave of interviews remeasured these things to assess *changes* in attitudes and behavior during the intervening period. Changes between Wave 1 to Wave 2 then could be related to new victimizations occurring during the period between the interviews. Panel data are not a perfect solution to the confounding problem. A special difficulty is that the consequences of other events that take place between the two waves of interviews can be confused with "victimization effects," especially if they co-occur to some extent with victimization. One candidate in this category is contact with the police. And, because there is inevitably error in the measurement of variables, our Wave 1 data do not fully "adjust" Wave 2 data for "true" levels of fear during the first period, and some variance in the Wave 2 measures really reflects prior levels of fear.

There were a number of different measures of "fear." The *attitudinal* measures reflected the distinction between "worry" and "concern" about crime. Following Furstenberg (1971) and others, we distinguished between how worried people were about being victimized and how concerned they were regarding the level of crime in their neighborhood. Measures of the two are of course correlated, but some people feel relatively immune to crime around them (because, for example, they do a lot to protect themselves), so responses to the two differ. Separate "worry" and "concern" measures were created for personal and property crime. Methodological research by Rosenbaum and Baumer (1981) indicates the personal-property crime distinction is a prominent dimension in any set of crime-related attitudes. There were also indicators of defensive and preventive *behavior* with respect to personal and property crime.

The analytic scales measuring worry, concern, and behavior each combined responses to several survey questions. *Worry about personal victimization* was measured by combining responses to questions about fear of going out after dark, fear of walking in nearby areas, and the extent to which respondents were worried about being robbed and assaulted in their neighborhood. A measure of *worry about property crime* was based on questions about burglary and auto theft. *Concern about personal crime problems* was measured by responses to questions about "how big a problem" robbery, assault by strangers, and sexual assaults were in the area. The *concern about property crime* scale combined responses to questions about the extent of local burglary, auto vandalism, and auto theft problems. There were two self-reported measures of crime-related behaviors. Respondents were asked whether or not they tried to go out with others for safety reasons, if they avoided nearby areas, and if they avoided certain types of people when they saw them, and how often they simply stayed home because of crime? Responses to these questions formed a measure of *defensive actions against personal crime*. Also, those interviewed were quizzed about various *household crime prevention efforts*. A score was given each respondent reflecting whether or not their household had installed special locks, lights, timers, and so on.

Except for the household crime prevention measure, all of these scales were single factored. Their reliabilities (Cronbach's Alpha) ranged from .70 to .85, and were very similar for the two waves of the survey. Household crime prevention was measured by a simple count of the extent of adoption of six different tactics. More details about the measures can be found in Annan, 1985.

Victimization was measured by yes-no responses to 17 "screener" items. Each asked about specific recent experiences, and they covered both completed and attempted incidents in a variety of crime categories. This report uses indicators of *personal victimization* (encompassing robbery, rape, actual assault, and purse snatching), *property victimization* (burglary, theft, vandalism, and auto theft), and *total victimization* (combining all of them). In the Wave 2 survey, 32% of those interviewed were classified as inter-wave victims of property crime, 5.3% as victims of personal crimes, and (because they overlapped) 33% as victims of either. The most frequent property victimization was simple theft (20%), followed by vandalism (11%), and burglary (10%). Among personal crimes, robbery was most frequent (2.4%).

FINDINGS: VICTIMIZATION AND FEAR

The first research question was, "Is there a general and consistent relationship between victimization and fear?" As indicated above, the complex connection between those factors and other features of people's lives clouds our view of their interrelationship.

Table 1 takes advantage of the panel nature of the data to examine the correspondence between recent victimization and measures of attitudes and behavior, controlling for past levels of fear and experiences with crime. In summary form, the statistical model analyzed in Table 1 is: Wave 2 = V2 + Wave 1 + V1.

The "Wave" variables are before and after consequences measures. The "V"s are before and after measures of victimization. Table 1 presents regression coefficients describing the relationship between "V2" victimization measures for total, personal and property crime, and the consequences measures discussed above. As victimization is a "count" measure, the unstandardized regression coefficients in Table 1 indicate the (estimated) extent of change in the outcome measures for each additional victimization.

The data in Table 1 document a strong and consistent pattern: net of past experiences and attitudes, recent victims report higher levels of worry and concern about crime. Also, even controlling for what they did in the past, recent victims report doing more to protect themselves from both personal and property victimization.

A detailed inspection of Table 1 suggests several things. Note, for example, that both personal and property crime had significant consequences for victims. The regression coefficients (which can be compared across rows) belie the proposition advanced by DuBow et al. (1979) and Garofalo (1977), that only personal, potentially violent encounters generate substantial fear or stimulate changes in behavior. Here the effects are of comparable magnitude. Direct experience with personal crime had somewhat greater consequences for the personal-crime outcomes, while the same was true for the property-crime indicators. The only nonsignificant coefficient in Table 1 relates personal victimization to household crime prevention efforts, somewhat unrelated phenomena.

If more detailed information were available about these incidents, so they could be weighted for seriousness and otherwise analyzed more closely, the relationship between victimization and fear probably would appear even stronger than suggested here. One measure of the serious-

TABLE 1: Relationship Between Recent Victimization and Fear of Crime

| Wave 2 Consequences | Regression Coefficients and Significance Levels Controlling for Wave 1 Scores and Pre-Wave 1 Victimization | | | |
	Total Victimization	Personal Victimization	Property Victimization	(N)
Personal Crime				
Worry about personal victimization	.09*	.12*	.09*	(1737)
Concern about area personal crime	.15*	.24*	.17*	(1680)
Defensive behavior	.03*	.05*	.02*	(1733)
Property Crime				
Worry about property victimization	.18*	.16*	.20*	(1733)
Concern about area property crime	.19*	.20*	.22*	(1704)
Household protection	.15*	.09	.17*	(1738)

ness of the predicament our respondents found themselves in that can be calculated from the data is the extent of *multiple* victimization during the period between the two surveys. Rifai (1976) found that elderly victims in Portland who had been victimized more than once had much higher anxiety scores than did nonvictims or one-time victims. Garofalo (1977) also found an added "multiple victim" effect on perceptions of future risk of victimization. Figure 1 illustrates the magnitude of the impact of multiple recent victimization in this data.

Figure 1 plots the distribution of "standardized and residualized" outcome measures against the frequency of recent victimization reported by our respondents in Houston and Newark. Victimization between the two waves of surveys has been categorized at the high end as "five or more incidents." The outcome measures arrayed across the bottom of Figure 1 have been adjusted statistically for their pretest level and for victimizations recalled prior to the first interview, just as they were in the regression analyses presented in Table 1. They have also been *standardized*, with a mean of zero for all respondents, so that the values for the various outcome measures are comparable. Figure 1 illustrates a fairly regular, "stairstep" distribution of Wave 2 fear levels; in each case, as levels of victimization between the waves of the survey mount, so do subsequent levels of worry, concern, and crime-related behavior.

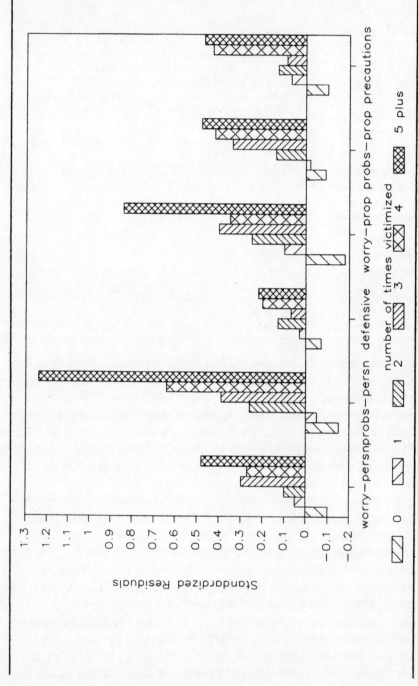

Figure 1: The Consequences of Victimization by Number of Wave 2 Victimizations

FINDINGS: DIFFERENTIAL IMPACT
OF VICTIMIZATION

The second research question was, "Are the consequences of victimization relatively evenly distributed, or are some victims more severely impacted?" Hypotheses were advanced that isolation, resources, personal vulnerability, and earlier levels of fear lead less advantaged victims on each dimension to be especially more fearful and more reclusive as a result of their experience.

Technically, these are hypotheses concerning "victimization-covariate interaction." The mediating factors discussed above—poverty, gender, age—are the covariates. The statistical model for testing such "special impact" hypotheses is as follows: Wave 2 = Wave 1 + V2 + V1 + C + C * V2. Using this model, one can control for a number of factors in order to detect any special impact of victimization on the groups detailed above. It controls for previous levels of fear (Wave 1), the fact that victims are more fearful (V2 and V1), and the fact that—for a variety of reasons—those groups have "baseline" levels of fear that vary greatly (measures of those are "C"s, for "covariates"). This leaves the factor "C * V2" (covariate-victimization interaction); if it is significantly related to Wave 2 measures of fear and behavior independently of the other factors, it is evidence that "being in that group *and* being victimized" has special consequences.

No extensive table details the findings of this analysis, for the results were uniform and simple: There was *no* evidence of a differential effect of victimization on the groups identified above. People who were isolated, vulnerable, and had fewer resources were more fearful when they were victimized, but the effect of that experience was the same for their counterparts. This (null) finding held for 53 of the 54 tests of "special consequences" hypotheses for groups (six outcome measures for each of eight groups); this is far fewer than we would expect by chance, which weighs very heavily against the proposition. The same "null" findings characterize the data with regard to the hypothesis that those who were more fearful before they were victimized were particularly effected by that experience. Of the six consequences measures, five showed no special interactive relationships with inter-wave victimization and earlier fear levels, and in the 18 tests the only significant coefficient (about the number expected by chance) was in the opposite direction.

The apparent wisdom of the "special consequences" hypothesis clearly calls for more research. Demands for special legislation punishing those who victimize specific classes of individuals have been justified, in part, by claims concerning the unique consequences of those crimes. Such claims also have been advanced to justify special services for selected victims of crime. In this case, however, analyses of the impact of various kinds of victimization, and detailed inspection of patterns for subgroups, could find no support for those claims.

Why should this be the case? Part of the problem may lie in the sparse representation of particular subgroups in this survey. For example, there were interviews with only 6 elderly victims of a recent (Wave 2) personal crime. However, redefining the "elderly" category to include those 50 and older—which increased the count substantially—did not change the conclusion. And, the no-effect finding held for elderly property crime victims, who were much more numerous.

The expectation that different types of people should be differently affected by victimization may also be true—for types of people or victimization not examined here. Certainly other hypotheses concerning the impact of victimization could be entertained. For example, Waller (1982, p. 176) advances the hypothesis that the impact of victimization will vary with one's "locus of control." The null finding reported here does hold for other measures of isolation, for race and linguistic groups, and for other consequences measures (such as "commitment to the neighborhood") as well. The victimization categories discussed above were highly aggregated. But, in addition to the simple classifications presented in Table 1, separate victimization-covariate analyses were done for experiences with burglary, vandalism, robbery, threats and intimidation, and simple theft. None showed any but random deviations from the pattern of null findings reported here.

Victimization also has other consequences than those measured here. The list of potential psychological consequences of victimization is a long one, including depression, anxiety, paranoia, loss of control, shame, embarrassment, vulnerability, helplessness, humiliation, anger, shock, feelings of inequity, awareness of mortality, tension, and malaise, as well as fear. Victimization can lead to such interpersonal problems as extreme mistrust of others, social isolation, difficulty in interacting with family and friends, divorce, and an inability to function appropriately at work. These consequences have been summarized in a recent report of the American Psychological Association's Task Force on the Victims of Crime (Kahn, 1984). It may be that differential, group-specific consequences of victimization are confined to some of those outcomes, and not to the attitudinal measures of worry or concern, or the crime-related behaviors examined here.

CONCLUSION AND IMPLICATIONS

Two general empirical findings were reported here. First, recent victimization was consistently related to measures of worry and concern about crime, and to crime-related defensive behaviors and household crime prevention efforts. Property victimization may have had more measured effects than personal victimization. There are reasons to expect this to be the case, including the fact that more of the property crimes measured in the survey took place in the respondent's immediate neighborhood. However, it may also be due to the more infrequent occurrence of personal victimization. Only 5% of these respondents reported being the recent victims of personal crimes, as compared to 32% for property crime, and—other things being equal—the latter is thus more likely to "explain" frequent behavior and normally distributed measures of worry and concern about crime.

Second, there was no evidence of any special impact of victimization on particular subgroups. There has been some speculation about factors that might amplify or ameliorate the impact of victimization on particular classes of persons. However, none of the hypotheses here were supported. Clearly, vulnerable groups such as women and the elderly are more fearful and more willing to report taking defensive actions. People who are socially isolated are more fearful, as are those with fewer resources for coping with the consequences of crime. And recent victims are more worried, more concerned about the amount of crime around them, and more likely to take actions to protect themselves and their families. However, these differences appear to be cumulative in an additive way, and did not multiply to the special disadvantage of particular groups.

What does all of this imply about the "irrationality" of fear of crime? The analysis reported here indicates a strong, consistent relationship between people's recent experiences with crime and their attitudes and behavior. That effect is cumulative with other features of their lives, but experience seems only to add to victim's stock of assessments of their environment and is not exaggerated in some fashion by their personal attributes. All of this seems quite "rational." Research does indicate that factors other than direct, personal experience with crime affect people's levels of fear. However, these factors include many that may signal danger, including street disorder and unpredictable social conditions. Hearing about nearby crime and victims who resemble themselves also spark fear in people, and that also seems to be a reasonable reaction. This research has found that, in addition, people who are victimized (a) think there is more crime around, (b) are more worried about being a victim, and (c) do things to protect themselves, probably as a consequence of their experience.

It is not clear that these necessarily are "negative" consequences of crime; in other contexts, the ability to alter one's behavior in light of experience is called "learning." Janoff-Bulman (1982, p. 1979) and others find that victims who identify shortcomings in their self-protective tactics are more likely to perceive they can avoid subsequent victimization. The benefits of learning appropriate levels of caution can flow both from direct experience (as reported above), and indirectly. As Tyler (1984) points out, learning from "socially transmitted experience" (as in a classroom, or from the neighborhood rumor spreader) is rational and cost-effective, especially when personal experience can be risky. People should not have to be burgled to act "rationally" to protect their homes from unlawful entry. "To be most adaptive, individuals should combine . . . socially acquired experiences with their own personal experiences to produce an overall judgment of risk" (Tyler, 1984, p. 29). Some "healthy anxiety" leading to awareness and caution probably is a good thing, when it is rooted one way or another in reality. It is when fear is incapacitating, or not linked to environmental conditions, that it can be dysfunctional.

REFERENCES

Annan, Sampson. 1985. *Fear Reduction Program: Technical Report.* Washington, DC: Police Foundation.

Antunes, George E., Fay Lomax Cook, Thomas D. Cook, and Wesley G. Skogan. 1977. "Patterns of Personal Crime Against the Elderly." *Gerontologist* 17, 4: 321-327.

Atkeson, B. M., L. S. Calhoun, D. A. Resick, and E. M. Ellis. 1982. "Victims of Rape." *Journal of Consulting and Clinical Psychology* 50: 96-102.

Bard, Morton, and Dawn Sangrey. 1979. *The Crime Victim's Book.* New York: Scribners.

Bard, Morton, and H. Connolly. 1983. *The Social and Psychological Consequences of Homicide.* New York: New York Academy of Sciences.

Baumer, Terry. 1978. "Research on Fear of Crime in the United States." *Victimology* 3, 3-4: 254-264.

Bourque, Blair B., G. B. Brumback, R. E. Krug, and L. O. Richardson. 1978. *Crisis Intervention: Investigating the Need for New Applications.* Washington, DC: American Institutes for Research.

Bureau of Justice Statistics, 1985. *Bulletin: Household Burglary.* Washington, DC: Author.

Burgess, Ann W., and Lynn L. Holmstrom. 1974. *Rape: Victims of Crisis.* Bowie, MD: Robert Brady.

Coates, D., Wortman, C., and Abbey A. 1979. "Reactions to Victims." In *New Approaches to Social Problems,* edited by I. Frieze, D. Bar-Tal, and J. S. Carrol. San Francisco: Jossey-Bass.

Cook, Fay Lomax, and Wesley G. Skogan. 1984. "Evaluating the Changing Definition of a Policy Issue in Congress: Crime Against the Elderly." Pp. 47-66 in *Public Policy and Social Institutions,* edited by Harrell Rodgers. New York: JAI Press.

DuBow, Fred, Edward McCabe, and Gail Kaplan. 1979. *Reactions to Crime: A Critical Review of the Literature.* Washington, DC: National Institute of Justice, US Department of Justice.

Friedman, Kenneth, Helen Bischoff, Robert Davis, and Andresa Person. 1982. *Victims and Helpers: Reactions to Crime.* New York: New York City Victim Services Agency (Report to the National Institute of Justice, US. Department of Justice.)

Furstenberg, Frank. 1971. "Public Reactions to Crime in the Streets." *American Scholar* 40 (Autumn): 601-610.

Garofalo, James. 1977. *Public Opinion About Crime: The Attitudes of Victims and Nonvictims.* Washington, DC: National Institute of Justice, US Department of Justice.

Garofalo, James, and John Laub. 1979. "The Fear of Crime." *Victimology* 3, 3-4: 242-253.

Janoff-Bulman, R. 1979. "Characterological versus Behavioral Self-Blame: Inquires into Depression and Rape." *Journal of Personality and Social Psychology* 37, 10: 1798-1809.

Janoff-Bulman, R. 1982. "Esteem and Control Bases of Blame: "Adaptive" Strategies for Victims versus Observers," *Journal of Personality* 50: 180-192.

Kahn, Arnold, ed. 1984. *Victims of Violence: Final Report of the APA Task Force on the Victims of Crime and Violence.* Washington, DC: American Psychological Association.

Karmen, Andrew. 1980. "Auto Theft: Beyond Victim Blaming." *Victimology* 5, 2-4: 161-174.

Kennedy, Leslie W., and Robert A. Silverman. 1984-1985. "Significant Others and Fear of Crime Among the Elderly." *International Journal of Aging and Human Development* 20, 4: 241-256.

Kennedy, Leslie W., and Robert A. Silverman. 1985. "Perception of Social Diversity and Fear of Crime," *Environment and Behavior* 17 (May): 275-295.

Knudten, Robert, Anthony Meade, Mary Knudten, and W. G. Doerner. 1977. *Victims and Witnesses.* Washington, DC: National Institute of Justice, US Department of Justice.

Lavrakas, Paul J. 1981. "On Households." Pp. 67-86 in *Reactions to Crime,* edited by Dan A. Lewis. Beverly Hills, CA: Sage.

Lebowitz, Barry. 1975. "Age and Fearfulness: Personal and Situational Factors." *Journal of Gerontology* 30: 696-700.

Maguire, Mike. 1980. "The Impact of Burglary on Victims." *British Journal of Criminology* 20 (July): 261-275.

Maguire, Mike. 1984. "Victims' Needs and Victim Services: Indications from Research." Paper presented at the Third International Institute on Victimology, Lisbon.

Mayhew, Pat. 1984. "The Effects of Crime: Victims, the Public, and Fear." Paper presented at the 16th International Symposium on Criminology, Strasbourg.

Ministry of the Solicitor General. 1983. *Who Are the Victims?* Ottawa: Research and Statistics Group, Ministry of the Solicitor General, Report No. 1.

Reiss, Albert J. Jr. 1982. "How Serious is Serious Crime," *Vanderbilt Law Review* 35 (April): 541-585.

Rifai, Marlene Young. 1976. *Older Americans Crime Prevention Research Project.* Portland, OR: Multnomah County Division of Public Safety.

Rifai, Marlene Young. 1982. "Methods of Measuring the Impact of Criminal Victimization Through Victimization Surveys." Pp. 189-202 in *The Victim in International Perspective*, edited by Hans Joachim Schneider. Berlin and New York: de Gruyter.

Riger, Stephanie. 1978. "Women's Fear of Crime," *Victimology* 3, 3-4: 254-264.

Riger, Stephanie. 1981. "On Women." Pp. 47-66 in *Reactions to Crime*, edited by Dan A. Lewis. Newbury Park, CA: Sage.

Rosenbaum, Dennis, and Terry Baumer. 1981. *Measuring Fear of Crime.* Evanston, IL: Westinghouse Evaluation Institute (Report to the National Institute of Justice, US Department of Justice).

Sales, E., M. Baum, and B. Shore. 1984. "Victim Readjustment Following Assault." *Journal of Social Issues* 40, 1: 117-136.

Shapland, Joanna. 1984. "Victims, the Criminal Justice System, and Compensation." *British Journal of Criminology* 24 (April): 131-149.

Sheppele, Kim L., and Pauline Bart. 1983. "Through Women's Eyes: Defining Danger in the Wake of Sexual Assault." *Journal of Social Issues* 39, 2: 63-80.

Silverman, Robert A., and Leslie W. Kennedy. 1985. "Loneliness, Satisfaction and Fear of Crime." *Canadian Journal of Criminology* 27, 1: 1-13.

Skogan, Wesley G. 1981. *Issues in the Measurement of Victimization.* Washington, DC: National Institute of Justice, US Department of Justice.

Skogan, Wesley G., and Michael Maxfield. 1981. *Coping With Crime.* Beverly Hills, CA: Sage.

Sparks, Richard F. 1981. "Surveys of Victimization: An Optimistic Assessment." Pp. 1-60 in *Crime and Justice: An Annual Review of Research Vol. 3,* edited by M. Tonrey, and N. Morris. Chicago: University of Chicago Press.

Sparks, Richard F., Hazel Genn, and David Dodd. 1977. *Surveying Victims.* London: John Wiley.

Taub, Richard, D. Garth Taylor, and Jan Dunham. 1984. *Patterns of Neighborhood Change: Race and Crime in Urban America.* Chicago: University of Chicago Press.

Taylor, Ralph, and Margaret Hale. 1985. "Testing Alternative Models of Fear." Unpublished paper, Department of Criminal Justice, Temple University.

Tyler, Tom R. 1984. "Assessing the Risk of Crime Victimization." *Journal of Social Issues* 40, 1: 27-38.

Waller, Irvin. 1982. "Victimization Studies as Guides to Action." Pp. 166-188 in *The Victim in International Perspective*, edited by Hans Joachim Schneider. Berlin and New York: de Gruyter.

Waller, Irvin, and Norman Okihiro. 1978. *Burglary: The Victim and the Public.* Toronto: University of Toronto Press.

Yin, Peter P. 1980. "Fear of Crime Among the Elderly." *Social Problems* 27 (April): 492-504.

Part III
The Sources of Information on Victimization

[9]

THE IMPACT OF A CRIME WAVE: PERCEPTIONS, FEAR, AND CONFIDENCE IN THE POLICE

MARY HOLLAND BAKER*
BARBARA C. NIENSTEDT
RONALD S. EVERETT
RICHARD McCLEARY

In 1980, Phoenix, Arizona, experienced a "crime wave." A structural equation model based on a two-wave survey of the population shows that the crime wave had a powerful impact that was almost a mirror image of what the fear of crime literature would predict. Demographic groups thought to be most fearful (e.g., women and the elderly) were least affected while groups thought to be least fearful (e.g., well-educated whites) were affected most. In addition to demographic factors, our analysis demonstrates that crime rate perceptions and confidence in the police are integral components of fear, especially in the context of a crime wave. These findings have important implications for crime policy specifically and for criminological research generally.

A "crime wave" ordinarily begins with an abrupt increase in reported crime. Crime and *reported* crime are not necessarily correlated, of course, so this distinction is crucial (Hindelang, 1974; 1976; Skogan, 1974). Crime-reporting institutions (media, police, etc.) play an essential role in any crime wave. A newspaper can start a crime wave independent of crime rates (Steffens, 1931). Similarly, the police find it all but impossible to suppress crime, but *reported* crime can be suppressed with relative ease (Kitsuse and Cicourel, 1963; Seidman and Couzens, 1974). In either case, crime waves are not necessarily a function of "real" crime increases but, rather, may be a function of media and/or police crime-reporting practices.

A final component of any "crime wave" definition is social reaction: crime waves are always public phenomena. Fishman's (1978: 531) statement of this point is typical:

* We are indebted to Thomas Epperlein and Hiroshi Nakajima for assistance in data collection and analysis.

320   THE IMPACT OF A CRIME WAVE

When we speak of a crime wave, we are talking about a
kind of social awareness of crime, crime brought to
public consciousness. It is something to be remarked
upon at the corner grocery store, complained about in a
community meeting, and denounced at the mayor's
press conference. One cannot be mugged by a crime
wave, but one can be scared. And one can put more
police on the streets and enact new laws on the basis
of fear. Crime waves may be 'things of the mind,' but
they have real consequences.

Research on crime waves has been largely qualitative,
focussing on the role of crime-reporting institutions (Molotch
and Lester, 1974; Tuchman, 1973) or on the consequences of
crime waves for social elites (Berk and Rossi, 1977; Sennet,
1969). The more general social reactions have not been widely
studied.

One likely reaction to a crime wave is, as Fishman notes, a
heightened level of fear. Fear of crime in turn has several
consequences which must be treated as indirect reactions.
Fear elicits avoidance behavior. It can, for example, inhibit
routine social interaction and alter life-styles (Hartnagel, 1979;
Wilson, 1975). Attitudinal consequences of fear may be less
tangible than these behavioral consequences but they are no
less important. Fear obviously affects the quantity and quality
of police-citizen interactions (O'Neil, 1979; Schneider et al.,
1975). But more importantly, individuals who are fearful lose
confidence in the ability of local governments to solve problems
(Conklin, 1971; Ennis, 1967; Smith and Hawkins, 1973). A crime
wave in this sense may have serious political consequences.
When the electorate believes, correctly or not, that the
government cannot control crime, crime becomes a political
issue, a basis for voting incumbent officials and administrations
out of office.

Figure 1 shows a structural model relating a crime wave to
perceptions of the crime rate, fear, and confidence in the police.
A crime wave affects perceptions of the crime rate by
definition. Reflecting Fishman's view, we further hypothesize
that a crime wave will directly affect fear of crime and
confidence in the police. Confidence in the police is also
expected to have a direct effect on fear, so the model implies
that factors which affect confidence in the police will have
indirect effects on fear.

The internal dynamics of this model are, with one
exception, identical to other models suggested in the literature
(Garofalo, 1981; Skogan and Maxfield, 1981; Hartnagel, 1979); we

Figure 1.   A Structural Model of the Implications
of a Crime Wave

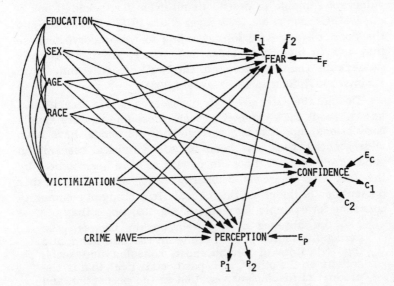

posit a direct impact of recent victimization on fear. Some research (Fowler and Mangione, 1974; Block and Long, 1973; Furstenberg, 1971) has found no correlation between victimization and fear of crime. This research is not based on an extensive multivariate causal model, however. We have included a direct path from victimization to fear in order to test for that effect when other variables and processes are controlled.

Several demographic variables are exogenous to this system. Prior research has shown that education, sex, age, and race are correlated with perceptions, fear, and confidence, but the precise causal mechanism for these correlations is unknown. One explanation is that these demographic variables measure the individual's perceived *risk* of victimization. Actual and perceived risk are negatively correlated for some groups, however. Men are victimized more frequently than women, for example, but women are more fearful than men (Clemente and Kleiman, 1977). Similarly, although age and victimization are inversely related, the elderly are more fearful than the young (Antunes *et al.*, 1977; Cook *et al.*, 1981; Goldsmith and Tomas, 1974). A related hypothesis that would seem to account for this anomaly is that perceived vulnerability to victimization, not

322   THE IMPACT OF A CRIME WAVE

(Kidder and Cohn, 1979; Skogan and Maxfield, 1981). Women and the elderly often perceive themselves as physically vulnerable, unable to defend themselves if attacked (Cook *et al.*, 1981; Gordon *et al.*, 1980; Riger *et al.*, 1978). Nonwhites and the poor are more fearful, according to this theory, because they live in high-crime areas and, hence, are more socially vulnerable than whites and the well-off (Clemente and Kleiman, 1977; Skogan and Maxfield, 1981).

Despite the extensive body of research in this area, little is known about the dynamics of fear. Most findings are simple correlations and, although variations of our model have been widely noted, none has been tested. Empirical research in general and tests of theory in particular have been limited by the fact that there is ordinarily little variance in either perceptions of the crime rate or fear. In a study of community cohesion, for example, Hartnagel (1979: 189) notes that:

> . . . the absence of any relationship between the perception or the fear of crime on the one hand, and the indicators of neighborhood cohesion and social activity on the other . . . is partly statistical; that is, the product of insufficient variation in the perception and fear of crime.

This conclusion is typical. Given the normal, static perceived level of crime, past research has been able to show only that some individuals are fearful while others are not. It has not explained the dynamic relationships between perceptions and fear, nor has it explained the processes which make people more or less fearful over time.

In light of this, the most important exogenous variable of our model is the crime wave. To the extent that a crime wave affects perceptions of crime, generating fear in individuals who would otherwise not be fearful, it is what Campbell (1969) calls a "natural experiment," a fortuitous opportunity to study the dynamics of fear.

I. THE CRIME WAVE

In 1979 and 1980, we conducted a two-wave survey of Phoenix households as part of a team policing experiment. Our survey instrument covered such topics as attitudes toward police, recent victimization experience, and perceptions of crime, safety, and police effectiveness.[1] The first survey wave, conducted in early September, 1979, had a sample of 572 respondents with 84.9 percent response. The second wave,

---

[1] These survey data are described in an appendix.

conducted in late July, 1980, had a sample of 635 respondents with 86.6 percent response. Interviews were conducted by telephone from a central location with close supervision. To ensure sampling of persons with unlisted phone numbers, phone numbers were selected by random digit dialing.

Table 1. Responses to Victimization Items Collected from Randomly Selected Phoenix Telephone Households in September, 1979 and July, 1980

	Sept 79	July 80
Has anyone in your household requested police assistance of any kind within the last six months?		
- yes	38.6%	36.5%
Has anyone in your household called the police to report a crime within the last six months?		
- yes	25.9%	22.2%
Household victimization within the last twelve months		
Break-in, burglary, etc.	13.0%	11.4%
Attempted break-in	10.3%	13.3%
Robbery	7.5%	6.8%
Physical assault	5.6%	6.5%
Vandalism of home, car, etc.	31.8%	30.8%

Table 2. Responses to Perceptual Items Collected from Randomly Selected Phoenix Telephone Households in September, 1979 and July, 1980

	Sept 79	July 80
Within the past year, has crime in your neighborhood increased, decreased, or stayed about the same?		
- increased	26.2%	35.6%
What about the City of Phoenix in general? Within the past year, has crime in Phoenix increased, decreased, or stayed about the same?		
- increased	61.5%	76.7%

Due to profound changes in attitudes and perceptions across the two survey waves, the data were useless for their intended purpose. Tables 1 and 2 illustrate the most important dimensions of the change. As shown in Table 1, victimization item responses remained constant across the two waves. As shown in Table 2, however, perceptions of the crime rate changed markedly. Prior research (e.g., Conklin, 1971; Fowler, 1974; Fowler and Mangione, 1974) suggests that these responses will be stable over time. The differences in Table 2 are remarkable in this broader context and, in the present context,

324   THE IMPACT OF A CRIME WAVE

they are central to our structural model. They measure the public reaction which defines a crime wave.

In fact, several UCR crime rates did increase substantially in the ten months between survey waves.[2] The conclusion drawn from Table 2 is that the public was aware of this UCR crime wave. But because victimization rates remained constant, public awareness could not have been due to aggregate personal experience. A plausible alternative hypothesis is that this effect was due to media crime reports. Although perceptions of crime may be influenced by a variety of sources (e.g., friendship networks), prior research demonstrates that media reports are a crucial source of crime information (Gordon and Heath, 1981). This is especially so when crime is an "emerging issue" as in the case of a crime wave (Hubbard *et al.*, 1975).

Local newspapers, radio, and TV gave the 1979-80 UCR rate increases prominent coverage. To capture the objective dimensions of this media campaign, we analyzed crime news printed on the front-pages ("A" and "B" sections) of Phoenix's two daily newspapers for the last six months of 1979 and the first six months of 1980. Our analysis shows that the quantity of crime reports did not increase substantially from September, 1979 to July, 1980. This is consistent with prior research (Hurley and Antunes, 1977; Jones, 1976; Davis, 1952) which has found no relationship between UCR rates and the quantity or frequency of media crime reports.

Qualitative differences from 1979 to 1980, on the other hand, were substantial. In the first six months of 1980, for example, the two papers carried 35 crime-related editorials versus 20 in the last six months of 1979. The editorials published in 1980 were also more likely to concern local issues and were more likely to be critical of local law enforcement agencies. Crime thus became an editorial issue in Phoenix during the first half of 1980.

More importantly, in the first six months of 1980, crime news began to reflect a crime wave theme. According to Fishman (1978), a "crime wave theme" is a journalistic device which links a set of apparently unrelated crimes together so that they are recognized as early signs of an emerging issue. Whatever the cause, the local media suddenly "discovered" in

---

[2] McCleary *et al.* (1982a; 1982b) argue that the increase in UCRs from late 1979 to 1980 is due to the retirement of the incumbent police chief in July, 1979. The ensuing administrative shake-up in the Phoenix Police Department led to changes in UCR coding procedures.

early 1980 that Phoenix was being ravaged by crime.[3] There were several important aspects of the media campaign, but coverage of crime statistics is most germane. In the last six months of 1979, the newspapers printed only two front-page articles about UCR increases. Both articles, moreover, were positive in tone, reporting local UCR increases but noting that these increases were smaller than increases in other large cities. During the first six months of 1980, on the other hand, eleven stories about the UCR increases appeared on the front page and all were negative in tone. An *Arizona Republic* story on May 26, for example, was run under the sarcastic headline "Crime pays . . ." And on April 26, a *Phoenix Gazette* story was headlined (with no apologies to Eliot) "April is the cruelest month" for robberies; on May 30, an *Arizona Republic* story noted in its headline that robberies were "plaguing" the city. These stories did not report specific crimes but, rather, reported "trends." In May and June, robbery stories in both papers began to carry running counts in their headlines; "35th armed robbery this month . . ." Finally, although Phoenix has a relatively low homicide rate, both papers gave prominent coverage to a slight rise in UCR homicides. In June and July, three front-page stories reported homicide "trends." An editorial decried the "trend," attributing it to lenient judges, pampered criminals, and a general breakdown in the moral fabric of society.

Given this media campaign, the differences in Table 2 are not surprising. We cannot, of course, attribute the differences in Table 2 solely to the media campaign but, given the consistent body of research in this area (especially Hubbard *et al.*, 1975), media effects appear to be the most plausible explanation for these differences.

II. A TEST OF THE MODEL

Our model of the effects of the crime wave (Figure 1) was tested with the survey data. Operational definitions of the variables are given in an appendix. Estimates of the model

---

[3] Two factors explain this runaway media campaign. First, in 1980, an election was held on a 40 million dollar bond issue to build more jails in Phoenix. Both papers took strong editorial stands supporting the bond issue, and insiders have claimed that the media campaign was part of this editorial stand. Second, in late 1979, long-standing relationships between local police and the media broke down. Personnel changes at the papers brought new reporters to the "police beat" while incumbent chiefs of three local police departments simultaneously retired. The new chiefs had relatively little experience dealing with "police beat" reporters and vice versa. The runaway media campaign was a spontaneous result of these two coincidental factors.

326   THE IMPACT OF A CRIME WAVE

parameters, calculated with LISREL IV (Joreskog and Sorbom, 1980), are given in Table 3. The model is a viable portrait of the effects of the crime wave. The rho coefficient for the model (see Burt, 1973; Tucker and Lewis, 1973) is .94 and, in our experience, this value is quite high. The model also explains 25 percent of the variance in fear of crime.

Before we discuss the parameter estimates and implications of this model, we must clarify several statistical assumptions of the model.

Exogenous Correlations

Since victimization is related to age, sex, race, and education, all of these correlations are included in the model. The correlation between crime wave and victimization is not included. Had a "real" crime wave occurred, our crime wave variable would be correlated with victimization. Because the two survey waves were random samples, we expected our crime wave variable (a dummy measuring the survey wave) to be uncorrelated with demographics. Age, race, and sex were hypothesized to be uncorrelated with each other, but all were expected to be correlated with education. All exogenous correlations were tested for significance with an F-statistic (Blalock, 1979: 417) and, except for the age-race correlation, our hypotheses were supported.[4] Given the higher birth rate and shorter life-expectancy of blacks and Hispanics, minorities have a younger mean age than the white population (U.S. Bureau of the Census, 1980). We included the age-race correlation in our model to reflect this empirical result.

Interactions

Prior research (e.g., Clemente and Kleiman, 1977; Skogan and Maxfield, 1981) found no interactions between demographics and perceptions, fear, or confidence. We conducted logistic regressions for endogenous variables to test this assumption. None of our equations had significant multi-way interactions, so the linear assumption is empirically justified.

---

[4] Correlations among the exogenous variables are

	Sex	Age	Race	Educ.	Victim.	Cr. Wv.
Sex	1.000					
Age	−.065	1.000				
Race	−.018	.174	1.000			
Educ.	.055	−.096	.259	1.000		
Victim.	.073	−.163	−.119	−.083	1.000	
Cr. Wv.	−.028	−.059	.007	.043	−.021	1.000

Causal Direction

Prior research does not clearly specify the causal relationship between fear and confidence. To test the validity of our model, we estimated reciprocal effects for each endogenous variable pair. It seems certain from this analysis that perceptions precede fear in causal ordering. The estimated effect from perceptions to fear was strong and significant, while the effect from fear to perceptions was weak and insignificant. The results for confidence-fear and perceptions-confidence were more ambiguous but supported our model nevertheless.[5] We include confidence as an effect of perceptions and fear as an effect of confidence because this is the most empirically and theoretically viable specification.

Given these assumptions, our final model leads to a set of findings about the crime wave specifically and about the dynamics of fear generally. Direct effects of the model are given in Table 3. The correlations in this table are simply the zero-order correlations among the exogenous variables. The standardized parameters are maximum likelihood estimates of the latent endogenous variables (Perception, Fear, and Confidence) regressed on the exogenous variables and on the other latent variables. These maximum likelihood estimates are interpreted as path coefficients. The measurement level parameters refer to the regression of the observed indicators $(P_1, P_2, C_1, C_2, F_1,$ and $F_2)$ on the corresponding latent constructs (Perception, Fear, and Confidence). These coefficients are (confirmatory) maximum likelihood factor loadings. Finally, since our most important findings concern fear, we have decomposed the total effects for fear in Table 4.

Crime Wave

The crime wave had a significant effect on perceptions of crime (p = .25), as expected, but it had no significant direct effect on fear or confidence. These latter findings are contrary

---

[5] To estimate one of the reciprocal effects, we excluded a statistically insignificant exogenous variable. For the confidence-fear estimate, both parameters were insignificant. However, the effect for the direction shown in Figure 1 was much larger than the effect running in the opposite direction.

328   THE IMPACT OF A CRIME WAVE

Table 3. Zero-Order Correlations and LISREL IV Estimates for the Figure 1 Model Parameters

to ——	Correlations				Standardized Parameters		
	Sex	Age	Race	Victim	Perception	Confidence	Fear
From Education	(.05)*	(-.09)	(.26)	(-.08)	.10*	.05*	-.17
From Sex	(1.00)	—	—	(.06)	-.14	-.11	-.43
From Age		(1.00)	(.17)	(-.16)	-.04	.28	.21
From Race			(1.00)	(-.12)	.14	.16	-.09
From Victimization				(1.00)	.36	-.01*	-.05*
From Crime Wave					.25	.02*	.02*
From Perception						-.28	.34
From Confidence							-.20

Measurement-level parameters for *Perceptions:* $P_1 = .50$; $P_2 = .26$; $e_P = .88$;
     for *Fear:* $F_1 = .74$; $F_2 = .76$; $e_F = .75$;
     for *Confidence:* $C_1 = .66$; $C_2 = .76$; $e_C = .89$;

* not statistically significant at $P_{.05}$

Table 4. Decomposition of Total Effect for Exogenous Impacts on Fear of Crime

Variable	Indirect Effect[a] (Perception)	Indirect Effect[a] (Confidence)	Indirect Effect[b] (Total)	Direct Effect (Total)	Total Effect
Education	.03	-.01	-.03	-.17	-.20
Sex	-.05	.02	-.03	-.43	-.46
Age	-.01	-.06	-.09	.21	.12
Race	.05	-.03	.00	-.09	-.09
Victimization	.12	.00	.11	-.05	.06
Crime Wave	.08	.00	.09	.02	.11

[a] Calculated with the two-step path from the exogenous variable to confidence to fear; the three-step path from the exogenous variable to perception to confidence to fear is not included.
[b] Since three-or-more-step paths are not given here, the total indirect effect is not the sum of indirect effects through perception and confidence.

to our expectations and, given the literature's preoccupation with direct effects on fear, may be surprising. Perceptions had a powerful effect on fear (p = .34), so the indirect effect of the crime wave on fear is substantial; see Table 4. The zero-order correlations reported in the literature are no doubt due to this strong indirect effect. Finally, the crime wave had no indirect effect on fear through confidence in the police.

Victimization

Consistent with prior research (Block and Long, 1973; Fowler and Mangione, 1974; Furstenberg, 1971; 1972), we found no direct effect of recent victimization experience on fear (p = −.05). A partial explanation may be that most of our victims were victims of property crime (see Table 1), whereas our fear of crime indicators involve fear of assaultive crime. Recent victimization experience has a direct effect on perceptions of the crime rate nevertheless and, through perceptions, a strong indirect effect on fear. Victimization, in fact, is the single most important cause of crime rate perceptions (p = .36). At the same time, it has no direct effect on confidence in the police.

Race

The direct effect of race on fear is negative. Nonwhites are more likely to be afraid than whites, controlling for the effects of other exogenous variables and perceptions. However, Table 4 reveals a positive indirect effect of race on fear through perceptions. Whites are more likely to perceive increasing crime rates and, as a result, become fearful. When combined into a single effect, the opposite-signed direct and indirect effects of race on fear cancel each other. This would explain why some research has found no race effect on fear. The effect will not be apparent unless perceptions are controlled. Race also has a positive effect on confidence in the police. Whites have more confidence than nonwhites, leading to a small negative indirect effect of race on fear. Nonwhites have less confidence in the police and, as a result, are more fearful.

Age

Controlling for all other independent variables, the *direct* effect of age on fear is stronger than the *total* effect of age on fear. The primary mediating factor here is confidence in the police. Age has a strong direct effect on confidence (p = .28). The elderly have more confidence in the police and, as a result, are less fearful than would otherwise be expected.

330   THE IMPACT OF A CRIME WAVE

Sex

Sex has the largest single direct effect on fear (p = −.43). This direct effect accounts for most of the total effect of sex on fear. Women are also more likely to perceive rising crime rates and, as a result, sex has a small indirect effect on fear through perceptions. Sex has no effect on confidence in the police, so there is no indirect effect on fear through this variable. The zero-order correlation between victimization and sex is positive, so even though women are more fearful than men, they are less likely to be victimized.

Education

Education has a direct negative effect on fear. Since we are not controlling for occupation or income, education is our primary SES indicator. Less educated individuals are more likely to live in high-crime areas, so the direct inverse relationship between education and fear is not surprising. Education has a small positive indirect effect on fear through perceptions. Better educated individuals are more likely to perceive rising crime rates and, thus, become fearful. The relationship between education and perception is particularly important here because better educated people are more likely to read newspapers. The direct effect of education on confidence is insignificant, so there is no indirect effect on fear through this variable.

Perceptions

As noted, perception of rising crime rates is due to the strong direct effects of the crime wave and victimization; the next most important causes are sex and race. As an independent variable, perception is the second most important cause of fear (after sex) and is an important cause of confidence (p = −.28). Individuals who perceive rising crime rates lose confidence in the police.

Confidence

Only three variables have significant direct effects on confidence. These are perceptions, age, and race. Whites, the elderly, and people who believe that crime is not on the rise have more confidence in the police, controlling for other variables. Confidence in the police, moreover, has a substantial negative effect on fear (p = −.20). Individuals who have more confidence in the police are less fearful.

III. DISCUSSION

Our findings have two policy implications. First, because confidence in the police reduces fear among the elderly, fear of crime among the elderly might be reduced by programs designed to increase their confidence in the police. Second, whites have significantly more confidence in the police than nonwhites and, through an indirect effect, less fear of crime. An implication of this finding is that programs designed to improve police-minority relations will also reduce fear of crime among minorities.

But our findings have more important implications for theory. From the beginning, we were guided by the fear of crime literature and many of our results are consistent with this literature. Concerning the direct effects of exogenous variables on fear, for example, we found nothing new. As shown in Table 4, however, these same exogenous variables often have indirect effects on fear—through changing perceptions of the crime rate—that run counter to the direct effects. Individuals who ordinarily are not fearful become fearful when they perceive rising crime rates. And because the crime wave and prior victimization variables are important causes of perceptual change, they are essential to our understanding of fear.

The elderly are an exceptional group in this sense. Fear among the elderly is not due to perceptions of the crime rate. It is therefore likely that a "crime wave" would have less impact on fear among the elderly than among the young.

Blacks and Chicanos are more fearful than whites, and the less educated are more fearful than the better educated. Our findings again support prior research on this point. The direct effects of race and education and indirect effects through perceptions have opposite signs, however. Whites and the better educated are more likely to perceive rising crime rates and, while not ordinarily fearful, they are more likely than nonwhites and the less educated to be affected by crime waves.

Finally, we found that recent victimization experience has no direct effect on fear. Victims are more likely to perceive rising crime rates, however, and by means of indirect effects, become fearful. A crime wave will thus affect the fears of these individuals.

But while many of our findings are consistent with the fear of crime literature, other findings contradict previous research. By virtue of an indirect effect, for example, we found that recent victims *are* significantly more fearful; that minorities *are*

332   THE IMPACT OF A CRIME WAVE

more fearful than whites but that this fear is due in no small part to lack of confidence in the police; and that, when confidence in the police is controlled, the elderly are more fearful than previous research has suggested. We would not have been able to spot these inconsistencies with prior research had we not used a relatively sophisticated causal model. Our most important finding is that perceptions of the crime rate and confidence in the police are important in the causal modeling of fear. Without much exaggeration, we may say that fear of crime cannot be measured outside a model that simultaneously accounts for perceptions and confidence. These variables deserve further investigation.

APPENDIX
DESCRIPTION OF THE VARIABLES ˎ
(See Figure 1.)

Exogenous variables include the sex, age, race, education, and recent victimization experience of the respondent, and the crime wave. These variables are operationalized as

Sex: male = 1, female = 0

Age: in years

Race: Anglo white = 1, all other = 0

Education: years schooling completed (zero to seventeen)

Victimization: burglary, attempted burglary, robbery, attempted robbery, or physical assault in the last twelve months = 1, all other reports = 0

Crime Wave: a dummy variable, = 0 for the pretest (September, 1979), = 1 for the posttest (July, 1980)

Endogenous variables include perception of the crime wave, confidence in the police, and fear of crime. Two items measure the degree to which a respondent is aware of the crime wave:

P_1: *Within the past year, do you think crime in Phoenix has increased, decreased, or stayed about the same?*

decreased or stayed the same = 0, increased = 1

P_2: *Within the past year, do you think crime in your neighborhood has increased, decreased, or stayed about the same?*

decreased or stayed the same = 0, increased = 1

Two items measure a respondent's fear-related confidence in the police:

BAKER, NIENSTEDT, EVERETT & McCLEARY 333

C_1: *How would you rate the speed of the Phoenix Police Department in responding to emergency calls for assistance? Excellent, good, fair, or poor?*

excellent = 1, good = 0, fair or poor = −1

C_2: *How would you rate the speed of the Phoenix Police Department in responding to general service or non-emergency calls for assistance? Excellent, good, fair, or poor?*

excellent = 1, good = 0, fair or poor = −1

Two items measure the level of a respondent's general fear of crime:

F_1: *How safe would you feel walking alone at night in your neighborhood? Would you feel very safe, somewhat safe, or not safe at all?*

very safe = −1, somewhat safe = 0, not safe at all = 1

F_2: *Think of the worst area within a mile of your house. How safe would you feel walking alone at night in this area? Would you feel very safe, somewhat safe, somewhat unsafe, or not safe at all?*

very safe = − 1, somewhat safe or somewhat unsafe = 0, not safe at all = 1

REFERENCES

ANTUNES, G.E., F.L. COOK, T.D. COOK and W.G. SKOGAN (1977) "Patterns of Personal Crime against the Elderly," 17 *Gerontologist* 321.

BERK, R.A. and P.H. ROSSI (1977) *Prison Reform and State Elites*. Cambridge, MA: Ballinger.

BLALOCK, H.M. (1979) *Social Statistics*, Revised 2nd Ed. New York: McGraw-Hill.

BLOCK, M.S. and G.J. LONG (1973) "Subjective Probability of Victimization and Crime Levels: An Econometric Approach," 11 *Criminology* 87.

BURT, R.S. (1973) "Confirmatory Factor-Analytic Structures and Theory Construction Processes," 2 *Sociological Methods and Research* 131.

CAMPBELL, D.T. (1969) "Reforms as Experiments," 24 *American Psychologist* 409.

CLEMENTE, F. and M.B. KLEIMAN (1977) "Fear of Crime in the United States: A Multivariate Analysis," 56 *Social Forces* 519.

CONKLIN, J.E. (1971) "Dimensions of Community Response to the Crime Problem," 18 *Social Problems* 373.

———(1975) *The Impact of Crime*. New York: Macmillan.

COOK, F.L., W.G. SKOGAN, T.D. COOK and G.E. ANTUNES (1981) *Criminal Victimization of the Elderly*. New York: Oxford University Press.

CROUSE, T. (1972) *The Boys on the Bus*. New York: Ballantine.

DAVIS, F.J. (1952) "Crime News in Colorado Newspapers," 57 *American Journal of Sociology* 325.

ENNIS, P.H. (1967) "Attitudes towards the Police, Law Enforcement, and Individual Security," in *Criminal Victimization in the United States: A Report of the National Survey*. Washington, D.C.: U.S. Government Printing Office.

FISHMAN, M. (1978) "Crime Waves as Ideology," 25 *Social Problems* 531.

FOWLER, F.J. (1974) *Citizen Attitudes toward Local Government Services and Taxes*. Cambridge, MA: Ballinger.

334 THE IMPACT OF A CRIME WAVE

FOWLER, F.J. and T.W. MANGIONE (1974) *The Nature of Fear*. Cambridge, MA: Survey Research Program, Harvard-MIT Joint Center for Urban Studies.
FURSTENBERG, F.F. (1971) "Public Reaction to Crime in the Streets," 40 *American Scholar* 601.
—— (1972) "Fear of Crime and its Effects on Citizen Behavior," in A. Biderman (ed.), *Crime and Justice: A Symposium*. New York: Nailburg Publishing Company.
GAROFALO, J. (1981) "The Fear of Crime: Causes and Consequences," 72 *The Journal of Criminal Law and Criminology* 839.
GOLDSMITH, J. and N. TOMAS (1974) "Crimes against the Elderly: A Continuing National Crisis," 236 *Aging* 10.
GORDON, M.T. and L. HEATH (1981) "The News Business, Crime and Fear," in D.A. Lewis (ed.), *Reactions to Crime*. Beverly Hills: Sage.
GORDON, M.T., S. RIGER, R.K. LeBAILLY and L. HEATH (1980) "Crime, Women, and the Quality of Urban Life," 5 *Signs* 144.
HARTNAGEL, T.F. (1979) "The Perception and Fear of Crime: Implications for Neighborhood Cohesion, Social Activity, and Community Affect," 58 *Social Forces* 176.
HINDELANG, M.J. (1974) "Public Opinion Regarding Crime, Criminal Justice, and Related Topics," 11 *Journal of Research in Crime and Delinquency* 101.
—— (1976) *Criminal Victimization in Eight American Cities: A Descriptive Analysis of Common Theft and Assault*. Cambridge, MA: Ballinger.
HUBBARD, J., M. DeFLEUR, and L. DeFLEUR (1975) "Mass Media Influences on Public Conceptions of Social Problems," 23 *Social Problems* 22.
HURLEY, P. and G.E. ANTUNES (1977) "The Representation of Criminal Events in Houston's Two Daily Newspapers," 54 *Journalism Quarterly* 756.
JONES, E.T. (1976) "The Press as Metropolitan Monitor," 40 *Public Opinion Quarterly* 239.
JORESKOG, K.G. and D. SORBOM (1980) *LISREL IV: Analysis of Linear Structural Relationships by the Method of Maximum Likelihood*. Chicago: International Educational Services.
KIDDER, L.H. and E.S. COHN (1979) "Public Views of Crime and Crime Prevention," Chapter 10 in I.H. Frieze, D. Bar-Tal, and J.S. Carrol (eds.), *New Approaches to Social Problems*. San Francisco: Jossey-Bass.
KITSUSE, J. and A.V. CICOUREL (1963) "A Note on the Use of Official Statistics," 11 *Social Problems* 131.
McCLEARY, R., B.C. NIENSTEDT and J.M. ERVEN (1982a) "Uniform Crime Reports as Organizational Outcomes: Three Time Series Quasi-Experiments," 29 *Social Problems* 361.
—— (1982b) "Interrupted Time Series Analysis of Crime Statistics: The Case of Organizational Reforms," in J. Hagan (ed.), *Methodological Advances in Criminological Research*. Beverly Hills: Sage.
MOLOTCH, H. and M. LESTER (1974) "News as Purposive Behavior: The Strategic Use of Routine Events, Accidents, and Scandals," 39 *American Sociological Review* 101.
O'NEIL, M.J. (1979) "A Little Help from our Friends: Citizen Predisposition to Intervene in Spouse Abuse," 1 *Law and Policy Quarterly* 177.
RIGER, S., M.T. GORDON and R. LeBAILLY (1978) "Women's Fear of Crime: From Blaming to Restricting the Victim," 3 *Victimology* 3.
SCHNEIDER, A.L., J.M. BURCAT, and L.A. WILSON II (1975) "The Role of Attitudes in the Decision to Report Crimes to the Police," Chapter 4 in W.F. McDonald (ed.), *Criminal Justice and the Victim*. Beverly Hills: Sage.
SEIDMAN, D. and M. COUZENS (1974) "Getting the Crime Rate Down: Political Pressure and Crime," 8 *Law and Society Review* 457.
SENNET, R. (1969) "Middle Class Families and Urban Violence: The Experience of a Chicago Community in the Nineteenth Century," in J. Thernstrom and R. Sennet (eds.), *Nineteenth Century Cities*. New Haven: Yale University Press.
SINGER, S.L. (1977) "The Concept of Vulnerability and the Elderly Victim in an Urban Environment," in J.E. Scott and S. Dinitz (eds.), *Criminal Justice Planning*. New York: Praeger.
SKOGAN, W.G. (1974) "The Validity of Official Crime Statistics: An Empirical Investigation," 55 *Social Science Quarterly* 25.
SKOGAN, W.G. and M.G. MAXFIELD (1981) *Coping with Crime*. Beverly Hills: Sage.
SMITH, P.E. and R.O. HAWKINS (1973) "Victimization, Types of Citizen-Police Contacts, and Attitudes toward the Police," 8 *Law and Society Review* 135.

STEFFENS, L. (1931) *The Autobiography of Lincoln Steffens.* New York: Harcourt-Brace.

TUCHMAN, G. (1973) "Making News by Doing Work: Routinizing the Unexpected," 79 *American Journal of Sociology* 110.

TUCKER, L. and C. LEWIS (1973) "A Reliability Coefficient for Maximum Likelihood Factor Analysis," 38 *Psychometrika* 1.

U.S. BUREAU OF THE CENSUS (1980) *Statistical Abstract of the United States*, 101st Ed. Washington, D.C.: U.S. Government Printing Office.

WILSON, J.Q. (1975) *Thinking about Crime*. New York: Basic Books.

[10]

Living With Television: The Violence Profile

by George Gerbner and Larry Gross

Does TV entertainment incite or pacify (or both)?
New approach to research uses Cultural Indicators
as a framework for a progress report on a long-range
study of trends in television content and effects.

The environment that sustains the most distinctive aspects of human existence is the environment of symbols. We learn, share, and act upon meanings derived from that environment. The first and longest lasting organization of the symbolic world was what we now call religion. Within its sacred scope, in earlier times, were the most essential processes of culture: art, science, technology, statecraft, and public story-telling.

Common rituals and mythologies are agencies of symbolic socialization and control. They demonstrate how society works by dramatizing its norms and values. They are essential parts of the general system of messages that cultivates prevailing outlooks (which is why we call it culture) and regulates social relationships. This system of messages, with its story-telling functions, makes people perceive as real and normal and right that which fits the established social order.

The institutional processes producing these message systems have become increasingly professionalized, industrialized, centralized, and specialized. Their principal locus shifted from handicraft to mass production and from traditional religion and formal education to the mass media of communications—particularly television. New technologies on the horizon may enrich the choices of the choosy but cannot replace the simultaneous public experience of a common symbolic environment that now binds diverse communities, including large

George Gerbner is Professor and Dean and Larry Gross is Associate Professor at The Annenberg School of Communications, University of Pennsylvania, Philadelphia. They are also co-editors (with William H. Melody) of *Communications Technology and Social Policy: Understanding the New "Cultural Revolution"* (Wiley, 1973). For collaboration and assistance in the continuing study from which the findings reported here are based, the authors wish to give acknowledgment and thanks to Michael F. Eleey, Suzanne K. Fox, Marilyn Jackson-Beeck, Stephen D. Rappaport, Thomas M. Wick, and Dr. Nancy Signorielli.

Journal of Communication, Spring 1976

groups of young and old and isolated people who have never before joined any mass public. Television is likely to remain for a long time the chief source of repetitive and ritualized symbol systems cultivating the common consciousness of the most far-flung and heterogenous mass publics in history.

> *Our long-range study of this new symbolic environment*
> *developed from, and still includes, the annual Violence*
> *Index and Profile of TV content and its correlates in*
> *viewers' conceptions of relevant aspects of social reality.*

The research began with the investigation of violence in network television drama in 1967-68 for the National Commission on the Causes and Prevention of Violence (4) and continued through 1972 under the sponsorship of the Surgeon General's Scientific Advisory Committee on Television and Social Behavior (5). The study was broadly conceived from the beginning and both reports showed the role and symbolic functions, as well as the extent, of violence in the world of television drama. A conference of research consultants to the National Institute of Mental Health in the spring of 1972 recommended that the Violence Index developed for the report to the Surgeon General be further broadened to take into account social relationships and viewer conceptions. Implementing that recommendation, we issued the Violence Profile (fifth in our series of reports), including violence-victim ratios and eventually viewer responses. The then Secretary of Health, Education, and Welfare Caspar W. Weinberger reported to Senator John O. Pastore in the fall of 1973 that our research was "broadened to encompass a number of additional dimensions and linked with viewers' perceptions of violence and its effects. as recommended by NIMH consultants and as incorporated by Dr. Gerbner in his renewal research" (16).

The "renewal research" to which Secretary Weinberger referred is our present project, Cultural Indicators. Conducted under a grant from the National Institute of Mental Health. it consists of periodic study of television programming and of the conceptions of social reality that viewing cultivates in child and adult audiences. Although the study of violence is a continuing aspect of the research,[1] the project is also developing indicators of other themes, roles, and relationships significant for social science and policy.

The pattern of findings that is beginning to emerge confirms our belief that television is essentially different from other media and that research on television requires a new approach. In this article we shall sketch the outlines of a critique of modes of research derived from experience with other media and advance an approach we find more appropriate to the special characteristics, features, and functions of television. We shall illustrate the design and some

[1] Several additional events influenced the further fate and development of the Violence Profile. Senator Pastore and Chairman Torbert Macdonald of the House Communications Subcommittee continued to take an active interest in it. The research director of the studies for the Surgeon General. Eli A. Rubinstein, continued to press for follow-up research (14). Douglass Cater and Stephen Strickland wrote a book on the report and argued for "ongoing research capable of undergirding large public policy investigations" (1,p.133). And, finally, a committee of the Social Science Research Council especially formed and funded by NIMH to study the Violence Profile recommended continued use and further development (15).

contributions of the approach taken in the Cultural Indicators project by presenting the latest Violence Profile (No. 7 in the series), including indicators of some conceptions television cultivates in its viewers.[2]

> *The confusing state of television research is*
> *largely due to inappropriate conceptions of the problem.*

The automobile that burst upon the dusty highways of the turn of the century was seen by most people as just a horseless carriage rather than as a prime mover of a new way of life. Similarly, those who grew up before television tended to think of it as just another in the long series of technological innovations in mass communications. Consequently, modes of thinking and research rooted in experience with other media have been applied to television. These earlier modes of study were based on selectively used media and focused on attitude or behavior change. Both assumptions are largely inadequate to the task of conceptualizing and investigating the effects of television.

We begin with the assertion that television is the central cultural arm of American society. It is an agency of the established order and as such serves primarily to extend and maintain rather than to alter, threaten, or weaken conventional conceptions, beliefs, and behaviors. Its chief cultural function is to spread and stabilize social patterns, to cultivate not change but resistance to change. Television is a medium of the socialization of most people into standardized roles and behaviors. Its function is, in a word, enculturation.

The substance of the consciousness cultivated by TV is not so much specific attitudes and opinions as more basic assumptions about the "facts" of life and standards of judgment on which conclusions are based. The purpose of the Cultural Indicators project is to identify and track these premises and the conclusions they might cultivate across TV's diverse publics.

We shall make a case for studying television as a force for enculturation rather than as a selectively used medium of separate "entertainment" and "information" functions. First, we shall suggest that the essential differences between television and other media are more crucial than the similarities. Second, we will show why traditional research designs are inadequate for the study of television effects and suggest more appropriate methods. Third, we will sketch the pattern of evidence emerging from our studies indicating that "living" in the world of television cultivates conceptions of its own conventionalized "reality."

> *The reach, scope, ritualization, organic connectedness,*
> *and non-selective use of mainstream television makes*
> *it different from other media of mass communications.*

TV penetrates every home in the land. Its seasonal, cyclical, and perpetual patterns of organically related fact and fiction (all woven into an entertainment fabric producing publics of consumers for sale to advertisers) again encompass

---

[2]A summary of the cultivation studies also appears in our article in the April 1976 *Psychology Today* (10).

Journal of Communication, Spring 1976

essential elements of art, science, technology, statecraft, and public (as well as most family) story-telling. The information-poor (children and less educated adults) are again the entertainment-rich held in thrall by the myths and legends of a new electronic priesthood.

If you were born before, say, 1950, television came into your life after the formative years as just another medium. Even if you are now an "addict," it will be difficult for you to comprehend the transformations it has wrought. Could you, as a twelve-year old, have contemplated spending an average of six hours *a day* at the local movie house? Not only would most parents not have permitted such behavior but most children would not have imagined the possibility. Yet, in our sample of children, nearly half the twelve-year-olds watch at least six hours of television every day.

Unlike print, television does not require literacy. Unlike the movies, television is "free" (supported by a privately imposed tax on all goods), and it is always running. Unlike radio, television can show as well as tell. Unlike the theater, concerts, movies, and even churches, television does not require mobility. It comes into the home and reaches individuals directly. With its virtually unlimited access from cradle to grave, television both precedes reading and, increasingly, preempts it.

Television is the first centralized cultural influence to permeate both the initial and the final years of life—as well as the years between. Most infants are exposed to television long before reading. By the time a child reaches school, television will have occupied more time than would be spent in a college classroom. At the other end of the lifelong curriculum, television is there to keep the elderly company when all else fails.

All societies have evolved ways of explaining the world to themselves and to their children. Socially constructed "reality" gives a coherent picture of what exists, what is important, what is related to what, and what is right. The constant cultivation of such "realities" is the task of mainstream rituals and mythologies. They legitimize action along socially functional and conventionally acceptable lines.

The social, political, and economic integration of modern industrial society has created a system in which few communities, if any, can maintain an independent integrity. We are parts of a Leviathan and its nervous system is telecommunications. Publicly shared knowledge of the "wide world" is what this nervous system transmits to us.

Television is the chief common ground among the different groups that make up a large and heterogeneous national community. No national achievement, celebration, or mourning seems real until it is confirmed and shared on television.

Never before have all classes and groups (as well as ages) shared so much of the same culture and the same perspectives while having so little to do with their creation. Representation in the world of television gives an idea, a cause, a group its sense of public identity, importance, and relevance. No movement can get going without some visibility in that world or long withstand television's power to discredit, insulate, or undercut. Other media, used selectively and by special interests or cultural elites, cultivate partial and parochial outlooks. Television spreads the same images and messages to all from penthouse to tenement. TV is the new (and only) culture of those who expose themselves to information only when it comes as "entertainment." Entertainment is the most broadly effective educational fare in any culture.

All major networks serving the same social system depend on the same markets and programming formulas. That may be one reason why, unlike other media, television is used non-selectively; it just doesn't matter that much. With the exception of national events and some "specials," the total viewing audience is fairly stable regardless of what is on. Individual tastes and program preferences are less important in determining viewing patterns than is the time a program is on. The nearly universal, non-selective, and habitual use of television fits the ritualistic pattern of its programming. You watch television as you might attend a church service, except that most people watch television more religiously.

Constitutional guarantees shield the prerogatives of ownership. Technological imperatives of electronics have changed modern governance more than Constitutional amendments and court decisions. Television, the flagship of industrial mass culture, now rivals ancient religions as a purveyor of organic patterns of symbols—news and other entertainment—that animate national and even global communities' senses of reality and value.

> *These considerations led us to question*
> *many of the more common arguments raised*
> *in discussions of television's effects.*

An important example is the concern over the consequences of violence on television. The invention and development of technologies which permit the production and dissemination of mass mediated fictional images across class lines seems invariably to raise in the minds of the established classes the specter of subversion, corruption and unrest being encouraged among the various lower orders—poor people, ethnic and racial minorities, children and women. The specter arises when it seems that the lower orders may presume to imitate—if not to replace—their betters. Whether the suspect and controversial media are newspapers, novels, and theater, as in the nineteenth century, or movies, radio, comic books, and television as in the twentieth, concern tends to focus on the possibilities of disruption that threaten the established norms of belief, behavior, and morality.

In our view, however, that concern has become anachronistic. Once the industrial order has legitimized its rule, the primary function of its cultural arm becomes the reiteration of that legitimacy and the maintenance of established power and authority. The rules of the games and the morality of its goals can best be demonstrated by dramatic stories of their symbolic violations. The intended lessons are generally effective and the social order is only rarely and peripherally threatened. The *system* is the message and, as our politicians like to say, the system works. Our question is, in fact, whether it may not work too well

Journal of Communication, Spring 1976

in cultivating uniform assumptions, exploitable fears, acquiescence to power, and resistance to meaningful change.

Therefore, in contrast to the more usual statement of the problem, we do not believe that the only critical correlate of television violence is to be found in the stimulation of occasional individual aggression. The consequences of living in a symbolic world ruled largely by violence may be much more far-reaching. Preparation for large-scale organized violence requires the cultivation of fear and acquiescence to power. TV violence is a dramatic demonstration of power which communicates much about social norms and relationships, about goals and means, about winners and losers, about the risks of life and the price for transgressions of society's rules. Violence laden drama shows who gets away with what, when, why, how and against whom. "Real world" *victims* as well as violents may have to learn their roles. Fear—that historic instrument of social control—may be an even more critical residue of a show of violence than aggression. Expectation of violence or passivity in the face of injustice may be consequences of even greater social concern. We shall return to this theme with data from our studies.

The realism of TV fiction hides its synthetic and functionally selective nature.

The dominant stylistic convention of Western narrative art—novels, plays, films, TV dramas—is that of representational realism. However contrived television plots are, viewers assume that they take place against a backdrop of the real world. Nothing impeaches the basic "reality" of the world of television drama. It is also highly informative. That is, it offers to the unsuspecting viewer a continuous stream of "facts" and impressions about the way of the world, about the constancies and vagaries of human nature, and about the consequences of actions. The premise of realism is a Trojan horse which carries within it a highly selective, synthetic, and purposeful image of the facts of life.

A normal adult viewer is not unaware of the fictiveness of television drama. No one calls the police or an ambulance when a character in a television program is shot. "War of the Worlds"-type scares are rare, if they occur at all. Granting this basic awareness on the part of the viewers, one may still wonder how often and to what degree all viewers suspend their disbelief in the reality of the symbolic world.

Surely we all know that Robert Young is not a doctor and that Marcus Welby is an M.D. by only poetic license. Yet according to the Philadelphia Bulletin (July 10, 1974) in the first five years of the program "Dr. Welby" received over a quarter of a million letters from viewers, most containing requests for medical advice.

Doctor shows are not the only targets of such claims. A former New York City police official has complained that jury members have formed images and expectations of trial procedures and outcomes from television which often prejudice them in actual trials. In a courtroom incident related to us by a lawyer, the counsel for the defense leapt to his feet, objecting, "Your Honor, the

Prosecutor is badgering the witness!" The judge replied that he, too, had seen that objection raised on the Perry Mason show but, unfortunately, it was not included in the California code.

> *Anecdotes and examples should not trivialize the real point,*
> *which is that even the most sophisticated can find many*
> *important components of their knowledge of the real world*
> *derived wholly or in part from fictional representation.*

How often do we make a sharp distinction between the action which we know is not "real" and the accumulation of background information (which is, after all, "realistic")? Are we keenly aware that in the total population of the television world men outnumber women four to one? Or that, with all the violence, the leading causes of real life injury and death—industrial and traffic accidents—are hardly ever depicted?

How many of us have ever been in an operating room, a criminal courtroom, a police station or jail, a corporate board room, or a movie studio? How much of what we know about such diverse spheres of activity, about how various kinds of people work and what they do—how much of our real world has been learned from fictional worlds? To the extent that viewers see television drama—the foreground of plot or the background of the television world—as naturalistic, they may derive a wealth of incidental "knowledge." This incidental learning may be effected by bald "facts" and by the subtle interplay of occurrence, co-occurrence, and non-occurrence of actors and actions.

In addition to the subtle patterns against whose influence we may all be somewhat defenseless, television provides another seductively persuasive sort of imagery. In real life much is hidden from our eyes. Often, motives are obscure, outcomes ambiguous, personalities complex, people unpredictable. The truth is never pure and rarely simple. The world of television, in contrast, offers us cogency, clarity, and resolution. Unlike life, television is an open book. Problems are never left hanging, rewards and punishments are present and accounted for. The rules of the game are known and rarely change. Not only does television "show" us the normally hidden workings of many important and fascinating institutions—medicine, law enforcement and justice, big business, the glamorous world of entertainment, etc.—but we "see" the people who fill important and exciting roles. We see who they are in terms of sex, age, race, and class and we also see them as personalities—dedicated and selfless, ruthless and ambitious, good-hearted but ineffectual, lazy and shiftless, corrupt and corrupting. Television provides the broadest common background of assumptions not only about what things are but also about how they work, or should work, and why.

The world of television drama is a mixture of truth and falsehood, of accuracy and distortion. It is not the true world but an extension of the standardized images which we have been taught since childhood. The audience for which the message of television is primarily intended (recall that an au-

Journal of Communication, Spring 1976

dience of about 20 million viewers is necessary for a program's survival) is the great majority of middle-class citizens for whom America is a democracy (our leaders act in accordance with the desires of the people), for whom our economy is free, and for whom God is alive, white, and male.

> *The implications for research are far-reaching and call into question essential aspects of the research paradigm stemming from historic pressures for behavior manipulation and marketing efficacy.*

They suggest a model based on the concept of broad enculturation rather than of narrow changes in opinion or behavior. Instead of asking what communication "variables" might propagate what kinds of individual behavior changes, we want to know what types of common consciousness whole systems of messages might cultivate. This is less like asking about preconceived fears and hopes and more like asking about the "effects" of Christianity on one's view of the world or—as the Chinese *had* asked—of Confucianism on public morality. To answer such questions, we must review and revise some conventional articles of faith about research strategy.

First, we cannot presume consequences without the prior investigation of content, as the conventional research paradigm tends to do. Nor can the content be limited to isolated elements (e.g., news, commercials, specific programs), taken out of the total context, or to individual viewer selections. The "world" of television is an organic system of stories and images. Only system-wide analysis of messages can reveal the symbolic world which structures common assumptions and definitions for the generations born into it and provides bases for interaction (though not necessarily of agreement) among large and heterogeneous communities. The system *as a whole* plays a major role in setting the agenda of issues to agree or disagree about; it shapes the most pervasive norms and cultivates the dominant perspectives of society.

Another conventional research assumption is that the experiment is the most powerful method, and that change (in attitudes, opinions, likes-dislikes, etc., toward or conveyed by "variable X") is the most significant outcome to measure. In the ideal experiment, you expose a group to X and assess salient aspects of the state of the receivers before and after exposure, comparing the change, if any, to data obtained from a control group (identical in all relevant ways to the experimental group) who have not received X. No change or no difference means no effect.

When X is television, however, we must turn this paradigm around: stability may be *the* significant outcome of the sum total of the play of many variables. If nearly everyone "lives" to some extent in the world of television, clearly we cannot find unexposed groups who would be identical in all important respects to the viewers. We cannot isolate television from the mainstream of modern culture because it *is* the mainstream. We cannot look for change as the most significant accomplishment of the chief arm of established culture if its main social function is to maintain, reinforce, and exploit rather than to undermine or alter conventional conceptions, beliefs, and behaviors. On the contrary, the relative ineffectiveness of isolated campaigns may itself be testimony to the power of mainstream communications.

Neither can we assume that TV cultivates conceptions easily distinguishable from those of other major entertainment media. (But we cannot emphasize too strongly the historically novel role of television in standardizing and sharing with all as the common norm what had before been more parochial, local, and selective cultural patterns.) We assume, therefore, that TV's standardizing and legitimizing influence comes largely from its ability to streamline, amplify, ritualize, and spread into hitherto isolated or protected subcultures, homes, nooks, and crannies of the land the conventional capsules of mass produced information and entertainment.

> *Another popular research technique which is inappropriate is the experimental or quasi-experimental test of the consequences of exposure to one particular type of television programming.*

Much of the research on media violence, for example, has focused on the observation and measurement of behavior which occurs after a viewer has seen a particular program or even isolated scenes from programs. All such studies, no matter how clean the design and clear the results, are of limited value because they ignore a fundamental fact: the world of TV drama consists of a complex and integrated system of characters, events, actions, and relationships whose effects cannot be measured with regard to any single element or program seen in isolation.

> *How should, then, the effects of television be conceptualized and studied?*

We believe that the key to the answer rests in a search for those assumptions about the "facts" of life and society that television cultivates in its more faithful viewers. That search requires two different methods of research. The relationship between the two is one of the special characteristics of the Cultural Indicators approach.[3]

The first method of research is the periodic analysis of large and representative aggregates of television output (rather than individual segments) as the system of messages to which total communities are exposed. The purpose of message system analysis is to establish to composition and structure of the symbolic world. We have begun that analysis with the most ubiquitous, translucent, and instructive part of television (or any cultural) fare, the dramatic programs (series, cartoons, movies on television) that populate and animate for most viewers the heartland of the symbolic world. Instead of guessing or assuming the contours and dynamics of that world, message system analysis maps its geography, demography, thematic and action structure, time and space

[3]For a more detailed description of the conceptual framework for this research see "Cultural Indicators: The Third Voice" (8).

Journal of Communication, Spring 1976

dimensions, personality profiles, occupations, and fates. Message system analysis yields the gross but clear terms of location, action, and characterization discharged into the mainstream of community consciousness. Aggregate viewer interpretation and response starts with these common terms of basic exposure.

The second step of the research is to determine what, if anything, viewers absorb from living in the world of television. Cultivation analysis, as we call that method, inquires into the assumptions television cultivates about the facts, norms, and values of society. Here we turn the findings of message system analysis about the fantasy land of television into questions about social reality. To each of these questions there is a "television answer," which is like the way things appear in the world of television, and another and different answer which is biased in the opposite direction, closer to the way things are in the observable world. We ask these questions of samples of adults and children. All responses are related to television exposure, other media habits, and demographic characteristics. We then compare the response of light and heavy viewers controlling for sex, age, education, and other characteristics. The margin of heavy viewers over light viewers giving the "television answers" within and across groups is the "cultivation differential" indicating conceptions about social reality that viewing tends to cultivate.

Our analysis looks at the contribution of TV drama to viewer conceptions in conjunction with such other sources of knowledge as education and news. The analysis is intended to illuminate the complementary as well as the divergent roles of these sources of facts, images, beliefs, and values in the cultivation of assumptions about reality.

> *We shall now sketch some general features of the*
> *world of network television drama, and then report*
> *the latest findings about violence in that world.*

As any mythical world, television presents a selective and functional system of messages. Its time, space, and motion—even its "accidents"—follow laws of dramatic convention and social utility. Its people are not born but are created to depict social types, causes, powers, and fates. The economics of the assembly line and the requirement of wide acceptability assure general adherence to common notions of justice and fair play, clear-cut characterizations, tested plot lines, and proven formulas for resolving all issues.

Representation in the fictional world signifies social existence; absence means symbolic annihilation. Being buffeted by events and victimized by people denotes social impotence; ability to wrest events about, to act freely, boldly, and effectively is a mark of dramatic importance and social power. Values and forces come into play through characterizations; good is a certain type of attractiveness, evil is a personality defect, and right is the might that wins. Plots weave a thread of causality into the fabric of dramatic ritual, as stock characters act out familiar parts and confirm preferred notions of what's what, who's who, and who counts for what. The issue is rarely in doubt; the action is typically a game of social typing, group identification, skill, and power.

Many times a day, seven days a week, the dramatic pattern defines situations and cultivates premises about society, people, and issues. Casting the symbolic world thus has a meaning of its own: the lion's share of representation goes to the types that dominate the social order. About three-quarters of all leading characters are male, American, middle- and upper-class, and in the prime of life. Symbolic independence requires freedom relatively uninhabited by real-life constraints. Less fully represented are those lower in the domestic and global power hierarchy and characters involved in familiar social contexts, human dependencies, and other situations that impose the real-life burdens of human relationships and obligations upon freewheeling activity.

Women typically represent romantic or family interest, close human contact, love. Males can act in nearly any role, but rare is the female part that does not involve at least the suggestion of sex. While only one in three male leads is shown as intending to or ever having been married, two of every three females are married or expect to marry in the story. Female "specialties" limit the proportion of TV's women to about one-fourth of the total population.

Nearly half of all females are concentrated in the most sexually eligible young adult population, to which only one-fifth of males are assigned; women are also disproportionately represented among the very young and old. Children, adolescents, and old people together account for less than 15 percent of the total fictional population.

Approximately five in ten characters can be unambiguously identified as gainfully employed. Of these, three are proprietors, managers, and professionals. The fourth comes from the ranks of labor—including all those employed in factories, farms, offices, shops, stores, mining, transportation, service stations, restaurants, and households, and working in unskilled, skilled, clerical, sales, and domestic service capacities. The fifth serves to enforce the law or preserve the peace on behalf of public or private clients.

Types of activity—paid and unpaid—also reflect dramatic and social purposes. Six in ten characters are engaged in discernible occupational activity and can be roughly divided into three groups of two each. The first group represents the world of legitimate private business, industry, agriculture, finance, etc. The second group is engaged in activity related to art, science, religion, health, education, and welfare, as professionals, amateurs, patients, students, or clients. The third makes up the forces of official or semiofficial authority and the army of criminals, outlaws, spies, and other enemies arrayed against them. One in every four leading characters acts out a drama of some sort of transgression and its suppression at home and abroad.

Violence plays a key role in such a world. It is the simplest and cheapest dramatic means available to demonstrate the rules of the game of power. In real life much violence is subtle, slow, circumstantial, invisible, even impersonal. Encounters with physical violence in real life are rare, more sickening than thrilling. But in the symbolic world, overt physical motion makes dramatically visible that which in the real world is usually hidden. Symbolic violence, as any show of force, typically does the job of real violence more cheaply and, of course, entertainingly.

Journal of Communication, Spring 1976

Geared for independent action in loosely-knit and often remote social contexts, half of all characters are free to engage in violence. One-fifth "specialize" in violence as law breakers or law enforcers. Violence on television, unlike in real-life, rarely stems from close personal relationships. Most of it is between strangers, set up to drive home lessons of social typing. Violence is often just a specialty—a skill, a craft, an efficient means to test the norms of and settle any challenge to the existing structure of power.

> *The Violence Profile is a set of indicators*
> *tracing aspects of the television world and*
> *of conceptions of social reality they tend*
> *to cultivate in the minds of viewers.*

Four specific types of indicators have been developed. Three come from message system analysis: (1) the context of programming trends against which any aspect of the world of television can be seen; (2) several specific measures of violence given separately and also combined in the Violence Index; and (3) structural characteristics of the dramatic world indicating social relationships depicted in it, (in the present report, "risk ratios"). The fourth type of indicator comes from cultivation analysis and will be shown in this report as the "cultivation differential." Although the Violence Profile is the most developed, the Cultural Indicators project is constructing similar profiles of other aspects and relationships of the media world.

Before we present the indicators, let us briefly note the definitions, terms, and some procedures employed in generating the TV violence measures.[4]

Message system analysis has been performed on annual sample-weeks of prime time and weekend daytime network dramatic programming since 1967 by trained analysts who observe and code many aspects of TV content. The definition of violence employed in this analysis is "the overt expression of physical force against self or other, compelling action against one's will on pain of being hurt or killed, or actually hurting or killing." The research focuses on a clear-cut and commonly understood definition of violence, and yields indicators of trends in the programming context in which violence occurs; in the prevalence, rate, and characterizations involved in violence; and in the power relationships expressed by the differential risks found in the world of television drama.

All observations are recorded in three types of unite: the program (play) as a whole, each specific violent action (if any) in the program, and each dramatic character appearing in the program.

"*Program*" means a single fictional story presented in dramatic form. This may be a play produced for television, a feature film telecast during the period

---

[4]For a more detailed methodological description and all tabulations not included here, see "Violence Profile: A Technical Report" (3), available for $12.00 (checks to be made out to the Trustees of the University of Pennsylvania) from The Annenberg School of Communications. University of Pennsylvania, Philadelphia, PA 19174.

of the study, or a cartoon story (of which there may be one or more in a single program).

Violent action means a scene of some violence confined to the same parties. If a scene is interrupted (by flashback or shift to another scene) but continues in "real time," it is still the same act. However, if a new agent of violence enters the scene, that begins another act. These units are also called violent episodes.

Characters analyzed in all programs (whether violent or not) are of two types. Major characters are the principal roles essential to the story. Minor characters (subjected to a less detailed analysis) are all other speaking roles. (The findings summarized in this report include the analysis of major characters only.)

Samples of programming. Network dramatic programs transmitted in evening prime time (8 p.m. to 11 p.m. each day), and network children's dramatic programs transmitted weekend mornings (Saturday and Sunday between 8 a.m. and 2 p.m.) comprise the analytical source material.[5] With respect to four basic sample dimensions (network, program format, type and tone), the solid week sample is at least as generalizable to a year's programming as larger randomly drawn samples (2).

Coder training and reliability. For the analysis of each program sample, a staff of 12 to 18 coders is recruited. After about three weeks of training and testing, coders analyze the season's videotaped program sample.

During both the training and data-collection phases, coders work in independent pairs and monitor their assigned videotaped programs as often as necessary. All programs in the sample are coded by two separate coder-pairs to provide double-coded data for reliability comparisons. Final measures, computed on the study's entire corpus of double-coded data, determine the acceptability of information for analysis and provide guidelines to its interpretation (11, 12).

Three sets of violence measures have been computed from the direct observational data of the message system analysis. They show the percent of programs with any violence at all, the frequency and rate of violent episodes, and the number of roles calling for characterizations as violents, victims, or both. These measures are called *prevalence*, *rate*, and *role*, respectively. Each is given separately in all the tabulations that follow.

For ease of illustration and comparison, the three types of measures are also combined to form the Violence Index. The Index itself is not a statistical finding but serves as a convenient illustrator of trends and facilitates gross comparisons. The Index is obtained by adding measures of prevalence, rates (doubled to raise their relatively low numerical value) and roles. The formula can be seen on Tables 1 through 4.

[5]In 1967 and 1968, the hours included were 7:30 to 10 p.m. Monday through Saturday, 7 to 10 p.m. Sunday, and children's programs 8 a.m. to noon Saturday. Beginning in 1969, these hours were expanded until 11 p.m. each evening and from 7 a.m. to 2:30 p.m. Saturday and Sunday. As of 1971 however, network evening programming has been reduced by the FCC's prime-time access rule. The effective evening parameters since 1971 are therefore 8 to 11 p.m. Monday through Saturday and 7:30 to 10:30 p.m. Sunday.

Journal of Communication, Spring 1976

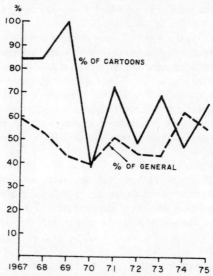

Figure 1: "Action" (crime, western, adventure) programs as percent of cartoon and of other (general) programs analyzed

Before presenting the trends indicated by the measures just discussed, let us glance at the first indicator, that of program mix. "Action" programs contribute most violence to the world of television drama. Figure 1 shows that such programs comprise more than half of all prime-time and weekend daytime programming, and their proportion of the total has not changed much in recent years. In fact, while general (non-cartoon) crime and adventure plays dropped from their 1974 high of 62 percent to 54 percent in 1975, cartoon crime and adventure rose in the same period from 47 percent to 66 percent of all cartoons.

These programming trends foreshadow the violence findings that follow. We can summarize them by noting that there has been *no significant reduction in the overall Violence Index despite some fluctuations in the specific measures and a definite drop in "family hour" violence, especially on CBS, in the current season.* The "family hour" decline has been matched by a sharp increase in violence during children's (weekend daytime) programming in the current season and by an even larger two-year rise in violence after 9 p.m. EST.

Figure 2 shows these trends in greater detail. Figure 3 provides similar information for each network separately, showing that late evening violence shot up on all three networks in the past two or three years (with minor dips on CBS and ABC in 1975), and that children's (weekend daytime) programs became more violent on ABC and NBC in the past season. Figure 4 is a direct comparison of the Violence Index for each network, showing remarkable long-term stability and similarity among them. Figure 5 is a direct comparison of the "family hour" Violence Index for each network, showing little change over a two-year period for ABC and NBC, substantial reduction for the second year in a row for CBS.

Tables 1 through 4 (found at the end of the article) present all measures for the different hours of programming. They show how the specific measures of prevalence, rate, and role fluctuate and combine each year to make up the composite Violence Index. More complete tabulations, including network and format breakdowns, can be found in the Technical Report (3).

The indicators reflected in the Violence Index are clear manifestations of what network programmers actually do as compared to what they say or intend to do. Network executives and their censorship ("Standards and Practices") offices maintain close control over the assembly line production process that results in the particular program mix of a season (6). While our data permit many specific qualifications to any generalization that might be made, it is safe to say that network policy seems to have responded in narrow terms, when at all, to very specific pressure, and only while the heat was on. After nine years of investigations, hearings, and commissions (or since we have been tracking violence on television), eight out of every ten programs (nine out of every ten weekend children's hour programs) still contain some violence. The overall rate of violent episodes, 8 per hour, is, if anything, higher than at any time since 1969. (The violence saturation of weekend children's programs declined from the 1969 high but increased from its 1974 low to 16 per hour, double that of overall programming, as can be seen on Table 4.) Between six and seven out of every ten leading characters (eight and nine for children) are still involved in some violence. Between one and two out of every ten are still involved in killing.

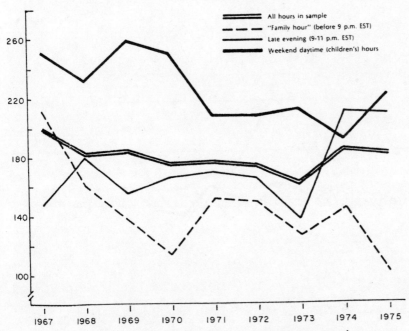

Figure 2: Violence Index for different hours of dramatic programming

Journal of Communication, Spring 1976

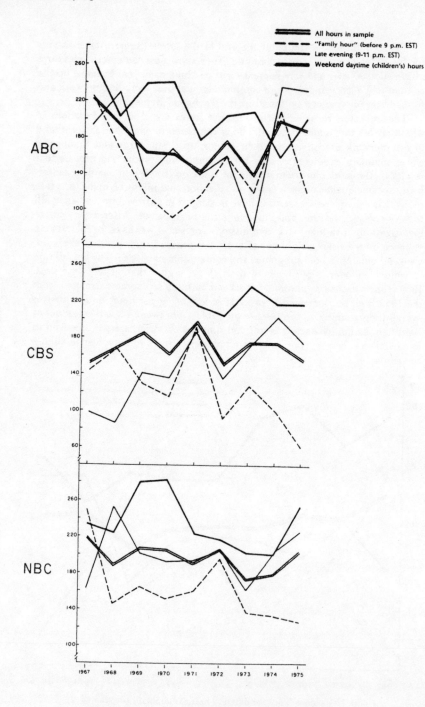

Figure 3: Violence Index for different hours by network

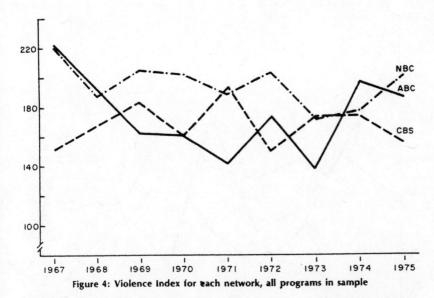

Figure 4: Violence Index for each network, all programs in sample

Reductions have been achieved in the portrayal of on-screen killers (especially during weekend children's hours) and in "family hour" violence (especially by CBS), but, as we have noted, a sharp rise in late evening and general children's violence has canceled out any overall gains from the latter.

It is clear, at least to us, that deeply rooted sociocultural forces, rather than just obstinacy or profit-seeking, are at work. We have suggested earlier in this article, and have also developed elsewhere (9, 10), that symbolic violence is a demonstration of power and an instrument of social control serving, on the whole, to reinforce and preserve the existing social order, even if at an ever increasing price in terms of pervasive fear and mistrust and of selective aggressiveness. That maintenance mechanism seems to work through cultivating a sense of danger, a differential calculus of the risks of life in different groups in the population. The Violence Profile is beginning to yield indicators of such a mechanism, and thereby also of basic structural and cultivation characteristics of television programming.

The structural characteristics of television drama are not easily controlled. They reflect basic cultural assumptions that make a show "entertaining"—i.e., smoothly and pleasingly fitting dominant notions (and prejudices) about social relations and thus demonstrating conventional notions of morality and power.

The most elementary—and telling—relationship involved in violent action is that of violent and victim. The pattern of those who inflict and those who suffer violence (or both) provides a differential calculus of hazards and opportunities for different groups of people in the "world" of television drama. Table 5[6] presents a summary of the scores of involvement and what we call risk ratios. The character score is the roles component (CS) of the Violence Index; it is the percent of all characters involved in any violence plus the percent involved in

[6] All tables appear at the end of the article.

Journal of Communication, Spring 1976

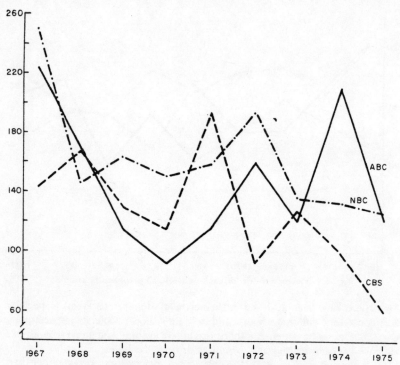

Figure 5: Violence Index for each network, family hour only

any killing. The violent-victim and killer-killed (risk) ratio are obtained by dividing violents and victims, or killers and killed within each group. The plus sign means more violents or killers in the group; the minus sign means more victims (hurt) or killed.

We see that the 1967–75 totals show 1.19 male and 1.32 female victims for every violent male and female. Even more striking are the differential risks or fatal victimization. There were nearly two male killers for every male killed; however, for every female killer one woman was killed.

Table 5 also shows the differential risks of involvement and victimization attributed to other groups, projecting assumptions about social and power relations. Old men, married men, lower class, foreign, and nonwhite males were most likely to get killed rather than to inflict lethal injury. "Good guys" were of course most likely to be the killers.

Among females, more vulnerable than men in most categories, both young and old women as well as unmarried, lower class, foreign, and nonwhite women bore especially heavy burdens of relative victimization. Old, poor, and black women were shown *only* as killed and never as killers. Interestingly, "good" women, unlike "good" men, had no lethal power, but "bad" women were even more lethal than "bad" men. The victimization of the "good" woman is often the curtain-raiser that provokes the hero to righteous "action."

The pattern of relative victimization is remarkably stable from year to year. It demonstrates an invidious (but socially functional) sense of risk and power. We do not yet know whether it also cultivates a corresponding hierarchy of fear and aggression. But we do have evidence to suggest that television viewing cultivates a general sense of danger and mistrust. That evidence comes from the fourth and final element of the Violence Profile, the component we call the cultivation differential.

> *The cultivation differential comes, of course, from the cultivation analysis part of the Cultural Indicators research approach.*

It highlights differences in conception of relevant aspects of social reality that television viewing tends to cultivate in heavy viewers compared to light viewers. The strategy is obviously most appropriate to those propositions in which television might cultivate conceptions that measurably deviate from those coming from other sources. Furthermore, the independent contributions of television are likely to be most powerful in cultivating assumptions about which there is little opportunity to learn first-hand, and which are not strongly anchored in other established beliefs and ideologies.

The obvious objection arises that light and heavy viewers are different prior to—and aside from—television. Factors other than television may account for the difference.

The point is well taken. We have found, as have others, that heavy viewing is part and parcel of a complex syndrome which also includes lower education, lower mobility, lower aspirations, higher anxieties, and other class, age, and sex related characteristics. We assume, indeed, that viewing helps to hold together and cultivate elements of that syndrome. But it does more than that. Television viewing also makes a separate and independent contribution to the "biasing" of conceptions of social reality within most age, sex, educational, and other groupings, including those presumably most "immune" to its effects.

Our study of TV's contribution to notions of social reality proceeds by various methods, each comparing responses of heavy and light viewers, with other characteristics held constant. Of the different methods used in cultivation analysis, only adult survey results are included in this report; the others are still in the process of development and summarization. These surveys were executed by commercial survey research organizations. For details of sampling, etc., the reader is referred to the Technical Report (3).

To probe in the direction of the pattern suggested by our message analysis, we obtained responses to questions about facts of life that relate to law enforcement, trust, and a sense of danger. Figure 6 presents the results of the first question asking what proportion of people are employed in law enforcement. The "television answer" (slanted in the direction of the world of television) was five percent. The alternative answer (more in the direction of reality) was one percent.

As Figure 6 shows, the heavy viewers (those viewing an average of four hours a day or more) were always more likely to give the television answer than

Journal of Communication, Spring 1976

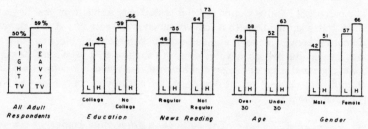

Figure 6: Percent giving the "television answer" to a question about the proportion of people employed in law enforcement

the light viewers (those viewing an average of two hours a day or less). Figure 7 shows similar results for the question "Can most people be trusted?" and Figure 8 for the question "During any given week, what are your chances of being involved in some type of violence?" One in ten (the "television answer") or one in a hundred?"

Let us take education as probably the best index of a complex of social circumstances that provide alternative informational and cultural opportunities. Those of our respondents who have had some college education are less likely to choose the "television answer" than those who have had none. But *within* each group, television viewing "biases" conceptions in the direction of the "facts" it presents. When we compared light and heavy viewers within the "college" and the "no college" groups, we got a typical step-wise pattern of the percentage of "television answers." Regular reading of newspapers makes a similar difference.

Both college education and regular newspaper reading seem to reduce the percentage of "television answers," but heavy viewing boosts it within both groups. This appears to be the general pattern of TV's ability to cultivate its own "reality."

An exaggerated impression of the actual number of law enforcement workers seems to be a consequence of viewing television. Of greater concern, however, would be the cultivation of a concomitantly exaggerated demand for their services. The world of television drama is, above all, a violent one in which more than half of all characters are involved in some violence, at least one-tenth

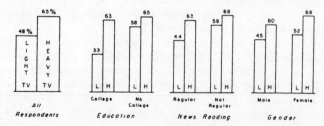

Figure 7: Percent responding "Can't be too careful" to the question "Can most people be trusted?"

in some killing, and in which over three-fourths of prime-time hours contain some violence. As we have suggested, the cultivation of fear and a sense of danger may well be a prime residue of the show of violence.

Questions about feelings of trust and safety may be used to test that suggestion. The National Opinion Research Corporation's 1975 General Social Survey asked "Can most people be trusted?" Living in the world of television seems to strengthen the conclusion that they cannot. Heavy viewers chose the answer "Can't be too careful" in significantly greater proportions than did light viewers in the same groups, as shown in Figure 7. Those who do not read newspapers regularly have a high level of mistrust regardless of TV viewing. But, not surprisingly, women are the most likely to absorb the message of distrust.

Focusing directly on violence, we asked a national sample of adults about people's chances of being involved in violence in any given week. Figure 8 shows the patterns of overestimations in line with television's view of the world. It may explain why in recent surveys, such as the Detroit study conducted by the Institute of Social Research (13), respondents' estimates of danger in their neighborhoods had little to do with crime statistics or even with their own personal experience. The pattern of our findings suggests that television and other media exposure may be as important as demographic and other experiential factors in explaining why people view the world as they do.

Television certainly appears to condition the view of the generation that knew no world without it. All the figures show that the "under 30" respondents exhibit consistently higher levels of "television responses," despite the fact that they tend to be better educated than the "over 30" respondents. We may all live in a dangerous world, but young people (including children tested but not reported on here), the less educated, women, and heavy viewers within all these groups sense greater danger than light viewers in the same groups. College education (and its social correlates) may counter the television view, but heavy exposure to TV will counteract that too.

Fear is a universal emotion and easy to exploit. Symbolic violence may be the cheapest way to cultivate it effectively. Raw violence is, in comparison, risky and costly, resorted to when symbolic means fail. Ritualized displays of any violence (such as in crime and disaster news, as well as in mass-produced drama)

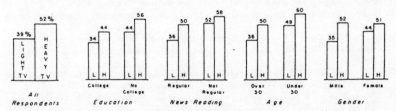

Figure 8: Percent giving the "television answer" (exaggerating) their own chances of being involved in violence

Journal of Communication, Spring 1976

may cultivate exaggerated assumptions about the extent of threat and danger in the world and lead to demands for protection.

What is the net result? A heightened sense of risk and insecurity (different for groups of varying power) is more likely to increase acquiescence to and dependence upon established authority, and to legitimize its use of force, than it is to threaten the social order through occasional non-legitimized imitations. Risky for their perpetrators and costly for their victims, media-incited criminal violence may be a price industrial cultures extract from some citizens for the general pacification of most others.

As with violence, so with other aspects of social reality we are investigating, TV appears to cultivate assumptions that fit its socially functional myths. Our chief instrument of enculturation and social control, television may function as the established religion of the industrial order, relating to governance as the church did to the state in earlier times.

REFERENCES

1. Cater, Douglass, and Stephen Strickland. *TV Violence and the Child; The Evolution and Fate of the Surgeon General's Report*. New York: Russell Sage Foundation, 1975.
2. Eleey, Michael F. "Variations in Generalizability Resulting from Sampling Characteristics of Content Analysis Data: A Case Study." Unpublished manuscript, Annenberg School of Communications, University of Pennsylvania, 1969.
3. Gerbner, George, and Larry Gross, with the assistance of Michael F. Eleey, Suzanne K. Fox, Marilyn Jackson–Beeck, and Nancy Signorielli. "Violence Profile No. 7: A Technical Report." Annenberg School of Communications, 1976.
4. Gerbner, George. "Dimensions of Violence in Television Drama." Chapter 15 in *Violence and the Media* edited by Robert K. Baker and Sandra J. Ball, a staff report to the National Commission on the Causes and Prevention of Violence, U.S. Government Printing Office, 1969.
5. Gerbner, George. "Violence in Television Drama: Trends and Symbolic Functions." In G. A. Comstock and E. A. Rubinstein (Eds.) *Television and Social Behavior*, Vol. 1. Washington D.C.: U.S. Government Printing Office, 1972.
6. Gerbner, George, Larry Gross, and William H. Melody. *Communications Technology and Social Policy*. New York: John Wiley and Sons, 1973.
7. Gerbner, George. "The Structure and Process of Television Program Content Regulation in the U.S." In G. A. Comstock and E. A. Rubinstein (Eds.) *Television and Social Behavior*, Vol. 1. Washington, D.C.: U.S. Government Printing Office, 1972.
8. Gerbner, George. "Cultural Indicators: The Third Voice." In *Communications Technology and Social Policy*. New York: John Wiley and Sons, 1973.
9. Gerbner, George. "Scenario for Violence." *Human Behavior*, October 1975.
10. Gerbner, George, and Larry Gross. "The Scary World of Television," *Psychology Today*, April 1976.
11. Krippendorff, Klaus. "Bivariate Agreement Coefficients for the Reliability of Data." In E. F. Borgatta and G. W. Bohrnstedt (Eds.), *Sociological Methodology*. San Francisco: Jossey Bass, 1970.
12. Krippendorf, Klaus. "A Computer Program for Agreement Analysis of Reliability Data, Version 4." Mimeographed. Annenberg School of Communications, July 1973.
13. "Personal Safety a Major Concern: Public Perceptions of Quality of Life in Metropolitan Detroit Examined in ISR Study." *ISR Newsletter*, Winter 1976, p. 4.
14. Rubinstein, Eli A. "The TV Violence Report: What's Next?" *Journal of Communication*, Winter 1974, pp. 80-88.
15. Social Science Research Council. "A Profile of Television Violence." Report submitted by the Committee on Television and Social Behavior of the SSRC, July 1975.
16. Weinberger, Caspar W. Letter to Senator John O. Pastore dated November 13, 1973.

Living With Television: The Violence Profile

Table 1: Violence measures for all programs in sample

	1967	1968	1969	1970	1971	1972	1973	1974	1975	TOTAL
SAMPLES (100%)	N	N	N	N	N	N	N	N	N	N
Programs (plays) analyzed	96	87	121	111	103	100	99	96	111	924
Program Hours Analyzed	62.0	58.5	71.8	67.2	70.3	72.0	75.2	76.0	77.3	630.2
Leading characters analyzed	240	215	377	196	252	300	359	346	364	2649
PREVALENCE	%	%	%	%	%	%	%	%	%	%
(%P) Programs containing violence	81.3	81.6	83.5	77.5	80.6	79.0	72.7	83.3	78.4	79.8
Program hours containing violence	83.2	87.0	83.2	78.3	87.2	84.2	79.7	86.8	83.0	83.6
RATE	N	N	N	N	N	N	N	N	N	N
Number of violent episodes	478	394	630	498	483	539	524	522	626	4694
(R/P) Rate per all programs (plays)	5.0	4.5	5.2	4.5	4.7	5.4	5.3	5.4	5.6	5.1
(R/H) Rate per all hours	7.7	6.7	8.8	7.4	6.9	7.5	7.0	6.9	8.1	7.4
Duration of Violent Episodes (hrs)	..	..	..	..	..	..	3.2	3.8	3.6	10.6
ROLES (% OF LEADING CHARACTERS)	%	%	%	%	%	%	%	%	%	%
Violents (committing violence)	55.8	49.3	46.5	52.0	46.0	39.3	34.5	40.8	43.1	44.6
Victims (subjected to violence)	64.6	55.8	58.9	56.6	50.8	49.7	48.2	51.2	53.8	54.0
(%V) Any involvement in violence	73.3	65.1	66.3	62.8	61.5	58.3	55.7	60.7	64.8	62.9
Killers (committing fatal violence)	12.5	10.7	3.7	6.6	8.7	7.7	5.8	9.8	6.3	7.7
Killed (victims of lethal violence)	7.1	3.7	2.1	4.6	3.2	4.7	3.3	5.8	3.8	4.2
(%K) Any involvement in killing	18.7	11.6	5.6	8.7	9.9	9.7	7.5	13.6	9.1	10.2
INDICATORS OF VIOLENCE										
Program Score: PS=(%P)+2(R/P)+2(R/H)	106.6	104.1	111.4	101.3	103.7	104.8	97.3	107.9	105.8	104.8
Character V-Score: CS = (%V) + (%K)	92.1	76.7	71.9	71.4	71.4	68.0	63.2	74.3	73.9	73.0
Violence Index: VI = PS + CS	198.7	180.9	183.3	172.7	175.1	172.8	160.5	182.2	179.7	177.8

Journal of Communication, Spring 1976

Table 2: Violence measures for family hour only

	1967	1968	1969	1970	1971	1972	1973	1974	1975	TOTAL
SAMPLES (100%)	N	N	N	N	N	N	N	N	N	N
Programs (plays) analyzed	38	36	38	35	28	27	32	29	31	294
Program Hours Analyzed	30.0	27.0	27.3	26.0	25.0	23.5	29.0	27.0	21.5	236.3
Leading characters analyzed	103	102	130	76	78	98	110	109	105	911
PREVALENCE	%	%	%	%	%	%	%	%	%	%
(%P) Programs containing violence	78.9	75.0	63.2	57.1	75.0	74.1	56.3	69.0	51.6	66.7
Program hours containing violence	86.7	83.3	74.3	67.3	86.0	85.1	70.7	77.8	60.5	77.1
RATE	N	N	N	N	N	N	N	N	N	N
Number of violent episodes	240	123	122	86	110	122	147	108	77	1135
(R/P) Rate per all programs (plays)	6.3	3.4	3.2	2.5	3.9	4.5	4.6	3.7	2.5	3.9
(R/H) Rate per all hours	8.0	4.6	4.5	3.3	4.4	5.2	5.1	4.0	3.6	4.8
Duration of Violent Episodes (hrs)	..	..	..	..	..	..	0.9	1.0	0.5	2.4
ROLES (% OF LEADING CHARACTERS)	%	%	%	%	%	%	%	%	%	%
Violents (committing violence)	58.3	39.2	36.2	32.9	37.2	37.8	29.1	29.4	16.2	35.0
(%V) Victims (subjected to violence)	68.9	46.1	40.8	39.5	38.5	40.8	33.6	36.7	27.6	41.4
Any involvement in violence	75.7	56.9	49.2	40.8	50.0	50.0	40.9	45.0	36.2	49.5
Killers (committing fatal violence)	22.3	10.8	6.2	3.9	9.0	4.1	6.4	12.8	1.0	8.6
(%K) Killed (victims of lethal violence)	7.8	4.9	3.1	1.3	2.6	3.1	4.5	7.3	0.0	4.0
Any involvement in killing	28.2	12.7	9.2	3.9	10.3	5.1	10.0	16.5	1.0	11.0
INDICATORS OF VIOLENCE										
Program Score: PS=(%P)+2(R/P)+2(R/H)	107.6	90.9	78.5	68.7	91.7	93.5	75.6	84.4	63.7	84.0
Character V-Score: CS = (%V) + (%K)	103.9	69.6	58.5	44.7	60.3	55.1	50.9	61.5	37.1	60.5
Violence Index: VI = PS + CS	211.5	160.6	137.0	113.4	151.9	148.6	126.5	145.9	100.9	144.5

Table 3: Violence measures for late evening (9-11 p.m. EST)

	1967	1968	1969	1970	1971	1972	1973	1974	1975	TOTAL
SAMPLES (100%)	N	N	N	N	N	N	N	N	N	N
Programs (plays) analyzed	26	21	26	26	34	33	30	29	35	260
Program Hours Analyzed	25.0	24.0	30.5	28.0	30.3	33.0	27.5	33.0	39.5	270.7
Leading characters analyzed	75	60	88	56	91	119	104	115	133	841
PREVALENCE	%	%	%	%	%	%	%	%	%	%
(%P) Programs containing violence	69.2	76.2	80.8	69.2	76.5	69.7	63.3	86.2	85.7	75.4
Program hours containing violence	76.0	89.6	84.4	80.4	87.6	79.8	79.1	92.4	92.4	85.1
RATE	N	N	N	N	N	N	N	N	N	N
Number of violent episodes	87	99	110	116	129	172	130	220	284	1347
(R/P) Rate per all programs (plays)	3.3	4.7	4.2	4.5	3.8	5.2	4.3	7.6	8.1	5.2
(R/H) Rate per all hours	3.5	4.1	3.6	4.1	4.3	5.2	4.7	6.7	7.2	5.0
Duration of Violent Episodes (hrs)	--	--	--	--	--	--	1.3	1.8	1.9	5.0
ROLES (% OF LEADING CHARACTERS)	%	%	%	%	%	%	%	%	%	%
Violents (committing violence)	38.7	55.0	34.1	46.4	44.0	37.8	32.7	56.5	51.1	44.0
Victims (subjected to violence)	42.7	55.0	44.3	50.0	48.4	45.4	36.5	61.7	59.4	49.7
(%V) Any involvement in violence	56.0	68.3	52.3	57.1	59.3	55.5	41.3	71.3	68.4	59.1
Killers (committing fatal violence)	5.3	16.7	5.7	14.3	15.4	16.0	12.5	16.5	16.5	13.6
Killed (victims of lethal violence)	4.0	5.0	2.3	12.5	5.5	8.4	6.7	10.4	9.8	7.4
(%K) Any involvement in killing	9.3	16.7	6.8	21.4	17.6	19.3	14.4	24.3	23.3	17.6
INDICATORS OF VIOLENCE										
Program Score: PS=(%P)+2(R/P)+2(R/H)	82.9	93.9	96.4	86.4	92.6	90.5	81.5	114.7	116.3	95.7
Character V-Score: CS = (%V) + (%K)	65.3	85.0	59.1	78.6	76.9	74.8	55.8	95.7	91.7	76.7
Violence Index: VI = PS + CS	148.2	178.9	155.5	165.0	169.5	165.3	137.2	210.4	208.1	172.4

Journal of Communication, Spring 1976

Table 4: Violence measures for weekend daytime (children's) hours

	1967	1968	1969	1970	1971	1972	1973	1974	1975	TOTAL
SAMPLES (100%)	N	N	N	N	N	N	N	N	N	N
Programs (plays) analyzed	32	30	57	50	41	40	37	38	45	370
Program Hours Analyzed	7.0	7.5	14.0	13.2	15.0	15.5	18.7	16.0	16.3	123.2
Leading characters analyzed	62	53	159	64	83	83	145	122	126	897
PREVALENCE	%	%	%	%	%	%	%	%	%	%
(%P) Programs containing violence	93.8	93.3	98.2	96.0	87.8	90.0	94.6	92.1	91.1	93.2
Program hours containing violence	94.0	92.2	97.6	95.6	88.5	92.3	94.6	90.6	89.8	92.7
RATE	N	N	N	N	N	N	N	N	N	N
Number of violent episodes	151	172	398	296	244	245	247	194	265	2212
(R/P) Rate per all programs (plays)	4.7	5.7	7.0	5.9	6.0	6.1	6.7	5.1	5.9	6.0
(R/H) Rate per all hours	21.6	22.9	28.4	22.5	16.2	15.8	13.2	12.1	16.2	18.0
Duration of Violent Episodes (hrs)	..	..	..	..	..	..	1.0	0.9	1.2	3.2
ROLES (% OF LEADING CHARACTERS)	%	%	%	%	%	%	%	%	%	%
(%V) Violents (committing violence)	72.6	62.3	66.7	79.7	56.6	43.4	40.0	36.1	57.1	54.8
Victims (subjected to violence)	83.9	75.5	81.8	82.8	65.1	66.3	67.6	54.1	69.8	70.9
Any involvement in violence	90.3	77.4	88.1	93.8	74.7	72.3	77.2	64.8	84.9	79.9
(%K) Killers (committing fatal violence)	4.8	3.8	0.6	3.1	1.2	0.0	0.7	0.8	0.0	1.2
Killed (victims of lethal violence)	9.7	0.0	1.3	1.6	1.2	1.2	0.0	0.0	0.8	1.3
Any involvement in killing	14.5	3.8	1.9	3.1	1.2	1.2	0.7	0.8	0.8	2.3
INDICATORS OF VIOLENCE										
Program Score: PS=(%P)+2(R/P)+2(R/H)	146.3	150.7	169.1	152.8	132.2	133.9	134.4	126.6	135.3	141.1
Character V-Score: CS = (%V) + (%K)	104.8	81.1	89.9	96.9	75.9	73.5	77.9	65.6	85.7	82.3
Violence Index: VI = PS + CS	251.2	231.8	259.0	249.7	208.1	207.4	212.3	192.1	221.1	223.4

Table 5: Risk ratios for all programs studied 1967-75

Groups	Male Characters				Female Characters			
	N	Character score	Violent–victim ratio	Killer–killed ratio	N	Character score	Violent–victim ratio	Killer–killed ratio
All characters	2010	80.0	−1.19	+1.97	605	48.9	−1.32	1.00
Social age								
Children-adolescents	188	64.9	−1.03	+0.00	77	46.8	−1.39	0.00*
Young adults	431	81.2	−1.21	+3.07	209	59.8	−1.67	+1.29
Settled adults	1068	80.8	−1.15	+1.98	267	37.8	1.00	1.00
Old	81	58.0	+1.03	−2.00	22	50.0	−2.25	−0.00*
Marital status								
Not married	1133	83.6	−1.16	+2.24	306	57.2	−1.51	−1.43
Married	462	66.9	−1.33	+1.57	252	39.3	−1.11	+1.40
Class								
Clearly upper	196	87.2	−1.28	+1.15	70	52.9	−1.64	+1.33
Mixed; indeterminate	1744	78.7	−1.19	+2.36	517	48.2	−1.26	1.00
Clearly lower	70	91.4	−1.11	−1.33	18	55.6	−2.67	−0.00*
Nationality								
U.S.	1505	75.0	−1.19	+2.39	503	46.1	−1.39	−1.08
Other	276	96.7	−1.22	+1.13	66	60.6	−1.55	+3.00
Race								
White	1533	77.6	−1.20	+2.12	541	49.9	−1.29	+1.07
Other	264	83.3	−1.27	+1.33	50	38.0	−2.43	−0.00*
*Character type**								
"Good" (heroes)	928	69.3	−1.26	+3.47	314	43.3	−1.56	−6.00
Mixed type	432	71.1	−1.31	+1.09	156	43.6	−1.37	1.00
"Bad" (villains)	291	114.1	−1.03	+1.80	41	82.9	+1.14	+2.00

* Group has neither violents nor victims. If 0.00 is preceded by a sign, group has either no violents or no victims; +0.00 means only violent(s) but no victims(s); −0.00 means only victim(s) but no violent(s).

** This classification was introduced in 1969.

Note: Character score is the percent of characters involved in any violence plus the percent involved in any killing. V–v ration is of violents (+) and victims (−). K–k ration is of killers (+) and killed (−).

Journal of Personality and Social Psychology
1979, Vol. 37, No. 2, 170–179

Television Viewing and Fear of Victimization:
Is the Relationship Causal?

Anthony N. Doob and Glenn E. Macdonald
University of Toronto
Toronto, Canada

Previous findings have suggested that people who watch a lot of television are more likely to fear their environment than are those who report being less frequent viewers of television. From this simple correlation, previous authors have suggested that television causes people to overestimate the amount of danger that exists in their own neighborhoods. The present study attempted to replicate this finding and to determine if the apparent effect was due to a previously uncontrolled factor: the actual incidence of crime in the neighborhood. Respondents to a door-to-door survey indicated their media usage and estimated the likelihood of their being a victim of violence. Neighborhoods were chosen so as to include a high- and a low-crime area in downtown Toronto and a high- and a low-crime area in Toronto's suburbs. Pooling across the four areas sampled, the previous findings were replicated. However, the average within-area correlation was insignificant, suggesting that when actual incidence of crime is controlled for, there is no overall relationship between television viewing and fear of being a victim of crime. A multiple regression analysis and a canonical correlation analysis confirmed these findings.

A variety of social problems have been attributed to television viewing. It is said that television makes people more violent, that it lowers the level of literacy in the population, and that it distorts the viewer's perception of the world. There is little denying that the picture of reality that comes into people's homes

We wish to thank Julian Roberts for his help and useful suggestions at all phases of this work and Bob Gebotys for his help in analyzing the data. The Metropolitan Toronto Police were very open and helpful to us in providing the data necessary for choosing our experimental neighborhoods. The research was supported by the (Ontario) Royal Commission on Violence in the Communications Industry, and a version of this study is published in Volume V of that commission's report. We wish to thank Mr. C. K. Marchant, the Director of Research of that commission, for his help and encouragement throughout all phases of the work. The data analysis was supported, in part, by funds provided to the Centre of Criminology, University of Toronto, by the Ministry of the Solicitor General, Canada.

Requests for reprints should be sent to Anthony N. Doob, Department of Psychology, University of Toronto, Toronto, Ontario, Canada M5S 1A1.

is not an accurate reflection of their own society. That we learn from television, as we learn from every other medium, seems intuitively plausible independent of research results. Gerbner and Gross (1974, 1976a, 1976b; Gerbner et al., 1976), however, have suggested something even more serious than simple learning effects: that people not only learn factual information, such as the proportion of people involved in law enforcement, but that they generalize from the information that they get from television. In particular, Gerbner and his associates show that those who watch a lot of television are more likely to feel that they might be involved in some kind of violence during a given week than do those who watch relatively little television. This same pattern of results shows up in a variety of questions having to do with the viewers' perceptions of various aspects of the society in which they live. As Gerbner et al. (1976) point out, "Their heightened sense of fear and mistrust is manifested in their typically more apprehensive responses to questions about their own personal safety, about crime and law enforcement, and about trust in people" (p. 9).

Obviously, heavy television viewing is not independent of other social factors. Gerbner and Gross (1976a) have found that "heavy viewing is part and parcel of a complex syndrome which also includes lower education, lower mobility, lower aspirations, higher anxieties, and other class, age, and sex-related characteristics" (p. 191).

Because of the problem of confounding variables, Gerbner has been careful to break down his data on various other characteristics of television viewers such as age, sex, educational level, news reading, news magazine reading, prime-time viewing, and viewing or nonviewing of TV news. The notable finding in all of these comparisons is that although there may be main effects of some of these other characteristics, in all cases, heavy viewers are more likely than light viewers to feel that they might be involved in some violence.

No list of possible confounding variables can be complete. The worry of any researcher doing correlational research and wishing to make a causal statement is that some other variable would, in fact, account for the effect apparently demonstrated. We felt that there is one quite plausible factor that might account for the correlation between viewing and fear of violence: People who watch a lot of television may have a greater fear of being victims of violent crimes because, in fact, they live in more violent neighborhoods.

The study that this explanation suggests, then, is quite obvious: A survey of the television viewing habits of people and their perception of being involved in violence should be performed in both high- and low-crime neighborhoods. Pooling across neighborhoods, we should be able to replicate Gerbner's and his associates' findings; within neighborhoods, however, the effect should be substantially reduced or eliminated.

Method

For purposes of efficient distribution of resources, the Metropolitan Toronto Police have divided Toronto into approximately 210 patrol areas. The size of these patrol areas varies not only as a function

of the resident population but also as a function of the number of calls of all types that the police receive in the area: Busy areas thus tend to be smaller in terms of the size of the population served and in terms of geographic area. The police identified for us the 10 patrol areas with the highest number of reported assaults and woundings and the 14 areas with the lowest number of reported assaults and woundings for the 7-month period ending 2 months before the beginning of the survey. From these data, four geographic areas, approximately equal in size, were chosen. Two (one within the city of Toronto, the other suburban) were high in reported crime; two (one city, one suburban) were low in reported crime. It is difficult to estimate the exact rates of crime for the four areas. However, very rough estimates would suggest that the rates of assaults and woundings per 100,000 resident population for the 7-month period for the four designated areas would be the following: high-crime city, 614; low-crime city, 8; high-crime suburb, 195; low-crime suburb, 6. It must be emphasized that these are very rough figures: The low-crime areas each had only two reported assaults (and no woundings) for the entire 7-month period; hence the estimates are bound to be unstable. There were eight patrol areas constituting the high-crime city area; one patrol area was sampled for the high-crime suburban area and two each for the low-crime areas.

Obviously, the four areas differ considerably on a large number of social variables other than reported crime rates. The high-crime city area contains a portion of the downtown commercial/entertainment district of the city, the largest block of public housing in the metropolitan area, and much of the poorest portion of the population. The low-crime city area is largely expensive, single, detached houses and is one of the more exclusive residential areas. The high-crime suburban area contains a high concentration of low-rise public housing and is generally fairly poor. The low-crime suburban area is mostly single, detached, middle-class housing.

Random households were chosen within each of these areas. Interviewers, employed by a commercial survey company, did a door-to-door survey. The person who answered the door was asked to list all of the people over 18 years of age living in the household. One of these people was then chosen at random by the interviewer. If this person could not be interviewed at that time or at some mutually acceptable time, the interviewer went on to the next randomly chosen household, and the procedure was repeated. The effect of this selection procedure was an oversampling of women (70.5%) and, presumably, a general oversampling of those who spend much of the time at home. Although this effect would be unfortunate if one were interested in estimating population values for the measures that were taken, it was less relevant in our study, where we were interested in the relationship between television viewing and fear of criminal victimization.

Table 1
*Mean Fear-of-Crime Factor Scores for Each
of the Sampled Areas*

Area	City		Suburb	
	M	n	M	n
High crime	.28	83	.15	69
Low crime	−.34	71	−.13	77

Note. The higher the number, the more fear.

Respondents were first asked to indicate those programs that they had watched during the previous week. According to our interviewers, very few people had any difficulty in doing this. They were then asked to complete a 37-item fixed-alternatives questionnaire. This questionnaire consisted of six questions dealing directly with the person's estimate of his or her own likelihood of being a victim of a crime; four questions dealing with estimates of the likelihood of particular groups of people being victims; four questions dealing with the perception of crime in general being a problem and there being a need for more police personnel; two questions dealing with the necessity to arm oneself; eight questions of a factual nature dealing with crime; three questions dealing with society's response to crime; four questions dealing with the respondents' view of Toronto with respect to crime; three questions dealing with the respondents' prediction of their response to a request for help; and three questions dealing with media usage. The whole interview took approximately 45 minutes on the average.

For purposes of analyzing the types of television, we decided to use the number of programs watched as an index of total viewing. In addition, programs were coded by a research associate into violent and nonviolent types before the tabulation of the other data. It should be pointed out that this last measure is, necessarily, somewhat subjective. However, as will be seen, this turns out not to be a serious problem in understanding the results.

Results

In order to reduce the number of measures to a somewhat workable number, a factor analysis was performed[1] on the 34 opinion questions. Using a varimax rotation, only one factor accounted for a substantial amount of the common variance. The percentages of the common variance accounted for by the first 4 of the 11 factors were 35.9%, 12.5%, 10.8%, and 8.4%. The questions that loaded highest on the first factor are shown in Table 4; they were the six questions related to the

respondents' estimates of their own chances of victimization, two of the questions dealing with the chances of victimization of particular groups, and one of the questions dealing with crime as a general problem. Generally speaking, it seems fair to label this factor "fear of crime." Each of the next three factors had substantial loadings from only one or two questions.

As one would expect, the residents of the four areas differed significantly on their overall fear of crime. The average factor scores for the four areas are shown in Table 1. Analysis of variance on the factor scores revealed a main effect for high-/low-crime area that was highly significant, $F(1, 296) = 17.79$, $p < .01$. Neither the city/suburb effect nor the interaction was significant. It is clear, then, that people who live in high-crime areas, are, in fact, more afraid.

The four areas sampled also differed on their exposure to the various media. Table 2 presents these data. Overall, people in high-crime areas watched more television and, generally speaking, tended to watch more violent television. Although there were interactions between the two factors on these two measures, for the purposes of this article, these interactions are not very important. As one might expect, since the areas differed on so many dimensions, there were also effects on self-report of exposure to radio news: People living in low-crime areas tended to report listening to radio news more frequently. Furthermore, the reported frequency of newspaper reading was higher in low-crime areas and in the city.

Gerbner and his associates (Gerbner & Gross, 1974, 1976a, 1976b; Gerbner et al., 1976) do not directly present measures of association between the total amount of tele-

---

[1] The input for the factor analysis consisted only of those 300 respondents (of the total of 408) who answered every question. Most of the other 108 respondents failed to answer only a few of the questions. The proportion of complete questionnaires varied somewhat from area to area. The numbers of complete/total questionnaires are as follows: high-crime city, 83/119, or 70%; low-crime city, 71/118, or 60%; high-crime suburb, 69/85, or 81%; low-crime suburb, 77/86, or 90%.

Table 2
Media Usage for the Four Areas

| | High-crime area | | Low-crime area | | F value | | |
Medium	City(119)	Suburbs(85)	City(118)	Suburbs(86)	High/low crime	City/ suburb	Inter- action
Total TV	36.25	31.71	18.89	25.03	25.21**	<1	4.98*
TV violence	6.97	3.73	2.11	3.33	23.25**	2.72	18.11**
TV news	3.07	2.99	3.72	3.74	2.83	<1	<1
Radio news	5.07	4.96	5.44	5.37	9.79**	<1	<1
Newspaper reading	4.78	4.58	5.26	4.80	6.89**	6.01*	<1

Note. For TV viewing, numbers refer to mean number of programs watched during the previous week. The other measures are mean values on a scale where 1 equals never and 6 equals daily. *n*s are in parentheses.
* $p < .05$.
** $p < .01$.

vision viewed by their respondents (in re-sponse to the question "How many hours a day do you usually watch television? Please include morning, afternoon, and evening") and their fear of being a victim of a violent crime (in response to the question "During any given week, what are your chances of being involved in some type of violence—about a 50–50 chance, about a 1-in-10 chance, or about a 1-in-100 chance?"). However, estimating from the data that are presented in the various reports, we calculated a phi coefficient of .13 and a contingency coefficient of the same value.

Looking at our data, then, we calculated the (Pearson) correlation between our fear-of-crime factor scores and our various mea-sures of media usage. These correlations are presented in the first column of Table 3. It

is quite clear that the basic effect is much the same as that found by Gerbner and his associates: Across the four areas, those who watched the most television (or violent tele-vision) tended to be those who were the most afraid. However, the effect *within* area is not quite so simple: Although the effect would appear to hold in the high-crime area of the city, it tended to disappear for the other areas. Indeed, the average correlations (last column of Table 3) indicate that there is es-sentially no relationship between media usage and fear of crime when the effect of neigh-borhood is removed. We have suggested that the artifact that created the first two correla-tions in the first column might be labeled "actual incidence of crime." However, in terms of the focus of this article (the rela-tionship of media usage to fear of crime), the

Table 3
Correlations Between Media Usage and Fear-of-Crime Factor Scores for all Subjects (Pooled), for Each of the Four Areas, and for the Average of the Four Areas

| | Pooled across all areas | High crime | | Low crime | | Average correlation |
Medium		City(83)	Suburb(69)	City(71)	Suburb(77)	
Total TV	.18**	.24*	.16	.06	−.09	.09
TV violence	.18**	.22*	−.03	.14	−.04	.07
TV news	.05	.14	−.04	.05	.06	.05
Radio news	.05	.18	−.09	−.02	.21	.07
Newspaper reading	−.07	−.20*	−.14	.09	.15	−.03

Note. Positive correlations indicate more fear associated with higher media usage. *n*s are in parentheses.
* $p < .05$.
** $p < .001$.

Table 4
Fear-of-Crime Questions and the Correlations Between Responses to Each Question and Total TV Viewing and TV Violence for the Four Areas Pooled and the Average of the Four Areas Calculated Individually

Question	Total TV		TV violence		High TV viewing associated with
	Pooled	Average within area	Pooled	Average within area	
1. To what extent are crimes of violence a serious problem in your neighborhood? (399)	.07	−.02	.16*	0	Serious problem
2. What do you think the chances are that if you were to walk alone at night on the residential streets of your neighborhood each night for a month that you would be the victim of a serious crime? (391)	.18*	.10*	.19*	.05	High probability (1 in 10)
3. If a child were to play alone in a park each day for a month, what do you think the chances are that he would be the victim of a violent crime? (382)	.12*	.02	.22*	.12*	High probability (1 in 10)
4. If you were to walk by yourself in a park close to your home each night for a month, what do you think the chances are that you would be the victim of a serious crime? (391)	.10*	.02	.14*	.04	High probability (1 in 10)
5. What do you think the chances are that an unaccompanied woman would be the victim of a violent crime late at night in a Toronto subway station? (389)	.10*	.04	.09	.04	High probability (1 in 10)
6. What do you think the chances are that you, one of your family, or one of your close friends might be the victim of an assault during the next year? (385)	.13*	.02	.12*	−.02	High probability (1 in 10)
7. How likely do you think it is that you or one of your close friends would have their house broken into during the next year? (405)	−.04	−.07	.01	−.01	Extremely unlikely
8. Do you ever decide not to walk alone at night because you are afraid of being the victim of a violent crime? (402)	.05	.06	−.04	−.04	Very often
9. Is there any area around your home (i.e., within a mile) where you would be afraid to walk alone at night? (403)	.12*	.05	.02	−.06	Yes

Note. ns of respondents for each question are in parentheses.
* *p* < .05.

name given to this variable is unimportant: When the effect of neighborhood is removed, the "effect" of television is reduced to almost nothing.

Clearly, however, the artifact (whatever it is called) measures in only the crudest way the amount of crime that a person is exposed to. For example, a person living in one part of what we have labeled as a high-crime section of the city might, in fact, be quite safe: The crimes might well be in a different section of that patrol area. However crude the measure might be, the size of the correlations does drop dramatically.

It should be pointed out that correlations are responsive to effects other than the strength of the relationship between two variables. In particular, as McNemar (1962) points out, "the magnitude of the correlation coefficient varies with the degree of heterogeneity (with respect to the traits being correlated) of the sample" (p. 144). Given that we have divided our overall sample (into the four areas) in a manner that clearly relates to both of the variables (see Tables 1 and 2), this curtailment of the variance could be a problem. It turns out, however, not to be a serious problem in this case. The ratios of the standard deviations of the "curtailed" distribution (average of the four areas' standard deviations) to the uncurtailed distribution (standard deviation for the four areas pooled) are .965, .917, and .844 for the factor scores, total TV viewing scores, and TV violence scores, respectively. McNemar (1962) indicates that "formulas for 'correcting' for double curtailment are not too satisfactory" (p. 145). However, correcting for the curtailment of the range for the most curtailed distribution (TV violence) would only raise the average correlation between fear and amount of violent TV watched (averaged across the four areas) from .07 to .09.

The data look very much the same when analyzed question by question. The nine questions with the highest weight on the first factor of the factor analysis are shown in Table 4. In addition, the overall correlations for all subjects pooled across areas are shown in the first column (for each question with total TV viewing) and the third column (for

Table 5
Stepwise Multiple Regression Summary[a]

Variable	R when entered[b]	F when entered[c]	F in final equation[d]
High/low crime	.234	17.234**	16.704**
City/suburb	.235	.186	.051
Interaction: Crime × City/Suburb	.251	2.335	2.322
Sex	.350	19.858**	21.176**
Age	.376	6.605*	5.206*
Total TV	.385	2.363	.058
TV violence	.391	1.703	1.537
Radio news	.401	2.637	3.002
Newspaper reading	.403	.389	.389

[a] Variables entered in the order indicated.
[b] R achieved with this and all variables above it included.
[c] Equivalent to a test of the significance of the partial correlation between this variable and fear of crime with all variables listed above it partialed out.
[d] Equivalent to a test of the null hypothesis that the beta for this measure in the final equation involving all nine variables is zero.
* $p < .05$ ($df = 1$ and ≥ 290 for all Fs).
** $p < .01$.

the responses to each question and violent TV). All of the significant correlations are in the direction consistent with the Gerbner (Gerbner & Gross, 1974, 1976a, 1976b; Gerbner et al., 1976) findings (i.e., more TV associated with higher likelihood of victimization, etc.). Generally speaking, it is clear that the correlations tend to decrease substantially in size when they are run within the four areas and then pooled.

An alternative method of analyzing these data is in a stepwise multiple regression analysis using the fear-of-crime factor scores as the criterion and various other social and media exposure data as predictors. In order to control for neighborhood, this was entered first into the regression equation (coded as three variables: high/low crime, city/suburb, and their interaction). Next, two subject characteristics, sex and age, were entered, since both of them related to the fear-of-crime measure. (Not surprisingly, women and older people reported higher levels of fear than did men and younger people.) After these more "basic" variables had been entered, total TV viewing and TV violence were entered. Finally, the frequency of listen-

Table 6
Standardized Canonical Variate Coefficients

Variable	High score indicates	Variate 1	Variate 2	Variate 3
Outcome set				
Question 1	No problem	.536	−.102	.339
Question 2	Low chance	.064	−.108	.266
Question 3	Low chance	.365	−.012	−.773
Question 4	Low chance	.107	−.175	.283
Question 5	Low chance	−.159	−.059	−.806
Question 6	Low chance	.394	.216	.541
Question 7	Unlikely	−.420	.131	.131
Question 8	Never	−.501	−.451	.417
Question 9	No	.028	−.577	−.281
Predictor set				
Total TV	Much	.079	.088	−.063
TV violence	Much	−.136	−.017	.335
Radio news	Little	−.177	−.194	.430
Newspaper reading	Little	−.014	−.168	.032
High/low crime area	High	−.609	.472	−.178
City/surburb	City	−.279	−.145	−.845
Interaction: Crime × Location	High suburb/ low city	.465	−.283	−.236
Age	Older	.010	.163	.096
Sex	Female	.229	.889	−.110
Canonical correlation		.608	.468	.305
p value[a]		<.001	<.001	<.002

[a] Using Wilks' lambda. Using the method of the greatest characteristic root, the third pair of canonical variates is not significant. For a discussion of this problem, see Harris (1976).

ing to radio news and newspaper reading were entered into the equation.

The results are shown in Table 5. It is clear that after the subject characteristics had been entered, the media questions had no significant predictive value. Most relevant to the Gerbner results is of course the lack of importance of total TV viewing when it first entered the equation.

Finally, a canonical correlation analysis was done, using the nine fear-of-crime questions (see Table 4) as the criterion set and the same nine variables as in the multiple regression analysis (see Table 5) as the predictor set. Three significant canonical correlations were found. The variates associated with these correlations are shown in Table 6.

The first pair of canonical variates suggests that those who do not see crimes of violence as a problem in their neighborhood (Question 1), who do not think that a child playing alone in a park is in danger (Question 3), and who do not think that they themselves are likely to be victims of an assault (Question 6), but who are afraid that their houses will be broken into (Question 7) and who do not walk alone at night (Question 8), tend to be females living in low-crime (city) areas.

The second pair of canonical variates appears to indicate that people who have areas near them that they will not walk in at night (Question 9) and who fear walking alone at night (Question 8), but who do not think that they will be victims of a violent crime (Question 6), tend to be females living in high-crime (city) areas who listen to a lot of radio news.

The third set of variates suggests that those who think that unaccompanied female subway riders (Question 5) and children playing alone in parks (Question 3) are vulnerable to attacks, but who themselves do not feel vulnerable (Question 6) and do not worry about walking alone at night (Question 8), since their neighborhoods are safe (Question 1), tend to be suburban (low-crime area) residents who watch a lot of violent TV and do not listen to radio news.

The total amount of television watched did not seem to be important, and the amount of violent television watched entered into the interpretation only in the third canonical variate. Even in this case, it appears that the amount of violent TV watched related positively to the perceived vulnerability of particular groups (female subway riders and children playing alone in parks) but negatively to the perceived likelihood of the respondents themselves being victims of violent crime.

In summary, then, looking at these data from three somewhat different points of view, it appears that the amount of television watched did not relate to the amount of fear a person felt about being a victim of crime when other, more basic variables were taken into account.

Other Findings

As indicated earlier, we asked 25 other questions. Most of these questions related, directly or indirectly, to the respondents' views of the nature and frequency of crime or violence around them. In 14 of the questions, there was a significant relationship (pooled or calculated individually and then averaged) between TV viewing and the response to the question. The questions and the relationship of each question to TV viewing are shown in Table 7. What is noteworthy about these correlations is that there is generally not a substantial drop when the correlations are computed within area and then averaged (column 2 of Table 7). Thus, it appears that the relationship between total TV viewing and responses to these questions is not mediated by the area in which the respondent resides. These were the only other questions that correlated with TV viewing, and, at least from our point of view, they are qualitatively different from those that were large contributors to the "fear index" (see Table 4). Because it is not of central interest

to this study, we did not look at other possible factors that might account for the correlations that we have presented.

Discussion

A number of things are reasonably clear from these data. First of all, the basic findings of Gerbner and his associates (Gerbner & Gross, 1974, 1976a, 1976b; Gerbner et al., 1976) are replicable: People who watch a lot of television are more likely to indicate fear of their environment. It is equally clear, however, that this relationship disappears when attempts are made to control for other variables, including the actual incidence of crime in the neighborhood. Thus, it would appear that television itself is not likely to be a direct cause of people's fear of being victims of crime.

Although clearly at the level of speculation, it is interesting to note that Gerbner's (Gerbner & Gross, 1974) own data on this issue were collected by telephone interview in four cities: Philadelphia, Chicago, Los Angeles, and Dallas. One can assume that there exists in these cities some variability in the dangerousness of different neighborhoods. Since households for that survey were selected randomly from telephone books, it seems reasonable to expect that neighborhoods differing in actual dangerousness would be included from each city. This variation could be sufficient to produce the apparently small correlation that Gerbner found. More interesting, however, is the possibility that for some unspecifiable reason, the relationship only holds in high-crime areas, or in high-crime cities in particular. As shown in Table 3, we, too, got significant correlations within the high-crime area of the city of Toronto. One possible admittedly post hoc explanation for this result is that television violence in the form of police shows and so forth deals mostly with high-crime city neighborhoods. It is possible that people outside of such areas do not feel that the violence on television has any relevance for them; hence, there is no relationship between the amount of television watched and the perception of the likelihood of being a victim.

Table 7
Questions Associated Significantly With TV Viewing: Correlations Between Responses to
Each Question and Total TV and TV Violence for the Four Areas Pooled and the
Average of the Four Areas Calculated Individually

Question	Total TV		TV violence		High TV viewing associated with
	Pooled	Average within area	Pooled	Average within area	
10. Would you imagine that you would be more likely to be seriously harmed by someone you knew previously or by a complete stranger? (400)	.12*	.09*	.04	.06	Previously known
12. How dangerous do you think it is for a female driver of a car to pick up a male hitchhiker who is a stranger? (404)	.09*	.06	.06	.06	Dangerous
13. Do you think that it would be a good idea to spend more money on police patrols of your area of the city? (403)	.11*	.06	.12*	.08	Definitely yes
17. Do you think that it is useful for people to keep firearms in their homes to protect themselves? (405)	.31*	.20*	.25*	.11*	Definitely yes
20. Should women carry a weapon such as a knife to protect themselves against sexual assault? (405)	.18*	.17*	.19*	.18*	Definitely yes
21. Some people have suggested that one way to reduce the incidence of violent crime is to encourage people to stay away from areas thought to be high in crime. Do you think that this is a good way of dealing with the problem of crime? (403)	.09*	.07	.09*	.06	Definitely yes
22. What proportion of murders in Toronto do you think are committed by people who could be classified as mentally ill? (381)	.11*	.10*	.08*	.09*	High proportion
23. Approximately what proportion of assaults in Toronto are directed against members of racial minorities (i.e., nonwhites) by whites? (359)	.10*	.12*	.09*	.11*	High proportion
24. What proportion of serious assaults in Toronto do you think are carried out by nonwhites? (364)	.08	.11*	.08	.12*	High proportion
25. How many murders do you think took place in metropolitan Toronto during 1975? (372)	.17*	.16*	.16*	.13*	Large number

TELEVISION VIEWING AND FEAR OF VICTIMIZATION   179

Table 7   *(continued)*

Question	Total TV		TV violence		High TV viewing associated with
	Pooled	Average within area	Pooled	Average within area	
26. During the last 5 years, how many people do you think were murdered in the TTC subway? (384)	.15*	.12*	.09*	.08*	Large number
31. If you were walking alone on a residential street at night and someone asked you for directions, would you stop and give him the directions? (404)	.10*	.11*	0	0	Definitely not
32. If a person were to have an epileptic seizure on the street in front of you, how likely do you think most people would be to help? (405)	.10*	.07	.08	0	Very likely
33. If, in the middle of the night, a stranger knocked on your door and asked to use your telephone to call someone to help him start his car that had apparently stalled on your street, which of the following would you be most likely to do? (404)	.11*	.12*	.05	.03	Not help

Note. ns of respondents for each question are in parentheses.
* $p < .05$.

The second general point that should be made about our data is that although the correlation between TV viewing and fear dropped off when neighborhood was used as a controlling factor, this same factor did not eliminate the relationship between TV viewing and other factors (see Table 7). It is possible that the questions listed in Table 7 are, in fact, related to television viewing because they deal with matters of a more factual nature than the questions having to do with the person's own level of fear. Thus, television may well act as a source of information with regard to questions of fact, whereas it does not change people's views of how afraid they should be.

References

Gerbner, G., & Gross, L. *Trends in network television drama and viewer conceptions of social re-*

ality, 1967–1973. Violence profile number 6. Washington, D.C.: Educational Resources Information Center, 1974.

Gerbner, G., & Gross, L. Living with television: The violence profile. *Journal of Communication,* 1976, *26,* 172–199. (a)

Gerbner, G., & Gross, L. The scary world of TV's heavy viewer. *Psychology Today,* April 1976, pp. 41–45; 89. (b)

Gerbner, G., Gross, L., Eleey, M. F., Fox, S., Jackson-Beeck, M., & Signorielli, N. *Trends in network television drama and viewer conceptions of social reality, 1967–1975. Violence profile number 7.* Philadelphia, Pa.: The Annenberg School of Communications, University of Pennsylvania, 1976.

Harris, R. J. The invalidity of partitioned-U tests in canonical correlation and multivariate analysis of variance. *Multivariate Behavioral Research,* 1976, *11,* 353–366.

McNemar, Q. *Psychological statistics* (3rd ed.). New York: Wiley, 1962.

Received February 24, 1978 ∎

[12]

BASIC AND APPLIED SOCIAL PSYCHOLOGY, 1987, 8(1 & 2), 97–123

Television Viewing and Fear of Crime: Where Is the Mean World?

Linda Heath and John Petraitis
Loyola University of Chicago

Although Gerbner and Gross (1976) maintained that television viewing cultivates impressions of the real world that are distorted in the direction of the TV version of reality, several studies (e.g., Doob & Macdonald, 1979) have found no relationship between viewing and perceptions of crime in the respondent's neighborhood. It is possible, however, that TV viewing may not affect perceptions of crime in the respondent's immediate environment but may affect perceptions of crime in more distant settings. In two separate studies, we examined the effects of TV viewing on perceptions of crime in the immediate neighborhood and on perceptions of crime in more distant, urban settings. Study 1, based on 372 nationwide telephone interviews, found that the total amount of TV viewed is related to fear of distant urban setting (i.e., New York City) but not to fear of respondent's own city or to fear of respondent's immediate neighborhood. Study 2, based on a survey of 192 undergraduates, found that the total amount of TV viewed is related to fear of distant urban setting (i.e., NYC) and to fear of less distant urban setting (i.e., downtown Chicago) but not to fear of respondent's immediate neighborhood. The implications of these studies for clearing up past confusions in the cultivation hypothesis literature are discussed.

The notion that daily bombardment by mass media images affects our views of the world has great intuitive appeal. Gerbner and Gross (1976) gave this notion scientific status with their research on the cultivation hypothesis. Basically, the cultivation hypothesis posits that television shapes and misshapes the audience's conceptions of the real world. Frequent exposure to TV "cultivates" views of the real world that are distorted toward the views of the imaginary world of TV. One portion of the TV view of the world that has received substantial attention in regard to the cultivation hypothesis is criminality.

Violence profiles (Gerbner & Gross, 1976; Gerbner et al., 1976) document that one aspect of the imaginary world of TV is rampant crime. For instance,

---

Requests for reprints should be sent to Linda Heath, Department of Psychology, Loyola University of Chicago, 6525 North Sheridan Road, Chicago, IL 60626.

police are present in TV dramas in numbers that far outdistance their prevalence in even the most crime-ridden cities (Gerbner et al., 1977). TV characters have a far greater chance of becoming a crime victim than the rest of us
(Gerbner et al., 1977), and TV criminals are much more likely to attack strangers than are criminals who commit their illegal acts without the benefit of
cameras (Gerbner et al., 1977). Based on items such as "What percent of employed men are law officers?" and "Can you trust most people?", Gerbner et
al. (1976) and Gerbner et al. (1977) contended that frequent exposure to the
TV version of crime cultivates a view of the world as a mean, scary place.

However plausible, this notion is not easily translated into research terms.
Difficulties lie in the myriad demographic variables that are confounded with
TV viewing. For example, frequent TV viewing is more prevalent among
women, the elderly, the less educated, and lower income populations (Comstock, Chaffee, Katzman, McCombs, & Roberts, 1978).[1] These confound-
ings are particularly problematic for cultivation studies because these factors
are also strong independent predictors of fear of crime. Hughes (1980),
Hirsch (1980), and Wober and Gunter (1982) have all found that the cultivation effect disappears when multiple demographic controls are entered simultaneously into analyses.

In a similar vein, Doob and Macdonald (1979) hypothesized that frequent
TV viewers report higher levels of fear of crime not because they view more
TV, but rather because they live in neighborhoods that are objectively more
dangerous. The demographic correlates of viewing (i.e., sex, age, education,
income) all operate in the direction that would lead to residence in less afflu-
ent (and therefore more crime-ridden) neighborhoods. To test this hypothesis, Doob and Macdonald assessed reported TV viewing and fear of crime in
urban and suburban areas with high and low crime rates. Their measure on
fear of crime consisted of a factor-analytically derived scale that was based
on items such as "To what extent are crimes of violence a serious problem in
your neighborhood?" and "What do you think the chances are that if you
were to walk alone at night on the residential streets of your neighborhood
each night for a month that you would be the victim of a serious crime?"

Doob and Macdonald found that, although analysis of the overall sample
confirmed the cultivation hypothesis, analyses within geographic subgroups
showed a significant relationship between viewing and fear of crime only for
residents of a high-crime, urban area. Although Doob and Macdonald focused on the lack of relationship between viewing and fear for the other three
neighborhoods, Gerbner, Gross, Morgan, and Signorielli (1980) focused on
the persisting relationship within the high-crime, urban neighborhood.
Gerbner et al. (1980) discussed this persisting effect as evidence of "reso-

---

[1]Hughes (1980) maintained that the common factor underlying these demographic relationships is time available for viewing.

nance" whereby TV images that match real-world experience provide a "double dose" of that reality, producing even more profound cultivation effects. Gerbner et al. (1980) also examined the relationship between viewing and fear within urban, suburban, and rural areas and found that the relationship is strongest within the major urban areas, which they interpreted as further evidence of resonance.

Another interesting aspect of Doob and Macdonald's data is that the relationship between viewing and certain fear items (that were not included in the Fear of Crime Scale) persisted even within geographic subgroups. Analyses of 14 items that do not load on the main Fear of Crime factor showed that, for 10 of these items, the relationship between viewing and fear did not dissipate within geographic subgroups. For example, responses to the item "How many murders do you think took place in metropolitan Toronto during 1975" correlated .17 ($p < .05$) with TV viewing in the total sample and .16 ($p < .05$) averaged across the four subgroups. Doob and Macdonald (1979) considered the items that do not load on the main factor to be related more to factual information than to fear. They stated: "Television may well act as a source of information in regard to questions of fact, whereas it does not change people's views of how afraid they should be" (p. 179).

Another interpretation of these findings, however, is that TV does increase fear of crime but only fear of crime as presented on television. As Doob and Macdonald (1979) noted, TV crime drama "deals mostly with high-crime city neighborhoods" (p. 177). Perhaps, then, the cultivation hypothesis is correct but in a more circumscribed sense. Frequent exposure to the TV version of crime (i.e., big-city, violent crime) could increase viewer's apprehension associated with big cities but not with their own neighborhoods (unless, of course, they happen to live in a big city or in a high-crime neighborhood). This pattern of geographic location mediating effects of media crime reports on fear has already been demonstrated in regard to newspapers (Heath, 1984). Readers of newspapers that carried high proportions of sensational, nonlocal news reported less fear of crime in their immediate neighborhoods than did readers of papers with less sensational nonlocal news. The presence of distant heinous crimes seemed to reassure the readers in regard to proximate danger.

This geographic explanation is consistent with the pattern of results obtained by Doob and Macdonald (1979). Their Fear of Crime Scale is primarily a measure of fear of neighborhood crime. Four of the 9 items that load on the Fear of Crime factor directly reference neighborhood locations, and 3 other items could be interpreted as assessing neighborhood-based fear. On the other hand, only 1 of the 14 nonscale fear items taps neighborhood fear. The distinction between neighborhood-based fear and big-city fear could, therefore, explain both the persisting relationship between viewing and fear of crime within the high-crime, urban area and the relationship between viewing and nonscale items in Doob and Macdonald's data.

100   HEATH AND PETRAITIS

Additionally, this distinction between neighborhood-based and more general big-city fear corresponds to the support or lack of support found for the cultivation hypothesis in other research (see Table 1). Gerbner and his associates have consistently found a significant first-order relationship between TV viewing and fear of neighborhood-based crime, but when they have examined the cultivation hypothesis within demographic groups, the effects have been mixed (e.g., Gerbner et al, 1977; Gerbner, Gross, Jackson-Beeck, Jefferies-Fox, & Signorielli, 1978; Gerbner et al., 1980). Employing multiple control variables simultaneously eliminates the relationship between TV viewing and neighborhood-based fear of crime (e.g., Hirsch, 1980; Hughes, 1980; Wober & Gunter, 1982).

The relationship between TV viewing and general fear of crime, however, appears to be more robust. Gerbner et al. (1977), Gerbner et al. (1980), Hawkins and Pingree (1981), and Pingree and Hawkins (1981) have employed demographic and media-exposure controls simultaneously and have found support for the cultivation hypothesis in regard to nonneighborhood crime. That TV should be more powerful in cultivating perceptions about non-immediate rather than immediate events is not surprising. In many cases, direct experience has a much more powerful impact on perceptions than does indirect experience (e.g., Fazio & Zanna, 1978). In fact, Gerbner and Gross (1976), in an early statement regarding the cultivation hypothesis, made precisely the same point: "The independent contributions of television are likely to be most powerful in cultivating assumptions about which there is little opportunity to learn first-hand, and which are not strongly anchored in other established beliefs and ideologies" (p. 191).

Another dimension that geographic specification captures is personal versus societal risk. Tyler and Cook (1984) found that mass media affects judgments of general societal prevalence of a problem but not judgments of personal vulnerability to the problem. Tyler and Cook demonstrated this effect in regard to home health care fraud, drunk driving accidents, and natural disasters. They further suggested, however, that mass media presentations that respondents see as applicable to themselves may affect personal as well as societal risk assessments. One factor that could lead to perceptions of applicability to self is the immediacy of the geographic location portrayed in the media message.

In two studies, we examined the cultivation hypothesis using this distinction between fear of crime in immediate and non-immediate environments. We hypothesized, based on previous research patterns and puzzles, that TV viewing would cultivate impressions of a mean world "out there"—in distant urban settings—but would not affect perceptions of danger in the immediate environment.

TABLE 1
Cultivation Hypothesis Research

Author(s)	Independent Variable(s)	Dependent Variable(s)	Controls	Effect
Neighborhood-Based Fear-of-Crime Measure				
Gerbner and Gross (1976)	Total daily viewing	Chances of being personally involved in violence	Separately for education, news reading, sex, and age	Positive (cultivation differential in right direction)
Gerbner et al. (1978)	Total daily viewing	Afraid to walk "around here" (within a mile) alone at night	Separately for age, sex, and education	Zero order positive ($p < .05$); ns within controls
	Crime drama viewing	Safe to walk around here alone at night	Separately for age, sex, and education	Zero order no relationship; mixed effects within controls
	Total daily viewing (children)	Afraid to walk alone in city at night	Separately for grade, sex, parents' education	Zero order positive ($p < .01$); mixed effects within controls
Gerbner et al. (1980)	Total daily viewing	Chances of being involved in crime, neighborhood safety	Separately for age, sex, education, race, newspaper reading, urban proximity, income	Zero order positive ($p < .001$); generally positive relationships within controls
		Perceptions of Danger Index (*mixed* neighborhood and general fear items)	Simultaneously for first five above by urban–suburban and income	Positive ($p < .001$) for all except high-income city group
Doob and Macdonald (1979)	Total daily viewing Total crime drama viewing	Fear of Crime Scale (mostly neighborhood based)	Simultaneously for Urban–Suburban × High–Low Crime interaction (sex, age, radio news, newspapers)	Overall no relationship; relationship within urban/ high-crime group
Hirsch (1980)	Total daily viewing	Afraid to walk around here (within a mile) alone at night	Simultaneously for age, sex, education, race	Negaive ($p < .05$)

(Continued)

101

TABLE 1 *(Continued)*

Author(s)	Independent Variable(s)	Dependent Variable(s)	Controls	Effect
Hughes (1980)	Total daily viewing		Simultaneously for age, sex, race, income, education, employment, church volunteer, city size	No relationship
Wober and Gunter (1982)	Total number of fiction programs/week	Local fear ("in my own neighborhood," "my home")	Simultaneously for locus of control, cynicism, satisfaction, age, socio-economic status (SES)	No relationship
General Fear-of-Crime Measure				
Gerbner et al. (1977)	Total daily viewing (adults)	Violence and Law Enforcement Index	Simultaneously for sex, age, education, newspaper reading, TV news	Positive ($p < .05$)
	Total daily viewing (children)	Violence and Law Enforcement Index	Simultaneously for sex, age, newspapers, father's education, SES, IQ	Positive ($p < .005$)
Doob and Macdonald (1979)	Total viewing (number of programs) Total crime drama viewing (number of programs)	13 nonneighborhood-based fear items	Simultaneously for urban–suburban, high–low crime rate	Positive for total TV and nine items ($p < .05$); positive for TV crime drama and seven items ($p < .05$)
Pingree and Hawkins (1981)	Total viewing by content type	Violence in Society Scale	Simultaneously for other types of programming, origin of programming	Positive ($p < .001$) for crime/adventure viewing
Hawkins and Pingree (1981)	Total viewing by content type	Violence in Society Scale	Simultaneously for SES, total viewing of other content types	Positive ($p < .001$) for crime/adventure viewing

STUDY 1

Method

Participants

Telephone interviews were conducted with 372 respondents in 26 medium-size cities in the United States.[2] Telephone numbers were selected via a variant of random digit dialing. Base numbers were selected from telephone directories, with the last digit being changed by an increment or decrement of one to produce the target telephone number. A different base number was used to generate each target number. This method has the advantage of including respondents with unlisted telephone numbers in the target population and is more cost-efficient than straight random digit dialing. Interviews were conducted by seven female undergraduates who had been trained in telephone survey techniques.

The first adult to answer the telephone was invited to participate in a ½-hr interview about media habits and views on crime. This procedure resulted in an oversampling of women (68% of the sample) that would have been problematic had we been seeking population estimates for our variables. Given our current interests, however, such oversampling was less problematic and, in fact, increased the comparability to the Doob and Macdonald (1979) sample, which was 70% female. Respondents ranged in age from 16 to 83 years, with a median age of 36 years. High-school graduation represented the median as well as the modal educational achievement of our respondents. Most respondents were employed (41%) or were homemakers (30%), and 51% had total annual household incomes of less than $20,000.

Materials

A standard interview schedule was constructed as part of a large effort to assess the factors that possibly contribute to perceptions of crime and fear of crime. The interview schedule measured demographics (e.g., sex and education), crime victimization experience, and, of special interest to this study, fear of crimes in the respondent's own neighborhood, in the respondent's own city, and in New York City. Further, the interview schedule measured exposure to the TV version of the world in two ways. First, respondents were asked to indicate how many hours they had spent watching TV the previous weekday. They were then asked to indicate their typical amount of viewing.

---

[2]This sample was also used in Heath (1984). Completion rate among potential respondents was 61%, which is comparable to other recent surveys about crime (e.g., Doob & Macdonald, 1979; Tyler, 1980). The demographics for this randomly drawn sample matched the overall demographics for the cities we contacted, except for the oversampling of women.

104   HEATH AND PETRAITIS

This procedure was followed to allow respondents to anchor their viewing report to a specific, recent time; it would also allow respondents to correct reports that they judged to be atypical. Respondents also indicated their total weekend viewing, and these figures were used to compute average daily viewing — that is, [(Typical Viewing × 5) + Weekend Viewing] / 7.

In addition to being asked to indicate total average daily viewing, respondents were asked to indicate whether they watched certain types of programs (e.g., comedies, talk shows, crime dramas) *often, sometimes, seldom,* or *never.* The categories for frequency of viewing crime drama were collapsed (*often/sometimes, seldom/never*) to form our second measure of exposure to the TV version of crime — general crime drama viewing.

Three items measured fear of crimes that could occur close to the respondent's home. Two of these items concerned risk of victimization to the "average person" in the respondent's *city,* assessing the fears that the average person in that city would have something stolen or would be mugged. The third neighborhood-based item on fear of crime was the classic "How safe do you feel out on the streets in your *neighborhood* alone at night?" To assess the role of TV in shaping perceptions of crimes in distant, urban settings, these same three questions regarding fear of crime were asked in reference to NYC. That is, respondents were asked to indicate the likelihood that the average person in NYC would have something stolen or would be mugged in a year's time and to indicate how safe they would feel out alone on the streets of NYC at night. Responses to these items had four levels, ranging from *very unlikely* (unsafe) to *very likely* (safe). Although the direction of the responses was counterbalanced in the original interview schedule, all items have been recoded so that a high score indicates high fear.

Results and Discussion

Multivariate analyses of variance (MANOVAs) were performed with TV viewing, education, and sex serving as independent variables.[3] Because we

---

[3]Because the three independent variables are non-orthogonal and because the independent variables do not have a clear causal ordering, the classic experimental approach was used. Strong correlations among the independent variables could therefore suppress main effects. Because all main effects were significant, suppression due to non-orthogonality appeared not to be a problem in these analyses.

Crime victimization experience was examined as a possible factor in determining fear of crime. A three-level variable was constructed, composed of no victimization (to self or others), minor victimization (to self or others), and major or multiple victimization (to self or others). This victimization variable did not enter into any significant main effects or interactions when included with television exposure (i.e., total TV or crime drama), sex, and education in MANOVAs of local fear and NYC fear items. Similarly, victimization (scaled as a continuous variable) did not account for a significant proportion of the variance when entered as a covariate. Therefore, crime victimization is not discussed as a possible contributor to fear of crime in this study. Similarly, income and age did not explain significant proportions of variance in these analyses once education entered the equation and are therefore not discussed further.

had two operationalizations of exposure to TV, two sets of analyses were done—one with total TV viewing as the operationalization of TV exposure and another with crime drama viewing serving that function. In regard to total TV viewing, respondents were categorized according to Gerbner's framework as *light viewers* if they watched some television but less than 2 hr a day, as *moderate viewers* if they watched between 2 and 4 hr a day, and as *heavy viewers* if they watched more than 4 hr a day.[4]

NYC Fear

Total TV viewing. As predicted, total TV viewing is related to fear of distant, urban settings. The MANOVA of the three items that measure perceptions of crime in NYC revealed significant main effects for sex, $F(3, 301)$ = 18.75, $p < .001$, education, $F(6, 600) = 7.43$, $p < .001$, and total TV, $F(6, 600) = 3.40$, $p < .01$, as well as a marginal Sex × Total TV interaction, $F(6, 600) = 1.86$, $p < .10$. Women reported higher levels of fear than did men on all three urban fear measures, as is indicated by univariate analyses on the NYC fear items, all $Fs(1, 303) \geq 3.70$, $ps < .06$ (see Table 2 for means). Respondents who had completed education beyond high school reported less fear than did respondents with less education on all three NYC fear items, all $Fs(2, 303) \geq 9.40$, $ps < .001$. Finally, respondents who viewed more than 4 hr of TV daily reported marginally greater likelihood of theft, $F(2, 303) = 2.68$, $p < .07$, greater perceived risk of mugging, overall $F(2, 303) = 7.32$, $p < .001$, and higher fear on NYC streets, $F(2, 303) = 5.32$, $p < .005$, than did respondents who viewed less TV (see Table 2).

The effect of TV viewing on big-city, urban fear depended somewhat on the sex of the respondent. An examination of the univariate effects for dependent variables in this analysis indicated that, although the multivariate Sex × Total TV interaction is only marginally significant, Sex interacts reliably with Total TV in the item on likelihood of theft, $F(2, 303) = 4.54$, $p < .05$. As Table 3 indicates, the cultivation effect is only evident among male respondents, with heavy viewers reporting greater perceived risk than moderate or light viewers, cellwise $Fs(1, 303) = 6.76$ and 8.64 respectively, $ps < .01$.[5] The absence of a cultivation effect among female respondents might,

---

[4]Respondents who never watch TV (Study 1, $n = 11$; Study 2, $n = 4$) were removed from these analyses because, as Hirsch (1980) showed, they cannot be combined with light viewers based on either demographics or perceptions of crime and because there were too few of them to constitute a separate group. The demographic composition of nonviewers in Study 1 (i.e., high education, very low income) led us to suspect that this group was composed primarily of undergraduate and graduate students.

[5]The Sex × Total TV interaction for the likelihood of NYC mugging variable was marginally significant, $F(2, 303) = 2.77$, $p < .10$, and the cell means followed the same pattern as those for the item on likelihood of theft did.

TABLE 2

Mean NYC Fear by Sex, Education, and Average Total Daily TV Viewing

Item		Sex		Education			Average Total Daily TV Viewing		
		Male	Female	Less Than High School	High School Graduate	More Than High School	Less Than 2 hr	2 to 4 hr	Over 4 hr
NYC theft likelihood	M	3.53	3.75	3.80$_a$	3.84$_a$	3.50	3.62$_a$	3.67$_{a,b}$	3.78$_b$
	SD	.72	.48	.40	.38	.70	.66	.55	.44
	n	102	232	45	141	153	143	98	94
NYC mugging likelihood	M	2.91	3.40	3.60$_a$	3.41$_a$	2.99	3.12$_a$	3.21$_a$	3.46
	SD	.92	.71	.58	.68	.90	.83	.81	.74
	n	104	226	45	140	150	138	98	94
Fear of NYC streets at night	M	3.15	3.81	3.72$_a$	3.78$_a$	3.42	3.49$_a$	3.63$_{a,b}$	3.77$_b$
	SD	.97	.46	.62	.59	.82	.81	.71	.55
	n	104	239	46	146	151	142	101	96

Note. Means that share a common subscript do not differ reliably (at $p < .05$).

TABLE 3
Mean Likelihood of NYC Theft by Total
TV Viewing and Sex

		Sex	
		Male	Female
Total TV Viewing			
Light	M	3.46	3.71
	SD	.80	.54
	n	52	91
Moderate	M	3.44	3.79
	SD	.72	.41
	n	32	66
Heavy	M	3.89	3.76
	SD	.32	.47
	n	18	75

however, be an artifact attributable to the overall high level of perceived task of NYC theft among women.

Crime drama viewing. Analysis of the three items relating NYC fear to sex, education, and crime drama viewing revealed (as did the analysis incorporating total TV viewing) that women and lower educational groups express more fear and risk associated with NYC than do men and more educated respondents (refer to Table 2 for these main effects). Although crime drama viewing did not produce a significant main effect on the NYC fear items, as with total TV viewing, the effect of crime drama viewing was somewhat dependent on sex, $F(3, 301) = 2.79, p < .05$. Univariate analyses of the three NYC fear items indicated that, as with total TV viewing, the cultivation effect is apparent among men but not among women for two of three NYC items: NYC theft likelihood, $F(1, 303) = 6.94, p < .01$, and NYC mugging likelihood, $F(1, 303) = 4.07, p < .05$ (see Table 4). That is, cellwise comparisons showed that men who reported watching crime dramas often or sometimes expressed greater likelihood of NYC mugging, $F(1, 303) = 5.27, p < .05$, than did men who watched crime dramas seldom or never. Crime drama viewing did not, however, reliably affect women's estimates of mugging in NYC, $F(1, 303) = .84$, ns. Cell means for the NYC theft item followed the same pattern, although cellwise comparisons were not significant for either men or women.

Local Fear

Total TV viewing. In regard to local fear, women were consistently more fearful than men, $F(3, 316) = 14.81, p < .001$. As Table 5 indicates, women expressed greater likelihood of local theft, greater likelihood of

TABLE 4
Mean NYC Crime Likelihood by Crime Drama Viewing and Sex

Crime Drama Viewing		NYC Theft Likelihood		NYC Mugging Likelihood	
		Male	Female	Male	Female
Often/sometimes	M	3.70	3.76	3.11	3.45
	SD	.61	.45	.95	.72
	n	40	101	41	100
Seldom/never	M	3.40	3.73	2.79	3.36
	SD	.79	.51	.88	.69
	n	60	127	61	122

TABLE 5
Mean Local Fear by Sex and Education

Item		Sex		Education		
		Male	Female	Low	Middle	High
Local theft likelihood	M	2.98	3.30			
	SD	.88	.68			
	n	110	238			
Local mugging likelihood	M	2.22	2.74	2.87$_a$	2.71$_a$	2.36
	SD	.92	.91	.97	.88	.95
	n	110	240	45	148	157
Fear of neighborhood streets at night	M	1.59	2.25	2.53	2.10	1.86
	SD	.77	1.05	1.14	1.05	.92
	n	110	242	45	150	157

Note. Means with a common subscript are not reliably different (at $p < .05$). Statistics are provided only for overall effects that reach conventional levels of statistical significance.

mugging in their cities, and greater fear on the streets of their neighborhood at night, all $Fs(1, 318) \geq 3.35$, $ps < .001$, than did men. Education level was also related to local fear, $F(6, 630) = 2.99$, $p < .01$, with reported fear of neighborhood streets decreasing as education increased, $F(2, 318) = 5.09$, $p < .01$, and with the highest education group reporting a lower perceived risk of local mugging than other groups, $F(2, 318) = 5.48$, $p < .01$. As predicted, however, total TV viewing was not related to fear of local or neighborhood crime in either a direct or interactive fashion.

General crime drama viewing. This analysis again revealed the significant effects of sex and education in locally based fear (see Table 5 for means). In addition, however, this analysis revealed a significant effect for crime drama viewing, $F(3, 316) = 2.90$, $p < .05$. The univariate examination revealed no relationship between crime drama exposure and fear of the streets in the immediate *neighborhood* but did reveal that respondents who viewed crime drama often or sometimes reported greater perceived likelihood of mugging in their *cities* (Ms = 2.69 and 2.48, respectively), $F(1, 318)$ = 4.92, p < .05, and greater likelihood of theft in their *cities* (M = 3.27 and 3.11, respectively), $F(1, 318)$ = 3.89, p < .05, than did respondents who watched crime dramas seldom or never.

The sex and crime drama main effects, however, were subsumed under a two-way interaction, $F(3, 316)$ = 2.83, p < .05. Univariate analyses revealed this interaction for the item on local mugging likelihood, $F(1, 318)$ = 4.10, p < .05, for the item on fear on neighborhood streets at night, $F(1, 318)$ = 5.96, p < .05, and marginally for the item on local theft likelihood, $F(1, 318)$ = 3.37, p < .07. As Table 6 indicates, the cultivation hypothesis was confirmed for men, cellwise $F(1, 318)$ = 7.05, p < .01, but not for women, cellwise $F(1, 318)$ = .45, ns, in regard to local, city-based mugging. In regard to fear on the streets, however, women who watched less crime drama expressed marginally more fear than did women who watched more crime shows, $F(1, 318)$ = 3.35, p < .10, whereas crime drama viewing did not affect men's fear on neighborhood streets, $F(1, 318)$ = 1.00, ns. The marginal interaction regarding perceptions of local mugging likelihood followed the pattern for local theft likelihood, with the cultivation hypothesis being supported among men and no viewing effect being evident among women.

Although the general pattern of results for the total TV viewing analyses supports our reformulation, the crime drama viewing analyses do not. With the exception of the marginally significant reversal for neighborhood street fear experienced by women, the analyses show that crime drama viewing is related to both fear of distant, urban environments and to fear of closer environments (specifically, the respondent's city). These findings are consistent with most interpretations of the cultivation hypothesis and suggest that our introduction of geographic specifications is unwarranted.

TABLE 6
Mean Local Crime Likelihood by Crime Drama Viewing and Sex

Crime Drama Viewing		Local Mugging Likelihood		Fear on Neighborhood Streets	
		Male	Female	Male	Female
Often/sometimes	M	2.50	2.77	1.69	2.12
	SD	.89	.91	.81	1.09
	n	42	103	42	104
Seldom/never	M	2.03	2.69	1.52	2.34
	SD	.93	.90	.74	1.01
	n	63	130	63	131

There is, however, another interpretation of these results. The results found no relationship between crime drama exposure and fear of the respondent's own *neighborhood* but did reveal a relationship between exposure to TV crimes and perceptions of crimes in the respondent's *city*. This pattern of findings suggests that watching crime dramas may not affect fear of the environment immediately outside the respondent's front door but that crime dramas may affect fear of the city in general or fear of other, non-immediate areas in the city. Apparently, our measures did not exclusively assess neighborhood-based and NYC-based fear of crime. Rather, it appears as though our measures assessed a city-based fear as well. This interpretation suggests that our introduction of geographic specifications was warranted and that exposure to crime dramas does shape perceptions of crime in non-immediate settings but that these settings are closer to the respondent's immediate neighborhood than we originally assumed.

A final explanation exists for the results of the crime drama viewing analyses. The results may be spurious, reflecting the instability of an independent variable that was based on a single item (i.e., "How often do you watch crime dramas?"). Additional research is needed to determine whether one formulation of the cultivation hypothesis (the more inclusive interpretation or the geographically specific reformulation) is more plausible than the other or whether both are inadequate because empirical support is based on unreliable findings.

The results of these analyses also suggest that the effects of crime drama viewing may be different for men than for women. Watching crime dramas might have less of an impact on women than it does on men. It is also possible, however, that given the consistently higher fear scores for women (especially for the NYC fear items), our measures of NYC fear were not sensitive enough and reached a statistical ceiling, making it impossible to decompose the variance in women's NYC fear responses. Again, additional research must be specifically designed to address these possibilities.

Our interpretation of these findings is, admittedly, post hoc and fails to explain adequately why crime drama viewing is not related to NYC fear for women. Therefore, additional research was conducted to determine the effects of TV viewing (both total TV and crime drama viewing) on perceptions (for both men and women) of crime in distant urban settings, in less distant urban settings, and in the immediate neighborhood.

STUDY 2

In Study 2, we specifically attempted (a) to construct a more stable measure of crime drama viewing; (b) to construct more sensitive measures of neighborhood-based fear of crime, of own-city-based fear of crime, and of other-city-based fear of crime; and (c) to eliminate an additional confounding factor by examining TV effects for residents of high-crime as well as low-crime neighborhoods.

Method

Participants

Eighty-nine male and 103 female undergraduates from Loyola University of Chicago participated in this study and earned credit points toward their introductory psychology course. All participants lived in Chicago or in the surrounding suburbs at the time of Study 2.

Materials

This study used a more thorough questionnaire to assess TV viewing habits, perceptions of crime in the immediate neighborhood and perceptions of nonneighborhood crime, crime victimization experience, neighborhood crime rates, and demographics.

Exposure to TV was measured in three ways. As in Study 1, respondents were asked to indicate how many hours they watch TV on a typical weekday and over a typical weekend. These figures were combined and were used to compute average total daily viewing.

In addition to the total TV measure, we also assessed exposure to crime dramas in two ways. As in Study 1, respondents were asked "How often do you watch crime dramas, in general?" (this variable is called *general crime drama viewing* throughout this study). This single-item measure was supplemented in Study 2 by having respondents indicate how often they watch each of seven prime-time crime programs: "Hill Street Blues," "Magnum, P.I.," "Remington Steel," "Hardcastle and McCormick," "Miami Vice," "A-Team," and "Simon and Simon."[6] These responses were then combined to form the second index of crime drama viewing—called *specific crime show viewing*.

Study 2 contained 20 items that measured both neighborhood and nonneighborhood fear. These 20 items assessed perceptions of crime and fear of crime in the respondents' various neighborhoods, in other neighborhoods throughout Chicago (including downtown), and in NYC. Respondents estimated the likelihood that the "average person" from each of these three geo-

---

[6]Respondents also indicated how often they watched four additional prime-time crime programs ("Cagney and Lacy," "T. J. Hooker," "Scarecrow and Mrs. King," and "Hawaiian Heat") and three syndicated reruns ("Rockford Files," "Kojak," and "Barnaby Jones"). Because fewer than 13% of respondents reported watching any of these programs either often or sometimes, responses on these programs were not used to construct the specific crime show viewing variable.

graphic locations would have something stolen or would be the victim of mugging and estimated the safety of an unaccompanied teen-age girl on the streets in the respondents' own neighborhood, on other streets in Chicago, and on the streets of NYC. Respondents also estimated their own chances of having something stolen or being mugged while in their neighborhoods or elsewhere in Chicago and estimated their own levels of safety when walking alone and when walking accompanied during the daytime and nighttime in all geographic locations. Finally, respondents estimated whether their own neighborhood streets had crime rates that were higher, lower, or about the same as those in other neighborhoods in Chicago.

Because perceptions of crime and fear of crime could be shaped by personal experiences with crime, respondents were asked to indicate whether they or someone in their family had been the victim of a serious crime, like a mugging, or a less serious crime, like a purse snatching. They were also asked to name the two streets that intersected closest to their homes so that we could determine in which police district each respondent lived. This last question was used along with police records of violent crimes in that district to estimate the actual levels of crime that each respondent faces daily in his or her own neighborhood.[7] Respondents in this study lived in 89 police districts throughout Chicago and in the surrounding suburbs. These districts were rank-ordered for the number of murders per 1,000 residents, and a median split was performed to categorize a respondent's neighborhood as having relatively high or low crime.

Results and Discussion

Study 2 had three operationalizations of TV exposure—total TV, general crime drama viewing, and specific crime drama viewing. In regard to total TV, recall that in Study 1 respondents were categorized according to the Gerbner formulation as light viewers (if they viewed some but less than 2 hr a day), as moderate viewers (2 to 4 hr) and as heavy viewers (more than 4 hr). As anticipated, however, our sample of college undergraduates in Study 2 did not have enough viewers who watched more than 4 hr of TV a day ($n = 30$) to use this framework for reliable statistical analyses. Therefore, respondents in Study 2 were categorized as *light viewers* if they watched some

---

[7]Police districts/neighborhoods were also coded for the number of rapes, robberies, and assaults per 1,000 residents in 1983, and correlations were computed between the prevalence of each category of crime. All correlations were highly significant (all $ps < .001$) and positive (ranging from $r = .58$ for rape rate and assault rate to $r = .94$ for rape rate and robbery rate). Because murder rates were so highly correlated with assault rates ($r = 68$), rape rates ($r = 73$), and robbery rates ($r = 84$), and because local murders are more likely to capture the attention of neighborhood residents, we decided to use murder rates as the index of neighborhood crime rate.

TELEVISION AND FEAR OF CRIME   113

but less than 2 hr a day ($n = 95$) and as *heavy viewers* if they typically watched more than 2 hr a day ($n = 90$).

The second operationalization of TV viewing was general crime drama viewing based on the same single-item measure of crime drama exposure that was used in Study 1. As in Study 1, responses were collapsed into two levels (never/seldom, sometimes/often).

Finally, responses to the seven items that assessed frequency of viewing particular crime shows were averaged to create a 4-point scale of specific crime drama exposure ranging from *never watch any of the seven crime shows* (1) to *always watch each of the seven crime shows* (4). The distribution of these averages was then trichotomized, classifying respondents as *light* (range = 1.4 to 2.9) as *moderate* (range = 3.0 to 3.4), and as *heavy* (range = 3.5 to 4.0) viewers of these crime shows.

We hypothesized that all three measures of TV exposure (total TV viewing, general crime drama viewing, and specific crime show viewing) would be positively related to fear of urban settings (both distant and less distant) but would not be related to fear of the immediate neighborhood. To test this hypothesis, it was first necessary to determine if urban and neighborhood fears are separate and distinct kinds of fear. Therefore, principal-components factor analysis with varimax rotation was performed on all 20 items on crime perception and fear. The factor analysis was restricted only to respondents who answered all 20 items ($n = 148$).

All 20 items loaded on four factors, with 15 items loading on the first two factors.[8] These two orthogonal factors accounted for 27.9% and 15.8% of the shared variance, respectively. Table 7 lists all the items that had factor loadings greater than .5 for each factor along with their factor loadings.

The results of the factor analysis support a distinction between immediate and non-immediate fear. As can be seen in Table 7, the eight items that loaded highest on the first factor were only those items that referred to crime outside the respondent's neighborhood—that is, throughout Chicago, in downtown Chicago, and in NYC. Conversely, the second factor had its highest loadings on items that specifically referred to the respondent's neighborhood and did not have substantial loadings on items that referred to other places in Chicago or in NYC. The results of the factor analysis also support our interpretation of the results in Study 1 by showing that city-based items are not appropriate indices of neighborhood-based fear. As anticipated,

---

[8]The third and fourth factors accounted for 10.8% and 6.4% of the shared variance, respectively. Items that loaded on the third factor assessed the respondents' sense of safety for walking alone at night in downtown Chicago, for walking accompanied at night in downtown Chicago, and for walking accompanied at night in NYC. Items that loaded on the fourth factor measured the respondents' sense of safety for walking alone during the daytime in downtown Chicago and for walking alone during the daytime in NYC.

The Fear of Crime

TABLE 7
Factor Loadings and Items for Urban Fear and Neighborhood Fear

Item	Factor 1 Loading	Factor 2 Loading
1. How likely is it that the average person in New York City would be mugged or seriously assaulted in a year's time?	.79650	
2. How likely is it that the average person in Chicago would be mugged or seriously assaulted in a year's time?	.78558	
3. How likely is it that the average person in Chicago would have something stolen from them in a year's time?	.76345	
4. How likely do you think it is that the average person in New York City would have something stolen from them in a year's time?	.76170	
5. How safe do you think a teen-age girl would be in downtown Chicago alone out on the streets at night?	.55175	
6. How safe do you think a teen-age girl would be in New York City alone out on the streets at night?	.53766	
7. How safe would you feel out on the streets of New York City alone at night?	.52759	
8. How likely do you think it is that you would be the victim of a serious assault or mugging in downtown Chicago in a year's time?	.50247	
9. How safe do you think a teen-age girl would be in your neighborhood alone out on the streets at night?		.78607
10. How likely do you think it is that the average person in your neighborhood would be mugged or seriously assaulted in a year's time?		.78454
11. How likely do you think it is that the average person in your neighborhood would have something stolen from them in a year's time?		.73971
12. How likely do you think it is that you would be the victim of a mugging or serious assault in your neighborhood in a year?		.73633
13. Do you think the crime rate in your neighborhood is higher, lower, or about the same as the average crime rate in Chicago?		.67831
14. How safe do you feel out on the streets in your neighborhood alone at night?		.61941
15. How safe would you feel out on the streets in your neighborhood at night if you were not alone?		.52713

Note. Only factor loadings greater than .5 are listed.

none of the city-based fear items had substantial loadings on the Neighborhood Fear factor. The city-based items were, however, closely aligned with the NYC-based items on the Urban Fear factor.

Based on the factor analysis results, two factor scales were constructed. Each scale consists of the sum of the Z-score transformations of all 20 fear items weighted by the appropriate factor score coefficients. The factor scale based on the first factor extracted is labeled *Urban Fear*. The factor scale based on the second factor is labeled *Neighborhood Fear*. Because we used a varimax rotation and constructed full factor scales, the correlation between these scales is forced to zero.

Urban Fear

Total TV viewing. As predicted, total TV viewing is positively related to fear of non-immediate, urban environments. The three-way analysis of variance (ANOVA)[9] on Urban Fear factor scores using sex, total TV viewing, and neighborhood crime rate as independent variables revealed significant main effects for total TV, $F(1, 136) = 3.91$, $p < .05$, and sex, $F(1, 136) = 19.84$, $p < .001$, but not for neighborhood crime rate, $F(1, 136) = .72$, ns. The analysis revealed that heavy viewers reported significantly higher levels of fear than light viewers ($Ms = .20$ and $-.13$, respectively), and women reported more fear than men ($Ms = .36$ and $-.33$, respectively). The analysis revealed no significant interactions involving TV and no significant interaction between sex and neighborhood crime rate.

General crime drama viewing. As predicted, and consistent with the findings in Study 1, general exposure to crime dramas is positively related to fear of non-immediate urban settings. The ANOVA on Urban Fear factor scores revealed a significant main effect for general crime drama viewing, $F(1, 141) = 6.01$, $p < .05$, indicating that viewers who generally watched crime dramas often or sometimes reported more fear of urban settings than did viewers who watched this type of program seldom or never ($Ms = .15$ and $-.15$, respectively).

Specific crime show viewing. The relationship between Urban Fear factor scores and viewing of specific crime programs was similar to the rela-

----

[9]MANOVAs were also performed in Study 2. The results from the MANOVAs were very comparable to the findings from the ANOVAs and were consistent with our predictions. As predicted, the MANOVAs revealed no significant main effects or interactions for any measure of TV exposure on local fear but did reveal main effects for specific crime show viewing and general crime drama viewing on nonlocal fear and marginal interactions between total TV and specific crime show viewing and urban fear. For more information on the findings using the MANOVA strategy, contact the first author.

tionships between Urban Fear and both total TV and general crime drama viewing. An ANOVA on the Urban Fear scores revealed a marginally significant effect for specific crime show viewing, $F(2, 136) = 2.88, p < .06$, a significant effect for sex, and no effect for neighborhood crime rate. Heavy viewers reported marginally more fear than moderate viewers ($Ms = .22$ and $- .10$, respectively), cellwise $F(1, 136) = 3.27, p < .10$.

In addition, a significant interaction existed between specific crime show viewing and neighborhood crime rate, $F(2, 136) = 3.97, p < .025$, and a marginal interaction existed between crime show viewing and sex, $F(2, 136) = 2.53, p < .10$. Although cellwise comparisons on the Crime Show $\times$ Crime Rate interaction revealed no relationship between TV and urban fear for residents of low-crime neighborhoods, largest cellwise $F(1, 136) = 1.06$, ns, comparisons did reveal that in high-crime areas, heavy viewers of crime dramas reported significantly more fear than light viewers, cellwise $F(1, 136) = 8.18, p < .01$, and marginally more fear than moderate viewers, cellwise $F(1, 132) = 3.45, p < .10$ (see Table 8). In addition, cellwise comparisons uncovered no relationship between crime show viewing and urban fear for women, largest cellwise $F(1, 50) = 1.35$, ns, but did find that among men, heavy viewers reported significantly more fear than either moderate viewers, cellwise $F(1, 136) = 4.82, p < .05$, or light viewers, cellwise $F(1, 136) = 9.90, p < .01$ (see Table 9 for means). These findings indicated that higher levels of exposure to specific crime programs are associated with higher levels of urban fear, especially for men and residents of high-crime neighborhoods.

Neighborhood Fear

Total TV viewing. As predicted, there was no main effect of total TV viewing on viewers' fear of their immediate, local environments, $F(1, 136) = 1.09$, ns. The ANOVA on the Neighborhood Fear factor scores revealed that women reported significantly more fear than men ($Ms = .23$ and $- .19$, re-

TABLE 8
Mean Urban Fear by Neighborhood Crime Rate and
Crime Show Viewing

Neighborhood Crime Rate		Crime Show Viewing		
		Light	Moderate	Heavy
High	M	- .24	- .05	.43
	SD	1.19	.99	.88
	n	26	18	28
Low	M	.19	- .14	.00
	SD	.86	.86	.88
	n	26	24	26

TABLE 9
Mean Urban Fear by Crime Show Viewing and Sex

		\multicolumn{3}{c}{Crime Show Viewing}
Sex		Light	Moderate	Heavy
Male	M	−.72	−.48	.05
	SD	1.01	.89	.89
	n	21	22	30
Female	M	.45	.32	.44
	SD	.80	.72	.88
	n	31	20	24

spectively), $F(1, 136) = 11.08$, $p < .001$, and respondents reported more local fear if they lived in high-crime rather than low-crime neighborhoods ($Ms = .36$ and $−.29$, respectively), $F(1, 136) = 21.70$, $p < .001$.

Although the analysis revealed no significant two-way interactions, the three-way interaction was significant, $F(1, 136) = 6.84$, $p < .01$. Cellwise comparisons on the low-crime neighborhood cells revealed no significant differences due to viewing among either men or women. Cellwise comparisons involving high-crime areas, however, uncovered different patterns. Men in dangerous neighborhoods who were heavy viewers reported marginally more fear than light viewers ($Ms = .11$ and $.04$, respectively), cellwise $F(1, 136) = 3.49$, $p < .10$. Women in dangerous neighborhoods who were heavy viewers, on the other hand, reported significantly less fear than light viewers ($Ms = .09$ and $.98$, respectively), cellwise $F(1, 136) = 8.01$, $p < .01$. That is, women who were heavy viewers and lived in high-crime areas reported unexpectedly *low* levels of fear, a finding that runs counter to any formulation of the cultivation hypothesis.

Crime drama viewing. As predicted, general crime drama viewing showed no relationship to fear of the immediate neighborhood, $F(1, 141) = 0.12$, ns. The pattern of findings for the general crime drama viewing analyses strongly supports our hypothesis. General exposure to crime dramas was not related to viewers' fear of their immediate neighborhoods but was related to fear of other neighborhoods in their own city and to fear of more distant urban settings. Using the same measure, Study 2 replicated the findings of the crime drama analyses in Study 1 and suggested that our original findings were not the products of an unreliable or insensitive measure of exposure to TV.

Specific crime show viewing. The analysis of Neighborhood Fear factor scores and specific crime show viewing is entirely consistent with our predictions. Neighborhood Fear scores showed no significant main effect for specific crime show viewing and no significant interaction involving TV. The lack of any relationship between exposure to several specific crime shows and Neighborhood Fear was highly consistent with the findings in Study 1 and with the other analyses in Study 2.

Study 2 predicted that (a) urban fear and local fear are separate, distinct constructs and that (b) heavier doses of TV viewing would be positively related to fear of distant and not so distant urban settings but would not be related to fear of the respondent's immediate neighborhood. The overall pattern of findings from this study strongly supported these predictions. First, the results of the factor analysis on the 20 original items on fear of crime and perceptions of crime (see Table 7) supported our contention that fear of distant urban settings and fear of the immediate neighborhood are substantially different, and, therefore, they cannot be treated equivalently in studies analyzing the relationship between TV and fear of crime.

Second, the results of Study 2 support our predictions for the relationship between TV and fear of distant, urban settings. Total TV viewing and general crime drama viewing were significantly related to Urban Fear factor scores (built with items that referred to distant NYC and to less distant places in Chicago), with more frequent viewers reporting higher levels of urban fear. In addition, although the relationship between specific crime show viewing and urban fear was only marginally significant ($p < .06$), the relationship between crime show viewing and urban fear was significant for men and for residents of high-crime neighborhoods.

Finally, the predictions in regard to neighborhood-based fear were also supported in Study 2. The original cultivation hypothesis predicted that higher levels of viewing (either total viewing or crime drama viewing) would be related to higher levels of fear of crime, including fear of neighborhood-based crime. No such relationship was found in this study. In fact, the only significant relationship found in the analyses of local fear worked in the opposite direction.

GENERAL DISCUSSION

Is Gerbner's assertion that TV viewing cultivates a view of the world as a mean, scary place warranted? The answer, according to these studies, is, "It depends." It depends on the geographic specification of "the world." It depends on the measure of "TV viewing." It depends perhaps on the sex of the respondent. And, finally, it may depend on the actual crime rate in the respondent's own neighborhood. Each of these qualifiers is now discussed in turn.

Geographic Specification of "The World"

The first qualifier for the cultivation effect involves the location of "the world." In our initial reformulation of the cultivation hypothesis, we predicted that viewing would affect perceptions of crime in distant urban settings but would not affect perceptions of crime in the respondent's own city or in the respondent's own neighborhood. The results of these studies clearly demonstrate that the geographic location of fear is a pivotal variable for the cultivation hypothesis. The results, however, lead us to modify our initial reformulation of the cultivation hypothesis. Although TV viewing does not influence perceptions of crime in the immediate neighborhood, we now believe that TV viewing (especially crime drama viewing) influences perceptions of crime in the respondent's own city as well as in more distant cities.

This geographic specification also brings some order to the conflicting results of prior research (see Table 1). Given the documented effects of direct experience compared with indirect experience (e.g., Fazio & Zanna, 1978), the cultivation hypothesis has in essence been put to a very stringent test by use of items on neighborhood-based fear of crime. Although Gerbner and Gross (1976) originally acknowledged this limitation of the cultivation hypothesis, they later claimed to have demonstrated cultivation effects at this specific, neighborhood level (e.g., Gerbner et al., 1978; Gerbner et al., 1980). This expansion of the cultivation hypothesis led other researchers (e.g., Doob & Macdonald, 1979; Hirsch, 1980, 1981; Hughes, 1980) to focus on the more inclusive formulation rather than on the original formulation of the cultivation effect, producing temporary confusion and conflict in the area.

TV World Exposure

"Exposure to the TV view of the world" has been operationalized in previous research as total hours viewed on the previous day, total number of programs viewed per week, average daily viewing, total number of violent shows viewed, and general exposure to various types of programming (see Table 1). The definition (or operationalization) of "TV viewing" embodies certain assumptions about the underlying dynamics of the cultivation effect. Does cultivation operate through social learning of specifics regarding the nature of crime? If so, then measurements of "exposure to the TV world" should arguably be based only on crime drama viewing in research that investigates cultivation effects on perceptions of crime. If the underlying process is social learning, viewing "The Golden Girls" or "Cosby" provides little information to be incorporated into perceptions of crime.

If, however, one assumes that the underlying dynamic is other than social learning (e.g., passivity, relative deprivation) or is a more subtle form of so-

120   HEATH AND PETRAITIS

cial learning (e.g., learning the world is chaotic and hostile), then total TV viewing could be the appropriate measure. Although viewing "Cheers" or "Rhoda" does not present direct images of crime, these shows could convey a sense of chaos and underlying hostility. Similarly, "Dallas" and "Family Feud" both emphasize material possessions and could, therefore, trigger feelings of relative deprivation, leading to perceptions of the world as a generally unfair, mean place.

The results of these studies suggest that measures of crime drama exposure provide more sensitive and more appropriate operationalizations of "TV viewing." The results of Study 1 found that our simple, single-item measure of crime drama viewing was related to NYC-based and city-based fear of crime. The total TV measure, however, was not related to city-based fear but was related to NYC fear. We believe the relationship between total TV and NYC fear is attributable to the high levels of crime drama that contribute to the montage of "total TV." Our total TV measure combined talk shows, game shows, "sitcoms," and other program types, including crime dramas. In fact, our total TV measure was significantly correlated with our specific crime show measure in Study 2 ($r = +.38$, $p < .001$). Because this confounding is significant and positive, we would expect the effects of crime drama viewing to "spill over" into the total TV analyses. But, because this confounding is not perfect, we would also expect the "effects" of total TV to be less robust than the effects of crime drama viewing measures. This is exactly what we found. This suggests that measures of crime drama viewing are more appropriate operationalizations of "TV viewing" and that the relationship between total TV viewing measures and fear of crime can be attributed to the high levels of crime programs in the TV diet.

Sex of the Respondent

Another qualifier to be applied to the cultivation hypothesis involves the sex of the respondent. Throughout these studies, sex of respondent interacted with media exposure in relation to fear of crime. As was mentioned previously, the confirmation of the cultivation hypothesis among men but not among women could be attributable to a ceiling effect among female respondents. This ceiling effect could be artifactual or real. An artifactual ceiling implies that our measures of fear of crime are simply not sensitive enough to reveal a cultivation effect among women, even if the effect exists. This was a distinct possibility in Study 1. In Study 2, however, our indices of fear were constructed through factor analysis. Even when using more sensitive indices of fear, we still found no relationship between specific crime show viewing and urban fear for women.

Another possible explanation for the inconsistent relationship between viewing and fear for women hinges on a real ceiling effect. It is possible that women's fear is really at a maximum level even without considering cultivation effects. That is, women might be so terrified of crime that no further increase in fear is possible. This explanation is unsatisfactory, however, because the mean fear factor scores for women in Study 2 did not approach the statistical ceiling on our Urban Fear and Neighborhood Fear factors.

A final explanation for these findings for women's fear argues that women's fear is at neither an artifactual nor a real ceiling, but rather that it is a true effect. Perhaps TV simply does not affect women's fear in a fashion that is comparable to the effects of TV on men's fear. For example, women might be less affected by TV than men because disproportionately fewer characters in crime dramas are women.

Neighborhood Crime Rate

The final qualifier involves neighborhood crime rate. Doob and Macdonald (1979) hypothesized that Gerbner's cultivation studies found positive relationships between viewing and fear because viewing was confounded with neighborhood crime rates. These researchers argued that more frequent viewers report more fear because they tend to live in more dangerous neighborhoods and not because they watch more TV. Doob and Macdonald tested this hypothesis and found that after controlling for neighborhood crime rates, the relationship between viewing and fear generally disappeared. The relationship did *not* disappear in high-crime areas, however. We found similar patterns. In our second study, we found that specific crime drama viewing was related to urban fear for residents of high-crime neighborhoods but was not related to urban fear for residents of low-crime neighborhoods. These findings lend support to Gerbner's notions of "resonance" whereby similarities between "real-world experiences" and "TV experiences" interact to produce more pronounced media effects.

The findings regarding neighborhood location also lend credence to Tyler and Cook's (1984) suggestion that media messages judged to be personally applicable may indeed affect personal-risk assessments, although general media messages do not affect personal risk. Personal applicability is not limited to but does appear to include geographic similarity.

These studies also raise two additional methodological issues. First, the interactions involving sex, crime rates, and media exposure raise issues with the statistical assumptions of previous research on the cultivation hypothesis. Although Gerbner and his associates have examined media effects using the "cultivation differential" within demographic groupings, other researchers (e.g., Hirsch, 1980; Hughes, 1980) have entered demographics into regression or partial-correlation analyses of media effects. This procedure assumes there are no interactions between demographics and media effects. As this research and Gerbner's investigations regarding "resonance" and "main-

122   HEATH AND PETRAITIS

streaming" show, however, interactions among demographics (in this case, sex and neighborhood crime rate) and media effects do exist. Ignoring these interactions could mask true cultivation effects.

Finally, these studies address the issue of the direction of causality between TV exposure and fear. Cultivation researchers suggest that TV viewing is related to fear because TV viewing (specifically, crime drama viewing) cultivates fear, making TV the cause and fear the effect. Critics argue, however, that viewing might be related to fear only because fearful people stay home and watch more TV, making fear the cause and TV viewing the effect.

Historically, this had been a plausible explanation for the relationship between fear and TV viewing. Selective exposure, however, is not an adequate explanation for our findings. Repeatedly, we found that respondent's neighborhood fear is not related to TV viewing, suggesting that fear of the immediately threatening environment does not systematically increase TV exposure. At the same time, however, we found that TV is related to fear of distant settings. It is highly unlikely that fear of environments 20 or 1,000 miles away causes increased TV exposure and that fear of the immediate environment does not. It seems much more plausible (and much more consistent with our hypothesis) to argue that TV viewing causes perceptions of distant and not so distant settings but does not cause perceptions of the viewer's immediate world. Although we have not eliminated all possible third-variable explanations, we have demonstrated that the selective exposure explanation is inadequate.

In summary, these studies show that although cultivation effects are not universal, exposure to the TV version of reality is related to perceptions of the world "out there." "Out there" includes distant and non-immediate urban settings, but *excludes* the typical immediate neighborhood. Our findings also suggest that "out there" *does* include immediate neighborhoods if those neighborhoods look like the crime-ridden neighborhoods depicted on TV. Although frequent TV viewers come to believe in the "mean" world, most of them do not live in it. Rather, frequent viewers tend to see their own worlds as havens in the midst of the violence "out there."

ACKNOWLEDGMENTS

Study 1 was supported by National Science Foundation Grant DAR 8011225 and by a University of Minnesota Graduate School grant to the first author. Study 2 was supported by a Loyola University grant to the first author.

The authors thank Amy Blythe, Teresa Crimmins, Allison Langley, and Kristen Ragozzino for assistance in data collection in Study 1; Natalia Bandura, Tom Gasior, Jeff Pawlak, and Christopher Willson for assistance

TELEVISION AND FEAR OF CRIME 123

in data collection and data analysis in Study 2; and Anthony Doob, George Gerbner, Michael Morgan, and Steven Brown for helpful comments on earlier drafts of this article.

REFERENCES

Comstock, G., Chaffee, S., Katzman, N., McCombs, M., & Roberts, D. (1978). *Television and human behavior*. New York: Columbia University Press.

Doob, A. N., & Macdonald, G. E. (1979). Television viewing and fear of victimization: Is the relationship causal? *Journal of Personality and Social Psychology, 37,* 170–179.

Fazio, R., & Zanna, M. P. (1978). Attitude qualities relating to the strength of attitude–behavior relationship. *Journal of Experimental Social Psychology, 14,* 398–408.

Gerbner, G., & Gross, L. (1976). Living with television: The violence profile. *Journal of Communication, 26,* 173–199.

Gerbner, G., Gross, L., Eleey, M. F., Fox, S., Jackson-Beeck, M., & Signorielli, N. (1976). *Trends in network television drama and viewer conceptions of social reality. Violence profile no. 7.* Philadelphia: University of Pennsylvania, Annenberg School of Communications.

Gerbner, G., Gross, L., Eleey, M. F., Jackson-Beeck, M., Jefferies-Fox, S., & Signorielli, N. (1977). TV violence profile no. 8: The highlights. *Journal of Communication, 27,* 171–180.

Gerbner, G., Gross, L., Jackson-Beeck, M., Jefferies-Fox, S., & Signorielli, N. (1978). Cultural indicators: Violence profile no. 9. *Journal of Communication, 28,* 176–207.

Gerbner, G., Gross, L., Morgan, M., & Signorielli, N. (1980). The "mainstreaming" of America: Violence profile no. 11. *Journal of Communication, 30,* 10–27.

Hawkins, R. P., & Pingree, S. (1981). Uniform messages and habitual viewing: Unnecessary assumptions in social reality effects. *Human Communication Research, 7,* 291–301.

Heath, L. (1984). Impact of newspaper crime reports on fear of crime: Multimethodological investigation. *Journal of Personality and Social Psychology, 47,* 263–276.

Hirsch, P. (1980). The "scary world" of the nonviewer and other anomalies: A reanalysis of Gerbner et al.'s findings on the cultivation analysis, Part I. *Communication Research, 7,* 403–456.

Hirsch, P. (1981). On not learning from one's own mistakes: A reanalysis of Gerbner et al.'s findings on the cultivation analysis, Part II. *Communication Research, 8,* 3–37.

Hughes, M. (1980). The fruits of cultivation analysis: A reexamination of some effects of television viewing. *Public Opinion Quarterly, 44,* 287–302.

Pingree, S., & Hawkins, R. (1981). U.S. programs on Australian television: The cultivation effect. *Journal of Communication, 31,* 97–107.

Tyler, T. (1980). Impact of directly and indirectly experienced events: The origin of crime-related judgments and behaviors. *Journal of Personality and Social Psychology, 39,* 13–28.

Tyler, T. R., & Cook, F. L. (1984). The mass media and judgments of risk: Distinguishing impact on personal and societal level judgments. *Journal of Personality and Social Psychology, 47,* 693–708.

Wober, M., & Gunter, B. (1982). Television and personal threat: Fact or artifact: A British survey. *British Journal of Social Psychology, 21,* 239–247.

[13]

Feeling Safe by Comparison: Crime in the Newspapers*

ALLEN E. LISKA, *State University of New York, Albany*

WILLIAM BACCAGLINI, *New York State Division for Youth*

Fear of crime has emerged as a significant social issue. Survey research suggests that it has significantly increased since the mid-1960s and that it has become a component of the stresses, strains, and health of contemporary urban life. Causal research, for the most part, treats fear as a characteristic of individuals and examines how it is affected by other individual characteristics, such as age, sex, class, and race. Our research treats fear as a characteristic of social units (cities) and examines how it is affected by the structural and cultural characteristics of those units, such as crime rates and the newspaper coverage of crime. The sample consists of the 26 cities used in the National Crime Survey (NCS). Data on the fear of crime are obtained from the NCS; data on structural characteristics are obtained from a variety of sources, including the Uniform Crime Reports (UCR), NCS, and the U.S. census; and data on newspaper coverage are obtained from a content analysis of the newspapers of the 26 cities. The results show that the effect of newspaper coverage is complex, with some forms of coverage increasing fear and other forms of coverage decreasing fear, and that the effect of official crime rates is mediated through the newspaper coverage of crime.

Over the last fifteen to twenty years fear of crime has emerged as an important research topic. Surveys (Harris, Gallop, National Opinion Research Center [NORC], and the National Crime Survey [NCS]) report that a high percentage of the U.S. population fear criminal victimization and that this percentage has increased since the mid-1960s (Hartnagel 1979; Baumer 1985; Skogan and Maxfield 1981; Miethe and Lee 1984; Warr and Stafford 1982; Yin 1985).

Since the 1960s considerable causal research has appeared. Most studies examine the variation in fear between individuals and link it to personality and socio-demographic characteristics. The best of these studies use multivariate statistical techniques and large samples, frequently analyzing NORC and NCS data. They generally report that fear is highest among the lonely, dissatisfied, alienated, and anxious, and among females, the elderly, non-whites, and the poor (see Yin 1985; Kennedy and Silverman 1985; Miethe and Lee 1984; see Baumer 1985 for recent reviews of this large literature).

A few studies examine the variation in fear across sites and situations. They report that the fear of crime varies significantly between macro units, such as neighborhoods (Taylor, Gottfredson, and Brower 1984; Skogan and Maxfield 1981; Hough and Mayhew 1985) and cities (Garofalo 1979; Skogan and Maxfield 1981; Liska, Lawrence, and Sanchirico 1982). Variation across these macro units is particularly important because a persistent high level of fear in a neighborhood or city can become a part of its culture, thereby constraining and altering its patterns of social life, such as its social solidarity, social cohesiveness, migration patterns, and business activity (Hartnagel 1979; Conklin 1975; Skogan and Maxfield 1981). Variation in fear across such units is the subject of this paper.

---

* This research was supported by a grant from the National Institute of Aging (AGO5R014067). Correspondence to: Liska, Department of Sociology, State University of New York, Albany, 12222.

Social Structure

Some research examines the effects of structural characteristics of macro units, such as crime rates, social disorganization, and racial composition, on fear. While it seems reasonable to assume that variation in the fear of crime across macro units should reflect similar variation in their crime rates, studies of neighborhoods (Skogan and Maxfield 1981; Taylor, Gottfredson, and Brower 1984) and cities (Garofalo 1979; Liska, Lawrence, and Sanchirico 1982) show that the effect of crime rates on fear is weak. These findings are consistent with those from studies of individuals. They show that those who experience victimization, directly or vicariously through the communicated experiences of interpersonal others, experience somewhat higher fear than those who do not, but that these relationships are weak (Yin 1985; Kennedy and Silverman 1985; Meithe and Lee 1984; Baumer 1985).

Unable to clearly connect fear to crime rates at either the macro or micro levels, some researchers (Garofalo and Laub 1979; Taylor and Hale 1986) argue that "the fear of crime is more than fear of crime," meaning it is part of a psychological syndrome of anxiety, worry, and nervousness, termed "urban unease," associated with the disorganization and the physical and social disabilities of contemporary urban life. Symbols of disorder and crime, such as teenagers on the street, abandoned buildings, graffiti, use of illegal drugs, public drunkenness, and vandalism, are thought to increase urban unease and, with it, the fear of crime. While the findings of these studies also are mixed, they do suggest some interesting directions for research. Some studies examine the effects of perceptions of instability (Taylor and Hale 1986; Skogan and Maxfield 1981), and others examine the effects of objective indicators of instability and disorganization, such as the presence of street gangs, large size buildings, physical decay, vacant buildings, and ethnic heterogeneity (Skogan and Maxfield 1981; Smith and Gray 1985).

Still other researchers argue that many of the above conditions are not just associated with general social disorganization, leading to general unease and anxiety, but that they are directly associated or perceived to be directly associated with street crimes, leading directly to the fear of crime. This argument is explicitly made in regard to race. Swigert and Farrell (1976) argue that public belief systems and stereotypes link non-whites with dangerous street crime in the U.S. Lizotte and Bordua (1980) argue that just the presence of non-whites may heighten whites' perception of their risk of victimization. Liska, Lawrence, and Sanchirico (1982) argue that the visibility and day-to-day presence of non-whites, as measured by the percentage of non-whites and segregation, increases the fear of crime of whites and non-whites.

Culture

Cultural theory suggests that once beliefs, values, ideas, and ideologies become norms in a macro unit, they can persist over time and generations through the normal processes of socialization. To some extent, beliefs and fear of crime may also be part of the socialization process. Little research has been directed toward this issue, with the exception of some research on the mass media.

This research examines the extent to which official crime rates affect the coverage of crime in the media and the extent to which the latter in turn affects people's attitudes, ideas, beliefs and fears about crime (see Graber 1980; Garofalo 1981 for reviews). Few firm conclusions have come from this work. Although it seems reasonable to assume that crime rates affect media coverage of crime, a considerable proportion of the variation in media coverage between cities is unaffected by crime rates; and although it seems reasonable to assume that people's images of crime are influenced by the mass media, research reports are mixed. Studies report numerous inconsistent findings regarding the effects of media coverage on people's perceptions of the crime rate, images of the typical offender and victim, and evaluations of the seriousness of crime relative to other social problems (Graber 1980; Rochier 1973; Gordon and Heath 1981, Baker et al. 1983; Skogan and Maxfield 1981; Garofalo 1981). Much of this research is not directly focused on the fear of crime and examines variation in coverage between only a few cities (Skogan and Maxfield 1981; and Gordon and Heath 1981) or over time in only one city (Baker et al. 1983) or state (Davis 1952)

We know of only one study that examines the relationship between fear of crime and the media coverage of crime among a substantial number of cities. Heath (1984) studied the effect of newspaper coverage of crime on fear in 26 different cities. The findings are mixed but intriguing; two are particularly noteworthy: the total number of crime stories did not affect fear; the proportion of crime stories in which the crimes are local, the proportion in which crimes are random (not stating whether or not the victim took some action that made him or her more or less vulnerable), and the proportion in which crimes are sensational (bizarre or violent) interact to affect fear, especially fear downtown. When the proportion of local crime stories was high, the proportions that are random and sensational increased fear; when the proportion of local crime stories was low, they decreased fear. Heath (1984) argues that it is the relative, and not the absolute, number of stories about crimes that people cannot avoid by taking rational evasive action, and it is the relative number of stories about sensational crime that are important. If they occur in one's own city they produce fear; if they occur elsewhere, people feel safe by comparison.

While Heath's study makes a major contribution to understanding the relationship between crime in the newspaper and fear of crime, it includes some significant sampling and measurement problems that may account for some of the findings. The sample of newspapers and respondents is very small. Only seven editions from each city over a month are content analyzed, and only 15-18 people from each city are interviewed. The characteristics of crime stories are measured as proportions, i.e., the proportions that are local, random, and sensational. This procedure obscures the effect of the absolute number of local, random, and sensational crime stories, and it assumes that a paper that reports two local crimes and one non-local crime has the same effect on fear as a paper that reports 200 local and 100 non-local crimes. The proportions are equal. While the absolute number of crime stories or even types of crime stories, like robbery, may not be very important, the absolute number of local, random, and sensational crime stories may be more important than the proportions of local to non-local, random to non-random, and sensational to non-sensational stories.

Our research builds on this study. First and foremost, we were intrigued by the above interaction effect, but we also felt that the general finding needed further and firmer empirical support. We thus examined the extent to which fear is affected by both the number of local crime stories and the number of non-local crime stories, and by both the number of violent crime stories and the number of non-violent crime stories. Following Heath (1984), we hypothesized that fear is affected more by the number of violent than non-violent crime stories and that fear is positively affected by the number of local stories and negatively affected by the number of non-local stories. We further hypothesized that fear is affected more by the number of initial crime stories than by the number of follow-up stories, and more by the number of crime stories that appear in the first part of the paper than the number that appear in the back sections. Stories in the front section are accessible and formulated to attract attention and thus are more likely to be read than are stories in the back sections.

Additionally, we examined the extent to which crime rates influence newspaper coverage and the extent to which coverage in turn mediates the effect of crime rates on fear. Some research (Davis 1952; Baker et al., 1983) suggests that newspaper coverage of crime is only weakly linked to the crime rate and thus that newspaper coverage of crime can mediate only a small proportion of the effect of crime rates on fear.

To determine the generalizability and scope conditions of our findings, we further examined these effects and mediation processes by social status (race, age, and gender). We hypothesized that the newspaper effect on fear is strongest for statuses least likely to experience victimization directly or vicariously through the victimization of friends and family, namely, for whites, the elderly, and females (see Miethe, Stafford, and Long 1987). These statuses are more likely to rely on the media for crime information.

In sum, the focus of this paper is on the newspaper coverage of crime: (1) the extent to which the characteristics of coverage affect fear; (2) the extent to which the characteristics of coverage mediate the effect of crime rates on fear; and (3) the extent to which these effects and mediational processes are contingent on social status.

Methods

Sample

The sample consists of the 26 major U.S. cities included in the National Crime Survey, which is sponsored and directed by the Bureau of the Census. The survey, conducted during 1974 and 1975, includes about 10,000 respondents 16 years of age and older from each of the 26 cities. While the number of cities is not large, it is the largest sample of cities for which data on fear of crime are available.

Measures

Fear of crime. Over the last five years most measures of fear, including the NCS measures, have been criticized for emphasizing general fear rather than fear of specific crimes; for not distinguishing the affective-emotional component (feeling of anxiety associated with being in a dangerous situation) from the cognitive component (beliefs about the risk of being victimized); for measuring only the cognitive component; and for using single, rather than multiple, item scales (Ferraro and LaGrange 1987). While we generally agree with these criticisms, we also feel that there is much to be learned by studying the cognitive component of fear, especially as a part of the NCS dataset. The cognitive component is very important; indeed, it may play a critical role in constraining social behavior (Liska, Reed, and Sanchirico 1988). We also feel that these criticisms of the fear measure should be balanced against the other virtues of a study. What is sometimes forgotten is the size and scope of the NCS study. It is the only U.S. study that measures fear over a substantial number of cities. As such it is the only U.S. study that allows significant macro questions to be addressed systematically, such as the effect of crime reported in the media on the variation of fear across cities. We think that these questions are important enough to warrant the use of items that measure general rather than specific fear of crime and that do not clearly distinguish the affective and cognitive components.

The fear level of each city is measured by adding the means of the following two items in the NCS: "How safe do you feel or would you feel being out alone in your neighborhood at night?" "How safe do you feel or would you feel being out alone in your neighborhood during the day?" Responses were coded as very safe, safe, unsafe, or very unsafe. Although the term, crime, is not included in the items, they are preceded by items on crime trends, which are introduced with the phrase, "Now I'd like to get your opinions about crime in general." It is therefore unlikely that respondents could be thinking about dangers other than crime in answering these items. The two items correlate .91 across the 26 cities.

Crime rates. Crime counts were collected and rates were calculated from the NCS and the Uniform Crime Reports for the years, 1973 and 1974, directly preceding the years during which the fear data were collected. So as to emphasize serious crimes, only the seven index crimes were used. We examined both absolute crime counts and crime rates, because there is no research on the extent to which people, in thinking about the crime problem, mentally standardize crime by the population of their city. It seems reasonable that they do, but only to some extent. Two homicides, for example, probably have more effect on people in a small town than in a large city. However, cognitive standardization is probably quite rough so that two homicides may have no more impact on people in a city of 1/2 million than in a city of one million. Because the cities in our sample are all among the very largest in the United States, we feel that standardizing crime by the population is probably inappropriate. Yet, because there is no data on this issue, we examined the effects of both absolute counts and rates on fear.

Media. The crime stories of the largest circulating daily newspaper in each of the 26 cities were content analyzed. Twenty-five editions of the leading newspaper from each city were selected randomly from a sampling frame of 365 days preceding the quarter in which the NCS data on fear were collected in that city.

Very little work has examined either the way in which people actually read newspapers or the manner in which crime stories are distributed throughout them. Nonetheless, it seems reasonable to assume both that a story's placement in the paper affects its readership and impact on fear (Swanson 1955) and that stories that appear towards the front or in the first section receive the largest general readership. Because newspapers differ in style and format (that is, in the use of the front page, the number of sections, and the number of pages), it is difficult to establish criteria for dividing newspapers into parts or sections that are meaningful for all of them. In the interest of reflecting the style and format of most newspapers, we analyzed separately those stories appearing in the first fifteen pages and those appearing in the balance of the paper. Each newspaper was coded for the total number of crime articles in the first fifteen pages and in the total newspaper, for the total number of specific crime articles, and for the total number of multiple crime articles. Eighteen crime story categories, including ten single crime categories (e.g., murder, rape, robbery) and eight multiple categories (e.g., murder-rape, murder-robbery) are used.

Each crime article was also coded as local or non-local and as an initial report or a follow-up of a crime previously reported. The number of cities included in the study made it difficult to distinguish local from non-local crime stories based upon our familiarity with either the perceived or real geographic boundaries of each study area. Consequently, an alternative strategy was used. Stories were treated as non-local when the byline indicated that the original source is either a wire service or another newspaper outside of the area. Stories not so designated were additionally reviewed to identify information that might indicate they are non-local (i.e., specific mention of another city or known area outside the city boundaries). All articles not classified as non-local using this two-step process were considered to be local.

Statuses. The statuses (race, age, and gender) of respondents were measured by items in the NCS questionnaire.

Control Variables. Liska, Lawrence, and Sanchirico (1982) report that the racial structure of a city (percent non-white, and segregation) affects the fear of crime; and considerable research links racial structures and crime rates (Blau and Blau 1982). Hence, to estimate the effect of crime rates on fear, the racial structure of a city should be controlled. Percent non-white was taken from the U.S. Census, and city segregation was measured as the dissimilarity between distributions of non-white and white households among city blocks, that is, the extent to which the racial composition of city blocks reflects the racial composition of the city as a whole.

Analysis

Since the fear items refer to neighborhoods it might be argued that the analysis should be on the neighborhood rather than the city level. High fear may be a rational response to high crime levels of some neighborhoods and a somewhat irrational response to psychological factors and the social characteristics of other neighborhoods. This question, however, can also be studied with city level crime rates, assuming that individuals, and thus neighborhoods, are randomly sampled (which they are in the NCS). If the variance in neighborhood level crime rates affects the between-neighborhood variance in fear, then the variance in city level crime rates should affect the between-city level variance in fear. Equally important, the crime content of newspapers, which is the subject matter of this research, is a city level characteristic, which requires that the analysis be at the city level.

The analysis was divided into two parts. First, we examined the extent to which characteristics of newspaper coverage affected the fear of crime and the extent to which these effects were contingent on social status. Second, we examined the extent to which newspaper coverage mediated the effect of crime rates on fear and the extent to which the mediational process was contingent on social status.

Results

First, consider the variation in both the fear of crime and newspaper coverage of crime between these cities. To appreciate the between-city variation in fear, it is simplest to examine the percentage feeling unsafe. The percentage feeling very unsafe during the day varies from 0.4 percent to 5.3 percent with a mean of 2.4 percent; and the percentage feeling very unsafe during the night varies from 12 percent to 30 percent with a mean of 22 percent. Fear of crime in large cities is clearly a night time phenomenon that varies considerably from city to city. While we used eighteen different single and multiple crime categories in the causal analysis, in the interest of brevity we here collapse them into eight categories.

Most of the categories used here are self-explanatory (see Table 1). Homicide, rape, assault, and robbery refer to stories that report single (e.g., homicide) or multiple crimes (e.g., homicide and rape). Multiple crime stories are categorized by the most serious crime. For example, a homicide-rape story is classified as a homicide. Multiple crime stories constituted

Table 1 • Univariate Characteristics of Crime Stories

	Means	SD	Range	Number
Homicide	71.0	16.6	36-104	1,848
Rape	4.1	2.1	1-9	108
Assault	3.2	2.2	0-10	84
Robbery	25.2	12.5	9-65	656
Drugs	11.7	7.6	2-28	306
Family	5.9	5.77	1-27	155
White Collar	33.1	15.5	9-67	863
Multiple-Other	4.5	1.9	1-9	116
Other	78.2	21.6	38-116	2,033
Total	237.3	59.5	122-359	6,169

a very small fraction of the crime stories; nonetheless, they are analyzed separately. "Family" refers to stories about crimes between family members, such as a family disturbance, that do not fall under any of the other categories; "multiple-other" refers to stories that reported two or more crimes that are not easily classified under any of the other categories; and "other" refers to a myriad of other crimes, including kidnapping and motor vehicle theft.

There is considerable variation across the cities in all of the categories, and homicide stories are by far the most common type of crime story, with a mean of 71.1, a standard deviation of 16.5, and a range of 36 to 104 (based on a random sample of 25 editions from each city). To obtain a yearly estimate, multiply them by 14.6.

Effects of Media Coverage

Because the sample includes only 26 cities, the effects of all the characteristics of coverage cannot be examined simultaneously. Thus, using correlations and regressions, we first located the most important characteristics of coverage. The pattern of correlation is clear and confirmed by various regressions. Of the various types of crime stories, homicide stories show by far the strongest relationship to fear. (This finding is consistent with findings on public perceptions of the seriousness of crime: Homicide by far shows the highest seriousness and the strongest consensus [Sellin and Wolfgang 1964; Rossi et al. 1974]). This relationship is positive for stories in the first fifteen pages of the paper and negative for stories in the remainder of the paper. The positive relationship in the first fifteen pages is stronger for local stories than for non-local stories and for initial reports than for follow-ups. For example, the correlation between fear and all homicide stories on the first fifteen pages is .19. For initial homicide stories on the first fifteen pages the correlation is .33, and for local initial stories on the first fifteen pages the correlation is .59.[1]

To clarify the pattern, we estimated a series of regressions: first, regressing fear on both initial and follow-up homicide stories on the first fifteen pages, and, second, regressing fear on both local and non-local homicide stories for the first fifteen pages (Table 2, panels 1 and 2, respectively). As expected, the effect of local stories is strongly positive (beta = .49), and the effect of non-local stories is moderately negative (beta = −.25); and the effect for initial stories (beta = .35) is stronger than the effect of follow-ups (beta = −.05).[2] To further clarify the findings, we disaggregated local and non-local stories into initial and follow-up stories (Table 2, panel 3). Again, as expected, initial local stories have by far the strongest positive effect, and, interestingly, the negative effect of non-local stories is mainly the effect of follow-up stories rather than initial stories. It may very well be that in order for non-local homicides to be followed-up in the media they must be sensational. Since sensational stories probably have a stronger effect than non-sensational stories do (Heath 1984), it follows that follow-up non-local stories have a stronger comparative effect than initial non-local stories do.

We also hypothesized that media effects may be stronger for those categories of people least likely to directly or vicariously experience victimization (whites, females, and the elderly). With one exception, there is little empirical support for this hypothesis; indeed, the above pattern of findings is evident for whites and non-whites, for males and females, and for the young, the middle-aged, and the aged (Table 3).[3]

These findings significantly extend those from Heath's study. Both her and our studies

1. For the other index violent crimes (rape, robbery and assault) the correlation between fear and initial local stories is weaker (approximately .15), and for the other crimes it is much weaker.

2. With a small sample size of 26 cities, critical values of statistical significance are difficult to reach. Hence, we report whether or not b estimates exceed a liberal level (b > 1.0 SE), a somewhat moderate level (b > 1.5 SE), and a more traditional level (b > 2.0 SE) of statistical significance. Using a one-tailed test, the significant SE values are 1.318 at the .10 level, 1.711 at the .05 level, and 2.064 at the .025 level when two independent variables are used, and 1.321, 1.717, and 2.074, respectively, when four independent variables are used.

3. The exception is the effect of follow-up local stories. Conforming to our hypothesis, they showed much greater

Table 2 • *Effect of Media Coverage of Homicide on Fear of Crime*

	b	Beta
Initial Report	.019[b]	.35
Follow-up Report	.002	−.05
(R²)		(.11)
Local Report	.015[a]	.49
Non-Local Report	−.009[c]	−.25
(R²)		(.35)
Initial Local Report	.038[a]	.47[a]
Follow-up Local Report	.005	.12
Initial Non-Local Report	−.003	−.03
Follow-up Non-Local Report	−.011[c]	−.26
(R²)		(.44)

Notes:
   a. b > 2 times SE.
   b. b > 1.5 times SE.
   c. b > 1 times SE.

report that the total number of crime stories did not affect fear and that local and non-local stories differentially affected fear. Heath found that the effect of the proportion of stories about random and sensational crimes depends on the proportion that is local. When the latter was high, the effect of the proportion of stories about random or sensational crimes was positive; and when the latter was low, the effect of the proportion of stories about random or sensational crimes was negative. These conclusions are unnecessarily limited by expressing the variables as proportions. For very violent crimes (homicide) our findings clearly show that the effect of coverage on fear simply depends on whether crime is local or non-local. Local homicide stories increased fear, and non-local homicide stories decreased fear. This pattern of findings holds for both racial groups, both genders, and all three age categories, while it is somewhat tempered by whether the local or non-local crime story was an initial report or a follow-up.

In sum, while homicide constituted only .02 percent of all index crimes, it constituted 29.9 percent of all crime stories. (This is consistent with Graber's [1980] extensive content analysis of the crime news in the Chicago Tribune. Homicide constituted 0.2 percent of the reported index crimes in Chicago and 26.2 percent of the crime stories in the Tribune.) It is very clear that fear was much more affected by homicide stories than by any other kind of crime story. It is equally clear that the effect is positive for only initial local reports in the first part of the newspaper, which constituted only 10 percent of all homicide stories and only 2.9 percent of all crime stories sampled; hence, while crime stories fill newspapers, fear of crime is positively affected by only a small proportion of them. It is also clear and equally interesting that fear was affected negatively by non-local homicides. It appears, as Heath (1984) suggests, that crime in other cities makes people feel safe by comparison.

Mediational Effects

We first examined the effects of homicide (absolute counts and rates), percent non-white, and segregation on fear for the total sample, and then by race, gender, and age. The effects of

effect on fear of crime by whites than by non-whites, by females than males, and by the aged than the young or middle-aged.

Table 3 • Effect of Media Coverage of Homicide on Fear

| | Race | | | | Gender | | | | Age | | | | | |
| | Non-White | | White | | Female | | Male | | Young | | Middle-Aged | | Old | |
	b	Beta	b	Beta	b	Beta	b	Beta	b	Beta	b	Beta	b	Beta
I	.028ᵃ	.44	.012ᶜ	.25	.019ᵇ	.35	.018ᵇ	.32	.020ᵃ	.40	.015ᶜ	.25	.018ᵇ	.30
F	−.009ᶜ	−.24	.003	.12	.00	.00	−.004	−.11	−.005	−.17	.00	.00	.002	.06
(R²)		(.14)		(.09)		(.12)		(.09)		(.15)		(.06)		(.11)
L	.013ᵃ	.37	.015ᵃ	.57	.015ᵃ	.51	.013ᵃ	.41	.010ᵇ	.36	.016ᵃ	.49	.016ᵃ	.51
NL	−.011ᶜ	−.29	−.002	−.19	−.058ᶜ	−.17	−.010ᵇ	−.29	−.006ᶜ	−.21	−.11ᵇ	−.29	−.005	−.14
(R²)		(.28)		(.42)		(.33)		(.31)		(.21)		(.39)		(.31)
IL	.051ᵃ	.55	.026ᵇ	.37	.032ᵇ	.41	.048ᵃ	.57	.036ᵃ	.49	.040ᵃ	.45	.029ᵇ	.34
FL	−.003	−.07	.010ᵇ	.30	.007	.19	−.001	−.02	−.001	−.03	.006	.15	.011ᶜ	.24
INL	.002	.02	−.005	−.07	.002	.03	−.012	−.14	.002	.03	−.012	−.13	.003	.03
FNL	−.019ᵃ	−.36	−.006	−.15	−.009ᶜ	−.22	−.010ᶜ	−.22	−.011ᶜ	−.28	−.011ᶜ	−.22	−.009	−.19
(R²)		(.48)		(.44)		(.40)		(.35)		(.36)		(.45)		(.35)

Notes:
I = initial report; F = follow-up report; L = local report; NL = non-local report.
a. b > 2 times SE.
b. b > 1.5 times SE.
c. b > 1.0 times SE.

Table 4 • *Effect of Media Coverage of Homicide Controlling for Racial Structure and Homicide Counts*

Total

	b	Beta	b	Beta
HM	.030[a]	.35	.010	.12
SEG	.001	.01	.001	.03
% NW	.012	.64	.010[a]	.55
IL			.027[a]	.34
FNL			-.009[b]	-.19
(R²)	(.60)		(.71)	

Race

	Whites				Non-Whites			
	b	Beta	b	Beta	b	Beta	b	Beta
HM	.020[b]	.31	.006	.09	.043[a]	.45	.018[c]	.19
SEG	-.006[c]	-.20	-.005[c]	-.18	.012[a]	.32	.012[a]	.34
% NW	.010[a]	.56	.008	.47	.008[a]	.35	.005[b]	.24
IL			.025	.36			.035[a]	.37
FNL			-.006[c]	-.16			-.012[b]	-.24
(R²)	(.45)		(.57)		(.55)		(.71)	

Table 4 • Effect of Media Coverage of Homicide Controlling for Racial Structure and Homicide Counts (continued)

Gender

	Females				Males			
	b	Beta	b	Beta	b	Beta	b	Beta
HM	.024[b]	.30	.006	.08	.037[a]	.43	.020[b]	.24
SEG	.001	.02	−.001	.04	.002	.05	−.001	−.03
% NW	.010[a]	.57	.009[a]	.48	.013[a]	.65	.001[a]	.57
IL			.028[a]	.37			.024[a]	.29
FNL			−.007[c]	−.16			−.008[b]	−.18
(R²)	(.48)		(.60)		(.67)		(.76)	

Age

	Young				Middle Aged				Old			
	b	Beta	b	Beta	b	Beta	b	Beta	b	Beta	b	Beta
HM	.029[a]	.37	.015	.20	.032[a]	.35	.013[c]	.14	.021[b]	.24	.003	.04
SEG	.006[b]	.20	.007[b]	.21	−.001	−.03	.001	−.02	−.005	−.16	−.005	−.14
% NW	.016[a]	.58	.009[a]	.51	.014[a]	.66	.012[a]	.58	.012	.61	.010[a]	.52
IL			.020[a]	.27			.027[a]	.30			.028[a]	.33
FNL			−.006[c]	−.14			−.101[b]	−.21			−.007[c]	−.15
(R²)	(.65)		(.72)		(.62)		(.73)		(.45)		(.55)	

Notes:
I = initial report; F = follow-up report; L = local report; SEG = segregation; %NW = percent nonwhite; Hm = Homicide counts (for b move decimal two places to the left).
a. b > 2 times SE.
b. b > 1.5 times SE.
c. b > 1.0 times SE.

homicide counts and rates are similar, with the effect of counts being somewhat stronger; hence, we focused on counts. For the total sample, homicide counts and percent non-white show a strong effect and segregation shows no effect (Table 4, first half of each panel). This pattern of findings is not contingent on gender and age but is partially contingent on race. The effect of segregation was negative for whites and positive for non-whites, which is consistent with findings reported by Liska, Lawrence, and Sanchirico (1982).

Now, to what extent is the consistently strong effect of local homicide counts mediated by the coverage of local homicide? Drawing on the previous analysis, we included both initial coverage of local homicide on the first fifteen pages and follow-up coverage of non-local homicide on the first fifteen pages in the equations. We included the former because it shows the strongest effect in the previous analysis and, theoretically, it is the logical mediator of the effect of the local homicide count on fear; and we included the latter to observe whether its moderately strong negative effect holds up when the local homicide count and the racial composition variables are included in the equation.

The findings are very clear. With these two newspaper coverage variables in the equations, the effect of the homicide count on fear drops substantially for the total sample and for each racial, gender, or age subsample. For the total sample the beta drops from .35 to .12; for whites it drops from .31 to .09; for non-whites it drops from .45 to .19; for females it drops from .30 to .08; for males it drops from .43 to .24; for the young it drops from .37 to .20; for the middle-aged it drops from .35 to .14; and for the elderly it drops from .24 to .04. (This pattern is exactly the same when homicide rates are substituted for homicide counts.) Of the two newspaper coverage variables, initial local coverage is the major mediator. The homicide count is most highly correlated with it (r = .50), and it shows the strongest effect on fear (e.g., beta = .34 for the total sample).

Note, however, that follow-up non-local coverage, too, plays some mediating role. This occurs because the local homicide count is negatively linked to it. As the local homicide count increases, the non-local homicide coverage decreases (-.25). Because of limits on the total space devoted to crime coverage, especially for the first fifteen pages (Graber 1980), a high local homicide count leaves little space for the coverage of non-local homicide. Therefore, by decreasing non-local coverage, which decreases fear, the local homicide count indirectly increases fear. For example, for the total sample the homicide rate beta drops from .35 (statistically significant) to .18 (not significant) when initial local coverage is included in the equation and to .12 (not significant) when initial local coverage and follow-up non-local coverage are both included in the equation.

It is further interesting to note that, while the newspaper coverage effect is not contingent on status, the mediational effect of newspaper coverage is partially contingent on status. Upon controlling for newspaper coverage, the homicide count shows little to no effect for whites, females, and the old (the statuses least likely to experience victimization directly or indirectly through communication with friends and relatives), but still shows a moderate effect, which is statistically significant, for non-whites, males, and the young (the statuses most likely to experience victimization directly or indirectly through communication with friends). For the latter statuses the homicide count affects fear both through direct experience and communicated experience of friends and relatives, and through the newspaper coverage of homicide.

Discussion

In sum, our research shows that among crime stories it is homicide stories that have the strongest effect on the fear of crime. Local stories have a positive effect that is accentuated both for stories in the first part of the newspaper and for initial stories; and non-local stories have a negative effect that is accentuated both for stories in the first part of the newspaper and for follow-up stories. The strong effect of the homicide count on fear is mediated by the initial coverage of local homicide and by the follow-up coverage of non-local homicide in the first part of the paper. This pattern of findings holds for whites and non-whites, males and females, and the young, the middle-aged, and the elderly; however, the mediation effect is weakest for those statuses most likely to experience victimization directly or indirectly through communication with friends and relatives.

These findings have important implications. They suggest that, while crime stories flood newspapers, fear is affected positively by only initial local homicide stories in the first part of the newspaper, which constitute only 10 percent of all homicide stories and 2.9 percent of all crime stories.

And, as suggested by Heath (1984), it seems that the newspaper coverage of crime in other cities makes people feel safe by comparison. This process may explain the low level of fear in small urban and rural areas where homicide rates are not always that much lower than those in large urban areas. Because rural communities may not experience enough homicides to fill the space devoted to crime coverage in their newspapers, a higher proportion of the homicide coverage in rural newspapers may be of non-local homicides, generally homicides in the largest city of the state. Reading about urban homicides and crime in the newspaper, and hearing about it on the radio and TV, rural residents may feel safe by comparison. That is, they may feel safe, not because crime in their locality is low, but because it seems lower than elsewhere. This process also may explain the inconsistent findings in the literature regarding the effect of media coverage of crime on fear. Most studies simply do not distinguish local from non-local coverage. If the effect of local coverage is positive and the effect of non-local coverage is negative, then their net effect, as suggested by our research, may well be small and insignificant.

Generally, beliefs about crime may be part of urban culture in the sense that they vary between social, political, and geographical units and in the sense that they are partially shaped by the media coverage of crime, which is only moderately related to the crime count in these units. The newspapers in some cities report a higher number of local homicide stories, especially in the first part of the paper, than do the newspapers of other cities. This coverage pattern probably contributes substantially to the image of some cities as high crime and dangerous places and to the image of others as low crime and safe places in much the same way that media coverage contributes to the image of some cities as clean, conservative, progressive, polluted, or politically corrupt. A city's social image or reputation as crime-ridden and dangerous not only affects the fear of crime, as suggested by this research, but also probably affects general patterns of social life, such as economic development, migrations, residential patterns, politics, and cultural activities.

Appendix A: Correlation Matrix[a]

	Fear	IL	FL	INL	FNL	HM	SEG	%NW
Fear	—							
IL	.59*	—						
FL	.43*	.52*	—					
INL	−.10	.10	−.16	—				
FNL	−.41*	−.24	−.22	.39*	—			
HM	.44*	.49*	.09	−.29	−.33*	—		
SEG	.18	.02	−.30	.11	−.09	.10	—	
%NW	.69*	.26	.17	−.01	−.17	.15	.22	—

Notes:

    a. For the description of variables, see the legend for Table 4.

    * Significant at the .05 level.

References

Baker, Mary Holland, Barbara C. Nienstedt, Ronald S. Everett, and Richard McCleary
    1983   "The impact of a crime wave: perceptions, fear, and confidence in the police." Law and
            Society Review 17:319-33.
Baumer, Terry L.
    1985   "Testing a general model of fear of crime." Journal of Research on Crime and
            Delinquency 22:239-56.
Blau, Judith R. and Peter M. Blau
    1982   "Metropolitan structure and violent crime." American Sociological Review 47:114-28.
Conklin, John E.
    1975   The Impact of Crime. New York: MacMillan.
Davis, F. James
    1952   "Crime news in Colorado newspapers." American Journal of Sociology 57:325-30.
Ferraro, Kenneth F. and Randy LeGrange
    1987   "The measurement of the fear of crime." Sociological Inquiry 57:70-101.
Garofalo, James
    1979   "Victimization and the fear of crime." Journal of Research in Crime and Delinquency
            16:80-97.
    1981   "Crime and the mass media: a selective review of research." Journal of Research in
            Crime and Delinquency 18:319-50.
Garofalo, James and John Laub
    1979   "The fear of crime: broadening our perspective." Victimology 3:242-53.
Gordon, Margaret T. and Linda Heath
    1981   "The news business, crime, and fear" In Reactions to Crime, ed. Dan A. Lewis, 227-50.
            Beverly Hills, Calif.: Sage.
Graber, D.A.
    1980   Crime News and the Public. New York: Praeger
Hartnagel, Timothy F.
    1979   The perception and fear of crime: implications for neighborhood cohesion, social activity
            and community affect." Social Forces 58:176-93.
Heath, Linda
    1984   "Impact of newspaper crime reports on fear of crime: multi-methodological
            investigation." Journal of Personality and Social Psychology 47:263-76.

374   LISKA/BACCAGLINI

Hough, M. and P. Mayhew
      1985   Taking Account of Crime: Key Findings From the British Crime Survey. London: HMSO.
Kennedy, Leslie W. and Robert A. Silverman
      1985   "Significant others and fear of crime among the elderly." Journal of Aging and Human Development 20:241-56.
Law Enforcement Assistance Administration
      1978   National Crime Surveys. Ann Arbor, Mich.: Inter-University Consortium for Political and Social Research.
Liska, Allen E., Joseph J. Lawrence, and Andrew Sanchirico
      1982   "Fear of crime as a social fact." Social Forces 60:760-71.
Liska, Allen, Mark Reed, and Andrew Sanchirico
      1985   "Fear of crime and constrained behavior: specifying and estimating a reciprocal effects model." Social Forces 66:827-37.
Lizotte, Alan J. and David Bordua
      1980   "Firearms ownership for sport and protection: two divergent models." American Sociological Review 45:229-44.
Miethe, Terance D. and Gary R. Lee
      1984   "Fear of crime among older people: a reassessment of the predictive power of crime-related factors." The Sociological Quarterly 25:397-415.
Miethe, Terance D., Mark C. Stafford, and J. Scott Long
      1987   "Social differentiation in criminal victimization: a test of routine activities/lifestyle theories." American Sociological Review 52:184-94.
Roshier, B.
      1973   "The selection of crime news by the press." In The Manufacture of News, ed. S. Cohen and J. Young, 28-39. London, England: Constable.
Rossi, Peter H., Emily Waite, Christine E. Bose and Richard Berk
      1974   "The seriousness of crimes: normative structure and individual differences," American Sociological Review 39:224-37.
Sellin, Thorsten and Marvin E. Wolfgang
      1964   The Measurement of Delinquency. New York: Russell Sage Foundation.
Skogan, Wesley G. and Michael G. Maxfield
      1981   Coping with Crime: Individual and Neighborhood Reactions. Beverly Hills: Sage.
Smith, D.J. and J. Gray
      1985   Police and People in London. Aldershot: Gower.
Swanson, Charles E.
      1955   "What they read in 130 daily newspapers." Journalism Quarterly 32:411-21.
Swigert, Victoria L. and Ronald A. Farrell
      1976   Murder, Inequality and the Law: Differential Treatment in the Legal Process. Lexington, Mass.: Heath.
Taylor, Ralph B., Stephen D. Gottfredson, and Sidney Brower
      1984   "Black crime and fear: defensible space, local social ties, and territorial functioning." Journal of Research in Crime and Delinquency 21:303-32.
Taylor, Ralph and Margaret Hale
      1986   "Testing alternative models of fear and crime." Journal of Criminology and Criminal Law 77:151-89.
Warr, Mark and Mark Stafford
      1982   "Fear of victimization: a look at proximate causes." Social Forces 61:1033-43.
Yin, Peter
      1985   Victimization and the Aged. Springfield, Ill.: Charles C. Thomas.

[14]

BRIT. J. CRIMINOL.   VOL. 33   NO. 1   WINTER 1993

FEAR OF CRIME: READ ALL ABOUT IT?

The Relationship between Newspaper Crime Reporting and Fear of Crime

PAUL WILLIAMS* and JULIE DICKINSON**

This article reports a three-stage study of the relationship between newspaper reporting of crime and fear of crime. The first stage measured the amount of space and prominence given to crime, particularly violent crime, in ten British daily newspapers. The second stage of the study was a questionnaire survey of the relationship between newspaper reporting of crime and fear of crime. A significant positive correlation was found which appeared to be independent of demographic factors associated with readership. The third stage examined qualitative aspects of reporting styles in these newspapers. Consistent differences were found between newspapers. Those newspapers classified as 'broadsheets' carried proportionally fewer crime reports and reported crimes in a less sensational fashion than the 'tabloids', particularly low-market ones.

Fear of crime (FOC) has been identified as a problem in its own right. A Home Office working party recently noted that 'fear of crime will grow unless checked. As an issue of social concern, it has to be taken as seriously as . . . crime prevention and reduction' (Home Office 1989: ii). Moore and Trojanowicz (1988) argue that reasonable fears concerning crime can be harnessed to fight the threat of crime, but when these fears become unreasonable they amount to a counterproductive response and become a social problem.

Research has highlighted many sources of fear of crime, such as being a victim, environmental characteristics (e.g. living in a high crime rate area), and physical vulnerability (see Skogan 1986; Box *et al.* 1988; Parker and Ray 1990), but most people have been neither a victim nor a witness of crime. This suggests that the perception that individuals have of the 'crime problem' must be due largely to indirect sources. The purpose of this paper is to examine the links between FOC and one of those sources—newspapers.

Crime and the News

Crime reporting in the news media has been a focus of concern because of the assumption that the salience given to certain types of crime, notably those involving sex or violence, creates a distorted picture of reality which is reflected in the beliefs of news consumers (see Roshier 1973; Meyer 1975; Winkel and Vrij 1990; Marsh 1991). News is clearly vulnerable to distortion, for everyday events cannot simply be mirrored by newspapers. There are so many events that could be reported that journalists must be selective and it is this process of selection which is the first stage of 'creating news' (Tuchman 1978). Lester has argued that selection is determined by a 'template . . . [of]

* Sussex Police, Malling House, Lewes, East Sussex.
** Department of Occupational Psychology, Birkbeck College, Malet Street, London WC1E 7HX.
This research was carried out while the first author, a police officer, was a student and the second author a lecturer at Sussex University. We are grateful to an anonymous reviewer for suggestions incorporated in the text.

PAUL WILLIAMS AND JULIE DICKINSON

. . . official and unofficial values, norms and beliefs' (1980: 5), including beliefs about commercial viability (cf. Humphries 1981). Fishman (1978), for example, described how a 'crime wave' against the elderly of New York was 'created' by reporters who began to search for and highlight more cases of attacks on the elderly. As Lichtenstein *et al.* note, 'Fear sells' (1978: 575).

The frame context in which the news is presented (e.g. reporting style, page format) can vary from one newspaper to another to such an extent that Quinney (1970) has suggested that an individual's conception of crime may depend upon the newspaper he or she reads. This relationship will be investigated in this study. However, it is important to note than the relationship between news reporting and public opinion is not necessarily that of a biased press shaping unresisting wills (cf. Smith 1984). The consumer is also actively involved in investing news with meaning and may, for example, choose which newspaper to buy on the basis of how accurate and truthful he or she believes the reporting to be.

Before examining the relationship between FOC and newspaper crime reporting in more detail, the complex nature and etiology of FOC and the problems of measuring crime reporting in newspapers will be considered.

Fear of Crime

Garofalo defined FOC as an 'emotional reaction characterized by a sense of danger and anxiety . . . produced by the threat of physical harm . . . elicited by perceived cues in the environment that relate to some aspect of crime' (1981: 840). Garofalo and Lamb (1978) saw FOC as part of the wider concept of 'quality of life', that is, as more diffuse than a fear of some specific danger in one's immediate environment. Skogan (1984) identified two components in FOC: an evaluative aspect (assessment of risk) and an emotional element (what the individual perceives to be the personal threat of crime). Garofalo (1981) related FOC to three sources of information about crime: direct experience, interpersonal communication about another's experience, and the mass media. Skogan's (1984) review of research pointed to the interactional nature of FOC in the findings that FOC is closely associated with personal vulnerability and the perceived seriousness of the consequences resulting from criminal victimization.

Much evidence of FOC in Britain has been gathered by successive editions of the British Crime Survey (BCS). The 1984 BCS (Maxfield 1987; Box *et al.* 1988) found that respondents made alarmingly high estimates of crime rates—far in excess of actual risks. Pessimistic estimates were made particularly by women, the elderly, and those on lower incomes. As with most surveys of this kind, the main measures of FOC were the extent to which people worry about becoming a victim, and the anxiety felt about their personal safety in various situations, such as when walking alone at night. On these measures also it was women, the elderly, and those from lower-income households who were most worried and felt most unsafe.

Many studies have sought to disentangle the most important mediating factors influencing the individual's FOC. Toseland (1982) found that twelve variables accounted for 45.7 per cent of the variance in subjects' FOC: sex, area of residence (e.g. in a city/rural), satisfaction with the neighbourhood, age, health, education, social class, marital status (married/never having married/widowed), experience of burglary, helpfulness of people in the neighbourhood, number of persons living with the

34

NEWSPAPER CRIME REPORTING AND FEAR OF CRIME

respondent, and race. The most important demographic predictors were sex, area of residence, age, health, and whether the individual lives alone. Psychosocial variables (e.g. satisfaction with the area of residence) were also important.

It appears that FOC is very much a matter of vulnerability. Junger (1987), for example, placed much emphasis on women's inability to handle dangerous situations in accounting for their high FOC. However, Maxfield (1987) reminds us to talk not of being vulnerable but of feeling vulnerable.

FOC is not manifest only in measures of personal fear and risk assessments. It is marked also by increased estimates of the crime rate for the general population (Baker *et al.* 1983).

A major source of data concerning FOC in Britain has been a recent survey in Bristol (Last and Jackson 1989). Women, the elderly, and those living in poorer districts were again shown to have higher levels of FOC as indicated by personal and general risk assessments, anxiety, and behavioural consequences. Respondents were asked about what they perceived to be the main source of their knowledge of the risk. Acknowledging the dubious validity of relying on respondents' subjectivity, the authors noted that approximately 70 per cent identified the mass media.

Analyses of Crime Reporting in Newspapers

Most analyses of newspaper crime reporting have been concerned with the potentially distorted impression created by the high proportion of reports of violent crimes (e.g. Davis 1952; Roshier 1973). Ditton and Duffy (1983) analysed the crime content of three Scottish newspapers in terms of the numbers and page areas of crime reports. They found that 6.5 per cent of the news involved crime and that 45.8 per cent of this was violent and sexual crime. These proportions were compared to police statistics that show just 2.4 per cent of crime in the locality to be violent and/or sexual. They suggested, however, that readers may be 'sufficiently intelligent and discerning to appreciate that frequency and type of coverage does not necessarily reflect, pro rata, frequency and type of incidence' (1983: 164). They called for research into qualitative aspects of reporting such as sensationalism) and for research to determine whether the misrepresentations of crime in newspapers influence the general perceptions of readers.

Smith (1984 supported Ditton and Duffy's arguments but cautioned against overestimating the influence of newspapers while ignoring factors in the social and physical environments and interpersonal rumour. Shapland (1985) also pointed out the dangers of the rationale behind Ditton and Duffy's study, which assumed that newspaper reporting is a major influence on public opinion about crime, ignoring the mutual interaction between newspapers and readers. Winkel and Vrij (1990) found that identifying with the victim or perceiving a similarity between one's own neighbourhood and the locale of the reported crime heightens FOC in response to newspaper reports of crime.

There has been a recognition that quantitative content analyses can offer more than these studies suggest, although little research has been conducted in this area. Davis and Turner suggested that it might be a good idea to investigate 'the influence of eyecatching devices' such as headlines and pictures (1951: 330). Indeed, Emig (1928) concluded that 192 of 375 subjects based their opinions about news on reading and skimming headlines and English defined the reader as a 'shopper of headlines' (1944:

217). Deichsel and Stone identified headlines as very useful for studies of salience and attention orientation, noting that 'many readers only remember . . . at headline level' (1975: 114). Research on the Von Restorff effect confirms that distinctive material is easier to learn and recall (Hall 1966). 'Serial learning theory' research shows that recall of a news item is greater if it is favourably situated or if it is read first or last (Booth 1970). Booth's research has also shown how recall is increased when news items are larger and when they appear with photographs. Photographs are important in catching the reader's attention and in reinforcing the accompanying message. Any multiple-channel presentation is more likely to have a strong impact than a single-channel display (cf. Hartman 1961).

Content analyses have also ignored more qualitative aspects of reporting. Priyadarsini noted that many crime reports are far from dispassionate, are 'highly graphic' and involve 'sensational portrayals' and 'embellished descriptions' (1984: 320). Heath (1984) is one of the few to have addressed qualitative aspects of presentation—specifically the geographical locality, randomness (lack of victim precipitation), and sensationalism of the crime reported. She found that random and sensational crimes lead to increased fear (especially if committed locally). However, this study ignored reporting style.

Overall, then, content analyses have looked at superficial and easy-to-measure quantitative aspects of newspaper crime reporting, while ignoring more subtle, qualitative dimensions.

The Relationship between Newspaper Crime Reporting and FOC

The main question is whether people base their own subjective assessments of the probability of crime on the frequency with which various types of crime are reported in newspapers. Tversky and Kahneman (1973, 1974) suggested that, when assessing probability, people 'rely on heuristic principles which reduce . . . complex tasks . . . to simple judgemental operations' (1974: 1124). Such principles, or 'rules of thumb', can also lead to systematic errors.

One such heuristic principle, 'availability', saves individuals from the need to review all the evidence before resolving a problem. However, because we tend to use only the information which is most readily retrievable (because of its familiarity, salience, or recentness), this can lead to biases. The implications for risk assessment are that an event is judged more likely or frequent if it is easier to imagine or recall relevant instances (Slovic *et al.* 1977). Taylor and Fiske (1978) developed this idea, suggesting that information is more readily available if it is encoded through more than one mode (e.g. iconic and semantic), or is encoded differently from other stimuli (e.g. in images as opposed to semantic encoding).

When Lichtenstein *et al.* (1978) applied these ideas to judging frequencies of different causes of death, two kinds of biases were identified: the tendency to overestimate small frequencies and underestimate large ones, and the tendency to exaggerate the frequencies of some specific causes because of disproportionate exposure to, or memorability and imaginability of, events—especially influential were memorable characteristics such as sensationalism and vividness. They concluded that 'the consistent errors people make can be predicted from the salient features of the events' (1978: 571). Some risks may be overestimated, they stated, because of the extensive media

NEWSPAPER CRIME REPORTING AND FEAR OF CRIME

coverage they receive. Saliency, however, is not just a characteristic of the stimulus. Taylor and Thompson (1982) pointed out that although the phenomenon of salience occurs when a person's attention is drawn to one part of the environment, the effect also depends upon characteristics of the perceiver. Thus the saliency of a robbery might be increased if the perceiver lives in the same locality.

The above review shows that research on the causes of FOC has tended to concentrate on demographic factors affecting perceived vulnerability rather than on factors affecting perceived frequencies of crime. While newspaper reports have been suggested as a source of beliefs about such frequencies, research into the effects of newspaper crime reporting has been hampered by variation in measures of news content. It seems apparent that, although some research has been carried out on the possible effects of newspaper crime reporting on FOC, (a) quantitative measures taken in content analyses have lacked thoroughness and ingenuity and have ignored many aspects of reporting; (b) virtually no qualitative content analyses have been undertaken; (c) analyses have largely ignored the British press; and (d) few attempts appear to have been made to relate newspaper reporting of crime to the readers' FOC. The purpose of this study was to attempt to rectify these failings and, in so doing, to take a more integrative and multidimensional approach to the subject.

The first part of the research project involved a detailed quantitative content analysis of the major national daily newspapers of Britain. Measurements of frequencies and areas of crime reports were taken to show how different newspapers vary in the attention they devote to crime, and highlighted particularly the disproportionate predominance given to personal violence crimes (PVCs). A number of new measures were designed to incorporate those findings that suggest the importance of vivid and salient reports. It was particularly felt that the content analysis should take into account the salience of crime articles on a page, the salience of the headlines, the use of photographs, and the positioning of crime reports on the front pages. Since people are more anxious about PVC victimization, less attention was given to reports of property crimes.

A questionnaire survey was than carried out to determine whether readers of newspapers which give more attention to crime (particularly PVC) and report it in a more salient way, rated higher on cognitive, affective, and behavioural measures of FOC. Possible confounding variables (sex, age, socioeconomic status, and educational background) were controlled. A qualitative analysis was also undertaken to assess how *frightening* and *sensationalized* the reporting styles appeared.

The overall hypothesis was that readers of newspapers containing more salient crime reports would have greater FOC.

Stage 1: Quantitative Content Analysis

Every copy of the ten most popular British national daily newspapers (*The Times, The Guardian, The Independent, The Daily Telegraph* (broadsheets); *Daily Express, Daily Mail, Today* (mid-market tabloids); *Daily Mirror, The Sun, Daily Star* (low-market tabloids)[1] published during a four-week period commencing 19 June 1989 was subjected to a detailed quantitative content analysis to measure the following aspects of salience:

[1] The *Daily Record* was not included because it is published only in Scotland.

PAUL WILLIAMS AND JULIE DICKINSON

(a) proportion of each paper's newshole given over to crime;[2]
(b) proportion of each paper's newshole given over to personal violence crimes (PVCs);
(c) proportion of crime news area given over to PVC reports;
(d) proportion of front page news area given over to PVC reports;
(e) salience of PVC reports on pages in general;
(f) salience of PVC reports on front pages;
(g) salience of PVC report headlines;
(h) number, size, and relative area of photographs accompanying PVC reports.

A quantitative measure of the salience of the PVC reports was created by comparing the proportionate page area devoted to PVC reports with the proportionate page area devoted to all other reports. This was calculated according to the following formula:

$$\left(\frac{\text{mean area of PVC reports}}{\text{mean page area}}\right) - \left(\frac{\text{mean area of all other reports}}{\text{mean page area}}\right).$$

This formula is responsive to (a) the area of the PVC report (larger ones appearing more salient), (b) the size of the page (the smaller it is, the more prominent the report), and (c) the confounding effect of competing articles on the same page (the larger they are, the less the impact of the PVC report).

A measure of the salience of the PVC report headlines was devised to be sensitive to factors similar to these, and was calculated by the following formula:

$$\left(\frac{\text{mean area of PVC headlines}}{\text{mean page area}}\right) - \left(\frac{\text{mean area of all other headlines}}{\text{mean page area}}\right)$$

No account was taken of the content of photographs or the occasional use of colour photographs by the *Daily Express*, *Today*, and *Daily Mirror* newspapers, though these factors almost certainly add to the impact of the photographs and the accompanying stories.

Stage 2: Questionnaire Survey

Design

A questionnaire survey was carried out to measure the following variables:

(a) perceptions of risks to the population at large;
(b) anxiety about personal victimization and safety;
(c) avoidance strategies.

Age, sex, educational background, and socioeconomic status were also measured.

Subjects

Two hundred and ninety subjects completed the questionnaire. They were all from the Worthing/Littlehampton area of West Sussex, England. Sex ratios (160 female, 130

---

[2] 'Newshole' refers to that area of the newspaper which contains reports of news events. 'Crime' refers to crime occurring in Britain which is recordable by the Home Office.

NEWSPAPER CRIME REPORTING AND FEAR OF CRIME

male), mean age (50.9 years), and a distinctive bimodal age distribution were all in keeping with the population sampled according to local census information.

Materials

Five hundred envelopes were delivered to randomly selected addresses. Each envelope contained an introductory letter, two questionnaires, and a return 'Freepost' envelope.

Procedure

One thousand questionnaires were printed (see Appendix A). The first nine questions assessed respondents' personal anxiety in three different situations: walking alone at night, at home at night, and driving alone at night. Question 10 was devised to measure respondents' worries about becoming the victim of specific crimes. Question 11 was designed to tap into respondents' assessments of risks of victimization for the local population. Questions 12–14 were designed to measure how FOC might influence how often respondents go out in the evening after dark. Question 15 recorded which newspapers were read and to what extent and questions 16–19 collected demographic information.

Envelopes were delivered to 500 addresses in the Worthing/Littlehampton area in early December 1989. Streets and houses were randomly selected from the local road index on a fixed ratio basis.

As each envelope was delivered, the researcher assessed the value of the property within three categories (0–£80,000; £80,000–£150,000; £150,000 upwards), and marked the return envelope with a corresponding symbol. This was designed as a measure, albeit crude, of socioeconomic status. Researcher reliability had previously been tested against local estate agents' figures and found to be approximately 95 per cent accurate. The introductory sheet stipulated that the questionnaires be completed only by adults over 17 years old and respondents were invited to volunteer for 'further research' by completing a tear-off strip to return with the completed questionnaire(s). This was to recruit volunteers for the qualitative analysis stage of the study (see below). The postal survey method was used as a cheap and time-effective way of tapping into the feelings of a representative sample, while not increasing personal anxiety among respondents as face-to-face interviews might have done.

Stage 3: Qualitative Analysis

Design

A qualitative analysis of PVC reports from each paper was conducted to measure two further independent variables: the fearfulness and the sensationalism of the reporting styles.

Subjects

Of 290 subjects who completed the questionnaire survey of FOC, 127 volunteered to take part in 'further research'. Twenty of these were selected to judge qualitative

PAUL WILLIAMS AND JULIE DICKINSON

aspects of newspaper reporting styles. Five were randomly selected from each category—readers of broadsheets, mid-market tabloids, and low-market tabloids—and five were non-readers. The sample was adjusted by further random selection to give equal numbers of males and females. Seventeen of the twenty responded.

Materials

Fifty PVC reports were randomly selected from the supply of newspapers used in the quantitative analysis with the provisos that five were from each newspaper and that twenty covered two stories common to each of the ten newspapers. The headlines and opening sentences (to a maximum of eighty words) were transposed into the same typed format. Two short questions were placed under each report, requesting respondents to judge (on a 1–7 scale) the 'fearfulness' and 'sensationalism' of reporting style. Examples are given in Appendix B.

Procedure

Ten reports (one from each newspaper) were sent to each of the subjects, together with a letter explaining what was required of them—namely, the judging of the style of the reporting. In answering how frightening the style was, they were instructed to ignore their own personal circumstances in relation to the victim. As for sensationalism, judges were instructed to assess whether the report was portraying 'the plain facts' or whether the facts had been 'emphasized, exaggerated, or dramatized in some way'. Anonymity and confidentiality were assured. A 'Freepost' envelope was enclosed for return of judgement sheets.

Results

Quantitative content analysis

(a) Proportion of newshole given to crime   Table 1 shows the area of crime news calculated as a percentage of the total newshole for each newspaper. On average, 12.7 per cent of event-oriented news reports were about crime. Tabloids (particularly low-market ones) devoted most newshole space to crime.

(b) Proportion of newshole given to personal violence crime   Overall, 8.2 per cent of event-oriented news stories reported PVCs. The percentages for each newspaper are shown in Table 2. Tabloid newspapers (particularly low-market ones) gave the highest priority to PVCs.

(c) PVC reports as proportion of crime news   On average, newspapers devote 64.5 per cent (with little variation) of the space that they allocate to crime reporting to stories dealing with PVCs. This compares with official figures suggesting that only 6 per cent of crime involves personal violence (Mayhew 1989).

(d) Proportion of front-page news given to PVC   The analysis showed that, on average, 13.9 per cent of front-page space is devoted to reporting PVCs. The pattern of results

NEWSPAPER CRIME REPORTING AND FEAR OF CRIME

TABLE 1   *Proportion of Newspaper Newsholes Devoted to Crime*

Newspaper	Mean newshole area (cm²)	Mean crime area (cm²)	Crime area / Newshole area (%)	Rank
Times	11,777	748	6.4	(3)
Independent	10,251	591	5.8	(2)
Guardian	10,583	543	5.1	(1)
Telegraph	10,392	942	9.1	(4)
Mail	5,286	1,024	19.4	(7)
Express	4,465	775	17.4	(6)
Today	5,725	803	14.0	(5)
Mirror	4,346	1,151	26.5	(8)
Sun	4,284	1,304	30.4	(10)
Star	4,015	1,129	28.1	(9)
			$\bar{X} = 12.7$	

TABLE 2   *Proportion of Newspaper Newsholes Devoted to Crimes Involving Personal Violence*

Newspaper	Mean newshole area (cm²)	Mean PVC area (cm²)	PVC area / Newshole area (%)	Rank
Times	11,777	503	4.3	(3)
Independent	10,251	305	3.0	(1)
Guardian	10,583	348	3.3	(2)
Telegraph	10,392	627	6.0	(4)
Mail	5,286	733	13.9	(7)
Express	4,465	480	10.7	(6)
Today	5,725	489	8.5	(5)
Mirror	4,346	747	17.2	(8)
Sun	4,284	815	19.0	(9)
Star	4,015	768	19.1	(10)
			$\bar{X} = 8.2$	

for the various newspapers was similar to that portrayed for the proportion of the overall newshole devoted to PVC shown in Table 2. The rank order of the newspapers from the one with the smallest proportion of the front page devoted to PVC to that with the largest was as follows (mean proportions in brackets): *Guardian* (0.8 per cent), *Independent* (1.9 per cent), *Telegraph* (4.2 per cent), *Times* (5.2 per cent), *Today* (16.7 per cent), *Mail* (17.9 per cent), *Star* (18.8 per cent), *Express* (21.0 per cent), *Mirror* (25.9 per cent), *Sun* (26.8 per cent).

(e) Salience of PVC news reports   Table 3 shows the salience scores for each newspaper. Tabloids (particularly low-market ones) had the most salient PVC reports. Low-market tabloid newspapers PVC reports were, on average, almost twice the size of non-PVC reports, whereas in broadsheets PVC reports are, on average, less than three-quarters of the size of non-PVC reports.

41

The Fear of Crime

PAUL WILLIAMS AND JULIE DICKINSON

TABLE 3 *Salience of PVC Reports*

Newspaper	Page area (cm²)	Area of each PVC report (cm²)	Area of each non-PVC report (cm²)	Salience scores	Rank
Times	1,924	112.8	147.5	−1.81	(2)
Independent	2,038	81.3	161.6	−3.94	(1)
Guardian	1,953	120.7	148.2	−1.41	(4)
Telegraph	1,957	91.2	124.1	−1.68	(3)
Mail	955	194.0	143.0	5.34	(5)
Express	913	240.0	149.9	9.87	(9)
Today	936	230.7	164.2	7.11	(7)
Mirror	978	197.0	94.0	10.53	(10)
Sun	917	144.8	83.9	6.64	(6)
Star	917	188.3	101.0	9.52	(8)

(f) Salience of PVC news reports on front pages The results were very similar to those in Table 3. The rank order of the newspapers for the salience of the PVC news reports on the front pages (scores in brackets) was: *Guardian* (−11.7), *Independent* (−3.07), *Telegraph* (0.32), *Times* (2.91), *Today* (3.76), *Mail* (10.12), *Express* (15.8), *Sun* (17.95), *Mirror* (25.22), *Star* (28.36).

(g) Salience of PVC news report headlines The rank order of the newspapers from those with the least salient PVC news report headlines to those with the most salient headlines was as follows (salience scores in brackets): *Independent* (−0.005), *Times* (−0.002), *Telegraph* (0.001), *Guardian* (0.002), *Today* (0.01), *Star* (0.011), *Sun* (0.011), *Mail* (0.011), *Mirror* (0.014), *Express* (0.019). Whereas the PVC report headlines of the broadsheets are of a similar size to the non-PVC ones, tabloid news report headlines are approximately one-third larger than non-PVC equivalents.

(h) Number, size, and relative area of photographs accompanying PVC reports Details of the use of photographs (including sketches, diagrams, and maps) are shown in Table 4. Tabloids were more likely than broadsheets to accompany PVC stories with photographs. On the whole tabloid photographs were smaller than broadsheet photographs, but when page area is taken into account tabloid photographs take up a larger proportion of the page.

Questionnaire survey

In all, 290 (29 per cent) of the 1,000 questionnaires were returned. These were from 201 (40.2 per cent) of addresses, indicating that eighty-nine households returned more than one questionnaire each. As census information suggests that 32 per cent of the residences in the area are occupied by single individuals, approximately 160 of the 500 addresses were likely to contain only one occupant. This means that the 290 questionnaires were returned from a probable sample of 840 subjects able to respond, suggesting a real response rate of 34.5 per cent. Respondents were representative of the population on all confirmable demographic variables: sex ratio, mean age, age distribution, and socioeconomic status (according to the most recent census data).

42

NEWSPAPER CRIME REPORTING AND FEAR OF CRIME

TABLE 4   *Photographs Accompanying PVC Reports*

Newspaper	Page area (cm²)	Mean no. of PVC photos	Rank	Mean area of PVC photos (cm²)	Area of PVS photos page area (%)	Rank
Times	1,924	0.79	(3)	103.67	5.39	(4)
Independent	2,038	0.42	(2)	100.48	4.93	(3)
Guardian	1,953	0.36	(1)	125.00	6.40	(5)
Telegraph	1,957	1.46	(4)	81.16	4.15	(1)
Mail	955	2.09	(6)	70.19	7.35	(7)
Express	913	2.38	(8)	40.84	4.47	(2)
Today	936	1.48	(5)	101.49	10.84	(10)
Mirror	978	2.54	(10)	75.83	7.75	(8)
Sun	917	2.33	(7)	66.22	7.22	(6)
Star	917	2.42	(9)	81.94	8.94	(9)

Note: 'Photographs' includes sketches, diagrams, and maps.

The responses to questions 3, 6, and 9 in the questionnaire provided information on another variable which has been related to FOC—personal or vicarious experience of crime itself (cf. Taylor and Hale 1986; Box *et al.* 1988; Parker and Ray 1990). A total of 226 of the 290 respondents answered question 3 (they could give more than one answer). Twelve (4.1 per cent of all respondents) attributed their unease to personal experience of assault and thirty-one (10.7 per cent) to vicarious experience. Higher percentages of respondents attributed their fear of assault to television or radio coverage (41.4 per cent) and press coverage (39 per cent). Question 6 was answered by 155 respondents. Fourteen (4.8 per cent of all respondents) attributed not feeling 'very safe' in their home at night to personal experience of burglary or assault and thirty-four (11.7 per cent) to vicarious experience. Again, higher percentages attributed their fear to television or radio (24.1 per cent) and press (23.8 per cent) coverage. The discrepancy in attributed source of FOC was more marked in the answers to question 9 of the sixty people who feared being assaulted when driving alone at night. None had personal experience of assault and only three (1 per cent of all respondents) had vicarious experience, while forty-five (15.5 per cent) had seen or heard of such assaults on the television or radio and forty-four (15.2 per cent) had read about them in the press. These results are in keeping with Last and Jackson's (1989) finding that the majority of people attribute their knowledge of the risk of crime to information in the mass media.

As the percentage of the sample with personal or vicarious experience of crime was small, and as the data collected related to self-reported experience and were unspecific to the type of assault or burglary, this variable was not included in further analysis of the causes of FOC. This is not to dismiss the importance of personal and vicarious experience of crime or the possibility that low-market tabloid readers might experience more crime;[3] but the sample size did not allow a thorough investigation of this factor.

Only two questions appeared to pose particular difficulties to respondents: 10.3 per cent of respondents, mainly males, failed to answer the question about how much they

[3] We are grateful to an anonymous reviewer for suggesting this possibility.

PAUL WILLIAMS AND JULIE DICKINSON

worried about sexual assault; and 7.2 per cent mostly older respondents, failed to estimate the risk of local population victimization.

Newspaper readership pattern   Table 5 shows the newspaper readership pattern for the survey respondents. The newspapers are grouped in terms of broadsheets (*Times, Guardian, Independent, Telegraph*), mid-market tabloids (*Express, Mail, Today*), and low-market tabloids (*Mirror, Sun, Star*).

TABLE 5   *Newspaper Readership Pattern for Survey Respondents*

Newspaper 'always' or 'nearly always' read	No.
Broadsheet	49
Mid-market tabloid	80
Low-market tabloid	69
None	28
Others ('occasional' or multiple readers)	64
Total	290

Broadsheet = *Times, Guardian, Independent, Daily Telegraph*; mid-market tabloid = *Daily Express, Daily Mail, Today*; low-market tabloid = *Daily Mirror, Sun, Daily Star*.

The newspaper readership groups varied significantly in their assessments of victimization risks for the local population. Fig. 1 shows that the estimates for both PVCs and non-PVCs of low-market tabloid (LMT) readers were almost twice as high as those of mid-market tabloid (MMT) readers and three times as high as those broadsheet (BS) readers.

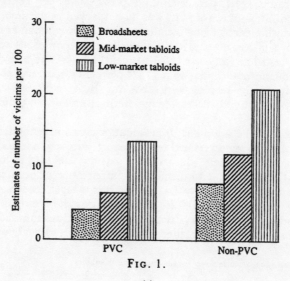

FIG. 1.

NEWSPAPER CRIME REPORTING AND FEAR OF CRIME

Personal worries expressed by respondents followed a similar pattern, but this was significant only in relation to fear of assault, wounding, and car theft. Table 6 shows the mean level of worry about personal victimization expressed by the different newspaper readership groups.

TABLE 6   *Readers' Fears about Being a Victim of Crime*

| | Worry about personal victimization (on 1–7 scale) among readers of: | | | | |
	Broadsheet	Mid-market tabloid	Low-market tabloid	F	p
PVC					
Assault/wounding	2.83	3.03	3.62	3.07 (2,187)	0.05
Sexual assault	2.56	3.25	3.60	2.43 (2,166)	ns
Robbery/mugging	3.15	3.38	3.86	2.43 (2,187)	ns
Non-PVC					
Burglary	3.61	3.68	4.03	1.04 (2.188)	ns
Property damage	3.00	4.20	3.55	0.70 (2,187)	ns
Theft from car	2.81	3.15	3.91	4.76 (2,138)	0.01

ns = not significant.

The responses to the questions about personal safety when walking alone and in the home at night showed that broadsheet readers felt most safe and low-market tabloid readers least safe (see Figs. 2 and 3). The variance was statistically significant for concern about walking alone at night ($x^2 = 18.26$, $df = 9$, $p = 0.03$) but not for safety felt at home ($x^2 = 14.38$, $df = 9$, $p = 0.11$). However, newspaper readership did not predict how often respondents went out after dark. Broadsheet readers had gone out, on average, 2.53 times in the previous week compared with 2.94 times for mid-market tabloid readers and 2.55 times for low-market tabloid readers.

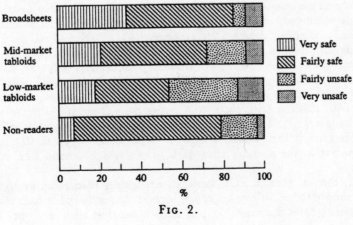

FIG. 2.

PAUL WILLIAMS AND JULIE DICKINSON

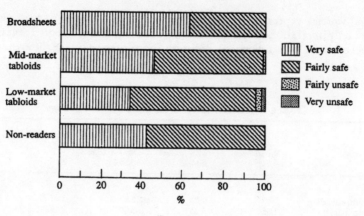

FIG. 3.

In view of the differences among groups of readers, a demographic analysis of the groups was carried out. Age bore no relation to the type of newspaper read and sex differences did not vary in a linear fashion across groups. However, education and socioeconomic status (SES) were important. Broadsheet readers left full-time education at a mean age of 17.35 years, mid-market tabloid readers at 16.22 years and low-market tabloid readers at 15.54 years. This was statistically significant $(F(2,193) = 7.63, p < 0.001)$. It was also found that broadsheet readers had the highest SES and low-market tabloid readers the lowest $(F(2,195) = 10.05, p < 0.001)$.

A series of further tests was carried out to determine whether the different demographic variables were related to the varying FOC levels of the newspaper readership groups. Although sex ratios did not vary significantly among the newspaper readership groups $(x^2 = 5.47, df = 2, p < 0.1)$, women formed the majority of mid-market and low-market tabloid readers and it is, therefore, possible that higher levels of FOC among women (Maxfield 1987; Junger 1987) may have accounted for some of the variance in FOC associated with newspaper readership. Sex differences were found in the responses to the questionnaire. Women were significantly more worried than men about being wounded/assaulted (men: 2.47, women: 3.79, $t(275) = 6.44, p < 0.001$), being sexually assaulted (men: 1.25, women: 4.43, $t(222) = 16.56, p < 0.001$), being robbed/mugged (men: 2.57, women: 4.22, $t(275) = 8.47, p < 0.001$), and being the victim of non-PVC crime (men: 3.00, women: 3.49, $t(269) = 2.38, p = 0.018$). (Scores on a 1–7 scale where 7 = 'very worried'.) They also gave higher estimates of the number of people per 100 of the local population who would be victims of PVC (men: 8.50, women: 14.80, $t(245) = 3.56, p < 0.001$) and non-PVC (men: 11.50, women: 16.20, $t(266) = 2.23, p = 0.27$). They felt less safe walking alone at night $(x^2 = 71.85, df = 3, p < 0.001)$, less safe in their homes at night $(x^2 = 26.03, df = 3, p < 0.001)$, and were less likely to go out in the evening after dark (men: 3.45, women: 2.22, $t(270) = 4.04, p < 0.001$).

However, the variance in FOC between newspaper readership groups cannot be attributed simply to sex differences as the highest proportion of female readers was in the mid-market tabloid group (65 per cent, compared with 44.9 per cent in the

46

NEWSPAPER CRIME REPORTING AND FEAR OF CRIME

broadsheet group and 52.2 per cent in the low-market tabloid group), yet this newspaper group was associated with FOC levels between those of the broadsheet and low-market tabloid groups.

Age was generally found to be correlated with worry about victimization but not with risk assessment. Table 7 provides details. Again, though, the affect on FOC levels for the three newspaper readership groups runs contrary to what was found as broadsheet readers were significantly older than tabloid readers (59.5 years compared with 49.7 years).

TABLE 7   *Age Correlations with Various FOC Measures*

FOC measure	r	$p <$
Victimization worry		
assault/wounding	0.157	0.01
sexual assault	0.126	0.05
robbery/mugging	0.163	0.01
burglary	0.255	0.01
damage to property	0.157	0.01
theft of car	−0.042	ns
Risk assessment		
assault/wounding	−0.009	ns
sexual assault	0.010	ns
robbery/mugging	−0.053	ns
burglary	−0.032	ns
damage to property	−0.061	ns
theft of car	−0.056	ns
Out in evening after dark in last 7 days	0.312	0.01

ns = not significant.

Education had no significant effect on any of the FOC measures but socioeconomic status (SES) was related to most FOC measures. Of the 290 respondents, thirty-five fell into the high SES group (judged by cost of housing), ninety-five into the medium SES group, and 160 into the low SES group. The SES groups varied significantly in their anxiety about walking alone at night ($x^2 = 29.97$, d$f = 6$, $p < 0.001$) and being a victim of PVC ($F(2,257) = 4.89$, $p = 0.008$). They also varied in their assessments of risk of PVC ($F(2,266) = 5.45$, $p = 0.005$) and non-PVC ($F(2,266) = 4.80$, $p = 0.009$) for a sample of 100 people in the local area. In all these cases the highest SES group expressed least fear and the lowest SES group most fear.

As the type of newspaper read did vary with SES it is possible that the variance in FOC associated with newspaper readership is related to SES. To test this association further, a series of one-way analysis of variance tests were conducted to measure SES effects on FOC within the two readership groups that had a large enough spread of readers across the different SES groups: broadsheets (high SES = 17 subjects, medium SES = 21 subjects, low SES = 11 subjects) and mid-market tabloids (high SES = 10 subjects, medium SES = 33 subjects, low SES = 37 subjects). On none of the thirteen tests for each of the two newspaper groups carried out on the answers to questions about worry about victimization, assessment of risk, and number of times out after dark (see Table 7 for a detailed list of the measures) were significant results found. Thus SES

PAUL WILLIAMS AND JULIE DICKINSON

appears to have no effect independent of newspaper readership, at least for the broadsheet and mid-market tabloid groups.

The reverse of this analysis was carried out holding the largest SES group (low SES: broadsheet readers = 11, mid-market tabloid readers = 37, low-market tabloid readers = 54) steady and analysing the variance caused by newspaper readership groups. Estimates of risk for both PVCs $(F(2,93) = 4.85, p < 0.01)$ and non-PVCs $(F(2,93) = 7.28, p < 0.001)$ varied significantly, with broadsheet readers giving the most conservative estimates and low-market tabloid readers the most pessimistic ones. These results suggest that there is a newspaper effect quite separate from SES influence on perceptions of crime rates.

Qualitative analyses

Fig. 4 shows the mean judging scores for reports from each newspaper on the 'fearfulness' and 'sensationalism' of the reporting styles. The mean scores for each newspaper group are also included. Analyses of variance between the newspaper groups were carried out on the scores for 'fearfulness' and 'sensationalism'. Significant differences were found between the newspaper groups on judgements of 'fearfulness' $(F(2,157) = 4.88, p = 0.009)$ and 'sensationalism' $(F(2,157) = 28.72, p < 0.001)$. It can clearly be seen that broadsheet newspapers were judged to have the least fearful/sensational reporting styles and low-market tabloids to have the most fearful/sensational reporting styles.

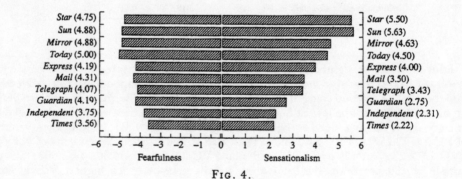

FIG. 4.

Overall results

Table 8 brings together all of the quantitative and qualitative rankings that have been shown in the newspaper analyses. There is a strong tendency for the broadsheet newspapers to have rankings within the 1–4 range; for mid-market tabloids to rank between 5 and 7; and for low-market tabloids to rank 8–10: 82.5 per cent of all rankings are consistent with this analysis and 92.5 per cent are not further than one ranking away from these ranges.

NEWSPAPER CRIME REPORTING AND FEAR OF CRIME

TABLE 8   *All Quantitative and Qualitative Rankings for All Newspapers*

Newspaper	Rankings								Mean rankings for newspaper groups
Times	3	3	4	2	4	2	3	4	
Independent	2	1	2	1	2	1	2	3	
Guardian	1	2	1	4	1	4	1	5	
Telegraph	4	4	3	3	3	3	4	1	2.59
Mail	7	7	6	5	6	8	6	7	
Express	6	6	8	9	7	10	8	2	
Today	5	5	5	7	5	5	5	10	6.46
Mirror	8	8	9	10	9	9	10	8	
Sun	10	9	10	6	8	6.5	7	6	
Star	9	10	7	8	10	6.5	9	9	8.42

The survey results showed that broadsheet readers demonstrated lowest and low-market tabloid readers highest levels of FOC on all measures except the behavioural one. While a strong relationship was found between newspaper readership groups and socioeconomic status, there was evidence that newspaper readership was related to FOC independently of socioeconomic status.

Discussion

The results show both that different newspaper groups differ greatly in how they report crime news (particularly news of crimes involving personal violence) and that the corresponding readership groups vary on most levels of FOC. The variance was in the direction predicted, namely, that people who read newspapers which contain more salient crime reports show more FOC.

There are some problems in comparing the results of the quantitative analysis in this study with previous analyses, because of differences in measurement, but the disproportionate emphasis given to violent crime found by Davis (1952), Roshier (1973), and Ditton and Duffy (1983) was confirmed in the British press. The fact that, on average, 64.5 per cent of crime news in British newspapers deals with PVCs may well enhance readers' fears. However, it may not be realistic to expect newspapers to reflect crime types and frequencies accurately when the disproportion may be a reflection of the information that is disseminated by official agencies, particularly the police.

There is evidence that newspapers 'construct' news (cf. Tuchman 1978; Lester 1980) in the differences found between newspapers. That the comparable figure for broadsheet reporting of crime as a percentage of newshole size was approximately half the average, whereas that for low-market tabloids was over twice the average, shows the disparity between what different newspapers regard as newsworthy.

All the salience measures must be regarded with some caution in that their precise influence has not been thoroughly tested. There is a need for experimental research to extend Booth's (1970) research on recall, to determine accurately the full impact of various aspects of salience on the reader.

When qualitative aspects of newspaper crime reports were examined, the same

PAUL WILLIAMS AND JULIE DICKINSON

pattern emerged: the tabloids (again, the low-market ones in particular) were judged to have the most 'sensationalized' and 'fearful' reporting styles. This analysis was essentially exploratory as little previous research has examined qualitative aspects of reporting style. Following Heath's (1984) finding that sensational crimes produced more fear and Lichtenstein *et al.*'s (1978) finding that sensational causes of death were more memorable and led to exaggerated estimates of the frequency of the cause, it was hypothesized that a sensationalized crime news report would be likely to increase FOC and attract and hold the reader's attention, making the information more available to recall. As tabloids, particularly the low-market ones, were judged to have more sensational reporting styles and low-market tabloid readers showed the highest FOC and highest estimates of the likelihood of crime, there is some support for the hypothesis that sensationalized reports increase FOC and raise estimates of the likelihood of crime. However, when the estimates of sensationalism are compared with those of fearfulness, it appears that sensationalism does not bring with it a comparable increase in fearfulness. There appears to have been a dual feeling expressed whereby judges were saying, 'I find this report frightening, but I know that it is sensationalized'. Perhaps this is one aspect of readership 'discernment' (cf. Ditton and Duffy 1983). Readership gullibility may have been previously overstated.

The questionnaire survey demonstrated that newspaper readership group quite accurately predicts FOC. Using measures of personal safety, worry about personal victimization and estimates of risk, broadsheet readers displayed least and low-market tabloid readers most FOC. Only as a predictor of behavioural differences (measured by how often respondents go out after dark) did newspaper readership fail. This may have been due, however, to the confounding effect of age: broadsheet readers were almost ten years older, on average, than tabloid readers and age was most strongly associated with restrictions in the number of times respondents went out in the evening after dark.

The results in the survey on demographic factors were in line with data recently collected in Britain (Maxfield 1987; Last and Jackson 1989). It was found that women, the elderly, and those from low-income households felt most worried and most unsafe and gave the most pessimistic risk estimates of victimization. As in other studies, behavioural restrictions are not clearly attributable to FOC. For example, women possibly go out less in the evenings because they are less likely to be car owners/drivers, and the elderly may be less likely to go out because of invalidity.

When the relationships between newspaper readership and the various indices of FOC are considered in detail it becomes clear that newspaper readership was strongly related to feelings of personal safety (whether walking alone at night or while at home at night), if not to behavioural measures. The picture was not so decisive when it came to personal anxiety about being a victim of crime. The variance in respondents' worries about PVC victimization followed the predicted pattern, but worries about non-PVC crime, especially car theft, did not. (Worry about burglary and damage to property was in the expected direction, but not significantly so.) The most striking evidence of the predictive strength of newspaper readership for FOC was displayed in readers' assessments of victimization risks for the local population. For both PVCs and non-PVCs, the readers of low-market tabloids gave estimates that were approximately three times those of the broadsheet readers.

Notwithstanding the strength of this evidence in support of the hypothesis, the possibility has to be examined that the variances might be due to other factors that

NEWSPAPER CRIME REPORTING AND FEAR OF CRIME

were common to the newspaper readership groups. The most likely factors (based on the evidence of, among others, Toseland 1982; Maxfield 1987; Last and Jackson 1989) would be age, sex, and socioeconomic status. If age were very important, one would expect that the readership group expressing least FOC (broadsheet readers) would be the youngest. However, they were, on average, almost a decade older than tabloid readers. Similarly, if sex were important, the readership group with the highest proportion of female readers—mid-market tabloids—should have displayed the highest FOC. This was not the case. Socioeconomic status, however, was both a good predictor of FOC levels and closely associated with newspaper readership patterns (higher SES subjects being most likely to read broadsheets and least likely to read low-market tabloids). Tests devised to tease out the predictive strength of newspaper readership independent of socioeconomic status showed that newspaper readership did have an independent effect. When newspaper group was controlled no significant socioeconomic status differences were found. However, when socioeconomic status was controlled significant newspaper group differences were found in assessment of the risks of crime. Since sample sizes restricted a thorough examination of the relative effects of newspaper readership and socioeconomic status, the conclusion that newspaper readership affects FOC independently of socioeconomic status must be tentative.

Despite many significant results, the survey findings must be treated with caution. To categorize respondents solely as young or old, male or female, broadsheet or tabloid reader is tempting but dangerous. Individual FOC results represent an interaction of many factors, of which only some have been measured in this survey. It could be, for example, that newspaper readership and socioeconomic status jointly reflect of some other factor not examined. It may also be that people with high FOC actively seek out newspapers with the most salient crime coverage—either to support their view of reality or for excitement (in the same way that some people often stay up to watch late-night horror movies despite being terrified by them). There is clearly a need for longitudinal studies of the effects of newspaper readership to disentangle the problem of cause and effect.

In conclusion, it can be stated that the reporting of crime by the British daily press varies enormously. Those papers that report most crime (particularly crimes involving personal violence) and in the most salient fashion (visually and stylistically) have readers who have the highest FOC levels. However, the causal link between newspapers and FOC is not clear. In any case, newspapers represent just one source of information that people receive about crime. It may well be the case that newspaper influence interacts with, or is related to, other sources of influence about crime, such as rumour. There is an argument in this paper for some newspapers in particular to report crime in a more dispassionate, objective, and responsible fashion, but there is also clearly a need for further research to pin down more precisely what it is about newspaper reports that is influential and to measure the impact that those feaures have upon the reader.

REFERENCES

BAKER, M. H., NEINSTEDT, B. C., EVERETT, R. S., and McCLEARY, R. (1983), 'The Impact of a Crime Wave: Perceptions, Fear and Confidence in the Police', *Law and Society Review*, 17/2: 319–35.

PAUL WILLIAMS AND JULIE DICKINSON

BOOTH, A. (1970), 'The Recall of News Items', *Public Opinion Quarterly*, 34/4: 606–10.

BOX, S., HALE, C., and ANDREWS, G. (1988), 'Explaining Fear of Crime', *British Journal of Criminology*, 28: 340–56.

DAVIS, F. J. (1952), 'Crime News in Colorado Newspapers', *American Journal of Sociology*, 57: 325–30.

DAVIS, F. J., and TURNER, L. W. (1951), 'Sample Efficiency in Quantitative Newspaper Content Analysis', *Public Opinion Quarterly*, 25: 762–3.

DEICHSEL, A., and STONE, P. J. (1975), 'Newspaper Headlines: A Multinational Content Analysis Project on Textual Indicators from Mass Media', *Social Science Information*, 14/1: 112–16.

DITTON, J., and DUFFY, J. (1983), 'Bias in Newspaper Reporting of Crime News', *British Journal of Criminology*, 23/2: 159–65.

EMIG, E. (1928), 'The Connotation of Newspaper Headlines', *Journalism Quarterly*, 4: 53.

ENGLISH, E. (1944), 'A Study of the Readability of Four Newspaper Headline Types', *Journalism Quarterly*, 21: 217–19.

FISHMAN, M. (1978), 'Crime News as Ideology', *Social Problems*, 25: 531–43.

GAROFALO, J. (1981), 'The Fear of Crime: Causes and Consequences', *Journal of Criminal Law and Criminology*, 72/2: 839–59.

GAROFALO, J., and LAMB, J. (1978), 'The Fear of Crime: Broadening our own Perspective', *Victimology*, 2: 242–53.

HALL, J. F. (1966), *The Psychology of Learning*. Philadelphia: Lippincott.

HARTMAN, F. R. (1961), 'Single and Multiple Channel Communication: A Review of Research and a Proposed Model', *Audio Visual Communication Review*, 9: 235–62.

HEATH, L. (1984), 'Impact of Newspaper Crime Reports on Fear of Crime: A Multimethodological Investigation', *Journal of Personality and Social Psychology*, 47/2: 263–76.

HOME OFFICE (1989), Standing Conference on Crime Prevention, Report of the Working Group on Fear of Crime (11/12/89). London: HMSO.

HUMPHRIES, D. (1981), 'Serious Crime, News Coverage and Ideology: A Content Analysis of Crime Coverage in a Metropolitan Paper', *Crime and Delinquency*, 27/2: 191–205.

JUNGER, M. (1987), 'Women's Experiences of Sexual Harassment', *British Journal of Criminology*, 22/4: 358–83.

LAST, P., and JACKSON, S. (1989), The Bristol Fear and Risk of Crime Project (A Preliminary Report on Fear of Crime). Bristol: Avon and Somerset Constabulary.

LESTER, M. (1980), 'Generating Newsworthiness: The Interpretive Construction of Public Events', *American Sociological Review*, 45: 984–94.

LICHTENSTEIN, S., SLOVIC, P., FISCHOFF, B., LAYMAN, M., and COMBS, B. (1978), 'Judged Frequency of Lethal Events', *Journal of Experimental Psychology: Human Learning and Memory*, 4/6: 551–78.

MARSH, H. L. (1991), 'A Comparative Analysis of Crime Coverage in Newspapers in the United States and other Countries from 1960 to 1989: A Review of the Literature', *Journal of Criminal Justice*, 19: 67–80.

MAXFIELD, M. (1987), *Explaining Fear of Crime: Evidence from the 1984 British Crime Survey*, Home Office Research and Planning Unit Paper no. 43. London: HMSO.

MAYHEW, P. (1989), *The 1988 British Crime Survey*, Home Office Research Study no. 111. London: HMSO.

MEYER, J. C. (1975), 'Newspaper Reporting of Crime and Justice: Analysis of an Assumed Difference', *Journalism Quarterly*, 52/4: 731–4.

NEWSPAPER CRIME REPORTING AND FEAR OF CRIME

MOORE, M. H., and TROJANOWICZ, R. C. (1988), 'Policing and the Fear of Crime', in *Perspectives in Policing*, vol. 3. Washington US Department of Justice.

PARKER, K. D., and RAY, M. C. (1990), 'Fear of Crime: An Assessment of Related Factors', *Sociological Spectrum*, 10: 29–41.

PRIYADARSINI, S. (1984), 'Crime News in Newspapers: A Case Study in Tamil Nadu, India', *Deviant Behaviour*, 5: 313–26.

QUINNEY, R. (1970), *The Social Reality of Crime*. Boston: Little, Brown.

ROSHIER, R. (1973), 'The Selection of Crime News by the Press', in S. Cohen and J. Young, eds., *The Manufacture of News*. Beverly Hills: Sage.

SHAPLAND, J. (1985), Review of Ditton and Duffy's 'Bias in Newspaper Reporting of Crime News', *British Journal of Criminology*, 25: 83–5.

SKOGAN, W. G. (1984), *The Fear of Crime*. The Hague: Research and Documentation Centre, Ministry of Justice.

—— (1986), 'Fear of Crime and Neighbourhood Change', in A. J. Reiss and M. Tonry, eds., *Crime and Justice: A Review of Research*, vol. 8: *Communities and Crime*. Chicago: University of Chicago Press.

SLOVIC, P., FISCHOFF, B., and LICHTENSTEIN, S. (1977), 'Behavioural Decision Theory', *Annual Review of Psychology*, 28: 1–39.

SMITH, S. J. (1984), 'Crime in the News', *British Journal of Criminology*, 24/3: 289–95.

TAYLOR, R. B., and HALE, M. (1986), 'Testing Alternative Models of Fear of Crime', *Journal of Criminal Law and Criminology*, 77: 151–89.

TAYLOR, S. E., and FISKE, S. T. (1978), 'Salience, Attention and Attribution Theory: Top of the Head Phenomenon', *Advances in Experimental Social Psychology*, 11: 249–86.

TAYLOR, S. E., and THOMPSON, S. C. (1982), 'Stalking the Elusive "Vividness" Effect', *Psychological Review*. 89/2: 155–81.

TOSELAND, R. W. (1982), 'Fear of Crime: Who is most Vulnerable?', *Journal of Criminal Justice*, 10: 199–209.

TUCHMAN, G. (1978. *Making News*. New York: Free Press.

TVERSKY, A., and KAHNEMAN, D. (1973), 'Availability: A Heuristic for Judging Frequency and Probability', *Cognitive Psychology*, 5: 207–32.

—— (1974). 'Judgement under Uncertainty: Heuristics and Biases', *Science*, 185: 1124–31.

WINKEL, F. W., and VRIJ. A. (1990), 'Fear of Crime and Media Crime Reports: Testing Similarity Hypotheses'. *International Review of Victimology*, 1: 251–66.

APPENDIX A

QUESTIONNAIRE

PLEASE COMPLETE THIS QUESTIONNAIRE IN THE ORDER IT IS PRESENTED BY RINGING THE APPROPRIATE ANSWER ((a))—UNLESS OTHERWISE DIRECTED.

1. How safe do you feel walking (a) VERY SAFE
   alone at night in the area of (b) FAIRLY SAFE
   your home (within ½ mile)? (c) FAIRLY UNSAFE
                       (d) VERY UNSAFE

(if (a), go on to Q4)

53

PAUL WILLIAMS AND JULIE DICKINSON

2. Why don't you feel VERY   (a) MIGHT BE ASSAULTED/MUGGED/ATTACKED
   SAFE? (if more than one   (b) FEAR OF DARK
   reason, underline main one) (c) OTHER FEAR/REASON (specify).............................
                                            (if (b) or (c), go on to Q4)

3. Why do you feel this way? (if (a) IT HAS HAPPENED TO ME BEFORE
   more than one reason,   (b) IT HAS HAPPENED TO A FRIEND/RELATIVE/
   underline main one)   NEIGHBOUR
                              (c) I HAVE SEEN/HEARD ABOUT IT ON
                                  TV/RADIO
                              (d) I HAVE READ ABOUT IT IN THE PRESS
                              (e) OTHER REASON (specify).......................................

4. How safe do you feel in your (a) VERY SAFE
   home at night?   (b) FAIRLY SAFE
                              (c) FAIRLY UNSAFE
                              (d) VERY UNSAFE
                                            (if (a), go on to Q7)

5. Why don't you feel VERY   (a) MIGHT BE BURGLED/ATTACKED
   SAFE? (if more than one   (b) RISK OF HOUSE FIRE
   reason, underline main one) (c) OTHER FEAR/REASON (specify).............................
                                            (if (b) or (c), go on to Q7)

6. Why do you feel this way?   (a) IT HAS HAPPENED TO ME BEFORE
   (if more than one reason,   (b) IT HAS HAPPENED TO A FRIEND/RELATIVE/
   underline main one)   NEIGHBOUR
                              (c) I HAVE SEEN/HEARD ABOUT IT ON
                                  TV/RADIO
                              (d) I HAVE READ ABOUT IT IN THE PRESS
                              (e) OTHER REASON (specify) ....

7. How safe do you feel driving (a) NOT APPLICABLE
   alone in your car at night? (b) VERY SAFE
                              (c) FAIRLY SAFE
                              (d) FAIRLY UNSAFE
                              (e) VERY UNSAFE
                                            (if (a) or (b), go on to Q10)

8. Why don't you feel VERY   (a) MIGHT BE ASSAULTED/MUGGED/ATTACKED
   SAFE? (if more than one   (b) MIGHT HAVE ACCIDENT
   reason, underline main one) (c) FEAR OF THE DARK
                              (d) OTHER FEAR/REASON (specify) ....
                                            (if (b), (c) or (d), go on to Q10)

9. Why do you feel this way?   (a) IT HAS HAPPENED TO ME BEFORE
   (if more than one reason,   (b) IT HAS HAPPENED TO A
   underline main one)   FRIEND/RELATIVE/NEIGHBOUR
                              (c) I HAVE SEEN/HEARD ABOUT IT ON
                                  TV/RADIO
                              (d) I HAVE READ ABOUT IT IN THE PRESS
                              (e) OTHER REASON (specify).......................................

NEWSPAPER CRIME REPORTING AND FEAR OF CRIME

10. To what extent are you worried that the following might happen to you? (ring any number on each scale, from 1 [not worried] to 7 [very worried])

  (i) being wounded/assaulted
     (not sexually)   1 — 2 — 3 — 4 — 5 — 6 — 7
 (ii) being sexually assaulted   1 — 2 — 3 — 4 — 5 — 6 — 7
(iii) being robbed/mugged   1 — 2 — 3 — 4 — 5 — 6 — 7
(iv) having your house burgled
    (whilst out)   1 — 2 — 3 — 4 — 5 — 6 — 7
 (v) having damage inflicted to
    your property   1 — 2 — 3 — 4 — 5 — 6 — 7
(vi) having your car stolen (if
    applicable)   1 — 2 — 3 — 4 — 5 — 6 — 7

11. *Imagine* a sample of *100* people living in the Worthing/Littlehampton area. How many of them do you think have been/will be victims during *1989* of the following crimes:

    woundings/assaults (not sexual) ....
    sexual assaults ....
    robberies/muggings ....
    house burglaries (whilst out) ....
    criminal damage to property ....
    thefts of cars ....

12. Thinking of the last 7 days. On how many occasions have you gone out in the evening after dark? ....

13. How many of these journeys have been made alone (ignore taxi drivers, bus drivers/passengers etc.)? ....

14. How many of these journeys have been made wholly or party by:

    foot..
    pedal cycle ....
    motor cycle/moped..
    car..
    taxi/minicab..
    bus ....
    other (specify . . . .)..

15. Which of the following newspapers do you read, and how often? (Indicate in the space provided: 'always', 'nearly always' or 'occasionally')

    Daily Express..
    Daily Mail ....
    Daily Mirror..
    Daily Star..
    The Daily Telegraph..
    The Guardian ....
    The Independent..
    The Sun..
    The Times ....
    Today..
    Evening Argus ....
    Arun Gazette ....
    Worthing Herald..

PAUL WILLIAMS AND JULIE DICKINSON

16. Do you watch BBC's *Crime-watch UK*?

    (a) Yes, always.

    (b) Yes, sometimes.
    (c) No, never.

17. How old are you?   . . . .
18. What sex are you?   . . . .
19. At what age did you leave full-time education?   . . . .

YOUR HELP IN COMPLETING THIS QUESTIONNAIRE HAS BEEN OF GREAT ASSISTANCE—THANK YOU.

Appendix B
Qualitative Analysis—Newspaper Report Examples

SEX MONSTER SHOOTS 2 ON TOP OF CLIFFS
COUPLE AMBUSHED IN SEASIDE HORROR

A brutal sex killer who executed a devoted husband and wife on a remote clifftop path was being hunted in a massive police dragnet last night.

The fiend ambushed ramblers Peter and Gwenda Dixon—called 'the loveliest couple in the world' by relatives—as they strolled at a seaside beauty spot.

Mrs Dixon, a 52-year-old secretary, was stripped half naked and detectives believe she was sexually assaulted.

MANIAC MURDERS 'PERFECT COUPLE'
POLICE IN HUNT FOR HOLIDAY RAMBLERS' KILLER

Police were hunting last night a 'cruel and clinical maniac' after they revealed the last moments of murdered nature lovers Peter and Gwenda Dixon.

The devoted couple were blasted with a shotgun as they strolled along a coastal path at a Pembrokeshire beauty spot.

Mrs Dixon, 52, was partially stripped—and may have been sexually abused—while her 50-year-old husband's wrists were bound with rope.

WALKERS TOLD TO AVOID CLIFFTOP AFTER DOUBLE KILLING

Holidaymakers were yesterday warned to stay away from a remote coastal path in West Wales near where a middle-aged couple were found shot dead.

Detectives are hunting the killer of Peter Dixon and his wife Gwenda, who were attacked as they walked a remote clifftop path near Little Haven, Dyfed.

The couple, from Witney, near Oxford, were shot several times at close range and their bodies dragged into dense scrub in the Pembrokeshire National Park.

Part IV
The Methods of Surveying

[15]

The Measurement of Fear of Crime *

Kenneth F. Ferraro, *Northern Illinois University*
Randy LaGrange, *University of North Carolina at Wilmington*

The volume of research on fear of crime in the United States is substantial and continues to regularly appear in sociology and criminology journals. Despite the amount of research on the subject, the measurement procedures most frequently used are suspect because of theoretical and methodological shortcomings. We present a conceptual definition of fear of crime and then systematically review the way it has been measured in research over the last fifteen years. The review indicates that while omnibus fear of crime and risk of crime measures are only moderately correlated, a substantial number of studies have used risk measures and generalized to fear. Suggestions for future research are offered.

Introduction

Decades of rising crime rates and extensive media coverage have made crime salient in the public's mind and fueled a substantial research agenda. The results of several studies conducted in the late sixties and the report of the President's Commission on Law Enforcement and the Administration of Justice (1967) made fear of crime the focus of widespread national attention (Wilson, 1975). These findings provided the impetus for nearly two decades of serious study of reactions to crime. During this time, several national and local opinion polls have found that crime ranks highly as one of America's most enduring and serious social problems (Beardwood, 1968; Erskine, 1974; Gallup, 1982; Skogan and Maxfield, 1981; TIME, 1985). While this body of research has aided our understanding of reactions to crime, it lacks consistency in how these reactions—especially fear of crime—have been conceptualized and measured.

In order to accurately describe, explain, or predict the occurrence of any given phenomenon, the variables under consideration must be adequately measured. Indeed, it can be said that "measurement is the basis of all science." Measurement problems beset a wide variety of research issues and hinder the process of the cumulative development of scientific knowledge. Fear of crime is one of these areas that has suffered from measurement problems. The research is replete with methodological problems that impede our ability to make useful generalizations. The purpose of this paper is to critically review and assess the measurement procedures that have been employed in empirical studies on fear of crime.

Conceptualization: The Omnibus Variable Problem

Prior to accurately measuring fear of crime one must first come to terms with its conceptual definition. Though such a statement may seem pedantic, a substantial body of the research on fear of crime has not manifested a rigorous concern for conceptual issues. As DuBow et al. (1979:1) have stated, " 'fear of crime' refers to a wide variety of subjective and emotional assessments and behavioral reports. There is a serious lack of both consistency and specificity in these reports." Indeed, even a casual review of the literature indicates that the phrase "fear of crime" has acquired so many divergent meanings that its current utility is negligible.

A major problem in conceptualizing and measuring fear of crime is the confounding of fear of crime with risk of or vulnerability to crime (Miethe and Lee, 1984). As Yin (1980:496) states in a review of the literature, "Though fear of crime is almost never explicitly defined by researchers, their measurements suggest that such fear is implicitly defined as the perception of the probability of being victimized."

Figure 1 is presented to delineate the types of crime perceptions that are variously referred to as "fear of crime." This figure is designed primarily to differentiate risk from fear and is adapted from the work of DuBow et al. (1979). The vertical axis refers to the *level of reference* of the perceptions. These range from the personal or self-oriented to the general or community-oriented. The horizontal axis refers to the *type* of perceptions ranging from cognitive to affective; the cognitive end of the continuum includes judgments of risk and safety while the affective end of the continuum includes fear reactions.

The crime perceptions identified in cells C and F refer to the varying emotional reactions generated by crime. The "values" referred to in Figure 1 represent a concern one has about crime, either for others (B) or for one's self (E). These generally take the form of public opinion regarding the seriousness of the crime problem or, on the personal level, an evaluation of one's intolerance of crime. "Judgments" are estimates of the rate of victimization for a social group (A) or the risk of victimization to the person making the judgment (D). It should not be inferred that judgments are reflections of actual realities of risk. Rather, all of these reactions are perceptions laden with subjective interpretations of reality. The major benefit of this taxonomy is that it differentiates judgments from values from emotions at both the individual and community levels. The concept of fear of crime is limited to the emotional reaction arising from crime, or symbols that a person associates with crime, to others (C) or to one's self (F). As we will point out later in this review, many researchers have not followed such a classification and have referred to fear of crime when actually measuring either judgments or values about crime.[1]

Figure 1
Classification of Crime Perceptions*

	Type of Perception		
	Cognitive		Affective
Level of Reference	*Judgments*	*Values*	*Emotions*
General	A. Risk to others; crime or safety assessments	B. Concern about crime to others	C. Fear for others' victimization
Personal	D. Risk to self; safety of self	E. Concern about crime to self; personal intolerance	F. Fear for self victimization

*Adapted from DuBow et al. 1979

Based on the premise that fear of crime is a negative emotional reaction to crime or the symbols associated with crime, it may be helpful to further describe the genesis of this emotional reaction. Physiologically speaking, fear involves a series of complex changes in bodily functioning that alerts an individual to potential danger. These bodily changes, especially in the endocrine system, can be either functional or dysfunctional to the individual (Silberman, 1981). On the one hand, fear may aid the responding capability of the individual to the point that he or she may be able to accomplish feats that were previously defined as impossible. However, fear can also be counterproductive. The bodily changes that can give added power can also result in physiological dysfunction and even incapacitation. This is most likely if the "fearful" stimuli persist without being resolved, as has been demonstrated in research on the stress process (Selye, 1956, 1974; Stagner, 1981). In comparison to the activities of everyday life, the most potent forms of fear involve an intense emotional and physiological reaction to potential danger.

Erving Goffman (1971:4) has described two basic modes of activity which differentiate fear reactions from everyday life:

> They go about their business grazing, gazing, mothering, digesting, building, resting, playing, placidly attending to easily managed matters at hand. Or, fully mobilized, a fury of intent, alarmed, they get ready to attack or to stalk or to flee.

In addition, Goffman asserts that we make use of "dissociated vigilance" to monitor the environment while engaging in everyday activities. Humans can sometimes anticipate danger in certain environments and estimate risk (i.e., a judgment in Figure 1). When estimated risk increases, one is likely to increase the monitoring of the environment. The added information guides the subsequent activity whether it is a return to previous activity, additional monitoring, or preparation for fight or flight.

Knowledge of the environment also influences the estimate of risk and concomitant levels of fear. Specifically, familiarity with an environment increases one's assessment of its safety (DuBow et al. 1979; Silberman, 1981). People who live in high crime areas oftentimes do not feel there is a high risk of victimization. Instead, "strange" people or environments are more likely to be evaluated as dangerous and provocative of fear of crime. Thus, fear of crime, as it frequently has been measured, actually may be indicating fear of strangers and inflating fear of crime with the amount of contact with strangers in a neighborhood—obviously higher in urban areas (Garofalo and Laub, 1978).

Fear of crime may be part of a more general tendency to be fearful which detracts from one's quality of life. Erikson's (1976:234) research on disaster victims indicates that the typical individual experienced " . . . a sense of vulnerability, a feeling that one has lost a certain natural immunity to misfortune, a growing conviction, even, that the world is no longer a safe place to be." Fear reactions may also be accompanied by feelings of violation, helplessness, anger, outrage, and frustration (DuBow et al. 1979).

It is this tendency to be afraid regardless of the circumstances that is most likely to be dysfunctional to individuals. It should be expected that people will be fearful when confronted by a dangerous object; fear may at times be a wholly appropriate reaction (Sarnoff and Zimbardo, 1961). However, fear of crime may also be deleterious to the individual if it is aroused by stimuli that are fundamentally innocuous. Our objective is not to extend this line of thinking into discussions of the "rationality" of fear. Rather, our purpose is to illustrate that fear, as an emotional reaction, is both an effect and a cause in its relationship to judgments of risk. Fear is influenced by judgments of risk, but also affects such judgments. To assume, however, that when one measures judgments of risk that one is measuring fear of crime is both invalid and obscures the processes that generate these perceptions. Fear of crime refers to the negative emotional reaction generated by crime or symbols associated with crime and is conceptually distinct from either judgments (risks) or concerns (values) about crime.

Another major problem with the conceptualization of fear of crime is the generic reference of the term "crime." Crime refers to a wide variety of activities including violent personal crime, property crime, organized crime,

74 KENNETH F. FERRARO AND RANDY LAGRANGE

occupational crime, public order crime, political crime, etc. While there is some value in having an overall indicator of fear of crime, it should be obvious that the fear of being victimized varies by the type of crime considered. Most research indicates that violent personal crimes, such as assault, robbery, and rape are the most frightening.

A welcomed trend in research on fear of crime has been the tendency of researchers to provide specific types of crimes for respondents to estimate their fears. Most studies, however, possess only *implicit* referents which are usually violent personal crimes. In order to get the most valid and reliable indicators of fear of crime, it is best to specify the type of crime to the respondent rather than leave it up to the respondent's own inference. A conceptual reference of crime is needed, and if the respondent is not provided with one, he or she will select one. Unfortunately, the selection procedure will probably not be a random function, thereby posing threats to the measurement properties of the instrument. If omnibus estimates of fear of crime are desired, it would be far more desirable to transform a set of individual items about specific crimes into an unobserved variable either by weighted or unweighted mathematical functions.[2] While we do not generally advocate the use of omnibus measures, there may be specific reasons for wanting to do so—perhaps if one is interested in the way a particular crime is related to the complex of residual categories of crime (e.g., Warr, 1984).

Review of the Literature

The Appendix summarizes the results of a review of the empirical research on fear of crime.[3] The entries are presented in alphabetical order with the author's name and year of publication appearing in the left-hand column. The center column lists the purported measure(s) of fear of crime utilized in each study. Whenever possible, each fear of crime measure has been recorded verbatim in the Appendix in order to preserve the operational integrity of the original work. In the few instances when the article did not provide sufficient information concerning the measurement procedures, the implied measure(s) was included in the table. Finally, the right-hand column of the Appendix notes if fear of crime was measured by a single indicator—or a series of single-item indicators—or whether a composite measure of fear of crime was constructed.

Focusing attention first upon the far right-hand column, it is readily apparent that fear of crime is frequently measured and analyzed as a single-item indicator. Indeed, more than forty percent of the forty-six studies reviewed rely solely upon a single-item indicator of fear of crime. (Thirteen additional studies, or 28.3 percent, employ more than one "fear" measure yet analyze them individually rather than as a multiple-item construct.) The methodological adequacy of this type of measurement strategy is questionable for certain types of analyses. In light of the substantial advance in sophistication of social science measurement, the desirability of multiple-item indices over single-item indicators is well documented (Bohrnstedt and Borgatta, 1981:10).[4] This is especially true when one is attempting to measure abstract theoretical constructs such as fear of crime (Miethe and Lee, 1984). Relating this knowledge to the problem at hand, any purported single-item measure of the rather complex concept of fear of crime must be viewed with some degree of caution, and study results should be assessed accordingly.

It may appear that the suggestion to use multiple indicators contradicts the suggestion to examine specific types of crime. These are really two separate issues. Throughout this essay we note the value of measuring fear of specific *types* of crime. This has been approached by a few researchers with one question per type of crime (e.g., Warr, 1984). We feel that this is an acceptable, though not ideal, practice. However, one could also use multiple indicators for a given type of crime. The objectives of the latter strategy are to enhance the psychometric properties of the measuring instruments and examine some of the range of emotional reaction typically characterized as fear. Fear may range from relatively diffuse states such as anxiety to relatively acute states such as trauma. Very little attention has been given to a consideration of the range of variation in emotional reaction. Unfortunately, when researchers have used multiple measures to form indexes, they have most frequently blended types of crime rather than degrees of fear.

Obviously, multiple-item indices are not a panacea to social measurement. Unless properly constructed and tested, one cannot be assured that composite indices and measurement scales possess appropriate psychometric properties. Interestingly, of the thirteen studies reviewed in the Appendix which utilize a fear of crime index, only two report reliability coefficients (Lee, 1982b; Miethe and Lee, 1984). This raises an empirical dilemma regarding the adequacy of the measurement process and the meaningfulness of study results. As Cohen and Cohen (1975:372) have stated, "unreliability in a partialled variable may yield grossly inaccurate results when it is ignored." At the very least researchers should heed the appeal of Bohrnstedt and Carter (1971:143):

> Our plea is for sociologists engaged in substantive research to confront the unreliability of their measurement instruments . . . we do not feel it is either unrealistic or unreasonable to expect sociologists to recognize explicitly the error existent in their instruments and to take this error into account in their analyses. At the very minimum, researchers ought to report the reliability of their measuring instruments.

Lest the reader feel that we are unduly critical of researchers who have not reported reliabilities because of the lack of methodological sophistication of the times, we would like to point out that nine of the eleven studies that use an index without reporting a reliability have been published since 1980.[5] Clearly, then, the vast majority of the fear of crime research falls prey to criticisms of its measurement sophistication and design.

Purported Measures of Fear of Crime

The main contention of this paper is that much of the fear of crime research suffers from measurement problems. Conceptual cloudiness and inappropriate operationalization taints the majority of this literature thereby distorting the meaning and the utility of the fear of crime concept. A careful scrutiny of the *item content* of fear of crime indicators offers testimony to their lack of conceptual clarity and specificity. A few examples should illustrate this point.

Consider the following question: "How safe would you feel walking alone at night in your neighborhood?" While such a question has been used to measure fear of crime (e.g., Baker et al. 1983), it more accurately measures the risk to self of walking alone at night in one's neighborhood. This is not an emotional reaction to crime, but rather a judgment about the likelihood of criminal victimization for the individual. A person who says he or she would not feel very safe may not be afraid at all, but simply aware of the relative risk. Thus, such a person may avoid walking alone in their neighborhood at night and not really manifest any fear of crime. A related question is "How likely it is that a person walking around here at night might be held up or attacked?" (e.g., Block, 1971; Erskine, 1974; Mirande, 1980). Note that the respondent is asked to make a *risk assessment of the community in general*; the level of personal fear is left unmeasured.

It should be assumed that measures which do not differentiate emotional reactions from judgments are invalid measures. People have perceptions of their risk of victimization; however, the perceived risk of victimization is vastly different from the feeling of fear of victimization. Warr and Stafford (1983) provide evidence that risk of victimization, in and of itself, is not even a strong predictor of fear of victimization.

Another measure commonly employed in fear of crime research is the National Crime Survey (NCS) question: "How safe do you feel or would you feel being out alone in your neighborhood at night?" (e.g., Baumer, 1985; Garofalo, 1979; Liska et al. 1982; Maxfield, 1984; Riger et al. 1978). Despite the popularity of this item, it is, nonetheless, inherently flawed. Garofalo (1979:82) identifies four fundamental problems with this question that detract considerably from its utility: (1) the word "crime" is not even mentioned leaving the thrust of the question more implicit than explicit;[6] (2) the geographical frame of reference is the neighborhood, which means different things to different people; (3) the respondents are asked to think about their perceived safety when *alone at night in their neighborhood*—there are few instances when this actually occurs; and (4) the part of the question that asks "do you feel or would you feel" mixes actual with hypothetical assessments of safety which are not necessarily equivalent. There is a fifth problem with the NCS question similar to that noted in the above example. That is, the item fails to differentiate relatively objective risk judgments from emotional fears of crime, thus rendering the question conceptually vague and largely invalid.[7]

Finally, the question "Is there any area right around here—that is, within a mile—where you would be afraid to walk alone at night?" has become a standard in the fear of crime literature. According to our review, it is the most frequently employed single-item indicator and has been utilized in ten different studies listed in the Appendix (Braungart et al. 1980; Clarke and Lewis, 1982; Clemente and Kleiman, 1976, 1977; DeFronzo 1979; Erskine, 1974; Jeffords, 1983; Lebowitz, 1975; Lee, 1982a, 1982b).

Contrary to the common problems cited thus far, this indicator does venture away from purely judgmental, objective assessments of one's personal risk of victimization to touch more upon fear. This is accomplished through a subtle yet important shift in wording from the idea of "safety" to feelings of being "afraid." Unfortunately, the lack of specificity in the remainder of the question overrides its apparent usefulness. For example, several of the criticisms Garofalo (1979) levels against the NCS question have equal applicability here: (1) the question, in itself, does not explicitly specify "fear of what" (fear of crime? fear of traffic? fear of becoming lost?); (2) the frame of reference is vaguely defined by the term "neighborhood"; (3) the likelihood of being alone on the neighborhood streets at night is such an unlikely event for most of us, especially for the elderly to whom much of this research has been directed, that it fails to touch base with everyday life experiences. In short, the continued use of this question as an indicator of fear of crime is difficult to justify.

Figure 2 seeks to further clarify some of these measurement problems in the context of our conceptual framework presented earlier. Applying the general model presented in Figure 1, the selected examples in Figure 2 illustrate which crime perceptions are most fully tapped by different "fear of crime" indicators. For instance, in the upper left-hand corner (cell A), the question "Do you think that people in this neighborhood are safe inside their homes at night?" (Clarke and Lewis, 1982) is a combination of judgments, or risk assessments, and a general referent (i.e., "people in this neighborhood"). Clearly the measure is conceptually distinct from the meaning which many researchers attach to it and probably is equally inappropriate as a "surrogate"

78   KENNETH F. FERRARO AND RANDY LAGRANGE

indicator of fear. By comparison, the lower right-hand corner of Figure 2 (cell F) comes closest to the conceptual domain commonly assumed to represent fear of crime. The personal level of reference is crossed with stated feelings of fear. The series of indicators employed by Warr and Stafford (1983) to measure the amount of fear for sixteen different types of victimization are good examples and provide useful measures of fear of crime.

Figure 2
Examples of Crime Perceptions

Level of Reference	Type of Perceptions		
	Cognitive		Affective
	Judgments	*Values*	*Emotions*
General	A. Do you think that people in this neighborhood are safe inside their homes at night? (Clarke and Lewis, 1982)	B. Choose the single most serious domestic problem (from a list of ten) that you would like to see government do something about. (Furstenberg, 1971)	C. I worry a great deal about the safety of my loved ones from crime and criminals. (Lee, 1982a)
Personal	D. How safe do you feel or would you feel being out alone in your neighborhood at night? (Liska et al. 1982)	E. Are you personally concerned about becoming a victim of crime? (Jaehnig et al. 1981)	F. How afraid are you of becoming the victim of (*sixteen separate offenses*) in your everyday life? (Warr and Stafford, 1983)

Discussion

Assuming we have adequately documented the weak conceptual development and the pervasive measurement problems of the research on fear of crime, some important implications arise. To the extent that this general body of literature is subject to questions of its sophistication and appropriateness, what we "know" about the phenomenon—its causes, consequences, geographic and demographic distribution—is also open to question. Another way of approaching this issue is to ask: What are the substantive consequences of using different measures of "fear of crime"? A few studies give some hints of the potential problems when one generalizes to fear from an item that actually measures a judgment or value.

To begin, research by Lee (1982a) reveals that the correlation between a fear of crime measure (i.e., emotion)[8] and risk assessments of the community (i.e., judgment) range in absolute value between .32 and .48. Even less encouraging is the correlation between the most frequently used measure in the Appendix and Lee's fear of crime measure: r = .28. Assuredly, these correlations are statistically significant; but more importantly, they reveal that *fear of crime and perceived risk of crime are only moderately related*. Based on Lee's research, one could reasonably conclude that perceived risk of crime is a poor surrogate of fear since it can, at best, explain only about twenty to twenty-five percent of the variance in fear.

The works of Warr and Stafford (1983) and Warr (1984) offer additional insight into this issue. These articles are based on data which assess both *risk* of victimization and *fear* of victimization for each of sixteen different offenses. (Thus, while most of Lee's measures are omnibus, Warr's are offense specific.) Because the data are offense specific, correlations between fear and risk for each type of crime were computed by Warr (1984:690). These correlations (between fear and risk) range between .9 and − .6 for the sixteen offenses. These results show more dramatically the problems with (1) lumping types of crime into one measure and (2) using risk measures to show fear.

The results also indicate that subject characteristics affect the relationship between fear and risk. As Warr (1984:694) notes, " . . . perceived risk of victimization does not have a uniform impact on fear among all age/sex groups." Thus anyone willing to tolerate the measurement error inherent in interpreting risk measures as fear should also realize that the error is not random, but related to subject characteristics and probably community type and test conditions as well.

In short, it appears that different measures of fear, or purported fear, of crime yield inconsistent empirical relationships. Not only are the distinctions outlined in Figure 1 helpful for conceptual purposes but meaningful in an observable way as well. The practical implications of the measurement problems are also important. Theory development and testing are hindered. More directly, recommendations for social policy may be hampered and specific efforts to reduce fear of crime may be misguided.

For example, consider the quite common and altogether unstartling observation that many people report feelings of apprehension when walking the streets of their neighborhood alone at night. Measures of this caliber partially ensure discovering elevated levels of fear simply by the dangerous scenario presented. Images of bad-guys lurking in the streets are created, and only the most courageous of souls would dare travel at night. Perhaps a more realistic and more revealing question would be "Who wouldn't be afraid to walk the streets alone at night?" It is worthy of note that several studies have found that even among "high fear" groups (e.g., the elderly), the oft-stated feelings of fear are significantly reduced when the home is the locational reference rather than the neighborhood (Davis and Brody, 1979). In other words, fear of crime may not be as problematic in the *everyday lives* of people as public opinion polls typically suggest (LaGrange and Ferraro, 1986). The standard recommendation for reducing fear—that is, increasing patrol strength on the streets—may be less effective than many believe. Other security measures such as replacing old locks, installing burglar alarms, or establishing community watch programs where residents keep an eye on their neighbors would prove less expensive and perhaps more effective in allaying feelings of fear.

Our earlier admonition that global fear of crime measures mask important differences in the degree of fear of specific crimes should not be ignored. Not all criminal offenses pose similar levels of threat to the public, partly because of differences in the likelihood of victimization (e.g., mugging versus kidnapping), and partly because of variation in the seriousness of offenses (e.g., property destruction versus sexual assault). It is generally agreed that the category of offenses called street crime, such as robbery, rape and aggravated assault, evokes the greatest fear among the public. James Q. Wilson (1975:23) writes that "predatory crime does not merely victimize individuals, it impedes and, in the extreme case, even prevents the formation and maintenance of community." McIntyre (1967) warns us that street crime reduces social interaction and the level of mutual trust, while Garofalo and Laub (1978) speak of its erosive effects on the "quality of life" of the community. Therefore, it is not surprising that assessments of the public's fear of crime generally have been assessments of their fear of street crime.

However, not everyone shares equally high levels of fear of predatory crime, nor is fear of predatory crime always the highest among the list of victimization fears. For example, Sundeen and Mathieu (1976) discovered that residents in retirement communities (i.e., an age-segregated environment) tend to fear consumer fraud more than predatory crime. In contrast, Wolf (1977) found that residents of the community at large (i.e., an age-integrated environment) have a greater fear of burglary and vandalism. Brodyaga et al. (1975) found that only murder ranks higher among the fears of women than rape, providing an additional crime in the overall fear of crime equation that rarely applies to men (Riger et al. 1978:278). Although global single-item indicators of fear of crime may serve as a useful barometer of the public's concern in general, they do not speak to the complexities of fear of crime as a social problem, nor do they immediately lend themselves to specific policy implementation. Since vague measures often raise more questions than they answer, researchers are advised to be more vigilant in their pursuit of appropriate fear of crime indicators.

Suggestions for Future Research

Recognizing these problems should issue a call for a new wave of research that improves upon this weakness in research design. Though the type of research we would consider valuable should be somewhat obvious, we would like to, nevertheless, offer some specific suggestions for future research on this topic.

First, measures of fear of crime should tap the emotional state of fear rather than judgments or concerns about crime. The phrase "how afraid" is a helpful way to examine this emotional reaction. Second, questions that attempt to measure fear of crime should make explicit reference to crime. Many researchers have based their studies upon implied meanings which are probably not valid indicators. Third, as mentioned earlier, general referents about crimes are often vague; if there is no clear crime referent, one could certainly not expect respondents' fear reactions to be reliable or valid. Thus, we recommend that specific victimizations or categories of victimizations be used to assess an individual's fear reactions.[9] This procedure should enhance object consistency upon which the fear reactions are predicated. Fourth, questions intended to measure fear of crime should be stated in a nonhypothetical format. More than ten different questions cited in the Appendix ask the respondent to estimate how they *would* feel under certain circumstances. We suggest that researchers should avoid the use of the word "would" in questions attempting to measure fear of crime. Rather, it is better to obtain specific reports about how individuals feel in everyday situations. Fifth, the qualifying phrase, "in your everyday life" brings a touch of reality to the questions regarding fear of crime. Respondents can better relate to this type of question than more abstract, hypothetical, or perhaps unlikely situations such as "when walking alone at night in your neighborhood.'' If we are truly interested in measuring fear of crime, our efforts will best be targeted toward examining the world of everyday life, not hypothetical situations.

With these suggestions in mind, the careful reader will already note that a few research studies meet all, or at least most, of these criteria. We would like to offer such studies as exemplars for the measurement of fear of crime. Two studies conducted during the mid-1970s demonstrate the value of assessing fear of specific victimizations rather than fear of crime in general. Sundeen and Mathieu (1976) asked their respondents to indicate how fearful they were of being victimized for each of four specific offenses, and Lalli and Savitz (1976) used 13 offenses to measure fear. These investigations saw the importance of a crime referent for assessing fear. Lalli and Savitz (1976:405) made use of a ''fear ladder'' for measuring fear of victimization for each of the offenses. During the personal interview a card displaying an eleven-step ladder ranging from a bottom rung indicating ''no fear'' (0) to a top rung indicating ''extreme fear'' (10) was used.

The works of Warr and Stafford (1983) and Warr (1984) are more recent examples of appropriate measurement coupled with sound scientific analyses. In these studies, respondents were asked to describe how afraid they were of becoming a victim to each of sixteen different criminal offenses. The questions tapped the emotional reaction of fear in a direct way and were based on specific victimizations. Even a casual glance at their research findings will show the crudeness of attempting to only apply omnibus measures for fear of crime. Fear reactions vary substantially by the perceived seriousness of the crime and the individual's judgment of the risk of victimization. These studies provide better measures of fear of victimization than most of the other studies and are good baselines for further analyses. As others replicate and extend their work, we will be in a much better position to understand the etiology and reduction of fear of crime.

Theoretical Epilogue

It should be readily apparent that the methodological problems in research on fear of crime have obscured theoretical development in this subject. Researchers' proclivity to term various types of perceptions about crime (i.e., cells A, B, D, and E in Figure 1) as the fear of crime has all too frequently resulted in misspecification of models and/or a confounded variable problem. We exhort researchers to use the categorical descriptions in Figure 1, or similar terms, rather than the omnibus concept of fear of crime. This will hopefully lead to more fruitful discussions of the relationships between these concepts as well as other theoretically relevant concepts (e.g., perceived seriousness of a crime). A few scholars (e.g., Furstenberg, 1971; Warr and

Stafford, 1983; Warr, 1984) have engaged in this endeavor and their work deserves serious consideration.

APPENDIX
Summary Table of Fear of Crime Studies

Study	Purported Measure (s) of Fear of Crime		Use of Measure(s)
Baker et al. (1983)	1.	How safe would you feel walking alone at night in your neighborhood?	Additive index (no reported reliability)
	2.	Think of the worst area within a mile of your house. How safe would you feel walking alone at night in this area?	
Balkin (1979)	1.	How safe do you feel being out alone in your neighborhood during the day?	Single item
Baumer (1985)	1.	How safe do you feel or would you feel being out alone in your neighborhood at night?	Single item
Block (1971)	1.	How likely is it that a person walking around here at night might be held up or attacked?	Single item
Braungart et al. (1980)	1.	Is there any area right around here—that is, within a mile—where you would be afraid to walk alone at night?	Single item
Clarke and Lewis (1982)	1.	Is there any area right around here—that is, within a mile—where you	Single item

84   KENNETH F. FERRARO AND RANDY LAGRANGE

APPENDIX (continued)

Study	Purported Measure (s) of Fear of Crime	Use of Measure(s)
	would be afraid to walk alone at night?	
	2. Do you think that people in this neighborhood are safe inside their homes at night?	
	3. Respondents chose their three most serious problems from a list of ten items with one being ''fear of being victimized.''	
Clemente and Kleiman (1976)	1. Is there any area right around here—that is, within a mile—where you would be afraid to walk alone at night?	Single item
Clemente and Kleiman (1977)	1. Is there any area right around here—that is, within a mile—where you would be afraid to walk alone at night?	Single item
Cutler (1980)	1. Is there any area right around here—that is, within a mile—where you would be afraid to walk alone at night?	Single item
DeFronzo (1979)	1. Is there any area right around here—that is, within a mile—where you would be afraid to walk alone at night?	Single item
Erskine (1974)	1. In the past year, do you feel the crime rate in your neighborhood has been increasing, decreasing, or has	Single item

APPENDIX (continued)

Study	Purported Measure (s) of Fear of Crime	Use of Measure(s)
	it remained about the same as it was before?	

2. Would you say that there is more crime in this community now than there was five years ago, or less?

3. Is there more crime in this area than there was a year ago, or less?

4. Would you say there is more crime or less crime in this area than there was a year ago?

5. Is there any area around here—that is, within a mile —where you would be afraid to walk alone at night?

6. Compared to a year ago, do you personally feel more worried, less worried, or not much different about your personal safety on the streets?

7. Compared to a year ago, are you personally more worried about violence and safety on the streets, less worried, or do you feel about the same as you did then?

8. How likely is it that a person walking around here at night might be held up or attacked?

9. What about walking alone

86   KENNETH F. FERRARO AND RANDY LAGRANGE

APPENDIX (continued)

Study	Purported Measure (s) of Fear of Crime	Use of Measure(s)
	(in your neighborhood) when it is dark—how safe do (would) you feel?	
	10. Have there been any times recently when you might have wanted to go somewhere in town but stayed home instead because you thought it would be unsafe to go there?	
	11. Compared to a year ago, do you feel more afraid and uneasy on the streets today, less uneasy, or not much different from the way you felt a few years ago?	
	12. Do you feel it is safe to walk in the streets alone in your neighborhood?	
Furstenberg (1971)	1. Respondents selected single most serious domestic problem from a list of ten they would like to see the government do something about.	Additive index of eight different offenses (no reported reliability)
	2. Respondents rated the possible risk of their being victimized on eight different offenses.	
Garofalo (1979)	1. How safe do you feel or would you feel being out alone in your neighborhood at night?	Single item
Hartnagel	1. The degree of personal	Single item

APPENDIX (continued)

Study	Purported Measure (s) of Fear of Crime	Use of Measure(s)
(1979)	safety the respondents felt in their own neighborhoods.	
	2. The safety of the city as a whole as respondents rated it.	
Hepburn and Monti (1979)	1. Have you been afraid that someone will hurt you or bother you at school?	Single item
Hunter and Baumer (1982)	1. Respondents were asked to estimate the risk of being the victim of robbery, assault, and theft (street crime).	Additive index of five questions (no reliability reported)
	2. Respondents were asked how worried they were of street crime.	
Jaehnig et al. (1981)	1. Are you personally concerned about becoming a victim of crime?	Single item
Janson and Ryder (1983)	1. A question asking respondents what are their three greatest problems.	Additive index of the three items (no reliability reported)
	2. Is living in a high crime neighborhood a serious problem to you?	
	3. Does crime in the streets cause you any special difficulties in getting around?	
Jeffords (1983)	1. Is there any area within one mile of your home where you would be afraid to walk alone at night?	Single item

88   KENNETH F. FERRARO AND RANDY LAGRANGE

APPENDIX (continued)

Study	Purported Measure (s) of Fear of Crime	Use of Measure(s)
	2. Would you be afraid to walk alone within one block of your home at night?	
	3. Are you afraid to be alone at night?	
Kennedy and Krahn (1984)	1. How safe do you feel walking alone in your neighborhood at night?	Single item
Kennedy and Silverman (1985)	1. How safe do you feel walking alone in your neighborhood at night?	Single item
Lalli and Savitz (1976)	1. Adults were asked to rate the intensity of their "fear," "concern," or "worry" of being victimized to *each of twelve* different offenses and one specific dangerous locale.	Single item
	2. Youth were asked a similar question involving eight different offenses.	
Lawton and Yaffe (1980)	1. A scale derived from ten closed-ended and sixteen open-ended questions concerning personal anxiety over crime (individual items not reported).	Additive index (no reliability reported)
Lebowitz (1975)	1. Is there any area right around here—that is, within a mile—where you would be afraid to walk alone at night?	Single item

THE MEASUREMENT OF FEAR OF CRIME   89

APPENDIX (continued)

Study	Purported Measure (s) of Fear of Crime	Use of Measure(s)
Lee (1982a)	1. Is there any area near your home—that is, within a mile—where you would be afraid to walk alone at night?	Single item
	2. How about during the day? Is there any area near your home where you would be afraid to walk alone in the daytime?	
	3. There are times during the night when I'm afraid to go outside.	
	4. If someone assaulted me, I could protect myself.	
	5. In terms of crime, do you think that your neighborhood is a very safe place in which to live?	
	6. When I am away from home, I worry about the safety of my property.	
	7. I worry a great deal about my personal safety from crime and criminals.	
	8. I worry a great deal about the safety of my loved ones from crime and criminals.	
	9. I worry a great deal about the safety of my property from crime and criminals.	
	10. Even in my home, I'm not	

90   KENNETH F. FERRARO AND RANDY LAGRANGE

APPENDIX (continued)

Study	Purported Measure (s) of Fear of Crime	Use of Measure(s)

safe from people who want to take what I have.

11. There is a reason to be afraid of becoming a victim of crime in my community.

12. My neighborhood is a very safe place in which to live.

13. Please tell us whether crime or fear of crime has been a serious problem for you in the past year.

Lee
(1982b)

1. Is there any area near your home—that is, within a mile or so—where you would be afraid to walk alone at night?

Single item and additive index of seven items (alpha of .842)

2. a) When I am away from home, I worry about the safety of my property.

b) I worry a great deal about my personal safety from crime and criminals.

c) I worry a great deal about the safety of my loved ones from crime and criminals.

d) I worry a great deal about the safety of my property from crime and criminals.

e) Even in my own home, I'm not safe from people who want to take what I have.

APPENDIX (continued)

Study	Purported Measure (s) of Fear of Crime	Use of Measure(s)
	f) There is reason to be afraid of becoming a victim of crime in my community.	
	g) Crime or fear of crime has been (no problem/a problem/a serious problem) for me in the past year.	
Lewis and Maxfield (1980)	1. How much of a problem does (burglary, robbery, assault, and sexual assault) represent?	Single item
	2. Estimate on a scale of one to ten the likelihood of being victimized for each of the above four offenses.	
	3. How safe do you feel in your neighborhood at night?	
Lindquist and Duke (1982)	1. Respondents were asked if fear of crime was a personal problem.	Single item
Liska et al. (1982)	1. How safe do you feel or would you feel being out alone in your neighborhood at night?	Single item
Maxfield (1984)	1. How safe do you feel, or would you feel, being out alone in your neighborhood at night?	Single item
Miethe and Lee (1984)	1. a) I worry a great deal about my personal safety from crime and criminals.	Additive index of violent crime (alpha of .753)
	b) I worry a great deal about	

92   KENNETH F. FERRARO AND RANDY LAGRANGE

APPENDIX (continued)

Study	Purported Measure (s) of Fear of Crime	Use of Measure(s)
	the safety of my loved ones from crime and criminals.	
	2. a) I worry a great deal about the safety of my property from crime and criminals.	Additive index of property crime (alpha of .745)
	b) When I am away from home, I worry about the safety of my property.	
Mirande (1980)	1. How likely is it that a person walking around at night might be held up or attacked?	Single item
Norton and Courlander (1982)	1. Fearfulness of vandalism.	Additive index of eight items derived from factor analysis (no reliability reported)
	2. Safety in neighborhood during the day.	
	3. Safety in neighborhood at night.	
	4. Concern over home being broken into while away.	
	5. Security in home at night.	
	6. Fear of crime preventing you from action.	
	7. Worry about assault.	
	8. Worry about robbery.	
Ollenburger (1981)	1. Do you secure your home and other structures on the premises from burglary?	Additive index (item-level correlations reported)
	2. Are you or any members of your household afraid to go out in your neighborhood after dark?	

APPENDIX (continued)

Study	Purported Measure (s) of Fear of Crime		Use of Measure(s)
	3.	All things considered, would you say that (your town) is safer from crime, about as safe, or not as safe, as it was a few years ago?	
Pollack and Patterson (1980)	1.	A "fear of property loss" scale was constructed from eleven items (only two of the items were reported as examples).	Additive indices (no reliabilities reported)
	2.	A "fear of personal assault" scale was constructed from sixteen items (only two items were reported).	
Riger et al. (1978)	1.	How safe do you feel being out alone in your neighborhood at night?	Single item
	2.	How often do you think of your own safety?	
	3.	Do you ever feel afraid that someone might deliberately harm you?	
	4.	The last time you worried about rape, how afraid or scared did you feel?	
	5.	Do you fear for the safety of others who live in your home?	
	6.	Indicate the extent of your worry to the following activities: (twelve different activities such as (1) being	

APPENDIX (continued)

Study		Purported Measure (s) of Fear of Crime	Use of Measure(s)
		home alone after dark and (2) riding with male strangers alone after dark).	
Shotland et al. (1979)	1.	Two hypothetical situations (one concerning rape, the other burglary) were presented to college females to measure their fear.	Single item
Smith and Patterson (1984)	1.	Respondents were asked how likely they thought it was that they would be the vicims of a) robbery, b) burglary, and c) vandalism during the next year.	A latent variable was created with three indicators (LISREL)
Stafford and Galle (1984)	1.	Are you afraid to go out into your neighborhood after dark by yourself?	Single item
Sundeen and Mathieu (1976)	1.	Respondents were asked to indicate how fearful they were of being victimized of each of four specific offenses: burglary, robbery, car theft, and consumer fraud.	Single item
Taylor et al. (1984)	1.	How safe would you feel being out alone in your neighborhood during the day?	Additive index (no reliability reported)
	2.	How safe would you feel being out alone in your neighborhood at night?	
Thomas and Hyman (1977)	1.	This city's downtown section just isn't safe at night anymore.	Additive index (no reliability reported)

APPENDIX (continued)

Study	Purported Measure (s) of Fear of Crime	Use of Measure(s)

2. I don't really feel that the threat of criminal behavior is any greater today than in the past.

3. The danger of becoming the victim of a criminal offense seems to be lower in this city than in many parts of the country.

4. I avoid shopping in the downtown section of this city because of the crime problem.

5. During recent years I have become more afraid of being victimized by criminals than I ever was before.

6. My family and I feel reasonably safe and secure in the community.

7. Crime is such a problem that this city is not a safe place to raise children.

8. The threat of crime has become so great that nobody can feel safe in his own home anymore.

9. Crime has become such a problem in my neighborhood that I'm afraid to go out at night.

Warr   1. Respondents were asked to   Single item
(1984)   describe how afraid they

96   KENNETH F. FERRARO AND RANDY LAGRANGE

APPENDIX (continued)

Study	Purported Measure (s) of Fear of Crime	Use of Measure(s)
	were of becoming a victim to each of sixteen different offenses.	
Warr and Stafford (1983)	1. Respondents were asked to describe how afraid they were of becoming a victim to each of sixteen different offenses.	Single item
Wiltz (1982)	1. What is the likelihood of your being victimized in the future?	Single item
	2. What is the possibility of being burglarized?	
	3. What is the possibility of having your purse snatched?	
Yin (1982)	1. How safe do you feel it is to be out alone in your neighborhood during the day?	Additive index (no reliability reported)
	2. How safe do you feel it is to be out alone in your neighborhood at night?	

ENDNOTES

*This paper was originally prepared for presentation at the annual meeting of the Southern Sociological Society, Charlotte, N.C., April, 1985. We extend our appreciation to Margaret Lyons and Ranie Huffman for library research assistance and to Kenneth Bechtel, Linda Ferraro, Joseph Harry, William Minor, Mark Warr, and two anonymous reviewers for helpful comments on earlier drafts of this paper. We thank Amber Oldham for manuscript preparation. Please direct all correspondence to Kenneth F. Ferraro, Department of Sociology and Center for Governmental Studies, Northern Illinois University, DeKalb, IL 60115.

[1]Most of the articles reviewed include the phrase "fear of crime" in the title. In some cases the conceptual inconsistency is more subtle. For example, Mullen and Donnermeyer (1985)

THE MEASUREMENT OF FEAR OF CRIME   97

attempt to focus on perceived safety from crime in their paper entitled "Age, trust, and perceived safety from crime in rural areas." However, in their attempt to compare their findings to previous studies on fear of crime, the authors imply that the fear of crime and perceived safety from crime concepts are simply opposite of each other. While it might be argued that fear of crime is the opposite of a *feeling* of safety, the authors mistakenly assume that fear of crime is the opposite of a *cognitive assessment* of safety as measured in their research.

[2]The work of Smith and Patterson (1984), applying a MIMIC model to the study of victimization, is a good work to consider on this topic. It does not deal with fear of crime as previously defined, but rather personal judgments about crime (cell D in Figure One). It is not an exemplar for the measurement of fear of crime, but the method of analysis deserves consideration. The authors use three indicators to create a latent variable with LISREL, called perceived risk, and then model the relationship between the indicators, the latent variable, and the exogenous variables. Clearly, confirmatory factor analytic models are advantageous for a number of reasons, especially when the variables of interest are theoretical constructs.

[3]The studies reviewed here were derived from a complete search of the *Social Science Index* as well as a number of pieces located during the process of researching the subject. Although this review is by no means exhaustive, it is extensive and includes the main empirical works that occupy the nucleus of the fear of crime literature.

[4]Smith (1981:296) has examined the interplay between the operational reliability of a variable and the number of items used, contending that "not only is reliability increased by using more than one item, but also validity tends to increase with larger numbers of items used." Thus, for any given variable (y), there is an underlying true score component (t) and an error component (e). The influence of item-specific errors generally decreases as items are added to the scale since error terms have a tendency to cancel each other out (Lord and Novick, 1968).

[5]At least Norton and Courlander (1982) used factor analysis to select the items to be used in their index.

[6]In all fairness we should note, as Garofalo (1979) does, that the introduction to the section in which the NCS question appears contains the following statement: "Now I'd like to get your opinion about crime in general." Hence, the location of the "fear" question in relation to the introductory statement is important and will largely influence whether the respondents are likely to be thinking specifically about crime and criminalization at the time that they answer it. For additional information on the NCS, consult the critique by Block and Block (1984).

[7]Despite the fact that the item has been repeatedly criticized, researchers continue to use it (e.g., Baumer, 1985; Maxfield, 1984).

[8]The fear of crime variable selected on the basis of face validity is number 7 in the Appendix under Lee (1982a). Risk assessments are best measured with items 5 and 11 in the same section of the Appendix.

[9]If measures of fear of specific victimizations are not available or desirable, at least categories of victimization should be used as referents. For instance, Miethe and Lee (1984) have argued that it is essential to differentiate violent crime from property crime when studying fear of crime.

REFERENCES

Baker, Mary H., Barbara C. Nienstedt, Ronald S. Everett, and Richard McCleary
    1983   "Impact of a crime wave: Perceptions, fear and confidence in the police." Law and Society Review 17:319–335.
Balkin, Steve
    1979   "Victimization rates, safety, and fear of crime." Social Problems 26:343–358.

Baumer, Terry L.
  1985   "Testing a general model of fear of crime: Data from a national sample." Journal of
          Research in Crime and Delinquency 22:239-255.
Beardwood, Roger
  1968   "The new Negro mood." Fortune 77 (January):146-151.
Block, Carolyn Rebecca, and Richard L. Block
  1984   "Crime definition, crime measurement, and victim surveys." Journal of Social Issues
          40:137-160.
Block, Richard L.
  1971   "Fear of crime and fear of police." Social Problems 19:91-101.
Bohrnstedt, George W., and Edgar F. Borgatta
  1981   Social Measurement: Current Issues. Beverly Hills, Calif.: Sage Publications.
Bohrnstedt, George W., and T. M. Carter
  1971   "Robustness in regression analysis." Pp. 118-146 in Herbert L. Costner (ed.),
          Sociological Methodology 1971. San Francisco, Calif.: Jossey-Bass.
Braungart, Margaret M., Richard G. Braungart, and William J. Hoyer
  1980   "Age, sex, and social factors in fear of crime." Sociological Focus 13:55-56.
Brodyaga, Lisa, Margaret Gates, Susan Singer, Marna Tucker, and Richardson White
  1975   Rape and Its Victims: A Report for Cities, Health Facilities, and Criminal Justice
          Agencies. Washington, D.C.: U.S. Government Printing Office.
Clarke, Alan H., and Margaret Lewis
  1982   "Fear of crime among the elderly." British Journal of Criminology 22:49-62.
Clement, Frank, and Michael B. Kleiman
  1976   "Fear of crime among the aged." Gerontologist 16:207-210.
  1977   "Fear of crime in the United States: A multivariate analysis." Social Forces 56:519-531.
Cohen, Jacob, and Patricia Cohen
  1975   Applied Multiple Regression/Correlation Analysis for the Behavioral Sciences. New
          York: Wiley.
Cutler, Stephen J.
  1980   "Safety on the streets: Cohort changes in fear." International Journal of Aging and
          Human Development 10:373-384.
Davis, Linda J., and Elaine M. Brody
  1979   Rape and Older Women. U.S. Department of Health, Education and Welfare.
          Washington, D.C.: U.S. Government Printing Office.
DeFronzo, James
  1979   "Fear of crime and handgun ownership." Criminology 17:331-339.
DuBow, Frederic, Edward McCabe, and Gail Kaplan
  1979   Reactions to Crime: A Critical Review of the Literature. Washington, D.C.: National
          Institute of Law Enforcement and Criminal Justice, U.S. Government Printing
          Office.
Erikson, Kai T.
  1976   Everything in Its Path. New York: Simon and Schuster.
Erskine, Hazel
  1974   "The polls: Fear of violence and crime." Public Opinion Quarterly 38:131-145.
Furstenberg, Frank F., Jr.
  1971   "Public reaction to crime in the street." American Scholar 40:601-610.
Gallup, George H.
  1982   The Gallup Report, Report Number 198. Princeton, N.J.: The Gallup Poll.

Garofalo, James
    1979   "Victimization and the fear of crime." Journal of Research on Crime and Delinquency 16:80-97.
Garofalo, James, and John Laub
    1978   "The fear of crime: Broadening our perspective." Victimology 3:242-253.
Goffman, Erving
    1971   Relations In Public. New York: Harper Colophon Books.
Hartnagel, Timothy F.
    1979   "The perception of fear of crime: Implications for neighborhood cohesion, social activity, and community affect." Social Forces 58:176-193.
Hepburn, John R., and D. J. Monti
    1979   "Victimization, Fear of Crime, and Adaptive Responses among High School Students." Pp. 121-132 in William H. Parsonage (ed.), Perspectives on Victimology. Beverly Hills, Calif.: Sage Publications.
Hunter, Albert, and Terry L. Baumer
    1982   "Street traffic, social integration, and fear of crime." Sociological Inquiry 52:122-131.
Jaehnig, Walter B., David H. Weaver, and Frederick Fico
    1981   "Reporting crime and fear of crime in three communities." Journal of Communication 31:88-96.
Janson, Philip, and Louise K. Ryder
    1983   "Crime and the elderly: The relationship between risk and fear." Gerontologist 23:207-212.
Jeffords, Clifford R.
    1983   "The situational relationship between age and the fear of crime." International Journal of Aging and Human Development 17:103-111.
Kennedy, Leslie W., and Harvey Krahn
    1984   "Rural-urban origin and fear of crime: The case for 'rural baggage'." Rural Sociology 49:247-260.
Kennedy, Leslie W., and Robert A. Silverman
    1985   "Significant others and fear of crime among the elderly." International Journal of Aging and Human Development 20:241-256.
LaGrange, Randy L., and Kenneth F. Ferraro
    1986   "The elderly's fear of crime: How serious is it?" Paper presented at the Annual Meeting of the Southern Sociological Society, New Orleans, La.
Lalli, Michael, and Leonard Savitz
    1976   "Fear of crime in the school enterprise and its consequences." Education and Urban Society 8:401-416.
Lawton, M. Powell, and Sylvia Yaffe
    1980   "Victimization and fear of crime in elderly public housing tenants." Journal of Gerontology 35:768-779.
Lebowitz, Barry
    1975   "Age and fearfulness: Personal and situational factors." Journal of Gerontology 30:696-700.
Lee, Gary R.
    1982a   "Sex differences in fear of crime among older people." Research and Aging 4:284-298.
    1982b   "Residential location and fear of crime among the elderly." Rural Sociology 47:655-669.

100   KENNETH F. FERRARO AND RANDY LAGRANGE

Lewis, D. A., and Michael G. Maxfield
  1980   "Fear in the neighborhoods: An investigation of the impact of crime." Journal of
          Research on Crime and Delinquency 17:160–189.
Lindquist, John H., and Janice M. Duke
  1982   "The elderly victim at risk: Explaining the fear-victimization paradox." Criminology
          20:115–126.
Liska, Allen E., Joseph Lawrence, and Andrew Sanchirico
  1982   "Fear of crime as a social fact." Social Forces 60:760–770.
Lord, Frederic M., and Melvin R. Novick
  1968   Statistical Theories of Mental Test Scores. Reading, Mass.: Addison-Wesley.
Maxfield, Michael G.
  1984   "The limits of vulnerability in explaining fear of crime: A comparative neighbor-
          hood analysis." Journal of Research in Crime and Delinquency 21:233–250.
McIntyre, Jennie J.
  1967   "Public attitudes toward crime and law enforcement." Annals 374:34–46.
Miethe, Terance, and Gary R. Lee
  1984   "Fear of crime among older people: A reassessment of the predictive power of crime-
          related factors." Sociological Quarterly 25:397–415.
Mirande, Alfredo
  1980   "Fear of crime and fear of the police in a Chicano community." Sociology and
          Social Research 64:528–541.
Mullen Robert E., and Joseph F. Donnermeyer
  1985   "Age, trust, and perceived safety from crime in rural areas." Gerontologist 25:
          237–242.
Norton, Lee, and Michael Courlander
  1982   "Fear of crime among the elderly: The role of crime prevention programs." Geron-
          tologist 22:388–393.
Ollenburger, Jane C.
  1981   "Criminal victimization and fear of crime." Research on Aging 3:101–118.
Pollack, Lance, and Arthur H. Patterson
  1980   "Territoriality and fear of crime in elderly and nonelderly homeowners." Journal of
          Social Psychology 111:119–129.
Riger, Stephanie, Margaret Gordon, and Robert Le Baily
  1978   "Women's fear of crime: From blaming to restricting the victim." Victimology
          3:274–284.
Sarnoff, Irving, and Philip G. Zimbardo
  1961   "Anxiety, fear, and social affiliation." Journal of Abnormal Social Psychology
          62:356–363.
Selye, Hans
  1956   The Stress of Life. New York: McGraw-Hill.
  1974   Stress Without Distress. Philadelphia, Penn.: J. B. Lippincott.
Shotland, R., Scott Hayward, Carlotta Young, Margaret Signorella, Kenneth Mindingall,
John Kennedy, Michael Rovine, and Edward Danowitz
  1979   "Fear of crime in residential communities." Criminology 17:34–45.
Silberman, Charles
  1981   "Fear." Pp. 5–21 in Robert C. Culbertson and Mark R. Tezak (eds.), Order Under
          Law: Readings in Criminal Justice. Prospect Heights, Ill.: Waveland Press, Inc.
Skogan, Wesley G., and Michael G. Maxfield
  1981   Coping with Crime: Individual and Neighborhood Differences. Beverly Hills, Calif.:
          Sage.

Smith, Douglas A., and E. Britt Patterson
    1984   "Applications and a generalization of MIMIC models to criminological research."
            Journal of Research in Crime and Delinquency 21:333-352.
Smith, Herman W.
    1981   Strategies of Social Research. Second edition. Englewood Cliffs, N.J.: Prentice-Hall,
            Inc.
Stafford, Mark C., and Omer P. Galle
    1984   "Victimization rates, exposure to risk, and fear of crime." Criminology 22:173-185.
Stagner, Ross
    1981   "Stress, strain, coping, and defense." Research on Aging 3:3-32.
Sundeen, Richard A., and James T. Mathieu
    1976   "The urban elderly: Environments of fear." Pp. 51-66 in Jack Goldsmith and
            Sharon S. Goldsmith (eds.), Crime and The Elderly: Challenge and Response.
            Lexington, Mass.: Lexington Books.
Taylor, Ralph B., Steven D. Gottfredson, and Sidney Brower
    1984   "Block crime and fear: Defensible space, local social ties, and territorial functioning."
            Journal of Research in Crime and Delinquency 21:303-331.
Thomas, C. N., and J. M. Hyman
    1977   "Perceptions of crime, fear of victimization, and public perceptions of police per-
            formance." Journal of Police Science and Administration. 5:305-317.
TIME
    1985   "Up in arms over crime." TIME 125: 28-34.
U.S. Government
    1967   The President's Commission on Law Enforcement and Administration of Justice:
            The Challenge of Crime in a Free Society. Washington, D.C.: U.S. Government
            Printing Office.
Warr, Mark
    1984   "Fear of victimization: Why are women and the elderly more afraid?" Social Science
            Quarterly 65:681-702.
Warr, Mark, and Mark Stafford
    1983   "Fear of victimization: A look at the proximate causes." Social Forces 61:1033-1043.
Wilson, James Q.
    1975   Thinking About Crime. New York: Vintage Books.
Wiltz, C. J.
    1982   "Fear of crime, criminal victimization and elderly blacks." Phylon 43:283-294.
Wolf, Robert
    1977   "An aid to designing prevention programs." Police Chief 44:27-29.
Yin, Peter
    1982   "Fear of crime as a problem for the elderly." Social Problems 30:240-245.
    1980   "Fear of crime among the elderly: Some issues and suggestions." Social Problems
            27:492-504.

[16]

Published as a separate and in *The Journal of Psychology*, 1976, **93**, 197-202.

METHODOLOGICAL PROBLEMS IN THE STUDY OF FEARS*

Virginia Polytechnic Institute and State University

JAMES W. CROAKE[1] AND DENNIS E. HINKLE

SUMMARY

The purpose of this paper is to elucidate methodological problems in the study of fears and to make suggestions that will facilitate future research. The most basic problem begins with a definition of "fear." Other considerations include methods of assessment, classification, and the instruments used.

A. INTRODUCTION

Since the systematic, large scale study of fears began in the early thirties (13), there have been conflicting results. While the most frequently cited studies are still those done by Jersild and his associates (14), there has been considerable recent research done in this area that has added further insight in the study of fears (5). Text writers, however, have become uncertain as to what studies should be reported and have tended to cite the classical studies even though they are 40 years old.

The purpose of the present paper is to elucidate current methodological problems in the study of fears and to make suggestions that will facilitate future research.

B. FEAR VS. ANXIETY

The specific design difficulties in the study of fear begin with defining the problem. Many studies that report fears may actually have investigated anxiety, and many reporting the results of anxiety studies may have been researching fears. Hersen (12) has presented evidence that there is a moderate relationship between fear and anxiety; however, while they are similar, they are also different phenomena. Croake and Knox (8) found that results are more consistent when investigators accept common definitions of fear (e. g., when the object that threatens is clearly in focus) and anxiety (e. g., when the object that threatens is not clearly in focus).

---

* Received in the Editorial Office on April 12, 1976, and published immediately at Provincetown, Massachusetts. Copyright by The Journal Press.
[1] Direct all correspondence to the first author at the address shown at the end of this article.

C. METHODS OF REPORTING

The methods of assessing an individual's fears have yielded varying results. For example, there seems to be an inconsistent relationship between what oneself reports as a fear and that which is observed by a nonrelated examiner (15). It has also been shown that there is a low correlation between what a parent reports as his child's fears and what the child actually reports (16, 21).

There is another dimension, however, to the problem of asking an individual to indicate his own fears. This procedure may produce results that are much different from those produced when the individual is asked to indicate fears that would be common with his peers. A method that attempts to reduce the social desirability factor in self-reporting involves asking the subject to check each item on a checklist even though such a check is not indicating a fear (e. g., "This is not a fear which I hold"). This method reduces the social recognition of marking a given item when the questionnaire or checklist is completed in the presence of one's peers, such as in a classroom setting (8).

While it has been reported that up to eight times as many fears were identified when an interview technique was used as compared to a checklist (18), the checklist is a more objective method of assessing an individual's fears. The length of the list and the nature of the items are important variables. The longer the list, the greater the number of reported fears (4). Obviously, one can only indicate those fears that appear on a given checklist; so, therefore, the number and variety of items become limiting factors.

D. CLASSIFICATION

For the past several decades, many long checklists of fears have been generated, and the lists of fears classified or categorized. For the most part, the method of determining the various categories has been logically based; i. e., the individual researcher developed the categories on the basis of what he seemed to think were the logical groupings of fears. This method of classification has resulted in many classification schemes which have varied from one researcher to the next. A given researcher may have categories unlike those found in the literature, or he may classify the same or similar items in a different category, which has made comparisons from one study to the next arduous (2).

More recently, individual researchers, concerned with this lack of a consistent classification scheme, have initially grouped fears together in categories that seem fitting to them and then have had other experts in the area or make logical changes. A final check on this cooperative approach has been to have experts independently group the fear items and statistically measure the degree of agreement using the coefficient of concordance (3). While this method may never result in unanimous agreement, the coefficient of concordance should indicate the strength of the agreement among the experts, and, hopefully through continual interaction, the experts will come closer to agreeing on the classification of fears.

E. UNEQUAL CATEGORIES

An accompanying problem in the logical classification of fears has been that of an unequal number of fears in the various categories. This has resulted in certain categories of fears being more popular simply because there have been more items to which the subject can respond. The usual method for dealing with this problem has been to assign weights to the various categories. For example, if the category "school" has 10 items and the category "political" has two items, then every time a subject indicates a political item as a fear, a weighting is assigned that is five times greater than that for a school item checked as a fear. This method of determining the weightings, and thus the most common fears, has not been questioned. It is possible that a more accurate method would be to have an equal number of items in each category; this procedure would tend not to favor items because they are presented more frequently or because they are disproportionately weighted (6).

F. POPULARITY AND INTENSITY

A second accompanying problem in the logical classification of fears, in addition to the initial problem of identifying fears, has been the task of determining the most common, the most popular, or the most intense fears. This problem is both semantic and methodological. "Most common," "most popular," and "most intense" are terms that have been used interchangeably but yet have been studied as separate phenomena. Thus the problem has been that an item on a checklist might be frequently selected without the investigator knowing how intensely it was felt. It seems necessary, therefore, for any checklist to incorporate both the recognition of a given item as a fear and the strength of the fear: e. g., "lightning" to be checked, if such a fear is felt, by use of a scale "rarely concerns me," "sometimes concerns me," "often concerns me," or "almost always concerns me" (7). It should be noted that while the use of such a scale overcomes the problem of determining fear intensity, it tends to compound the problem of using the logical approach to the classification of fears. For example, a researcher may want to use fear intensity for classification rather than classifying "types" of fears.

G. LOGICAL VS. EMPIRICAL CLASSIFICATION

The problems inherent in the logical classification of fears and other accompanying problems have been discussed above. A promising approach in solving many of the problems associated with the classification has been through the use of factor analysis. This method has become more popular in recent years (12, 17) because of the availability and easy utilization of factor analysis programs. Factor analysis is a well-recognized empirical/psychometric method of determining the number and nature of the constructs that underlie a large number of variables. In the context of this paper, factor analyzing a checklist of fears would result in clusters of fear items; each of these clusters contains items that are pairwise highly intercorrelated.

While factor analytic methodologies should not be viewed as utopian, such approaches can be used not only in determining the fear categories empirically, but also in validating the previously mentioned logical approach. The former strategy has been used more often. However, the latter combines the strengths of both the empirical approach and the logical approach, with the one validating the other. This latter procedure has been used in determining the construct validity of several fear checklists (9).

The factor analytic method used most often in the study of fears appears to be a principal component analysis with orthogonal rotation, sometimes referred to as a "little jiffy." Such a procedure can be on both checklists using a "yes-no" response mode and checklists with a "scaled" response mode. (The investigator is cautioned to consider the appropriate correlation coefficient when using one or the other of these scales—i.e., the tetrachoric coefficient in the former and the Pearson product-moment in the latter.) While this approach has been used primarily because of its ready availability, common factor analytic methodologies with oblique rotations should be considered as viable alternatives (9).

H. RELIABILITY AND VALIDITY

The problem of determining the reliability and validity of a measuring instrument (e. g., a fears checklist) is perennial. Many reliability studies have been conducted on the various scales: for example, the Louisville Behavior Check List (18), the Fear Survey Schedule II (10, 20), the Fear

Survey Schedule III (10), and the Temple Fear Survey Inventory (1). As new instruments are developed using more consistent classification schemes, reliability studies will, of necessity, be imperative.

Validity poses a greater problem. Studies have been done in an attempt to determine the concurrent validity of the Fear Survey Scale by correlating responses with the Taylor Manifest Anxiety Scale (10, 11), the Welsh-A-Scale (10, 19), and the Text Anxiety Scale (20). Such studies are limited because of the distinction that has been previously made regarding the differences between fear and anxiety. More appropriate approaches to concurrent validity would involve correlating the respective fear scales.

Age differentiation, as a method of determining construct validity, was found not to be promising because of the lack of the predictable line of best fit (linear or nonlinear) between age and the number or types of fears held (5). Use of factor analytic studies, cross-validated and/or double cross-validated, in determining the construct validity is a very promising method that should be seriously considered.

I. DEVELOPMENT OF NEW INSTRUMENTS

The methodological problems in the study of fears have been presented above, accompanied by suggestions for improvement. Implicit in the suggestions is the need for developing new instruments for assessing fears. Such development should take advantage of the 40 years of research in the area and begin the item selection by borrowing from existing instruments. This would avoid the problem of different research results as an artifact of item specificity and would make meaningful comparisons with various populations possible. A frequency count of the items checked by subjects in previous studies would eliminate those items and categories that are no longer appropriate.

Additional items would be generated as a result of interviewing people representing various age, sex, and socioeconomic strata. Interviews tap current fears which are possibly different from those mentioned by previous generations and allow items to be phrased as they are expressed by the subjects. This item pool should then be subjected to the appropriate factor analytic methodologies for the classification of the fears, as well as for cross-validation and double cross-validation studies. While these procedures would be a step toward the increased accuracy in the measurement of fears, there will always be a need to update the instrument as the fears in the population evolve.

202 JOURNAL OF PSYCHOLOGY

REFERENCES

1. BROWN, P. R., & REYNOLDS, D. N. A factor analysis of a 100-item fear survey inventory. *Behav. Res. Ther.*, 1969, 7, 399-402.
2. CROAKE, J. W. Fears of adolescence. *J. Adolescence*, 1967, 2, 459-468.
3. ――――. Dissonance theory and fear retention. *Psychology*, 1969, 6, 19-23.
4. ――――. Fears of children, *Hum. Devel.*, 1969, 12, 239-247.
5. CROAKE, J. W., & CATLIN, N. Adlerian theory and fears. *Internat. J. Sociol. Fam.*, 1975. 4,(1), 56-74.
6. CROAKE, J. W., KNOX, F. A reinvestigation of fear retention and dissonance. *Psychology*, 1971, 8, 51-54.
7. ――――. A second look at adolescent fears. *J. Adolescence*, 1971, 6, 223-227.
8. The changing nature of children's fears. *Child Stud. J.*, 1973, 3, 91-105.
9. CROAKE, J. W., HINKLE, D. E., & GLOVER, K. G. An empirical investigation of the classification of children's fears. Unpublished manuscript, Virginia Polytechnic Institute and State University, Blackburg, 1975.
10. GEER, J. H. The development of a scale to measure fear. *Behav. Res. Ther.*, 1965, 3, 45-53.
11. HERSEN, M. Fear scale norms for an in-patient population. *J. Clin. Psychol.*, 1971, 27, 375-378.
12. ――――. Self-assessment of fear. *Behav. Ther.*, 1973, 4, 241-257.
13. JERSILD, A. T., & HOLMES, F. B. A study of children's fears. *J. Exper. Educ.*, 1933, 2, 109-123.
14. JERSILD, A. T., MARKEY, F. V., & JERSILD, C. C. Children's fears, dreams, wishes, daydreams, likes, dislikes, pleasant and unpleasant memories. *Child Devel. Monog.*, 1933, 12, 144-159.
15. LANG, P. J. Fear reduction and fear behavior: Problems in treating à construct. In J. M. Shlien (Ed.), *Research in Psychotherapy* (*Vol. 3*). Washington, D. C.: Amer. Psychol. Assoc., 1968. Pp. 90-102.
16. LAPOUSSE, R., & MONK, M. A. Fears and worries in a representative sample of children. *Amer. J. Orthopsychiat.*, 1959, 29(4), 803-818.
17. MILLER, L. C., BARRETT, C. L., & Hampe, E. Factor structure of childhood fears. *J. Consult. & Clin. Psychol.*, 1972, 39, 264-268.
18. MILLER, L. C., BARRETT, C. L., HAMPE, E., & NOBLE, H. Revised anxiety scales for the Louisville behavior check list. *Psychol. Rep.*, 1971, 29, 503-511.
19. SCHROEDER, H., & CRAINE, Relationships among measures of fear and anxiety for snake phobias. *J. Consult. & Clin. Psychol.*, 36, 443.
20. SUINN, R. M. Changes in non-treated subjects: Data on a fear survey schedule and the test anxiety scale. *Behav. Res. Ther.*, 1969, 7, 205-206.
21. YARROW, M. R., CAMPBELL, J. D., & BURTON, R. V. Child Rearing. San Francisco: Jossey-Bass, 1968.

Seattle Veterans Administration Hospital
MHC (116M)
4435 Beacon Avenue South
Seattle, Washington 98108

[17]

International Review of Victimology, 1990, Vol. 1, pp. 153–167
0269-7580/90 $10
© 1990 A B Academic Publishers—Printed in Great Britain

NEW METHODOLOGICAL PERSPECTIVES FOR VICTIMIZATION SURVEYS: THE POTENTIALS OF COMPUTER-ASSISTED TELEPHONE SURVEYS AND SOME RELATED INNOVATIONS*

MARTIN KILLIAS

Institut de police scientifique et de criminologie, University of Lausanne, BFSH 1, 1015 Lausanne, Switzerland

ABSTRACT

Victimization surveys conducted outside the United States have largely followed the design of the American National Crime Survey (NCS). Due to financial constraints, however, they have consistently used far smaller samples, and they never adopted the panel design (bounding of interviews) of the NCS. Drawing on experiences from the Swiss Crime Survey, it is argued that computer-assisted telephone interviews (CATI) offer interesting solutions to the methodological difficulties resulting from these constraints. Also CATI may allow for a more precise location of incidents in time and space, and may be more efficient in controlling attrition rate (and interviewer behavior). Taken together, the suggested methodological innovations may result in more valid estimates of victimization rates.

INTRODUCTION

The Swiss Crime Survey, the first European victimization survey conducted by computer-assisted telephone interviews (CATI), was conducted in two parts. The first survey was carried out in French-speaking Switzerland in December 1984. In each. of 3,000 randomly selected private households, one person (selected according to the sampling quota) was interviewed on household and personal victimizations. Several months after the telephone interview, 95 victims of serious crimes and/or multi-victims as well as 95 non-victims (matched on sex, age, and place of residence) were personally interviewed in order to assess the reliability of the CATI method in gathering data on victimization. Since the results of this test were encouraging, the second survey was conducted in German- and Italian-speaking Switzerland in January 1987 using the same methodology and a random sample of 3.500 households[1]. Although the questionnaire of the second survey, containing some 600 variables, was somewhat more comprehensive than that of the first, an effort was made to keep the

*This research has been supported by grants from the Swiss National Science Foundation (projects nr. 1.830-0.83, 1.354-0.86).

154

two surveys as comparable as possible. Since the Swiss Crime Survey differs somewhat in design from more traditional models, the observations made in conducting this survey may be of interest to those considering similar victimization surveys in other countries (particularly if budgetary constraints are a major concern). The focus of this paper will be on the CATI technique and its implications for response rate and the location of victims.

THE NCS AND ITS ROLE IN EUROPE

Since the first American victimization surveys of the 1960s, there has been widespread application of similar surveys in a large number of countries. Due to the excellent methodological foundation of America's National Crime Survey (NCS), it was accepted by scholars as the model for victimization surveys. However, insufficient resources have not allowed this survey to be properly carried out in other countries, and those that have been conducted in Europe have never met the standards of the NCS and have required great methodological adaptations. In addition, the great respect in which the NCS is held may have been a contributory factor in the insensitivity of European and other scholars towards new areas of research within the scope of victimization surveys. Victimization surveys were considered for many years to be a means of counting crimes rather than as an instrument for collecting information on victims from their own perspective. Significantly, they were in many instances called crime surveys rather than victimization surveys as they focussed on the crime rather than the victim (Zauberman, 1985; p. 26). Interest in the victims was usually limited to geographical and social distribution of victimization and to the decision to report criminal offenses to the police.

Since 1973, when the first National Crime Survey was conducted nationwide in the United States, 65,000 households with 130,000 respondents have been interviewed every six months (Gottfredson and Hindelang, 1981). As far as sample size is concerned, the NCS is unique. Even the Canadian victimization survey of 1981 (Solicitor General 1985) covered a sample only half the size of the NCS. The 1984 British Crime Survey, which is among the largest surveys of this kind conducted outside the United States, is based on about 11,000 interviews (Hough and Mayhew, 1985). Only the Dutch victimization surveys of 1978 and 1979 (Van Dijk and Steinmetz, 1979) and the Swedish survey of 1978 (National Central Bureau of Statistics, 1981) were of comparable size. Other local and national victimization surveys seem to have been based on even smaller samples, ranging from as high as 4,000 in Denmark (Gottfredson, 1981; p. 722) to as low as 500 in Switzerland (Clinard, 1978; p. 171)[2].

In light of Europe's relatively low crime rates, samples of less than 5,000 interviewed persons do not yield sufficient data for reliable analyses.

This problem may be relatively unimportant if the survey is designed to corroborate the low crime rate shown by official data (as in the case of Clinard's study on Zurich). However, if the survey is designed to identify theoretically interesting differences between victims and non-victims, the absence of data on serious victimizations prevents any meaningful analysis. Comparing non-victims with victims of trivial offenses (who can always be found in sufficient numbers regardless of the sample size) is not a reasonable strategy since important differences only exist between victims of serious crimes and the rest of the population. Not surprisingly, European victimization surveys (except those in England and the Netherlands) have not contributed significantly to the understanding of victimization since they usually fail to identify relevant differences between victims and non-victims[3].

Assuming that funds for crime surveys will continue to be limited in Europe, it becomes necessary to find ways to increase the sample size while keeping within a restricted budget. Since the sample size is, among other things, a function of the cost per interview, interview techniques are of great importance. Mail questionnaires and telephone interviews are considerably cheaper than personal interviews, costing roughly 1/4 of the price. They allow therefore, for a sample size four to five times larger than surveys using personnal interviews. The use of either mail or telephone interviews may therefore be an acceptable way of increasing sample size and allowing for a more meaningful analysis of the given population.

THE IMPACT OF THE SURVEY METHOD ON RELIABILITY AND VALIDITY

Telephone survey methods were evaluated in the United States in the early years of the victimization surveys, and did not compare favorably to the personal interview[4]. However, computer-assisted telephone surveys[5] do not share any of the limitations of regular telephone surveys. The results of experiments conducted in the 1960s using telephone survey methods are not relevant given the progress in computer technology over the last decade. In addition, tests on the reliability of data gathered on the phone tend to corroborate the merits of computer-assisted telephone surveys. A pretest within the framework of the Canadian Victimization Survey used this method for one half of the sample while the other half of the respondents were interviewed personally; this procedure yielded the same number of victimizations regardless of the method (Evans and Leger, 1979). In our own research, 95 of the most seriously victimized persons and 95 matched non-victims were recontacted for a personal interview several months after the telephone interview. This control revealed that 3.6 per cent (N = 7) of the total number of offenses (N = 195) reported during the telephone interview had been inappropriately

156

classified. In 11 out of 95 cases, the exact number of victimizations of the same type for a given person (i.e. concerning multi-victims) did not match; 16 additional victimizations (or 8 per cent) were revealed during the personal interview, whereas 5 incidents (or 2.6 per cent) were not mentioned. However, since multi-victims were over-represented among the 95 personally interviewed victims, the number of inaccuracies is surprisingly low given the frequent difficulty in assessing the precise number of victimizations experienced by multi-victims. Only 2 out of 95 non-victims turned out to be victims through newly reported victimizations; on the other hand, 2 out of 95 victims turned out to be non-victims. We may conclude, therefore, that the telephone method allows the identification of victims with considerable accuracy and that the inaccuracies generally occur in the number and kinds of victimizations rather than in the classification of respondents as victims or non-victims[6]. Some inaccuracies may be due to the fact that a second interview took place, with the respondent having another opportunity to remember victimizations. This is particularly true of this research, in which all victimizations experienced in the victim's lifetime were taken into account (see below). The reliability of the CATI method was also satisfactory in connection with measuring attitudes (such as the fear of crime[7]).

There are a number of reasons why CATI surveys compare favourably, in terms of reliability, with more classical methods such as personal interviews. First, the program usually does not allow illegal answers, i.e. if the interviewer, in entering the respondent's answer enters the wrong code by mistake, the error will be immediately deteted by the system. Second, the centralization of the interviewers in one laboratory allows for continuous supervision of the interviewers by the researcher. Thus if unforeseen difficulties arise or interviewer biases are detected, the researcher can intervene immediately and rectify the situation before it distorts the results of the survey. Moreover, the researcher in the CATI lab can also offer assistance to the interviewers in defining offenses in situations where the correct classification of an incident is not obvious. In view of the importance of interviewer effects (Skogan, 1981; pp. 27–28; Dodge, 1985; p. 4) we opted for a frequent change of staff which necessitated the employment of many relatively inexperienced interviewers requiring more supervision and assistance.

The opportunities for assistance and supervision offered by the CATI method are an advantage over the personal interview. In personal interviews the role of interviewer becomes much more crucial. Our experience has been that interviewers sometimes simplify, abbreviate, or otherwise distort questions concerning offenses; this, of course may elicit negative answers from the respondents. Permanent supervision in conjunction with informing interviewers of the crucial character of screening questions, prevented such tendencies from becoming pervasive. The interesting point here is that the tendency to simplify such 'difficult' questions did arise despite the fact that the interviewers were paid per hour and not per interview completed. Although some of these tendencies may be due to the fact that interviewing over the phone produced routine, and thus boredom, more rapidly than personal interviewing (where most of the time is taken up in finding the respondent), the important question is how interviewers behave in personal interview situations. Do they fully respect their instructions (Dodge, 1985; p. 4)? Even less may be known about the reliability of the responses in the case of mail surveys where wrong classifications may be rather frequent (Turner, 1981; p. 26). As found in our surveys, even among the generally well educated Swiss population, many respondents did not fully realize the difference between burglary, robbery and common theft, or between an accomplished offense and an attempt. In fact, it turned out that up to 24 per cent of the incidents would have been inappropriately classified within the frame of the screening questions if no follow-up questions had helped in identifying some misunderstanding of the offense definition, and if no assistance had been offered to the respondents.

Other advantages offered by the CATI technique must also be considered. Questionnaires used in victimization surveys tend to contain many follow-up questions which may be relevant to only a few respondents. For example, questions on the consequences of an injury suffered during a robbery can be asked only of the few victims of robberies who suffered personal injury. In addition, multi-victims and persons who suffered from more serious injuries will have to answer more questions than non-victims or victims of trivial offenses. This implies a highly complex questionnaire with a large number of filters. As we experienced during the personal follow-up interviews with 95 victims and 95 matched non-victims, the complexity of this kind of questionnaire can exceed the capacity of even well trained and highly motivated interviewers. This may explain why leading victimization surveys, such as the NCS and the British Crime Survey, tend to use shorter questionnaires and neglect certain important areas such as the long term consequences of victimization, the experiences of victims with the police, social services etc. Given the constraints on the number of filters in questionnaires used in personal interviews and mail surveys, it does not seem feasible that any substantial extension to such surveys can be considered in the future. The technical possibilities offered by CATI however overcome this restriction without any difficulty. Since the program provides the next appropriate question without the interviewer's intervention, there is virtually no restriction on the number of filters that can be introduced into the questionnaire. For example, in the case of the victimization survey in German and Italian-speaking Switzerland, though the number of variables totalled more than 600, many interviews did not last longer than 5 minutes since the majority of respondents had to answer relatively few questions. On the other hand, in the case of multi-victims, the interviews sometimes lasted up to one

158

TABLE 1

Comparison of three frequently used methods in victimization surveys.

Criteria of comparison	Computer-assisted telephone interview	Personal interview	Mail questionnaire
Complexity of the questionnaire's structure (number of filters)	High (unlimited number of filters is possible)	Medium	Low (the least competent respondent has to understand the structure of the questionnaire)
Problems of the understanding of the questionnaire (e.g. in connection with crime definitions)	The researcher can assist the interviewers who can offer any explanation to the respondent	The interviewer can assist the respondent; nobody can assist or control the interviewer	The respondent is alone. Misunderstandings may be frequent and often go unnoticed
Reliability and validity of the responses	High (interviewers undersupervision and assisted = presumably less interviewer effects)	High, but depending on the qualities of interviewers (interviewer effect)	Questionable; no control (e.g. on the identity of the person who filled out the questionnaire)
Errors of recording	Hardly possible	Possible	Possible
Response rate (= rate of interviews completed in a given sample)	Medium to high	Medium to high	Low to medium
Rapidity of data analysis	High	Low	Low
Cost per interview in Switzerland	approx. 15 US $	approx. 70 US $	approx. 10 to 15 US $

hour. This flexibility may be the most important advantage of CATI over mail and personal interviews (Block and Block, 1984; p. 158). In order to maximize this advantage, the CATI method requires a particular style and structure in its questionnaire. As Sparks (1982; pp. 78–79) has pointed out, it may not be appropriate to use questionnaires designed for personal interviews when the interview is conducted over the phone.

Table 1 summarizes the different aspects and advantages to the three methods most commonly used in victimological surveys: CATI, mail, and personal interview methods. Our point is not that CATI is superior in all respects and for all types of surveys; for victimization survey research, however, we feel that it offers many relevant advantages. Wherever a majority of households have telephones, researchers may be interested in considering CATI if financial constraints prevent them conducting personal interviews with large samples. Whatever the shortcomings of CATI, they are, in our view, less significant than those of other cheap techniques (such as mail questionnaires).

PROBLEMS RELATED TO THE RESPONSE RATE

Every researcher is concerned with biases in random samples which result from refusals of respondents or failures to complete the interview. In the case of the CATI survey, the researcher has the additional problem of households which do not possess a telephone. In Switzerland, according to unpublished estimates by the Federal Office of Statistics, less than 5 per cent of all households have no telephone. It must also be considered that it is notoriously difficult to interview persons who cannot be contacted by phone, no matter what method is being used. Of the total number of sample households with telephones in German-speaking Switzerland, 5.9 per cent could never be contacted, despite being called at various hours and days (many of these telephone numbers may be secondary residences). Another 5 per cent could not be interviewed due to language and other communication barriers. Finally, 17 per cent of the persons answering the call did not agree to participate in the survey, and one per cent, after having agreed to participate at the onset of the interview, interrupted the phone call in the course of the conversation. (Given the length of the interview, this rate was surprisingly low). This means that the effort to interview one person per household in the sample set was successful in 71.3 per cent of the cases in German-speaking Switzerland. This rate is lower than that achieved in Great Britain and Australia where such research is carried out by government agencies, but considerably higher than in other surveys[8] including the victimization survey in French-speaking Switzerland. It can therefore be concluded that the response rate is a function of the efforts undertaken to obtain the participation of the persons selected and not of the survey methodology. A comparison of several victimization surveys may illustrate this point (Table 2).

160

TABLE 2
Response rate in victimization surveys.

Place and year of survey	Method of survey	Response rate	Sample size number of persons interviewed	Source
Switzerland (German and Italian-speaking parts), 1987	Computer-assisted telephone interviews	69%	3,500	Killias (1989)
Switzerland (French-speaking parts), 1984	"	approx. 60%	3,000	Killias (1989)
Canada, 7 cities, 1981	"	no indication	61,000	Solicitor General (1985)
Australia, 1979	Personal interviews	91%	18,700	Braithwaite J. (1984)
England & Wales, 1984	"	77%	11,030	Hough & Mayhew (1985)
Zurich, Switzerland, 1973	"	69%	482	Clinard (1978)
Stuttgart, West Germany, 1973	"	68%	1,073	Stephan E. (1976)
Tokyo, Japan, 1977	"	66%	661	Kühne & Miyazawa (1979)
Finland, 1973	"	approx. 50%	2,014	Aromaa (1984)
Sweden, 1978	"	no indication	10,307	National Central Bureau of Statistics (1981)
Netherlands, 1978	"	"	11,000	Van Dijk & Steinmetz (1979)
France, 1986	"	"	d11,000	Lévy et al. (1986)
Baden-Wurtemberg, West Germany, 1981	Mail interviews	59%	2,200	Arnold (1986)
Canton of Uri, Switzerland, 1984	"	53%	265	Stadler (1987)
Netherlands, Cities of more than 25,000, 1973	"	47%	4,699	Fiselier (1978)

Concerning the response rate, an interesting observation was made during the 190 follow-up interviews in French-speaking Switzerland. The willingness to respond to a second (personal) interview turned out to be much higher among victims than among non-victims, the proportion of refusals being about three times higher among the latter. Victims may, therefore, be much more motivated to give their time to a project which they view as in their interests[9]. Also talking to someone who displays interest can be rewarding to victims who resent the lack of interest and sympathy shown by others[10]. Thus, victimization surveys will tend to overestimate the crime rate since more victims respond than non-victims, particularly when the overall response rate is low. It seems that many experts on victimization surveys are not sufficiently aware of this problem. This is illustrated by the fact that in many instances, the response rate is not even indicated in research reports. Thus it is of the utmost importance that substantial resources should be available to achieve a high response rate. Therefore government agencies such as the British Home Office Research and Planning Unit or the American Bureau of Justice Statistics, may be in a better position than University research centers to conduct victimization surveys when the response rate is a major concern.

THE REFERENCE PERIOD

In the late 1960s, considerable research was conducted on the issue of memory decay and telescoping effects (Skogan, 1981; pp. 15–24). This research led to the introduction of two characteristics of NCS design, namely the reduction of the reference period to 6 months and the panel design, which allows the bounding of interviews (Fienberg, 1980; p. 35). It is estimated that the bounding of interviews results in a reduction in the number of victimizations to be taken into account by about one third (Skogan, 1981; pp. 19–21)[11]. Telescoping, therefore, seems to be a major factor in distortion if no measures are taken to prevent it. To the author's knowledge, the panel design of the NCS has, unfortunately, never been replicated in victimization studies outside the United States. Even more unfortunate, this omission has not resulted in any modification of the format employed for the screening questions. These questions usually are formulated as: Have you, during the past twelve (or 6 or 24) months, been a victim of...?[12]. Without the panel design of the NCS, this kind of screening question results in considerable over-reporting. In addition, it gives the impression that any victimization which occurred outside the reference period is not important. This can lead the victim to feel that the researcher is insensitive. Instead, screening questions in victimization surveys should follow a more natural format, asking at first whether the respondent has ever been victimized and, if so, when the event occurred. Indeed, since many respondents have some difficulty with the definition of

162

offenses, the separation of the latter from the location of an incident in space and time will facilitate the screening questions to be answered. Thus, although the location of incidents in time should not be abandoned, it should not be raised during the screening questions.

In addition, by taking into account all incidents which come to the victim's mind, the researcher obtains a certain number of important secondary advantages:

(1) There is no risk that persons who have been seriously victimized immediately before the reference period will be considered non-victims, thus reducing the risk that differences between victims and non-victims on several attitudes, e.g., fear of crime, will disappear due to inappropriate measurement of the independent variable.

(2) The suggested format of the screening questions allows the researcher the chance (and the choice) to take into account, within the framework of the follow-up questions, certain offenses which happened before the reference period. If the purpose of the research is only to estimate rates of victimization, such events are, of course, of little interest. But if the research should address other relevant questions as well, such as the long-term impact of victimization, the ways of coping with crime, the feelings of the victim on the way his/her case has been handled by the authorities, insurance companies, social workers et al., then more remote events should not be totally dismissed. At the very least those crimes which affect the victim's life for longer periods of time, such as rape, robbery and burglary, should be taken into account beyond the reference period (Kilpatrick et al., 1987). In the Swiss victimization surveys, for example, victims of burglaries were considered for detailed questioning if the burglary had occurred within the last 3 years before the interview while rape and robbery were considered without any time limit. This procedure by no means excludes the computation of rates based on incidents which happened during a specific time limit. (Indeed, the Swiss surveys have been conducted shortly before or after the New Year in order to facilitate the location of incidents in time.)

(3) Including more remote incidents has the important advantage of increasing substantially the number of victims of serious crime in the sample. For example, in the case of both Swiss Crime Surveys there was a total sample of 6,500 respondents, with 130 victims of rape (including attempts and sexual assault) and 102 victims of robbery (including attempts) but for the 12 months preceding the interview the corresponding figures were 12 cases of rape (including attempts and sexual assault) and 28 victims of robbery. Obviously, any meaningful analysis (e.g. of the distribution of risk as a function of geography, social background and lifestyle variables) is impossible with the rates based on 12 months alone. By taking into account more remote victimizations, this kind of analysis becomes feasible. As additional

investigation revealed, there seems to be no significant memory decay in cases of serious vicimization, at least not for a period of three to five years before the interview. Furthermore, there was no tendency for more remote incidents to be reported to the police more frequently (Killias, 1987; p. 325). Again, this holds true for serious crime (robbery, rape, burglary, etc). It may well be that trivial offenses tend to be forgotten rather rapidly; but since the researcher has no interest in taking into account minor remote victimizations this is not viewed as a serious problem.

Even though remote victimizations are relevant under certain conditions and should not, therefore, be totally dismissed from victimization surveys, the figures given above may give an idea of the feasibility of available alternatives when remote victimizations are not to be considered. If, as in Switzerland, the actual incidence of rape (including attempts), is about 10 in a sample of 6,500 and within a set reference period of 12 months, then any meaningful analysis of the impact of social background and lifestyle would require a sample of at least 30,000 which is simply not available in any European country. Some researchers have attempted to solve this problem by extending the scope of the definition of the most serious crimes, such as rape. In the British Crime Survey, for example, any form of sexual harassment was considered, which resulted in a remarkably low reporting rate (10 per cent, compared to 61 per cent for completed or attempted rape in the NCS and close to 40 per cent in the Swiss studies)[13]. In other studies, such as in those by Clinard (1978), Stephan (1976) and Kühne and Miyazawa (1979; p. 88), the strict limitation to the preceding 12 months in the screening questions may have produced strong telescoping effects which, due to their exceptionally small sample size (482, 741 and 661 respectively), resulted in unrealistically inflated estimates of the crime rate[14]. Therefore, a different approach to the problem of locating incidents in time would not only allow a more meaningful analysis, given the actually limited sample size, but may also result in considerably more precision in the estimates of crime rates. In this respect, some improvement in the questionnaire may indeed be a valid alternative to the panel design, as Sparks (1982; p. 76) has suggested. But even if the current NCS design is preferable, it seems obvious that it will continue to be out of range of the research budgets available to most researchers outside the United States.

CONCLUSIONS

The high prestige of the National Crime Survey has resulted in victimization surveys throughout the world being very similar in design to the NCS. However, as a result of financial constraints, surveys in other countries have used far smaller samples, and the panel design (bounding of interviews) has not been replicated in any victimization survey conducted outside the United States. It seems likely that these two crucial features of

164

the NCS methodology will continue to be unavailable in other countries. Therefore, researchers outside the United States should seriously consider alternatives to the current methodology of victimization surveys, such as computer-assisted telephone interviews (CATI) and more sophisticated questionnaires which allow a different approach to locating incidents in time and space. Such suggestions have been made in the American literature over the last ten years[15], but have not received much attention among researchers outside the United States. Studies outside the United States have also been plagued by problems related to the attrition rate; indeed, possible distortions due to low response rates need to be addressed in future research. Taken together, the suggested methodological innovations may contribute to increased precision of estimates of victimization rates[16], as well as improving the analytical power of crime surveys in the future.

NOTES

1. For further details see Killias (1989, chapter 2) and the technical reports on the two surveys: *Les Romands face au crime* (The French Swiss in the face of crime), Research Report to the Swiss National Science Foundation (project nr. 1.830–0.83), University of Lausanne, 1986; *Les Suisses allemands et les Tessinois face au crime* (The German and Italian Swiss in the face of crime), project nr. 1.354–0.86, University of Lausanne, 1987.
2. Concerning the size of other European samples in victimization surveys, see OECD/OCDE 1976; p. 52–65.
3. Concerning the absence of any correlation between victimization and the fear of crime in European research see e.g. Villmow (1979).
4. For early and more recent evaluation studies see Skogan (1981; p. 27). Particularly relevant are the encouraging results found by Tuchfarber and Klecka (1976).
5. On the methodology of computer-assisted telephone surveys, see Frey (1983).
6. Although there is no easy answer to this issue, it seems that though victimization surveys do rather well in identifying victims and non-victims, they face considerable difficulties in assessing the exact number of incidents experienced by multi-victims (Sparks, 1982; p. 86; Gottfredson, 1984; p. 43). If reliability is the major concern, priority should be given to assess prevalence rates of victimized households and individuals rather than to the computation of crime (i.e. incidence) rates.
7. Fear of crime was measured, among other things, by the usual question concerning fear while walking alone at night around one's place of residence (Gamma = .986, $p < .000$, for the association between fear as measured at the first and at the second interview).
8. Some surveys (not listed in table 2) suffered from response (completion) rates below 50 per cent, e.g., the survey by Sparks et al. (1977; p. 30) in London (41 per cent, personal interviews), and the Reactions to Crime Project (48 per cent, telephone interviews; see Skogan, 1980).
9. This hypothesis received some support from a study (Grandjean, 1988; p. 37–39) which compared 200 Swiss banks that were victims of hold-ups over the last few years with 200 banks that were not victimized in this way (matched pairs). After 6 weeks, 67 per cent of the victimized agencies had returned the (mail) questionnaire, against 56 per cent of the control group; after several reminders, the difference disappeared almost completely and was no longer statistically significant (85 and 82 per cent, respectively). Thus at first

contact and before additional efforts are made, victims are more motivated to participate. A similar result was found by Fiselier (1978; pp. 50–51, p. 267) in a victimization survey conducted through the mail in Holland. When persons who had not returned their questionnaires were interviewed, the number of victims turned out to be significantly lower than in the group of the respondents (32 against 41 per cent).

10. In a study undertaken in Hamburg, West Germany, a correlation was observed between the seriousness of victimization and the willingness to respond to additional questions. (Sessar, 1986; p. 384; note 32).

11. In the victimization survey conducted in German and Italian-speaking Switzerland, the usual 12-months limit was introduced into the screening question concerning common theft (since the more remote victimizations are not very relevant in connection with this offense). In addition, respondents were asked, within the framework of follow-up questions concerning common theft, when the incident they had reported had occurred. Interestingly, 24 per cent of the cases turned out to have occurred more than 12 months ago.

12. See, e.g., Dodge (1985; p. 5) concerning the NCS, with a limit of 6 months. Twelve months is the most common reference period. The French victimization survey included 24 months (Levy et al., 1986). Some questionnaires, such as the one used for the 1981 BCS (question no. 27), provide for the possibility of indicating older victimizations at the end of the questionnaire. This solution, however, does not prevent the difficulties discussed here, since the respondent may not be aware of this possibility when answering the screening questions. The same procedure was used by Arnold (1986) and by Stadler (1987).

13. Question no. 26 on the 1981 BCS questionnaire reads: '...since the first of January, 1981, have you been sexually attacked. assaulted or interfered with?'. Concerning the reporting rates see: Hough and Mayhew (1985; p. 62); Jamieson and Flanagan (1987; p. 155); Killias (1989; p. 120).

14. According to these studies, the rate of burglary is, per 100.000 households, 5,400 in Zurich, 7.100 in Stuttgart (West Germany), and 6.200 in Tokyo. whereas the rate for American central cities within an SMSA was 3,300 in 1984 (Flanagan and McGarell 1986; p. 249), and 2.100 for Zurich according to the Swiss Crime Survey (Killias, 1989; p. 66).

15. On telephone interviews as a cheaper method allowing larger samples. see Tuchfarber and Klecka (1976) and Block and Block (1984); on more sophisticated questionnaires as an alternative to the panel design, see Sparks (1982; pp. 76–79).

16. Even when the reporting of offenses by victims is taken into account, the estimated victimization rates differed dramatically from estimates derived from police statistics in the case of most European surveys; however, there is much more correspondence between the two data sources in England (Hough and Mayhew, 1985), Holland (van Dijk and Steinmetz, 1979) and Switzerland (Killias, 1989; pp. 45–52), suggesting the greater reliability of these surveys.

REFERENCES

Arnold, H. (1986). Kriminelle Viktimisierung und ihre Korrelate. Ergebnisse international vergleichender Opferbefragungen. *Zeitschrift für die gesamte Strafrechtswissenschaft*, **98/4**. 326–347.

Aromaa. K. (1984). Three Surveys in Finland. In *Victimization and Fear of Crime: World Perspective* (R. Block, ed.). GPO; Washington DC.

Block, C.R. and Block, R.L. (1984). Crime Definition, Crime Measurement, and Victim Surveys. *Journal of Social Issues*, **40/1**, 137–160.

166

Braithwaite, J. and Biles, D. (1984). The Australian Experience. In *Victimization and Fear of Crime: World Perspective* (R. Block, ed.). GPO; Washington DC.

Clinard, M.B. (1978). *Cities with Little Crime. The Case of Switzerland.* Cambridge University Press; Cambridge.

van Dijk, J.J.M. and Steinmetz, C.M.D. (1979). *The RCD Victim Surveys: 1974–1979.* Research and Documentation Centre, Ministry of Justice; The Hague.

Dodge, R.W. (1985). *Response to Screening Questions in the National Crime Survey* (Bureau of Justice Statistics, Technical Report). GPO; Washington DC.

Evans, J.L. and Leger, G.J. (1979). Canadian Victimization Survey: A Discussion Paper. *Canadian Journal of Criminology,* 21/2, 166–183.

Fienberg, S.E. (1980). Victimization and the National Crime Survey: Problems of Design and Analysis. In *Indicators of Crime and Justice: Quantitative Studies* (S.E. Fienberg, A.J. Reiss, eds.) pp. 33–40. GPO; Washington DC.

Fiselier, J.P.S. (1978). *Slachtoffers van delicten. Een onderzoek naar verborgen criminaliteit.* Ars Aequi Libri; Utrecht.

Flanagan, T.J. and McGarell, E.F. (eds.) (1986). *Sourcebook of Criminal Statistics – 1985* GPO; Washington DC.

Frey, J.H. (1983). *Survey Research by Telephone.* Sage Publications; London.

Gottfredson, M.R. (1981). On the Etiology of Criminal Victimization. *Journal of Criminal Law and Criminology,* 72/2.

Gottfredson, M.R. (1984). *Victims of Crime: the Dimensions of Risk* HMSO; London.

Gottfredson, M.R. and Hindelang, M.J. (1981). Sociological Aspects of Victimization. *Annual Review of Sociology,* 7, 107–126.

Grandjean, C. (1988). *Les effets des mesures de sécurité: l'exemple des attaques à main armée contre les établissements bancaires en Suisse.* Rüegger; Grüsch (Switzerland).

Hough, M. and Mayhew, P. (1985). *Taking Account of Crime: Key Findings from the Second British Crime Survey.* Home Office Research Study no 85. HMSO; London.

Jamieson, K.M. and Flanagan, T.J. (eds.) (1987). *Sourcebook of Criminal Justice Statistics – 1986.* GPO; Washington DC.

Killias, M. (1987). Nouvelles perspectives méthodologiques en matière de sondage de victimisation. L'expérience des enquêtes suisses. *Déviance et Société* 11/3, 311–330.

Killias, M. (1989). *Les Suisses face au crime: Leurs expériences et attitudes à la lumière des enquêtes suisses de victimisation.* Rüegger; Grüsch (Switzerland).

Kilpatrick, D.G. et al. (1987). Criminal Victimization: Lifetime Prevalence, Reporting to Police, and Psychological Impact. *Crime & Delinquency,* 33/4, 479–489.

Kühne, H.-H. and Miyazawa, K. (1979). *Kriminalität und Kriminalitätsgekämpfung in Japan,* Bundeskriminalamt; Wiesbaden.

Levy, R., Perez-Diaz, C., Robert. Ph. and Zauberman, R. (1986). *Profils sociaux de victimes d'infractions. Premiers résultats d'une enquête nationale.* CESDIP; Paris.

National Central Bureau of Statistics (1981). *Official Statistics of Sweden, Living Conditions Report nr. 24: Victims of Violence and Property Crime 1978,* Stockholm.

OCDE/OECD (1976). *Origines des données pour l'élaboration d'indicateurs sociaux de la violence subie par les individus.* Paris.

Sessar, K. (1986). Neue Wege de Kriminologie aus dem Strafrecht. In *Gedächtnisschrift für Hilde Kaufmann,* (H.J. Hirsch, G. Kaiser and H. Marquardt, eds.) pp. 373–391, de Gruyter; Berlin/New York.

Skogan, W.G. (1980). The Center for Urban Affairs Random Digit Dialing Telephone Survey. In *Methodological Overview of the Reactions to Crime Project* (M.G. Maxfield and A. Hunter, eds.) pp. 173–225, Center for Urban Affairs, Northwestern University; Evanston (Illinois).

Skogan, W.G. (1981). *Issues in the Measurement of Victmization.* GPO; Washington DC.

Solicitor-General Canada (1985). *Canadian Urban Victimization Survey,* No. 5.

Sparks, R.F. (1982). *Research on Victims of Crime. Accomplishments, Issues, and New Directions.* National Institute of Mental Health; Rockville (Maryland).

Sparks, R.F., Genn, H.G. and Dodd, D.J. (1977). *Surveying Victims. A Study of the Measurement of Criminal Victimization, Perception of Crime, and Attitudes to Criminal Justice.* Wiley; Chichester/New York.

Stadler, H. (1987). *Kriminalität im Kanton Uri. Eine Opferbefragung.* Huber Druck AG; Entlebuch (Switzerland).

Stephan, E. (1976). *Die Stuttgarter Opferbefragung.* Bundeskriminalamt; Wiesbaden.

Tuchfarber, A.J. and Klecka, W.R. (1976). *Random Digit Dialing. Lowering Costs of Victimization Surveys.* Police Foundation; Cincinnati (Ohio).

Turner, A.G. (1981). The San José Recall Study. In *The National Crime Survey: Working Papers, vol I: Current and Historical Perspectives* (R.G. Lehnen and W.G. Skogan, eds.) pp. 22–27. GPO; Washington DC.

Villmow, B. (1979). Die Einstellung des Opfers zu Tat und Täter. In *Das Verbrechensopfer* (G.F. Kirchhoff and K. Sessar, eds.) pp. 199–218. Studienverlag Brockmeyer; Bochum.

Zauberman, R. (1985). Sources d'informations sur les victimes et problèmes méthodologiques dans ce domaine. In *Recherches sur la victimisation, 16ème conférence de recherches criminologiques* pp. 21–66. Council of Europe; Strasbourg.

[18]

0091-4169/81/7202-0818
THE JOURNAL OF CRIMINAL LAW & CRIMINOLOGY
Copyright © 1981 by Northwestern University School of Law

Vol. 72, No. 2
Printed in U.S.A.

METHODOLOGICAL PROBLEMS IN VICTIM SURVEYS AND THEIR IMPLICATIONS FOR RESEARCH IN VICTIMOLOGY*

ANNE L. SCHNEIDER**

The purpose of this paper is to examine several of the more serious methodological problems in victimization surveying, with particular attention to the implications of certain measurement problems for basic research in victimology. Most of the paper deals with three aspects of measurement error: the amount of error contained in survey-generated estimates of victimization; the net direction of that error; and the correlates of error. Errors in survey data concerning the identification of persons as victims will be the primary focus.

OVERVIEW OF THE MAJOR METHODOLOGICAL PROBLEMS

As in any kind of survey approach, regardless of the specific topic under consideration, most of the methodological problems in victimization surveying fall into one of three categories: problems of sampling, problems in measurement, and problems of inference.

A fundamental methodological problem in victimization research is that surveys of the general population are not productive. Crime, especially serious personal crime, is a relatively rare event. Only samples of considerable size yield enough victimization incidents of any particular type to permit detailed and meaningful study. Alternative methods of sampling, such as beginning with known victims from police files or from victim programs of some type, are more efficient in generating victims, but suffer from other kinds of problems. These samples contain only known victims, those who reported their victimization to the authorities or the program. The lack of representativeness of these victims vis-a-vis the total population of victims is further increased by difficul-

---

* This article benefited greatly from insightful reviews and comments by Michael Gottfredson, Al Biderman, James Garofalo, and David Griswold. All remaining errors are the author's responsibility.

** Institute of Policy Analysis, Eugene, Oregon.

ties in locating them for the survey interview.[1] Research results based on these samples may not be applicable to the full population of victims.

Another fundamental methodological problem with surveys of victims is that researchers often attempt to develop explanatory or predictive models, or they seek to test propositions derived from causal theories, using data from a survey of a single point in time rather than a panel design. The designation of certain variables as independent or as dependent may be arbitrary and the direction of causality impossible to ascertain. This problem is particularaly acute for studies in which victimization is the dependent variable and the respondent's attitudes or behaviors are used as explanatory variables. The behaviors and attitudes are measured at the current point in time, whereas the assumed victimization occurred prior to the interview. When victimization experiences are the independent variables, however, the problem is more tractable.

The third broad area of methodological problems, which is the central focus of this paper, concerns the amount of variance in the victimization variable that is true variance and the amount that is error. Whether the error is produced by a lack of reliability or by a lack of validity is not particularly important; what is important is that measurement error can influence the conclusions drawn from research studies. Unless the investigator is aware of the nature of the error and its implications, erroneous inferences can occur.

IMPLICATIONS OF MEASUREMENT ERROR

The implication of error for the research depends on whether it is random or directional, and whether it is correlated or uncorrelated with other variables of interest to the investigator. The primary impact of random error, that is, error which is not correlated with other variables of interest to the investigator and which has a mean of zero, is that it reduces the likelihood of finding significant differences between variables when, in fact, such differences exist.

In a similar way, random error reduces the strength of measures of association such as the correlation coefficient, regression coefficient, non-

---

[1] The lack of representativeness of the sample, beginning with victims known to authorities or known to victim-oriented programs, depends on the proportion of all victims known to these authorities, the response rate of persons contacted for the purpose of interviewing, and the extent to which persons actually interviewed differ from both the non-respondent and nonreported groups. The reverse records checks, especially London and San Jose, contain information on characteristics of victims who could not be located for interviews. *See* R. SPARKS, H. GENN & D. DODD, SURVEYING VICTIMS (1977); A. Turner, San Jose Methods Test of Known Crime Victims (Nat'l Inst. of Law Enforcement & Crim. Just. Statistics Div. Rpt. No. 1, 1972).

parametric measures of association (such as gamma, sommer's d, lambda, etc.), and other similar statistics. For example, the maximum correlation coefficient that can be obtained between two variables is estimated to be the square root of the product of the non-error variance (reliability) of the variables:[2]

$$r_{max_{ab}} = \sqrt{(rel_a) (rel_b)}$$

The principle is straightforward; measures of association are based on the extent to which one variable can explain the variance in another. If part of the variance is random error, then by definition, this portion of the variance cannot be explained by any other variable. Thus, the maximum variance available to covary with some other variable is reduced. The practical effect is that when the amount of error is high, even though randomly distributed, the researcher's measures of association and tests of significance are too conservative, and biased toward finding no relationships even if they exist.[3]

A second problem pertains to directional error, that is, the mean of the error is either positive or negative. If this error is not correlated with other variables, the implication is that the investigator's description of the concept measured by the variable will be distorted. For example, there is evidence that the amount of loss estimated in victimization surveys may be exaggerated. The mean of the error, then, would be positive, and one of the implications of the errror is an overestimate in the amount that victim compensation programs would cost.

Correlated error particularly concerns researchers who are examining relationships among variables. Two kinds of correlated error should be distinguished. First, the absolute amount of error in a variable can be correlated with other variables of interest to the investigator. For example, certain types of victims may make more errors in the recall of the crime than do other types of victims. Consequently, the amount of error differs, and the investigator is likely to find that relationships which hold for one type of victim may not hold for the other. Although this phenomenon could be produced by real differences, it is also produced by different validity of the data for different types of victims.

---

[2] *See* H. WALKER & J. LEV, STATISTICAL INFERENCE 303-05 (1953), for a discussion of this coefficient.

[3] The principle can be extended to multivariate models, and in general, variables with greater error will show lower regression coefficients than variables with less error. The significance of this finding is particularly important in studies where the researcher is attempting to compare the relative impact of variables with different error variances. For example, measures of attitudes, opinions, and perceptions contain more error than do factual attributes of victims such as race, sex, and employment, and more error than factual characteristics of offenses.

Other practical problems are introduced when the absolute amount of error is correlated with other variables. For example, attempts to replicate results, or to find consistent results in several different data sets, may be thwarted because of different amounts of error in the data being used. Attempts to demonstrate consistent patterns of relationships may be confounded for the same reason.

A second, and perhaps even more troublesome, type of correlated error exists when the direction of error in one variable is related to another variable being used by the researcher. Suppose, for example, that the problem of under-reporting of crime is related to age in such a way that older persons tend to forget incidents more than younger victims do. The result would be that the relationship between age and frequency of victimization is confounded with the relationship between age and memory decay.

IDENTIFICATION OF VICTIMS IN GENERAL POPULATION SURVEYS

Of all the methodological problems confronted by the field of victimology, none is more critical than a proper determination of who has been a victim of crime. Even assuming that the investigator can settle such issues as which behaviors or events constitute victimization, there still are problems in developing adequate measures. The problems of non-recall and telescoping have been recognized for years as major contributors to the misidentification of victims as nonvictims and vice versa, but the enormous difficulties in studying these problems have generally thwarted efforts to develop estimates of validity for the categorization of persons.[4] If researchers obtained a true measure of victimization, then the data from surveys and police records could be compared directly to the true measure and the extent of error could be determined. Figure 1

---

[4] The early pilot studies, P. ENNIS, CRIMINAL VICTIMIZATION IN THE UNITED STATES: A REPORT OF A NATIONAL SURVEY (Nat'l Opinion Research Center 1967); Reiss, *Public Perceptions and Recollections About Crime, Law Enforcement, and Criminal Justice*, in 1 STUDIES IN CRIME AND LAW ENFORCEMENT IN MAJOR METROPOLITAN AREAS § 2 (1967); A. Biderman, (A Pilot Study of) Public Survey Approaches to Crime Phenomena—Report on a Design for National Study (BSSR 382, April 1966), identified most of the methodological problems in victim surveys. At this time, there have been four reverse records checks and one forward records check of crime victims. A reverse records check begins with a sample of known victims and measures the efficiency of the survey technique in capturing the events and information about them. A forward records check begins with the general population. Persons who say they were victims are tracked through the official records. The reverse records checks were done by R. SPARKS, H. GENN & D. DODD, *supra* note 1, in three areas of London, and A. Turner, *supra* note 1, for the LEAA in San Jose. Two additional reverse records checks were done by the LEAA in Washington, D.C. and Baltimore. Very little information is available about the latter two. The forward records check was conducted by A. Schneider, The Portland Forward Records Check of Crime Victims—Final Report (Ore. Research Inst., April 1977), in Portland, Oregon, from victimization survey data that had been collected earlier for different purposes.

822   *ANNE L. SCHNEIDER*   [Vol. 72

FIGURE 1

TYPES OF ERRORS IN SURVEY AND POLICE DATA

	TRUF CATEGORIZATION	
	Victim in Reference Period	Not a Victim in Reference Period
SURVEY ESTIMATE		
victim in reference period	(a)	1. external forward telescoping 2. exaggeration or lying
not a victim in reference period	3. non-recall, lying, underestimate of situation 4. external backward telescoping	(c)

	TRUE CATEGORIZATION	
	Victim in Reference period	Not a Victim in Reference Period
POLICE ESTIMATE		
victim in reference period	(a)	5. exaggeration of situation, lying
not a victim in reference period	6. non-reporting by victim 7. non-recording by police	(c)

displays different kinds of misidentification problems that occur in survey data, and for comparison purposes, in police data.

In the first two-by-two table, the cases falling on the main diagonal (cells *a* and *c*) have been correctly classified, and those on the off-diagonal are incorrect. The sources of error for the incorrect categorization are shown in Figure 1. In the lower part of the figure, the two-by-two table shows the sources of error in police estimates. Again, cases falling in the main diagonal are correctly categorized, whereas those in the off-diagonal are incorrect. In addition to the types of error shown in Figure 1, there are some victims who do not report the crime either to the police or to the interviewer. These individuals would be categorized incorrectly in both the police and survey data.

Table A contains information from four reverse records checks, one forward records check, and other methodological studies that can be used to make rough judgments about the magnitude of error in the victimization surveys and in the police data. The amount of error in survey data depends, in part, on the survey methodology, such as the quality of interviewing, questioning procedures, length of reference period, and sampling frame. Thus, the four reverse records checks are not directly comparable to one another, and the forward records check is not comparable to any of the reverse records checks.[5] Nevertheless, the figures provide rough ideas of the amount of error in studies using victimization as an independent or dependent variable.

EXTERNAL FORWARD TELESCOPING

External forward telescoping occurs when respondents place an event forward in time, in the reference period, when in fact it occurred prior to the reference period. Estimates of the magnitude of external forward telescoping, measured as the proportion of persons categorized as victims who actually were victims prior to the reference period in

---

[5] The reverse records checks are not comparable to one another because: the length of recall period differs; the questioning procedure was different; the length of the interview varied; and the interviewing contact procedures differed. Perhaps most important, the surveys differed in the types of crimes covered. The San Jose results were weighted so that each offense contributed to the overall scores for the survey in relation to its contribution to the initial sample, but in none of the other studies was the sample weighted so that it reflected the original sample, correcting for non-response, or so that it reflected offenses as represented in official data. *See* R. SPARKS, H. GENN & D. DODD, *supra* note 1; A. Schneider, *supra* note 4; A. Turner, *supra* note 1. Since the amount and type of error differ by offense, this lack of equivalency is especially important but virtually impossible to correct in secondary analysis. The Baltimore and Washington studies were the first, and were not as accurate as the San Jose or London studies. For information on the NCS study comparing bounded and unbounded surveys, *see* H. Woltman & J. Bushery, A Panel Bias Study in the National Crime Survey (paper presented at the Am. Statistical Ass'n Meetings, Aug. 25-28, 1975); H. Woltman, J. Bushery & L. Carstensen, Recall Bias and Telescoping in the National Crime Survey (Census Bureau Statistical Methods Div. Memo, Sept. 23, 1975). The technique used to estimate external forward telescoping in this study was to compare the victimization rates of the bounded part of the sample with the unbounded portion. The difference, presumably, would represent the extent of external forward telescoping into the reference period. Of course, there are other operative factors in this comparison, such as population mobility rates of the bounded and unbounded portions with the corresponding likelihood of different rates of victimization. The Census Bureau report does not discuss how these other possible contaminating factors were dealt with. *See* Lehren & Reiss, *Response Effects in the National Crime Survey*, 3 VICTIMOLOGY 110 (1978).

unbounded surveys, range to 25% (see Table A) for reference periods of six months, and to 11% for a twelve-month reference period.[6]

TABLE A

ESTIMATES OF THE PERCENT OF ERROR IN SURVEY AND POLICE VICTIMIZATION DATA

TYPE OF ERROR	Portland FRC		London RRC		San Jose RRC		Washington RRC		Baltimore RRC	NCS Experiment
	6 mo.	12 mo.	6 mo.	12 mo.	6 mo.	12 mo.	6 mo.	12 mo.	6 mo.	6 mo.
SURVEY										
A. Non-victim identified as victim										
1. External forward telescoping	18%	11%		(>4%)	13%	-	-	(>4%)	-	24%
2. Exaggeration or lying		(32%) (3)								
B. Victim identifies as non-victim										
3. Forgetting, understatement, lying to interviewer	-	-	4%	8%	32%	33%	18%	30%	33%	
4. External backward telescoping	6%	3%			3%	5%				
POLICE										
A. Non-victim identified as victim										
5. Exaggeration or lying	-	-								
B. Victim identified as non-victim										
6. Non-reporting		51%								60-70%
6a. Victim claimed to have reported, but did not		(32%) (3)								
7. Non-recording		(32%) (3)								

NON-RECALL

The reverse records checks show that the proportion who fail to recall a known crime to the interviewer has ranged from 4% in Sparks'

---

[6] The 12-month external forward telescoping estimates for the London and Washington studies are not comparable to the other estimates because, in each case, the external forward telescoping was estimated by drawing a sample of known victims within 13 to 15 months prior to the interview date. The 4% estimate is the proportion of the 15-month sample base which were pulled into the 12-month part of the time period. Forward telescoping, however, can be more extreme than this example. If the sample had included incidents 16 to 20 months in the past, some of these incidents also would have been pulled in. Thus, the London and Washington information of 12-month external forward telescoping is an underestimate if the researcher is interested in determining the proportion of incidents actually recalled in a time period that do not belong in that time period.

London study[7] for the six-month time period to 33% in the Baltimore study.[8] Sparks reports that only 8% of his respondents failed to recall the incident during the twelve-month reference period.[9] This remarkably better recall rate, in comparison with American efforts, probably is due to the improved questioning procedures used in the London study,[10] and the extensive efforts to assist respondents in remembering key dates during the previous year.[11]

EXTERNAL BACKWARD TELESCOPING

A third source of error in victim survey estimates is produced by external backward telescoping, in which the respondent places the incident earlier, out of the reference period. The procedures currently followed in almost all victimization survey work indicate that these incidents would not be counted, and in some surveys, would not even be entered with the computerized data. Although these persons are victims, the usual assumption is that the investigator wishes to identify the persons who have been victims within a particular period.

The Portland Forward Records Check[12] and the London Reverse Records Check[13] both showed that 3% of the incidents which actually occurred during the twelve-month reference period were telescoped backward out of it. The Portland estimate for external backward telescoping in a six-month reference period was 6%,[14] and the San Jose data show 5% external backward telescoping for a six-month reference period.[15]

NOT REPORTING TO THE POLICE

Information in the lower portion of Table A shows that the major source of error in police data involves an undercounting of victims attributable to victims not reporting incidents. The extent of not reporting is 60-70% according to the National Crime Survey.[16]

THE SURVEY-POLICE GAP

Estimates are given in Table A for three other sources of error, all

---

[7] R. SPARKS, H. GENN & D. DODD, *supra* note 1.

[8] *See* notes 4-5 *supra*.

[9] Sparks, Genn & Dodd, *Crimes and Victims in London*, in SAMPLE SURVEYS OF THE VICTIMS OF CRIME 43-72 (W. Skogan ed. 1976).

[10] *Id*. at 1-15.

[11] *Id*. at 16-34.

[12] A. Schneider, *supra* note 4.

[13] Sparks, Genn & Dodd, *supra* note 9.

[14] A. Schneider, *supra* note 4.

[15] A. Turner, *supra* note 1, at 6-11.

[16] Lehren & Reiss, *supra* note 5.

of which are related to the common gap between survey and police estimates of crime.[17] The major contributor to the difference between survey and police estimates is lack of reporting, but even when only the incidents that survey respondents said were reported to the police are examined, the survey data often show a higher victimization rate than police records.

In the Portland Forward Records Check, 212 out of the original 972 incidents (22%) were found in the police records. Of the 760 which could not be found, 65% were not found due to the respondents' failure to report the incident. Of those which the respondent said were reported to the police, and for which a search was undertaken, 53% were located. An estimated additional 15% had not been located due to methodological problems or the importance of protecting the victim's identity.

Thus, approximately 68% of the victims identified in the survey were accounted for, leaving 32% who apparently were miscategorized either by the survey as victims or by the police data which said they were not. Three sources of error could account for the estimated 32% missing: (1) respondent's exaggeration of a situation as a crime when legally it would not qualify, or outright fabrication of incidents; (2) respondent's telling the interviewer that the incident was reported when, in fact, it was not; (3) the police not recording the incident because it did not have the elements of an offense or for other reasons.

ESTIMATING THE ERROR

Unfortunately, the data shown in Table A cannot be used to develop estimates of the amount of error to be expected in survey-generated identification of victims and non-victims. However, hypothetical populations with known distributions of victims and non-victims can be constructed. By applying various combinations of the error estimates to this distribution, and by choosing among the various assumptions, esti-

---

[17] The gap in victimization and official records is not found in all cities nor for all crimes. In Portland, Oregon, for example, the forward records check found one in five of the offenses and accounted for about two-thirds of all the incidents that respondents claimed to have reported. A. Schneider, *supra* note 4. Sparks estimates that only one in 14 of the incidents uncovered in the London survey made it into police records. R. SPARKS, H. GENN & D. DODD, *supra* note 1. For other cities, the survey may contain far too many reported incidents, whereas in some cities there is actually a negative gap, probably produced by the serious problems in calculation of rates for the official data with denominators that do not reflect the same population as counted in the numerator. *See* Skogan, *Comparing Measures of Crime Police Statistics and Survey Estimates of Citizen Victimization in American Cities*, 1974 PROC. SOC. STATISTICS SECTION AM. STATISTICAL ASS'N 44-52; Skogan, *Measurement Problems in Official and Survey Crime Rates*, 3 J. CRIM. JUST. 17-32 (1975); W. Skogan, Key Issues in the Measurement of Crime (paper presented to the Victimology Section, Congress of the Int'l Soc'y of Criminology, Lisbon, Sept. 6, 1978), for discussion of these problems.

mates of the validity of the data can be generated. Corresponding estimates of the maximum strength of association to be expected when
using the victimization variable can be generated.

'For example, consider an unbounded survey with a twelve-month
recall period, utilizing questioning procedures similar to San Jose and
NCS, which identifies 30% of the sample as victims and 70% as nonvictims.[18] Disregarding all other sources of error for now, what proportion
in each category have been misidentified due to the problems shown in
Table A? Of the 30% identified as victims, 11% of the victims may have
telescoped the incident forward into the recall period, and a similar proportion exaggerated or lied to the interviewer (see Table B). Thus, 22%
of the 30% (7%) are incorrectly identified as victims. The estimate of
actual victims could be obtained by assuming a 33% forgetting rate as
shown in the San Jose study, and by assuming external backward telescoping for 3% of the victims as estimated in the Portland and London
studies. The survey estimate of victims, minus those misidentified and
shifted to the non-victim category, should be increased to account for
those missed. The results of these calculations, shown in Table B, indicate that the survey underestimated victimization (30% versus 36%) but,
overall, 80% of the respondents were placed in the correct categories (the
main diagonal), and only 20% are in the incorrect categories (the off-
diagonal). The index of inconsistency is .34, the correlation coefficient
(which also is phi) is .55, and the maximum correlation coefficient to be
expected when using this hypothetical variable would be .74, assuming
that the variable contains no other error and that the variables with
which it is correlated contain all true variance and no error variance.[19]

Table C contains similar types of estimates for a variety of other
conditions and assumptions. The calculations in Table C are based on
estimates of the major measurement errors in victimization surveys, but
the accuracy of the estimates used to generate the figures in Table C are
not known. Furthermore, other assumptions could change the esti-

---

[18] A bounded interview, as that term is used here, refers to an interview that is bounded
by a prior interview in that it is conducted at the beginning of the reference period, such as
the procedure used in the NCS.

[19] The index of inconsistency is used in the San Jose Study. A. Turner, *supra* note 1.
Hindelang indicates that .20 or below is considered very good; .21 to .50 indicates some
problems with the data; and above .50 is an indication of serious problems. M. HINDELANG,
M. GOTTFREDSON & J. GAROFALO, VICTIMS OF PERSONAL CRIME: AN EMPRICIAL FOUN-
DATION FOR A THEORY OF PERSONAL VICTIMIZATION (1978). It is a measure of association
similar to phi and r, but reversed in its direction, and is asymmetrical rather than symmetri-
cal. Thus, it shows the degree of association between the "standard" and the measure to be
validated. The index can vary between zero and +1 with higher scores indicating more inconsistency. All of these statistics, except the simple percentage agreement, are influenced by
the marginal distribution and, unless the marginals are equal, the statistics cannot achieve
their maximum.

mates. Thus, the coefficients.in the table should be used only as rough indications of the amount of error variance in the data. Before summarizing the implications of these figures, the critical assumptions underlying the particular calculations in Table C should be reviewed.

TABLE B

VALIDITY ESTIMATES FOR HYPOTHETICAL SURVEY DATA

	TRUE CATEGORIZATION		
	Victim	Non-Victim	Totals
SURVEY RESULTS			
Victim	(a)	(b)	(a+b)
	23	07	30
Non-Victim	(d)	(c)	(d+c)
	13	57	70
Totals	(a+d)	(b+c)	
	36	64	100

ERROR ESTIMATES:

Cell b - External forward telescoping   = 11% of a+b
         - Exaggeration or lying = 11% of a+b } $= e_b$

Cell d - Forgetting = 33% of a+d
         - External backward telescoping =   3% of a+d } $= e_d$

TRUE SCORE ESTIMATES:

Cell b = $(a+b)(e_b)$ = 30 × .22 = .07
Cell a = $(a+b)$ − $[(a+b)(e_b)]$ = .30 − [(.30)(.22)] = .23
Cell a+d = $a/(1.0−e_d)$ = 23/64 = .36[20]

DEGREE OF FIT:

Percentage Agreement =. a+c = 80%
Correlation (r) (and phi) = $ac−bd/ \sqrt{(a+b)\ (a+d)(d+c)(b+c)}$ = .55

Index of Inconsistency = $N \dfrac{(N−(a+c))}{(N^2 − [(a+d)^2 + (b+c)^2])}$ = .34

r Max = .74

---

[20] Cell a + d is found as follows: If 33% of the true victims fail to recall the incident and 3% place it outside the reference period, then the actual number of victims in the survey is 100% − 36% ≈ 64%. Thus, the number of victims identified by the survey (cell a) is 64% of the total. The number of true victims is .23/.64 ≈ .36.

1.   The amount of non-recall in a twelve-month time period is the same as that in a six-month time period for survey procedures such as those used in the American pre-tests and the NCS (see Table B).[21]

2.   The amount of non-recall could be reduced substantially if questioning procedures were improved, which probably accounts for Sparks' improved recall rate, but telescoping will not be altered by improved questioning.

3.   Bounding of interviews with a prior interview completely eliminates external forward and backward telescoping.

4.   The non-recall and telescoping error for reported and unreported offenses are the same. There are studies, reviewed below, which show that memory bias is accentuated for incidents that were not reported to the police, but the differences are not particularly great. No adjustment has been made in Table C.

5.   For comparison purposes, the survey data showed a 30-70 split of victims and non-victims and the police data showed a 10-90 split.

Readers, of course, are free to make other assumptions, and by using the data in Table A would be able to generate other estimates of error in the survey or police data. With these caveats, the implications of the calculations shown in Table C include:

1.   For unbounded surveys, a twelve-month recall period may be better than a six-month recall period, because telescoping is more strongly related to the length of the recall period than is forgetting, at least for recall periods of six to twelve months.[22]

2.   Surveys using six-month recall periods that are not bounded by a prior interview, and do not use sophisticated methods of memory improvement may contain substantially more error than any of the other options. The maximum correlation coefficient obtainable for these surveys might be as low as .44.

3.   Police data in a community that only reports 30% of its crimes, and in which there is a 10% rate of not recording, is less valid than most

---

[21] *See* A. Turner, *supra* note 1; notes 4-5 *supra*.

[22] The 12-month recall period would still be superior to the six-month in unbounded surveys even if the rate of forgetting dropped to 18%, which is the estimate obtained from the Washington study, and the 12-month data stayed the same as in example A of Table C. A six-month, unbounded survey, with external forward telescoping of 24%, exaggeration of 11%, forgetting of 18%, and external backward telescoping of 6% would show a percentage agreement of 83.5; phi = .59; and the index of inconsistency would be .43. In addition, of course, a 12-month recall period is more productive than a six-month survey in terms of the sample size of victims, especially the less common ones.

TABLE C

COMPARISON OF VALIDITY ESTIMATES UNDER DIFFERENT
ASSUMPTIONS AND CONDITIONS[23]

	RELATIONSHIP TO "TRUE" DATA			
CONDITION	Percent Agreement	Index of Inconsistency	phi(r)	Maximum r Obtainable in Analysis
SURVEY DATA (12-MONTH)				
A. EFT = 11% Exaggeration = 11% Non-Recall = 33% EBT = 3%	80%	.34	.55	.74
B. Same, except Non-Recall = 8%	90%	.26	.76	.87
SURVEY DATA (6-MONTH)				
C. EFT = 24% Exaggeration = 11% Non-Recall = 33% EBT = 6%	59%	.82	.20	.44
D. Same, except Non-Recall = 4%	88%	.38	.71	.84
BOUNDED SURVEY (6-MONTH)				
E. Exaggeration = 11% Non-Recall = 33%	84%	.33	.67	.82
F. Exaggeration = 11 Non-Recall = 4%	96%	.10	.90	.95
POLICE DATA				
A. Non-reporting = 70% Non-recording = 10%	60%	.80	.31	.55
B. Non-reporting = 60% Non-recording = 10%	77%	.52	.47	.69
C. Non-reporting = 50% Non-recording = 10%	85%	.40	.57	.76

23 The coefficients shown in the table are very rough indications of the estimated error in categorization of respondents as victims or nonvictims. EFT refers to external forward telescoping; EBT refers to external backward telescoping. For each situation described in the rows

of the survey data, but may be more valid than the six-month un-bounded interview using no special recall devices to minimize non-recall.[24]

4. With the possible exception of surveys using six-month un-bounded reference periods and no special memory aides, data produced by surveys using six or twelve-month recall periods appear to be within the range of acceptable validity. The correlation coefficients tend to be at .70 or more, the index of inconsistency is in the .30s, and the maximum obtainable correlation coefficient is .75 or better.

5. Bounded surveys using the procedures adopted by the NCS with a six-month reference period can be expected to have a high degree of validity.

AMOUNT OF ERROR BY OFFENSE

If the error in victimization data were random and uncorrelated with all other variables of interest to the researcher, then its primary impact is attenuation of the estimates of the strength of association between variables and in the tests of significance. In other words, conclusions are biased against findings.

The errors discussed thus far, however, are correlated with the type of offense under consideration, and for that reason, introduce several additional problems. Offenses that contain substantial amounts of error, such as assaults, will be more susceptible to unnecessarily conservative conclusions than will offenses which contain less error, such as burglary. Theories of victimization that seem to work for one crime may not work for another simply because of differences in the error between offenses.

---

of the table, the initial set of estimates uses the highest error figures from Table A and the last situation uses the lowest set of error figures from Table A. The estimates for surveys are based on a 30-70 distribution of victims and nonvictims. Police estimates are based on the assumption that 10% of the population has reported an offense.

[24] This article does not focus on the utility of official data for victimology research, but the interested reader might notice that if the sample of known victims, such as police records or program files, covers 60% of the actual victims, and if this sample is combined with a sample from the general population, with corresponding re-weighting if needed in later phases of the study, then the validity of the victim to nonvictim variable might approach that of a 12-month unbounded survey—provided that there were no expected differences between reporting and nonreporting victims as well as victims who participate and those who do not. Sixty percent coverage from official files is difficult to obtain, and for incidents in which 60% coverage is obtained, the 10-90 split used in Table C is too low. If so, then the validity estimates would change and worsen if the proportion who are victims increases. For rare offenses with high coverage in official data, the costs of general population surveys may not be worth the marginal improvement in accuracy, especially since error also is a function of sample size and is not taken into account in the tables. To illustrate, an offense with a true victimization rate of 2% and a reporting rate of 50% would have a percentage agreement of 98%; phi of .70; and an index of inconsistency of .51.

TABLE D

OFFENSE-SPECIFIC ERROR IN VICTIM IDENTIFICATION

	Burglary	Larceny/ Theft	Robbery	Assault	Rape
1. External Forward Telescoping					
NCS (6 months)	17%	28%	47%	30%	
San Jose (6 months)	6%	17%	22%	16%	0
Portland (6 months)	9%	17%	-	-	-
Portland (12 months)	6%	21%	-	-	-
2. Non-Recall Washington (12 months)	12%	23%	9%	35%	-
Baltimore (6 months)	14%	25%	24%	64%	-
San Jose (6 months)	5%	22%	24%	49%	53%
San Jose (12 months)	10%	9%	24%	52%	33%
London (12 months)	4%	11%	------------------11%------------------		
3. External Backward Telescoping San Jose (6 months)	5%	4%	10%	6%	0
Portland (6 months)	4%	7%	-	-	-
Portland (12 months)	3%	6%	-	-	-
4. Nonreporting by victim to police (NCS)	52%	73%	47%	53%	47%

Table D contains estimates of the amount of external forward telescoping, non-recall, and external backward telescoping for burglary, larceny, robbery, assault, and rape. These errors all influence the accuracy of a survey's categorization of persons as victims of these offenses. In addition, the proportion of these offenses not reported to the police, based on NCS data, is shown in Table D.

The data show that survey identification of persons whose homes have been burglarized probably is more accurate than identification of any other offenses. The non-recall rate for burglaries is less than 15%. The amount of external forward telescoping is estimated to be less than 10% except for the NCS estimate. The amount of external backward telescoping is 5% or less. Assaults appear to suffer from the greatest amount of error. The non-recall rate is exceptionally high, and the rates of external forward and backward telescoping both are substantial. Data are far less accurate on incidents of rape, but the recall rate for rape appears as poor as that for assaults, although the telescoping may not be as severe. This finding could indicate that non-recall for the rape incidents is attributable not to actual lack of memory but to unwillingness to report the incident to the interviewer. Larcenies and theft seem to have about the same amount of error as robberies. Both have more error than burglaries but less than assault and rape.

The proportion of incidents reported to the police, according to survey respondents, varies substantially among the different offenses, with larcenies and thefts being especially underreported. As indicated by the last row of Table D, police data should be expected to omit about half the incidents of burglary (52%), robbery and rape (47%), and assault (53%), but to omit 73% of the larcenies and thefts. Because larcenies are particularly subject to external forward telescoping combined with relatively good recall in the surveys, and because they are not likely to be reported to the police, survey data often suggest that a much greater proportion of all incidents are larcenies than would be shown in the police data.

The major implications of the information in Table D can be summarized as follows: First, because of different errors in the data, survey information will not show the same patterns of offenses as police data. In particular, police data will indicate that a smaller proportion of all incidents are larcenies, whereas survey data will show that a larger proportion are larcenies.

Second, the strength of relationships between burglary and other variables should be closer to the true magnitude of the relationship, although still underestimated. The strength of relationships between the other crimes and other variables of interest would be seriously underestimated.

OTHER CORRELATES OF MEMORY RECALL BIASES

If certain types of victims tend to telescope forward more than others, then survey data will overestimate the victimization rates of these persons. Likewise, if certain types of victims telescope incidents out of the reference period to a greater extent than others, then these persons would be underrepresented in the survey data.

In the Portland Forward Records Check, several characteristics of victims were examined in order to determine whether some are more inclined to telescope than others. As shown in Table E, the age, race, sex, and educational level of the victims were not correlated significantly with the extent of forward telescoping. Two general tendencies, however, did not reach statistical significance. More serious crimes tended to be telescoped foward less than trivial incidents. There is a slight indication that men telescope forward less than women.

The absolute amount of either forward or backward telescoping appears to have weak, but statistically significant, relationships with some characteristics of victims and offenses (see Table F). More errors appear to be made by younger respondents than by older ones, and by women rather than men. The information suggests that errors are more likely to be made in reference to trivial incidents than to serious ones.

TABLE E

CORRELATES OF FORWARD TELESCOPING BY CRIME TYPE
FOR MATCHED CASES[25]
(Pearson Correlations)

Characteristic	All Crimes (n=203)	Property Crimes (n=181)	Personal Crimes (n=16)
Time between incident and interview	.68**	.70**	.03
Positive attitude toward police	.00	.02	−.31
Age	−.06	−.06	.33
Race (0=black; 1=white)	−.08	.11	‡
Sex (0=female; 1=male)	−.10	−.13*	−.21
Education	−.01	.04	−.08
Seriousness	−.11	−.08	.03

*P < .05
**P < .001
‡ Only one black respondent

Even though these relationships reach statistical significance, they are not very substantial. For instance, correlations of less than .15 explain less than 3% of the variance in telescoping. The period between the date of the incident and the interview correlates at .64 with the absolute amount of error. Of considerable interest is the fact that Sparks found only a .14 correlation between this period and the absolute amount of error in placement of the date.[26] The additional emphasis on accuracy of recall used in his questioning procedures might account for this substantial difference in results of the two studies. Moreover, Sparks did not find correlations between the absolute amount of error in recall of the date and age, race, sex, or other similar variables. This lack of correlation could be produced by differences in questioning proce-

---

25 Positive correlations mean that higher scores on the characteristic are related to forward telescoping; negative correlations mean that lower scores on the characteristic are related to forward telescoping. For example, for all crimes longer time between the incident and the interview is strongly related to forward telescoping.

26 Sparks, Genn & Dodd, *supra* note 9.

TABLE F

CORRELATES OF ERROR IN RECALL OF INCIDENT DATE
(TELESCOPING) FOR MATCHED CASES[27]
(Pearson Correlations)

Characteristic	All Crimes (n=203)	Property Crimes (n=181)	Personal Crimes (n=16)
Time between incident and interview	.64**	.65**	−.02
Positive attitude toward police	.07	.08	.10
Age	−.12*	−.11	22
Race (0=black; 1=white)	−.04	−.03	‡
Sex (0=female; 1=male)	−.14*	−.16*	−.30
Education	−.04	−.04	−.03
Seriousness	−.12*	−.08	−.02

*P < .05
**P < .001
‡ Only one black respondent

dures, if such procedures are most effective on persons who otherwise would be most likely to err. Thus, the improved surveying technique could not only reduce error, but might result in the error being more evenly distributed across different kinds of respondents.

Perhaps the most widely known error in the victimization surveys is the relationship between failure to recall incidents of assaultive violence and the relationship of the victim to the offender. The San Jose study showed that incidents in which the victim knew the offender were far less likely to be reported during the interview. The Portland Forward Records Check showed the same pattern of bias for official data. Interview victimizations which involved family members, persons who knew each other, or juveniles were not as likely to be found in the records or, if found, were more likely to have been classified as a reduced crime type, e.g., malicious mischief rather than assault.

Sparks' study is the only one of the reverse records checks that reports whether the tendency not to recall the incident to the interviewer was related to characteristics of the victim. His conclusion was that

---

[27] Positive correlations mean that higher scores on the characteristic are related to greater error in recalling the incident date; negative correlations mean that lower scores on the characteristic are related to greater error. For example, for all crimes lower seriousness is related to greater error in recalling the incident date.

non-recall was not related to sex, age, race, migration patterns, employment, attitudes, perceptions about crime seriousness, or social class of the victim. Another technique that has been used to correlate memory decay in the form of either telescoping or forgetting is to examine the pattern of recall during the months covered in the reference period. The usual procedure is to assume that if there were no memory decay, each month in the recall period would contain an equal share of the total incidents recalled in the study. In some studies, the official data have been used to correct for actual trend, but in most instances these corrections have not been needed.

Two studies have examined the relationship between victim characteristics of age, race, sex, and education, and memory decay.[28] Both concluded that there were no sigificant relationships. A National Crime Survey methodological study found two statistically significant relationships. Incidents with weapons were less subject to memory bias than incidents without weapons. Incidents in which the suspect was a stranger were less subject to memory biases. These findings indicate that less salient incidents show a sharper memory decay due either to more forward telescoping or to more forgetting in the distant months.

Several investigations have been undertaken to determine whether incidents that respondents said were not reported to the police are more likely to be forward telescoped or forgotten than are incidents which were reported.[29] Although the evidence is not substantial, the nonreported incidents are subject to more memory bias than are the reported incidents. Therefore, the unreported incidents either are telescoped forward more than the reported ones, or they are forgotten easier, or both. If forward telescoping is the primary problem, then in unbounded surveys estimates of the proportion of incidents not reported will be inflated. If non-recall is the primary problem, then survey estimates of incidents not reported will be too low.

A further implication of different error patterns for incidents reported and not reported is that error estimates which rely on police data as the standard cannot be used without adjustments to estimate the error in survey data.

---

28 M. HINDELANG, CRIMINAL VICTIMIZATION IN EIGHT AMERICAN CITIES—A DESCRIPTION ANALYSIS OF COMMON THEFT AND ASSAULT ch. 2 (1976); A. Schneider & D. Sumi, Patterns of Forgetting and Telescoping in LEAA Survey Victimization Data (Inst. Pol'y Analysis, Nov. 1977).

29 *See* Gottfredson & Hindelang, *Victims of Personal Crimes—A Methodological Disquisition*, PROC. SOC. STATISTICS SECTION AM. STATISTICAL ASS'N (1975); A. Schneider & D. Sumi, *supra* note 28; H. Woltman & G. Cadek, Are Memory Biases in the NCS Associated with the Characteristics of the Criminal Incident (Census Bureau Memo, April 4, 1977).

DISCUSSION AND CONCLUSIONS

The implications of measurement error depend on both the amount and the nature of the error. The key consequence of random error is an attenuation of the strength of relationship and tests of significance which, in turn, produce no findings even when relationships exist. Probably the most important consequence of directional error, that is, error not correlated with other variables but which has a non-zero mean, is inaccuracy in descriptive studies of the phenomenon being measured. If the error is correlated with other variables used in the study, then the results may contain serious distortions, or even reversals, in the direction of the relationship among the variables.

Presuming that the estimates of error obtained from the reverse record checks, forward record check, and the NCS methodological studies are relatively accurate, the following conclusions are warranted:

1. Surveys using six-month reference periods, no bounding to eliminate telescoping, and no special memory aides other than the usual screening questions may contain considerable misidentification of respondents as victims during the reference period. The total amount of error in the six-month reference period appears to exceed that contained in the twelve-month surveys.

2. Sampling from files of known victims, such as police records of victim programs, and subsequent use of the information in conjunction with general population surveys to identify non-victims can be expected to produce data with accuracy approaching that of the surveys only if their coverage of all reported and unreported victims is considerably higher than indicated by the nonreporting rates shown in the NCS. The extent of coverage is open to speculation, but an unbounded survey using a twelve-month recall period should produce data that are as valid as police or program data which capture 40-50% of all the actual incidents. The choice of a data set is not the subject of this paper, and of course, should be guided by several additional considerations, such as size of the sample that can be generated, which is a major contributor to error, and the cost of the data.

3. The accuracy of survey data in categorizing respondents as victims varies by offense. Burglary victims are better-identified than any other type of personal, rather than commercial, victims. Victims of personal assault, especially if the offender is known to the victim, are identified with the least amount of accuracy. The implication here is clear that theories of assaultive violence may be more difficult to support from the data than are theories of property offenses such as burglaries. Although surveys seem not to be a particularly efficient way of recovering incidents of personal violence, especially between persons who are

known to one another, the same may be true for police data. The Portland Forward Records Check study indicated that these offenses, even though reported to the interviewer, were more likely not to be found in police files than were property offenses such as burglaries.

4.   Evidence is accumulating that different amounts and patterns of errors may be found for reported crimes than for unreported ones. Of particular concern, then, is the fact that all estimates of non-recall, and most estimates of telescoping, are based on reverse records checks which began with reported crimes. In addition, no victimization studies using truly short reference periods such as one day or one week have been undertaken, hence the amount of non-recall found in the reverse records studies is seriously underestimated.

Part V
Theoretical Models of Explanation

[19]

0091-4169/86/7701-151
THE JOURNAL OF CRIMINAL LAW & CRIMINOLOGY
Copyright © 1986 by Northwestern University, School of Law

Vol. 77, No. 1
Printed in U.S.A.

CRIMINOLOGY

TESTING ALTERNATIVE MODELS OF FEAR OF CRIME*

RALPH B. TAYLOR**
MARGARET HALE***

I. INTRODUCTION

Fear of crime is a significant social problem. Recognition of the serious impact that fear may have on individuals and communities has emerged among policymakers, crime prevention practitioners, as well as researchers.[1] As a social problem, several aspects of fear of crime are notable. By the late 1970's, fear of crime was "touching" more households than ever.[2] This increase in fear to some extent paralleled the rise in crime levels during the 1970's. However, the longstanding and deep-seated nature of the fear problem is reflected in the fact that at the national level, although fear goes up as crime goes up, fear does not fall as rapidly when crime declines.[3]

---

* Portions of this research were presented at the annual meetings of the American Society of Criminology, Denver, CO, November, 1983. This research was carried out under a summer research fellowship awarded the first author by the National Institute of Justice. The research was carried out while both authors were affiliated with the Center for Metropolitan Planning and Research of the Johns Hopkins University. Statements contained herein do not necessarily reflect the opinions or policies of the National Institute of Justice or the Department of Justice. We are indebted to ICPSR, University of Michigan, for providing the documented data set. The data were originally collected under a grant, "Safe and Secure Neighborhoods," Stephanie Greenberg, Principal Investigator. Request reprints from Ralph B. Taylor, Department of Criminal Justice, Gladfelter Hall, Temple University, Philadelphia, PA 19122.

** Associate Professor, Department of Criminal Justice, Temple University, Philadelphia, Pennsylvania. Ph.D., Johns Hopkins University, 1977; M.A., Johns Hopkins University, 1975; B.A., Dartmouth College, 1972.

*** Juvenile Services Administration, State of Maryland. Ph.D., Johns Hopkins University, 1984.

[1] Images of Fear: On the Perception and Reality of Crime, 270 HARPER'S 39 (1985).

[2] SOURCEBOOK OF CRIMINAL JUSTICE STATISTICS: 1981, at 181 (Figure 2.4) (T. Flanagan, D. Van Alstyne & M. Gottfredson eds. 1982).

[3] F. DUBOW, E. MCCABE & G. KAPLAN, REACTIONS TO CRIME (1979).

Such a pattern suggests that once the population is sensitized to fear-related issues, that awareness is unlikely to dissipate rapidly.

Partially in recognition of the severity and persistence of the fear problem, policies focusing directly on fear reduction have emerged in the last five years. Perhaps the clearest example of this is the recent field experiment conducted by the Police Foundation.[4] Following the Wilson and Kelling thesis that (1) minor "incivilities" inspire fear and that (2) the police could serve as the agents of order,[5] the project attempted to reduce fear levels by devoting police resources to community contact. Preliminary results suggest that fear levels may not have been reduced by the intervention, although it is difficult to pinpoint the exact "strength" of the treatment. Nonetheless, the important point is that policymakers are increasingly interested in implementing programs that deal directly with fear of crime.

In short, levels of fear of crime have increased and appear less variable than crime. Recognition of the "costs" of fear has widened to the point that programs targeted specifically at fear reduction have been implemented. Given these "real world" developments surrounding fear of crime, theoretical clarifications and empirical investigations of fear become all the more critical.

The way that fear is patterned, across people and places, however, continues to pose a conundrum for researchers. In fact, much of the theoretical attention to fear is an attempt to solve these riddles. Three points about the patterning of fear are significant.

First, the rank ordering of age-sex groups on fear levels is exactly opposite their ordering on victimization rates.[6] Young males are the least fearful but are victimized at the highest rate; elderly women are victimized at the lowest rate but are the most fearful. The notion of vulnerability, discussed below, is largely an attempt to resolve this discrepancy.

Second, many more people are fearful than are actually victimized, and fear levels are higher than would seem to be warranted by actual crime rates, even if we assume a liberal amount of unreported crime. This has led to a search for a crime "multiplier:" processes

---

[4] T. PATE, W. SKOGAN & L. SHERMAN, FEAR OF CRIME AND POLICING (FINAL REPORT) (1985).

[5] Wilson & Kelling, *Broken Windows*, 249 ATLANTIC MONTHLY 29 (March 1982). For a more detailed discussion of this model, see J. Greene & R. Taylor, A Closer Look at the Rationale Behind Community Policing (unpublished manuscript).

[6] M. HINDELANG, M. GOTTFREDSON, & J. GAROFALO, VICTIMS OF PERSONAL CRIME: AN EMPIRICAL FOUNDATION FOR A THEORY OF PERSONAL VICTIMIZATION (1978); M. MAXFIELD, FEAR OF CRIME IN ENGLAND AND WALES (1984); Cook & Skogan, *Crime Against the Elderly*, in PUBLIC POLICY AND SOCIAL INSTITUTIONS (H. Rogers ed. 1984).

operating in the residential environment that would "spread" the impacts of criminal events. The indirect victimization model, discussed below, is an example of a model constructed along these lines.

Third, the patterning of fear across areas does not match the patterning of crime levels. Although at least one study has found that actual victims of crime are more fearful than non-victims,[7] areas with higher crime or victimization rates do not always have residents who are more fearful.[8] This failure of fear levels to covary spatially with crime levels has led to an ongoing debate concerning the meaning or construct validity of fear of crime survey items.

Turning to the issue of construct validity, it is accepted that fear is "the emotional dimension of [people's] response to crime. . . ."[9] More recently, fear has been further circumscribed. Garofalo has suggested that fear taps the emotional response to possible violent crime and physical harm, while the term "worry" captures the emotional response to possible property crime (e.g., burglary, larceny).[10] Maxfield has concurred in the view that fear is linked to violent crime and worry to property crime.[11] The emotional "fear" and "worry" responses can be captured with items about " 'how afraid,' 'how uneasy' people feel about the occurrence of crime in general or a specific type of crime."[12] Most assume that the standard National Crime Survey "day fear" and "night fear" items ("How safe do you feel (or would you feel) alone at night in your neighborhood?") capture the fear people anticipate due to the possibility of violent crime.

A. THE DISORDER PERSPECTIVE

Nonetheless, despite these suggestions by researchers about how to tap fear of crime and what fear of crime questions "get at,"

---

[7] W. SKOGAN & M. MAXFIELD, COPING WITH CRIME (1981).

[8] W. SKOGAN & M. MAXFIELD, *supra* note 7; McPherson, Realities and Perceptions of Crime at the Neighborhood Level, 3 VICTIMOLOGY 319 (1978); Taylor, Gottfredson, & Brower, Predicting Block Crime and Fear, 23 J. RESEARCH CRIME & DELINQ. 331 (1984); R. Taylor, The Roots of Fear (1984)(unpublished paper presented at the meetings of the American Society of Criminology). The strength of the correlation of course depends upon the unit of aggregation. At the street block level, correlations of around .2 have been observed. At the neighborhood level, correlations of .6 have been observed but appear to be a result of spurious correlations, with social class being the cause of both fear and crime.

[9] F. DuBow, E. McCabe & G. Kaplan, *supra* note 3, at 4.

[10] Garofalo, *The Fear of Crime: Causes and Consequences*, 72 J. CRIM. L. & CRIMINOLOGY 839, 840 (1981).

[11] M. MAXFIELD, *supra* note 6.

[12] F. DuBow, E. McCabe & G. Kaplan, *supra* note 3, at 5.

the empirical patterning of the covariates of fear of crime have not fully supported these suggestions. Consequently, Garofalo and Laub have asked: Is "fear of crime" more than "fear" of "crime?"[13] In other words, is fear of crime part and parcel of the general "urban unease" experienced by residents, or is it something only, and distinctly, tied to crime? It may be that as problems intensify in a neighborhood, anxiety increases, and fear of crime is part of this anxiety. This is in fact the assumption adopted by those linking social incivilities (such as public drunkenness) and physical incivilities (such as abandoned houses or graffiti) to fear.[14]

This disorder perspective, however, has been stated differently by different researchers. Hunter proposed that social disorganization, stemming from community decline, gives rise to social and physical incivilities and crime.[15] Social and physical incivilities are fear-inspiring not only because they indicate a lack of concern for public order, but also because their continued presence points up the inability of officials to cope with these problems. But, based on an analysis of conditions in ten neighborhoods, Lewis and Maxfield have suggested a somewhat different conceptualization.[16] They proposed that crime and incivilities bear a *conditional* relationship to fear. If *both* crime and incivilities are high, they suggested, then and only then will fear levels be high.[17]

Despite the popularity of the disorder perspective, empirical work to date has focused almost exclusively on *perceptions* of disorder. The only study that has provided a comprehensive assessment

---

[13] Garofalo & Laub, *The Fear of Crime: Broadening Our Perspective*, 3 VICTIMOLOGY 242, 243 (1978).

[14] Social and physical incivilities are signs of lack of adherence to norms of public behavior. Social incivilities include such behaviors as public drinking, drunkenness or drug use, being noisy in public, or "hey honey" hassles. Physical incivilities include graffiti, litter, vacant houses, vacant or unkempt lots, houses and properties not well maintained, and abandoned cars. For a more extensive discussion of the conceptual status of incivilities, see Taylor, *Toward an Environmental Psychology of Disorder*, in HANDBOOK OF ENVIRONMENTAL PSYCHOLOGY (D. Stokols & I. Altman eds., in press). Hunter, Lewis and Maxfield, and Skogan and Maxfield have all suggested that fear may be partly attributable to actual and perceived disorder in the immediate urban environment. *See* A. Hunter, Symbols of Incivility (1978)(unpublished paper presented at the American Society of Criminology); Lewis & Maxfield, *Fear in the Neighborhoods: An Investigation of the Impact of Crime*, 17 J. RESEARCH CRIME & DELINQ. 160 (1980); W. SKOGAN & M. MAXFIELD, *supra* note 7.

[15] A. Hunter, *supra* note 14.

[16] Lewis & Maxfield, *supra* note 14.

[17] W. SKOGAN & M. MAXFIELD, *supra* note 7, at 110-15. Using the same data, Skogan and Maxfield reported a simple main effect between fear and perceptions of disorder (r = .66 at the neighborhood level). *Id.* at 111. They did not, however, report a partial correlation, controlling for social class variables, and thus it is not clear if the correlation is spurious.

of objective incivilities found that their impacts on fear were not large, nor were they apparent in all types of neighborhoods. Rather, in neighborhoods whose futures were uncertain, due to income levels that were neither so high as to guarantee stability nor so low as to guarantee continued dissolution, incivilities had a significant but not overwhelming impact on fear of crime levels.[18]

In sum, proponents of the disorder perspective have advanced several theoretical rationales to explain how and why fear of crime should be produced by social and physical incivilities. Links between fear and perceived incivilities have been observed but may be spurious (i.e., due to social class). There is some evidence for a conditional linkage between objective incivilities and fear. It remains to be seen whether, controlling for social class, perceived incivilities contribute to fear levels.

B. THE COMMUNITY CONCERN PERSPECTIVE

Another view, related to but distinct from the disorder perspective on fear, includes residents' perceptions of community dynamics. In Hunter's first explicit formulation of the impact of incivilities on fear, awareness of local disorder was expected to directly influence fear levels. Others have suggested, however, that community concern is part of the process.[19] Garofalo and Laub succinctly summarized this model. "[T]he fear of actual criminal victimization is inseparable from the unease generated by other minor forms in public deviance, and that the sum of these anxieties is the basis for the concern with community."[20] Lewis and Salem extended this argument to the neighborhood level.[21] According to their view, fear and community concern are intimately interwoven. They suggested that if crime was high or increasing in a neighborhood, *and* the neighborhood lacked certain structural characteristics such as strong local social ties and strong "vertical" ties to local power structures, then crime would inspire the perception of problems and consequent concern for where the community was headed. These evaluations, it was expected, would translate into fear.[22] Recent re-

---

[18] Taylor, Shumaker, & Gottfredson, *Neighborhood-level Links Between Physical Features and Local Sentiments*, 2 J. ARCH. PLAN. & RES. 261 (1985).

[19] J. CONKLIN, THE IMPACT OF CRIME (1975); J. JACOBS, THE DEATH AND LIFE OF THE GREAT AMERICAN CITY (1961); J. WILSON, THINKING ABOUT CRIME (1975); Garofalo & Laub, *supra* note 13.

[20] Garofalo & Laub, *supra* note 13, at 250.

[21] *See* D. LEWIS & G. SALEM, CRIME AND URBAN COMMUNITY: TOWARDS A THEORY OF NEIGHBORHOOD SECURITY—FINAL REPORT (1980).

[22] Taub, Taylor, and Dunham's finding that high or increasing crime translated into fear if other worrisome changes were happening in the neighborhood at the same time

sults which indicate that the neighborhood context has more of an impact on fear than direct victimization[23] and that the perception of neighborhood problems is a strong correlate of fear[24] support the community concern perspective. They give substance to the notion that fear of crime is a result more of community dynamics than of crime dynamics.

C. INDIRECT VICTIMIZATION PERSPECTIVE

But, this is not to say that crime and related dynamics can be ignored in considering the origins of fear. In fact, one popular approach, the indirect victimization perspective, has attempted to clarify the processes linking crime and fear. It has two major points. First, it interprets sociodemographic correlates of fear as reflections of vulnerability to violent crime.[25] According to this line of reasoning, increased age and being female are correlated with fear because they reflect a heightened physical vulnerability to crime. If older persons or women are in fact attacked, the possible harm is greater than would be the case for males or younger persons. Further, according to this view, being black and of a lower income group reflects heightened social vulnerability. Poor blacks are more vulnerable because they are likely to live in areas with higher offender and offense rates, making them more likely to be victimized.[26] Stated differently, this perspective provides an interpretation of the linkages between sociodemographic characteristics and fear and focuses on specific demographics.

The second point of this model is that a criminal event sends out "shock waves" that spread throughout the community via local social networks. People who hear about a crime become indirect victims in that their levels of fear increase. Local social contacts serve to amplify the fear-inspiring impact of local crime. The indirect victimization model thus attempts to bring crime and fear into correspondence by adding a crime "multiplier."

Some studies support the indirect victimization view. Tyler's analysis of two surveys—one a multi-city survey of approximately

---

would also support this perspective. R. TAUB, G. TAYLOR & J. DUNHAM, PATHS OF NEIGHBORHOOD CHANGE (1984).

[23] Taylor, Taub & Dunham, *City Residents and Social Theorists: Some Microanalytic Surprises on Crime and the Causes of Neighborhood Decline*, in METROPOLITAN CRIME PATTERNS (R. Figlio, S. Hakim & G. Rengert eds. 1986).

[24] W. SKOGAN & M. MAXFIELD, *supra* note 7.

[25] W. SKOGAN & M. MAXFIELD, *supra* note 7, at 69-78.

[26] Sparks has used the more common sense term "ecological vulnerability" to describe the hazards arising from location. *See* R. SPARKS, RESEARCH ON VICTIMS OF CRIME: ACCOMPLISHMENTS, ISSUES AND NEW DIRECTIONS (1982).

1600 residents and the other a localized survey of over 200 house-holds in Ventura, California—had mixed results.[27] Although crimes heard about from others significantly increased fear levels amoung the multi-city respondents, they did not significantly increase esti-mates of personal vulnerability to crime among the Ventura group. Skogan and Maxfield's re-analysis of the multi-city survey yielded similar findings: individuals who knew a local crime victim had higher fear levels, and fear was most increased if the crime heard about was a robbery or stranger-to-stranger assault.[28] The authors concluded that "some forms of vicarious experience with crime have a significant impact on the distribution of fear. . . . Unlike direct victimization, indirect exposure to crime is frequent and relatively widespread."[29] Thus, in the indirect victimization perspective, con-cern for specifying the crime-fear linkage, despite recognition that the connection is not straightforward, is the key focus.

D. ACHIEVEMENTS AND LIMITATIONS OF RESEARCH

What are the achievements and limitations of the fear of crime research? Two positive points are that (a) there is increasing atten-tion to better specifying the multi-link and possibly conditional na-ture of the relationship between crime factors and fear, and (b) there is increasing attention to the contextual, non-crime factors that may influence fear. Nonetheless, there are still several limita-tions, some methodological or analytical, some theoretical, which beset this area of research.

With regard to methodological or analytical matters, three points deserve mention. First, in much fear research the aggrega-tion problem has been ignored.[30] Most prior fear studies have been based on clustered sample surveys. In such cases, the variance of any particular item includes several sources of variation. More spe-cifically, if the sample includes respondents from different neighbor-hoods within one city, the total variance of an item $(x1)$ includes between-neighborhood sources of variance, individual-level sources of variation, and error. That is:

item   = between-neighborhood + within-neighborhood +   error
variance   variance   variance   variance.

Analysis of raw correlations can lead to misleading results because

---

[27] Tyler, *Impact of Directly and Indirectly Experienced Events: The Origin of Crime-related Judgments and Behaviors*, 39 J. PERS. & SOC. PSYCH. 13 (1980).

[28] W. SKOGAN & M. MAXFIELD, *supra* note 7, Tables 10-1 & 10-2.

[29] W. SKOGAN & M. MAXFIELD, *supra* note 7, at 180.

[30] For a discussion of this problem, see M. HANNAN, AGGREGATION AND DISAGGREGA-TION IN SOCIOLOGY (1971).

area and individual-level sources of variation are confounded.[31] Thus, if we want to examine the individual-level dynamics of fear and understand why some individuals are more fearful than others, it is important to focus exclusively on individual-level variation and covariation, unconfounded by neighborhood differences. Such work has not as yet been done.

Second, even though increasing theoretical attention has been given to the causal impacts of non-crime neighborhood factors on fear, few studies have incorporated objective features of the neighborhood context.[32] In order to develop a better understanding of the linkage between neighborhood context and fear, objective indicators need to be included.

A third matter concerns outcome measures. Most studies have only a very limited coverage of fear of crime, usually comprising one or two measures.[33] Although the tradition of investigating fear items which follow the National Crime Survey format is well established, items tapping "how uneasy" people might feel can tap fear of crime as well. It would be worthwhile for fear researchers to branch out and include several different types of items for outcome measures, for two reasons. Such a step makes it possible to build scales, which are less "noisy" than single items. In addition, it helps avoid developing an extensive research tradition limited to very narrow outcome measures.

Theoretical development in the fear of crime area has been significant, as exemplified by the consideration of a widening web of "causes" of fear of crime. Nevertheless, due to lack of attention to the *process* of theory construction and testing, theory development has been hindered. To date, two very general models of fear of crime have emerged.[34] One, proposed by Skogan and Maxfield includes fourteen concepts.[35] Predictor variables include "personal

---

[31] *See* M. HANNAN, *supra* note 30; Taylor, *Neighborhood Physical Environment and Stress,* in ENVIRONMENTAL STRESS 286, 310-17 (G. Evans ed. 1982).

[32] For example, the study by Taylor, Taub & Dunham, *supra* note 23, simply used dummy variables to capture the context of each neighborhood. Another example is the Northwestern RTC project, where, except for some detailed case studies, *see, e.g.,* Lewis & Maxfield, *supra* note 14, subjective indicators of neighborhood climate (most notably, residents' perceptions of various problems in their neighborhoods) rather than objective indicators were used. *See* W. SKOGAN & M. MAXFIELD, *supra* note 7.

[33] *See, e.g.,* W. SKOGAN & M. MAXFIELD, *supra* note 7, at 59-78.

[34] "Models," as we use the term here, denotes a "low-level" theory that includes specific concepts and perhaps variables. It is, however, more advanced than a "perspective," such as the three discussed above, in that the latter are open-ended in terms of the relevant concepts and may pay little attention to the specific structure of causal dynamics or level of analysis.

[35] W. SKOGAN & M. MAXFIELD, *supra* note 7, at 17 (Figure 1.1).

and household vulnerability," "city of residence," "neighborhood conditions," "media exposure," "victimization experiences," "personal communication networks," and others. Outcomes include "fear of crime," and "behavior." As an outcome, "behavior" is influenced by four sets of factors (e.g., "role constraints").

Garofalo has proposed a second general model of fear of crime.[36] It includes twelve categories of variables ranging from "position in social space," "other attitudes," "beliefs," "mediating factors" and "image of crime" to "fear of crime," "costs and options," and "social outcomes." The authors of both of these models are trying to capture the complex causal processes that inspire fear and its ensuing consequences. Regarding his model, Garofalo notes that "[i]t is complex, yet it is a simplication of even greater complexity."[37] This statement can be fairly applied to both models.

From a theory construction point of view, however, such model building is premature. Blalock makes several points regarding the process of theory construction which clarify the difficulties raised by models such as the two mentioned above. [38] First, he notes that

theories. . . must contain lawlike propositions that interrelate the concepts or variables two or more at a time. Furthermore, these propositions must themselves be interrelated. For example, if one proposition relates variables A and B, a second relates C and D, and a third E and F, then there must be additional propositions enabling one to make deductive statements connecting these three propositions.[39]

The two models noted above do not satisfy this condition. The authors of the models do not connect together all of the different propositions. Second, even if all connections were made so that the models were completely closed, each model would contain on the order of sixty or more hypotheses.[40] It is difficult to imagine how all of these hypotheses could be tested in one study, particularly when some of the concepts are community-level measures such as "social outcomes" in the Garofalo model.

One might nevertheless argue that these two models are useful because they include concepts that are related to fear of crime. That is correct. From a theory-construction point of view, however, they amount to a "dragnet approach."[41] Under such an approach all

---

[36] *See* Garofalo, *supra* note 10, at 843.

[37] Garofalo, *supra* note 10, at 842.

[38] H. BLALOCK, THEORY CONSTRUCTION (1969).

[39] H. BLALOCK, *supra* note 38, at 2.

[40] If N is the number of concepts, the number of pairwise connections are (N(N-1))/2.

[41] H. BLALOCK, *supra* note 38. Blalock explains:

[E]mpirically-minded quantitative sociologists sometimes in effect endorse an anti-

variables thought to be relevant to the phenomenon in question are "thrown in." Such "models," like those proposed by Skogan and Maxfield, and by Garofalo, are in effect untestable and useful only in the most preliminary stages of theory building.

A more appropriate process is one which is incremental.[42] Very simple models are first proposed and tested. Additional variables are gradually added, resulting in progressively more complex models which better capture the real-world dynamics of fear of crime. In short, although fear of crime is enmeshed in a complex web of causes and consequences, theoretical understanding of fear of crime will progress only if explicit, simple causal models are the starting point. In the fear of crime literature, such tests have not as yet been made.

E. SUMMARY

To summarize, the following points can be made. Fear of crime research has evolved in several directions in the last few years. Three "approaches" to understanding fear of crime have been suggested. The indirect victimization perspective recasts the sociodemographic correlates of fear into a vulnerability framework and attempts to specify the crime-fear link by examining the impact of local social ties. The perceived disorder approach argues that people are afraid because, in addition to crime, they witness signs of social and physical decay. This decay signals the impotence of the powers of the state, resulting in increased feelings of vulnerability. The community concern perspective builds on the disorder perspective by arguing that as a result of signs of physical and social decay people become concerned about the continued viability of their neighborhood and the quality of their neighbors. This heightened concern then translates into fear. None of these three approaches to fear of crime has been correctly tested. Proper testing of these approaches requires a data set that provides several objective meas-

---

theoretical position by throwing numerous variables into a regression equation with the idea of selecting out that subset which 'explains' the most variance. To be sure, this kind of dragnet approach is useful as an exploratory device... but... can hardly be judged an efficient procedure. . . .

Id. at 2-3.

[42] "In order to develop deductive theories, one must ordinarily begin with very simple models that are totally inadequate to mirror the real world. By adding new variables and complications, a few at a time, one can then construct more realistic theories by what amounts to an inductive process." H. BLALOCK, *supra* note 38, at 3-4. Blalock further explains that "if they are to be simple, . . . theories must omit numerous explanatory factors." *Id.* at 6-7.

ures of the immediate residential environment, several fear outcome measures, and an analysis that recognizes the aggregation problem.

The purpose of our analysis is to provide such tests of these three perspectives. For each perspective a model will be formulated and tested. Five questions about this model testing arise. First, overall, how well does the model do in explaining the outcome? Second, which of the particular hypotheses (causal pathways) predicted by each model are supported by the data? Third, how well does the model "fit" the data? Fourth, which types of predictors have the most impact on fear? And, lastly, how well do the models perform vis-a-vis one another? Before we can do any testing, however, we need to explicitly formulate each of the models we will be examining.

II. STATEMENT OF MODELS TO BE TESTED

A. INDIRECT VICTIMIZATION

The indirect victimization model, represented as a causal diagram, appears in Figure 1.[43] The model hypothesizes the following. People who are more vulnerable such as women, low income individuals, blacks, or the elderly, are more likely to be victimized or to see crime. Those who are victimized or who have witnessed crime will pass this information through their local social networks. Local social networks channel the impacts of victimization. Those with more local ties will therefore be more fearful. Likewise, those who are more vulnerable will be more fearful. In addition, those who have experienced or witnessed crime will have elevated fear levels.

B. PERCEIVED DISORDER

The perceived disorder model is depicted in Figure 2. It makes the following hypotheses. Socioeconomic status is associated in several ways with fear. First, those who have a lower socioeconomic status are likely to perceive more problems in their locale. In other words, lower socioeconomic status has an indirect effect on fear vis-a-vis impact on perceived problems. This results from living in less stable areas, from having less access to more desirable areas, and from having co-residents who rarely contribute to the upkeep of the locale and who may be less likely to observe the norms of public order than residents of higher socioeconomic status living in more stable locales. Lower socioeconomic status may also be directly

---

[43] This model is based in large part upon portions of the model presented by Skogan and Maxfield. *See* W. SKOGAN & M. MAXFIELD, *supra* note 7, at 17.

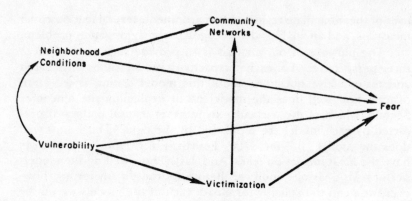

FIGURE 1
INDIRECT VICTIMIZATION MODEL

linked with higher fear levels. Due to less adequate police protection or to the diversity of the areas they live in, lower status residents may feel more vulnerable and thus more fearful.

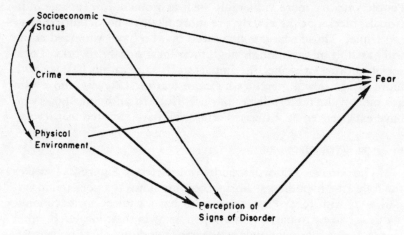

FIGURE 2
SIGNS OF DISORDER MODEL

Crime may contribute directly to increased fear. It may also contribute to fear via an increased perception of problems. Higher crime may be accompanied by higher rates of other disorderly behaviors. These disorders may result in residents perceiving more local problems.

Physical deterioration in the neighborhood may result in a

heightened perception by the residents of the seriousness or extensiveness of local problems. For example, survey respondents living in neighborhoods where vacant lots and houses are more extensive may report a higher incidence of physical upkeep problems than survey respondents living in neighborhoods where these problems are not as widespread. In addition, respondents in more dilapidated areas, with more vacant lots and houses, may also report a higher incidence of local social problems if vacant houses serve as havens for pushers or street people, and if vacant lots provide gathering places for youth groups.

The key causal sequence articulated by the disorder model is that both lower social class and a higher incidence of physical and social incivilities heighten the perception of local problems. This perception, in turn, elevates fear levels.

C. COMMUNITY CONCERN

The community concern model includes all of the hypotheses made by the disorder model. It differs, however, by adding several key hypotheses. (The model is presented as a causal diagram in Figure 3.) Specifically, the model makes the following additional pro-

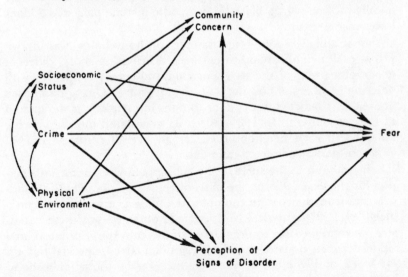

FIGURE 3
COMMUNITY CONCERN MODEL

posals. Witnessing crime or local physical and social problems may elevate levels of community concern. Such events may cause greater concern about the future of the neighborhood and the quality of present and future residents. This uncertainty and concern may lead residents to feel more vulnerable and thus heighten fear. The model also allows that perceived problems, even if they do not induce higher levels of community concern, may still contribute to higher fear levels. It is expected, however, that perceived disorders will influence fear mostly via their impact on community concern. The key causal sequence in the community concern model leads from objective characteristics (e.g., crime, physical conditions, socioeconomic status) to perceived problems which in turn lead to concern, which in turn leads to fear.

III. Method

A. DATA SET

The data come from a study of six Atlanta neighborhoods.[44] The six neighborhoods were selected in physically adjacent pairs matched on racial composition and economic status. Further, one neighborhood in each pair had a "high" crime rate, defined by total Part I (serious) offenses per household, whereas the other had a "low" crime rate. The three neighborhood pairs included a white middle-income pair, a black lower-middle income pair, and a black lower-income pair.

A stratified, single-stage sample of households was drawn within each neighborhood to ensure a distribution across different geographic areas of the neighborhood and across properties with differing numbers of housing units per structure. One adult in each household contacted in the door-to-door interviews was designated as the respondent. In 1980, 80 to 93 completed interviews were obtained in each neighborhood, for an overall response rate of 77.3% and 523 completed interviews.

In addition to the surveys, the authors obtained crime information for the year 1978 on the basis of census blocks. Physical land-use data from a city-wide computerized file was also collected on a block level. The physical land use data obtained was quite extensive. Several measures were related to the concept of physical incivilities: vacant houses, vacant lots, residential/commercial mix on the block, and whether or not the street was on the neighborhood boundary. The presence of commercial properties is associated with incivilities because stores draw foot traffic, resulting in more

---

[44] This study was carried out by Stephanie Greenberg and her colleagues. *See* Greenberg, Rohe & Williams, *Safety in Urban Neighborhoods*, 5 POPULATION & ENVIRONMENT 141 (1982).

loiterers, litter, and other problems in these locations. The last measure may be associated with physical incivilities for two reasons. First, boundary streets tended to be wider, higher traffic-volume streets, often with commercial establishments on them. These kinds of streets would tend to have more loiterers, litter or graffiti. Second, Hunter has suggested that higher incidences of physical and social incivilities would be found at the edges of communities. He suggests that this occurs because boundary areas are less looked after and surveilled.[45]

In sum, the land-use information, although not providing an exhaustive measure of objective incivilities, included several key measures of incivilities or features linked to incivilities. In addition, the inclusion of these variables must be weighed against the fact that most prior studies on the fear of crime have included no objective measures of physical or social incivilities.

This Atlanta data set thus provides measures of all of the concepts that have been proposed in the above three models. Objective measures of crime, physical deterioration, and land use were available. The survey included items regarding witnessed victimization, fear, social ties, perceptions of problems, and community concern. It also included all of the sociodemographic information needed to develop fully specified models.

B. LOGIC OF ANALYSIS

In order to conduct this analysis, we first centered all survey, crime, and land use items by their respective neighborhood means.[46] Survey items were then transformed into individual-level deviations from their respective neighborhood means; land-use and crime data were transformed into block-level deviations from the respective neighborhood mean.

Using the deviation-scored variables, we built scales to reflect the concepts of interest. In most cases this was achieved via principal components analysis, although in a few instances we simply added up z-scored variables.[47]

We then began preparations for our path analysis. In the case of sociodemographics and vulnerability (the indirect victimization model suggests that women, blacks, and lower income persons are

---

[45] *See* A. Hunter, *supra* note 14.

[46] The only two exceptions to this were gender and race. Centering the latter item was not required, because the neighborhoods were either all black or all white. Centering the former item was judged inappropriate.

[47] For full details on all aspects of scale building, see R. Taylor & M. Hale, Testing Alternative Models of Fear of Crime (unpublished final report).

more vulnerable to fear), a composite was built for each outcome using the procedure suggested by Igra.[48] We regressed each outcome on the explanatory variables for each concept and constructed a single composite variable for each concept using the individual unstandardized b weights of the items.

In order to develop composites for each concept, only those scales or variables which reflected that concept and made a significant unique contribution ($p < .05$) to the outcome were used. In most instances this meant that a concept was represented by one scale or item. Unstandardized b weights were used to build two composites in cases where more than one scale made a significant unique contribution to the outcome.

The following example may clarify this procedure. Consider two disorder scales, one reflecting physical problems (x_1) and the other social problems (x_2), each of which correlates significantly ($p < .05$) with fear (y_1) such that $r_{x_1y_1} = .15$ and $r_{x_2y_2} = .17$, both with significant unstandardized b weights ($b_1 = .10$ and $b_2 = .13$) when regressed on fear. In such a case, we made up a problem composite (C) such that $C = .10X_1 + .13X_2$. It was this composite that was entered in the path analysis.

The models proposed are fully recursive. Once a path model was estimated, paths with standardized coefficients of less than .05 were eliminated, and the trimmed model was estimated. We assessed the goodness of fit of the models (trimmed or untrimmed) by using the standardized path coefficients to reproduce the original correlation matrices. In assessing goodness of fit, we used the standard criterion that the correlation reproduced by the model must be within ±.05 of the original correlation.[49] Of course, many models can fit one set of data. Acceptable fit does not tell us which model is "best"; it simply tells us that that model is one fitting the correlation matrix. Nevertheless, such evidence is important because it tells us that there is a correspondence between the theoretical structure and the observed patterns.

Two important and testable assumptions of path analysis are (1) additivity (i.e., no interactions) and (2) linearity. We tested for interactions by carrying out regressions with the interaction terms added after the other variables. In two cases a path analysis was rerun after logging the predictors (plus a constant) which had significantly interacted. We tested for curvilinearity by adding power (squared)

[48] Igra, *On Forming Variable Set Composites to Summarize a Block Recursive Model*, 8 Soc. Sci. Research 253 (1979).

[49] *See generally* F. Kerlinger & E. Pedhazur, Multiple Regression in Behavioral Research (1973).

terms after all linear main effects had been entered and found that the curvilinear form of the sociodemographic and/or vulnerability composites merited entry on several models. That is, the relation between the composites and the outcomes were curvilinear. In each such case, however, the curvilinearity was slight.[50]

C. PARTITIONING OF VARIANCE

As mentioned above, variables were centered by neighborhood means. The results of that decomposition follow.

1. Crime

The results of the partitioning of the variance of the crime data indicated that over 90% of the variation in all Type I offenses, with the exception of assault, was within-neighborhood variation. Stated differently, the bulk of the variation between the high- and low-crime areas occurred at the block level and not at the neighborhood level.

2. Other Variables

We carried out a similar decomposition for the other variables to be used in our fear models. The proportion of individual-level variation ranged from 50% to 100% across the items, and averaged 93%. That is, across all of these items—which reflect social dynamics, perceived problems, neighborhood expectations, fear, etc.— 93% of the variation is a property of individuals or blocks rather than a property of a particular neighborhood. Thus, after removing between-neighborhood variation from the data set, there is still considerable remaining variation.

---

[50] Four reasons convinced us the curvilinearity was modest. First, the tolerance of the power term was always much less than .01, suggesting that the curvilinearity represented a very small portion of the composite. Second, we compared the bivariate scattergrams of the composites with the outcomes. No marked curvilinearity was evident, and, in fact, the plots were quite elliptical. Third, when we logged the curvilinear predictor variables, no sizable increments in R^2 were observed. The changes were typically .2%-.3%. Finally, if we "forced" the (squared) term into the regression, "beta bounce" appeared—i.e., the beta for the composite became significant in the opposite direction. There were also very sizable increases in the standard error of the betas for these variables. This suggests that the power term was extremely colinear with the linear form of the variable and contributed little uniquely. For these reasons, we persisted in assessing and reporting recursive causal models, despite slight evidence of curvilinearity. Those who may disagree with our analyses, despite the above reasoning, should simply focus on the interpretation of our models' direct effects, which represent the betas we would have obtained as the final step in a multiple regression.

D.   OUTCOME MEASURES

One of the valuable features of this data set is that it includes several fear of crime variables. Two items assessed emotional reactions to possible person-to-person confrontation or violence. One item asked how fearful the respondent would be if approached at night by a stranger asking directions. Another asked how uneasy the respondent would be if he or she heard footsteps behind him or her while walking in the neighborhood at night. These items seem conceptually close to the standard National Crime Survey fear of crime items. In fact, these items may be better because the situation is described more specifically for the respondent.

Another five items asked about the possibility of personal harm but used a "worry" instead of an "afraid" standard. One item simply asked the respondent how worried he or she was about being a crime victim. The other four questions concerned street robbery. First, the respondent was asked how worried he or she was about being held up "within two blocks of home." Second, the question was repeated but the respondent was asked to consider a different location, i.e., "elsewhere in the neighborhood." Finally, substituting other household members for the respondent as the possible victim, these two questions were repeated. These items, although they use a "worry" standard, qualify as fear of crime items because they tap "the sense of danger and anxiety produced by the threat of *physical harm.*"[51]

The final item concerned what Maxfield and Garofalo call "worry:" the reaction to possible property loss.[52] In this item the respondent indicated how worried he or she was about a break-in while no one was home. Although this question tapped a reaction to possible property crime with no possibility of confrontation, rather than a reaction to possible violent crime, we decided to analyze this item along with the others. If it were a conceptually distinct reaction, it would not covary closely with the other items, and we could drop it from further consideration. If, however, it did covary closely with the other items, it would suggest that "worry" is not as distinct from "fear" as some researchers have proposed.[53] In this case, adding the item would help to build more reliable (i.e., internally consistent) scales.

We carried out a principal components analysis of these outcome measures. Two components, with eigenvalues greater than

---

[51] Garofalo, *supra* note 10, at 840 (emphasis supplied).
[52] *See* M. MAXFIELD, *supra* note 6; Garofalo, *supra* note 9.
[53] *See, e.g.*, M. MAXFIELD, *supra* note 6.

one, were extracted. These two components accounted for 52% of the covariation in the matrix. There were five items which loaded heavily (a > .40) on the first component. The coefficient alpha for the scale based on these five items was a respectable .87. The five items were: worry about a break-in while away, worry about being held up within two blocks of home, worry about being held up elsewhere in the neighborhood, worry about some member of the family being held up within two blocks of home, and worry about some family member being help up elsewhere in the neighborhood. This scale clearly taps anxiety or worry about street robbery. For shorthand we will label this a "worry" dimension, bearing in mind that our use of worry here is different from the connection made by Garofalo and Maxfield between worry and property crime.

Three items loaded heavily on the second component. These three items produced a scale with an acceptable Cronbach's alpha of .69. The three items on this scale were: worry about being a crime victim, fear if approached at night by a stranger asking directions, and unease when hearing footsteps behind while walking in the neighborhood at night. Because these three items seem to capture the more visceral aspect of emotional response to possible confrontation or harm, we label this second scale a "fear" dimension.

We think it is important that we have been able to identify two independent dimensions of fear of crime. The major difference between the two scales seems to be that the worry dimension captures a less immediate, less visceral aspect of the fear response, while the fear dimension captures a more aroused and intense aspect. Because it would be possible for the three models to be examined to perform differently for the two outcome dimensions, we thought it imperative to apply the models to both outcomes. If the models worked equally well with both outcome dimensions, this would underscore the generality of the models. Should the models work better for one outcome than another, this would reveal their limited applicability. In short, even though the analysis is lengthened considerably, it is important theoretically to pursue the application of the posited models to both outcome scales.

E.   OTHER SCALES

1.   Crime

Principal components analysis of serious crime rates yielded three components with eigenvalues greater than 1.0 which together accounted for 54% of the crime variation. The first component reflected crime related to commercial establishments or to the people they may attract—commercial burglaries, larcenies, and robbery. The crimes of auto theft and rape made up most of the second component. These crimes probably clustered because they occur on streets where there is little surveillance. Vigilant residents or pedestrian traffic would probably have interfered with the commission of both of these crimes. Thus, blocks with vacant or nonresidential land use should have had high scores on these crimes. The third component included residential burglaries, assaults and, to some extent, murders. This reflected blocks with a disorderly street life. Our interpretation of the first two crime components was supported by the patterns of correlations of crime-component scores with physical land-use variables. Thus, at the block level, we were able to identify three dimensions of crime variation. The other crime measure we used was a survey item in which the respondent indicated whether or not he or she had witnessed a street crime (e.g., mugging, pursesnatching) in the last six months.

2. *Community Networks*

Through principal components analysis, we identified three dimensions of local networks. The first dimension indicated the degree of involvement in neighborhood activities and likelihood of sharing information with neighbors (*localized orientation*). The second dimension consisted of several items reflecting a *perceived similarity* with co-residents. Finally, the third dimension contained items reflecting the availability of *local social ties* in the form of friends and relatives.

3. *Community Concern*

Two dimensions were identified by principal components analysis. One dimension reflected the perception of whether the neighborhood was deteriorating. People with a high score on this dimension felt that their neighborhood had worsened in the last two years, that it would be a worse place to live two years in the future, and that activities in the neighborhood were largely beyond their control. The second dimension reflected how the neighborhood compared to other neighborhoods. People with a high score on this dimension felt that their neighborhood was less safe compared to the rest of Atlanta. Additionally, such people planned on moving in the next two years, suggesting that they had a safer place to go.

4. *Perceived Problems*

Three clear dimensions were identified through principal components analysis. People with a high score on the first dimension perceived that a variety of *physical problems* afflicted their neighborhood such as vacant lots, empty houses, negligent slumlords, and neighbors who did not take care of lawns or garbage. The second dimension reflected *social problems* such as noisy neighbors, drugs, and loitering teens. The third component reflected problems stemming from *sex-related business* such as prostitution and adult bookstores.

5. Land Use

Principal components analysis of the land-use variables on deterioration and lack of upkeep yielded two dimensions. One component reflected blocks with a high incidence of vacant land or nonresidential land use. The second component reflected blocks at the boundary of neighborhoods with high-volume traffic arteries. In some analyses, we entered the boundary-block variable by itself because it correlated with some outcomes more clearly.

IV. Results and Discussion

We present all of our path analyses for Worry and for Fear sequentially. We report the indirect victimization model, the signs of disorder model, and finally the community concern model. We then make some comparisons across models.

In these analyses we employed the following conventions. First, correlations $> .07$ are significant at the $p < .05$ level (one-tailed test), and predictors with correlations this large or larger could be included in the path models. Second, higher scores on a variable or scale always mean more of the quality described by that variable or scale. Third, residuals which are reported are the square root of $(1 - R^2)$. Fourth, following Kerlinger and Pedhazur, if the correlations reproduced by the model are within $\pm.05$ of the original correlations, the model is accepted as providing a "good" fit with the data.[54] Fifth, pairwise deletion matrices are used thoughout with significance tests based on the smallest n. Finally, we report *adjusted* total R^2 for each outcome.

A. PREDICTING WORRY

1. Indirect Victimization Model

The zero order correlations for the indirect victimization model appear in Table 1. Vulnerability variables (i.e., race, age, income,

---

[54] F. Kerlinger & E. Pedhazur, *supra* note 49.

gender) do not merit entry in the matrix of predictors either alone or as a group.

TABLE 1
INDIRECT VICTIMIZATION MODEL PREDICTING WORRY

	SOCIO-DEMOGRAPHICS (SDW1C)	CRIME SEEN (VICTIM2)	COMMUNITY NETWORKS (COMMW1C)	WORRY (FWORRY1)
SDW1C	1.0	.052 (.052)	.091 (.091)	.184 (.207)
VICTIM2		1.0	.181 (.181)	.152 (.152)
COMMW1C			1.0	.276 (.274)

NOTE: Original correlations, and those reproduced by model (in parentheses). SDW1C and COMMW1C are composite variables. SDW1C = .162 (Number of adults in household) + .25 (renter status). COMMW1C = .25 (localized activities) − .08 (perceived similarities) + .1 (relatives and friends in neighborhood).

Two variables (shown along with their b and beta weights when the outcome is regressed on the cluster of sociodemographic variables) appear in the sociodemographic composite: number of adults in the household (b = .16; beta = .15; $p < .01$) and renter status (b = .25; beta = .12; $p < .05$). Thus, worry is higher both in houses with more adults and in rental households.

The community networks composite includes all three network dimensions. The b weights produced when the outcome is regressed on the three dimensions of this cluster are: localized activities (b = .24; $p < .001$), perceived similarities (b = −.08; $p < .05$), and nearby relatives and friends (b = .10; $p < .05$). Activities and local ties increase worry, similarity depresses it. Although all three contribute to worry levels, the first dimension—localized activities and information networks—clearly has the strongest impact. (Since these variables are principal components scores, b and beta weights are equivalent.)

The results of the path analysis appear in Figure 4. Overall, the model explains a significant amount (10.6%) of the varience in worry ($F(3,499) = 19.72$; $p < .001$).

Concentrating first on the direct effects on worry, we see that

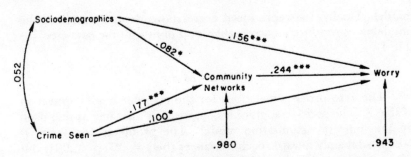

FIGURE 4
INDIRECT VICTIMIZATION MODEL PREDICTING WORRY

the strongest contribution, as measured by the path coefficient, is made by the networks composite (.24), followed by the sociodemographic composite (.16), and, finally, by crime (.10). In other words, localized activity patterns, information networks, and social ties contribute more to worry than do household makeup or crime. The worry factor includes two items specifically concerned with worry about family and friends, partially explaining why community networks play such a strong role. It also explains why the number of adults in the household is associated with worry, because there are more people about whom to worry.

Focusing on the indirect effects on worry, we see that 30% of the total causal impact of witnessed crime is channeled via community networks, in contrast to the 70% which is channelled as a direct effect. The effect of witnessed crime on networks is sizable and significant (.18), suggesting that witnessed crime leads to crimes being shared with others. Stated differently, this effect suggests that having seen street crime may act as a stressor, leading witnesses to inquire about local events from co-residents. Yet, even considering both direct and indirect effects, the total causal impact of witnessed crime is less than the impact of either of the other two predictors. (The total causal impact of networks was .24; sociodemographics' impact was .18; and witnessed crime was .14.) The bulk of the causal impact of the sociodemographic composite (92%) is in the form of its direct effect on worry, while only 8% is channeled via networks.

As expected, networks and to a lesser extent witnessed crime, contribute to worry. Contrary to expectations, vulnerability does not appear relevant. Also, as predicted by the model, some of the impact of crime is channeled via local social networks. However, the size of this pathway is smaller than anticipated by proponents of this model. Finally, the reproduced correlations demonstrate that the model does produce an acceptable level of fit with the data (see Table 1).

2. *Disorder Model*

The zero order correlations for the disorder model appear in Table 2. The sociodemographic composite is the same as that used in the indirect victimization model. The problems composite is weighted mainly toward social nuisances (beta = .27; p < .001) but also includes physical problems (beta = .08; p < .05).

TABLE 2
SIGNS OF DISORDER MODEL PREDICTING WORRY

	SOCIO-DEMOGRAPHICS (SDW1C)	CRIME SEEN (VICTIM2)	LIVE ON NBHD. BOUNDARY (V48DEV)	PERCEIVED PROBLEMS (PROBSW1C)	WORRY (FWORRY1)
SDW1C	1.0	.052 (.052)	.108 (.108)	.125 (.128)	.184 (.184)
VICTIM2		1.0	.089 (.089)	.295 (.295)	.152 (.152)
V48DEV			1.0	.105 (.104)	.082 (.041)
PROBSW1C				1.0	.282 (.279)
FWORRY1					1.0

NOTE: Original correlations, and those reproduced by model (in parentheses). SDW1C and PROBSW1C are composite variables. See TABLE 1 for description of SDW1C. PROBSW1C = .08 (physical problems) + .27 (social nuisance problems).

The results of the path analysis appear in Figure 5. The model explains a significant amount (10.1%) of worry ($F(4,498) = 13.99$; p < .001). Focusing first on the direct effects on worry, the problems composite has the biggest causal impact (.24), followed by sociodemographics (.15). Witnessed crime has a nonsignificant impact on worry in this model. Because living on the neighborhood boundary has less than a .05 direct impact on worry, we trimmed that path from the model.[55] The essential thesis that perceived signs of disor-

---

[55] Living on the neighborhood boundary was the only variable of all the objective indices of incivilities available that had a significant zero-order correlation with the outcome. Although we have very good measures of objective incivilities, those measures did not perform as well as anticipated. This in no way impugns, however, the qualities of those measures which were based on reliable land-use files.

der lead to worry is thus confirmed. The results, however, do not confirm the objective form of the theory.

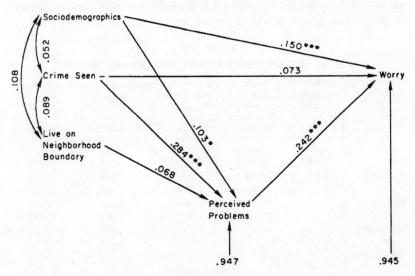

FIGURE 5
TRIMMED SIGNS OF DISORDER MODEL PREDICTING WORRY

A focus on indirect effects helps clarify the role of the witnessed crime. The indirect impact, channeled through perceived problems, constitutes almost half (58%) of the total causal impact of witnessed crime. Even if we consider both direct and indirect causal channels, however, witnessed crime has less of an impact on worry than does the sociodemographic composite. In contrast to witnessed crime, only 17% of the total causal impact of sociodemographics is channeled through problems. Witnessed crime (.28) and sociodemographics (.10) determine problems.

In short, perceived problems have a strong effect on worry. Witnessed crime has a weak direct effect on worry but a sizable indirect effect via perceived problems. Contrary to expectation, objective physical conditions have no significant effects on problems or worry. In light of this, the central thesis of the disorder model should be revised. The revised thesis is that witnessed street crime rather than social and physical incivilities causes perceived problems which lead to higher fear levels.

3. *Community Concern Model*

The zero order correlations for the community concern model

appear in Table 3. The relevant community concern scale is the negative comparision of the neighborhood with other areas. The sociodemographic and problems composite variables are the same as those that appear in the disorder model.

TABLE 3
COMMUNITY CONCERN MODEL PREDICTING WORRY

	CRIME SEEN (VICTIM2)	LIVE ON NBHD. BOUNDARY (V48DEV)	PERCEIVED PROBLEMS (PROBSW1C)	COMMUNITY CONCERN (FCOMCON2)	WORRY (FWORRY1)
SDW1C	.052 (.052)	.108 (.108)	.125 (.128)	.046 (.040)	.184 (.185)
VICTIM2	1.0	.089 (.089)	.295 (.295)	.167 (.163)	.152 (.151)
V48DEV		1.0	.105 (.085)	−.050 (−.068)	.082 (.048)
PROBSW1C			1.0	.376 (.378)	.282 (.279)
FCOMCON2				1.0	.124 (.093)
FWORRY1					1.0

NOTE: Original correlations, and those reproduced by model (in parentheses). SDW1C and PROBSW1C are composite variables; see TABLES 1 & 2 for description.

The results of the path analysis appear in Figure 6. Overall, the model explains a significant amount (9.4%) of worry (F(5,307) = 6.37; p < .001). The pattern of direct effects on worry is the same as in the disorder model because we trimmed out the direct effect of community concern due to a very small coefficient of .02. Problems have the biggest direct effect (.24), followed by sociodemographics (.15) and witnessed crime (.07).

Several features of this model are of interest. Most significantly, community concern is not linked to worry. Residents' concern and negative evaluations about the neighborhood do not "translate" into higher fear levels. Second, the prediction of community concern itself is intriguing. As anticipated, perceived problems strongly inspire (.37) community concern. Also, objective physical conditions such as living on a neighborhood boundary rather than an interior street surprisingly are negatively associated with concern—persons living on the boundary are less concerned. Witnessed crime contributes to concern predominantly by its impact

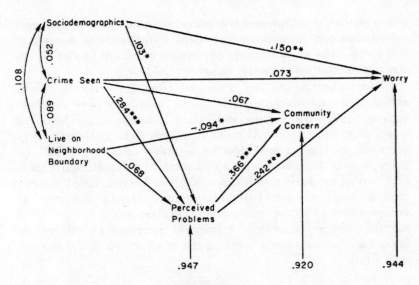

FIGURE 6
TRIMMED COMMUNITY CONCERN MODEL PREDICTING WORRY

on problems (87% of its total causal impact on concern). Finally, the model produces an acceptable fit with the data.

This analysis of the worry dimension yields several insights into the community concern model. First and most importantly, concern does not result in higher fear levels as previously hypothesized. Second, concern and perceived problems are strongly linked as hypothesized. Third, contrary to the hypothesis, incivilities do not inspire perceived problems and concern; crime witnessed, however, does heighten levels of concern, mainly through its impact on perceived disorder.

4. Summarizing Models Predicting Worry

All of the models explain roughly 10% of worry. In two of the models—indirect victimization, and disorder—the key mediating variables have the largest direct impact on the outcome. Significantly, this indicates that the social processes identified by the indirect victimization model and the psychological processes specified by the disorder model are key predictors of fear levels. The sizes of the direct impacts of these key variables also indicate, in the case of both models, that these processes mediate the impacts of objective conditions, such as witnessed crimes, on fear levels.

For the community concern model, however, this did not turn

out to be the case. Community concern, once we controlled for perceived disorder, made no independent contribution to predicting fear levels. The key mediating perception identified by this model was not relevant to the worry dimension of fear.

Two other points also emerged from the analyses. First, although several objective measures of incivilities were available such as abandoned housing and vacant lots, few were relevant to worry or even to perceived problems. This lack of relevancy suggests that the link between objective disorders or incivilities and the perception of these incivilities is by no means straightforward. Second, two types of crime variables could have been included in these models: crime measures based on crimes reported to the police or crimes witnessed by the respondents. Of these two, only the second merited entry in the models. Witnessed crime had a much greater impact on fear than crime rates on the block on which the respondent lived.

B. PREDICTING FEAR

The second dimension of fear of crime is the Fear scale. Applying the models to this second dimension is somewhat of an effort to replicate the results obtained with the Worry scale.

1. Indirect Victimization Model

The zero order correlations of the indirect victimization model predicting fear appear in Table 4. Two composite variables are included. Vulnerability includes being female (b = .26; beta = .15; p < .01) and lower income (b = −.04; beta = −.13; p < .01) and is significantly associated with higher fear levels. The sociodemographic composite is composed of households with more adults (b = .17; beta = .15; p < .01) and nonrental (i.e., homeowner) households (b = −.29: beta = .13; p < .05) and is associated with lower fear levels.

The results of the path model appear in Figure 7. Overall, the model explains a significant amount (6.9%) of the variation in fear (F(4,335) = 6.23; p < .001).

Turning first to the direct effects of the predictors of fear, we see that the sociodemographic composite has a significant path coefficient (−.18), as does vulnerability (.15). The direct effects of crime and community networks are not significant. No significant mediating path coefficients are observed. Therefore, the indirect victimization model in the prediction of fear is able to offer little more than a specification, under the concept of vulnerability, of

TABLE 4
INDIRECT VICTIMIZATION MODEL PREDICTING FEAR

	SOCIO-DEMOGRAPHICS	VULNERABILITY	CRIME	COMMUNITY NETWORKS: FRIENDS & RELATIVES	FEAR
	(IVSDW2C)	(VULNW2C)	(FCRIME2)	(FCOMNET3)	(FWORRY2)
IVSDW2C	1.0	−.249 (−.249)	−.026 (−.026)	.086 (.083)	−.222 (−.221)
VULNW2C		1.0	.007 (.007)	−.034 (−.021)	.192 (.191)
FCRIME2			1.0	.035 (−.002)	.084 (.087)
FCOMNET3				1.0	−.089 (−.087)
FWORRY2					1.0

NOTE: Original correlations, and those reproduced by model (in parentheses). Crime dimension used is concerned with rapes and auto thefts. IVSDWC and VULNW2C are composite variables. IVSDW2C = .17 (number of adults in household) − .29 (renter status). VULNW2C = .26 (female) + .04 (non-white) − .04 (income). Gender and race were not deviation scored.

some of the sociodemographic correlates of fear. Other demographics not tied to the concept of vulnerability, such as household size and rental status, have a slightly larger impact on fear.

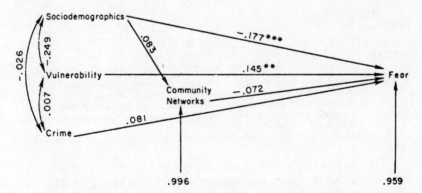

FIGURE 7
INDIRECT VICTIMIZATION MODEL PREDICTING FEAR

The results provide an interesting contrast to the results of the indirect victimization model predicting worry. In the analysis of worry, vulnerability was not relevant to the outcome, although social networks were relevant. We obtained the opposite pattern of results in the fear analysis. Vulnerability was relevant in the fear analysis; social networks were not.

2. Disorder Model

The zero order correlations for the disorder model appear in Table 5. Two composite variables are included. The sociodemographic composite includes four items: number of adults in the household (b = −.14; beta = −.13; p < .05), non-renter status (b = −.24; beta = −.11; p < .05), being male (b = −.23; beta = −.14; p < .01), and high income (b = −.03; beta = −.09; p < .05).[56] A problems composite includes physical (beta = .11; p < .01) and social nuisance problems (beta = .17; p < .001).

TABLE 5
SIGNS OF DISORDER MODEL PREDICTING FEAR

	SOCIO-DEMOGRAPHICS (SDW2C)	CRIME (FCRIME2)	LIVE ON NBHD. BOUNDARY (V48DEV)	PERCEIVED PROBLEMS (PROBSW2C)	FEAR (FWORRY2)
SDW2C	1.0	−.006 (−.006)	−.107 (−.107)	−.124 (−.124)	−.285 (−.284)
FCRIME2		1.0	.066 (.060)	.019 (.005)	.084 (.081)
V48DEV			1.0	.083 (.083)	(.090 (.047)
PROBSW2C				1.0	.199 (.196)
FWORRY2					1.0

NOTE: Original correlations, and those reproduced by model (in parentheses). SDW2C and PROBSW2C are composite variables. SDW2C = .14 (number of adults in household) − .24 (renter status) − .23 (female) + .03 (income). PROBSW2C = .11 (physical problems) + .17 (social nuisance problems). Crime dimension used is concerned with rapes and auto thefts.

The results of the full model appear in Figure 8. Overall, the model explains a significant amount (10.6%) of fear (F(4,332) = 9.86; p < .001).

The sociodemographic composite has the largest direct impact

---

[56] Variables included under the vulnerability concept in the indirect victimization model are included here under sociodemographics because this model and the community concern model do not use the vulnerability concept. Thus, all sociodemographics are treated as part of one cluster of variables.

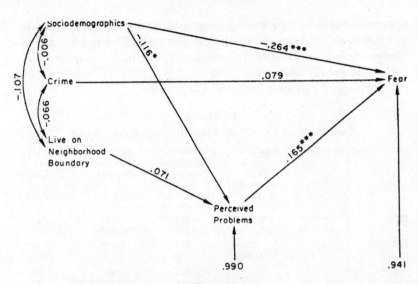

FIGURE 8
TRIMMED SIGNS OF DISORDER MODEL PREDICTING FEAR

(-.26) on fear. This path coefficient represents 93% of its total causal effect. Although still sizable and significant, the problems composite has a smaller direct effect (.17). Witnessed crime has a nonsignificant impact on fear (.08).

The level of perceived problems is determined in part by social class and demographic factors. Fewer problems are perceived by people in households with more adults, by people in owner-occupied households, and by males. Neither crime nor living on the neighborhood boundary is significantly associated with the perception of problems. Therefore, the central tenet of the disorder model is upheld: perceived problems contribute to fear. Objective conditions of disorder, however, neither contribute to fear nor to the perception of disorder, as the model anticipates.

Results with the Fear scale partially replicate the results predicting the Worry scale. In both analyses, perceived disorders are strongly tied to fear indices. What determines perceived disorder or problems, aside from social class factors, is less clear. Neither analysis linked objective measures of incivilities to perceived disorder.

3. *Community Concern Model*

The zero order correlations for the community concern model

appear in Table 6. The sociodemographic and problem composites are the same as those in the disorder model. The model also includes a community concern composite which contains both the "going downhill" dimension (beta = .2; p < .01) and the "negative comparison" dimension (beta = .13; p < .05).

TABLE 6
COMMUNITY CONCERN MODEL PREDICTING FEAR

	CRIME (FCRIME2)	LIVE ON NBHD. BOUNDARY (V48DEV)	PERCEIVED PROBLEMS (PROBSW2C)	COMMUNITY CONCERN (CMCNW2C)	FEAR (FWORRY2)
SDW2C	−.006 (−.006)	−.107 (−.107)	−.124 (−.124)	−.242 (−.243)	−.285 (−.287)
FCRIME2	1.0	.066 (.066)	.019 (.006)	.122 (.117)	.084 (.083)
V48DEV		1.0	.083 (.083)	−.022 (−.006)	.090 (.101)
PROBSW2C			1.0	.366 (.364)	.199 (.194)
CMCNW2C				1.0	.257 (.243)
FWORRY2					1.0

NOTE: Original correlations, and those reproduced by model (in parentheses). SDW2C, PROBSW2C, and CMCNW2C are composite variables. See TABLE 5 for a description of SDW2C and PROBSW2C. CMCNW2C = .21 (neighborhood going downhill + .13 (area dangerous, plan on moving).

The results of the path model predicting fear appear in Figure 9. Overall, the model explains a significant amount (11.8%) of the variation in fear (F(5,229) = 6.11; p < .001).

Sociodemographics, consisting of households with fewer adults, rental households, and women, all of which have higher fear levels, (−.23), and community concern, (.16), have significant direct impacts on fear. Crime and living on the neighborhood boundary, the objective incivilities measures used, have nonsignificant impacts.

Sociodemographics, crime and problems have sizable indirect effects on fear through community concern. Approximately 12% of the total causal effect of sociodemographics, 24% of the total causal impact of crime, and 33% of the total causal effect of problems are routed through concern. This is exactly what the model proposed. Both witnessed crime and perceived problems significantly exacerbate levels of concern. In short, the path analysis validates two central proposals of the community concern model: crime and

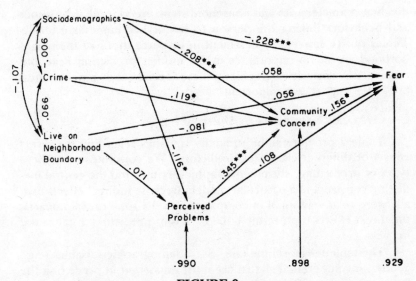

FIGURE 9
COMMUNITY CONCERN MODEL PREDICTING FEAR

problems feed community concern which in turn elevates fear levels.

The results differ somewhat from those predicting the Worry scale. In that analysis concern was not linked directly to the outcome as it is in the analysis of the Fear scale. Thus, the link of concern to the fear of crime is somewhat specific to the aspect of fear of crime examined. Both tests of the community concern model, however, make a firm connection between perception of local disorders and heightened community concern.

4. *Summing Up the Prediction of the Fear Scale*

In contrast to the consistency across models in predicting the Worry scale, the models vary in predicting the Fear scale, with adjusted R^2 ranging from 6% to 12%. The community concern model predicts the best; the disorder model predicts slightly less well; the indirect victimization model predicts least well.

Another difference in the models' abilities to predict Fear or Worry outcomes is that sociodemographics consistently exhibit the strongest direct effects in predicting fear, while aspects of local involvement (social networks) and perceptions consistently have the largest direct effects in predicting worry. This finding suggests that the more visceral, emotionally-laden component of fear reflects individual characteristics and household structure more than attitudes and behaviors linking the person to his or her immediate locale. This is not to say that involvement in or perceptions of the neighborhood are of no importance in the models predicting Fear, but relative to sociodemographics, these social and psychological processes appear less important.

C. OVERALL COMPARISON OF DIRECT EFFECTS

Table 7 provides some summary statistics regarding the direct effects of different classes of predictors. We concentrate on three types of predictors: sociodemographics, crime, and the central mediating construct in a particular model. Because indirect effects usually were relatively small in comparison to the total causal impacts, the direct effects capture the bulk of various predictors' total causal impacts.

The table tells a simple tale. Sociodemographic variables (e.g., gender, income, rental status) are most important in predicting the two dimensions of fear of crime (Worry and Fear). Across all models and both outcomes, sociodemographic variables explain, on average, 3.6% of the variance.[57] The key mediating variables identified by each of the models are the next strongest class of predictors. On average, they explain 2.1% of the outcome variance. In the models predicting the Worry scale these variables have the strongest average direct effect. In the models predictinq the Fear index they have the second strongest average direct effect. The crime variables are third in strength. On average, they explain .6% of the outcome variance and, for both outcomes, rank third (out of three classes of predictors) in the strength of their direct effects.

D. GOODNESS OF FIT

Throughout, we have included in the tables the correlations re-

---

[57] One reviewer has suggested that the sociodemographic variables outperform the mediating and crime classes of predictors due to their lower measurement error. We readily grant that crime, based on police reports or witnessed crime, and reports of attitudes and behaviors have more measurement error than do reports based on demographic characteristics such as age, sex, and household size. Nonetheless, if the reviewer's suggestion were correct, the sociodemographics should have contributed the strongest direct effects in the analyses predicting the Worry scale *and* the Fear scale. They did not. In the models predicting worry, variables based on survey responses provided larger direct effects in two out of three cases. Further, if the reviewer's suggestion were correct, land-use measures, based on *censuses of all parcels on all study blocks*, should have performed strongly. They did not. We therefore believe that it is incorrect to assume that the rank ordering of different classes of predictors, in terms of the size of their direct effects, is simply or largely a reflection of differential measurement error across the different types of predictors.

TABLE 7
SUMMARY ANALYSIS OF DIRECT EFFECTS

MODEL VARIABLE	WORRY		FEAR	
	Beta	Rank	Beta	Rank
INDIRECT VICTIMIZATION				
Sociodemographics	.16	2	.17	1
Crime	.10	3	.08	2
Prime Mediator	.24	1	.07	3
SIGNS OF DISORDER				
Sociodemographics	.15	2	.26	1
Crime	.07	3	.08	3
Prime Mediator	.24	1	.17	2
COMMUNITY CONCERN				
Sociodemographics	.15	1	.23	1
Crime	.07	2	.06	3
Prime Mediator	.00	3	.16	2
AVERAGE				
Sociodemographics	.15		.22	
Crime	.08		.08	
Prime Mediator	.16		.13	

NOTE: For the Indirect Victimization model, Community Networks was the prime mediating variable. Absolute values are reported for betas. Vulnerability is treated as a sociodemographic concept in the Indirect Victimization model.

produced by the path models. For all models, all reproduced correlations were within .05 of the original correlations. Our path analyses have thus confirmed that all of these models show a good fit with the data. Theoretically, this is important. This confirmation does not mean that these three models are the only ones which can accurately model the data, but these models successfully capture the intercorrelations between the key concepts. Thus, none of the three models can be rejected out of hand simply because of a lack of goodness of fit. There are, of course, other parameters by which to evaluate these models.

V. CONCLUSIONS

We have formulated three related but distinct perspectives which explain individual-level fear of crime—indirect victimization, disorder, and community concern—into testable causal models. In order for these models to be testable they have been presented in their most essential form. We have identified two independent dimensions of fear of crime: a visceral response to possible physical harm or confrontation; and a less emotional, more anxiety-related dimension. These two independent dimensions allow us to not only test but also to attempt to replicate the performance of each of the three models. We controlled for between-neighborhood sources of variation and examined covariation based on individuals and their immediate surroundings.

Several important points have emerged from our results. First, all of the models were successful in predicting significant portions of outcome variance and were successful at "fitting the data." Although some may consider the amount of outcome variation explained to be meagre, one must bear in mind that the models tested are "stripped down," as is necessary for an early stage of rigorous theory construction. Additionally, the sources of between-neighborhood covariation which can often "boost" results have been eliminated.

A second point that emerged is that none of the models were "perfect." The results did not support all the key hypotheses of any model in predicting both outcome dimensions. Rather, the following pattern emerged. In the indirect victimization model, social networks were relevant in predicting the Worry or anxiety dimension of fear of crime but were not relevant in predicting the more visceral Fear dimension. The measure of vulnerability was not relevant in predicting the Worry index but was relevant in predicting the Fear index. Thus, only one of the two tests (outcomes) supported each of the two key hypotheses of the indirect victimization model.

With the disorder model, perceived problems were linked to both fear scales. In both cases this linkage was strong. Thus, controlling for social class, land uses related to incivilities, and crime, perceptions of neighborhood problems are linked with fear of crime. This strong, replicated linkage supports Garofalo and Laub's notion that fear of crime is closely connected with a more general "urban unease."[58] This linkage is the first time this notion has been supported in an analysis that controls for between-neighborhood sources of variation in fear. Essentially, those who are more bothered by local social and physical problems are more fearful regardless of the qualities of the locale.

The sources of these perceived problems, however, are still unclear. In neither test were objective measures of land uses pertinent to incivilities (vacant houses, vacant lots, nonresidential land use, larger-volume arteries) related to perceived problems once social

---

[58] *See* Garofalo & Laub, *supra* note 13.

class and crime were controlled.[59] In the test with the Worry dimension, crime was linked to perceived problems, but this connection did not reoccur in tests with the Fear dimension. The unclear origins of perceived problems suggest that, at this level of analysis, these measures are capturing a largely subjective, idiographic appraisal of local conditions. If this is the case, and only further careful replications of what has been observed here will tell us if this is so, reappraisals should be made of the results of previous studies of fear of crime where perceived problems were interpreted as more or less veridical reports of neighborhood conditions and dynamics.[60] An important task for those working within the "perception of disorder" approach to fear of crime is to clarify the origins of these perceptions. Such information will have important implications for the ongoing discussion concerning the construct validity of fear of crime.

In the community concern model, concern was linked with fear of crime using the Fear index, but the two were not linked when the Worry index was examined. This suggests that present and future distress about the neighborhood feeds the more visceral aspect of fear of crime but not the less pressing, more anxiety-related aspects. Perhaps the relevance of community concern to fear is more specific than has heretofore been suggested. This model produced good results in indicating what gives rise to community concern. With both outcome dimensions we saw that the perception of local problems engendered community concern. In the model predicting the Worry index, crime also contributed to community concern.

Aside from these points specific to the particular models tested, the present pattern of results suggests some more general conclu-

---

[59] Again, these measures came from complete land-use files of all parcels on all study blocks. It is therefore acceptable to describe these measures as "objective," because measurement error was low to nonexistent in these files. One reviewer has suggested that this conclusion (objective conditions not linked to fear) is incorrect and that we have committed what is widely known as the "partialling fallacy." The reviewer suggested that we cannot deny a link between neighborhood conditions and the perception of neighborhood problems while controlling for social class, because social class variation gives rise to *both* the conditions and the perceptions. We think the reviewer's line of reasoning is correct *at the neighborhood or ecological level of analysis*. Our analysis here, however, is on individual-level variations in perceived problems and fear and the contributions to these variations of census-block-level exogenous conditions. At such a micro-ecological level it is much more difficult to make the same argument. One would have to assert that the social class of the individual resident largely determines conditions on the census block. The role of social class factors in determining both exogenous conditions and perceptions of conditions is undoubtedly much weaker at this micro-ecological level than it is at the ecological level.

[60] *See, e.g.,* W. SKOGAN & M. MAXFIELD, *supra* note 7; Taylor, Taub & Dunham, *supra* note 22.

sions. First, fear of crime at the individual level appears to be largely a function of the individual's position in the larger society. Social class and demographic characteristics have emerged as the strongest predictors of fear responses. Some of the variables included under sociodemographics, such as being female, relate to Skogan and Maxfield's concept of physical vulnerability.[61] Some of the other variables that have been included—lower income and rental status—relate to Skogan and Maxfield's concept of social vulnerability. A question that has previously been open is whether characteristics indicative of social vulnerability are correlated with fear because of where those socially vulnerable persons live or because of who they are. The results here, which control for between neighborhood sources of fear and block crime rates, suggest that the latter is more tenable. Social vulnerability correlates with fear partially because those characteristics of individuals, regardless of where they are living, are associated with certain perceptions and sentiments that are more fear-inspiring. It seems important for researchers to probe for the dynamics underlying the connection of social vulnerability to fear of crime. Characteristics of the previous habitats of the socially vulnerable and expectations based on prior residential settings may provide an answer.

Nonetheless, the performance of sociodemographic predictors should not obscure the consistent role played by residents' perceptions of local conditions and by involvement in locale. These factors reflect person-environment transactions and inform us about the congruence, or lack of congruence, between the resident and his or her immediate environment.[62] Community concern, for example, most clearly reflects such a lack of congruence. Thus, although fear, as argued above, is a reflection of relative position in the social order, it is also an indication of a presence or lack of congruence between individuals and where they live.

Finally, the results underscore the loose linkage between crime and fear. Crime rates and actual street crimes witnessed were available as crime measures. Crime was weaker as a predictor of fear of crime than perceptions of locale and sociodemographics.[63] This

---

[61] W. SKOGAN & M. MAXFIELD, *supra* note 7.

[62] For a discussion of congruence from a sociological perspective, see W. MICHEL-SON, MAN IN HIS URBAN ENVIRONMENT (1970). For a discussion from an environmental psychological perspective, see Stokols, *Introduction*, in PERSPECTIVES ON BEHAVIOR AND ENVIRONMENT (D. Stokols ed. 1977).

[63] Clearly, the measures of crime used in this study were not perfect. Police reports undercount actual crimes, the extent depending upon the actual crime involved. Respondents' recall of crimes witnessed was also probably less than perfect. Nonetheless, the measurement qualities of the items were certainly not noticeably inferior compared

pattern of results, coupled with the unclear origins of local perceptions (e.g., of disorder) and sentiments (e.g., community concern) that inspire fear, suggests that a more fruitful avenue for future research may involve pursuing links between fear and issues such as neighborhood change, rather than attempting to build a stronger case for the link between crime and fear.

---

to the qualities of the other classes of predictors used. Consequently, it would be incorrect to attribute the poor performance of crime predictors in this study, *relative* to other classes of predictors, to the measurement properties of the crime variables.

[20]

The Journal of Social Psychology, 129(2), 141–160

Fear of Crime in Residential Environments: Testing a Social Psychological Model

ADRI VAN DER WURFF
LEENDERT VAN STAALDUINEN
PETER STRINGER
Psychological Laboratory
University of Nijmegen, the Netherlands

ABSTRACT. We examined fear of crime in the residential environment from a theoretical and social psychological perspective by constructing a model that relates feelings of unsafety to attributions about self, the potential criminal, and the situation in which the criminal act might occur. Using data from a questionnaire field survey of 440 residents in four urban neighborhoods, the model was compared with a sociodemographic alternative (comprising such variables as gender, age, and educational level). LISREL, a relatively new method of analysis that takes measurement error into account, indicated that the model has superior explanatory power and greater interpretability. Multiple regression analyses confirmed these results and point to ways in which operationalization of the theoretical model might be improved.

FEAR OF CRIME has been studied from the perspective of a number of disciplines including criminology (e.g., Garofalo, 1979), sociology (e.g., Braungart, Braungart, & Hoyer, 1980), geography (e.g., Smith, 1986), and psychology (e.g., Tyler & Rasinski, 1984). Perhaps because of this pluralism, there has been little theorizing about the phenomenon and even less empirical research to test those theoretical ideas that have been proposed.

The research reported here was supported by the Foundation for Social-Spatial Research (S.R.O.) and funded by the Science Research Council (N.W.O.) in the Netherlands.

Adri van der Wurff is now at the Department of Psychology, University of Amsterdam; Leendert van Staalduinen is at the Research Centre for Applied Educational Studies, University of Twente; and Peter Stringer is at the Policy Research Institute, The Queen's University of Belfast and the University of Ulster.

Requests for reprints should be sent to Peter Stringer, Policy Research Institute, The Queen's University of Belfast and the University of Ulster, 105 Botanic Avenue, Belfast, BT7 1NN, Northern Ireland.

Typical studies draw on data from national surveys, interpret correlations between measured fear of crime and various background variables, and construct a "model" to explain fear of crime.

For example, Garofalo (1979) constructed a model that focused on gender and age as well as respondents' perceptions of the dangerousness of their residential environment. In this way, perception of the dangerousness of one's own residential environment was treated, without further elucidation, as a significant *predictor* variable for fear of crime, on the same level as gender or age. One might argue, however, that perception of danger is better treated as a *component* of the phenomenon.

In a somewhat earlier study, Garofalo (Garofalo & Laub, 1978) measured fear of crime by giving respondents a list of issues (e.g., traffic safety, noise, crime, litter) and asking them which of these was the most serious problem in their neighborhood. On this occasion, again without any further amplification, crime as a serious problem was equated with fear of crime and thus promoted to the position of the variable to be explained. In neither of these two approaches was there a justification for the implicit theoretical choices. Explicit theoretical choices would lend conceptual clarification and at least preclude arbitrary transpositions of dependent and independent variables.

The same pattern is found in many other studies (e.g., Hartnagel, 1979; Lavrakas, 1982; and Liska, Lawrence, & Sanchirico, 1982): a weakly reasoned operationalization of the concept of fear of crime, an exploratory application of techniques of multivariate analysis to an assortment of demographic, sociological, and sometimes psychological variables, and an attempt to construct an ad hoc model of fear of crime. For this reason Van der Wurff, Stringer, and Timmer (1986) have argued that the most appropriate contribution of psychologists to this field of research would lie in the development of a theoretical framework and a measuring instrument.

In Van der Wurff and Stringer (1986), a social psychological model is described that does include a more elaborate conceptualization of fear of crime and a number of possible explanatory factors. After a brief exposition of this model and an associated measuring instrument, the present report concentrates on the testing and evaluation of the model. Because of the lack of elaborated psychological theories in this area, a sociodemographic model will be used as an alternative hypothesis, in order to establish how much is to be gained by introducing psychological concepts. Earlier studies are in agreement in concluding that age and gender are important factors in predicting fear of crime (e.g., Baumer, 1978; Cozijn & van Dijk, 1976; Erskine, 1974; Jaycox, 1978; Skogan & Maxfield, 1981; and Smith, 1986; cf. also Braungart et al., 1980).

Much of the research to date has involved crime-victim surveys (for example, van Dijk, 1978a, 1978b; van der Heijden, 1984; Gaquin, 1978;

Kirchhoff & Kirchhoff, 1984; Maxfield, 1984). In large-scale survey studies
of this kind, the possibility of working with a precise and theoretically justified set of questions is extremely limited (cf. Gaquin). In much of the
American research, only a single question is used to measure fear of crime:
"How safe do you feel or would you feel being out alone in your neighborhood at night?" (Skogan & Maxfield, 1981). A more extensive and differentiated questionnaire would both increase the reliability of research findings and enable a more elaborated theoretical model to be tested. The questionnaire that was developed for the present study is described in Van der
Wurff and Stringer (1988).

Social Psychological and Demographic Models

Social Psychological Model

The social psychological model is illustrated in Figure 1. Besides fear of
crime, the model consists of four social psychological factors. It should be
emphasized that no causal, deterministic significance is ascribed to this

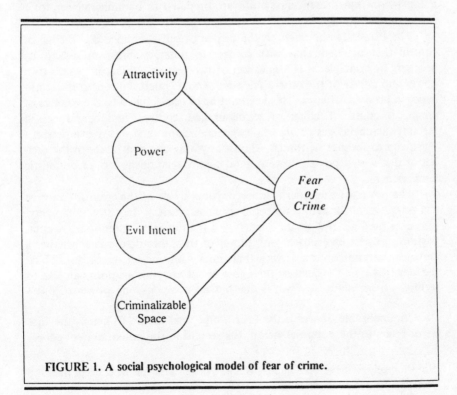

FIGURE 1. A social psychological model of fear of crime.

model. The four factors suggest a possible psychological background to fear of crime. Clearly, the Fear factor may also exert an influence on the other factors. Moreover, other possibly intermediary factors could also play a role. The present model should be understood as clarifying the question of which psychological components can contribute to the experience of fear of crime.

The Attractivity factor is intended to refer to the extent to which people see themselves or their possessions as an attractive target or victim for criminal activities. It involves the attribution of a characteristic to oneself and one's possessions. One thinks, for example, of the peculiar sensation one may have when walking on the street with a great deal of money. Another example would be the fear of burglary, which may be experienced if one keeps valuable articles in the house.

The Evil Intent factor relates to the wrongdoer's role in the phenomenon. It is represented by the extent to which a person attributes criminal intentions to another individual or to a particular group. Thus, one may be afraid of having one's pocket picked the moment one sees a gypsy. Or one can experience fear as a result of a feeling that society is in moral decay and a conviction that present-day youth are prepared to commit murder for a paltry sum of money.

The Power factor refers to the degree of self-assurance and feeling of control that a person has with respect to possible threat or assault by another. In principle, it is a question of two related subfactors: one's own power and power of the other. The first of these relates to a person's confidence in his own efficacy. This need not be directly related to the dangers of crime, of course. Feelings of self-assurance, control, and confidence in meeting the challenges of life will by generalization tend to lower a person's sensitivity to feelings of threat. Almost anything can contribute to the feeling of one's own power, from a good family relationship to an optimistic temperament.

The power of the other is the wrongdoer's side of the coin. It concerns characteristics attributed to potential criminals, such as their strength, agility, resources, and general ability to carry out their criminal intentions. A comparison of one's own power with power of the other determines whether a person faces confrontations with that other with confidence or not. Thus, the idea that even the smallest thief goes about carrying weapons can lead to feelings of uneasiness or fear, if one has no compensating power of one's own.

Criminalizable Space[1] is the fourth and final factor. Whereas the first factor refers to the potential victim, the second to the potential wrongdoer,

---

[1] Unfortunately we have been unable to find a better term for the concept than this neologism.

and the third to both these parties, the last factor has to do with the situation in which a crime may take place. The emphasis is on characteristics of place and time and on the presence of others. It is a question of the extent to which a situation lends itself to criminal activities in the eyes of a possible victim—of how much the situation facilitates crime or the criminal. A criminalizable situation might, for example, include walking at night through a poorly lit pedestrian subway or through a dark wood, although estimates of criminalizability for any one situation can naturally vary between individuals. The interest here is in the extent to which people have a general tendency to heed the criminalizability of the situations into which they venture.

The subjective nature of the four factors is already evident from the examples: The individual's own estimate is the primary consideration. For one person, power may be directly related to muscle girth; for another, it may be based on ideas about one's position in society (e.g., "I'm always the underdog"). Of course, more general stereotypes may also exist, particularly of wrongdoers or of criminalizable places. One thinks, for example, of unsavory, strange men in silent alleys at night (cf. Knapen & Lochtenberg, 1978). The four factors can operate independently of one another, as well as in combination. Two-way relationships are possible: The experience of fear of crime can itself influence perceptions, so that more criminalizable situations and more sinister types are seen, and one feels even more powerless.

One final point has to do with the parametric nature of the model. By means of an empirical test of the model, it is possible to derive estimates of the relative weight of the factors, rather than assuming their importance a priori.

Demographic Model

The demographic model is derived from the following variables: gender, age, educational level, income, the size of the individual's circle of acquaintances in the neighborhood, household composition (one person/several people), and participation in nondomestic activity (in the form of work or study). Figure 2 illustrates the model. Gender and age were selected because of their demonstrated relationship to fear of crime. The remaining variables were chosen on the basis of a speculative assumption that they might show a similar, positive relationship. The inclusion of these extra variables is aimed at making the demographic model as strong an alternative as possible to the social psychological model.

The status of two variables (size of the individual's circle of acquaintances in the neighborhood and household composition) needs some further explanation. Although they may be regularly used as indicators for sociological or social psychological variables (as, respectively, integration in the

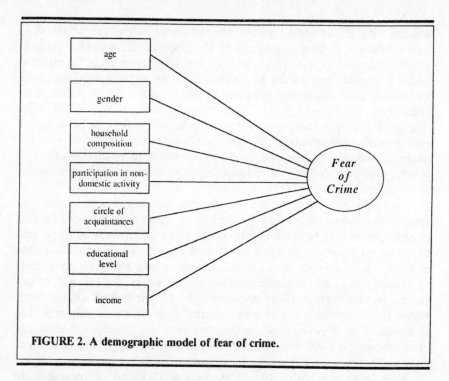

FIGURE 2. A demographic model of fear of crime.

neighborhood and independence), they are not used in this sense here. There is no evidence for such an interpretation. More generally, of course, it is self-evident that the influence of demographic variables on fear of crime will be one of mediating psychological processes. As long as these processes have not been specified, however, they play no role in the demographic model.

The two models do not have the same a priori explanatory power. This is most readily apparent if their potential for practical application is compared. Even if gender and age are strong predictors of fear of crime, no interventions can be based on these demographic variables alone. Auxiliary interpretations are needed that use, for instance, the concept of vulnerability (Perloff, 1983; Skogan & Maxfield, 1981). Any psychological model will by its very nature provide more immediate suggestions for relieving feelings of unsafety than will a purely demographic model.

Although the models do not offer the same type of explanation and do not operate on the same theoretical level, they are certainly comparable for statistical and practical purposes. The higher a priori explanatory power of the social psychological model is no guarantee of its worth as an empirical predictor. Demographic variables act as collectives, standing for large sets of associated intermediary variables, and, by their very lack of specificity, they may be better predictors than the social psychological model's variables. On the assumption that the factors in this model are more directly associated with the experience of fear of crime itself, however, the comparison between the psychological model and the demographic model should be to the former's advantage. The central hypothesis, then, is that the social psychological model has a higher explanatory value than the demographic model. Explanatory value will be evaluated in terms of the amount of explained variance of measured fear of crime.

Method

Instrument

A questionnaire was constructed consisting of (a) a number of questions on background variables; (b) six descriptions of situations, each followed by questions on associated feelings of unsafety; (c) both general and specific questions about feelings of unsafety in the neighborhood; and (d) questions to measure the variables in the social psychological model. The sequence of questions in the questionnaire was, with minor exceptions, as listed above.

The central measurement of fear of crime was formed by the six situational descriptions, each of which was followed by the same nine questions. The six descriptions are given in Table 1 (in an English translation of the Dutch originals). The descriptions were constructed systematically, with the help of a mapping sentence (cf. Canter, 1985; Levy & Guttman, 1982; Van der Wurff, van Staalduinen, & Stringer, 1986). By means of this technique, elements in the description were combined in various ways: contact (or not) with a possible aggressor; presence (or absence) of deviant behavior; sexual connotations (or not); during the day or in the evening; in one's own or strange surroundings. An attempt was made to choose situations that everyone might well have experienced or at least could easily imagine. All the situations have a certain ambiguity. In none is there an explicit mention of menace (though the third situation comes quite close): In each case, the respondent's perspective determines whether or not danger is perceived.

The questions accompanying the situational descriptions were, above all, intended to establish possible feelings of unsafety. The most important in this respect is the direct question, "How would you feel in such a situation?" The answer was given on a 5-point scale ranging from *completely safe* (1) to *very unsafe* (5). We refer to this question as the unsafety question.

Questions were also asked about how great the respondent thought the chance was of a negative outcome; how negative the outcome could be; what sort of outcome was imagined; what one would do in that situation; whether it would make a difference if one was with someone else; whether the respondent had ever experienced such a situation; if so, how often; and whether the respondent had felt unsafe then.

TABLE 1
Sketches of Six Situations

Situation	Description
The doorbell	One evening you're at home on your own. It's late. The doorbell rings, but you're not expecting anyone.
The car	One evening you go to put the dustbin out. A short way up the street you see two men walking around a parked car. When they see you looking at them, they begin to walk toward you.
To a party	You've been invited to a party in a neighborhood you don't really know. Early that evening you set out by bus. When you get off you still have a long way to walk. Suddenly you notice that you've lost your way. A group of youths is following you and begins to make unpleasant remarks at you.
The bus stop	One afternoon you're standing at the bus stop nearest home, when a group of 15- to 16-year-old boys comes along. They begin kicking the bus stop and daubing graffiti on the bus shelter.
The telephone	You're going out one evening. You're ready and are just about to leave when the telephone rings. You answer it, giving your name. But at the other end you hear only irregular breathing. You ask who's there. They hang up.
The cafe	You're travelling through a town where you've never been before. You have to ring home to say you'll be late getting back. Because you can't find a telephone box, you go into a cafe to ring from there. It turns out to be where a group of bikers meets.

The specific and general questions on feelings of unsafety in the neighborhood were distributed throughout the questionnaire. Questions used in previous studies as well as several newly formulated ones were used. Respondents were asked, inter alia, whether they ever felt unsafe in the neighborhood and, if so, how frequently. Elsewhere, the questionnaire ascertained how unsafe they felt in the neighborhood. In this way both the frequency and the intensity of feelings of unsafety in the residential environment were established. In addition, respondents indicated on a map those places in the neighborhood that they felt were safe or unsafe.

The questions concerning the social psychological model came at the end of the questionnaire. Each of the four factors was measured by means of a pair of questions. Table 2 gives a summary of the formulation that was used (translated from the Dutch). It is clear from this that the social psychological variables (e.g., Attractivity) should be conceived of as latent vari-

TABLE 2
Summary of the Questions Used to Measure the Factors in the
Social Psychological Model

Factor	Question
Attractivity	1. Do you think that people who are up to no good are likely to fix especially on *you* and *your* possessions? 2. Do you think there are people who are jealous of you?
Power	3. Do you think you're capable of chasing off a possible assailant? 4. Do you generally steer clear of rows?
Evil Intent	5. Do you generally trust strangers? 6. Do you distrust particular people in your surroundings?
Criminalizable Space	7. If you're on your way somewhere, do you ever imagine that someone could obstruct your path? 8. If you have to go somewhere, do you watch out that you take a safe route?

ables, measured in each case by two manifest variables. To prevent misunderstandings when presenting the results, we avoid the term factor in referring to these latent variables. The two components of the latent variable Power (one's own power and power of the other) were not measured separately; the relevant questions were intended to incorporate an implicit comparison between the two components on the part of respondents.

The remaining sections of the questionnaire were less extensive. Questions were asked about background variables, including place of residence, gender, age, income, and length of residence in the neighborhood. This set of questions included those that were important for the demographic model.

Survey

The questionnaire was used in a field survey. Interviews were carried out in two medium-sized cities in the Netherlands, in two neighborhoods per city. A random stratified sample of 110 residents was drawn from each of the four neighborhoods. The questionnaire was administered by trained interviewers. The majority of respondents gave the impression that they found the interview a pleasant experience. This emerged from debriefing talks with the interviewers and from the fact that 80% of respondents said that they would be willing to cooperate in a follow-up study.

Results

Global Test of the Questionnaire

The questionnaire was first examined for its adherence to a number of essential criteria for a measuring instrument. Three points were considered: the distribution of answers, their reliability, and their unidimensionality. Attention here is restricted to the six situational descriptions that constituted the central measurement of fear of crime and, for each description, to the unsafety question. Answers to this question showed a reasonable variation between situations. Table 3 summarizes the means, standard deviations, and modal answers. *Party* was the situation that elicited the most feelings of unsafety (and had the smallest standard deviation). *Telephone* had the lowest score. This is not to say, of course, that respondents would not find this situation annoying, only that they do not report reacting to it with fear. An analysis of variance showed the differences between situations to be significant, $F(5) = 206.24$, $p < .001$.

The reliability of the questions as an index of feelings of unsafety was also calculated. The unsafety question for the six situations gave rise to an alpha coefficient of 0.743 for their total.

The dimensionality of the six unsafety questions was examined by means of a factor analysis. The presence of more than one factor would point to multidimensionality rather than the desired unidimensionality. Analysis with a maximum likelihood estimation procedure produced only one factor. The average factor loading was 0.57 (see Table 4). It appears that the *Cafe* situation had a somewhat lower loading than the others.

Another way to test unidimensionality is by supposing that the questions satisfy the assumptions of the Rasch model (see, for example, Jansen, 1983; Van den Wollenberg, 1973). That is to say, they can be conceived of as six equivalent measures of one latent parameter: fear of crime. An analy-

TABLE 3
Degree of Safety in Six Situations

Situation	M	SD	Modal Answer
Doorbell	2.35	1.29	Entirely safe
Car	3.27	1.23	Rather unsafe
To a party	3.77	1.08	Rather unsafe
Bus stop	2.30	1.14	Fairly safe
Telephone	1.96	1.25	Entirely safe
Cafe	2.31	1.32	Entirely safe

TABLE 4
Summary of the Factor Loadings of the
Unsafety Questions for Six Situations

Situation	Factor loading
Doorbell	.66
Car	.71
To a party	.63
Bus stop	.61
Telephone	.47
Cafe	.36

Note. $\chi^2(9) = 16.35, p < .06$.

sis using the RADI program[2] showed that there was indeed no more than one dimension present, $\chi^2(9) = 16.16, p < .063$. A test for monotonicity did show, however, that the questions do not exhibit the same measurement behavior, $\chi^2(5) = 18.24, p < .003$. They are not straightforwardly interchangable, especially in the case of the *Cafe* situation. This is not important for the present study, however. Six situations were included to obtain as comprehensive a picture as possible. It is not important to discover post hoc that one of them might have been omitted.

In sum, the questionnaire seemed serviceable for its intended purpose—a differentiated measurement of feelings of unsafety. The next step was to test the social psychological model.

Model Testing

To analyze the data, we used two related types of analysis. The major emphasis was on linear structural analysis, a relatively new method that takes measurement error into account. A more traditional multiple regression analysis, which makes fewer assumptions and has a more direct link to the observed data, was also used for comparative purposes.

With the help of the LISREL VI computer program (Joreskog & Sorbom, 1983), a linear structural analysis of the results was carried out. This technique of analysis examines the interrelations between answers to concrete questions (in technical terms, scores on manifest variables) and the theoretical concepts (latent variables) that are associated with them in the

[2]RADI is a program for the dichotomous Rasch model developed by A. van den Wollenberg and M. Raaijmakers (University of Nijmegen).

specified model. The technique can be seen as a refinement and extension of path analysis and regression analysis (cf. Birnbaum, 1981; Duncan, 1975; Saris & Stronkhorst, 1984; for a clear exposition that emphasizes the relations of the technique to factor analysis, see McDonald, 1985). The analysis calculates a measure of fit between the proposed model and the optimal model derived from estimates of the various relationships. In the present case, the eight questions of the social psychological model were treated as manifest variables that were related pairwise to the four latent variables. The six unsafety questions were similarly related to the fear of crime latent variable. We assumed, thus, imperfect measurement of both independent and dependent latent variables. Following the convention in reporting analyses with LISREL, the rectangular boxes in Figures 3 and 4 represent graphically the manifest variables that were used to measure the latent independent variables and the dependent variable.

The demographic model also included the latent variable fear of crime and the six unsafety questions. On the other side of the equation were the manifest sociodemographic variables: gender, age, and so forth. The manifest demographic variables could be related directly to the fear variable: Answers to the age and gender questions need not be seen as possibly imperfect measurements of latent variables of age and gender.

In evaluating the results of a LISREL analysis, three measures are of particular importance. The adjusted goodness-of-fit index (AGFI), which is corrected for the number of degrees of freedom, indicates the agreement between the empirical results and the results expected by the model. It is also possible to work with chi-square values, but they are open to a number of objections (see Saris & Stronkhorst, 1984). The coefficient of determination (CoD) measures the proportion of variance of the fear variable accounted for. The parameter estimates for the relationships compose the third important outcome of the analysis. These values were standardized.

Figure 3 gives a summary of the results for the demographic model. The model's fit was sizable, $\chi^2(44) = 142.60$, $p < .000$ (AGFI = .907), but the amount of variance of the fear variable accounted for was not high (CoD = .404).[3] Gender, age, and participation in nondomestic activity had the greatest relative influence. (The negative parameter value of the last variable was caused by the direction of answers to the question).

In Figure 4, the results for the social psychological model are reported, $\chi^2(67) = 296.77$, $p < .000$ (AGFI = .867; CoD = .991; CoD_{adj} = .991). The fit was sizable, and the proportion of variance accounted for was very high.

---

[3]To correct for the number of predictors, a shrinkage formula can be applied: R^2_{adj} = $1 - ((N - 1) / (N - k - 1)) \times (1 - R^2)$, where N = number of observations, k = number of predictors, and R^2 = uncorrected CoD (Nunnally, 1978). The value is then CoD_{adj} = .391.

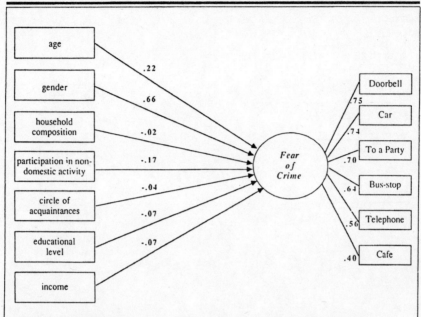

FIGURE 3. LISREL parameter estimates for the demographic model (standardized estimates; interaction and disturbance parameters have been left out).

Above all, Attractivity and Evil Intent had important roles to play. Here, too, negative parameter values were caused by the direction of the answers.

An alternative way of measuring fear of crime is with the two general questions on frequency and intensity of feelings of unsafety in the neighborhood. These can be used as the manifest variables for the latent variable fear. In this case, a reasonable fit could still be obtained (AGFI = .937 and .803 for the demographic and social psychological models, respectively), but the explanatory power dropped sharply (CoD = .172 and .202, respectively). The construction of a hybrid model, whereby the demographic variables are coupled with the four social psychological factors[4] but not directly to the fear variable, produced no improvement as far as the social psychological model was concerned, $\chi^2(116) = 635.89$, $p < .000$ (AGFI = .816; variance of the fear variable accounted for, .959).

---

[4]Income was coupled with Attractivity and Power, age with Power, gender with Power and Criminalizable Space, and the extent of the circle of acquaintances with Evil Intent and Criminalizable Space.

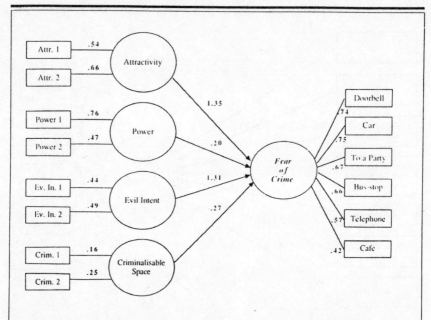

FIGURE 4. LISREL parameter estimates for the social psychological model (standardized estimates; interaction and disturbance parameters have been left out).

Multiple regression analysis tested the models in a more traditional way. Fear of crime was equated with the sum of equally weighted scores on the six unsafety questions. The seven demographic variables were treated in the same way as in the LISREL analysis, that is, the values of the independent variables were associated with scores on the relevant questions (using the normal dummy variable procedures). The social psychological variables were entered as eight separate independent variables.

Table 5 gives the results for regression analyses with all 15 independent variables in a forced-entry prediction model. A block-wise analysis was also carried out to show the effect of removal of the block of either demographic or social psychological variables, starting from the completed forced-entry model. Removal of the demographic variables resulted in a reduction of R^2 by 0.09, $F(7) = 6.32$, $p < .001$, and removal of the social psychological variables resulted in a reduction of 0.15, $F(8) = 9.34$, $p < .001$.

The results in Table 5 are consistent with those of the LISREL analysis: The social psychological model outperformed the demographic alternative. But there are interesting differences between the results of the two types of analysis. First, the amount of variance explained by the linear regression

TABLE 5
Regression Analysis Using Demographic and Social Psychological Variables as
Independent Variables and the Sum of Unsafety Scores as the Dependent Variable

Variable	Beta	t	p
Attractivity			
Question 1	.06	1.20	.23
Question 2	− .01	− .21	.84
Power			
Question 3	.15	3.08	.00
Question 4	.14	3.13	.00
Evil Intent			
Question 5	.07	1.52	.13
Question 6	.02	.45	.65
Criminalizable Space			
Question 7	.20	4.37	.00
Question 8	.16	3.33	.00
Gender	.33	5.83	.00
Age	.04	.66	.51
Educational level	− .04	− .78	.44
Income	− .03	− .70	.48
Circle of acquaintances	− .02	.66	.51
Household composition	− .05	− .10	.30
Activity	− .03	− .55	.58

Note. $R^2 = .33$; $F(15) = 10.90$, $p < .000$.

equations was much lower than the corresponding amount in the structural
equation analysis. Regression analyses with independent variables from only
one or the other model produced R^2 values of .18 for the demographic and
.24 for the social psychological model. Table 6 gives the detailed results for
the regression test of the social psychological model. These analyses indicated the extent of optimization in LISREL. The discrepancy was due in
part to the reduction of measurement error in the dependent variable.

A second set of differences points to a more fundamental issue. The relative strengths of the four social psychological factors were not the same in
the two analyses. Figure 4 illustrates the stronger influence of Attractivity
and Evil Intent in the LISREL analysis, whereas Power and Criminalizable
Space were the most important predictors of fear of crime in the regression
analyses. These differences in part result from the lack of covariance between the two items representing each of the factors Power and Criminalizable Space. Much of their variance was lost as error variance when they
acted as imperfect measures of the same concept in the LISREL analysis. In
the regression analysis, however, the predictive power of the individual

TABLE 6
Regression Analysis Using Social Psychological Variables as
Independent Variables and the Sum of Unsafety Scores as the Dependent Variable

Variable	Beta	t	p
Attractivity			
Question 1	.05	1.02	.31
Question 2	.00	.00	.99
Power			
Question 3	.22	4.40	.00
Question 4	.12	2.60	.01
Evil Intent			
Question 5	.10	2.10	.04
Question 6	.02	.42	.67
Criminalizable Space			
Question 7	.18	3.78	.00
Question 8	.25	5.19	.00

Note. $R^2 = .24$; $F(8) = 13.45$, $p < .000$.

items came through. Because Attractivity and Evil Intent were more consistently operationalized by their two respective items, they derived more weight as factors in LISREL than through their individual items in regression analysis.

Discussion

This study has made some progress both in operationalizing fear of crime and in analyzing it theoretically. The questionnaire appears to be suitable for a systematic and differentiated measurement of the phenomenon. There are still a number of scale characteristics to be determined, however. In particular, the relation between the responses to the situational descriptions and the other types of questions about feelings of unsafety needs to be examined. According to Furstenberg's (1971, 1972) expectations, there should be two distinguishable types of feeling of unsafety: a general concern about developments in the area of crime and a specific fear of being a victim. The six situations should measure specific fear, and a number of more general questions in the questionnaire should measure general concern.

Some indication of such a distinction can already be found in the observation that the models relating the latent variable fear to the general questions on frequency and intensity of feelings of unsafety in the neighborhood accounted for a considerably lower level of variance. If these general questions have more to do with concern, then models that relate concern to other manifest variables (for example, respondents' political preferences) should produce a better result. Another explanation for the lower level of variance accounted for could be that the frequency and intensity questions are less reliable than the situation questions, and therefore less systematic variance exists to be accounted for. Their alpha coefficient is .69, however, which is only marginally lower than the coefficient for the situation questions (.74). A purely methodological explanation does not suffice.

The differences between answers to the various situations need to be examined further. It has been noted that the *Cafe* situation departs somewhat from the other five. In addition, further attention should be given to whether the questionnaire elicits the same pattern of responses from men and women. But although a number of such points could be elucidated further, the results of the factor and Rasch analyses indicate the usefulness of the instrument described here.

The test of the models produced promising results. Social psychological concepts do seem to be able to clarify relationships that until now have generally been treated at a descriptive level. The social psychological and the demographic models in the LISREL analysis differed considerably in the proportion of variance of the Fear factor accounted for (99% vs. 40%). The variance accounted for by the social psychological model was also noticeably higher than that reached in earlier research using multiple regression analysis: 26% (Garofalo, 1979); 25% (Lavrakas, 1982); and an exceptional 59% (Liska et al., 1982). At this point, of course, one should note that the model is strongly optimalized and that the variance accounted for is the variance of the latent variable; 81.2% of the variance of the six unsafety questions is accounted for.

In this regard, more important than the precise level of the variance accounted for is the fact that such an optimalization is possible. Neither the demographic nor the social psychological model showed a perfect fit. In both cases gaps remain. Nevertheless, with the social psychological model it seems possible to build a structure of latent variables between the six unsafety questions and the eight questions measuring the social psychological variables. Furthermore, the structure agreed with the specified model and showed a strong relationship between the two sets of questions. With the demographic model there was a relation between the two sets of manifest questions, but the strength of the overall relation was much more limited.

All the latent variables of the social psychological model had a contribution to make. None of their standardized parameter values was under 0.20. Because parameter estimates may be naturally susceptible to chance fluctuations, values around 0.07, as in the demographic model, cannot be interpreted as an indication that the factor has even a limited influence. Furthermore, the parameter estimates for the relation between the six unsafety questions and the Fear factor seem very similar to the loadings found in the factor analysis (compare Table 4 and Figure 4).

The results of the regression analyses show that one should be careful in interpreting the LISREL parameter estimates, however. The introduction of error in the LISREL model—however appropriate on theoretical grounds—may lead to a distorted view of the relations involved. Further analysis needs to be done to investigate what individual items measure. For example, they may measure their respective constructs by tapping subdomains of meaning with no relation to each other. This would be like measuring wealth by asking, "Do you go skiing in December?" and "Do you go to the Seychelles in December?" Nevertheless, the regression analyses did make clear that the overall effect of the social psychological model was both greater and more uniformly spread over the variables included than was that of the demographic model, in which only gender played a significant role.

The interpretation of the results demonstrates best the advantages of these analyses. On the basis of the demographic model we can say, in general terms, that women and older people are more afraid of crime than men and younger people, respectively. On the basis of the social psychological model, we can indicate the importance of more variables, and we can relate these variables to other theoretical concepts (e.g., locus of control, self-image, or stereotyping). In addition, the social psychological model offers a more direct route to strategies for the reduction and prevention of fear. Thus, people who think that they are an attractive target for criminal acts will react most to information about how criminals choose their targets, whereas people who are low on power will benefit most from courses in self-defense. This is not to deny, however, that the demographic variables still have an important role to play. They can be measured with great reliability, and the variables of gender and age have an indisputably clear influence on the fear variable.

In constructing the social psychological model, the explanatory variables were linked as closely as possible to the fear variable, risking circularity: Feelings of unsafety could already be intimately embedded in the variables postulated for the social psychological model. However, inspection of the parameter values of the eight questions employed to operationalize the explanatory variables shows that the manifest variables with the strongest tendency toward circularity (such as the target question) did not always have the heaviest loadings (compare Figure 4 and Table 2). The possibility of reciprocal patterns of influence remains a problem for the social psychological model, however. If power has an influence on feelings of unsafety, then feelings of unsafety could well have an influence on the power variables. With the demographic model, the direction of these relations can only be one way.

The formulation of a social psychological model of feelings of unsafety in the residential environment can provide greater insight into both the nature of such feelings and the relationship between demographic variables and fear of crime. Feeling unsafe in a situation is not merely a global evaluation of that situation. It is possible to identify specific factors that have to do with respondents' views of themselves and of their physical and social surroundings. The increased specificity will be useful in answering such questions as why women are more fearful of crime than men. Data to follow them up are available; only further analyses are needed.

REFERENCES

Baumer, T. L. (1978). Research on fear of crime in America. *Victimology, 3*, 254–264.
Birnbaum, I. (1981). *An introduction to causal analysis in sociology*. London: Macmillan.
Braungart, M. M., Braungart, R. G., & Hoyer, W. J. (1980). Age, sex, and social factors in fear of crime. *Sociological Focus, 1*, 55–66.
Canter, D. (Ed.). (1985). *Facet theory*. Berlin: Springer.
Cozijn, C., & van Dijk, J. J. M. (1976). *Onrustgevoelens in Nederland* [Fear of crime in the Netherlands]. The Hague: Research and Documentation Center of the Ministry of Justice.
van Dijk, J. J. M. (1978a). Public attitudes toward crime in the Netherlands. *Victimology, 3*, 265–273.
van Dijk, J. J. M. (1978b). Publieke opinie en misdaad [Public opinion and crime]. *Justitiele Verkenningen, 9*, 4–41.
Duncan, O. D. (1975). *Introduction to structural equation models*. New York: Academic Press.
Erskine, H. (1974). The polls: Fear of violence and crime. *Public Opinion Quarterly, 38*, 131–145.
Furstenberg, F. F. (1971). Public reaction to crime in the streets. *American Scholar, 40*, 601–610.
Furstenberg, F. F. (1972). Fear of crime and its effects on citizen behavior. In A. Biderman (Ed.), *Crime and justice: A symposium*. New York: Nailburg.
Gaquin, D. A. (1978). Measuring fear of crime. *Victimology, 3*, 314–328.
Garofalo, J. (1979). Victimization and the fear of crime. *Journal of Research in Crime and Delinquency, 16*, 80–97.
Garofalo, J., & Laub, J. (1978). The fear of crime: Broadening our perspective. *Victimology, 3*, 242–253.
Hartnagel, T. F. (1979). The perception and fear of crime: Implications for neighborhood cohesion, social activity, and community affect. *Social Forces, 58*, 176–193.
van der Heijden, A. W. M. (1984). Onrustgevoelens in verband met criminaliteit: 1982–1984 [Feelings of fear as related to crime: 1982–1984]. *Maandstatistiek van Politie, Justitie en Brandweer, 28*, 8–14.
Jansen, P. (1983). *Rasch analysis of attitudinal data*. Doctoral (PhD) dissertation, University of Nijmegen, the Netherlands.
Jaycox, V. H. (1978). The elderly's fear of crime: Rational or irrational? *Victimology, 3*, 329–335.

160   *The Journal of Social Psychology*

Joreskog, K. G., & Sorbom, D. (1983). *LISREL VI user's guide.* Uppsala, Sweden: University of Uppsala.

Kirchhoff, G. F., & Kirchhoff, C. (1984). Victimological research in Germany: Victim survey and research on sexual victimization. In R. Block (Ed.), *Victimization and fear of crime: World perspectives* (pp. 57-64). Washington, DC: U.S. Government Printing Office.

Knapen, C., & Lochtenberg, B. (1978). Onrustgevoelens bij jonge vrouwen ten aanzien van criminaliteit en het beeld wat ze hebben van verkrachting. [Feelings of fear among young women as related to crime and their image of rape]. *Justitiele Verkenningen, 9,* 63-73.

Lavrakas, P. J. (1982). Fear of crime and behavioral restrictions in urban and suburban neighborhoods. *Population and Environment, 5,* 242-264.

Levy, S., & Guttman, L. (1982). Worry, fear and concern differentiated. In C. Spielberger, I. Sarason, & N. Milgram (Eds.), *Stress and anxiety* (Vol. 8, pp. 49-62). Washington: Hemisphere.

Liska, A. E., Lawrence, J. J., & Sanchirico, A. (1982). Fear of crime as a social fact. *Social Forces, 60,* 760-770.

Maxfield, M. (1984). *Fear of crime in England and Wales.* London: Her Majesty's Stationery Office.

McDonald, R. P. (1985). *Factor-analysis and related methods.* Hillsdale, NJ: Erlbaum.

Nunnally, J. C. (1978). *Psychometric theory.* New York: McGraw-Hill.

Perloff, L. S. (1983). Perceptions of vulnerability to victimization. *Journal of Social Issues, 39,* 41-61.

Saris, W., & Stronkhorst, H. (1984). *Causal modelling in nonexperimental research.* Amsterdam: Sociometric Research Foundation.

Skogan, W. G., & Maxfield, M. G. (1981). *Coping with crime: Individual and neighborhood reactions.* Beverly Hills, CA: Sage.

Smith, S. J. (1986). *Crime, space and society.* Cambridge, England: Cambridge University Press.

Tyler, T. R., & Rasinski, K. (1984). Comparing psychological images of the social perceiver: Role of perceived informativeness, memorability, and affect in mediating the impact of crime victimization. *Journal of Personality and Social Psychology, 46,* 308-329.

Van den Wollenberg, A. L. (1973). *The Rasch model and time limit tests.* Doctoral (PhD) dissertation, University of Nijmegen, the Netherlands.

Van der Wurff, A., van Staalduinen, L., & Stringer, P. (1986, July). *Designing facet designs: A methodology and a case study.* Paper presented at the IAPS-9 Conference, Haifa, Israel.

Van der Wurff, A., & Stringer, P. (1986). De duistere wereld van de angst voor misdaad [The dark world of fear of crime]. In J. von Grumbkow, D. van Kreveld, & P. Stringer (Eds.), *Toegepaste Sociale Psychologie II* (pp. 101-114). Lisse, the Netherlands: Swets & Zeitlinger.

Van der Wurff, A., & Stringer, P. (1988). Measuring fear of crime in residential surroundings. In D. Canter, C. Jesuino, L. Soczka, & G. Stephenson (Eds.), *Environmental social psychology* (pp. 135-148). Dordrecht: Kluwer.

Van der Wurff, A., Stringer, P., & Timmer, F. (1986). Feelings of unsafety in residential surroundings: Integrating divergent research. In M. Krampen (Ed.), *Environment and human action* (pp. 379-382). Berlin: Hochschule der Kunste.

Received May 24, 1988

[21]

VULNERABILITY, LOCUS OF CONTROL, AND WORRY ABOUT CRIME

VINCENT F. SACCO
Queen's University
and

WILLIAM GLACKMAN
Simon Fraser University

ABSTRACT

The concept of vulnerability has been widely used to explain the empirical relationship between certain sociodemographic characteristics and anxieties about criminal victimization. Building upon this conceptual base, the present study proposes a psychological operationalization of vulnerability. Specifically, the relationship between locus of control and worry about crime is explored through an analysis of data generated from a survey of urban residents. Attention is focused upon two particular issues. The first concerns the extent to which locus of control scores mediate the relationships involving sociodemographic indicators of vulnerability and worry about crime. The second issue relates to an investigation of the mechanisms that provide the theoretical and empirical linkage between locus of control and worry.

INTRODUCTION

An analytic theme that pervades much of the theoretical and empirical literature on public perceptions of crime relates to the attempt to understand public anxiety about criminal victimization as an expression of vulnerability to the experience of victimization. As with most concepts in this literature, however, vulnerability has rarely enjoyed consistent usage and there is, among researchers, nothing like a consensus regarding the way in which the term should be most appropriately defined or operationalized.

In general, the concept of vulnerability is meant to emphasize the feelings of susceptibility and openness to attack that influence the processes by which definitions of criminal danger are constructed and regarded as salient bases for action. In particular, the concept of vulnerability has served as a useful heuristic device for explaining the reasons why some social groups, such as women and the elderly, are more anxious about the prospects of victimization than the objective rates

This research was funded by the Social Sciences and Humanities Research Council of Canada.

of such behavior would seem to suggest is necessary.

To date. most of the empirical research that bears upon the vulnerability theme has emphasized the physical and social dimensions of this concept. Thus, it is argued that attitudinal and behavioural manifestations of concern with crime are most pronounced among certain social and demographic groups, because the members of such groups feel they possess physical, social, and economic characteristics that sensitize them to the potential risks and consequences of victimization episodes. A lack of physical or social resources may increase in an anticipatory way, it is argued, the perceived costs of potential criminal victimization and thereby promote worry and fear.

In contrast to this body of research, the present paper focuses attention upon some psychological dimensions of vulnerability. Specifically, interest is directed toward an examination of perceptions of personal powerlessness and the theoretical and empirical relationships that might link such perceptions to anxieties about crime.

The paper begins with a general discussion of the concept of vulnerability and a review of some of the major uses to which the concept has been put in the empirical literature.

This discussion is followed by an attempt to construct an argument that addresses the issue of powerlessness as a form of vulnerability and its theoretical relationship to perceptions of the threat and risk of crime and anxieties about crime. In this regard, some specific hypotheses are suggested.

Following that, data generated by a survey of urban residents are utilized for the purpose of empirically investigating these hypothesized relationships.

The paper concludes with a consideration of the substantive meaning of these findings and some of their implications for future research.

ON THE CONCEPT OF VULNERABILITY

A recent review of much of the empirical literature relating to the concept of vulnerability to stressful life events has been provided by Perloff (1983) who defines vulnerability as "a belief that one is susceptible to future negative outcomes and unprotected from danger or misfortune" (p. 43). As used by Perloff (and many other contemporary writers), the term denotes a type of expectation or awareness of the extent to which one may be particularly open to the risks or consequences of injurious life experiences. As such, the term suggests a distinctive posture toward the social and physical world which has important implications for the ways in which those worlds are understood as objects of thought and action. As a sensitizing concept, vulnerability forces a consideration of the ways in which individuals differentially anticipate criminal victimization rather than the ways in which they may be said to "react to crime."

The concept of vulnerability has been particularly useful in attempts to explain the manner in which crime-related anxieties are distributed across categories of sociodemographic membership. It has been demonstrated empirically by several researchers that, in particular, women, older persons, and those of lower socioeconomic status tend to be more likely than their comparison groups to express fear and worry about the possibilities of becoming crime victims (Baumer, 1978; Garofalo, 1981; Skogan & Maxfield, 1981). It should be pointed out in this regard that with respect to age and socioeconomic status these relationships tend

VULNERABILITY, LOCUS OF CONTROL, AND WORRY ABOUT CRIME

to be weaker and to be reported with less consistency than in the case of sex (Baumer, 1978; Dubow, McCabe, & Kaplan, 1979).

Nonetheless, with the exception of socioeconomic status, the significance of the empirical relationships involving sociodemographic membership and crime anxieties appeared paradoxical to early researchers. Although women and the elderly seemed to be most worried about crime, they were also least likely to be victimized (Hindelang, Gottfredson, & Garofalo, 1978). To the extent that such worries are conceptualized as, in some way, a response to crime, there appeared to be an irrational quality (Jaycox, 1978) to the fears women and older persons express.

To some extent, the concept of vulnerability provides a resolution of this paradox by emphasizing the anticipatory rather than the reactive nature of fear and worry. To the degree that people believe they are vulnerable, they may define the threat and risk of crime with a level of trepidation that does not (and would not be expected to) correspond in any precise way to the objective realities of threat and risk. Thus, the concept of vulnerability encourages a view of the fearing-crime process that places an analytic emphasis upon an understanding of the ways in which some people (and not others) acquire a sense of susceptibility. The sources of fear of crime must be sought therefore in the biographies, characteristics, and social circumstances of the fearful rather than in some external world of criminal risk.

The antecedants of perceived vulnerability have been discussed by a number of researchers (Baumer, 1978; Braungart, Braungart, & Hoyer, 1980; Garofalo, 1981; Hindelang et al., 1978; Stinchcombe et al., 1980). Most attention has focused upon the interplay of physical and social characteristics and their relationship to a belief in the susceptibility to victimization.

In this respect, Skogan and Maxfield (1981) have argued that heightened fear of crime among women and older persons is attributable, in large part, to a subjective sense of physical inefficacy. For many women and elderly, they suggest, confidence in the ability to resist personal crime is undermined by a perception of diminished strength, agility, and aggression *vis a vis* the young males who pose the modal threat with respect to such crimes. In a similar way Riger and Gordon (1981) concluded, "women's physiques rather than their psyches account for a substantial proportion of the differences between women's fear and that of men" (p. 81). Their research revealed most women in their sample were likely to judge themselves as less physically competent than the "average" woman or man and that these judgements were significantly related to fear scores. In a related study Cohn, Kidder, and Harvey (1978) found self-defense training had the effect of increasing women's sense of personal physical efficacy and thus of reducing their fear of victimization.

Skogan and Maxfield (1981) distinguished physical vulnerability from social vulnerability. While the former dimension is particularly relevant to women and the elderly, the latter is, they argued, more pertinent to an understanding of heightened fear of crime among racial and socioeconomic minorities. Their finding that blacks and the poor are more fearful than whites and the non-poor was explicable, they maintained, in terms of a lack of access to resources which would mitigate against the risk and the seriousness of the consequences of criminal victimization. According to Skogan and Maxfield:

CANADIAN JOURNAL OF COMMUNITY MENTAL HEALTH

> In part this is a direct function of income for people with little money simply cannot easily afford to replace stolen items or repair damage to their property. They may also find that time lost from work as a result of efforts to restore the equilibrium in the aftermath of victimization directly affects their pocket books. Private insurance does not help them much for they are among the least likely to be insured. Finally, survey measures of perception of the efficiency and efficacy of public services, including the police, indicate that blacks and the poor are less satisfied than their counterparts with those services (p. 74).

In general terms, then, researchers have argued that physical and social factors predispose individuals to anticipate the risks and consequences of criminal victimization in quite distinct ways. However, the emphasis in the empirical literature upon the physical and social character of vulnerability has not been balanced by equal attention to the psychological dimensions of this concept. To date, relatively little effort has been directed toward the analysis of the ways in which particular generalized world views or cognitive styles may be more specifically manifested in terms of a heightened concern about crime. In the next section, an attempt is made to provide a theoretical exploration of the relationships involving perceptions of crime and one such psychological construct. It will be argued that measures of powerlessness may be understood as indicators of an expression of psychological vulnerability which, like the forms of physical and social vulnerability discussed above, contribute to crime-related anxieties.

POWERLESSNESS AND VULNERABILITY TO CRIME

The concept of powerlessness has a very long and rich history in the social sciences. In sociological usage, the concept is generally understood as a variant of social alienation. The body of relevant psychological research has been more specifically focused upon locus of control. In each case, the accumulated literature is vast. The intention in the present section is not to review those more general literatures, since comprehensive reviews are readily available (Lefcourt, 1976; Lystand, 1972; Phares, 1976; Seeman, 1975), but to restrict discussion to a consideration of the extent to which generalized feelings of personal inefficacy may be related to anxieties about criminal victimization. It will be suggested that subjective powerlessness, like physical and social vulnerability, is indicative of a particular type of predisposition toward the risks, threats, and worries that individuals associate with crime.

It may be argued that, in a very real sense, criminal victimization represents a type of experience that brings the sense of personal power of those who anticipate such experiences into very sharp focus. Stripped to their barest essentials, personal victimizations represent situations in which a human agent pursues some course of action that is physically or materially threatening to the interests of another. It is, according to Stinchcombe et al. (1980), precisely from the unique situational and environmental characteristics of criminal victimization that a fear of crime derives, even though equally or more injurious encounters such as automobile or household accidents (which possess different characteristics) are not routinely viewed with fear.

However, as has been detailed above, individuals do not anticipate either the occurrence or the ability to manage the outcomes of such events with equal

VULNERABILITY, LOCUS OF CONTROL, AND WORRY ABOUT CRIME

trepidation. Thus, to the extent that people perceive themselves to be physically or socially resourceful, their fears are to a considerable extent ameliorated. To this might be added the hypothesis that to the degree that individuals are committed to a view that they are masters of their own fates, they are less likely to define their personal safety as problematic. Conversely, it may be argued that if individuals believe the course of their lives is determined by fate, chance, or the actions of others and that personal mastery is low, a sense of susceptibility to victimization is likely to be exacerbated. Thus, while vulnerability may relate to physical and social characteristcs, it may be maintained that, at another analytic level, the general view that one is lacking in personal power may express, in part, the psychological bases of vulnerability.

In general, therefore, it is expected that measures of generalized powerlessness would be related in significant fashion to indicators of crime-related anxieties. However, the need to specify with somewhat greater precision the form and meaning of these relationships suggests two additional issues that require elaboration. The first relates to the possible interrelationships which join powerlessness as a psychological source of vulnerability to the previously discussed sociodemographic indicators of physical and social vulnerability. The second concerns the nature of the intervening variables that might link measures of powerlessness to indicators of crime-related anxiety.

With respect to the former issue, it should be noted there is some evidence to suggest that those sociodemographic group members who are most concerned about crime are also those who express the most acute feelings of powerlessness. Thus the lack of personal power like the fear of victimization is related to being of lower socioeconomic status, older, and female (Lystad, 1972; Mirowsky & Ross, 1983; Seeman, 1975). The social distribution of powerlessness appears, however, to be more strongly related to socioeconomic variables than to either age or gender.

This distributional correspondence involving personal powerlessness and the concern about personal victimization raises the empirical possibility that measures of a generalized sense of personal influence may mediate the relationships between sex, age, and socioeconomic status on the one hand and fear of crime on the other. Put more succinctly, is psychological vulnerability the medium through which the effects of physical and social vulnerability are manifested? Alternatively, it is necessary to determine whether the effects of powerlessness upon fear are independent of the effects of sociodemographic vulnerability.

A second set of questions relates to the perceptual mechanisms which link perceptions of personal powerlessness to anxiety about crime. Two such mechanisms may be distinguished. The first which may be termed *threat* refers to the definition of the environment in which one lives and moves as more or less dangerous (Merry, 1981). The process of appraisal (Lawton, Nahemow, Yaffe, & Feldman, 1976) by which individuals attempt to assess environmental situations with respect to the threats they present reflects an understanding of the environment in terms of the meanings which environmental cues have for individuals. Thus, environments do not objectively threaten but are subjectively defined as doing so. Given this, it is not unreasonable to suggest those who feel a generalized sense of personal powerlessness may be more aware of, and sensitive to, learned cues denoting danger in the environment. If this is the case, it would be expected

CANADIAN JOURNAL OF COMMUNITY MENTAL HEALTH

that a measure of threat would mediate the effect of powerlessness upon fear.

A second possible explanatory mechanism may be termed *risk*. Whereas threat is addressed to a view of the external environment, risk refers to the individual's view of him- or herself in the context of that environment. Risk, therefore, expresses the individual's subjective probability of victimization (Block & Long, 1973). It may be argued that, given equal levels of threat, a differential in risk may explain a relationship between powerlessness and fear. To the extent that individuals perceive a lack of mastery over the experiences which affect them, they may overestimate the probability that they will become objects of criminal harm.

The present analysis uses data from a survey of a sample of residents in a western Canadian urban area for the purpose of investigating these issues. A discussion of the sample, measures, and analytic procedures used in this study follows.

THE RESEARCH

The data are drawn from the Vancouver Urban Survey conducted in Vancouver, British Columbia, from October to December, 1983. Respondents were selected using a two-stage cluster sampling procedure. The first stage involved the selection of sets of five households. In the second stage, a household member was selected through the use of a randomly assigned selection grid. The relevant universe for this study consisted of all Vancouver households in the 1981 census of Canada. The sampling procedures yielded 489 completed interviews.

Risk was operationalized in terms of the respondent's subjective probability of victimization relevant to several specific crimes.[1] A danger scale was constructed by factor analyzing four items which asked about the criminal threats they perceived in their local neighbourhoods.[2] Crime anxiety was defined for research purposes in terms of cumulative scores from items that asked respondents how much they "worry about the possibility" they could become victims of several specific crimes.[3] All measures were scored in a positive direction such that higher scores indicate greater values of the dimension in question.

Sex was treated as a dichotomous dummy variable (0 = Male, 1 = Female) while age was expressed as an interval level measure in yearly increments. An index of socioeconomic status was constructed by summing three traditional socioeconomic indicators. The first two indicators, education and income, had associated with them 12 and 48 categories respectively. The third item, occupational prestige, was operationalized in terms of the occupational prestige of the principle contributor to household income. This was accomplished through the assignment of scores derived from the Blishen scale of occupational prestige (Blishen & McRoberts, 1976). For each of the three measures combined to produce the socioeconomic index, higher scores reflected higher status rankings.

Feelings of personal powerlessness were assessed through the utilization of Levenson's (1974; 1981) locus of control scales which represent a significant modification of the locus of control measure previously introduced by Rotter (1966). The earlier measure was intended to assess the extent to which people believe they exercise control over their lives or the degree to which they feel their destinies are beyond their own control and are determined by fate, chance, or powerful others.

VULNERABILITY, LOCUS OF CONTROL, AND WORRY ABOUT CRIME

TABLE 1

Correlation Matrix

	Sex	Age	Socio-economic Status	Internal	Powerful Others	Chance	Threat	Risk	Worry
Sex	1.00								
Age	.039	1.00							
Socio-economic Status	-.103*	-.111**	1.00						
Internal	-.054	.024	.049	1.00					
Powerful Others	-.003	.061	-.150***	-.009	1.00				
Chance	.008	.101*	-.301***	-.094*	.599***	1.00			
Threat	-.094*	-.123**	-.106*	-.017	.136**	.135**	1.00		
Risk	.136**	.020	-.219***	-.067	.305***	.348***	.351***	1.00	
Worry	.217***	-.128**	-.122**	-.096*	.257***	.285***	.289***	.670***	1.00
X	.573	41.560	2.007	37.447	24.594	23.779	1.779	13.481	16.090
S.D.	.495	18.078	1.000	5.296	7.001	7.155	.831	10.601	11.517

* $p < .05$
** $p < .01$
*** $p < .001$

In a critique of the Rotter scale, Levenson (1974) argued that the construct employed too broad a definition of external control and that it was necessary to empirically distinguish belief in chance expectancies from a powerful others orientation. Levenson's modification involved the construction of three new scales (Internal, Powerful Others, and Chance). These I, P, and C scales comprise three eight-item subscales with Likert formats which are presented to subjects as a unified scale of 24 items. A detailed discussion of scale reliability, scoring procedures, and empirical correlates may be found elsewhere (Levenson, 1981).

Because the measures employed in this analysis may be treated either as dichotomous dummy variables or internal level measures, correlation and regression procedures were employed for the purpose of investigating the issues discussed above.

FINDINGS

Univariate and bivariate data relating to the variables used in this analysis may be found in Table 1. An examination of the univariate distributions of the I, P, and C scales indicates that, consistent with earlier research, the mean value of the former scale is significantly higher than the means of either of the latter two. As Levenson notes:

> Such a finding is expected for two reasons: 1) For most Western societies belief in personal control is given cultural perception, and b) a certain degree of personal means-end connection is basic to survival and coping in the world (1981, p. 22).

More germane to the central concerns of this research, however, the data in the body of Table 1 indicate moderate associations involving both external control orientations and worry about crime. The relationship involving the Internal Control scale is considerably weaker.

It should also be noted that sex is not significantly related to any of the subscales, age is significantly related (in a positive direction) to only the C scale, and socioeconomic status is negatively related to both the P and C scales. The presence of significant relationships involving external control measures and age and socioeconomic status and the absence of significant relationships involving internal control and these same variables may seem paradoxical. However, as Levenson (1981) points out, high scores on each subscale should only be interpreted as indicating high expectations of control by the source indicated. Similarly, low scores should only be interpreted as reflecting a tendency not to believe in that locus of control. Thus, it is not possible to interpret, for example, a low I score as indicating a subject believes in chance; it is only appropriate to suggest the subject does not perceive him- or herself as determining outcomes. Thus, any interpretation of bivariate relationships involving these scales must be informed by an awareness of the distinctiveness of these control dimensions.

Another notable and unexpected finding is the relationship between age and worry. Contrary to expectations, in this sample worry about crime decreases rather than increases with age. As indicated above, however, the empirical relationships between age and measures of crime anxiety have been less consistently reported in the research literature than those involving sex or socioeconomic status.

Table 2 permits an assessment of the extent to which the zero-order relationships involving the sociodemographic variables and worry about crime are mediated by the locus of control measures. The entry of those control variables has no effect on the zero-order association between sex and worry; and in the case of age, there is some suggestion that the zero-order relationship is being suppressed by the external locus of control measures. With respect to the socioeconomic measure, it does appear, however, that the P and C scales mediate the effect of this variable upon worry. The third-order partial reduces the original relationship to well below statistical significance.

Table 3 contains the structural equation coefficients used to estimate the path effects diagrammed in Figure 1. At the bottom of the table are the R^2 values associated with the addition of subsequent sets of variables. The difference in the R^2 values for the equation containing only the sociodemographic variables and the equations containing those variables and I, P, and C scores is significant ($R^2_1 - R^2_2 = .093$, $F(3,485) = 18.235$, p. $< .001$). Thus, the measure of psychological vulnerability adds significantly to the variation in worry that is accounted for by physical and social vulnerability. A test for first-order interaction between each of the control scales and each sociodemographic variable proved to be non-significant ($F(9,480) = 2.29$, $p < .001$). It can be concluded, therefore, that the effects of powerlessness are additive with respect to the sociodemographic measure.

The model of path effects provided in Figure 1 is intended to convey an hypothesized set of casual relationships among the variables. Effect coefficients were derived according to the procedures described by Alwin and Hauser (1975).

As Figure 1 illustrates, the fully recursive model distinguishes four types of variables which were entered into regression equations in sequential fashion. The

VULNERABILITY, LOCUS OF CONTROL, AND WORRY ABOUT CRIME

TABLE 2

Correlations Involving Sex, Age, Socioeconomic Status, and
Worry about Crime, Controlling for Locus of Control Measures: r

	Worry about Crime Controlling for				
	Zero-Order	Internal	Powerful Others	Chance	Third-Order Controls
Sex	.217***	.213***	.225***	.224***	.223***
Age	-.128**	-.127**	-.149***	-.165***	-.164***
Socioeconomic Status	-.122**	-.118**	-.087*	-.039	-.042

*   *p* ‹ .05
**   *p* ‹ .01
*** *p* ‹ .001

TABLE 3

Structural Equation Coefficients for Predictor Variables
and Worry about Crime: Beta and R^2

Sex	.211***	.216***	.196***	.138***
Age	-.150***	-.168***	-.137**	-.120***
Socioeconomic Status	-.117**	-.034	-.018	.043
Internal		-.059	-.060	-.041
Powerful Others		.146**	.127*	.044
Chance		.198***	.183***	.062
Threat			.209***	.039
Risk				.607***
$R_2 =$	.079	.172	.213	.491

*   *p* ‹ .05
**   *p* ‹ .001
*** *p* ‹ .0001

FIGURE 1

Worry about Crime: Model of Path Effects

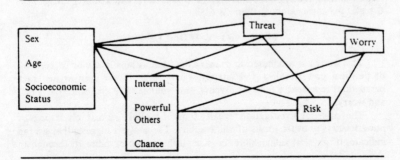

CANADIAN JOURNAL OF COMMUNITY MENTAL HEALTH

TABLE 4

Worry about Crime: Decomposition of Path Effects

Predetermined Variable	Total Effect	Locus of of Control	Indirect Effect Via Threat	Risk	Direct Effect
Sex	.211	-.005	.020	.058	.138
Age	-.150	.018	-.031	-.017	-.120
Socioeconomic Status	-.117	-.083	-.016	-.061	.043
Internal	-.059		.001	-.019	-.041
Powerful Others	.146		.019	.083	.044
Chance	.198		.015	.121	.062
Threat	.209			.170	.039
Risk	.607				.607

sociodemographic indicators of physical and social vulnerability were entered first, followed by the I, P, and C scales. In both cases, the variables were entered in blocks. In the final two stages, threat and risk were entered individually. The regression coefficients for the model are contained in Table 3 while the effect coefficients themselves may be found in Table 4.

An examination of the effects coefficients reaffirms the results of the correlational analysis. It will be noted that with respect to sex and age most of the effect is direct (65% and 80% respectively) and thus not mediated by other variables in the model. With respect to socioeconomic status, however, a considerable proportion of the effect (71%) is mediated by locus of control scores.

The effect coefficients in Table 4 also permit an empirical examination of a second set of issues raised earlier. Specifically, these issues relate to the mechanisms which intervene in the locus of control-worry relationship. It was suggested the effects of locus of control might be mediated either by the perception of threat (environmental appraisal) or by the perception of the risk (the extent to which one views oneself as a potential object of criminal harm). It is apparent from Table 4 that while both external control measures have moderate total effects, their direct effects upon worry are considerably smaller. In both cases, the indirect effect is attributable primarily to the influence of risk. With respect to the P scale, 57% of the effect is conveyed via risk and in the case of the C scale, the corresponding figure is 61%.

SUMMARY AND DISCUSSION

This study has attempted to examine the relationships involving perceptions of personal powerlessness and anxiety about crime. It has been argued such perceptions represent a form of psychological vulnerability that exacerbates fear and worry.

The empirical investigation revealed some of the linkages that join feelings of powerlessness to other forms of vulnerability. The analysis suggests that sex (an indicator of physical vulnerability) does not influence worry indirectly through an

VULNERABILITY, LOCUS OF CONTROL, AND WORRY ABOUT CRIME

effect upon external control. There was evidence, however, that the effect of socioeconomic status (an indicator of social vulnerability) upon worry largely results from the fact that socioeconomic status affects external control and external control affects worry. This suggests that a lack of social resources adequate to protect oneself from the occurrence or consequences of criminal victimization may reflect the more generalized condition of life in the lower socioeconomic strata; and that these conditions find expression in a perception of diminished control over life experiences. The finding that age was not related to worry in the predicted direction calls into question the assumption that age, like sex, may be an indicator of physical vulnerability. The analysis also revealed belief in external control has an effect upon worry over and above the effects attributable to the sociodemographic indicators of vulnerability; and the effects of the external control are additive with respect to the indicators of physical and social vulnerability.

This examination also suggests quite strongly that belief in external control affects worry largely through an effect upon risk. Thus, a sense that what happens to one is dependent upon chance or the actions of powerful others increases the subjective probability of victimization, and it is out of this view of oneself as a likely object of criminal harm that worry emanates.

Most generally, these findings point to the complexity and the multidimensional nature of vulnerability to victimization. While there is value to be derived from approaches which emphasize the physical and social character of this concept, it would appear there are distinct and equally salient psychological dimensions as well.

The results of this research suggest two important directions which might be taken by future investigators. The first relates to the conceptual and operational meaning of vulnerability. There is a need to refine and make explicit the empirical character of this concept and to clarify and distinguish among its various manifestations. With respect to vulnerability as a psychological construct, some research energy could be directed toward the development of a set of locus of control measures that relate directly and specifically to criminal victimization. Such specialized scales have proven fruitful in the investigation of other specific activity domains such as health care and alcohol use (Lefcourt, 1981).

A second set of research implications concerns the need to focus attention upon the social psychological processes by which individuals acquire a sense of their own vulnerability. While the claim is frequently made in the literature that an understanding of differentials in socialization is essential to comprehensive theory of public anxiety about crime, there has to date been little systematic attempt to explore these processes (Burt & Estep, 1981).

In any case, it is clear that the concept of vulnerability holds considerable promise in the study of crime perceptions and that it is likely to continue to be a central organizing theme of research in this area.

RESUME

On a largement utilisé le concept de vulnérabilité pour expliquer le lien empirique qui existe entre certaines caractéristiques sociodémographiques et les anxiétés concernant la victimisation criminelle. A partir de ce fondement conceptuel, la présente étude propose une formulation des étapes psychologiques de la vulnérabilité. On explore spécifiquement la relation entre le lieu de

CANADIAN JOURNAL OF COMMUNITY MENTAL HEALTH

contrôle et le souci concernant le crime à partir d'une analyse de données receuillies dans un sondage auprès de résidents urbains. On porte une attention particulière à deux aspects. D'abord la relation entre les indicateurs sociodémographiques de vulnérabilité et la préoccupation par rapport au crime se fait à partir de l'étendue des scores du lieu de contrôle. On examine ensuite les mécanismes qui fournissent un lien théorique et empirique entre le lieu de contrôle et la préoccupation par rapport au crime.

NOTES

1. For each of five offences, respondents were asked to indicate "how likely you think it is that these crimes will actually happen to you in the next year." Items were accompanied by a ten-point scale ranging from "not at all likely" to "extremely likely." The crimes about which respondents were asked were: (a) break and enter while away, (b) break and enter while home, (c) use of a weapon to take something by force, (d) cheat or con out of a large amount of money, and (e) sexual assault. Responses were combined into an additive index (Cronbach's Alpha = .83).

2. The danger scale included the following items: (a) "In your neighbourhood, how likely is it that a house or apartment other than yours would be broken into?"; (b) "In your neighbourhood, how likely is it that a car parked on the street at night would be broken into?"; (c) "In your neighbourhood, how likely is it that a woman would be threatened if she were walking alone on the street at night?"; (d) "Placing the rate of crime five years ago at the centre of the scale, can you show me with the help of this card where, in your opinion, the rate of crime is today in this neighbourhood?". The first three items employed 11-point scales ranging from "not at all likely" (0) to "extremely likely" (10). The remaining item was accompanied by an 11-point scale ranging from -5 (much lower) to + 5 (much higher). The factor analysis yielded a strong single factor solution with an associated Conbach's Alpha value of .78.

3. The crimes about which respondents were asked were identical to those used in the risk index. Also, a similar set of response categories was employed. In this case the 10-point scale ranged from 0 = worry - "not at all" to 10 = worry - "a great deal." The index constructed by summing responses to the worry items had an associated alpha value of .80.

REFERENCES

Alwin, D.F., & Hauser, R.M. (1975). The decomposition of effects in path analysis. *American Sociological Review, 40*, 37-47.

Baumer, T.L. (1978). Research on fear of crime in the United States. *Victimology, 3* (3-4), 254-264.

Blishen, B.R., & McRoberts, H.A. (1976). A revised socioeconomic index for occupations in Canada. *Canadian Review of Sociology and Anthropology, 13*(1), 70-79.

Block, M.K., & Long, G.J. (1973). Subjective probability of victimization and crime levels: An econometric approach. *Criminology, 11*, 87-93.

Braungart, M.P., Braungart, R.G., & Hoyer, W.J. (1980). Age, sex and social factors in fear of crime. *Sociological Focus, 13*(1), 55-66.

Burt, M.R., & Estep, R.E. (1981). Apprehension and fear: Learning a sense of sexual vulnerability. *Sex Roles, 7*, 511-522.

Cohn, E., Kidder, L.H., & Harvey, J. (1978). Crime prevention vs. victimization prevention: The psychology of two different reactions. *Victimology, 3*(3-4), 285-296.

Dubow, F., McCabe, E., & Kaplan, G. (1979). *Reactions to crime: A critical review of the literature.* Washington, DC: U.S. Department of Justice.

VULNERABILITY, LOCUS OF CONTROL, AND WORRY ABOUT CRIME

Garofalo, J. (1981). The fear of crime: Causes and consequences. *Journal of Criminal Law and Criminology, 72*(2), 839-857.

Hindelang, M., Gottfredson, M., & Garofalo, J. (1978). *Victims of personal crime: An empirical foundation for a theory of personal victimization.* Cambridge, MA: Ballinger Publishing.

Jaycox, V. (1978). The elderly's fear of crime: Rational or irrational. *Victimology, 3*(3-4), 329-334.

Lawton, M.P., Nahemow, L., Yaffe, S., & Feldman, S. (1976). Psychological aspects of crime and fear of crime. In J. Goldsmith & S.S. Goldsmith (Eds.), *Crime and the elderly* (pp. 21-29). Lexington, MA: Lexington Books.

Lefcourt, H.M. (1976). *Locus of control: Current trends in theory and research.* Hillsdale, NJ: Erlbaum.

Lefcourt, H.M. (1981). Overview. In H.M. Lefcourt (Ed.), *Research with the locus of control construct: Vol. 1. Assessment methods* (pp. 1-11). New York: Academic Press.

Levenson, H. (1974). Activism and powerful others: Distinctions within the concept of internal-external control. *Journal of Personality Assessment, 38*, 377-383.

Levenson, H. (1981). Differentiating among internality, powerful others and chance. In H.M. Lefcourt (Ed.), *Research with the locus of control construct: Vol. 1. Assessment methods* (pp. 15-63). New York: Academic Press.

Lystad, M.H. (1972). Social alienation: A review of current literature. *Sociological Quarterly, 13*, 90-113.

Merry, S.E. (1981). *Urban danger: Life in a neighborhood of strangers.* Philadelphia: Temple University Press.

Mirowsky, J., & Ross, C.E. (1983). Paranoia and the structure of powerlessness. *American Sociological Review, 48*, 228-239.

Perloff, L.S. (1983). Perceptions of vulnerability to victimization. *Journal of Social Issues, 39*(2), 41-61.

Phares, E.J. (1976). *Locus of control in personality.* Morristown, NJ: General Learning.

Riger, S., & Gordon, M.T. (1981). The fear of rape: A study in social control. *Journal of Social Issues, 37*(4), 71-92.

Rotter, J.B. (1966). Generalized expectancies for internal vs. external control of reinforcement. *Psychological Monographs, 80*, 1-28.

Seeman, M. (1975). Alienation studies. In A. Inkeles, J. Coleman, & N. Smelser (Eds.), *Annual review of sociology* (Vol. 1) (pp. 91-123). Palo Alto: Annual Reviews.

Skogan, W., & Maxfield, M. (1981). *Coping with crime.* Beverly Hills: Sage.

Stinchcombe, A.L., Adams, R., Heimer, C.A., Scheppele, K.L., Smith, T.W., & Taylor, D.G. (1980). *Crime and punishment: Changing attitudes in America.* San Francisco: Jossey-Bass.

[22]

BLOCK CRIME AND FEAR: DEFENSIBLE SPACE, LOCAL SOCIAL TIES, AND TERRITORIAL FUNCTIONING

RALPH B. TAYLOR
STEPHEN D. GOTTFREDSON
SIDNEY BROWER

Why do some blocks have more crime, or their residents have higher fear levels, than other blocks? In an effort to answer this question we proposed a model that incorporated physical defensible space features, local social ties, and territorial functioning. The model was tested using data from a multistage, stratified sample of 687 Baltimore households on 63 blocks. At each household, surveys were completed and on-site physical features were photographed and subsequently rated. Records of police activity on each block were also obtained. Our model explained significant portions of crimes of violence to persons (18%) and block fear (37%). It was also able to predict a significant amount (13%) of the variation in individual-level fear. At the block level: defensible space features dampened crime and fear but not as strongly as expected; and local social ties dampened crime and fear directly, and indirectly via an enhancement of territorial functioning. A model predicting individual fear levels, controlling for block context, was also supported. Our successful modeling of block dynamics suggests that these entities may profitably be treated as small-scale social units or groups. The pattern of findings has also confirmed suggestions made by others that physical factors alone cannot be relied on to preserve local order and feelings of security. Finally, the block-level linkages between local social ties and territorial attitudes clarify how territorial attitudes reflect, and may contribute to, the development of group-based norms regarding appropriate behaviors in on-block settings.

As crime in the urban residential environment has mounted in the last twenty years or so, so has concern about crime control. Ironically, this

This research was carried out under grant 78-NI-AX-0134 from the National Institute of Justice, Department of Justice. Points of view or opinions stated in this document are

JOURNAL OF RESEARCH IN CRIME AND DELINQUENCY, Vol. 21 No. 4, November 1984 303-331
© 1984 Sage Publications, Inc.

304   JOURNAL OF RESEARCH IN CRIME AND DELINQUENCY

increasing concern has been paralleled by an increasingly pessimistic view about the realistic possibilities of controlling crime through policing (e.g., Larson, 1975). Consequently, attention has turned to possible nonpolice methods of controlling crime. These methods fell, broadly speaking, into two groups. The first group is community crime prevention efforts (e.g., Podolefsky and DuBow, 1981; Podolefsky, 1983; Lavrakas, 1982; Taylor and Shumaker, 1982) in which citizens are mobilized for the purpose of being "the eyes and ears" of the police, watching out for neighbors and their property, and taking appropriate action where necessary. A second group of efforts has centered around understanding the "naturally" varying physical, social, and socioeconomic features that are associated with high or low crime.

The latter area of inquiry spans a sizable literature in the areas of criminology, economics, geography, planning, psychology, and sociology. (See Harries, 1979, Taylor, 1982, 1983, for reviews.) Of particular interest in this area are the roles played by site level or small-area level physical features, which, if they are relevant to crime, might then be changed so as to reduce crime. Consider the following two examples. In an Atlanta study of three matched pairs of high and low crime neighborhoods, Greenberg, Rohe, and Williams (1982) found that boundaries of high crime neighborhoods were high volume arteries that tended to draw vehicular and pedestrian traffic, thereby increasing passers-through in a locale. Fowler et al. (1979) carried out a demonstration project in a Hartford neighborhood and found that the implementation of physical changes such as reducing traffic flow by making street changes, and adding symbolic gateways, subsequent to organizational efforts and policing changes, resulted in less crime. Thus, if physical factors contribute to crime perhaps they can be changed and crime reduced. This possibility appeared in the ideas of Jacobs (1961), later elaborated by Newman (1972, 1979) into defensible space theory and research. The models we propose and test here may, in one sense, be seen as an attempt to revise and amplify this theory by incorporating

those of the authors and do not necessarily represent the official position or policies of the U.S. Department of Justice. Portions of an earlier version of this paper were presented at the Annual Meeting of the American Psychological Association, New York, September, 1979. David Haines, Fred Heinzelmann, Hal Proshansky, Amos Rapoport, Richard Titus and Lois Verbrugge provided helpful advice during the course of the project. Patty O'Brien provided programming and data processing assistance. Request reprints from Ralph B. Taylor, Department of Criminal Justice, Temple University, Philadelphia, PA 19122.

considerations from theory and research in human territoriality and social networks.

Defensible space research itself, despite its theoretical and empirical flaws, which are discussed in Taylor, Gottfredson, and Brower (1980) and Mayhew (1979), has developed considerably since its inception. Based on personal observations, Jacobs (1961) made several suggestions about how physical redesign might reduce crime: For example, buildings should be oriented toward the street to provide more natural surveillance, and outdoor spaces should be placed in proximity to intensively used areas. Newman (1972) went further to suggest that if public space could be segmented into small, controllable areas, this would encourage residents to exercise territorial control over these locations and, this in turn would result in less crime. Graphically, his argument can be stated as follows:

design features———→stronger territorial————————►less crime and
                             attitudes and behaviors   antisocial behavior

Newman analyzed archival data from New York City housing projects and found links between design variables (e.g., number of floors in building) and crime outcomes (e.g., indoor robbery rate). Note that in this study, and subsequent ones of this ilk, the hypothesized mediating constructs are not measured. Despite the controversy that surrounded these initial findings (see Taylor et al., 1980 for a discussion), several subsequent researchers have also established links between design features and crime at the site (e.g., Ley and Cybriwsky, 1974; Pablant and Baxter, 1975), street (e.g., Bevis and Nutter, 1977), and neighborhood level (e.g., Greenberg et al., 1982; Fowler et al., 1979). Thus, the focus on design as a covariate of crime has been substantiated.

Nonetheless, there has also been a growing recognition that the link between physical design and crime is modest, and in many cases conditioned by other factors. Links between design and crime are usually betas or correlations of less than .20 (e.g., Brown, 1979). Many instances have come to light of potentially defensible spaces going undefended, due to other social and cultural factors (Merry, 1981a, 1981b). This has led to a wider consideration of possible factors, that may help to explain variation in crime rates at the site or block level. It is in this context that we have proposed an expanded defensible space model, which appears in Figure 1. The model attempts to improve upon earlier formulations by treating human territorial functioning in a

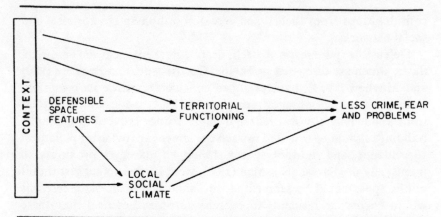

Figure 1   Conceptual Model

fashion consistent with empirical work, and by incorporating local social ties.

One assumption of the model is that sociocultural context variables have an influence on territorial functioning. Support for this assumption comes from work by Brower (1980) and others (Scheflen, 1971), which has indicated that different cultural or ethnic groups utilized different systems of territorial attitudes and behaviors in order to maintain control. Further, extensive work in criminology and geography (see Harries, 1980, for review) has linked crime and economic and cultural factors, pointing to other ways that sociocultural context may be influential. Below we detail the rationales for our hypotheses and causal ordering.

Rationale for Hypotheses

Defensible space features, which in the residential environment would include real barriers, symbolic barriers, and surveillance opportunities, may have three types of causal impacts.

(a) They may have a direct effect on crime and related outcomes. This expectation is supported by the above described research on crime and environment (see also Taylor, 1982, 1983). And although this impact is modeled as a direct effect, we do not assume architectural determinism (see Broady, 1972). Rather, it is more likely that the effect is carried via offenders' or coresidents' expectations based on physical features. For example, Brower et al. (1983) found that the presence of fences or ornamentation suggested to observers that the owner of the property would respond more readily to intrusions.

(b) Defensible space features may support local coresident interaction. This hypothesis was originally suggested by Jacobs (1961) and Newman (1972). The underlying expectation is that to the extent an area is defensible, residents will feel more protected, use the space more, and thus be more likely to come into contact with coresidents.

(c) Defensible space features may strengthen territorial functioning. This hypothesis was originally suggested by Newman (1972). A major aspect of territorial functioning is concern over boundary regulation (Brower, 1980; Sundstrom, 1977; Taylor, 1978); who has access to which spaces when. Boundaries are more salient, and more defensible, the better they are demarcated from adjoining spaces (Newman, 1979). Such salience increases the ease of maintaining access control, and may also facilitate the emergence of stronger, more proprietary attitudes.

Local social ties may have a direct and indirect impact on crime and related outcomes. The expectation of a direct impact is supported by studies such as Maccoby et al. (1958), in which it was found that if there were stronger ties between coresidents, they were more likely to intervene if they witnessed delinquent behavior. And this theme about the potential of social ties to increase adherence to norms of prosocial behavior is evident in both the informal control literature (Janowitz, 1975), and the social networks literature (Wheeldon, 1969). Ties may have an indirect effect on crime and related outcomes via a bolstering of territorial functioning. Territorial functioning is concerned, to a large extent, with control over who has access to which particular spaces, and what activities go on there. As local social ties increase, it becomes easier to discriminate between strangers, and people who live nearby and thus "belong." It becomes easier to predict what kind of activities will go on there. In addition to the benefits accruing to territorial functioning at the individual level, at the group level increased levels of friendship or acquaintanceship imply more widely shared norms between coresidents. These understandings facilitate access control and regulation over activities.

Finally, the impact of territorial functioning on crime and related outcomes has been suggested by Jacobs (1961) and Newman (1972). And Newman and Franck (1980) observed such an impact in their housing project study. It remains to be seen if such a linkage holds up in the everyday residential environment.

Human territorial functioning has been discussed in a variety of ways. Newman's (1972) original use of the term, for example, suggested that it was an undifferentiated instinct that could be activated by certain contextual features (Taylor et al., 1980). A substantial volume of empirical research, however, has supported a more careful, circumscribed view of human territorial functioning (Sundstrom, 1977; Taylor, 1978). It is this view that we espouse here. Human territorial functioning is viewed as an interrelated set of attitudes and behaviors concerned with (a) who has access to particular delimited or bounded spaces, (b) what activities are appropriate or permissible in those spaces, and (c) who has control over and/or responsibility for the people, conditions, and activities in those spaces. Stated differently: Territorial functioning refers to a system of person-place or group-place bonds concerned with issues of control, social legibility of setting, and quality of setting.

Thus for each of the causal links in our revised defensible space model, there is conceptual and sometimes empirical support, although the empirical support in several instances tends to be rather spotty or limited.

Rationale for Causal Ordering

Our model (Figure 1) presents a particular causal ordering. Obviously, other alternative causal orderings of the same concepts are also possible. Thus what rationale can we offer for our particular causal model?

The inclusion of defensible space features as the "first" concept in the model is warranted inasmuch as these are largely physical "givens" in the environment. That is, they reflect relatively fixed microfeatures in the locale. Of course design features can be altered, but this occurs rarely, and only with considerable expense. Thus, given the physical nature and relative permanence of defensible space features, they appear at the front end of the model.

Local social ties appear before, and feed into territorial functioning for several reasons. Territorial functioning is viewed not as a solipsistic or individuocentric system, but rather as a permeable, group-influenced system. The view that territorial functioning is a product of group dynamics is an assumption deeply embedded in the work on territorial behavior and social dominance (e.g., Sundstrom and Altman, 1974). Other treatments of urban territorial functioning (Brower, 1980) have also found evidence for such an assumption. Thus social ties come "second" in the model simply because they must come "before" the concept of territorial functioning.

Rationale for Dependent Variables

Crime is a powerful and omnipresent stressor, and thusly, of considerable practical interest. It is also the concept that has been the main dependent variable in most defensible space work. Whereas past studies of this ilk have focused primarily on property crimes, we will focus on crimes of violence to persons: mugging, assault, aggravated assault, purse-snatch, threatening with a weapon, and so on. These crimes are of interest because they occur on the street, where territorial control might be expected to operate in a deterrent manner. Although many assaults do occur inside the home, most of the assaults we will be discussing here probably occurred outside. We used calls for service data and not actual crime data; thus people were calling in assaults they witnessed on the street. Also, when we looked at the particular types of calls in this category, most of the calls were for the kinds of assaults that were most likely to occur on the street, such as muggings, yokings, and so on. Thus although some of the assaults we will be examining probably occurred inside homes, a large proportion occurred on the street, and this proportion is probably larger than it would have been had we used crime reports instead of calls for service. And although such crimes may be committed by persons from outside of a block, if these crimes do happen frequently on a block, this is strong evidence that residents are not exercising jurisdictional control over that domain.

Fear of crime is our second outcome of interest. It is a topic that has been widely investigated (e.g., Furstenburg, 1971; Baumer, 1979; Garofalo and Laub, 1978; Hartnagel, 1979; Skogan and Maxfield, 1981; Lewis and Maxfield, 1980). This research has suggested that "fear of crime" is more than "fear" of "crime." Rather than being solely a straightforward estimate of the risk of victimization, it is also a reflection of community concern. We measured fear using the two standard NCS items ("How safe would you feel being out alone in your neighborhood during the day? How about at night?"). And, in keeping with the idea that "fear of crime" is more than "fear" of "crime," the block-level correlation between fear and crimes of violence to persons, although positive and statistically significant by a one-tailed test, was modest ($r = .22$; $p < .05$; $n = 63$).

Some may be concerned about predicting fear at the street block, or small-group level. They may feel that fear of crime is primarily an individual-level, affective response. Our justification for treating fear at the group level stems from the notion that fear—in addition to being a quality of individuals—is at the same time a social fact, and a property

310   JOURNAL OF RESEARCH IN CRIME AND DELINQUENCY

of groups and sites (Liska et al., 1982). Thus it can appropriately be modeled at the group level, where that group might be a block, a neighborhood, or even a city (see Liska et al., 1982), as well as the individual level.

Units of Analysis

We examine grouped data: 687 households grouped onto 63 street blocks. The street block is the two facing sides of the street, extending between and bounded by cross streets. The street is a viable, loosely-knit, face-to-face social group. Levels of acquaintanceship may be minimal, as when people simply see one another in their daily comings and goings—or they may be stronger, as when people know about and trust one another. As such a group then, it is appropriate to use the street block as the unit of analysis. There is also considerable precedent for this treatment in other areas of urban research (e.g., Unger and Wandersman, 1983; Brower, 1980).

Because we are dealing with grouped data, and because people living on the same block are more like one another than persons living on different blocks, we have an aggregation problem (Blalock, 1964; Hannan, 1971a, 1971b; Taylor, 1982: 310-317). A correlation (r) between two variables (x,y) contains both between-block variance, and pooled, within-block, or individual-level variance. That is, the overall correlation (r_{xy}) has a between block ($r_{\bar{x}\bar{y}}$) and a within-block ($r_{(x-\bar{x})(y-\bar{y})}$) component. It is inappropriate and sometimes misleading to test a model simply using the overall correlation. The data must be decomposed.

Consequently, we have carried out separate block-level and individual-level analyses. Crime and fear of crime are modeled at the block level. The block is in some ways comparable to the project building, which has been the level of analysis at which defensible space research has been couched (Newman and Franck, 1982). In addition, we also carried out an individual-level or site-level analysis of fear of crime, using pooled, within-block residuals. Such an analysis opens up a new area of inquiry in that it asks whether or not the proposed dynamics shown in Figure 1 operate at the individual or parcel level, as well as at the group or block level.

Summary

(a) Past research, conducted primarily in the public housing context, has suggested that defensible space features may contribute to less crime. We seek to determine if this is also the case in the everyday residential envrionment. (b) We also incorporate local social ties and territorial functioning into our predictions, and hypothesize that ties may reduce crime directly, and indirectly, via a strengthening of territorial functioning. (c) We also broaden the range of outcomes that have been considered in this research genre to include fear of crime. (d) And finally, we test our model at both the street block, which amounts to a group-level analysis, and at the individual level. The data are decomposed so that these two levels of testing are independent.

METHOD

Site Selection

The initial step in developing our sampling frame was to define Baltimore City neighborhoods. For this task we used information from the local Community Association Directory, Baltimore City District Planners, and local community leaders. Planners also rated the defined neighborhoods (n = 238) on income and percent rental dwelling units (% RDU) dimensions. The results of this rating task showed good reliability between raters, and good external validity when compared with 1970 census information. (The 1970 data were the only ones that were available for each neighborhood.)[1] Examination of the bivariate scattergram of the neighborhoods on these two dimensions suggested three types of neighborhood: low-income, predominantly rental; medium income, predominantly homeowned; and mixed.[2] We used a probability proportional to size (PPS) strategy to sample the neighborhood, treating number of households as the size measure (Sudman, 1976). Given the large number of mixed neighborhoods (123) we decided to include twice as many from that group, as compared to the other two groups of neighborhoods, in our sample. This resulted in a sample of three low-income, rental; six mixed; and three medium-income, homeowned neighborhoods using a probability proportional to size (PPS) strategy.

To select blocks, neighborhood leaders in each sampled neighborhood were contacted and interviewed.[3] We asked these leaders to nominate examples of two types of blocks within their neighborhood: blocks where people looked out for each other and worked together (socially organized or cohesive) and blocks where people went their own way (socially unorganized or noncohesive). Our purpose in gathering these nominations was to obtain blocks with varying social climates.

(Checks on data indicated that this stratification was successful.) Leaders in each neighborhood were readily able to nominate several examples of each type of block.

We then assessed the block-level defensible space features of each block in our pool of 104 blocks. Subsequently, defensible space scales were constructed, and blocks were put into either a "high" or "low" group using a median split.

Thus our multistage stratified sample consisted of 12 strata: 3 neighborhood types (low-income, rental; mixed; medium-income, home-owned) × 2 types of social blocks (organized or unorganized) × 2 types of physical blocks (high versus low defensible space). For Survey 1 (see below for description of Survey I and Survey II), four blocks were sampled from each of the mixed (i.e., those that were neither low income, predominantly rental, or medium income, predominantly homeowned) neighborhood strata and 2 from each of the other strata (i.e., strata involving predominantly low-income rental housing, or medium-income, homeowned housing), yielding a total of 32 blocks. Thirty-one blocks were selected for Survey II using the same procedures.[4] For Survey I, we attempted to obtain 40 completed interviews from each stratum. Because Survey II used a sampling interval that was twice as large as that used in Survey I, the Survey II cases were reweighted appropriately. In Survey II we sought 20 interviews per stratum.

Household and Respondent Selection

All blocks were block-listed by field workers; that is, all occupied housing units were counted. The total number of occupied housing units in each stratum was then determined, and designated households were selected using a random start and the appropriate sampling interval. At this level, our primary sampling unit was the household, and not the individual.

When field workers arrived at a designated household and found someone at home, they attempted to complete a screener that asked just a few short questions.[5] If there was just one head of household, and he/she was married, the designated respondent became either the head or his/her spouse. Multiple heads of households were enumerated, and then one was randomly selected following the procedure suggested by Kish (1949).

If no contact was made at a designated household after three attempts at various times during the week, an alternative household was assigned to the interviewer. Or, if the interviewer was unable to survey the designated respondent after a week of trying, an alternative household was assigned.[6]

Survey Procedures

Survey I was completed in the summer of 1979; Survey II was completed in the early summer of 1980. Survey I took about an hour to complete, and Survey II took approximately 40 minutes to complete. Survey II was a shorter version of Survey I, including only items that initial analysis of Survey I indicated were important. Fully informed consent was obtained from all respondents, and all respondents were paid for their participation.

Each survey included sections on household composition, residence history, demographics, local social ties, perception of local crime and problems, fear, neighborhood identification, and territorial attitudes.

Respondents: A Sketch of the Sample

The following characteristics describe the full (Survey I and II) sample of 687 households. Of the households, 53% were owner occupied and 47% were rented; 39% were white and 61% were nonwhite, and average household size was slightly over three persons; the median household size was two. Average respondent age was 44 years (median = 40), and average educational level was 11th grade. Average length of residence in the neighborhood was 16 years (median = 12), and 22.2% of the sample was unemployed at the time of their interview.[7]

Site-Level Assessments

After a household was interviewed, color slides were taken of the front and rear of the house. The physical features shown in these slides were subsequently rated by two independent raters. Details regarding interrater reliability are described in analyses that use those variables.

Police Data

Police calls for service data for calendar year (CY) 1978 were obtained for every study block from the Baltimore City Police Department. We also obtained, for each block, Part I crime data for calendar year (CY) 1978 and 1979.[8] (Calls for service data for 1979 were not available in time to be included in these analyses.) In our analysis, we focus on police calls relevant to crimes of violence against persons.[9] Volume of calls for service in this category correlated most strongly with the Part I (serious) crime of aggravated assault. Crime levels were transformed into rates using occupied households as the denominator.

Transforms

Variables with the skewness of greater than 1 were normalized via a log transform, and subsequently analyzed. For the analyses we report here, this transform was carried out only on the crime data. One was added to each score before transforming.

Multicollinearity

We carried out the Haitovsky test, as recommended by Rockwell (1975) on our block level matrix of significant ($p < .05$) predictors of crimes of violence, and significant predictors of fear. The results indicated that the predictors exhibited multicollinearity (i.e., the hypothesis that the matrix was singular could not be rejected). As Gordon (1968) stated, multicollinearity can result in unstable beta weights as similar variables fight for the same "chunk" of explained variance. Thus we followed his recommended procedure and inverted each correlation matrix of predictors, and began eliminating variables which had the most shared variance with the other predictors (i.e., C_{ii} on the inverse was large). Redundant predictors (beginning with the most redundant) were eliminated, and the resulting inverse reexamined after each deletion, until the matrix of predictors "passed" the Haitovsky test. The variables that ended up being eliminated were some territorial behavior measures (levels of gardening), photographic measures of dwelling unit upkeep, some social network variables, and a socioeconomic variable.

One may object that this procedure may result in path models that are misspecified. That is, if we ignore a particular exogenous (socioeconomic) variable that is a cause of one or more of the endogenous variables in the model, the resulting coefficients may be misleading. To guard against this possibility we also ran the regressions for the path analyses, including the exogenous variable that had been eliminated by the Rockwell procedure. In both of the block-level models, the only variable that we "put back in" to avoid misspecification was homeownership. The inclusion of the extra exogenous variable made very little differences in the results, and we discuss those differences in the results section.

Measuring Defensible Space Features and Territorial Markers

At all surveyed households, slides were taken of the front and back. These slides were subsequently rated independently by two raters, using closed-ended rating scales. Defensible space features that we measured were surveillance opportunities, real barriers, and symbolic barriers. Territorial markers that we measured included gardening and ornaments. The endpoints of the real barriers scale were as follows: "There is no barrier that restricts and directs access from the alley/sidewalk, and no defined point of entry onto the property" (low real barriers), and "There is a barrier more than 20" in height, either continuous or with a controlled point of entry through the barrier" (high). The endpoints of the symbolic barrier scale were as follows: "One can't tell for sure where the property ends and the public sidewalk/alley begins" (low symbolic barrier), and "The boundary line of the property is defined by an edge feature more than 20" in height" (high). Mid scores on this scale were attuned to changes in texture, level, materials, and low barriers. We combined real and symbolic barriers to yield an additive scale. For the latter interrater reliability ($r_{intraclass}$) was .98, and internal consistency (Cronbach's alpha) was .92. The endpoints of the gardening scale were as follows: "There is little or no attempt at landscaping" (or gardening), and "Half the site or more is given over to high-demand gardening" (high). Interrater reliability was .85.

Analysis Overview

Data were analyzed by recursive causal models, using the decomposition approach suggested by Alwin and Hauser (1975). Causal modeling is the only analysis that would allow us to directly test all of our hypotheses. An alternative approach, such as hierarchical stepwise regression (Cohen and Cohen, 1975) would not have provided us with information about the mediating or indirect path coefficients hypothesized by our model. Thus recursive path analysis provided the best approach to testing our model.

Our causal model is linear and fully recursive; that is, all causal effects are assumed to occur, and to be unidirectional. Such an assumption denied (in the model) the existence of possible feedback loops, or of dynamic interchange. Other investigators, examining other versions of defensible space theory have made a similar assumption (Newman and Franck, 1982).

Furthermore, to make our model fully recursive, we "pulled apart" the territorial cluster of predictors. In the two block level models, we assumed that attitudes about block spaces preceded attitudes toward the larger neighborhood. In the case of the individual level model, we assumed that social dynamics, such as recognition, preceded attitudes such as responsibility. We carried out the analysis on standardized variables, and thus report path coefficients. We use $\sqrt{1-R^2}$ for the residual path coefficient.

Given our low number of cases (63), we decided to adopt an alpha level of .10 in the two models of block level outcomes. This gives us an acceptable of level of power $(1-\beta > .80)$ for detecting medium-sized effects $(r = .30)$ (Cohen, 1977). Given this alpha, coefficients $> |.17|$ are significant at $< .10$; and coefficients $> |.21|$ are significant at $< .05$. Paths with coefficients of less than $|.05|$ were trimmed from the model.

In the model of individual level fear, coefficients $> |.07|$ are significant at $p < .05$, and coefficients $> |.10|$ are significant at $p < .01$.

Predicting Crimes of Violence to Persons

Variables included. In the reduced, nonmulticollinear matrix of predictors, the following variables were included: real and symbolic barriers in front, proportion of respondents who belong to an organization to which coresidents also belong (SOCIAL TIES). Two measures of territorial functioning were included: the extent to which respondents felt responsible for what happened on the sidewalk in front of their house and the alley behind their house (NEAR HOME RESPONSIBILITIES), and the proportion of respondents who were able to provide a neighborhood name (NEIGHBORHOOD IDENTIFICATION). The latter was residualized with respect to race, owner/renter status, trust in neighbors, and gardening in back.

Results with reduced matrix. Results of our path model predicting crimes of violence to persons appear in Figure 2. The zero order correlations among variables in this model appear in Table 1. In parentheses in Table 1, we report the correlations reproduced by the model. For all correlations, the reproduced values are within ±.05 of the original correlations, confirming that the model "fits" the data (Kerlinger and Pedhazur, 1973). The model explains 18% of the

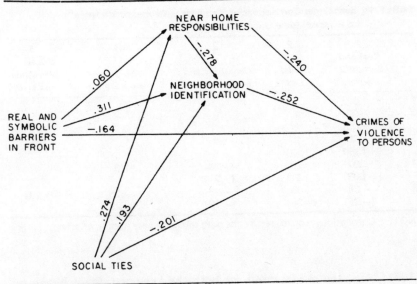

Figure 2   Path Analysis of Crimes of Violence to Persons

variance in crimes of violence ($F(4,58) = 3.19$; $p < .05$). (Throughout we report adjusted total R^2.)

Real and symbolic barriers have a sizeable, and almost significant, direct impact on crimes of violence ($p_{ji} = -.164$), which represents 64% of their total causal impact. Real and symbolic barriers also significantly bolster neighborhood-level identification, ($p_{ji} = .311$), but not near-home responsibility ($p_{ji} = .060$). The fact that real and symbolic barriers do not support feelings of territorial responsibility for near-home spaces is not surprising as the latter spaces (sidewalk, alley) are beyond the area bounded by the defensible space features. Thus defensible space strengthens some aspects of territorial functioning, at the same time that it has a direct impact on crime.

The hypothesized direct impact of social ties appears, and is significant ($p_{ji} = -.201$). This confirms the notion that informal social control may directly reduce crime-related outcomes. The direct effect of local ties comprises 68% of its total causal influence. Thus 32% of its causal impact is mediated by territorial functioning. Our expectation that local ties would strengthen territorial functioning receives very strong support. Local ties significantly enhance territorial responsibility for near-home spaces ($p_{ji} = .274$), and neighborhood identification ($p_{ji} =$

TABLE 1: Zero-Order Correlations of Variables in Crimes of Violence to Persons Model (n = 63)

	1 *Real and Symbolic Barriers*	2 *Social Ties*	3 *Neighborhood Identification*	4 *Near Home Responsibility*	5 *Crimes of Violence to Persons*
1	1.0				
2	.02 (.00)	1.0			
3	.30 (.29)	.12 (.12)	1.0		
4	.07 (.07)	.28 (.27)	−.20 (−.21)	1.0	
5	−.26 (−.25)	−.30 (−.30)	−.28 (−.32)	−.25 (−.23)	1.0

NOTE: Correlations reproduced by the path model appear in parentheses.

.193). Thus, the model confirms both the expected direct impact of social ties, as well as the expected indirect effect.

Both territorial variables exhibit a significant dampening impact on calls for crimes of violence: $p_{ji} = -.24$ for responsibility, $p_{ji} = -.252$ for neighborhood identification.

Results with homeownership included as exogenous variable. The inclusion of homeownership as an exogenous variable changed the results of our path analysis. The direct effect of homeownership on crimes of violence was of moderate negative size ($p_{ji} = -.12$), but did have a significant impact on social ties ($p_{ji} = .46$). Not surprisingly then, this reduced the direct effect of social ties on crime somewhat from −.20 to −.15. It did not reduce the significant impacts of social ties on territorial functioning. Homeownership also had a significant impact on near home responsibility ($p_{ji} = .21$), and a moderate nonsignificant impact on neighborhood identification ($p_{ji} = -.15$). Nonetheless, the direct effects of the two territorial variables on crime were not diminished substantially ($p_{ji} = -.22$ for near home responsibility; $p_{ji} = -.27$ for neighborhood identification). Finally, the inclusion of homeownership reduced slightly from −.16 to −.12, the direct coefficient of real and symbolic barriers on crimes of violence. In sum, the only substantive change caused by the inclusion of the homeownership variable was to reduce the coefficient of the direct effect of social ties on crime somewhat, rendering it nonsignificant. Effects of social ties on territorial functioning remained significant, and effects of territorial functioning on crimes of violence remained significant.

Predicting Block-Level Fear

Variables in the model. The reduced, nonmulticollinear matrix of predictors included three exogenous variables: the proportion of respondents on the block who were black (RACE), REAL AND SYMBOLIC BARRIERS IN FRONT, and SURVEILLANCE OPPORTUNITIES IN FRONT, two physical, defensible space measures. The social variable included was the proportion of occupied addresses on the street where the respondent knew someone by face or name (SOCIAL TIES). This information had been obtained in the interview by showing each respondent a schematic including all of the houses on the block, with his/her address clearly marked, and asking for each address if the respondent knew someone there by face or name. The same two territorial variables were included in this model as in the crime model: NEAR HOME RESPONSIBILITY and NEIGHBORHOOD IDENTIFICATION. The outcome (FEAR) was the summed response to the day fear and night fear questions. All variables were block level means, except for RACE, which was a proportion.

The additional exogenous variable included in the nonreduced matrix of predictors was the proportion of respondents who were homeowners.

Results with reduced matrix of predictors. The results of our path model predicting block fear appear in Figure 3. The original correlations and the correlations reproduced by the path model appear in Table 2. Reproduced correlations match the original ones confirming the "fit" of our path model. The model explains 37% ($F(6,56) = 5.59$; p $<.001$) of the variance in fear.

Of the causal impact of real and symbolic barriers, 62% is in the form of a direct impact on fear. The coefficient for this direct effect is sizable ($p_{ji} = -.164$). The remaining causal impact of real and symbolic barriers (27% of total effect, 71% of total indirect effect on fear) is channeled via territorial functioning. And the expected enhancement of territorial functioning by defensible space features is evident with neighborhood identification ($p_{ji} = .319$). The path coefficients of surveillance opportunities are all very small or essentially zero. Thus this type of defensible space feature failed to demonstrate the hypothesized impact.

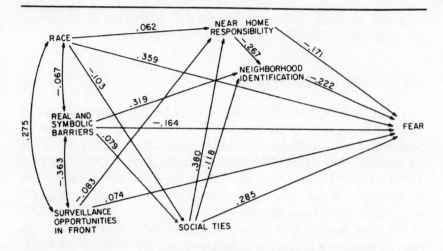

Figure 3 Path Analysis of Block Fear

Of the causal impact of local ties on fear, 81% is direct, and the coefficient for this path ($p_{ji} = -.285$) is significant and in the hypothesized direction. Thus knowing more people on the street has a direct dampening influence on fear. And the indirect influence of local ties on fear via territorial functioning appears as expected. The impact of acquaintanceship on feelings of territorial responsibility for near-home spaces is sizable and significant ($p_{ji} = .38$). Thus one of the important mediating paths hypothesized by the model is substantiated.

The impacts of the two territorial variables on fear are significant and in the hypothesized direction ($p_{ji} = -.171$, $p_{ji} = -.222$). Thus territorial functioning has a significant, direct impact on fear.

Contrary to expectations, increasing feelings of near-home responsibility have a dampening impact on neighborhood-level identification ($p_{ji} = -.267$). Thus territorial functioning at the block and neighborhood level appears to operate in a disjunctive fashion instead of in a mutually supportive fashion.

The bulk of the causal impact of racial composition (94%) is in the form of a significant direct impact on fear ($p_{ji} = .359$). Predominantly white blocks exhibited lower fear levels. The coefficients describing the impacts of race on the intervening social and territorial variables are modest.

Results with homeownership included as exogenous variable. When we carry out path analyses including homeownership as an exogenous

TABLE 2: Zero-Order Correlations of Variables in Block-Level Fear Model (n = 63)

	1 Race	2 Real and Symbolic Barriers in Front	3 Surveillance Opportunities	4 Social Ties	5 Neighborhood Identification	6 Near Home Responsibility	7 Fear
1	1.0						
2	.07	1.0					
3	.28	−.36	1.0				
4	−.10 (−.11)	.07 (.10)	−.03 (−.06)	1.0			
5	.00 (−.03)	.30 (.32)	−.06 (−.09)	.04 (.04)	1.0		
6	.00 (−.03)	.07 (.05)	−.08 (−.08)	.38 (.38)	−.20 (−.22)	1.0	
7	.42 (.42)	−.32 (−.32)	.27 (.29)	−.41 (−.41)	−.25 (−.23)	−.25 (−.28)	1.0

NOTE: Correlations reproduced by the path model appear in parentheses

variable, the model changes very little. The direct effect of SOCIAL TIES on FEAR remains very strong ($p_{ji} = -.293$), and the effect of SOCIAL TIES on NEAR HOME RESPONSIBILITY remains very strong ($p_{ji} = .324$). Finally, the territorial variables retain their significant effect on FEAR ($p_{ji} = -.184$ for NEAR HOME RESPONSIBILITY, −.220 for NEIGHBORHOOD IDENTIFICATION).

One change, and it is small, is a slight increase in the direct effect of REAL AND SYMBOLIC BARRIERS IN FRONT on FEAR ($p_{ji} = -.180$).

Summary on Block-Level Models

Defensible space features in the form of real and symbolic barriers have significant impact on fear, and a moderate impact on crimes of violence. Surveillance opportunities were not relevant to these two outcomes. Social ties strongly dampened crime and significantly dampened fear. Ties significantly enhanced territorial functioning. Territorial functioning significantly dampened both crime and fear. Both path models, although trimmed, showed acceptable levels of fit. Examination of the models including homeownership demonstrated that the models based on the reduced matrix of predictors were not misspecified.

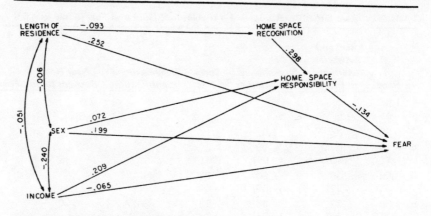

Figure 4 Path Analysis of Individual Fear

Predicting Individual-Level Fear

Variables in model. All significant zero order predictors constituted a nonmulticollinear matrix of predictors, thus all were included in the path model. Three exogenous variables were included: length of residence on the block (LENGTH OF RESIDENCE), SEX (males coded 0, females coded 1), and household INCOME. No physical or social variables were included. Two territorial variables merited entry: ability to distinguish between strangers and persons who belong in backyard, and on front porch or steps (HOME SPACE RECOGNITION) and feelings of responsibility for what goes on in these spaces (HOME SPACE RESPONSIBILITY). Coefficient alpha for the RECOGNITION scale was .83; for RESPONSIBILITY .87. The outcome is FEAR (alpha = .64). All variables are pooled, within-block residuals; that is, individual deviations from their respective block mean.

Results. The results of our path model predicting fear at the individual level appear in Figure 4. The zero order correlations of the variables in the model appear in Table 3 as well as the correlations reproduced by the path model. All reproduced correlations are acceptably close to the original, indicating that the model fits the original data. The model explains a significant 14% of the variation in individual level fear (F(5,614) = 19.23; p < .001).

Several demographic variables are included in the model. Length of residence works contrary to the expected direction, revealing a positive

TABLE 3: Zero-Order Correlations of Variables in Individual-Level Fear Model
(n = 687)

	1 Length of Residence	2 Sex	3 Income	4 Home Space Responsibility	5 Home Space Recognition	6 Fear
1	1.0					
2	−.01	1.0				
3	−.05	−.24	1.0			
4	.07 (.04)	.02 (.02)	.19 (.19)	1.0		
5	.09 (.09)	.01 (.00)	.01 (.00)	.30 (.30)	1.0	
6	.24 (.25)	.21 (.21)	−.15 (−.15)	−.14 (−.13)	−.06 (−.02)	1.0

NOTE: Correlations reproduced by path model are in parentheses.

direct impact on fear; p_{ji} = .25. This result becomes more sensible, however, when we recall that all variables in this model are individual deviations from block means. Thus, a positive score on LENGTH OF RESIDENCE means that respondent has lived on that block longer than the average of all respondents. In short, length of residence is probably working as a proxy for age here. And, other studies have demonstrated that the elderly, as compared to the nonelderly, have a higher fear of crime (DuBow et al., 1979). These more stable, older residents also demonstrate weaker territorial attitudes, which would be in keeping with their lower level of environmental mastery.

Being female has strong direct impact of fear (p_{ji} = .20), which is consonant with other studies that have also found women to be more fearful than men (DuBow et al., 1979). Women felt a significantly stonger sense of territorial responsibility for home spaces perhaps because many of them may spend more time at home (p_{ji} = .072). And, as territorial responsibility had a significant dampening effect on fear (p_{ji} = −.13), this means that the indirect impact of sex on fear (via territorial responsibility) was opposite to its direct effect. Of course, the size of the direct effect far outweighs the size of this indirect effect.

The final demographic variable, income, showed a much smaller direct impact on fear than sex (p_{ji} = −.07), although the sign of the path is in the expected direction. Much larger (and highly significant) was income's bolstering of territorial responsibility (p_{ji} = .21). And via this pathway, income had a dampening impact on fear. Thus in this instance, as with length of residence, the sign of the direct and indirect pathways are similar.

With regard to the territorial variables, the responsibility variable had a significant dampening impact on fear ($p_{ji} = -.13$). Ability to distinguish between strangers and insiders had a negligible direct impact on fear, but did dampen fear via its significant impact on responsibility ($p_{ji} = .30$).

In sum, the individual-level model differs from the two block-level models in that it includes demographic factors, and excludes social and physical variables. The individual and block models are similar, though, in that territorial functioning is included in all of them. Thus, territorial functioning is relevant to fear at the individual as well as the group level of analysis.

The individual-level model is also interesting in that length of residence, sex, and income all had significant impacts on one of the mediating territorial variables. (Income's impact on territorial functioning could be reflecting its link with homeownership.) Thus features of the individual are associated with less fear, in part, because these characteristics predispose the person toward stronger territorial attitudes. Thus being younger, a woman, and of higher income, are all associated with stronger territorial functioning.

One last noteworthy, and understandable difference between the individual model and the block models is the locus of the particular territorial variables included. In the block models the spaces in question were near-home, public spaces, such as sidewalk or alley. In the individual model, the referent shifts to more proximal home spaces, such as backyard, and front yard, or steps. Thus the "public" spaces are relevant to group functioning, and the more "private" outdoor spaces are relevant to individual level functioning.

DISCUSSION

We have developed and tested a model (Figure 1) concerned with explaining variations in crime and fear. Our model has incorporated as explanatory variables measures of physical defensible space features, local social climate, and territorial functioning. The inclusion of all three types of explanatory constructs has been supported. The concepts varied, however, in their predictive power. Turning in the strongest performance were the territorial variables, which demonstrated significant direct effects in all three models. In the two block-level models, the inclusion of a further exogenous variable to control for possible misspecification of the model did not diminish these impacts. Turning in a strong performance, social factors significantly boosted territorial functioning in both block-level models, and social factors had a significant dampening effect on fear, even with the inclusion of homeownership. Performing somewhat more weakly than expected were the physical defensible space features, which had sizable, but largely nonsignificant direct effects on the block level outcomes. They did, however, significantly boost neighborhood identification. This is probably due to the fact that blocks with more extensive real and symbolic barriers were also blocks that were of somewhat higher physical quality, and this increased quality was associated with feelings of greater satisfaction and attachment (Fried, 1982).

Nonetheless, our findings regarding the size of the effects of defensible space physical features may seem disappointing to some. We would therefore hasten to point out that the effect sizes observed here are comparable to what has been recently observed in other studies, (e.g., Newman and Franck, 1982; Brown, 1979).

Second, it is inevitable that the size of the direct effects should diminish as relevant mediating social and territorial variables are carefully measured and incorporated into the model. And finally, the pattern of physical effects is in keeping with the current wisdom (e.g., Merry, 1981a, 1981b), that physical features "can't do it all" when it comes to ensuring safety and security. More specifically, they cannot even do most of it; they play a minor, although significant, role in comparison to the influence of social and territorial variables.

The larger context proved relevant as well. In the nonreduced block fear and block crime models, homeownership significantly enhanced territorial responsibility. We think that homeownership is operating here as a proxy for contextual stability, indicating how social and territorial aspects of the block are supported by a steady-state background. Cultural factors proved relevant as well, with the inclusion of race in the fear model. More predominantly white blocks had significantly lower fear levels, and significantly higher levels of territorial responsibility. Thus we agree with both Merry and Podolefsky that we must consider the larger sociocultural context and how it contributes to the dynamics of interest.

Shifting into a more speculative vein, the following points are suggested by our analyses. We have confirmed that blocks function as small-scale social units. Social climate and strength of territorial

The Fear of Crime

functioning on the block are both conditioned by the larger sociocultural context—racial composition, neighborhood stability, and so on. As social bonds—perhaps even of a superficial nature such as acquaintanceship—evolve, residents' interest and involvement in the public spaces of the block is increased. The social bonds serve to permit a wider range of secure residential functioning. Individual residents can increase the orbit of their activities—and duties—and along with this, their expectations. They take more of a proprietary interest in and concern for near-home spaces such as sidewalks in front of the house, and alleys behind the house. Nominally public places—where strangers may come and go unhindered with few strictures regarding appropriate behavior—become somewhat transformed. Partially shared expectations emerge regarding what is and what is not appropriate behavior in these settings. Residents develop an involvement in these near-home settings and feel some level of responsibility for seeing that these norms are respected. Feeling responsible for what happens in these near-home, public spaces suggests a willingness to exercise informal social control, to intervene, or at least summon assistance in instances where the loosely agreed upon norms are flagrantly violated—that is, excessive noise at 3 a.m., youths spray painting cars, and so on. The social ties would be relevant again at this point inasmuch as they provide reassurance to a resident that should he or she adopt an enforcement role, coresidents may support him or her; or, at the very least, he or she knows who his or her nonsupporters would be.

The above scenario, which of course ignores how, over time, high levels of threat (crime) may "atomize" bonds of community (Conklin, 1975) or cause a restriction in the range of territorial functioning, suggests several practical ways that change agents—be they governmental or volunteer—may encourage forces supportive of local order. At the contextual level, matters such as increasing homeownership are one obvious strategy, one which has been promoted in Baltimore and many other urban areas. At the block level, strategies to assist in the development of coresident bonds—neighborhood membership drives, "get together" events such as bake sales and bazaars—would be helpful. Wandersman and his colleagues (e.g., Unger and Wandersman, 1983) have considered the virtues of block organization themselves, and this is one possible strategy for improving social climate. Territorial functioning can be enhanced by supporting behaviors that may result in strengthened attitudes. For example, clean-up and beautification contests and projects may result in a more concerned and involved attitude toward the public spaces adjacent the home. Strategies such as these are suggested by our findings.

Of course, as our study is limited, further clarifying research efforts are needed. Our study is only cross-sectional. (Some may feel that in light of this, our path analyses are inappropriate. Nonetheless, these analyses were the only way we could test all the links posited by our model. And had we done regression analyses, which may have been more acceptable to some, our conclusions would have been little changed, albeit less specific.) Offsetting this limit are the facts that (a) we have systematically sampled a broad range of environment;[10] (b) we have employed confirmatory as opposed to exploratory path analyses, and have tested for possible problems of misspecification and multi-collinearity, and (c) we have carried out analyses using decomposed data to avoid the aggregation problem. Our results are the first systematic examination of physical, social, and attitudinal (territorial) variables as relevant to crime and fear at the level of the street block.

NOTES

1. The correlation between neighborhood median household income and percentage of rental dwelling units, was -.45.

2. There were 16 low-income, predominantly rental neighborhoods, 123 mixed neighborhoods, and 49 medium-income, homeowned neighborhoods. Higher-income neighborhoods (1970 median income > $14,000) were excluded from the sample in consideration of the outcomes of interest.

3. At the time of the project the third author and other project staff (Whit Drain) were affiliated with the Baltimore City Department of Planning. Their close working relationships with community groups allowed us to pinpoint leaders in the sampled neighborhoods. In cases where leadership was shared, both leaders were interviewed.

4. The reason 31 blocks were sampled for Survey II instead of 32 is as follows. The low-income rental, low-defensible space, high social cohesion stratum included one very large block, and after putting this block in the Survey II frame, there were no more blocks to choose from in that stratum. Thus we double sampled from this last remaining block, treating it really as two blocks, and thereby maintaining the appropriate weighting across strata. Thus, with this one exception, blocks were perfectly distributed across strata (for each survey, 4 from each stratum containing a mixed neighborhood, and 2 from each other stratum).

5. Field workers worked evenings and weekends, as well as weekdays. At each designated household (if necessary), at least one contact attempt was made at each of these three time periods.

6. In some strata, the desired number of interviews fell below the expected number, because on some blocks we ran out of alternate addresses before the desired number of interviews was obtained. In Survey I, we sought to obtain 15 cases per block, for 480 completes. We ended up with 447. In Survey II we sought 7 or 8 interviews per block, for a

total of 240. We actually obtained 240 interviews. Examination of the "shortfall" of completed surveys, by block, in Survey I, indicated that it was not patterned by strata, thus suggesting that the nature of the final respondent pool probably did not produce serious bias.

7. Several factors preclude any serious attempts to validate our sample by comparing it with census data. First, our sample deliberately ignored some areas (high income neighborhoods) and, although our primary sampling unit was the neighborhood, respondents were not picked in proportion to neighborhood size. These two factors make it unlikely that our sample means or proportions will closely match population parameters. Nevertheless, on several parameters, our sample appears quite close to the city population, as described by the 1980 Census. In the city the owner/renter split is 47%/53% (close to our 53%/47% split). The proportions of white to black households is 44%/56%, which is not far from our 39%/61% figure for households. Our average household size of 3 is only slightly larger than the city average of 2.74, and the discrepancy is probably explained by our excluding upper income areas. Our average age of 44 almost exactly matches the 1970 SMSA adult mean of 43. Our median length of residence (12 years) closely matches that observed (13 years) in a large 1976 survey of Baltimore area households (Vergrugge and Taylor, 1976). Thus, despite the nature of our sampling procedure, our resulting sample closely resembles the city population on several parameters.

8. Part I offenses, as defined by the FBI, include criminal homicide, forcible rape, robbery, aggravated assault, burglary, commercial and residential larceny/theft, and motor vehicle thefts.

9. Crimes of violence to persons include aggravated assault by an armed person, common assault, cutting assault, murder, rape, shooting, and yoking. The other categories of police activity were crimes against property in private spaces (house and yard), crimes against property in public spaces, disturbing the peace and social nuisances (exposure, intoxicated persons, disorderlies, family disturbance), and other.

10. Our sample, albeit systematically drawn, was not random. It was, rather, an analytic sample drawn so as to maximize variation on certain parameters: contextual stability, social variation, and physical variation. Consequently one might expect that our pattern of results might not be highly generalizable to other samples. But, generalizability is always an empirical issue, and thus one cannot claim a priori that our results—given the nature of our sample—will necessarily have low generalizability. In addition, other studies of this ilk, that have assessed one or more of the hypotheses tested in this study, have already obtained comparable results. Thus we feel that despite our special sample, our pattern of findings have a good chance of being broadly applicable.

REFERENCES

Alwin, D. F. and R. M. Hauser
    1975   "The decomposition of effects in path analysis." Amer. Soc. Rev. 40: 37-47.
Baumer, T. L.
    1978   "Research on fear of crime in the United States." Victimology 3 (3-4): 254-264.
Bevis, C. and J. B. Nutter
    1977   "Changing street layouts to reduce residential burglary." Paper presented to the Crime Prevention Through Environmental Design Panel at the annual meeting of the American Society of Criminology, Atlanta.

Blalock, H. M., Jr.
  1964   "Causal inferences in non-experimental research." Chapel Hill: Univ. of North
         Carolina Press.
Broady, M.
  1972   "Social theory in architectural design," in R. Gutman (ed.) People and
         Buildings. New York: Basic Books.
Brower, S. N.
  1980   "Territory in urban settings," in Altman et al. (eds.) Human Behavior in the
         Environment: Advances in Theory and Research Vol. 4. New York: Plenum.
Brower, S., K. Dockett, and R. B. Taylor
  1983   "Resident's perceptions of site-level features." Environment and Behavior 15:
         419-437.
Brown, B. B.
  1979   "Territoriality and residential burglary." Paper presented at the annual meeting
         of the American Psychological Association, New York.
Cohen, J. and P. Cohen
  1975   Multiple Regression/Correlation Analysis in the Behavioral Sciences. Hills-
         dale, NJ: Erlbaum.
Conklin, J. E.
  1975   The Impact of Crime. New York: Macmillan.
Dubow, F. L., F. McCabe, and G. Kaplan
  1979   Reactions to Crime: A Critical Review of the Literature. Washington:
         Government Printing Office.
Fowler, F., M. E. McCalla, and T. Mangione
  1979   The Hartford Residential Crime Prevention Program. Washington: Govern-
         ment Printing Office.
Fried, M.
  1982   "Residential attachment: sources of residential and community satisfaction." J.
         of Social Issues 38: 107-119.
Furstenberg, F. F.
  1971   "Public reaction to crime in the streets." Amer. Scholar 40: 601-610.
Garofalo, J. and J. Laub
  1978   "The fear of crime: broadening our perspective." Victimology 3: 242-253.
Gordon, R. A.
  1968   "Issues in multiple regression." Amer. J. of Sociology 73: 592-616.
Greenberg, S. W., W. M. Rohe, and J. R. Williams
  1982   "Safety in urban neighborhoods." Population and Environment 5: 141-165.
Hannan, M. T.
  1971a "Problems of aggregation," in H. M. Blalock, Jr. (ed.) Causal Models in the
         Social Sciences. Chicago: Aldine.
  1971b Aggregation and Disaggregation in Sociology. Lexington, MA: D. C. Heath.
Harries, K. D.
  1980   Crime and Environment. Springfield, IL: Charles C Thomas.
Hartnagel, T. F.
  1979   "The perception and fear of crime: implications for neighborhood cohesion,
         social activity and community affect." Social Forces 58: 176-193.
Jacobs, J.
  1961   The Death and Life of the American City. New York: Vintage.

Janowitz, M.
    1975   "Sociological theory and social control." Amer. J. of Sociology 81: 82-108.
Kerlinger, F. N. and E. J. Pedhazur
    1973   Multiple Regression in Behavioral Research. New York: Holt, Rinehart &
            Winston.
Kish, L.
    1949   "A procedure for objective respondent selection within the household." J. of the
            Amer. Stat. Assn. 44: 380-387.
Larson, R. C.
    1975   "What happened to patrol operations in Kansas City? A review of the Kansas
            City preventive patrol experiment." J. of Criminal Justice 3: 267-297.
Lavrakas, P. J.
    1982   Citizen Self Help and Neighborhood Crime Prevention. Skokie, IL: Center for
            Urban Affairs, Northwestern University.
Lewis, D. A. and M. G. Maxfield
    1980   "Fear in the neighborhoods: an investigation of the impact of crime." J. of
            Research in Crime and Delinquency 17: 160-189.
Ley, D. and R. Cybriwsky
    1974   "The spatial ecology of stripped cars." Environment and Behavior 6: 653-668.
Liska, A. E., J. J. Lawrence, and A. Sanchirico
    1982   "Fear of crime as a social fact." Social Forces 60 (3): 760-770.
Maccoby, E. E., J. P. Johnson, and R. M. Church
    1958   "Community integration and the social control of juvenile delinquency." J. of
            Social Issues 14: 38-51.
Mayhew, P.
    1979   "Defensible space; the current status of a crime prevention theory." Howard J.
            of Penology and Crime Prevention 18: 150-159.
Merry, S. E.
    1981a   "Defensible space undefended: social factors in crime control through environ-
            mental design." Urban Affairs Q. 16: 397-422.
    1981b   Urban Danger: Life in a Neighborhood of Strangers. Philadelphia: Temple
            Univ. Press.
Newman, O.
    1972   Defensible Space. New York: MacMillan.
    1979   Community of Interest. New York: Doubleday.
Newman, O. and K. Franck
    1980   Factors Influencing Crime and Instability in Urban Housing Developments.
            Washington: Government Printing Office.
    1982   "The effects of building size on personal crime and fear of crime." Population
            and Environment 5: 203-220.
Pablant, P. and J. C. Baxter
    1975   "Environmental correlates of school vandalism." J. of the Amer. Institute of
            Planners (July): 270-277.
Podolefsky, A.
    1983   Case Studies in Community Crime Prevention. Springfield, IL: Charles C
            Thomas.
Podolefsky, A. and F. Dubow
    1981   Strategies for Community Crime Prevention: Collective Responses to Crime
            in Urban America. Springfield, IL: Charles C Thomas.

Rockwell, R. C.
  1975   "Assessment of multicollinearity: the Haitovsky test of the determinant." Soc. Methods and Research 3: 308-320.
Scheflen, A. E.
  1971   "Living space in an urban ghetto." Family Process 10: 429-450.
Skogan, W. and M. G. Maxfield
  1981   Coping with Crime. Beverly Hills, CA: Sage.
Sudman, S.
  1976   Applied Sampling. New York: Academic.
Sundstrom, E.
  1977   "Interpersonal behavior and the physical environment," in L. Wrightsman Social Psychology. Monterey, CA: Brooks/Cole.
Sundstrom, E. and I. Altman
  1974   "Field study of territorial behavior and dominance," J. of Personality and Social Psychology 30: 115-124.
Taylor, R. B.
  1978   "Human territoriality: a review and a model for future research." Cornell J. of Social Relations 13: 125-151.
  1982   "The neighborhood physical environment and stress," in G. W. Evans (ed.) Environmental Stress. New York: Cambridge Univ. Press.
  1983   "Conjoining environmental psychology, personality, and social psychology: natural marriage or shotgun wedding?" in N. R. Feimer and G. S. Geller (eds.) Environmental Psychology: Directions and Perspectives. New York: Praeger.
Taylor, R. B., S. D. Gottfredson, and S. N. Brower
  1980   "The defensibility of defensible space," in T. Hirschi and M. Gottfredson (eds.) Understanding Crime. Beverly Hills, CA: Sage.
Taylor, R. B. and S. A. Shumaker
  1982   "Community crime prevention in review: problems, progress and prospects in theory, research, programs, and evaluations." Paper presented at the annual meeting of the Law and Society Association, Toronto.
Unger, D. and A. Wandersman
  1983   "Neighboring and its role in block organizations: an exploratory report." Amer. J. of Community Psychology 11 (3): 291-300.
Verbrugge, L. M. and R. B. Taylor
  1976   Consequences of Population Density: Testing New Hypothesis. Occasional Paper. Baltimore, MD: Center for Metropolitan Planning and Research, Johns Hopkins University.
Wheeldon, P. D.
  1969   "The operation of voluntary associations and personal networks in the political processes of an inter-ethnic community," in J. C. Mitchell (ed.) Social Networks in Urban Situations. Manchester, England: Manchester Univ. Press.

Part VI
Policies to Reduce Fear

[23]

The Howard Journal Vol 23 No 3. Oct 84

Fear of Crime: The Effect of Improved Residential Security on a Difficult To Let Estate

PATRICIA ALLATT

Research Fellow, University of Durham

Abstract: An experiment in improved residential security on a difficult to let housing estate with a high burglary rate was evaluated by means of a two stage tenant survey of a target and control estate for the effect upon residents' perception of crime, fear of crime and alterations in behaviour. The results were set against the real risk of crime as recorded in police statistics. On the target estate the risk of burglary remained high but static and other types of property crime increased. Fear of burglary, however, fell significantly. There was a reduction in fear across a range of subgroups examined. On the control estate the risk of burglary increased but there was no significant change in the level of fear.

Crime has several facets: victimisation, that is, the crime itself, fear of crime and the extent to which an individual's behaviour alters in order to improve security (Brill 1979). An evaluation of an experiment in crime prevention on a difficult to let housing estate in the north-east of England sought to monitor the effects of improved residential security for a whole neighbourhood on these aspects of crime.

The experiment was initiated by Northumbria Police and the evaluation commissioned and funded by the Home Office Research Unit (now the Home Office Research and Planning Unit). The research was executed by the North East Centre for Community Studies, Newcastle-upon-Tyne Polytechnic.

There were two prongs to the evaluation. The first comprised an analysis of police burglary figures over five years for a target estate (where the security of all dwellings had been improved by fitting locks and window bolts on all ground floor points of entry), for a control estate and for two residential areas adjacent to the target estate. The second component was a two-stage tenant survey of target and control estates conducted prior to and one year after the security improvements of Spring 1980. A major focus here was upon the experience and fear of burglary and the impact of such fear upon behaviour.

The details of the evaluation are set out in an earlier paper (Allatt 1984) in which the results of the first aspect of the study are described: namely, the effect of the improved security of a neighbourhood upon the incidence of burglary and other predatory property crimes. Suffice it to say here that in the year following the security improvements police figures show that on the target estate burglary was at least contained and that, when measured against the increase on the control estate, there was a lower incidence of burglary than might otherwise have been expected. Burglary was, furthermore, not overwhelmingly displaced to adjacent areas although there was a rise in other property crimes on the target estate.

Fear of Crime

An evaluation of enhanced security, however, should not be confined to burglary rates. Studies in North America since 1967 (Maxfield 1984) and the recent British Crime Survey (Hough and Mayhew 1983) show that fear of crime can amount to a social problem in its own right. Furthermore, burglary and street crime provoke the most fear (Hough and Mayhew 1983). However, although victims of crime tend to be more fearful than those without such experience (Skogan and Maxfield 1981), and worry about burglary, whilst widespread, is greater in urban areas where the risk is greater (Hough and Mayhew 1983), fear of crime is not necessarily related to the incidence or experience of crime.

This disjunction between incidence, experience and fear may carry important individual, social and political consequences. The impact of fear can undermine the quality of individual and community life thereby exacerbating conditions in which crime may flourish (Maxfield 1984). Furthermore, if the apprehension of victimisation is higher than its probability of occurrence, unwarranted fear of crime may exist which may result in a demand for a more punitive system than would be otherwise acceptable (Clarke, in B.B.C.1 'War on Crime' 14 July 1981). Clarke's observations followed a discussion of attack in the street but they apply equally to burglary.

Hough and Mayhew (1983) have noted the possibility that 'some crime prevention measures can have the effect of reducing fear whether or not they reduce crime itself' (p. 27), and refer to studies of the installation of 'entry-phones' in burglary prone blocks of flats which resulted in a lessening of fear. The focus of this paper, therefore, is upon the second aspect of the evaluation of target hardening: the impact of the security measures upon residents' perceptions, especially upon their perceptions of crime on the estates, fear of burglary and their reaction to such fear, and, for the residents of the target estate, the impact of increased security upon their views of the unpopular public housing estate on which they lived.

Target and Control Estates

Scotswood, in the West End of Newcastle, and Springwell, in the Wrekenton area of Gateshead were selected as target and control estates respectively since they were sufficiently similar for the purposes of the experiment (Allatt 1984). As noted above, the target estate was subject to intensive security enhancement whereby all ground floor points of entry were fitted with security devices (see Allatt 1984). It was believed that changes in anxiety about and perceptions of crime expressed by people on the target estate which were not mirrored by trends on the control estate could be attributed to the security enhancement programme.

A 50% random sample of dwellings (396 target, 379 control), stratified by street, was drawn from local authority housing lists and a respondent randomly selected from household members over 16 years of age. Interviews took place in two stages, between 25 February and 16 June 1980, and 16 March and 10 July 1981.

The response rate for the two estates was similar but, as expected, suffered from attrition over the two stages of interviewing. The high response rate of 85% (338) on the target estate and 85% (322) on the control dropped to 61% (205) and 62% (199), respectively, of the original respondents. No substitution was made either of households or within households. The analysis, therefore, was confined to those interviewed at both stages and therefore comprised household members of approximately one-quarter (26%) of the households rather than approximately half the households of each estate.

The Effect of Security Enhancement

Unfortunately for the evaluation, the introduction of community policing on the target estate towards the end of the surveyed period, that is, prior to the second interview, posed difficulties in attributing any decline in fear solely to security enhancement. Moreover, as the analysis was confined to those respondents retained at both stages of interviewing, there was a consequent loss of generalisability of the data to the estates. This limitation, however, was modified by the fact that while victims of burglary were more likely to be among the lost cases, those expressing fear were not, nor were those subject to attempted burglary. In many respects, as a group, those still available and willing to be interviewed at the second stage were very similar to the lost cases.[1] In sum, the losses over the year were proportionately more amongst the young adult single, those most dissatisfied with the target estate and the victims of burglary. As noted above, these individuals were omitted from the analysis.

Perception of Crime

On both estates respondents felt that crime on their estate was extensive; considering that in the year prior to the security enhancement the actual risk of burglary (excluding attempts) was 1 in 5 on the target estate and 1 in 12 on the control, these perceptions were grounded in reality. The average annual risk for England and Wales has been estimated at 1 in 35 (Winchester and Jackson 1982, p. 1) and, in the British Crime Survey at 1 in 40[2] (Hough and Mayhew 1983, p. 17). Hough and Mayhew, (1983, p. 18) however, point out that burglary is a phenomenon of the inner city, the risk there being double that in other areas of conurbations and, at 1 in 12, five times those of elsewhere. On the target estate in this study, therefore, the risk of burglary was even greater.

In the year following the experiment the perception of the crime rate on the target estate remained high. In response to the question: 'Just thinking about this area, would you say that there is much crime round here?', 81% (166) in the pre-security and 79% (162) in the post-security interviews said there was a great deal or quite a lot of crime. With regard to burglary the constancy of these perceptions was correct. The chance of being burgled remained at 1 in 5 even after the security improvements, and displacement crime (those crimes to which it was thought a frustrated burglar might turn his attention such as theft of vehicles and burglary in other premises) almost doubled (Allatt 1982, 1984).

On the control estate, in line with an increase in burglary during the survey period, the feeling among respondents that crime was extensive rose from the lower base of 58% (118) in 1980 to 83% (165) in 1981. This increase was accounted for almost solely by those who felt there to be a great deal of crime, rising from 15% (30) to 38% (76). In fact, while displacement crime had shown little absolute change, rising 19% from 36 to 43, burglary had risen substantially, the chance of being burgled moving from 1 in 12 to 1 in 7 — a risk, it should be noted, which was still not as great as for those on the target estate although perception of crime as extensive now matched the perceptions of the target estate respondents.

Burglary dominated the perception of crime. On both estates and at both stages of the survey it was the crime most frequently mentioned. When asked: 'What kinds of crime do you think are committed round here?' burglary was cited by the majority of respondents: by 91% (186) of the respondents on the target estate prior to the installations and 89% (182) subsequently. On the control estate, where although the burglary rate rose it still did not reach the same level as that of the target estate, the pre-experimental citation was 69% (138) rising to 93% (186) at the post-experimental stage. This perceptual dominance over other crimes was attested by the fact that at both stages of the evaluation and on both estates the next most frequently cited crime, vandalism,[3] was mentioned at a much lower rate — target: 28% (57) rising to 59% (120); control: 32% (64) rising to 54% (107). Local youths from school age to the early twenties, were seen as the perpetrators of crime and some residents on the target estate believed that the people from whom they had most to fear were neighbours.

Factors in Fear

There was a generalised sense of fear among the residents of both estates. When asked the question which is thought to tap a sense of personal safety (Maxfield 1984): 'How safe do you think it is to be on the streets in this area after dark?' only 53 respondents (26%) on the target estate, for example, said they felt safe. Questions on victimisation, however, which are felt to tap respondents' fears and anxieties (Maxfield 1984) were the major focus of this study, and they indicated that on both estates burglary was the most dominant fear amongst those fearing victimisation; the proportions ranged from 79% to 90% on the two estates over the two stages of the study.

The security experiment appeared to have an impact on these levels of anxiety, with a significant reduction on the target estate and no significant change on the control. Thus in response to the question: 'Have you ever been worried in the last year of becoming a victim of any type of crime?' between 50% and 60% of the respondents over the two stages and on both estates said they had been afraid. In the year following the upgrading of security, however, within this range there was a marked divergence between the estates. On the target estate fear of becoming a victim dropped significantly, the proportion of the fearful falling from 59% (121) to 50% (102) (McNemar Test: $Chi^2 = 4.70$, df = 1, p ‹·05). On the control the proportion who feared victimisation rose from 56% (112) to 61% (121) (McNemar Test: $Chi^2 = 1.25$, df = 1, not significant).

Similarly when fear of burglary was examined independently there was a significant reduction in fear on the target estate and a rise on the control with an even more marked divergence between the estates; the proportions of those fearing burglary fell from 53% (109) to 40% (81) (McNemar Test: $Chi^2 = 9.11$, df = 1, p ‹·05) on the target estate, while rising from 48% (96) to 54% (107) on the control (McNemar Test: $Chi^2 = 1.59$, df = 1, not significant).[4] In a smaller study undertaken by Northumbria Police (Northumbria Police 1982) a reduction in fear similarly followed enhanced security.

Finally, for a substantial proportion on both estates the fear was sufficient to adversely affect their living patterns. A few were made ill by worry, several more said they could not sleep, whilst the majority said social and family life was affected; for example, they could never or only rarely go out, husband and wife could not go out together and families could not be visited. Again the same pattern emerged of a statistically significant reduction in such destructive worry on the target estate and no change on the control. Thus on the target estate there was a fall among those so affected from 40% (81) to 31% (63) (McNemar Test: $Chi^2 = 3.91$, df = 1, p ‹ .05); whilst on the control estate there was a small, although statistically insignificant, rise from 29% (58) to 35% (69) (McNemar Test: $Chi^2 = 1.49$, df = 1, not significant).

In sum, the fact that many respondents saw and continued to see burglary as extensive did not necessarily mean that they feared it; and it seemed that the installation of security devices had a significant impact on the level of anxiety that had obtained.

Fear, Security, Successful and Unsuccessful Burglary

A major difficulty in the evaluation of action projects of this kind lies in ensuring that the conditions for the measurement of experimental effects are fulfilled (see Allatt 1984). In this case, despite the brief to secure all the dwellings on the estate, only 82% had been fitted by the deadline of 31 March 1980 and fitting continued up to and beyond the second stage of interviewing. Furthermore, at the second interview it was discovered that on some dwellings not all ground floor points of entry had been fitted with security devices.

Because the extent to which dwellings had been made secure was unknown, and the implications this might have for a respondent's fear, an assessment of all security was made irrespective of whether devices were fitted by tenant or local authority. Two crude categories of dwelling were distinguished: those with total ground floor security and those with less than total. It was found that approximately 40% of each subgroup expressed fear: 39% (50) of those with total security, 41% (31) of those with less than total. Amongst the fearful, 62% had total security. The factors behind this were not explored. It is possible that the unafraid among those with incomplete security were less afraid initially and had not bothered to be in when workmen came to fit the devices. Alternatively, the majority of dwellings on the estate were more secure than formerly even if all ground floor points of entry were not covered. It does not seem, however, that the impact of less than total security distorted the results.

Comparison of the relationships between fear and burglary revealed differences (*Table 1*). For both estates and for both years the burgled comprised a small proportion of both fearful and non-fearful groups. However, on the target estate, both before and after the introduction of the security devices, the burgled were not significantly more likely to be anxious than those who had not been burgled (Before: $Chi^2 = 0.06$, df = 1, not significant; after: $Chi^2 = 0$, df = 1, not significant). This finding contrasts with that of the British Crime Survey in which the burgled were significantly more likely to be anxious (Maxfield 1984). In the study reported here, after the devices were installed the number of worried declined in both groups and the difference between them narrowed.

On the control estate there was, similarly, no significant difference in worry dependent upon the experience of burglary either before the intallation period ($Chi^2 = 0.02$, df = 1, not significant) or after it ($Chi^2 = 0.68$, df = 1, not significant). In the post-installation period, worry among non-victims increased slightly and that among victims substantially. Numbers, however, were small and the results consequently tentative. The pre-test interview (see Campbell and Stanley 1969) might have raised anxiety by making respondents more aware of their fears especially as no action was taken to quell them as was the case on the target estate. The rise in fear among the burgled on the control estate could also suggest that intervention on the target estate not only led to a general reduction in anxiety, but that without such intervention anxiety among the burgled might have shown a steeper increase than among the non-burgled.

While the effect upon anxiety among victims of attempted burglary shows a similar pattern (*Table 2*), a comparison of *Tables 1* and *2* suggests that the experience of unsuccessful burglary raises more fear than successful burglary. While still fewer than on the target estate, the number of attempted burglaries on the control estate increased during the experimental year. Furthermore, the proportions of the anxious among the victims increased from 57% (8) to 70% (14) whilst anxiety among those who had not been victims of attempts rose only slightly, comprising approximately half in both years. These changes, however, were not statistically significant. (Before: $Chi^2 = 0.19$, df = 1, not significant; after:

175

TABLE 1

Comparison of Fear of Burglary by Experience of Burglary

	Target Estate						Control Estate					
	Pre-Installation			Post-Installation			Pre-Installation			Post-Installation		
	Yes	No	Total	Yes	No	Total	Yes	No	Total	Yes	No	Total
Fearful	No. %	No. %	No.	No. %	No. %	No.	No. %	No. %	No.	No. %	No. %	No.
Burgled	16 (57)	12 (43)	28	10 (42)	14 (58)	24	4 (40)	6 (60)	10	13 (65)	7 (35)	20
Not Burgled	93 (53)	84 (47)	177	71 (39)	110 (61)	181	92 (49)	97 (51)	189	94 (53)	85 (47)	179
Total	109 (53)	96 (47)	205	81 (40)	124 (60)	205	96 (48)	103 (52)	199	107 (54)	92 (46)	199

TABLE 2

Comparison of Fear of Burglary by Attempted Burglary*

Fearful	Target Estate						Control Estate					
	Pre-Installation			Post-Installation			Pre-Installation			Post-Installation		
	Yes No. %	No No. %	Total No.	Yes No. %	No No. %	Total No.	Yes No. %	No No. %	Total No.	Yes No. %	No No. %	Total No.
Attempts No	33 (70)	14 (30)	47	20 (57)	15 (43)	35	8 (57)	6 (43)	14	14 (70)	6 (30)	20
Attempts	70 (47)	79 (53)	149	55 (34)	106 (66)	161	87 (47)	97 (53)	184	92 (52)	86 (48)	178
Total	103 (53)	93 (47)	196	75 (38)	121 (62)	196	95 (48)	103 (52)	198	106 (54)	92 (46)	198

Note:
* Those experiencing both burglary and attempted burglary are excluded.

Chi^2 = 1.74, df = 1, not significant). In contrast, on the target estate, while the upgrading of security appears to have had a marked effect in reducing anxiety irrespective of the experience of an attempt — the proportion of the fearful dropping 12–13 percentage points for both groups – at both stages those experiencing attempts were more afraid (Before: Chi^2 = 6.62, df = 1, p < .025; after: Chi^2 = 5.49, df = 1, p < .025).

In sum, the evidence suggests that the experiment achieved fear reduction on the target estate relative to the control estate. Fear was not related to the experience of burglary on either target or control estates. Experiencing an attempted burglary was associated with greater fear on the target estate but not on the control estate.

Fear Among Subgroups

The focus of the analysis was on the overall effects of enhanced residential security upon fear and the evidence of the British Crime Survey suggests that fear of burglary is less subject to variation by age, sex and social isolation than is fear of street crime (Maxfield 1984). There were, nonetheless, indications that the effect differed, to some extent, according to the social characteristics of the subgroups in the sample. The effects by gender, age and household composition are, therefore, briefly noted. This is not so much to draw out the differences but rather to emphasise the generalised effect improved security had across all group. Within this broad brush effect, however, there were potentially important findings, to be treated with caution because of the loss of representativeness inherent in research designs of this kind. These losses, it will be recalled, were not more likely to be among those expressing most fear *per se* but rather among the burgled and young adults.

Prior to the installations similar proportions of males (52% (47)) and females (54% (61)) were anxious. Following the installations the decline in anxiety was slightly greater for males than females, a reduction of 15% and 12% respectively. On the control estate the originally lower proportions of the anxious rose, females showing a greater increase than males (males rising from 48% (45) to 50% (47), females 49% (51) to 57% (60)).

For all age groups on the target estate fear of burglary declined, although most markedly, between 30% and 50%, for the middle aged and older age groups (46–55, 56–65 and over 65s). Several studies have suggested that fear of crime is greater among the elderly than the young (see Clarke and Lewis 1982). Such studies, however, have not sufficiently distinguished between fear for personal safety and fear of burglary; according to Maxfield's (1984) analysis of the data of the first British Crime Survey fear of burglary, as opposed to fear for personal safety, is lower for the elderly than for other age groups. This finding is reflected in the experiment reported here. Following the enhancement of security respondents over 65 years of age moved from the position of second least anxious group on the estate, 50% (16) of whom worried about burglary, to the least anxious group, 25% (8) of whom worried. It was not, moreover, this oldest age group as such which felt threatened, but older women living alone, a finding that is echoed elsewhere. Thus Clarke and Lewis (1982) in their study of fear among the elderly found that those with a socially supportive network, measured by contact with their neighbours, exhibited less fear of crime.

On the control estate the situation was more complex, anxiety declining in some age groups but increasing in others. Within this situation, and in contrast with the target estate, anxiety rose amongst the elderly and those between 46 and 55 years of age. Like the target estate, however, anxiety among those over 65, relative to other age groups on the estate, was low, rising over the period of the evaluation from the lowest position at 33% (9) of the group to next lowest at 48% (13).

Given the small numbers and the effect of the attenuation of the original sample upon the assessment of the impact of the enhanced security, these data must be treated with caution. Nonetheless, earlier unqualified statements that the elderly fear burglary (Hough and Mayhew 1983; Skogan and Maxfield 1981) warrant closer scrutiny. Studies such as that of Clarke and Lewis (1982) and Maxfield's (1984) later analysis of the data of the British Crime Survey are steps in this direction.

Finally it was felt that the number of adults in a household, connoting availability or assurance of defence if necessary, would be related to the expression of fear by an individual, and that solitary adults caring for children might similarly have a heightened sense of fear. Following the installation of the devices on the target estate fear among those living alone was contained while increasing on the control, respectively remaining at 48% (11) and rising from 37% (10) to 70% (19). On both estates however the most anxious were lone adults with children of school age and under. Again on the target estate fear among this group declined by half, falling by 31% from 62% (16) to 31% (8), while on the control estate the percentage decline, from 61% to 54%, reflected an absolute change of one, from 8 to 7. Although these numbers are too small to sustain elaborate arguments, the finding is important in view of the large proportion of such households living on difficult to let estates. On the target estate in the first year, they comprised 15% (50) of the 50% sample, that is approximately 1 in 7 of all households on the estate. On the control estate the comparable figure was 9% (25) of all households.

In sum, whilst reduction in anxiety was related to household composition and age, and anxiety as a proportion of their respective groups was much reduced for the middle aged, the elderly and solitary carers, it would seem that the upgrading of security had a general effect of reducing anxiety across a range of subgroups.

Attitudes to the Experiment

Despite the deficiencies in the execution of the scheme noted above (and see Allatt 1984), when compared with the upward trend of burglary on the control estate the enhancement of security had been effective. Nonetheless, burglary on the target estate did not decline; it was still, not surprisingly, perceived as the dominant crime and, among the now reduced group of anxious residents, continued to be the dominant fear. These factors, however, did not mean that the security devices were seen as having no effect by either the unworried or the worried. When asked if the devices had helped to prevent burglary, of the 197 respondents who replied, 64% (126) felt they had done so, 18% (36) that they had had no effect and a further 18% (35) did not know. Similarly, even amongst those fearful of being burgled, over half, 57% (44), felt the devices had been a deterrent, 24% (19) felt they had not and 19% (15) did not know. Those responding negatively observed that burglary had continued, there were other ways of gaining entry or that a determined burglar could always get in. Ten complained about the lack or inadequacy of the installations.

One of the interests informing this study was whether improved security might have some beneficial effect upon residents' satisfaction with their houses and their views of the estate. For the majority of all respondents on the estate the disposition towards the house had not changed. However, following the question: 'Do you think the locks and security catches have helped to prevent break-ins?' respondents were asked, 'Has it changed your attitude to your house?' and 33% (65/196) said they were more or slightly more satisfied. The predominant reason for the increased satisfaction was the enhanced security; 49 respondents said they felt safer, 16 that they now felt able to leave the house unattended (15 said they had always felt safe). Of this now more satisfied group 19 were still anxious about burglary. Overall, 25% (20) of those still fearful felt their safety to be enhanced.

However, despite this predominantly positive feeling of increased protection provided by the security devices, the satisfaction rarely extended to an enhancement of respondents' views of the estate. Approximately 92% (173) said they felt exactly the same, many of whom hated it; 6% (11) said they were more satisfied. Of the remaining 3 respondents who answered this question two were less satisfied and one did not know.

Although the estate was still viewed by the same proportion of respondents (50%) as having more crime than others, the proportions of those with other views had changed. Fewer, 10% (21) as opposed to 29% (60), now thought that the crime level was the same as on other estates. Conversely, more respondents 29% (59) as opposed to the previous 10% (21), thought the crime level to be lower; and indeed, although it was unknown as to whether respondents were aware of the fact, the burglary rate had more than doubled on the adjacent estate (see Allatt 1984). Perceptions therefore were changing, to some extent for the better, as regards the comparative criminal activity if not the desirability of residence on this estate.

Nonetheless, despite this more favourable comparison of the crime rate, as noted earlier crime on the estate was seen as extensive by approximately 80% of the respondents both before and after the installations; and, although there was probably a lower incidence of crime than might otherwise have been expected, the burglary rate did not decline and other property crime increased (see Allatt 1984). The data suggest therefore that it is possible to reduce fear by security enhancement even when there is no reduction in crime itself.

Conclusion

According to the evidence of the British Crime Survey in some areas fear of crime appears to be a serious problem which needs to be tackled separately from crime itself (Hough and Mayhew 1983, p. 26). Maxfield (1984) has also observed that:

While some research at the national level will continue to be informative, smaller scale studies in inner cities, especially in neighbourhoods where crime and fear are most acute, is [sic] especially needed. (p. 44)

The Northumbria Police Security Experiment meets these criteria, falling as it does within the developing Home Office tradition of the situational approach to crime prevention and set in a local context specifically selected because of a high burglary rate. It is an example of the shift advocated by Taylor and Coles (1983, p. 338), and which they see as implicit in the finding of the British Crime Survey, from the 'traditional criminological search for causes and cures ... to prevention ... not psychologically understanding the criminal but technically obstructing crime'.

This type of intervention to reduce fear has an additional advantage: fear reduction is not divorced from crime prevention thereby meeting the criticism (however unjustified this may be given that fear is excessive in relation to the risk of victimisation) that fear reduction campaigns alone lull people into a false sense of security while crime continues unabated.

Whether the reduction in fear was due to the fact that something was seen to be done by the authorities or that the presence of the devices produced a definite increase in the sense of security, the results of the experiment are encouraging. However, a note of caution must be raised. The evaluation of fear only covered the year immediately following the installations. In the following year the burglary rate began to climb, the housing authority had difficulties with maintenance (from a conversation with McCalman 1983) and a police survey of the security devices revealed many to be ineffective (Northumbria Police 1982, Part II). From the standpoint, therefore, of both benefit to the residents and the cost-effectiveness of the exercise for future policy decisions on implementation, a follow up evaluation (an exercise rarely undertaken) would provide valuable information.[5]

Notes

[1] The most marked differences were first, a reduction in the number of 18 to 22 year olds as a proportion of the sample, from 30% to 11% on the target estate and from 26% to 20% on the control; second, a reduction in

the proportion of the single, from 30% to 14% on the target estate and from 20% to 12% on the control. The representation of the other age groups and marital statuses remained broadly similar at both stages. Understandably, those who were most satisfied with the estate tended to be more represented amongst the retained cases, increasing from 20% to 31% on the target estate and 32% to 42% on the control, whilst the *very* dissatisfied on the target estate, although not so much on the control, tended to be among the lost, dropping from 49% to 31% on the target and 29% to 24% on the control. Other levels of satisfaction remained similar.

2   This statistic includes both burglary and attempted burglary, the latter comprising rather more than a third of the total (Hough and Mayhew 1983, p. 17).

3   The respondent's definition of vandalism was used and respondents were not confined to one response.

4   The British Crime Survey revealed that 60% of the sample were worried about becoming the victim of a crime and of this worried group 44%, that is 26% of the total sample, were worried about burglary. In comparison with the present local study, therefore, a real risk of 2.5% (1 in 40) yields 26% worry as opposed to a real risk of 20% (1 in 5) yielding the proportionately lower 50%–59%. This suggests that even in a threatening environment there are individuals who are resilient to fear and circumstances conducive to such resilience.

5   The report on which this article is based is subject to Crown Copyright, as was Allatt (1984), cited in this article. Reference to Crown Copyright was inadvertently omitted from the issue of the *Journal* in which the earlier article appeared.

References

Allatt, P. (1982) 'An experiment in crime prevention on a difficult to let estate', report for the Home Office (unpublished).

Allatt, P. (1984) 'Residential security: containment and displacement of burglary', *Howard Journal of Criminal Justice*, 23, 99–116.

Brill Associates, W. (1979) *Planning for Housing Security: Site Security Analysis Manual*. Prepared for the U.S. Department of Housing and Urban Development, Washington D.C., G.P.O. cited Perlgut, D. (1982) 'Public housing and crime prevention in Australia', in: M. Hough and P. Mayhew (Eds.), *Crime and Public Housing* (Research and Planning Unit Paper No. 6), London: Home Office.

Campbell, D.T. and Stanley, J.C. (1969) *Experimental and Quasi-Experimental Designs for Research*, Chicago: Rand McNally.

Clarke, A.H. and Lewis, J. (1982) 'Fear of crime among the elderly, an exploratory study', *British Journal of Criminology*, 22, 49–62.

Hough, M. and Mayhew, P. (1983) *The British Crime Survey: First Report* (Home Office Research Study No. 76), London: H.M.S.O.

Maxfield, M.G. (1984) *Fear of Crime in England and Wales* (Home Office Research Study No. 78), London: H.M.S.O.

Northumbria Police (1982) 'Prevention of fear, Part I. Felling; Part II. Scotswood', Northumbria Police (unpublished).

Skogan, W.G. and Maxfield, M. (1981) *Coping with Crime: Individual and Neighbourhood Reactions*, London: Sage.

Taylor, L. and Coles, B. (1983) 'Crime and the fear of crime', *New Society*, 63, 336–8.

Winchester, S.W.C. and Jackson, H.M.A. (1982) *Residential Burglary: The Limits of Prevention* (Home Office Research Study No. 74), London: H.M.S.O.

[24]

THE BRITISH JOURNAL

OF

CRIMINOLOGY

| Vol. 31 | Winter 1991 | No. 1 |

THE EFFECTIVENESS OF A POLICE-INITIATED
FEAR-REDUCING STRATEGY

TREVOR BENNETT*

The paper presents the results of a quasi-experimental evaluation of the impact of a policing initiative which aimed to reduce fear of crime and to improve the quality of life of residents in two chosen areas. The results show that the programme was fully implemented during the experimental period. There was no evidence that the programme achieved its major outcome goal of directly reducing the fear of crime. There was evidence, however, that the programme achieved its secondary goals, improving some aspects of the quality of life in the programme areas. The results showed significant improvements, in both programme areas, in respondents' involvement with neighbours in home protection, in satisfaction with the police, and in contact with the police. The results also showed significant improvements in at least one of the programme areas in satisfaction with the area, sense of community, and informal control of crime.

Introduction

There is a growing body of evidence to support the view that the police may play an important role in controlling fear of crime. Correlational studies conducted in the USA have found that the presence of the police on the streets is associated with feelings of safety (Balkin and Houlden 1983) and that residents who have high confidence in the police are generally less fearful than those with low confidence (Baker *et al.* 1983). Research has also shown a relationship between the perceived adequacy of police protection and the subjective likelihood of personal victimization (Baumer 1985).

Research which has evaluated the effectiveness of various policing strategies has also shown that the police might be in a position to control fear of crime. An evaluation of a policing programme in Baltimore, Maryland which included directed patrol and problem-orientated policing found reductions in fear of crime (Cordner 1986). Fewer respondents assessed their fear of crime as 'very high' following the implementation of

---

* Institute of Criminology, University of Cambridge.

TREVOR BENNETT

the programme than did before the programme. The results of a quasi-experimental evaluation of a foot patrol experiment in Newark, New Jersey showed that residents exposed to an increase in the number of foot patrol officers in their area became less fearful over the experimental period (Pate *et al.* 1986). A similar study of the impact of increased foot patrols in Flint, Michigan found that almost 70 per cent of survey respondents reported that they felt safer during the programme than they did before (Trojanowicz 1986). Research on the effectiveness of community-orientated policing programmes has also reported reductions in fear of crime. An evaluation of the Cincinnati Team Policing Experiment showed that following the implementation of decentralized policing the percentage of residents reporting that they felt 'very unsafe' walking in the neighbourhood at night was lower (Schwartz and Clarren 1977).

Some studies, however, have reported a failure of certain policing strategies to reduce fear. The Kansas City Preventive Patrol Experiment, which involved intensifying the number of routine preventive vehicle patrols by two to three times the usual level per beat, showed that fear of crime was not affected by the experimental conditions (Kelling *et al.* 1974); and the results of the Wilmington Split-Force Experiment showed that the proportion of respondents who felt 'unsafe' or 'very unsafe' in their neighbourhood remained constant during the course of the programme (Tien *et al.* 1978). The available research evidence on the ability of the police to control fear of crime, then, is not unanimous. What is significant at this stage is that there are a number of studies which show that under some circumstances and in some conditions the police might be effective in reducing that fear.

Support for the view that the police might have a role to play in the control of fear of crime can also be found in the results of British research. The results of the second British Crime Survey (BCS) relating to fear of crime in the general population were analysed and published in two papers: one by Maxfield (1987) and another by Box *et al.* (1988). The first of these studies (Maxfield 1987) concluded that the police might have a role to play in reducing fear of crime in providing the public with better information about the real risks of victimization and controlling levels of incivilities on the streets. The second (Box *et al.* 1988) analysed the same data using a different method and showed a direct relationship between public confidence in the police and fear of crime. The conclusion to this article expressed a need for the police to become involved with their local communities in controlling public disorder and fear of crime (ibid. p. 353).

The main impetus for the project reported in the present paper was the publication of a North American study which produced some of the strongest evidence to date on the ability of the police to control fear of crime. The research was conducted in Newark, New Jersey and Houston, Texas and comprised a collaborative effort by the National Institute of Justice (who funded the project), the Newark and Houston Police Departments, and the Police Foundation (who evaluated the programme). The programme involved seven policing experiments designed specifically to reduce fear of crime (details of the experiments are provided in Pate *et al.* 1986). The results of a rigorous quasi-experimental evaluation of the programmes showed that three of the experiments resulted in statistically significant reductions in fear of crime. The greatest impact on fear resulted from the implementation of police–community stations (local police 'shops' designed to improve police–public contact) and from citizen contact patrols (local police making proactive contacts with residents and shopkeepers) (Pate *et*

2

A POLICE-INITIATED FEAR-REDUCING STRATEGY

al. 1986). The third programme which was shown to reduce fear was a co-ordinated initiative involving elements of each of the separate programmes.

The involvement of the police in the control of fear of crime has a broader context which is identified in much of the research literature. The beginning of the period of collaboration between the police and the public in fear reduction coincided with an increase in concern over the effectiveness of traditional policing methods, a concern stimulated in part by a series of research findings which showed that innovations in policing were largely ineffective in reducing crime or improving clear-up rates (see Clarke and Hough 1980, 1984). It also came at a time when the nature of the police's role was undergoing a general reappraisal, which led to calls for a more community-orientated style of policing (see Goldstein 1987).

The aim of the current research was to replicate one of the Newark and Houston experiments in a police force area in Britain in order to determine whether the successes shown in the North American experiments could be repeated over here. The major aim of the experiment was to evaluate the direct impact of the programme on fear of crime. A further aim was to determine whether the programme had any other impact on community life which might benefit the community or which might instigate mechanisms which could lead to a reduction in fear of crime in the future.

There were few precedents for this type of work in Britain. At the time of setting up the project there had been very few experimental or quasi-experimental evaluations of police effectiveness relating to police service delivery. Further, there were no examples (to my knowledge at the time) of the kinds of policing programmes conducted in Newark and Houston being implemented in this country (see, though, as a possible exception Murray 1988).

The programme chosen for evaluation was the citizen contact patrols experiment (hereafter referred to as 'contact patrols'). The main reasons for this choice were that the programme resulted in the greatest number of positive findings in the Police Foundation evaluation and that it was relatively easy and inexpensive to implement in this country.

A small number of police forces in England were approached to see if they would be willing to host the experiment. The West Midlands force and the Metropolitan Police both agreed to take part and to make available the necessary resources to implement contact patrols.

Methods

The research aimed to implement and evaluate one contact patrols programme in each of two police force areas. The methods used in the research addressed both implementation and effectiveness.

It was important to the research that residents in the selected programme sites experienced fairly high levels of fear of crime. The areas chosen were selected on the basis of their potential level of fear of crime, estimated from known victimization rates and from signs of disorder (the two main correlates of fear). The areas chosen were also influenced by the location of the particular division within each police force area whose officers were willing to launch the experiment. The West Midlands site comprised an estate of about 2,000 households in south Birmingham and the Metropolitan Police site comprised an estate also with about 2,000 households in Southwark in south London.

3

TREVOR BENNETT

The programme launched in the experimental areas was based on the design of the Newark and Houston programmes and comprised two main elements: continuous police presence (referred to as 'beat integrity' in the North American literature) and resident contacts. In order to achieve continuous police presence it was necessary to maintain at least one officer in the programme area for two daytime shifts per day. In order to achieve resident contacts the programme officers were instructed to contact one adult representative of each household during the course of the one-year period of the evaluation. Both elements were achieved by creating a police team of four constables and one supervising sergeant in each programme area. Most of the resident contacts were made by officers knocking on the doors of residents within the area and introducing themselves. The officer would then ask the residents whether they had any problems concerning crime or other aspects of life on the estate that the police might be able to help do something about (details of the programmes can be found in Bennett 1989). In order to monitor implementation effectiveness the officers making the resident contacts were asked to complete a contact card containing details of each contact. The implementation of the programme was also monitored by the supervising sergeant who collected data on time spent in the programme area and the number of resident contacts achieved.

The method used for evaluating the effectiveness of the programmes is referred to as a quasi-experimental design using an 'untreated control group design with pre-test and post-test samples' (Cook and Campbell 1979). The current research was based on a slightly modified design in order to achieve both cross-sectional (a random cross-section of residents) and panel samples (using the same respondents for both pre-test and post-test measurements). (Details of the sampling method along with relevant justifications can be found in Bennett 1989.) In order to achieve both a repeated cross-sectional and an embedded panel survey design the sampling frame generated for the pre-test surveys was used for the post-test surveys. The core of the method is to interview respondents at a point before the implementation of the experimental programme and again after the programme has been in operation for about one year. A comparison is made by interviewing a control sample of respondents living in similar areas without the experimental programme. The control areas were selected from among similar housing estates within the same police division as the experimental area by comparing the crime rates of potential areas with the experimental areas and by site visits using the same criteria of selection as used in choosing the experimental areas. In order to avoid the problem of something unusual happening in a single control area during the course of the experiment a composite control area was created from three nearby areas in London and two nearby areas in Birmingham.

The surveys were conducted by a market research company in London and by specially trained fieldworkers in Birmingham. In both areas a sample of about one in three households was chosen for interview. The interviewers were instructed to select one member of each household for interview, using an agreed randomizing procedure. The interview schedule comprised questions drawn from the survey instruments used in the first and second British Crime Surveys and from the questionnaires used in Newark and Houston (see Bennett 1989).

The first round of surveys (pre-test) was conducted in June and July 1987. The contact patrol programmes were launched in both London and Birmingham in August 1987. The second round of surveys (post-test) was conducted in August and September

4

A POLICE-INITIATED FEAR-REDUCING STRATEGY

TABLE 1 *Response Rates and Sample Size, Cross-Section Samples*

	Birmingham		London	
	Exp.	Con.	Exp.	Con.
Pre-test				
Total households	749	500	586	585
Ineligible	169	85	60	75
Eligible	580	415	526	510
Total interviewed	374	291	305	296
Response rate, %	65	70	58	58
Post-test				
Total households	749	500	586	585
Ineligible	211	126	40	44
Eligible	538	374	546	541
Total interviewed	368	278	304	345
Response rate, %	68	74	56	64

Exp. = experimental area; Con. = control area.

1988 after the programmes had been running for one year. Details of the surveys and the number of interviews achieved are shown in Table 1.

The response rates were calculated by dividing the total number of households interviewed by the total number of households eligible. Households were recorded as ineligible if the address was vacant or could not be found or if the residents had lived in the area for less than one year. The response rates in London (ranging from 56 per cent to 64 per cent) were consistently lower than those in Birmingham (ranging from 65 per cent to 74 per cent). The main reasons given for non-response by the market research company conducting the surveys in London were personal refusal and no contact after five or more call backs.

Results

The results of the research cover both implementation effectiveness and programme effectiveness.

Implementation effectiveness

Implementation effectiveness concerns the extent to which the programme had been implemented as intended and whether the 'intermediate goals' of the programme had been achieved (Horton and Smith 1988).

The two main programme elements were resident contacts and continuous police presence. The analysis of the contact cards completed by each officer making a contact with a member of the public showed a contact rate of 88 per cent in Birmingham (1,416 out of 1,616 eligible households were contacted) and 87 per cent in London (1,914 out of 2,204 eligible households were contacted). It took eight months to contact at least 50 per cent of the dwellings in the programme area in Birmingham and six months to contact at least 50 per cent of the dwellings in the programme area in London. The results also showed that the demographic distribution of contacts was fairly even across

5

TREVOR BENNETT

a range of variables with no statistically significant difference shown on any of the factors analysed.

The analysis of the completed time sheets relating to the number of hours that an officer was within the boundaries of the experimental area showed that there was at least one officer in the area for an average of 10.6 hours per day in Birmingham and 10.4 hours per day in London. There were only two days out of the year in Birmingham and eleven days out of the year in London (including weekends and holidays) in which there were no officers patrolling the area.

The overall impression given by these results is that the main programme elements were implemented effectively and constituted a programme capable of being evaluated in terms of its outcome effectiveness.

Programme effectiveness

In order to simplify presentation of the results, the following analysis concerns specifically the data produced from the cross-sectional samples. The analysis of data produced from the panel samples shows no major variations in the results obtained.

The primary element of programme effectiveness is the extent to which the programme was experienced by local residents. The level of contact between the police and the public was measured on the scale 'contact with the police' (see Table 6 below), generated from responses to five items concerning police–public contact. Improvements were recorded on all five items in Birmingham and on three of the five items in London. The major changes in both areas occurred on the item 'know some police officers by name or sight'. In Birmingham, the percentage of respondents who said that they knew a police officer by name or sight increased in the programme area by 35 percentage points from 15 per cent to 50 per cent over the experimental period, compared with a smaller increase in the control area of 3 percentage points from 10 per cent to 13 per cent. In London, the percentage who knew a police officer increased by 20 percentage points from 12 per cent to 32 per cent, compared with a reduction in the control area of 4 percentage points from 21 per cent to 17 per cent.

Further substantial improvements were recorded on the items 'saw police in last two weeks' (an increase of 24 percentage points in Birmingham but no change in London), 'noticed changes in policing in the last year' (an increase of 35 percentage points in Birmingham and 12 percentage points in London), 'noticed increased patrol in the last year' (an increase of 24 percentage points in Birmingham and 8 percentage points in London), and 'perceived patrol level as adequate' (an increase of 18 percentage points in Birmingham, but no improvement in London). The results suggest that the programme was experienced by residents in the experimental areas.

It was not a major aim of the project to reduce victimizations over the one-year experimental period. The primary aims of the programme were fear reduction and improved police–community relations, neither of which directly required reductions in local crime rates. Nevertheless, it was necessary for the research to observe the widest possible impact of the programme and an assessment of changes in victimization rates was built into the research design.

The mean victimization rate for residents in all areas is presented in Table 2. The table shows a general reduction in victimization in all areas over the experimental period, with the exception of a small increase in personal victimizations in Birm-

6

A POLICE-INITIATED FEAR-REDUCING STRATEGY

TABLE 2 *Mean Victimization Rate per Household in Relation to Specific Offence Types (Incidence of Victimization), Cross-Section Samples*

	Birmingham Exp.		Con.		London Exp.		Con.	
	Pre	Post	Pre	Post	Pre	Post	Pre	Post
n =	374	368	291	278	305	304	296	345
Theft of vehicle	0.07	0.07	0.07	0.04	0.07	0.04	0.04	0.05
Theft from vehicle	0.24	0.19	0.30	0.12	0.21	0.15	0.22	0.15
Criminal damage to vehicle	0.32	0.32	0.20	0.26	0.31	0.23	0.35	0.24
Burg. dwell. (comp.)	0.22	0.17	0.14	0.13	0.26	0.11	0.21	0.19
Burg. dwell. (att.)	0.30	0.23	0.31	0.21	0.18	0.16	0.25	0.14
Criminal damage to dwelling	0.28	0.22	0.26	0.27	0.58	0.34	0.13	0.11
All household offences	2.00	1.73	1.79	1.50 ns	2.11	1.35	1.59	1.19 ns
All personal offences	0.30	0.33	0.32	0.22 ns	0.23	0.19	0.23	0.16 ns

Weighted data.
Personal offences are weighted by a factor $= n_a/x_a$ where:
   $n_a =$ the number of adults in the household;
   $x_a =$ the mean number of adults for the whole sample.
Burg. dwell. (comp.) = burglary in a dwelling—completed offence.
Burg. dwell. (att.) = burglary in a dwelling—attempted offence.
The category 'All household offences' includes all household offences covered by the survey.
ns = the interaction term between area and period was not significant after controlling for demographic factors using multivariate analysis (see note 2 for details).

ingham. The bivariate statistics show that there was little difference in the reduction in victimization rates between experimental and control areas for all household and personal offences combined and for specific offence types. These figures match the general nationwide reduction in notifiable offences recorded by the police during the period 1987–8. The multivariate analysis supports this conclusion by showing no significant difference in the rate of change between the programme and non-programme areas in all household and personal victimizations combined.[1]

The major aim of the experiment was to assess the impact of the contact patrols programme on fear of crime. The results of this part of the analysis are shown in Table 3. (The scales presented in Table 3 and the following tables were constructed by extracting factors from clusters of variables using principal component analysis; for details of this method see Bennett 1990. Variables which correlated well were combined into a single scale by adding across the values of each variable.) Table 3 shows that there were reductions in worry about victimization and improvements in perceptions of personal safety in both the Birmingham and the London experimental areas. However, the improvements recorded in the scale scores were not great. This can be exemplified by looking at the results of some of the items which made up the 'perceptions of personal safety' scale. The percentage of respondents who felt 'safe' or 'very safe' after dark in the area increased from 45 per cent to 49 per cent (an increase of just 4 percentage points) in Birmingham and from 36 per cent to 37 per cent in London (an increase of only 1 percentage point). Similarly, the percentage of respondents who were

---

[1] The multivariate method of analysis used is a form of generalized log-linear modelling (see Payne 1986). The analysis involves constructing a linear model whereby a dependent variable (such as victimization) can be predicted or explained by a number of independent variables. Details of the statistical methods used can be found in Bennett (1989).

7

TREVOR BENNETT

TABLE 3 *Mean Scale Scores of Factors Relating to Perceptions of Crime in the Area,*
Cross-Section Samples

Scales n =[a]	Birmingham Exp.		Con.		London Exp.		Con.	
	Pre 374	Post 368	Pre 291	Post 278	Pre 305	Post 304	Pre 296	Post 345
Perceptions of personal safety	2.22	2.25 (+)[b]	2.20	2.27 ns (+)	2.13	2.16 (+)	2.19	2.17 ns (−)
Worry about victimization	2.17	2.34 (+)	2.11	2.31 ns (+)	2.20	2.24 (+)	2.14	2.08 ns (−)
Perceived probability of personal victimization	3.36	3.60 (+)	3.27	3.48 ns (+)	3.26	3.21 (−)	3.20	3.04 ns (−)
Perceived probability of area crime	1.70	1.96 (+)	1.69	1.89 ns (+)	1.73	1.88 (+)	1.94	2.02 ns (+)

NB: Weighted data.
[a] Unweighted sample totals.
   Actual numbers may very due to missing values.
[b] (+) = mean change in a favourable direction,
   (−) = mean change in an unfavourable direction,
   (=) = no change.
ns = the interaction term between area and period was not significant after controlling for demographic factors using multivariate analysis (see note 2 for details).
* = $p < 0.05$ = the interaction term between area and period was significant at the 5% probability level after controlling for demographic factors using multivariate analysis (see note 2 for details).

'not worried' about burglary increased from 39 per cent to 43 per cent in Birmingham and from 11 per cent to 15 per cent in London—an increase of 4 percentage points in each case.

In Birmingham, the improvements in the experimental area were matched by similar improvements in the control area. In London, the improvements in the experimental area were not matched by improvements in the control area over the same period. The results of the multivariate analysis showed that in neither city did the experimental area perform significantly better than the control area.[2] There is no evidence from these results, therefore, that the contact patrols programme had any direct impact on fear of crime.

Improvements were also recorded in the mean scale scores relating to perceived probability of area crime in the experimental areas of both Birmingham and London and in perceived personal victimization in Birmingham only. Once again, these improvements were matched by similar changes in the respective control areas. The results of the multivariate analysis failed to show any significant difference in performance between experimental and control areas in either city. There is no evidence from these results that the programmes influenced residents' perceptions of the risks of victimization.

[2] In order to determine a programme effect using multivariate analysis it was necessary to create a pooled data set comprising data from the pre-test and post-test surveys and from the experimental and control areas. Dummy variables were added to the data to indicate whether the survey was conducted in the pre-test or post-test period and whether the area was an experimental or control area. A programme effect was determined by the statistical significance of the contribution of the interaction between the dummy variable relating to survey period and the dummy variable relating to programme or non-programme area in explaining the dependent variable.

8

A POLICE-INITIATED FEAR-REDUCING STRATEGY

It was also an aim of the research to determine whether the programme had any other benefits for the police or the community. It is possible that the programme might fail to have a direct impact on fear of crime but instigate processes which might benefit the community in other ways, or which might lead to an impact on fear of crime in the future. The research was designed to investigate changes in a number of factors relating to police–public relations and community development. The findings relating to residents' perceptions of their area are presented in Table 4, which shows that there were general improvements in all scale scores in both experimental areas, with the exception of a slight worsening of signs of disorder in London. In Birmingham, there were similar or equal improvements during the same period in the control area. In London the control area performed less well than the experimental area in terms of both changes in satisfaction with the area and changes in the sense of community.

The impression given by these bivariate level results is that there is little overall difference between changes in the programme and non-programme areas. However, the results of the multivariate analysis showed that two of the changes were statistically significant. In Birmingham, the programme area performed significantly better than the non-programme area in changes in residents' satisfaction with the area; and in London, the programme area performed significantly better than the non-programme area in changes in sense of community. These findings provide some evidence that there might have been a programme effect in relation to residents' satisfaction with their area and in a general sense of community.

The difference in performance of the experimental and control areas in relation to these two scales can be examined in more detail by looking at changes in the items that made up the scale. 'Satisfaction with the area' was measured by four items. The percentage of respondents in Birmingham who said that they were 'very' or 'fairly' satisfied with their area increased from 52 per cent in the pre-test survey to 64 per cent in the post-test survey (an increase of 12 percentage points). The percentage of respondents who felt that the area was 'a real home' increased from 39 per cent to 46

TABLE 4   *Mean Scale Scores of Factors Relating to Perceptions of the Area, Cross-Section Samples*

Scales n =*	Birmingham Exp.		Con.		London Exp.		Con.	
	Pre 374	Post 368	Pre 291	Post 278	Pre 305	Post 304	Pre 296	Post 345
Satisfaction with area	2.01	2.21 (+)	2.00	2.10* (+)	1.79	1.84 (+)	2.05	2.04 ns (−)
Area problems: persons	2.39	2.51 (+)	2.37	2.45 ns (+)	2.27	2.35 (+)	2.43	2.55 ns (+)
Area problems: environment	1.84	1.93 (+)	1.76	1.82 ns (+)	1.54	1.57 (+)	1.89	2.04 ns (+)
Sense of community	1.96	2.04 (+)	1.92	1.99 ns (+)	1.71	1.86 (+)	2.00	1.98* (−)
Observed disorder: incivilities	1.56	1.59 (+)	1.52	1.52 ns (=)	1.51	1.56 (+)	1.60	1.64 ns (+)
Observed disorder: crimes	1.91	1.94 (+)	1.92	1.92 ns (=)	1.90	1.89 (−)	1.85	1.88 ns (+)

Notes: as for Table 3.

9

TREVOR BENNETT

per cent (7 percentage points); the percentage who felt that the area had become a 'better place to live' increased from 13 per cent to 18 per cent (5 percentage points); and the percentage who would feel 'sorry to move' increased from 18 per cent to 24 per cent (6 percentage points). 'Sense of community' was measured by five items. In London, percentage point improvements were recorded for two of these five items. The percentage of respondents who thought that 'people help each other' increased from 33 per cent to 36 per cent (3 percentage points) and the percentage of respondents who thought that it was 'easy to recognize strangers' increased from 41 per cent to 46 per cent (5 percentage points).

The results of the analysis of changes in informal social control are presented in Table 5. This table shows that there were improvements in social control on the 'control of crime' and 'involvement of neighbours in home protection' scales in Birmingham and on the 'control of incivilities' and 'involvement of neighbours in home protection' scales in London. No similar improvements were recorded in the control area in Birmingham and no improvements were recorded for 'involvement of neighbours in home protection' in London. The impression from this table that the programme areas generally performed better than the non-programme areas was reflected in the results of the multivariate analysis. Both improvements recorded in Birmingham at the bivariate level of analysis were found to be statistically significant at the multivariate level of analysis. In London, the improvement in 'involvement of neighbours in home protection' was found to be significant while the improvement in 'control of incivilities' was not.

More detail on these favourable changes can be revealed by looking at the change in responses to some of the individual items. In Birmingham, the percentage of respondents who said that they had taken action in response to signs of a burglary increased from 94 per cent to 96 per cent (2 percentage points) in the programme area, but decreased from 95 per cent to 92 per cent in the non-programme area. The percentage of respondents who asked their neighbours to watch their property when away increased from 72 per cent to 77 per cent (5 percentage points) in the programme area, but decreased from 74 per cent to 73 per cent in the non-programme area. In London, the percentage of respondents who asked their neighbours to look after their property while away increased from 69 per cent to 75 per cent (6 percentage points) in the

TABLE 5 *Mean Scale Scores of Factors Relating to Informal Social Control, Cross-Section Samples*

Scales n=ᵃ	Birmingham Exp.		Con.		London Exp.		Con.	
	Pre 374	Post 368	Pre 291	Post 278	Pre 305	Post 304	Pre 296	Post 345
Control of crime	1.84	1.85 (+)	1.87	1.79* (−)	1.72	1.68 (−)	1.79	1.77 ns (−)
Control of incivilities	1.33	1.33 (=)	1.31	1.27 ns (−)	1.20	1.30 (+)	1.34	1.37 ns (+)
Involvement of neighbours in home protection	1.75	1.84 (+)	1.81	1.80* (−)	1.55	1.67 (+)	1.77	1.73* (−)

Notes: as for Table 3.

A POLICE-INITIATED FEAR-REDUCING STRATEGY

programme area, but decreased from 65 per cent to 54 per cent (11 percentage points) in the non-programme area.

The final block of analysis concerned the impact of the programme on public satisfaction with the police. The results of this analysis are presented in Table 6. The table shows that there were substantial improvements in both satisfaction with the police and contact with the police in both programme areas; also that there were improvements of a smaller magnitude in both of these scales in the non-programme areas too. The results of the multivariate analysis show that the difference in improvements between the experimental and control areas was statistically significant. These results provide evidence of a potential programme effect in terms of public satisfaction with the police and level of contact between the police and the public.

The scale 'satisfaction with the police' comprised seven items. In Birmingham, there were improvements in the percentage of favourable responses in all seven items and in London there were improvements in four of the seven. The largest percentage-point changes occurred in both areas in relation to the item 'satisfied with the police'. In Birmingham the percentage of respondents who reported that they were 'very' or 'fairly' satisfied with the police increased from 37 per cent to 65 per cent (an increase of 28 percentage points), while in London the percentage of respondents in this category increased from 38 per cent to 50 per cent (an increase of 12 percentage points). Other striking improvements were shown in the results from the Birmingham surveys which showed a 20 percentage-point increase in the proportion of respondents who perceived the police as 'polite' and a similar 20 percentage-point increase in the proportion of respondents who perceived that the police were 'doing a good job'.

TABLE 6 *Mean Scale Scores of Factors Relating to Contact and Satisfaction with the Police, Cross-Section Samples*

Scales n=ᵃ	Birmingham Exp.		Con.		London Exp.		Con.	
	Pre 374	Post 368	Pre 291	Post 278	Pre 305	Post 304	Pre 296	Post 345
Satisfaction with the police	2.19	2.54 (+)	2.04	2.23* (+)	2.23	2.37 (+)	2.30	2.31* (+)
Contact with the police	2.03	2.78 (+)	1.56	1.65* (+)	2.29	2.62 (+)	2.25	2.38* (+)

Notes: as for Table 3.

The largely optimistic results on public satisfaction with the police obtained from the public attitudes surveys were reflected in similarly optimistic accounts from the officers involved in the project. Questionnaires completed by the contact patrol officers on three separate occasions throughout the experimental period revealed that the police sustained a belief that the programme would be effective in achieving its aims. Throughout the year the mean assessment score relating to perceived likely programme effectiveness remained above point 4 on a 5-point scale in Birmingham and above point 3 on the same scale in London for each of the three interviews. All of the programme officers in London and four out of five programme officers in Birmingham thought that the work they were currently doing was more satisfying than the work they were doing

TREVOR BENNETT

during the year preceding the programme. When asked to record their current level of job satisfaction on a scale of 1 (very satisfied) to 5 (very dissatisfied) all of the officers in Birmingham recorded that they were 'very satisfied' on at least two of the three questionnaires completed and all of the officers in London recorded that they were either 'fairly' or 'very' satisfied on at least two of the questionnaires completed.

Conclusion

The results of a quasi-experimental evaluation of the impact of a policing initiative which aimed specifically to reduce fear of crime and generally to improve the quality of life of residents in the programme areas have shown that both programmes achieved their implementation goals. In spite of this there was no evidence that the programme achieved its major outcome goal of directly reducing the fear of crime. There was evidence, however, that the programme achieved its secondary goals, improving some aspects of the quality of life in the programme areas. The results showed significant improvements in respondents' involvements with neighbours in home protection, in satisfaction with the police, and in contact with the police in both programme areas. The results also showed significant improvements in satisfaction with the area, sense of community, and control of crime in at least one of the areas.

There is strong evidence that the favourable changes reported above were the result of the contact patrols programme. The research used a quasi-experimental method based on comparisons between experimental and control groups over time. The statistical analysis was based on multivariate techniques which help eliminate the influence of extraneous variables. The research sites were closely monitored during the course of the experiment to ensure that there were no other major changes to the areas. There was no evidence of any noticeable changes in policing methods during the experimental period in the control areas which could have accounted for the results obtained. It is unlikely that many of the constables involved in policing the control areas would have been aware of the experiment, and even among those who were, few would have been aware of the full nature of the programme.

One possible reason why the contact patrols programme did not have a direct impact on fear of crime is that the major factors which affect fear are not easily controlled by the police. The results of research on the correlates of fear show that it is strongly related to perceptions of the likelihood of victimization and perceptions of social disorder within the local neighbourhood (Maxfield 1984, 1987). Without substantial changes in victimization rates and signs of incivility it might be difficult for the police to have any direct impact on fear of crime. The favourable findings of the Newark and Houston evaluation of the citizen contact patrols programme might be a result of the simultaneous reduction in victimization rates within the programme areas (Pate *et al.* 1986).

Nevertheless, it still might be possible for the police to have an indirect effect on fear of crime in the longer term by instigating some of the social processes which could perhaps reduce it. There is evidence from the current research that some of these social processes might have begun in the areas investigated. The increase in satisfaction with the area and general improvements in informal social control, sense of community, and involvement of neighbours in home protection may be the precursors to a strengthening of community bonds which might lead to future reductions in fear of crime.

A POLICE-INITIATED FEAR-REDUCING STRATEGY

The most striking finding of the research, which deserves special emphasis, is the impact of both programmes on public confidence in the police. It is not an insubstantial result that the police changed a situation of one third of the community being satisfied with local police performance to two thirds being satisfied in the course of a single year. Such changes cannot be taken lightly at a time when public confidence in the police is declining nationally (Mayhew *et al.* 1989) and at a time when many inner-city areas of the kind investigated are becoming increasingly difficult to police.

REFERENCES

BAKER, M. H., NIENSTEDT, B. C., EVERETT, R. S., and McCLERY, R. (1983), 'The Impact of Crime Waves: Perception, Fear and Confidence in the Police', *Law and Society Review*, 17: 319–35.

BALKIN, S., and HOULDEN, P. (1983), 'Reducing Fear of Crime through Occupational Presence', *Criminal Justice and Behaviour*, 10: 13–33.

BAUMER, T. L. (1985), 'Testing a General Model of Fear of Crime: Data from a National Sample', *Journal of Research in Crime and Delinquency*, 22/3: 239–55.

BENNETT, T. H. (1989), *Contact Patrols in Birmingham and London: An Evaluation of a Fear Reducing Strategy*. Report to the Home Office Research and Planning Unit. (The report is obtainable from the Institute of Criminology, University of Cambridge.)

—— (1990), *Evaluating Neighbourhood Watch*. Aldershot: Gower.

BOX, S., HALE, C., and ANDREWS, G. (1988), 'Explaining Fear of Crime', *British Journal of Criminology*, 28/3: 340–56.

CLARKE, R. V. G., and HOUGH, J. M. (1980), *The Effectiveness of Policing*. Aldershot: Gower.

—— and HOUGH, J. M. (1984), *Crime and Police Effectiveness*. Home Office Research Study No. 79. London: HMSO.

COOK, T. D., and CAMPBELL, D. T. (1979), *Quasi-Experimentation: Design and Analysis Issues for Field Settings*. Chicago: Rand McNally.

CORDNER, G. W. (1986), 'Fear of Crime and the Police: An Evaluation of a Fear-Reduction Strategy', *Journal of Police Science and Administration*, 14/3: 223–33.

GOLDSTEIN, H. (1987), 'Towards Community-Oriented Policing: Potential, Basic Requirements, and Threshold Questions', *Crime and Delinquency*, 33/1: 6–30.

HORTON, C., and SMITH, D. (1988), *Evaluating Police Work: An Action Research Project*. London: Policy Studies Institute.

KELLING, G. L., PATE, T., DIECKMAN, D., and BROWN, C. E. (1974), *The Kansas City Preventive Patrol Experiment: A Technical Report*. Washington, DC: Police Foundation.

MAXFIELD, M. G. (1984), *Fear of Crime in England and Wales*. Home Office Research Study No. 78. London: HMSO.

—— (1987), *Explaining Fear of Crime: Evidence from the 1984 British Crime Survey*. Research and Planning Unit Paper 43. London: Home Office.

MAYHEW, P., ELLIOTT, D., and DOWDS, L. (1989), *The 1988 British Crime Survey*. Home Office Research Study No. 111. London: HMSO.

MURRAY, J. D. (1988), 'Contact Policing and the Role of the Constable', *The Police Journal*, 41/1: 76–90.

PATE, A. M., WYCOFF, M. A., SKOGAN, W. G., and SHERMAN, L. W. (1986), *Reducing Fear of Crime in Houston and Newark*. Washington, DC: Police Foundation.

PAYNE, C. D. (1986), *The GLIM System: Release 3.77*. Oxford: Numerical Algorithms Group.

13

TREVOR BENNETT

Schwartz, A. L., and Clarren, S. N. (1977), *The Cincinnati Team Policing Experiment: A Summary Report*. Washington DC: Police Foundation.

Tien, J. M., Simon, J. W., and Larson, R. C. (1978), *An Alternative Approach to Police Patrols: The Wilmington Split-Force Experiment*. Cambridge, Mass.: Public Systems Evaluation.

Trojanowicz, R. C. (1986), 'Evaluating a Neighborhood Foot Patrol Program', in D. P. Rosenbaum, *Community Crime Prevention: Does It Work?* London: Sage.

[25]

VICTIMOLOGY: AN INTERNATIONAL JOURNAL
Volume 3, 1978, Numbers 3-4, Pp. 297-313
© Copyright 1979 Visage Press Inc. *Printed in U.S.A.*

Reducing Fear of Crime: Strategies for Intervention

JEFFREY HENIG
George Washington University

MICHAEL G. MAXFIELD
Northwestern University

Fear of crime in large cities may affect individual behavior independently of actual experiences with crime. Fear may produce as debilitating an effect on economic and social systems as crime itself. Fear affects nearly everyone in urban areas, while a smaller proportion of the population is actually victimized. Factors related to fear of crime include misperceptions of the threat of crime, urban social disintegration, and physical characteristics of the environment. Policies for reducing fear may be independent of crime reduction policies. Confidence building, community building, or physical rebuilding strategies may be developed. There may, however, be problems with each of these strategies: some may increase fear by calling attention to crime; others may increase carelessness by prompting people to abandon precautions which were responsible for reductions in crime.

INTRODUCTION

When we think of the impact of violent crime we most often consider its direct effects, its impact upon the individuals who are victimized. The indirect effects of crime on the commercial sector are no less serious. Owners of department stores, theaters, restaurants, and other establishments lose money because fearful customers avoid the downtown area and because their employees are unwilling to work late hours. There are costs to the municipal infrastructure as well: public transit facilities lie idle or under-utilized most of the night as individuals either avoid the areas serviced by mass transit routes or opt for the perceived safety of private automobiles.

There has, however, been relatively little attention devoted to fear of crime as a policy issue. Policy-makers and social scientists have devoted the bulk of their energies and resources to addressing the problems directly caused by crime. Yet the incidence of crime is only part of the problem. Official rates of violent crime in large cities have declined since

Prepared under Grant Number 77–NI–99–0018 from the National Institute of Law Enforcement and Criminal Justice, Law Enforcement Assistance Administration, U.S. Department of Justice. A previous version of this paper was prepared for Westinghouse Electric Corporation, supported by contract #J–LEAA–022–74, U.S. Department of Justice, Law Enforcement Assistance Administration. Portions of this paper were presented at the Community Crime Prevention Workshop, UPDATE '78: National Conference for Local Elected Officials, June 9, 1978. Points of view or opinions expressed are those of the authors and do not necessarily represent the official position or policies of the U.S. Department of Justice, or the Westinghouse Electric Corporation. The authors also wish to thank Leonard Bickman, Westinghouse Electric Corporation, for helpful comments and suggestions on an earlier version of this paper.

298   VICTIMOLOGY: AN INTERNATIONAL JOURNAL

1974 (FBI, 1977). The sharp increases in major crime during the 1960s
and early 1970s have slowed, and may now be reversing (Skogan, 1979).
The problem of fear remains. Scholars have begun to realize that fear of
criminal victimization does not automatically decline along with crime
rates. Recent public opinion polls have shown that while fear tends to go
up with increasing crime, declines in the crime rate are not always
accompanied by corresponding drops in levels of fear (Erskine, 1974).
Fear as a problem for urban decision-makers, merchants, and residents
ought to be regarded as at least partially independent of the actual threat
of crime. Policies which reduce crime are vital for the continued viability
of our central cities, but the effects of fear on the behavior of urbanites
must be considered as well.

     This paper represents an attempt to bridge the gap between existing
theoretical and empirical literature dealing with the fear of crime, and
the policy needs of urban decision-makers. A review of the social science
literature in this field reveals four basic conceptual approaches to
understanding the dynamics behind fear of crime. These approaches are
discussed in the next section. Based on each general approach, we develop
a set of more specific strategies which might be employed to reduce levels
of fear in central cities. These are not costless policies, however; some
would be quite expensive to implement. Another set of costs involves the
possibility of "backlash" effects. There is the possibility that some policies
directed at reducing fear may either increase the fear of crime, or, more
importantly, increase the actual rate of victimization. Accordingly, we
discuss costs and possible backlash effects which might be associated with
each set of strategies.

UNDERSTANDING FEAR OF CRIME: FOUR APPROACHES

     Several academic disciplines and ideologies have contributed to the
growing and increasingly diverse literature on fear of crime (see DuBow,
et al., 1978 for a comprehensive review of this literature). It is possible to
group these studies into four approaches defined according to the general
correlates of fear which they identify: (1) actual victimization or objective
probability of victimization; (2) psychological characteristics and misinformation; (3) social disintegration; and (4) physical features of the urban
environment.

Probability of Victimization—The Direct Approach

     It is easy to believe that crime rates and fear of crime are directly
related. The way to reduce fear, according to this approach, is to reduce
victimization itself. It is usually assumed that this can best be accomplished by devoting additional resources to existing law enforcement
agencies. There is some evidence that direct victimization does contribute
to feelings of fear by victims. A recent analysis of victimization surveys
conducted by the Census Bureau indicates that individuals who have
been the victims of rape, robbery, personal theft, or burglary are more
likely than non-victims to feel unsafe while walking the streets of their
neighborhood. Victims of assault, auto theft, and simple larceny showed
no more fear of crime than did non-victims (Skogan, 1977).

However, direct victimization accounts for only a portion of fear of crime in the general population. One need not be the victim of a crime to be affected by fear. For this reason, a number of studies have examined the impact of probability of victimization, rather than victimization itself, on the fear response. Those who are most likely to be victimized are not necessarily those who fear crime the most (Reiss, 1967; Conklin, 1975; Hindelang, et al., 1978; Lewis and Maxfield, 1978). Surveys conducted in 1966 by the President's Commission on Law Enforcement and Administration of Justice found that population groups with the highest objective crime risks, such as low-income blacks, did indeed reveal intense fear. On the other hand, many people who were less likely to become victims also expressed considerable fear (President's Commission, 1967). A Harris Poll in 1969 reported that: ". . . many people's fear of crime is exaggerated, and disproportionate to the amount of crime in their area—the people *least* in danger are the *most* afraid." (Rosenthal, 1969:20, emphasis in original). Women and the elderly are two subgroups in the population for which the disparity between objective probability and fear of victimization is particularly great (Boland, 1976; Hindelang et al., 1978).

There are two additional problems with the direct approach. First, we know little more about reducing actual crime than we know about reducing fear. Recent studies have seriously questioned the effectiveness of long-standing police practices (Kelling et al., 1974; Greenwood et al., 1975; Kansas City Police Dept., 1977). Secondly, if fear is out of proportion with the actual risk of victimization, reducing the threat of crime will not necessarily reduce fear levels. We add a caveat to this assessment later, but there is reason to believe that the direct approach of reducing crime will not be particularly effective in reducing fear.

Psychological Correlates of Fear

Several studies attempt to explain the phenomenon of fear by reference to neuroses or misinformation on the part of individuals. These studies employ a psychological approach to the problem, assuming that for some individuals and groups the fear of crime exceeds that which could be explained by objective risks. Strategies for reducing fear should therefore focus on correcting these misperceptions rather than on reducing the probability of victimization.

Beginning with the reports of the President's Commission, numerous studies have noted that fear of crime often manifests itself as xenophobia, fear of strangers (Brooks, 1974; Hackler, 1974; Conklin, 1975; Kim, 1976; Hindelang et al., 1978). Individuals also fear neighborhoods where there are many unfamiliar people on the street (Merry, 1976). These findings may be somewhat limited in applicability since they refer primarily to the presence of strangers in residential neighborhoods where unfamiliar persons are more obviously out of place. In downtown commercial shopping and business areas the presence of strangers is normal and may have a different impact.

Psychological approaches to fear reduction stress the importance of symbolic reassurances to those who are afraid. This can be done by either increasing symbols of security or by decreasing those associated with threats to security. If exposure to strangers cannot be eliminated, perhaps the perceived threat from strangers can be reduced. An example of this approach involves the symbolic role of police. Charles Bahn recommends that police officers be placed at fixed posts in cognitively central locations throughout the city. "Highly visible, constantly present, predictable, and well-known these officers would symbolize police presence and offer continuous reassurance" (1974:343). Bahn suggests that tall, red-haired policemen would be an added benefit because their greater visibility would increase the sense of omnipresent protection. This strategy does not assume that increased police presence reduces crime, but simply that it reduces the perceived threat of crime. Similar approaches would foster reassurance by decreasing the visibility of certain activities and types of individuals who are associated, correctly or incorrectly, with increased risk of crime. Loiterers, prostitutes, panhandlers and the like are associated with danger in the minds of many people. This question of civility is reflected in the study of a small industrial town in California which found that much fear of crime was simply fear of teenagers who lived in the area (Poveda, 1972). Areas where teenagers gathered, drinking beer and playing loud music, were identified as the most dangerous locations by residents of a small public housing project in a northeastern industrial city (Merry, 1976). Mangione and Fowler (1974) conclude that removing people and activities which are perceived as threatening might be one of the most effective strategies for reducing fear. A recent analysis of fear in four Chicago neighborhoods has shown that expressed concern about crime varies more closely with perceptions of incivility in the neighborhood than with neighborhood crime rates (Lewis and Maxfield, 1978)

Newspapers, television, and the movies are frequently singled out as prime contributors to overinflated estimates of crime (Bell, 1960; Dominick, 1973; Conklin, 1975; Fishman, 1977). The amount of crime a newspaper reports may bear only a tenuous relationship to the amount which is actually taking place. Referring to so-called crime waves, Conklin states, "Crime waves are probably created more easily by fluctuations in newspaper reporting of crime than by changes in official crime rates, since people have greater familiarity with and access to what they read in the papers than what appears in the annual FBI reports" (1975:23).

Social Disintegration

The third approach to the correlates of fear focuses on the social links which bind individuals into a communal network. This view draws attention away from individual perceptions to the role of the individual in the community as a whole. Some scholars believe that many symptoms of fear, tension, and crisis in the inner city can be attributed to a breakdown of the sense of community, or movement to "a community of limited liability" (Greer, 1962). "Community," as used in this context, refers to mutual observation of ". ... standards of right and seemly conduct in the public places in which one lives and moves" (Wilson, 1968:27).

Where social networks are strong, crime as well as feelings of insecurity may be reduced. Jane Jacobs, a principal advocate of this view, argues that peace and order do not derive from the activities of the police, but from an "... intricate, almost unconscious network of voluntary controls and standards among the people themselves" (1961:32). She recommends a variety of strategies designed to attract people and to increase the diversity of urban neighborhoods. These are preconditions for the generation of spontaneous street surveillance, an integral part of the informal control system. Implicit in much of what Jacobs says is a chain of causality linking increased community interaction to greater feelings of security and reductions in fear of crime. Research has shown that areas in which residents do engage in informal street surveillance are likely to have lower levels of crime than those in which such controls are absent (Springer, n.d.; Ley and Cybriwsky, 1974). A study of fear of crime among the elderly found that fear was lower in protective, age-homogeneous housing where social interaction is likely to be high (Gubrium, 1974). Kim (1976) presents survey data which suggest that fear of crime is lower where respondents believe that their neighbors: (1) are concerned about others, (2) are willing to help the police, and (3) would report a crime if they observed one.

Confidence that others will come to your aid if you are attacked may help reduce fear (Bickman et al., 1975). Studies of the circumstances under which individuals will intervene on behalf of other people in distress indicate that familiarity between victim and observer increases the chance of intervention. Hackler et al. demonstrate that even in circumstances where subjects and stooge "victims" had previously encountered one another only briefly, bystanders were more likely to intervene (1974). The authors also demonstrate that models of helping behavior increase the probability of intervention by individuals who observe the helping model. Programs directed at increasing citizens' reporting of crimes act to foster confidence that law enforcement, aided by reporting programs, is more effective. The study by Bickman et al. suggests that citizen crime reporting programs may also reduce fear by increasing actual and symbolic citizen involvement. The goal of these programs is to increase the likelihood of intervention on the part of individuals. To the extent that this is perceived by members of the community, feelings of safety may be increased, and fear reduced (1975: 58–61).

Physical Environment

The fourth general class of correlates of fear comes from the growing awareness of the effect of the physical environment on behavior and attitudes. The Crime Prevention Through Environmental Design (CPTED) program, under the National Institute of Law Enforcement and Criminal Justice, is a practical application of this theoretical approach. Basing its premises on the works of Jacobs, Oscar Newman, and others, the program seeks to establish strategies for restructuring the urban environment which will lead to the reduction of crime and fear.

One thrust of the CPTED approach is based upon the belief that physical changes can reduce opportunities for actual crime, and indirectly lead to a decrease in fear of crime. Poor lighting, blind spots,

302   VICTIMOLOGY: AN INTERNATIONAL JOURNAL

columns, and pillars behind which an assailant can hide are examples of physical attributes of the environment which may combine to produce a high risk of victimization and high levels of fear. Building designs and natural topography can either help or hinder natural surveillance which can have a related deterrent effect.

The distinction between public and private areas may be accentuated or blurred by CPTED modifications. In this way strategies can help to generate social ties and informal social controls. The design and use of sidewalks and parks, as well as the routing of neighborhood blocks can, according to Jacobs, reduce both crime and fear by: (1) attracting people, (2) circulating them throughout the area, and (3) distributing traffic more evenly throughout the day. Establishing clearly defined communal areas can serve the dual purpose of promoting surveillance and setting the stage for establishing interpersonal contacts. These can in turn help people distinguish their neighbors from potentially threatening strangers, and breed feelings of cohesion which can affect fear independent of any reduction in the incidence of crime. Such simple restructuring efforts as opening apartment or office doorways onto a common hallway may convert the area from an isolated private space into a more public area which facilitates informal surveillance (Rainwater, 1966).

A study of security and crime problems in Allentown, Pennsylvania by Barton-Aschman Associates found that well-lighted streets and sidewalks promoted feelings of safety, while areas containing numerous trees and shrubs affording easy concealment generated feelings of insecurity (1975). The authors of this study recommend environmental design strategies which increase intra-community interaction and alter neighborhood circulation and topography as a means of increasing security and reducing fear among residents of the neighborhood.

The four classes of fear reduction strategies discussed here are obviously interrelated. CPTED approaches alter characteristics of the physical environment which have effects on feelings of community, perceptions of risk, and the actual incidence of crime. As will be noted below, however, CPTED strategies are often very costly. Although these various approaches are related, they may be implemented separately. It should be possible to specify strategies for increasing the sense of community and natural surveillance independently of costly large-scale physical changes.

FEAR REDUCTION STRATEGIES FOR URBAN AREAS

Each of these general approaches to explaining fear suggests corresponding strategies to reduce fear of crime in urban areas. The approach which relates fear of crime directly to risk of victimization suggests that one set of strategies would aim at reducing crime. The other three approaches may be similarly translated into more specific strategies. Psychological correlates of fear may be affected by *confidence building* strategies. *Community building* strategies are directed at the problem of social disintegration. Characteristics of the physical environment may be altered by *physical rebuilding*. Because this paper is concerned specifically with fear reduction, we restrict our discussion to the last three categories, although problems concerning the relationship between crime and fear will continually emerge. These fear reduction strategies are not costless, and our discussion will evaluate some of the financial and other costs involved with each of these approaches to fear reduction.

Confidence Building Strategies

If fear of crime is caused largely by individual neuroses or by distorted information which exaggerates actual risk it may be possible to reduce fear by building the confidence of workers, shoppers and others who frequent downtown areas. We discuss five such strategies: (1) "Tell the Truth" campaigns, (2) Moderating the Media, (3) Show of Force, (4) Role Models, and (5) Crime Compensation Programs.

Tell the Truth Campaigns. Skogan suggests that "Perhaps information campaigns that 'tell the truth' about the crime problem and contribute more to a realistic public assessment of the nature of the crime problem in the United States might contribute to an overall reduction in the level of fear in urban communities" (1977:10). By reporting crime rates for downtown areas which more accurately reflect the incidence of crime relative to the population at risk, "tell the truth" campaigns may reduce fear of victimization among those who presently avoid traveling downtown. This type of strategy was used in Chicago to stimulate ridership on that city's rapid transit system. The Chicago Transit Authority (CTA) publicized the fact that following intensified police patrol on stations and trains the system had become one of the safest areas in the city. Official statistics indicated that the incidence of violent crime per passenger within the jurisdiction of the CTA was lower than in most areas in the city (Chicago Tribune, 9/25/75, 10/24/75, 3/7/76). Bill Veeck, owner of the Chicago White Sox baseball team, has made special efforts to point out that the area near his baseball stadium reports very few crimes compared to the nearby south-side ghettos, and has a crime rate that is extraordinarily low when computed for the population at risk (Chicago Tribune, 7/1/77).

Moderating the Media. Polite Society, Incorporated is an organization in the Chicago area formed in response to what its members feel to be too much violence on television. Similar actions on the part of concerned citizens in other cities could urge responsibility on the part of the media in the style and quantity of their coverage of crime and violence in the downtown area. Such efforts should be proceeded by monitoring media coverage to determine the magnitude of exaggeration. Does one television station feature more lurid coverage of crime stories? Do crimes in the downtown area get disproportionately more attention than similar crimes in other areas?

Show of Force. One response to reducing fear would be a variant on the general strategy of placing a policeman on every block. In spite of inconclusive evidence, most law enforcement agencies remain convinced that the best way to deter crime and generate feelings of security among citizens is to increase the number of policemen on patrol and to increase the general visibility of police. In response to a few highly publicized violent crimes on the city's transit system, the Chicago Police Department and a special crime commission have increased the number of uniformed officers randomly boarding buses and trains and riding for a few blocks. A number of uniformed but unarmed security personnel have also been added (Chicago Tribune, 6/23/78). The goal is not so much to reduce the already low rate of reported crime, but to provide visible symbols of reassurance for transit users. This program ". . . recognizes that the way people perceive crime is just as important as the actual incidence of crime" (Chicago Tribune, 6/26/78).

There are a number of ways to increase the visibility of police: moving to one-man patrol cars, increasing foot patrols, hiring civilian employees for administrative and para-police functions so that additional uniformed officers may be placed on patrol. The show of force strategy may also be implemented through private means. Many businesses hire security guards, install television surveillance cameras, and add other alarm systems. These strategies can be utilized more effectively by coordinating the various security forces of separate businesses and buildings, and by providing a central location for security personnel so that workers and shoppers would always know where they might go for help.

Role Models. Research on the conditions which promote helping behavior by bystanders indicates that intervention increases when models of helping behavior are present (Hackler et al., 1974). Feelings of security are also increased when individuals feel that someone is around to intervene on their behalf in threatening situations. This suggests that fear might be reduced by using models of helping behavior or "stooges" who act out distressing situations which have happy endings. This strategy might take two forms. First, conspicuous but odd or incongruous security personnel can be employed: middle-aged women or retired men for example. These individuals are members of groups generally considered to be most vulnerable to certain crimes, and their presence as confident, helpful security personnel can help convey the impression that downtown shopping areas are safe for everyone. The second type of role model would be a form of street theater where "dramas" are acted out by stooge victims and helpers to an audience which is unaware that the confrontation is staged. The goals of this strategy are twofold: (1) increase feelings on the part of the audience that people, strangers even, will come to their aid in a crisis; and (2) promote helping behavior on the part of those observing the role model.

Crime Compensation. Government-sponsored victim insurance is one method for dealing with fear of crime which is currently attracting some legislative attention. The reasoning behind this strategy is that if the perceived probabilities of becoming a victim cannot easily be lowered, then it should at least be possible to reduce the financial costs imposed by victimization. There is no evidence regarding whether such compensation would in fact reduce fear, and it is likely that the impact where violent crimes are concerned would be very slight. Since the majority of crimes committed in downtown areas are not crimes involving force, a compensation scheme might have some impact.

Confidence Building Strategies: Potential Costs. Each of these

REDUCING FEAR OF CRIME 305

confidence building strategies involves financial costs and the possibility of unforeseen negative consequences. A large scale show of force or crime compensation program is likely to be expensive. Providing a single additional patrolman in a typical large city at all hours requires adding sufficient manpower to cover three shifts, holidays, sick days, and weekends, plus additional capital expenses to back up the additional manpower, plus training expenses for new patrolmen. Richard Larson (1972) has estimated that ten additional patrol personnel are required to staff a single two-man patrol car around the clock. Considering direct salary and retirement benefits this can place the cost of one two-man car at over $200,000 per year. The total costs of crime compensation programs will also be very high. Since 1967 the New Jersey Crime Compensation Board has processed 12,951 claims, and paid a total of $11,388,000 in benefits (New York Times, 9/21/75).

There is some evidence that individuals may not fear victimization sufficiently to spend money on insurance premiums. The federal government has experimented with some programs for providing homeowners' and tenant insurance in high risk areas. Few buyers have taken out such policies despite very low premiums (New York Times, 4/14/76). There may be a threshold level of fear and crime necessary before individuals begin to participate in special insurance programs. On the other hand, highly publicized compensation or insurance programs may actually *increase* fear—an unintended outcome or "backlash" effect. People may interpret programs in this area as a last ditch effort to fulfill the government obligation of preserving life, limb, and the prevailing social order. It may be concluded, accurately or not, that cities have failed in their attempts to protect life and property with conventional police forces, and must now rely on insurance policies for "cooling out" the victims of crime.

Other confidence building strategies risk the danger of inducing backlash effects. In cases where elaborate and obvious attempts are made to reduce fear of crime there is the very real danger that the reverse will in fact occur. "Why," the average worker or shopper might ask, "would they be doing all this unless there really *is* a crime problem around here?" Aggressive advertising campaigns to tell the truth about crime rates might have just this result. Charles Bahn suggests that efforts to convince people that crime rates have fallen are often met with skeptical responses: ". . . since fear does not readily dissipate, some people suspect that the figures are being manipulated" (1974:341). Boosting the number or visibility of police entails a similar risk. The sound of frequent sirens and the sight of policemen challenging "suspicious looking" pedestrians can add to an atmosphere of tension and a feeling of being under siege.

The direct approach, show of force, and tell the truth strategies probably have the greatest potential for generating undesirable side effects and actually increasing fear, but other attempts to reduce fear may also backfire. Restricting press coverage of crime stories may clash with reporters' First Amendment rights. Role models demonstrating examples of helping behavior may sharpen the fears of downtown shoppers who had not previously witnessed a crime. In general these confidence building strategies attempt to change individual perceptions

306   VICTIMOLOGY: AN INTERNATIONAL JOURNAL

of crime and minimize the effects of fear on behavior. There remains the danger that attempts to convince people their fears are groundless will be instrumental in convincing them that their fears are justified.

Community Building Strategies

If social interaction builds interpersonal commitments which in turn generate feelings of security, less cohesive communities such as downtown central business districts could benefit by increasing the level of interaction among users. Community building strategies would focus on different groups: (1) interaction among workers and shoppers in downtown areas, and the surrounding inner-city community, and (2) interaction between the loosely defined downtown community and the law enforcement agencies empowered to protect it.

Increasing Interaction Among User Groups and The Inner City. The anonymity that pervades most downtown areas affects fear by decreasing the confidence that others will come to an individual's aid or summon help in event of a crisis. A measure similar to the Whistle-STOP program described by DuBow and Reed (1976) could increase the sense of community in general, and the feeling that others are available to help. This program was designed to increase citizen reporting and intra-community cooperation in the Hyde Park area surrounding the University of Chicago on the city's south side. The authors analyzed the impact of the program and report that certain categories of street crimes were significantly reduced and the citizen reporting of street crime increased. To the extent that there is a link between feelings of safety and reporting programs, this study is an indicator of the potential effectiveness of community-based programs directed at increased crime reporting. Downtown area businessmen could launch an "I Help a Friend" campaign to educate people regarding the best procedures for intervening in threatening situations and for summoning assistance. Participants in the program would be provided with tags or decals announcing their roles.

Workers in downtown areas represent a wealth of talents and resources generally inaccessible to inner-city residents. They may be a transient population in one sense, but daytime users have nearly as much stake in central areas as do the relatively small resident population. Members of the business and retail community could contact existing organizations in the surrounding area to establish programs for making these resources available. Several positive goals might be attained. Stereotypes of the inner city which feed off vague feelings of fear might begin to break down. Greater familiarity with the city might help shoppers and workers more accurately distinguish between relatively safe areas and those where the dangers are real.

If activity is increased in the late evening hours it would serve the added function of easing the fear generated by dark empty streets at night. Different activities aimed at different types of people could change the image of a deserted city. Existing facilities such as museums and theaters could extend hours and reduce admission prices to attract more patrons. Street theater and street musicians—traditionally harassed by police and resented by merchants—may perform positive functions by providing surveillance, attracting people, and creating a communal atmosphere. Area merchants and street artists in San Francisco seem to have struck mutually beneficial compromises concerning the location, timing, and noise levels of such activities.

Increasing Interaction With the Police. When people know and trust their police protectors they are likely to feel more secure. Research has shown that victims who received satisfactory service from responding police officers were less likely to exhibit increased fear as a result of their experience (Parks, 1976; Kim, 1976). This suggests that providing satisfactory police service to victims and potential victims may aid in reducing fear of crime.

Team policing and increased foot patrols are two approaches to policing that may help reduce fear levels. While the effectiveness of these techniques in reducing crime is yet to be proven, a number of law enforcement officials have suggested that they can help to increase interaction between citizens and the police. Although its exact format varies, team policing essentially involves the permanent assignment of patrolmen to a specific beat. The officers follow complaints from initial calls through clearance. When policemen are rotated among different beats and different shifts, it becomes more difficult for citizens to get to know them as individuals. Police in New York are now being instructed to introduce themselves to merchants and residents on their beats, reversing policies which isolated patrolmen from their clientele in attempts to avoid petty corruption (New York Times, 5/17/78).

Community-Building Strategies—Potential Costs. Some of the community-building strategies can be implemented at very low cost, and relatively quickly. As with confidence building strategies there are dangers that attempts to increase community interaction will backfire. The community-building strategies are based upon the presumption that shared interests and common purposes lie beneath the surface features of suspicion and mistrust. The class, race, and cultural differences that set off the downtown area from its lower class environs may, however, prove intractable. If this is the case, increasing interaction and exposure may aggravate suppressed resentments and sharpen already existing fears.

Fortress building is the counterpart to community building strategies and evolves from the premise that the central city harbors antagonisms which cannot be soothed. If efforts to integrate the central business district and the surrounding community fail, an alternate strategy is to reduce fear by sharpening the distinction between office and shopping complexes and their inner-city environment. This approach means depicting commercial and shopping areas as zones of safety in the middle of a dangerous city. Transportation corridors and express buses to outlying areas can be established to link the downtown area with safe residential communities and transportation nodes.

The symbolic importance of transportation to and from central business districts is illustrated by Richard Peck's (1976) science fiction view of the future of a large city. In a story he describes the perilous journey of a commuter train in the future, speeding out of the protected environment of the central business area, and moving through concentric rings populated by hostile lower class workers and derelicts, heavy industry, high-rise low-status white collar housing, and finally to the increasingly distant suburbs. Along the way the train's defenses are tested by invaders attempting to breach the city's force field, and by terrorists who erect a barricade and force the train to a stop. A premonition of this vision may be found in Chicago where rapid transit service from the North Shore suburb of Evanston gives one the feeling of watching the inner city on television as the train winds non-stop through public housing projects and dilapidated neighborhoods.

The fortress building response assumes that fear can be reduced only by sealing off the central business district and controlling access. The cost of this option comes not only in initial investments in defensive hardware, but more significantly in fundamental infringements on civil liberties and personal freedom of mobility.

Physical Rebuilding Strategies

It has been suggested that certain physical changes can improve the safety of downtown office shopping areas and reduce fear as well. Crime Prevention Through Environmental Design strategies can be grouped according to their general goals: (1) increase and redistribute circulation of people, (2) improve natural surveillance, and (3) provide better lighting and improve general appearance.

Improve Circulation. The intent of circulation changes is to minimize the amount of unused space, and to spread population flow evenly through time and space. This can eliminate the fear-inducing experience of walking down an empty corridor or street. An alternative to closing unused areas of large public buildings is to give them new and interesting uses which will attract more people. Since lunch hours in commercial and shopping districts are times of increased foot traffic, CPTED strategies may be most effective in providing mobile and novel eating places. Popular hot dog wagons and gourmet lunch carts are regular features around downtown parks and public squares in Washington, D.C. Some of the more open but little used areas in large buildings could accomodate sandwich vendors and lunch carts which would attract shoppers and workers alike. Musical groups might provide entertainment during lunch and evening shopping hours. These devices are particularly useful since they can be easily relocated to channel traffic to or away from certain areas, thus increasing the mobility of midday crowds.

Improve Natural Surveillance Opportunities. Professional security services and red-haired policemen cannot replace the need for natural surveillance. Structures which impede natural surveillance and reduce the effectiveness of security patrols can also increase individual fears. Many of the corridors in modern office buildings lack the natural surveillance opportunities which could be provided simply by installing windows in office doors. Eliminating what appear to be hiding places enhances feelings of safety. The subway stations of Washington, D.C.'s Metro system were designed with vaulted ceilings to avoid the hiding places afforded by supporting columns.

Improve Lighting and Appearance. People generally feel safer when streets and hallways are well-lighted. The Allentown, Pennsylvania study by Barton-Aschman Associates (1975) found that residents listed good lighting as an important factor increasing their feelings of safety. However, the same survey found that many of those who did fear crime felt that lighting in their neighborhood was already quite good. Jane Jacobs asserts that lighting is important only when accompanied by the assurance that people will be around to witness what occurs.

Upgrading maintenance throughout downtown areas can also help to reduce fear and increase the use of vacant space. The windows of vacant shops can be rented or donated for advertising purposes; they may be used to display art or as sources for public information. It is often possible to install plantings, fountains, large sculptures, and other such devices which have come to characterize suburban shopping malls.

Physical Rebuilding: Potential Costs. Extensive physical changes such as eliminating blind turns, re-routing pedestrian traffic, and improving lighting are potentially very costly modifications. Certainly some environmental changes can be incorporated into plans for redevelopment and new construction in downtown areas. Although the initial capital investment in physical changes is potentially high, these are one-time expenditures, and operating expenses can be considerably lower than, for example, augmenting the city police force.

Like the other approaches to fear reduction, environmental changes can also backfire. Many people find bright sodium vapor lights unsettling. On a lonely street better lighting may simply increase the feeling of being vulnerable and exposed. If vaulted ceilings serve to provide clear views for rapid transit passengers, they also make it easier for muggers to scan station platforms for police and witnesses. One problem which may occur with CPTED approaches and other strategies exists where attempts to convince law abiding citizens that an area is safe actually serve to *attract* criminals who sense a new area to be exploited. Any strategy devised to attract attention and crowds may attract criminals as well. Potential robbers and criminals are just as attracted to brightness and crowds as are office workers and shoppers.

The most serious undesirable effect of fear reduction campaigns in general is their potential for increasing carelessness. Many community building and other strategies depend on the alertness and cooperation of people. There is the chance that as fear reduction policies succeed individuals will begin to abandon the security procedures which had been responsible for declining crime rates in the first place. These concerns relate to the possibility that crime rates may be low in downtown areas *because* people avoid them. Since few are willing to venture into these areas at night their precautions may have deflated the crime rate below that for surrounding residential areas where there is nighttime traffic. In other words, the avoidance behavior influenced by fear may be responsible for the low crime rate in central business areas, in which case *reducing fear* may be followed by an *increase* in the incidence of crime. Research has shown that avoidance of certain places in the city at certain times of day is one of the most common behavioral reactions to crime

(Ennis, 1967; Reiss, 1967; Conklin, 1976; Merry, 1976; Garofalo et al., 1978). If fear of crime in downtown areas is sufficient to prevent people from going there during certain hours, then the incidence of crime will drop as potential victims stay away from the area. If fear reduction campaigns succeed, they may reduce avoidance behavior and increase the supply of victims. This means that the fears of people who avoid certain areas of the city may indeed be rational, and based upon the accurate perception that given a supply of unwary victims the incidence of downtown crime will jump.

SUMMARY AND CONCLUSION

There are no cost-free solutions to the problem of fear of crime and its impacts on the central business districts of large urban areas. Not only are fear and crime reduction programs expensive, they are potentially dangerous. Some approaches aimed at fear reduction may actually increase fear among certain people, while other strategies may increase the incidence of crime itself. This can occur in two ways: (1) the policies which are designed to attract people to downtown areas may also attract criminals, and (2) the increased feelings of security which follow from successful fear reduction campaigns attract more potential victims and may result in carelessness.

Social scientists and urban decision makers must begin to recognize that fear, as distinct from the actual threat of victimization, can be manipulated by an appropriate policy. The effects of fear on the aggregate urban economy are no less debilitating than the effects of crime itself. Avoidance behavior and costly protective devices accelerate the decline in patronage of central city shopping districts and increase the cost of doing business in those areas. Focusing on fear as a policy goal also reflects the difficulty of achieving meaningful reductions in the incidence of crime. Dramatic reduction of crime rates would require vast expenditures in dollars and in civil liberties foregone. Increasing the money and authority available to police to achieve such goals is not feasible in U.S. cities.

None of the strategies described here can be considered a complete answer to the problem of fear in large urban areas. We are limited in this assessment by the fragmentation of existing social science literature regarding fear. Little is known about fear of crime as such, and our limited knowledge is even less often formulated to facilitate the design of fear reduction policies. Because of this we should not too easily dismiss the conjecture that those who fear crime in central business districts are accurate in their perceptions of risk. These strategies for reducing fear are not intended to be a panacea in the same vein as performing paper and pencil manipulations of official crime statistics. They are simply possible solutions to the problem of fear of crime in large cities.

REFERENCES

Bahn, Charles
    1974   "The Reassurance Factor in Police Patrol." Criminology 12: 338–345.

Barton-Aschman Associates
    1975   "Security Problems and Strategies," Allentown Community

REDUCING FEAR OF CRIME 311

Development Project, First and Sixth Wards. Washington, DC: Barton-Aschman Associates.

Bell, Daniel
1960 The End of Ideology. New York: Free Press.
Bickman, L., S. K. Green, J. Edwards, S. Shane-DuBow, P. J. Lavrakas, N. North-Walker, and S. Borkowski
1975 "Towards Increasing Citizen Responsibility, Surveillance, and Reporting of Crimes." Prepared for NILECJ, Law Enforcement Assistance Administration, Department of Justice.

Boland, Barbara
1976 "Patterns of Urban Crime," in Wesley G. Skogan, ed., Sample Surveys of the Victims of Crime. Cambridge, MA: Ballinger.

Brooks, James
1974 "The Fear of Crime in the United States." Crime and Delinquency July:241–244.

Chicago Tribune
9/25/75 "Rapid Transit Called 'Safe' "
10/24/75 "CTA Holdups Cut 50%: Rochford"
3/7/76 "Despite Police Progress, Terror Still Rides the Subways"
7/1/77 "Veeck Springs to Sox Neighborhood's Defense"
6/23/78 "New Plan to Fight Crime on CTA"
6/26/78 "City Takes Action to Cut CTA Crime"

Conklin, John E.
1976 "Robbery, the Elderly, and Fear: An Urban Problem in Search of Solution," in Jack and Sharon S. Goldsmith, eds., Crime and the Elderly. Lexington, MA: Lexington Books.
1975 The Impact of Crime. New York: Macmillan.

Dominick, Joseph
1973 "Crime and Law Enforcement on Prime-Time Television." Public Opinion Quarterly. Summer.

DuBow, Fredric, Edward McCabe, and Gail Kaplan
1978 "Reactions to Crime: A Critical Review of the Literature." Draft working paper, Reactions to Crime Project, Center for Urban Affairs, Northwestern University.

DuBow, Fredric and David E. Reed
1976 "The Limits of Victim Surveys: A Community Case Study," in Wesley G. Skogan, ed., Sample Surveys of the Victims of Crime. Cambridge, MA: Ballinger.

Ennis, Phillip H.
1967 Criminal Victimization in the United States: A Report of a National Survey. Field Surveys II, President's Commission on Law Enforcement and Administration of Justice. Washington, D.C.: U.S. Government Printing Office.

Erskine, Hazel
1974 "The Polls: Fear of Violence and Crime." Public Opinion Quarterly 38:Spring.

Federal Bureau of Investigation
1977 Crime in America, 1976. U.S. Department of Justice. Washington, D.C.: U.S. Government Printing Office.

Fishman, Mark
1977 "Crime Waves as Ideology," Prepared for presentation at the Annual Meeting of the Society for the Study of Social Problems, Chicago.

Greenwood, Peter W. and Joan Petersilia
1975 The Criminal Investigation Process: Volume I: Summary and Policy Implications. Santa Monica: Rand Corporation, R–1776–DOJ.

Greer, Scot
1962 The Emerging City. New York: Free Press.
Gubrium, Jaber F.
1974 "Victimization in Old Age." Crime and Delinquency 20:245–250.

312   VICTIMOLOGY: AN INTERNATIONAL JOURNAL

Hackler, James C., Kwai-Yiu Ho, and Carol Urquhart-Ross
1974   "The Willingness to Intervene: Differing Community Character-
                istics." Social Problems 21:328–344.
Hindelang, Michael J., Michael R. Gottfredson, and James Garofalo
1978   Victims of Personal Crime. Cambridge, MA: Ballinger.
Jacobs, Jane
1961   The Death and Life of Great American Cities. New York:
                Vintage Books.
Kansas City Police Department
1977   Response Time Analysis: Executive Summary. Kansas City MO:
                Board of Police Commissions.
Kelling, George L., Tony Pate, Duncan Dieckman, and Charles E. Brown
1974   The Kansas City Preventive Patrol Experiment: A Technical
                Report. Washington, D.C.: Police Foundation.
Kim, Young Ja
1976   "The Social Correlates of Perceptions of Neighborhood Crime
                Problems and Fear of Victimization." Working Paper, Reactions
                to Crime Project, Center for Urban Affairs, Northwestern Uni-
                versity.
Larson, Richard C.
1972   Urban Police Patrol Analysis. Cambridge, MA: MIT Press.
Lewis, Dan A. and Michael G. Maxfield
1978   "Fear in the Neighborhoods: A Preliminary Investigation of the
                Impact of Crime in Chicago." Reactions to Crime Papers, Number
                1, Center for Urban Affairs, Northwestern University.
Ley, David and Roman Cybriwsky
1974   "The Spatial Ecology of Stripped Cars." Environment and
                Behavior 6:March.
Mangione, Thomas W. and Floyd J. Fowler
1974   "Correlates of Fear: A Prelude to a Field Experiment." Person-
                ality and Social Psychology Bulletin 1:371–373.
Merry, Salley Engle
1976   "The Management of Danger in a High Crime Urban Neighbor-
                hood." Paper presented at the Annual Meeting of the American
                Anthropological Association.
New York Times
9/21/75   "Follow Up: State Crime Compensation"
4/14/76   "Inexpensive Insurance Against Crime"
5/17/78   "Commissioner Tells Policemen to Meet People on the Beat"
Parks, Roger B.
1976   "Police Response to Victimization: Effects on Citizen Attitudes
                and Perceptions," in Wesley G. Skogan, ed. Sample Surveys of the
                Victims of Crime. Cambridge, MA: Ballinger.
Peck, Richard E.
1976   "Gantlet," in Ralph Clem, Martin Henry Greenberg, and Joseph
                Olander, eds. The City 2000 A.D.: Urban Life Through Science
                Fiction. Greenwich, CT: Fawcett Crest.
Poveda, Tony
1972   "The Fear of Crime in a Small Town." Crime and Delinquency
                18:147–153.
President's Commission on Law Enforcement and Administration of Justice
1967   Task Force Report: Crime and Its Impact—An Assessment.
                Washington, D.C.: U.S. Government Printing Office.
Rainwater, Lee
1966   "Fear and the House-As-Haven in the Lower Class." Journal of
                the American Institute of Planners 32:23–31.
Reiss, Albert J., Jr.
1967   Studies on Crime and Law Enforcement in Major Metropolitan
                Areas. Field Surveys III, Part 1, President's Commission on Law
                Enforcement and Administration of Justice. Washington, D.C.:
                U.S. Government Printing Office.

REDUCING FEAR OF CRIME 313

Rosenthal, Jack
1969   "The Cage of Fear in Cities Beset by Crime." Life 67, July 11.
Skogan, Wesley G.
1979   "Crime in Contemporary America," in Hugh Davis Graham and
              Ted Robert Gurr, eds., The History of Violence in America, 2nd
              Edition. Beverly Hills, CA: Sage.
1977   "Public Policy and the Fear of Crime in Large American Cities,"
              in John A. Gardiner, ed., Public Law and Public Policy. New York:
              Praeger.
Springer, Larry
n.d.   "Crime, Feelings of Safety, and Street Surveillance," Department
              of Geography, Virginia Polytechnic and State University,
              Blacksburg, VA, mimeo.
Wilson, James Q.
1968   "The Urban Unease: Community versus the City," Public
              Interest, Vol. 12.

For reprints of this article, contact Jeffrey Henig, Department of Political Science, George Washington University, Washington, DC 20052, or Michael G. Maxfield, Center for Urban Affairs, Northwestern University, Evanston, IL 60201.

[26]

Community Crime Prevention:
An Analysis of a
Developing Strategy

Dan A. Lewis
Greta Salem

Crime prevention strategies often aim at changing the motivations and pre-dispositions of offenders. A new approach has developed within the last dec-ade which focuses on changing the behavior of potential victims. The authors explore the theoretical foundations of the new strategies for reducing crime, commonly known as community crime prevention. They suggest that the in-novation is a result of a major shift in the research paradigm for studying the effects of crime.

The orientation underlying community crime prevention is labeled the "vic-timization perspective." Following a description of some limitations in that perspective, the authors offer, as an alternative, a perspective oriented toward social control. The social control perspective, which is based on the empirical findings of several recently completed research projects, offers a theoretical foundation both for a fresh approach to the study of the effects of crime and for the development of policies for community crime prevention.

Crime prevention for the first three-quarters of the twentieth century was premised on a set of principles that changed very little. Pre-venting crime meant modifying the predisposition of offenders to commit illegal acts. Whether they concentrated on altering the environmental fac-tors that influence offenders or on working directly with offenders in a therapeutic setting, most prevention strategies since the emergence of the Progressive Era sought to prevent crime by changing the victimizers. Those strategies, however, came under attack in the late 1960s. Critics noted the increasing crime rates as evidence that nothing appeared to work in preventing crime. As a consequence, many of the then-current prevention strategies fell into disrepute. The 1970s saw a change in the

DAN A. LEWIS: Assistant Professor of Education, Urban Affairs and Policy Re-search, Northwestern University, Evanston, Illinois. GRETA SALEM: Assistant Pro-fessor of Social Science, Alverno College, Milwaukee.

Prepared under Grant Number 78-NI-AX-0057 from the National Institute of Law En-forcement and Criminal Justice, Law Enforcement Assistance Administration, United States Department of Justice. Points of view or opinions in this document are those of the authors and do not necessarily represent the official position or policies of the Department of Justice.

D. A. Lewis, G. Salem

orientation of those concerned about crime prevention and crime control with the potential for significantly modifying social reform in America. Exemplified in the *community crime prevention* approach, the new orientation shifts the locus of attention from potential offenders and their motivations to potential victims and their environment. The rationale for this approach is summed up in the Hartford Crime Prevention Program.

1. The crime rate in a residential neighborhood is a product of the linkage between offender motivation and the opportunities provided by the residents, users, and environmental features of that neighborhood.

2. The crime rate for a specific offense can be reduced by lessening the opportunities for that crime to occur.

3. Opportunities can be reduced by: (a) Altering the physical aspects of buildings and streets to increase surveillance capabilities and lessen target/victim vulnerability, to increase the neighborhood's attractiveness to residents, and to decrease its fear-producing features; (b) Increasing citizen concerns about and involvement in crime prevention and the neighborhood in general; and (c) Utilizing the police to support the above.

4. Opportunity-reducing activities will lead not only to a reduction in the crime rate but also to a reduction in fear of crime. The reduced crime and fear will mutually reinforce each other, leading to still further reductions in both.[1]

Rather than attempting to alter the predispositions and motivations of the criminal, as Progressive reforms throughout the century had sought to do, community crime prevention strategies prevent crime by altering the relations between the criminal, victim, and environment, reducing the opportunity for victimization. Prevention in this new formulation is based on a theory of crime causation that signifies a radical departure from the motivational and socialization theories that dominated American criminology and crime prevention over the last half century. Crime is to be prevented, not by changing perpetrators, but rather by educating potential victims and thus limiting the opportunities for victimization.

This shift in conceptions of crime prevention grew out of research that focused on the victim rather than the offender. The authors of this literature, funded by the National Commission on Crime and the Administration of Justice, attempted to determine both the level of crime and the level of fear Americans were experiencing.[2] In recognition of its emphasis, we

---

1. Brian Hollander et al., *Reducing Residential Crime and Fear: The Hartford Neighborhood Crime Prevention Program: Executive Summary* (Washington, D.C.: Dept. of Justice, February 1980), p. 2.

2. Albert J. Reiss, Jr., *Studies in Crime and Law Enforcement in Major Metropolitan Areas*, Field Survey III, Vol. 1 (Washington, D.C.: Govt. Printing Office, 1967); Albert D. Biderman et al., *Report on a Pilot Study in the District of Columbia on Victimization and Attitudes toward Law Enforcement* (Washington, D.C.: Govt. Printing Office, 1967); Philip H. Ennis, *Criminal Victimization in the United States: A Report of a National Survey* (Washington, D.C.: Govt. Printing Office, 1967).

have labeled this orientation the "victimization perspective." The perspective has served as a conceptual framework for much research and policy of the past decade, and has had considerable effects on the writings and programs produced. In exploring that influence in the first section of the article, we will argue that there are inherent limitations in the framework that both constrain the focus of the research and explain the programmatic weaknesses of the policies it has spawned. The policy and conceptual weaknesses are addressed in an alternative framework, the "social control perspective," which we describe in the concluding section. There is much of value in the community crime prevention strategy; with the proper modifications, efforts of this type can greatly enhance the community's capacity to prevent crime.

THE VICTIMIZATION PERSPECTIVE

A shift in methodology reflected in the victimization perspective heralded a change in definition. Crimes, which until these studies were conducted had been conceived of as *acts* committed by offenders, were now defined as *events* in which offenders and victims participated. The structural characteristics of these events, in terms of time and space, became the variables that could account for them.

The notion of crime as event rather than act has important implications. Events shape the social world; as the events cluster in time and space, they have far-reaching consequences for those people who experience them. Victimizations are events that affect people and are important to that extent. Acts, on the other hand, are the behaviors of individuals. Predicting an act is a function of explaining what motivates or shapes the behavior of the actor, while predicting an event entails assessing the relative importance of the significant factors that constitute the event. Furthermore, events shape the behaviors of those who experience them. Fear of crime, according to the victimization perspective, is a consequence of experiencing or anticipating victimization.[3] The study of fear of crime, however, illustrates most vividly the limitations of that perspective.

Albert Biderman et al., Albert Reiss, and Philip Ennis all administered surveys designed to measure the amount of fear reported by respondents.[4] Fear, although measured differently in each survey, was implicitly defined as anticipation of the occurrence of a crime event. When anticipation was high, fear, by definition, was high as well. An increase in crime was assumed to generate an increase in fear. In taking as their task

3. Dan A. Lewis and Greta Salem, *Crime and the Urban Community* (Evanston, Ill.: Center for Urban Affairs, Northwestern University, 1980).

4. Biderman et al., *Report on a Pilot Study in the District of Columbia*; Reiss, *Studies in Crime and Law Enforcement in Major Metropolitan Areas*; Ennis, *Criminal Victimization in the United States*.

documenting the level of fear among respondents, all three researchers assumed that fear was related to the amount of crime to which respondents were exposed. Indeed, given the measures employed by the scholars, it would have been impossible to dissociate fear of crime from the anticipated crime events. For example, Biderman et al. measured "fear of personal attack" by one item:

> Would you say there has been an increase in violent crime here in Washington? I mean attacks on people—like shootings, stabbings and rapes? Would you say that there's now very much more of this sort of thing, just a little bit more, not much difference, or that there is no more than five years ago?[5]

To report an increase in violent crime events is to score high on fear of crime (or, in this case, attack). Reiss, while avoiding a direct discussion of fear, subsumed the topic in a more general discussion of "citizen perceptions about crime in their areas." Here again, anticipation of the crime event was synonymous with fear:

> When you think about your chances of getting robbed, threatened, beaten up, or anything of that sort, would you say your neighborhood is (compared to other neighborhoods in town): very safe, above average, less safe, or one of the worst?
> In what ways have you changed your habits because of fear of crime? (stay off streets, use taxis or cars, avoid being taken out, don't talk to strangers)[6]

Both Ennis and Biderman et al. developed measures of fear premised on the imputed relationship between a dangerous neighborhood and the level of fear among individuals in that neighborhood. Biderman et al. called this measure an "index of anxiety," and it comprised the following items:

> 1. What is it about the neighborhood that was most important? [This was asked only of those residents who indicated the neighborhood was more important than the house in selecting their present residence.] (Safety or moral characteristics, convenience or aesthetic characteristics)
> 2. When you think about the chances of getting beaten up would you say this neighborhood is very safe, about average, less safe than most, one of the worst?
> 3. Is there so much trouble that you would move if you could? [Again, a screen question asked only of those who did not say their neighborhood was very safe.]
> 4. Are most of your neighbors quiet or are there some who create disturbances? (All quiet, few disturbances, many disturbances)

---

5. Biderman et al., *Report on a Pilot Study in the District of Columbia*, p. 132; see also Appendix D, p. 11.
6. Reiss, *Studies in Crime and Law Enforcement in Major Metropolitan Areas*, pp. 4, 35 (App. A).

Community Crime Prevention   **409**

5. Do you think that crime has been getting better or worse here in Washington during the past year? (Better, worse, same)[7]

Ennis distinguished between "fear of crime" and "perception of risk." He measured fear by the following items:

1. How safe do you feel walking alone in your neighborhood during the day?
2. How safe do you feel walking alone in your neighborhood after dark?
3. How often do you walk in your neighborhood after dark?
4. Have you wanted to go somewhere recently but stayed home because it was unsafe?
5. How concerned are you about having your house broken into?[8]

Risk was measured by two items:

1. How likely is it a person will be robbed or attacked on the streets around here? (Very likely, somewhat likely, somewhat unlikely, or very unlikely)
2. Compared to other parts of this city (county) how likely is it that your home will be broken into? (Much more likely, somewhat more likely, somewhat less likely, much less likely, no real difference)[9]

Ennis distinguished between "feeling unsafe" (the report and assessment of the possibility that a crime will occur) and risk. But his fear measure seems as much an assessment of the neighborhood as it is a report on the respondent's sense of uneasiness.

As Terry Baumer has pointed out, there is little published information on how these early measures were developed,[10] but for our purposes it is their content rather than their methodological limitations that is of interest. This early work assumes an association between the respondent's fear (as a reported internal state) and the number of victimizations the respondent anticipates. Fear is assumed to be a consequence of the potential for victimization; thus, the question facing the researcher is how that fear is distributed within a given population. The neighborhood is seen as a setting within which victimization takes place. If the respondent scores high as an *anticipator* of victimization, he is defined as fearful. A neighborhood is fear inducing to the extent that it provides a context for criminal activity. Thus, victimizations become the catalyst for fear; and this assumption limits the range of variables related to the fear-producing process. It is assumed that only crime causes fear. Fear, from this perspective, is a *consequence*, a *response* in time, of contact with crime events. If direct victimization fails to account for particularly high levels of fear,

7. Biderman et al., *Report on a Pilot Study in the District of Columbia*, p. 121.
8. Ennis, *Criminal Victimization in the United States*, pp. 72–75.
9. Ibid., pp. 75–76.
10. Terry Baumer, "The Dimensions of Fear: A Preliminary Investigation" (Evanston, Ill.: Reactions to Crime Project, Center for Urban Affairs, Northwestern University).

then indirect contact, usually through the media or personal communication, is postulated as the mechanism through which the experience of crime has affected the respondent.

However, Ennis, Biderman et al., and Reiss, although focusing on different issues, all found that fear was not directly or straightforwardly related to the level of victimization. Although the amount of crime in an area generally predicted the level of fear among the area residents, there were enough anomalies in these findings to raise the question of what other factors besides the level of victimization affected the level of fear among respondents. Citizens least likely to be victimized (females and the elderly), for example, exhibited the highest levels of fear.[11] Furthermore, the relationship between victimization levels and citizens' assessments of the crime problem is inconsistent at best:

> We have found that attitudes of citizens regarding crime are less affected by their past victimization than by their ideas about what is going on in their community—fears about a *weakening of social controls* on which they feel their safety and the broader fabric of social life is ultimately dependent.[12]

> All of the factors discussed above—the ambiguous relationship between victimization and the fear of crime, the indications that crime is not generally perceived as an immediate threat, and the mixing of fear of crime with fear of strangers—point to the conclusion that what has been measured in research as the "fear of crime" is not simply fear of crime. Many of those involved in the study of the "fear of crime" probably recognize this conclusion, at least implicitly. But there are good reasons for making the conclusion explicit and exploring its ramifications.[13]

Crime and Community

When the victimization perspective is applied to the analysis of crime and community, other difficulties emerge. These are illustrated in John Conklin's study entitled the *Impact of Crime*.[14] Rejecting Emile Durkheim's concept of the functionality of deviance in strengthening communities, Conklin argues that fear of crime robs citizens of the capacity to trust, isolates them, and thus contributes to the decline of community. Crime in this analysis is implicitly defined as the number of victimizations in the community:

11. Fay Lomax Cook and Thomas Cook, "Evaluating the Rhetoric of Crisis: A Case Study of Criminal Victimization of the Elderly" (Chicago, Ill.: School of Social Work, Loyola University).

12. Biderman et al., *Report on a Pilot Study in the District of Columbia*, p. 160.

13. James Garofalo and John Laub, "The Fear of Crime: Broadening Our Perspectives," *Victimology*, vol. 3, nos. 3 and 4 (1978), pp. 242–53.

14. John E. Conklin, *The Impact of Crime* (New York: Macmillan, 1975).

Community Crime Prevention   411

> Little of the material we have examined . . . suggests that Durkheim was correct in arguing that crime brings people together and strengthens social bonds. Instead, crime produces insecurity, distrust, and a negative view of the community. Although we lack conclusive evidence, crime also seems to reduce social interaction as fear and suspicion drive people apart. This produces a disorganized community that is unable to exercise informal social control over deviant behavior.[15]

This scenario is predicated on the notion that people react to crime as individuals. Rather than collectively sanctioning the criminal behavior, as Durkheim would anticipate, citizens react individually to fear and seek to protect themselves (e.g., buying guns and locks, not going out), thus breaking down community cohesion.

Conklin's discussion of community hinges on the distinction he makes between *individual* and *collective* responses to crime. The importance of these responses in turn stems from Conklin's use of the victimization perspective, for the logic of responding individually hinges on the salience of the victimization experience. Individual responses are assumed to be the normal reactions to the fear, or experience, of victimization. Thus, the conclusion that individual responses have negative consequences hinges on the imputed salience of victimization. Interestingly enough, this line of reasoning makes the *response* to victimization, rather than victimization itself, the central phenomenon. Conklin goes on to argue that when a community can respond collectively, crime does integrate:

> Crime weakens the fabric of social life by increasing fear, suspicion, and distrust. It also reduces public support for the law, in terms of unwillingness to report crime and criticism of the police. However, under certain conditions people will engage in collective action to fight crime. They may work for a political candidate who promises to restore law and order. They may call meetings of community residents to plan an attack on crime. Sometimes they may even band together in a civilian police patrol to carry out the functions that the police are not effectively performing for them. Since people who perceive high crime rates often hold the police responsible for crime prevention, we would expect such patrols to emerge where people feel very threatened by crime, believe that the police cannot protect them, and think from past experience with community groups that the people themselves can solve the problem.[16]

The collective response, in terms of the victimization perspective, is an attempt to exert social control. Like fear, it is a *response* to crime, but when it will emerge and the shape it may assume in varying circumstances are left unspecified. Since crime and fear atomize communities, it is not at all clear when we should expect to see collective action develop, nor why

15. Ibid., p. 99.
16. Ibid., p. 185.

it emerges in some contexts but not in others. The victimization perspective describes the weakening of community solidarity as a *consequence* of crime and thus fear. The capacity of a community to exert social control is linked to the reduction of fear, as well as crime. The result is a strategy for crime prevention postulating that to build a community is to deter crime. This is the strategy currently referred to as community crime prevention.

Community crime prevention seeks to reduce the number of victimizations in a neighborhood by increasing the capacity of that neighborhood to respond collectively. This application of Durkheimian sociology to a new approach to studying crime (the victimization perspective) has resulted in several new crime prevention programs sponsored by federal agencies. The goal of increasing informal control through action by citizens is reminiscent of the activities derived from the social disorganization theories of the Chicago School of Sociology,[17] with, however, a major difference in assumptions. The Chicago sociologists regarded social disorganization as the cause of local problems, which they sought to assuage with strategies designed to induce social cohesion. The community crime prevention programs define victimizations and their negative consequences (fear, isolation, and distrust) as the problem, and aim to induce cohesion by reducing crime.

A Critique of Community Crime Prevention

The utility of Community Crime Prevention strategies depends in large degree on how well the victimization perspective captures the experience of citizens with crime. There are several key empirical questions about the relationship between victimizations, fear, and individual and collective responses that must be addressed. The victimization perspective posits the centrality of victimization events in community crime prevention. As individuals experience victimizations, they assess their risk as increased and their concerns rise. They react either individually, which is likely to increase their community's victimization level, or collectively with neighbors, which may reduce victimizations and improve social cohesion. Intervention strategies are aimed at increasing the likelihood that the citizen will participate in collective efforts, thus preventing victimizations and increasing community cohesion.

The policies that follow from this construction of the crime problem are designed to enable collective responses. The response rather than the crime itself becomes the focus of action. Thus, unlike the early reformers

17. James T. Carey, *Sociology and Public Affairs: The Chicago School* (London, England: Sage, 1975).

Community Crime Prevention 413

Figure 1. Community Crime Prevention Paradigm

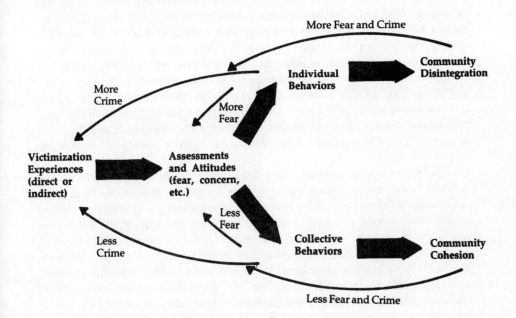

who were concerned with the motivation of the offenders, the current crime prevention strategists emphasize the responses of the victims. In encouraging collective responses, they assume that crime (as defined by the victimization perspective) is the most potent force in inducing fear and that citizens can be educated to respond collectively rather than individually when the threat of crime impinges on a community.

However, a five-year study, *Reactions to Crime*, conducted at the Center for Urban Affairs, Northwestern University, has produced findings that suggest that citizens define the crime problem in ways that are inconsistent with the assumptions of the victimization approach and thus are unlikely to respond to appeals based on those definitions. These findings have led us to construct an alternative framework for analysis of crime and community, which we have labeled the "social control perspective." Analyses conducted within the framework of this perspective, we argue, make it possible both to define the problems and to devise crime prevention strategies to elicit involvement in ways that are more consistent with the perceptions and interests of the neighborhood residents who are expected to participate. We report the relevant findings and describe the conceptual framework below.

414   **D. A. Lewis, G. Salem**

THE SOCIAL CONTROL PERSPECTIVE

Our examination of fear of crime in ten neighborhoods in Chicago, San Francisco, and Philadelphia revealed a broad range of concerns that included but were not limited to the crimes considered by those working within the victimization perspective.[18] Respondents questioned about crime problems described a range of what we have labeled "incivilities" as undesirable features of their communities—abandoned buildings, teenagers hanging around, illegal drug use, and vandalism.[19] In most instances, these other problems appeared to generate at least as much concern as did the crimes customarily considered by scholars examining fear of crime. And the concerns appeared to be equally potent in generating fear of crime.[20]

Furthermore, when asked what they were doing about crime in the neighborhood, respondents listed a wide range of activities, which went well beyond those offered by the crime prevention programs envisioned by criminal justice officials. Whereas law enforcement officials identify primarily those activities designed to diminish opportunities for victimization to occur, citizens include, in their definition of crime prevention, efforts to improve the neighborhood, to promote social integration, and to provide services for young people.[21] Local residents see physical, social, and service improvements in their neighborhoods as effective crime prevention mechanisms (see Table 1).[22] They recognize, as the victimization orientation does not, the importance of the community context in which events take place.

This was also underscored in our finding that levels of fear in some neighborhoods clearly defied expectations that high versus low levels of crime inevitably induce high versus low levels of fear.[23] In seeking to account for such deviations, we again turned to contextual variables; we found that the community's political and social resources appeared to constitute the prime mediating force between the perception of crime and other neighborhood problems and the subsequent expression of fear. Neighborhoods with political power, for example, appeared more capable

---

18. A more detailed discussion of the empirical data can be found in Lewis and Salem, *Crime and the Urban Community.*

19. Dan A. Lewis and Michael G. Maxfield, "Fear in the Neighborhoods: An Investigation of the Impact of Crime in Chicago," *Journal of Research in Crime and Delinquency,* July 1980, pp. 160–89.

20. Ibid.

21. Paul J. Lavrakas et al., *Factors Related to Citizen Involvement in Personal, Household and Neighborhood Anti-Crime Measures* (Evanston, Ill.: Center for Urban Affairs, Northwestern University, 1980).

22. Aaron Podolefsky and Frederic Dubow, *Strategies for Community Crime Prevention* (Springfield, Ill.: Charles C Thomas, forthcoming).

23. Lewis and Salem, *Crime and the Urban Community.*

Community Crime Prevention 415

of addressing local problems than did those without it; and this capacity often appeared to contribute to diminishing fear.

The power to react to community problems either was derived from well-established political connections or stemmed from the efforts of active community organizations. Neighborhoods without such power, even those in which only minimal problems were identified as cause for concern, exhibited fear levels that appeared to be higher than was warranted by the crime rate and perceived problems. Fear increased as a function of the perception of change in the area when local residents had little capacity to control that change.[24]

An additional means of support for local residents confronting crime and related problems was provided by high levels of social integration in the neighborhood. This could be induced intentionally, via such organizations as block clubs, or develop "naturally" where population movement was minimal and patterns of association within the neighborhood were well established. The value of the latter was illustrated by the comment of one respondent who noted, "We are like a family here, we take care of our own." Similarly a block club member pointed to the value of such organizing, saying, "On my block I'm known and I know everybody. I can feel safe walking on my block at twelve o'clock at night. I'm afraid on the bus, but when I reach my neighborhood, I'm not afraid."

Thus, both in the identification of forces that mediate between fear-producing conditions and subsequent expressions of fear, and in community residents' conception of crime problems and appropriate crime prevention activities, the neighborhood context assumes an importance that is overlooked by the research and crime prevention programs informed by the victimization perspective.

This perceptual gap separating researchers, crime prevention strategists, and citizens was also underscored in Aaron Podolefsky and Frederic Dubow's analysis of collective responses to crime.[25] They found that citizens were not likely to respond to inducements offered by independent crime prevention programs: Participation in such programs was more likely when they were adopted by an organization with multiple purposes and with which neighborhood residents were already associated. Because a large percentage of members of such organizations participate in crime prevention programs when they are adopted, success in crime prevention appears more likely when the program is aimed at organizations rather than at individuals. However, it was also found that crime serves only infrequently as an organizing impetus for neighborhood groups. Rather, such groups tend to unite around other issues and only take on crime and other social problems when they have achieved some organizational maturity.

24. Ibid.
25. Podolefsky and Dubow, *Strategies for Community Crime Control.*

Table 1. Collective Anticrime Activities[a]

Activity	Percentage of Total Activities	Category Percentage
Surveillance		13.54
Radio patrols	4.76	
Walking patrols (dog patrols)	4.55	
Tenant patrols	.11	
Neighborhood surveillance	4.12	
Protective behavior		8.57
Escorts, people with dogs walk together	.21	
Carry signalling devices, whistlestop	5.07	
Provide advice about home security	1.27	
Engrave objects (Operation ID)	.74	
Hire private police	.74	
Rent strike until safety of building improved	.11	
Anti-arson efforts	.32	
Stop muggings of elderly	.11	
Police/Criminal justice oriented		16.18
Pressure on police about policy	5.92	
Assist police	.74	
End police brutality	.11	
Encourage crime reporting	1.27	
Go to court to testify (about neighborhood kids)	.21	
Meet with or pressure public officials about crime	2.33	
Meet with police	5.60	
Promote awareness of crime		5.39
Promote awareness of crime	5.39	
Sanctions/Informal social control		1.48
Get rid of drug pushers, addicts, drunks	.53	
Talk to neighbors about crime problems	.42	
Get rid or stop introduction of pool halls, porno shops, halfway houses	.32	
Get rid of troublesome families	.21	
Improve or maintain the neighborhood		11.53
Improve or clean up neighborhood, property, buildings	8.25	
Street light programs	1.80	
Traffic control, speed bumps, stop signs	.95	
Get graffiti off walls	.11	
Reduce vandalism	.42	
Youth oriented		19.90
Provide positive youth activities	14.06	
Youth social control (off streets, out of trouble)	1.27	
Counseling kids	.74	
Dealing with juvenile delinquency	.63	

Community Crime Prevention **417**

Table 1. con't.

Teach children right and wrong—law	.74	
Parents work with kids	.95	
Deal with gang problems	1.48	
Promote social integration		7.99
Organize the neighborhood	4.60	
Look out for each other	1.80	
Develop community interest, get acquainted	1.59	
Provide general services		2.12
Help old people, people with problems	1.80	
Assist victims	.21	
Represent accused	.11	
Meetings		9.09
Hold meetings and discuss crime (often with police speaker)	9.09	
Miscellaneous		
Counsel or settle disputes	.42	
Strengthen families	.11	
Stop TV violence	.11	
Vague	1.06	

a_n = 946 activities.
Source: Podolefsky and Dubow, *Strategies for Community Crime Control.*

Furthermore, there is no systematic evidence that an individual's attitude toward crime is associated with participation in collective responses. Paul Lavrakas and his coauthors found no relationship between perceptions of crime in the neighborhood and collective participation in crime prevention activities,[26] nor did Podolefsky and Dubow find a connection between crime concerns and such participation.[27] Communities with higher concerns about robbery or burglary, for example, do not exhibit a higher incidence of burglary prevention programs. Instead, participation in crime prevention appears to be most closely associated with membership in community organizations with diverse purposes. Such involvement is not so much associated with attitudes toward crime as it is a function of the community's social composition (family income, number of children, and family status).

The theoretical underpinnings of the social control framework for the study of crime and community come from the Chicago School's orientation to the study of the city and community life. These theorists found an explanation for the distribution of crime and delinquency (and other

26. Lavrakas et al., *Factors Related to Citizen Involvement.*
27. Podolefsky and Dubow, *Strategies for Community Crime Control.*

forms of deviance) in what they saw as the disruptive effects of city life.[28] They argued that the changes induced by industrialization and the growth of urban populations led to social disorganization, which reflected the growing inability of the local urban community to regulate itself. Thus, crime and other forms of deviance were a product of local institutions' inability to exert social control, that is, to regulate the activities of residents.

In similar fashion, the social control perspective is based on the assumption that fear of crime is a problem in communities that do not have the capacity to regulate themselves. Fear is induced not only by crime, but also by many other signs of social disorganization that indicate to residents that their community is changing in threatening ways. The ability of local institutions to resist the disorganization process is a function of their capacity to assert the legitimacy of local standards and to affect those activities inside the neighborhood contributing to the disorganization process. When a community cannot assert its values, its residents become fearful. The social control perspective treats fear of crime as a reaction to the decline of a local area. Those who are fearful may in fact see that their risk of victimization is increasing, but they see this as a consequence of the moral decay of their community brought about by the invasion of forces viewed as disruptive to the social order. As these increase in number, fear increases.

Two factors mediate this relationship between fear and social disorganization. The first is political and refers to what Gerald Suttles has labeled *provincialism*.[29] Neighborhoods with a high degree of provincialism have the capacity to regulate the movement of populations and the use of land and to generate effective action by municipal agencies (i.e., building and sanitation departments). This capacity is especially effective in reducing fear when it is used to diminish the signs of social disorganization, as when abandoned buildings are removed from the neighborhood.

The second is a social dimension reflected in the level of social integration in the neighborhood. In communities with high levels of social integration, signs of social disorganization, although inducing perceptions of increased risk, do not engender increases in fear. The reason for this is that risk can be managed through knowledge of the area. For example, knowledge of boundaries between ethnic groups in conflict as well as of dangerous individuals and areas allows the citizen to move through the environment with relative safety, by careful avoidance of the persons and

28. Morris Janowitz, *The Last Half-Century: Societal Change and Politics in America* (Chicago: University of Chicago Press, 1978).
29. Gerald D. Suttles, *The Social Order of the Slum: Ethnicity and Territory in the Inner City* (Chicago: University of Chicago Press, 1968).

places that pose danger. Because they know the people and the areas to avoid, the citizens do not exhibit high levels of fear, even though their risk assessments are relatively high.

CONCLUSION: A COMPARISON

The social control perspective differs from the victimization perspective both in the independent variables identified as producing fear and in the way the major dimensions—crime, fear, responses, and community—are conceptualized. Because these differences are directly related to proposed interventions, they assume importance for both the policy makers who design programs and the citizens expected to participate in them. Table 2 presents the key hypothesized relationships of the independent, intervening, and dependent variables in the two perspectives, both illustrating how the central concepts are defined and linked and indicating differences in the conception of what constitutes a crime, in the relationship of crime and community, and in the types of responses induced.

According to the victimization perspective, a crime is an event defined by criminal statutes as illegal, which represents a joint experience for offender and victim. Fear is a consequence of either direct or indirect experience with the crime event. Persons respond to these events either individually or collectively: Individual responses, because they focus on individual protection, tend to lead to isolation, distrust, and thus deterioration of the community; collective responses, on the other hand, are efforts to decrease crime in the community, induce cohesion, and reduce the opportunities for victimizations to occur.

The social control perspective treats crime as an indicator of increased social disorganization reflecting a community's incapacity to exert social control. Fear is a response induced by the signs of social disorganization perceived in the environment. Local institutions rather than individuals respond to crime in efforts designed to increase political and social control in the community and to promote social integration among residents.

Whereas the victimization perspective looks at how a community is affected by crime or the response to it, the social control perspective sees the community as the context in which events occur, as a set of institutional relations through which local solidarity is maintained.

Intervention programs spawned by both perspectives seek to strengthen communities. While programs spawned by the victimization perspective seek to induce collective responses to crime which generate social cohesion, as we indicated before, the link between the problems perceived by residents and the types of responses desired does not appear to be consistent with the views of local residents. Because we believe the social control perspective is more consonant with the perceptions and expecta-

Table 2.   A Comparison of the Victimization and Social Control Perspectives

Concept	Victimization Perspective	Social Control Perspective
Crime	Crime is an event defined by criminal statutes as illegal. Crime is experienced by the individual. The potential victim is the key actor, for his victimization is the manifestation of crime.	Crime is an indication of the decline in the local moral order. The potential offender is the key actor in that decline. Crime demonstrates the lack of social control in the community.
Fear	Fear is a consequence of the experience of crime. That experience can either be direct victimization or the anticipation of victimization based on an assessment of local conditions.	Fear is a response to the decline in the moral order. That response is contingent upon the signs of disorganization perceived in the environment. Communities are generally fearful to the extent that these signs increase unchecked.
Responses	Citizens respond to crime individually or collectively. Individual responses are isolating and crime producing. Collective responses are crime reducing and community building. Most citizens react individually.	Local institutions, not individuals, respond to crime. Responses aim to strengthen the socialization and social control capacities of the community. Provincialism represents the control by the community of land and its use. Successful responses to disorganization and crime depend, structurally, on the level of provincialism in the community.
Community	Crime distintegrates the community. Community solidarity is disrupted by fear. Thus, because individual responses to crime decrease social cohesion and social control, it is difficult to unify communities in areas with high crime.	Community is the context in which crime affects the moral order. Community is a set of institutional relationships through which solidarity is maintained. Communities create crime by the way they are organized.
Intervention	Community crime prevention programs are designed to decrease victimization by increasing the potential victim's understanding of his risks and educating him about reducing those risks. Collective efforts by citizens reduce crime in the community by limiting opportunities for victimization.	Crime prevention programs are designed to increase the socialization and social control capacity of local institutions that support the conventional moral order. A strong emphasis is placed on working with adolescents who are in danger of becoming offenders.

Community Crime Prevention 421

tions of community residents, programs shaped by this perspective are designed to strengthen the capacity of the local community to exert social control.

The development of the victimization perspective and community crime prevention strategies offers a radical departure from offender-oriented prevention programming. The social control perspective modifies this innovative approach while leaving intact its emphasis on building community and increasing the participation of citizens in crime prevention efforts. Only further research and policy will test the utility of community crime prevention. However, these innovations offer the hope of crime prevention strategies that transcend the social reform failures of the 1960s and the repressive tactics of the 1970s.

[27]

BRIT. J. CRIMINOL.   VOL. 33   NO. 4   AUTUMN 1993

ENVIRONMENTAL IMPROVEMENTS AND THE FEAR OF CRIME

The Sad Case of the 'Pond' Area in Glasgow

GWYNETH NAIR,* JASON DITTON,* and SAMUEL PHILLIPS*

Studies investigating the positive effect that improved street lighting has on crime and the fear of crime have become remarkably popular. Impressive results have regularly been reported. However, while most use the 'before-and-after' interview format, many neglect to have a long enough follow-up period or to control for the effect that interviewing at different times of the year may have.

The study reported here is based on a twelve-month follow-up period, and controls exactly for time of year at follow-up interview stage. Further, in addition to relighting the area surrounding the homes of respondents, other external environmental improvements were effected, and the security precautions of the homes of respondents were substantially improved.

In spite of this, little improvement in victimization or fear of victimization could be documented. Some improvement might have been noticed had respondents been consulted when the nature and type of improvements were being planned. It is more likely that improved street lighting is no panacea for all ills, and may only be effective under certain conditions.

Improvements to street lighting, as a means of preventing both crime and the fear of crime, have become remarkably popular in the last five years. Prior to 1990, most of this research was carried out by Kate Painter in London (Painter 1988, 1989a, 1989b, 1991) and frequently reported dramatic reductions in criminal victimization following the installation of improved street lighting.

1991 was a watershed year in two senses. First, that year saw the publication of the reports from the five research studies, organized by the British Parliamentary Lighting Group, which were simultaneously conducted in different parts of Britain during 1990 and 1991 (Glasgow Crime Survey Team 1991; Barr and Lawes 1991; Herbert and Moore 1991; Davidson and Goodey 1991; Burden and Murphy 1991). Secondly, 1991 also witnessed the publication by the Home Office of the long-awaited Wandsworth study (Atkins *et al.* 1991).

Results from the five simultaneous studies conducted independently during 1991 were more mixed than those from studies carried out by Painter. Whilst all discovered reductions in fear amongst affected populations following improved street lighting (with more emphatic reductions noticed by several for women and the elderly), some discovered reductions in criminal victimization (Glasgow Crime Survey Team 1991; Barr and Lawes 1991) whilst others encountered increases (Herbert and Moore 1991; Davidson and Goodey 1991).

Probably the most significant limitation of both the early Painter studies and the

* The Criminology Research Unit at the University of Glasgow. The authors gratefully acknowledge the assistance of the Nuffield Foundation whose financial support made possible the research reported here.

British Parliamentary Lighting Group sponsored studies is the very short follow-up period—usually just six weeks. One American authority has claimed that the minimum period that should elapse before a follow-up survey should be contemplated is twelve months (Tien 1979: 24). Perhaps to take account of this view, Painter's most recent study (Painter 1991) reports a return to the site of an earlier study (Painter 1989*b*) to carry out just such a twelve-month review.

In that study, of forty-three householders interviewed during February 1989, forty were reinterviewed slightly over twelve months later in March 1990. Painter found very considerable improvements twelve months after, and because of, relighting (summarized on pp. 107–9 of Painter 1991). This seems to deal at least partly with criticisms of short follow-up, although no effective assessment of the 'taper-off' effect is possible as Painter usually reports the six-week-before data with the twelve-months-after data without giving the original six-week-after data. Full data are given for one score—the number of respondents who 'felt safer' at home after relighting—which was 62 per cent six weeks after relighting, and 77 per cent twelve months after relighting. Understandably, Painter feels that the effect of street lighting 'is consolidated and increased over the twelve-month period' (Painter 1991: 48).

Most recently, Atkins *et al.* (1991) reported the results of the huge Wandsworth study. Here, in stark contrast to the now conventional relighting of one or two dark alleys, the whole borough was relit with some 3,500 new street lights. The research team collected very detailed data on crimes reported to the police for all thirty-nine separate zones, monitoring each for the twelve-month period before and after each was relit. This was complemented with interviews (held seven weeks before and after relighting) with 248 householders in areas being relit, and with 131 householders in a control area.

A fourfold increase in intensity of street lighting was achieved, yet no evidence could be discovered to support the hypothesis that improved street lighting reduces crimes reported to the police. Interviewed householders reported a fall in personally remembered victimizations from 39 to 25, but the control group reported an even bigger percentage fall from 13 to 4. There was also very little evidence of general fear reduction, although 'there was clear evidence that the perceived safety of women walking alone after dark had been improved in the treated area' (Atkins *et al.* 1991: 20).

The study reported here was carried out in an area of Glasgow's Castlemilk housing scheme surrounding a small park called the Pond, and serendipitously offers a cautious development in the general area of the British study of the relationship between improved street lighting, crime, and the fear of crime. Serendipitous, as the study was originally envisaged as a then conventional (now outdated) simple before and after study in an area where the local authority had decided—independently of any involvement with the researchers—to improve local street lighting.

Originally, it had been planned crudely to control for extraneous influences by 'matching' before and after interviewing phases for identical lighting up times, with Phase I scheduled for the week beginning 12 November 1990 (sunset time 16.15), and Phase II scheduled for the week beginning 15 January 1991 (sunset time also 16.15). However, lighting improvements were not completed eventually until 8 August 1991. Although the initial plan, therefore, had to be suspended, this change offered the unexpected opportunity to reinterview in November 1991, which was both exactly

ENVIRONMENT AND THE FEAR OF CRIME

twelve months after the original 'before' interviews, and exactly three months after relighting. Since most of the victimization frequency and perceptual change questions on the main household questionnaire were of the 'in the last three months . . .' variety, this offered a unique chance to control for time of year in the assessment of attitudinal and perceptual change, although it can offer no assessment of the possible 'taper-off' effect described by Ramsay (1991: 17).

A random sample of one hundred addresses was taken from those streets bordering the Pond area, and interviewers used a table of random numbers to select a respondent from those living in each household successfully entered. In Phase I (November 1990) some sixty-nine individuals completed a long and detailed questionnaire. In November 1991 interviewers returned to the area and attempted to re-contact the original respondents. Interviewers were ultimately successful in carrying out repeat interviews with thirty-three respondents (48 per cent of the original number polled). The analysis which follows is restricted to those thirty-three respondents surveyed both before and after environmental improvements were effected.

In addition to being able to control for the time of year with the repeat interviews, this study also offers the opportunity to test just how malleable individuals' perceptions and attitudes are. Relighting was merely one of a whole range of general environmental and specific domestic improvements which were implemented at the same time. In the early summer of 1991 Glasgow District Council carried out an extensive programme of improvements in the Pond area: lighting was greatly enhanced, paths widened and resurfaced, and trees, bushes, and undergrowth drastically cut back. In addition, the local housing authority was in the midst of an extensive public housing rehabilitation project which involved very considerable improvements to the common areas of the tenement blocks (installation of remote door entry systems, for example), together with massive improvements to the flats within them. (In part, this explains the rather poor repeat interview success rate: some tenants had been decanted during Phase I interviewing, and some of those interviewed during Phase I were living temporarily elsewhere during Phase II, and the local Housing Officer was not prepared to release the information which would have allowed individuals to be traced accurately).

So, given the massive set of community and domestic enhancements affecting residents, and the short time elapsed since lighting improvements were effected (allowing no chance for beneficial effects to 'taper off') we would expect that if such environmental improvements do indeed have a beneficial effect on fear of crime and crime, then this clearly should be demonstrable.

Respondents ranged in age from 16 to 88, and three-quarters of those interviewed were women. They were mostly long-term residents of the area (mean length of residence was 19.8 years), and over 90 per cent rated it a 'good' or 'very good' place to live. Respondents were asked about a series of fourteen potential local problems, including street lighting quality, and asked to say (on both interview occasions) whether each had improved, stayed the same, or got worse over the previous three months. Before improvements were carried out, 17 per cent felt that there had been recent improvement in street lighting: afterwards 18 per cent felt that there had. Thus fewer than one respondent in five had apparently noted the relighting carried out three months previously. Those 'satisfied' with the Roads and Lighting Department rose from 19 per cent to 30 per cent of the total, although this department remained, with the police, at the bottom of a 'league' of eight local services so evaluated.

GWYNETH NAIR *ET AL.*

TABLE 1   *Worry about Victimization (%)*

	Before	After	Net change
Assault	15	9	−6
Sexual assault	15	9	−6
Harassment	18	12	−6
Break-In	24	24	0
Nuisance telephone call	18	21	+3

As Table 1 shows, there was a decrease in those worrying 'always' or 'sometimes' about being a victim of assault, sexual assault, and harassment. This decrease, in the case of sexual assault and assault, is almost entirely located among younger respondents in the 16–35 age group.

TABLE 2   *Precautions Taken after Dark (%)*

	Before	After	Net change
Avoid going out at all	36	33	−3
Avoid going out alone	42	51	+9
Avoid certain areas	70	79	+9
Carry a personal alarm	9	6	−3
Take a means of defence	3	12	+9

Respondents reported little relaxation in the precautions they took when going out alone after dark (see Table 2). A third still avoided going out at all, and over half, after environmental improvements, would avoid going out alone. Overall, this group seemed to feel less rather than more safe.

Changes in security precautions taken in the home, set out in Table 3, illustrate the extent of the home improvement scheme carried out by the District Council. Most homes were provided with door and window locks, an entryphone system on the common entry to the tenements, and a front door spyhole. Given the extent of this domestic property target-hardening, it is surprising that respondents felt if anything less safe at home (see Table 4). There had in fact been a 7 per cent swing towards 'unsafety' in respondents' perceptions.

TABLE 3   *Precautions in the Home (%)*

	Before	After	Net change
Door chains	12	33	+21
Door locks	24	82	+58
Window locks	33	70	+37
Spyhole	61	85	+24
Burglar alarm	6	9	+3
Entryphone	67	85	+18
Guard dog	6	21	+15

ENVIRONMENT AND THE FEAR OF CRIME

TABLE 4   *Feelings of Safety at Home (%)*

	Before	After	Net change
Very safe	70	70	0
Fairly safe	19	12	−7
Bit unsafe	0	9	+9
Very unsafe	11	9	−2

Lighting and other environmental improvements seemed similarly to have had only slight effects on perceptions of safety out of doors after dark, as Table 5 shows.

TABLE 5   *Feelings of Safety Outside (%)*

	Before	After	Net change
Very safe	31	30	−1
Fairly safe	19	21	+2
Bit unsafe	13	18	+5
Very unsafe	38	30	−8

This is reinforced by taped unstructured street interviews carried out with local residents (not questionnaire respondents).

'Would you walk through (the park) on your own?'
'Not at night, no.' (Woman, mid-30s)

'I never go through there after dark myself, never do. I think it's just too out of the way. There's still nothing round about here—even with the lights being on there's still nothing round about you.' (Woman, late 30s)

People had not been persuaded that the area was any safer than it was before: indeed those thinking that women, in particular, are unsafe after dark rose from 56 per cent to 64 per cent (see Table 6). Pedestrian interviewees too felt that there were particular dangers for women.

'I wouldna let my girlfriend go through at night—it's not safe.' (Man, early 20s)

TABLE 6   *Safety of Others (%)*

	Before	After	Net change
Children	31	31	0
Women	44	36	−8
Men	72	75	+3
Elderly	34	30	−4

GWYNETH NAIR *ET AL.*

One woman felt that far from dangers being alleviated by enhanced lighting, they may even have been increased:

'I think it's worse now. With the lights people can see you. When they couldn't see you they didn't know who you were. You could be anybody. Now they can see you're a lassie . . . Oh no, I wouldn't use it. I'd be safer without the lights than with the lights.' (Woman, late 20s)

The justification for reporting this study is, paradoxically, that it can be seen as a project that failed. Fortuitous circumstances enabled controlling for time of year; and simultaneous improvements to respondents' domestic environments as well as to the external local environment could have been expected to contribute greatly to enhanced feelings of safety. Furthermore, 'after' interviewing, at three months after the completion of relighting and other environmental improvements, should in theory have picked up perceptions at their most favourable point, before any 'taper-off' effect had time to mitigate impact. Yet results confounded expectations. The substantial fall in the fear of crime which might confidently have been predicted failed to materialize. What lessons can then be learned from the Pond study?

First, the effects of improved street lighting, while beneficial in many circumstances, cannot be guaranteed. Here they were tied to a whole range of environmental improvements, yet the complete package failed to produce a significant increase in local feelings of safety.

Secondly, we see what an intractable and resistant phenomenon the fear of crime really is. It is far from simple either to address or to solve. The possibility is even raised that the solution—for instance in the case of domestic target-hardening—might worsen the problem, underlining dangers and undermining feelings of safety.

One positive recommendation does emerge. Respondents and street interviewees called for greater local consultation before environmental improvements are undertaken. Several of those interviewed indicated that they rarely if ever used the routes through the park itself, and that, in their opinion, whilst the improvements were definitely improvements, the net effect had been to turn a poorly lit bad area into a well lit bad area. They frequently remarked that they would much have preferred to see environmental improvements on more heavily used pedestrian routes such as the paths leading away from the park, and towards the local shops.

We are left, though, with a central problem. If massive improvements to domestic safety measures coupled with enhanced local street lighting, path widening, and so on fail to make a significant impact on residents' fear of crime, what is there left to try?

REFERENCES

ATKINS, S., HUSAIN, S., and STOREY, A. (1991) *The Influence of Street Lighting on Crime and the Fear of Crime.* London: Crime Prevention Unit, Home Office, Paper No. 28.

BARR, R., and LAWES, H. (1991) *Towards a Brighter Monsall: Street Lighting as a Factor in Community Safety—The Manchester Experience,* Mimeo, Manchester University.

BURDEN, T., and MURPHY, L. (1991) *Street Lighting, Community Safety and the Local Environment,* Mimeo, Leeds Polytechnic.

ENVIRONMENT AND THE FEAR OF CRIME

DAVIDSON, N., and GOODEY, J. (1991) *Street Lighting and Crime: The Hull Project*, Mimeo, University of Hull.

FLEMING, R., and BURROWS, J. (1986) *The Case for Lighting as a Means of Preventing Crime*. London: Research and Planning Unit, Home Office, Research Bulletin No. 22: 14–17.

GLASGOW CRIME SURVEY TEAM (1991) *Street Lighting and Crime: The Strathclyde Twin Site Study*, Mimeo, Criminology Research Unit, Glasgow University.

HERBERT, D., and MOORE, L. (1991) *Street Lighting and Crime: The Cardiff Project*, Mimeo, University College of Swansea.

PAINTER, K. (1988) *Lighting and Crime Prevention: The Edmonton Project*, Mimeo, Middlesex Polytechnic.

—— (1989a) *Lighting and Crime Prevention for Community Safety: The Tower Hamlets Study 1st Report*, Mimeo, Middlesex Polytechnic.

—— (1989b) *Crime Prevention and Public Lighting with Special Focus on Women and Elderly People*, Mimeo, Middlesex Polytechnic.

—— (1991) *An Evaluation of Public Lighting as a Crime Prevention Strategy with Special Focus on Women and Elderly People*, Mimeo, Middlesex Polytechnic.

RAMSAY, M. (1991) *The Effect of Better Street Lighting on Crime and Fear: A Review*. London: Crime Prevention Unit, Home Office, Paper No. 29.

TIEN, J. M. (1979) *Street Lighting Projects*, National Evaluation Program, Phase 1 Report, LEAA. Hackensack, NJ: US Department of Justice.

Part VII
The Future?

[28]

International Review of Victimology, 1999, Vol. 6, pp. 83–99
0269-7580/99 $10
© 1999 A B Academic Publishers— Printed in Great Britain

AFRAID OR ANGRY?
RECALIBRATING THE 'FEAR' OF CRIME

JASON DITTON[1], JON BANNISTER[2], ELIZABETH GILCHRIST[3]
and STEPHEN FARRALL[4]

[1] *Law Department, Sheffield University, and Director, Scottish Centre for Criminology,
Charing Cross Clinic, 8 Woodside Crescent, Glasgow, G3 7UY, UK*
[2] *Department of Social Policy and Social Work, Glasgow University*
[3] *School of Psychology, University of Birmingham*
[4] *Centre for Criminological Research, Oxford University*

ABSTRACT

Studying the fear of crime is a research field that has grown enormously in the past two decades. Yet our empirical knowledge has grown at the expense of conceptual development. It is beginning to be suspected that 'fear' is a term encompassing a confusing variety of feelings, perspectives, risk-estimations, and which is thus means different things to different people. It is additionally suggested that what we know empirically may well be largely an artefact of the fact that the questions that are put repeatedly to respondents seldom vary, and the ways that those questions are put, and the settings in which they are put seldom change. The research project which is in part reported here initially used one set of respondents to develop new questions relating to their general and specific feelings about criminal victimisation, before testing them on another, much larger sample. This latter exercise confirmed that being 'angry' about the threat of criminal victimisation is more frequently reported than being 'afraid' of it. Little is known of the meaning or range of meanings that respondents infer with the term 'anger', but further research – which is needed – might well show that anger about crime is as complicated a concept as fear of crime has transpired to be. In any event, research into anger should benefit from the lessons learnt from three decades of research into fear.

BACKGROUND

'One of the principal reasons for conflicting findings concerning fear of crime lies in the confusion and lack of agreement in the construction of empirical instruments' (Hale, 1996; p. 80).

Fear of crime is now bigger than General Motors. In the last three decades or so, fear of crime has generated a phenomenal degree of interest among academics and policy makers. This is probably the main legacy of endless, and endlessly repeated, national crime surveys which have consistently identified it as a social problem of striking dimensions (Mayhew, 1985). Interestingly, recognition of the political power of the fear of crime was almost instant. Not long after the first National American Crime Survey (Lewis and Salem, 1986), it was recognised that problems posed by fear of crime might be greater than crime itself (Furstenberg, 1971). Prophetic indeed! Thirty years on, Hale (1996; p. 79) has estimated

84

that over two hundred related professional publications have appeared. Given the recency and exhaustiveness of Hale's review, there is little need to offer another here. This paper concentrates instead on empirically tested ways of developing fear of crime at the conceptual and methodological levels.

British national crime surveys are now conducted regularly and reported eloquently, with the latest full account from the English and Welsh crime survey being Hough (1995), and from the Scottish equivalent, Anderson and Leitch (1996). Repeated sweeps of these surveys – the main source of empirical information about the fear of crime – constitute a unique data resource. The preference for continuity coupled to the desire for historical and cross-border comparability has led to the retention of identical survey questions (often in the same sequence in the main questionnaire). This lends great credibility to subsequently illustrated trends. For example, it can be said, as it has recently, and with great confidence and uncanny precision, that the fear of crime fell between 1994 and 1996 in England and Wales as 'people are now less likely to feel unsafe on the streets. 54% of women felt very or a bit unsafe in 1994, falling to 47% in 1996' (Mirrlees-Black *et al.*, 1996; p. 1).

Yet, whilst the empirical grasp, such as this, of the minutiae of the phenomena grows continually, conceptual development has, relatively speaking, stagnated. This is the case in spite of increasing recognition by some – notably, Hough (1995) – that far from being a unitary or simple thing, 'fear' of crime is instead a highly complex interacting set of feelings and perceptions. It is even possible that, as Ferraro and LaGrange have noted, 'the phrase "fear of crime" has acquired so many divergent meanings that its current utility is negligible' (1987; p. 71).

This paper reports in part the result of a lengthy conceptual and methodological reassessment of people's fear of crime, and in particular concentrates on the degree to which the picture thus generated – of a population more or less worried, anxious, concerned, 'fearful' about possible victimisation – may in part be an artefact of the way that certain survey questions are routinely asked. It is similarly possible that the view presented here – that people are more angry about the threat of victimisation than they are afraid of it – is also artefactual.

METHOD

'Overall, reading the literature on the fear of crime produces a sense that the field is trapped within an overly restrictive methodological and theoretical framework. ... Too much reliance has been placed upon the use of surveys as a method and too great an emphasis given to research based upon responses to questions about feeling safe out at night. Any new research should look for a triangulation of methods. Ethnographic studies, life histories and individual and group interviews all have much to contribute and are currently relatively ignored as methods by researchers into fear.'

Surveys will still have an important role to play, not least in testing how far results from other approaches can be generalised, but they will be enriched rather than impoverished by the deeper insights from alternative approaches. Triangulation will allow the designers of survey questionnaires to become more sensitive in the design of their measures. In addition new research should not take fear as a given. What is needed is a strategy which begins by unpacking the concept of the fear of crime.' (Hale, 1996; p. 132).

The research in part reported here was funded within ESRC's *Crime and Social Order* research programme.[1] The project design emphasised an initial open-ended and qualitative investigation of people's general feelings about crime and a gradual compression and operationalisation of whatever was discovered into survey questions capable of administration in a standard crime survey.

All the research was conducted in the Strathclyde region of Scotland. This region enclosed a substantial part of the west of Scotland, nearly half the Scottish population, and Glasgow, Scotland's biggest city.[2] Research involved the following phases:

Initial quantitative trawl

Four sampling sites were selected in Glasgow along two dichotomies (outlying/inner city and poor/affluent). Within each area, a limited number of streets or blocks of flats were randomly selected. In each, starting points were also randomly selected, and thereafter researchers used random walk, calling at every fifth house. At each property to which entry was secured, the first person aged over 16 encountered was interviewed. Interview was by fixed schedule, and concentrated on individual concern about possible victimisation, and estimated risk of actual victimisation. Forty interviews was the target for each of the four locations, and, in the event, 168 individuals were successfully interviewed.

Quantitative follow-up

All 168 were classified in terms of their fear and risk self-ratings along two further dichotomies (high/low fear and high/low risk), producing four distinct groups. A considerably more extensive quantitative questionnaire was administered to a randomly selected 16 from each of these four groups.

86

Conceptual development

Qualitative interviewing

This group of 64 were also interviewed in an individual, open-ended and tape-recorded session, and the qualitative material transcribed and closely analysed.

Group Discussion

The range of feelings about crime revealed in phases 1 and 2 was extensively aired in two discussion groups, one male, the other female. The chief purpose of the discussion groups was to ask participants to arrange all the feelings about crime that interviewees had expressed into cognate groups. Members of discussion groups were provided with a pack of 'cards', with a previously respondent-expressed 'feeling' written on each. In discussion, these emerged uncontestedly as three cognate groups: 'thinking' about crime, 'afraid' about crime, and 'angry' about crime. This was confirmed by extensive analysis of the quantitative data from phases 1 and 2.

Operationalisation

Ferraro and LaGrange (1987) have suggested that future questions on the fear of crime should include more than one question per offence type, and DuBow *et al* (1979) further recommend that emotive, cognitive and affective dimensions of any topic should also be measured. Ferraro and LaGrange further indicate that feelings about crime should be separated along two dimensions: type of perception (from cognitive to affective), and level of reference (from general to personal). Indeed, they say (1987; p. 81):

' First, measures of fear of crime should tap the emotional state of fear rather than judgements or concerns about crime. The phrase "how afraid" is a helpful way to examine this emotional reaction. Second, questions that attempt to measure fear of crime should make explicit reference to crime. Many researchers have based their studies upon implied meanings which are probably not valid indicators. Third, as mentioned earlier, general referents about crimes are often vague; if there is no clear crime referent, one could certainly not expect respondents' fear reactions to be reliable or valid. Thus, we recommend that specific victimisations or categories of victimisations be used to assess an individual's fear reactions. This procedure should enhance object consistency upon which the fear reactions are predicated. Fourth, questions intended to measure fear of crime should be stated in a nonhypothetical format ... We suggest that researchers should avoid the use of the word "would" in questions attempting to measure fear of crime. Rather, it is better to obtain specific reports about how individuals feel in everyday situations. Fifth, the qualifying phrase "in your everyday life" brings a touch of reality to the questions regarding fear of crime. Respondents can better relate to this type of question than more abstract, hypothetical, or perhaps unlikely situations such as "when walking alone at night in your neighbourhood" ... '

Extensive piloting, with seemingly endless word exchange and result comparison, led eventually to the confirmation of three questions to be asked of any offence/offence group. For each, respondents were to be given the following possible answers on a card: '1 = not at all; 2 = hardly ever; (3 = don't know); 4 = some of the time; 5 = all the time'.[3] The three questions were: 'In your everyday life, do you THINK about [offence group]?'; 'In your everyday life, are you AFRAID of [offence group]?'; 'In your everyday life, does the thought of [offence group] make you ANGRY?'

'Angry' and 'think' about crime as possible general attitudes to the threat of victimisation were only operationalised as closed survey questions because they forced themselves onto the research agenda in both individual interview and group discussion. Before the survey results were to hand, nobody on the research team expected the responses to the 'angry' question to be as marked as they transpired to be.

Empirical confirmation

A completely new full crime survey questionnaire was developed, exhaustively piloted, and administered to a simple random intended sample of 1,600 Strathclyde region respondents aged 16 years or over in early 1996. Validity checks were conducted by the research team, not the company commissioned to conduct the survey itself. Further reports from the resulting data can be expected in due course. Initial papers (Farrall *et al.*, 1997; Gilchrist *et al.*, 1998) have outlined some initial doubts about the health of fear of crime research. This paper concentrates on the degree to which peoples' apparent 'fear' of crime can be reconstructed from asking the three questions noted above, each related to four offence groups: housebreaking, car crime, assault, and vandalism.[4]

In factor analysis, the 'think' and 'afraid' questions both loaded heavily on the same factor, collectively and across all offence types. Thus, this paper does not deal much with the 'think' data, and instead focuses more on the 'afraid' data, and a comparison of this with the 'angry' responses. The literature on 'afraid' of crime research has already been eloquently and exhaustively reviewed by Hale (1996) and the interested reader is directed there.

Anger as a response to actual victimisation has been noted, although only infrequently commented on, in a number of studies (Maguire, 1980; Kinsey and

88

Anderson, 1992; Ostrihanska and Wojcik, 1993 and Mawby and Walklate, 1997, amongst others), and in all these, victims report more initial anger than initial fear. However, we know of no literature on 'anger' about the threat of criminal victimisation to review.

RESULTS

As measured in the way already described, people seem to be more angry about, than afraid of crime. It should be recognised that the strength of this difference may reflect the relatively weak way that the afraid question was asked. Had the words 'anxious' or, particularly, 'worried' replaced 'afraid', many more respondents may have claimed to have experienced those feelings some or all of the time.

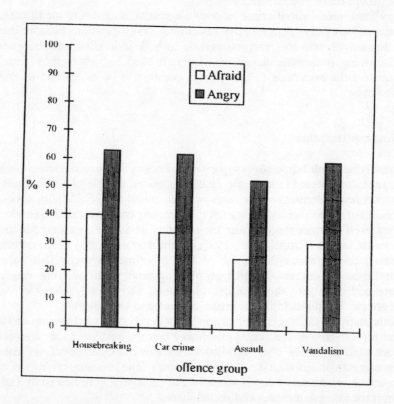

Figure 1. Percent 'Afraid' and 'Angry'

Nevertheless, Figure 1 illustrates the response differences given the way that the two questions were actually asked.

Figure 1 is constructed from row 9 of Table 1. The data sums, for each, those who claimed that they were 'angry' or 'afraid' either 'some of the time' or 'all the time'. The achieved sample, when weighted for gender and age group (by 1991 Census for Strathclyde), and for chance of selection, numbered 1,638. Sample and sub-sample sizes are given on the bottom line of each cell of Table 1. The N for car crime is smaller as 546 respondents had 'no household vehicle', and were subsequently excluded from the car crime data.

In Table 1, respondents are separated by gender, and also by age groupings. It can be seen that the overall finding – that feelings of 'anger' are more widespread than are feelings of being 'afraid' – (the final row, and Figure 1) is supported in every age and gender category. That is, feelings of 'anger' are more frequent than feelings of 'afraid' across the board. Generally speaking (rows 7 and 8) females are more afraid than males, and they are also angrier. For both genders, feelings of anger exceed feelings of being afraid.

This pattern holds for the young (16–35) and the middle aged (35–59), but is partly reversed for the old (60+). Here, anger is in excess of fear for both genders, but old men are consistently angrier than old women. All the differences between proportions afraid and angry are statistically significant at at least $p<0.001$, with 34 of the 36 cells significant at $p<0.00001$, 1 at $p<0.0001$, and only one at $p<0.001$.

Further analysis indicated not only that more people are angry than are afraid (the data shown in Table 1), but also that people who are more angry than they are afraid are much more angry than people who are more afraid, are afraid. This is a second, distinct sense in which anger outweighs fear, and data are in Table 2. Here, the data reported as percentages within each cell are, respectively, the percentage being more afraid than angry ('Afr'), then, in brackets, the percentage being equally afraid and angry ('(=)'), and then the percentage being more angry than afraid ('Angry'). The second line of data in each cell is simply the number of respondents to whom the percentages refer. So, for example, in the first cell of the bottom row, row 9 of Table 2, of the 1575 respondents to which the cell refers, 7% were more afraid then angry about housebreaking, 53% were equally afraid and angry about housebreaking, and 42% were more angry than afraid about housebreaking.

The only statistically significant gender differences were for those aged 60+ for housebreaking ($p<0.001$; 2df), for those aged under 34 for car crime ($p<0.01$; 2df), and for all three age groups for assault (for all, $p<0.001$; 2df). The only significant age difference was for housebreaking ($p<0.001$; 4df) where the numbers being both more afraid than angry, and more angry than afraid both increase with age (and at the expense of the numbers being equally so). Overall, it is clear from Table 2 that angry is 'stronger' than afraid: the percentages being angrier than afraid are much larger in all cells than the percentages that represent those that are more afraid than angry.

90

TABLE 1
Percent 'Afraid' and 'Angry' some or all of the time

		House-breaking	Car crime	Assault	Vandalism
1. Male, 16–34	% Afraid: % Angry	27:50	34:55	20:49	27:57
	significance	****	****	****	****
	% both (N)	23 (272)	29 (208)	19 (261)	26 (261)
2. Female, 16–34	% Afraid: % Angry	49:72	42:67	35:64	40:70
	significance	****	****	****	****
	% both (N)	46 (282)	39 (198)	31 (274)	39 (282)
3. Male, 35–59	% Afraid: % Angry	39:63	34:61	23:50	30:57
	significance	****	****	****	****
	% both (N)	33 (296)	30 (225)	23 (294)	28 (296)
4. Female, 35–59	% Afraid: % Angry	52:73	36:70	36:59	36:68
	significance	****	****	****	****
	% both (N)	48 (309)	34 (239)	32 (300)	33 (303)
5. Male, 60+	% Afraid: % Angry	31:67	41:70	13:55	21:61
	significance	***	****	**	****
	% both (N)	28 (158)	41 (93)	12 (148)	21 (155)
6. Female, 60+	% Afraid: % Angry	40:59	20:53	23:48	35:55
	significance	****	****	****	****
	% both (N)	34 (241)	20 (105)	21 (221)	32 (232)
7. Male	% Afraid: % Angry	33:59	34:60	20:51	27:58
	significance	****	****	****	****
	% both (N)	28 (731)	31 (525)	19 (707)	26 (716)
8. Female	% Afraid: % Angry	48:69	35:66	33:58	37:65
	significance	****	****	****	****
	% both (N)	44 (844)	34 (546)	29 (806)	35 (828)
9. All	% Afraid: % Angry	41:64	35:63	27:55	32:62
	significance	****	****	****	****
	% both (N)	37 (1575)	33 (1072)	24 (1512)	31 (1544)

* = $p<0.01$; ** = $p<0.001$; *** = $p<0.0001$; **** = $p<0.00001$; all df = 1.

TABLE 2
Percentages 'more afraid than angry', 'equally afraid and angry' and 'more angry than afraid'

		House-breaking	Car crime	Assault	Vandalism
1. Male, 16–34	Afr (=) Angry	5 (50) 34	2 (59) 39	7 (57) 36	5 (47) 48
	N	272	208	261	261
2. Female, 16–34	Afr (=) Angry	4 (58) 38	8 (53) 39	8 (42) 50	3 (56) 41
	N	282	198	274	282
3. Male, 35–59	Afr (=) Angry	7 (50) 43	6 (55) 39	4 (50) 47	5 (54) 41
	N	296	225	294	296
4. Female, 35–59	Afr (=) Angry	10 (49) 40	4 (44) 52	11 (47) 42	7 (46) 48
	N	309	239	300	303
5. Male, 60+	Afr (=) Angry	5 (40) 55	9 (50) 41	5 (39) 56	11 (42) 48
	N	158	93	148	155
6. Female, 60+	Afr (=) Angry	11 (52) 37	6 (53) 41	11 (55) 34	9 (49) 42
	N	241	105	221	232
7. Male	Afr (=) Angry	6 (52) 43	5 (50) 40	6 (50) 45	6 (49) 45
	N	731	525	707	716
8. Female	Afr (=) Angry	8 (54) 38	6 (49) 45	10 (48) 42	6 (50) 44
	N	844	546	806	828
9. All	Afr (=) Angry	7 (53) 40	5 (53) 42	8 (49) 43	6 (50) 44
	N	1575	1072	1512	1544
	Z score	Z = 18.9	Z = 17.1	Z = 19.0	Z = 20.7
	2-tailed p =	.0000	.0000	.0000	.0000

Z scores from Wilcoxon Matched-Pairs Signed-ranks test

Some further illumination of this relationship can also be discovered by reintroducing the 'think' data. For each of the four offence groups, those who are more afraid than angry 'think' about the offence type more than those for whom the degree of anger and afraid is equal, who in turn think about it more than those who are more angry than afraid (for all, $p<0.0001$; 2df; all by Kruskal-Wallis 1-way anova). In turn, the angry think about each offence group more than the non-angry ($p<0.0001$; 1df for all), and the afraid think about each offence group

92

more than the non-afraid (again, p<0.0001; 1df for all). Finally, the afraid think about each offence group significantly more than the angry for housebreaking (p<0.001; 2df), car crime and vandalism (both p<0.0001; 2df), but not for assault.

Actual experience of past year victimisation was collected using standardised British Crime Survey (and Scottish Crime Survey) 'screener' questions.[6] These varied in number for the different offence groups (six separate questions to establish housebreaking victimisations; four for car crime; five for assault; and two for vandalism). These screeners generated 638 victimisations in total: 169 for housebreaking, 260 for car crime, 125 for assault, and 84 for vandalism. These overall data are in row 9 of Table 3 (and are broken down by gender in rows 7 and 8) and by gender and standardised age groups in rows 1 through 6.

Data in Table 3 relate to being 'afraid' of victimisation, and equivalent data for being 'angry' about it are given in Table 4. Each of these tables can be read as follows: for example, at the foot of the 'housebreaking' column in Table 3 (i.e., at row 9), data relate to 169 victims and 1438 non-victims. Further, 58% of the housebreaking victims, but only 38% of the housebreaking non-victims claimed to be afraid of housebreaking some or all of the time (and p<0.0001).

Table 3 and the 'afraid' data first. Victims are more likely to be afraid than non-victims (row 9), and this holds for gender. Female victims are more afraid than female non-victims (row 8) and male victims are more afraid than male non-victims (row 7). Male victims are less likely to be afraid than female victims. Male victims are more afraid than male non-victims, and female victims are more afraid than female non-victims in all age groups.[7] The frequency of significant differences is lower than in Table 1, with 17 of the 36 cells being ns., 8 significant at p<0.01, 1 at p<0.001, 2 at p<0.0001, and just 8 at p<0.00001.

Now Table 4, and the 'angry' data. Much the same as with the 'afraid' data. Victims are more likely to be angry than non-victims (row 9), and this holds for gender. Female victims are more angry than female non-victims (row 8) and male victims are more angry than male non-victims (row 7). With two exceptions,[8] this holds for all age groups. Frequency of significant differences is again lower even than in Table 3, with 24 of the 36 cells being ns., 5 significant at p<0.01, 4 at p<0.001, 2 at p<0.0001, and only 1 at p<0.00001.

By visual comparison of Tables 3 and 4, it can be seen that, overall, more victims are angry than are afraid, and this is also true for non-victims (rows 9). This holds for all females separately (rows 8) and for all males separately (rows 7). With two exceptions,[9] this pattern holds also for males and females in all age groups.

It does not seem to be the case that respondents are either angry about everything – or angry about nothing. Nor does anger exclude fear, or *vice versa*. One thing is very clear: being 'angry' and being 'afraid' are not mutually exclusive. Each question seems to tap very different sets of feelings, and further research may show where the boundary, or boundaries, between them lie.

TABLE 3
Victims and Non-Victims: Percent 'Afraid' some or all of the time

		House-breaking	Car crime	Assault	Vandalism
1. Male, 16–34	Victim:Non-Victim	55:24	36:26	26:17	78:23
	significance	**	ns	ns	***
	(n) (N)	(24) (250)	(67) (142)	(60) (217)	(11) (262)
2. Female, 16–34	Victim:Non-Victim	74:46	77:30	49:33	84:36
	significance	*	****	ns	***
	(n) (N)	(29) (258)	(52) (148)	(33) (249)	(23) (266)
3. Male, 35–59	Victim:Non-Victim	48:38	44:31	24:22	52:28
	significance	ns	ns	ns	*
	(n) (N)	(42) (260)	(57) (169)	(23) (277)	(27) (269)
4. Female, 35–59	Victim:Non-Victim	77:49	53:32	71:35	60:34
	significance	*	*	ns	ns
	(n) (N)	(38) (279)	(48) (193)	(3) (309)	(10) (304)
5. Male, 60+	Victim:Non-Victim	33:29	68:33	0:18	48:19
	significance	ns	*	ns	ns
	(n) (N)	(22) (143)	(20) (73)	(1) (163)	(5) (160)
6. Female, 60+	Victim:Non-Victim	55:39	43:16	35:21	88:33
	significance	ns	ns	ns	*
	(n) (N)	(13) (232)	(14) (93)	(5) (236)	(7) (228)
7. Male	Victim:Non-Victim	46:31	44:29	25:18	58:24
	significance	*	*	ns	****
	(n) (N)	(89) (656)	(144) (384)	(84) (662)	(44) (697)
8. Female	Victim:Non-Victim	72:45	63:28	49:31	79:34
	significance	****	****	ns	****
	(n) (N)	(80) (781)	(116) (436)	(41) (805)	(40) (810)
9. All	Victim:Non-Victim	58:38	52:29	33:25	68:30
	significance	****	****	ns	****
	(n) (N)	(169) (1438)	(260) (820)	(125) (1466)	(84) (1506)

n = n victimised; N = N non-victimised; ns = not significant; * = p<0.01; ** = p<0.001; *** = p<0.0001; **** = p<0.00001; all df = 1.

94

TABLE 4
Victims and Non-Victims: Percent 'Angry' some or all of the time

		House-breaking	Car crime	Assault	Vandalism
1. Male, 16–34	Victim:Non-Victim	70:50	65:51	72:44	78:57
	significance	ns	ns	**	ns
	(n) (N)	(24) (256)	(68) (143)	(62) (206)	(11) (258)
2. Female, 16–34	Victim:Non-Victim	89:70	78:63	77:63	98:68
	significance	ns	ns	ns	*
	(n) (N)	(32) (257)	(52) (146)	(33) (252)	(23) (263)
3. Male, 35–59	Victim:Non-Victim	84:60	69:58	41:52	65:58
	significance	*	ns	ns	ns
	(n) (N)	(42) (257)	(60) (169)	(21) (276)	(27) (276)
4. Female, 35–59	Victim:Non-Victim	88:72	82:67	81:60	90:67
	significance	ns	ns	ns	ns
	(n) (N)	(36) (276)	(47) (192)	(3) (304)	(10) (299)
5. Male, 60+	Victim:Non-Victim	86:65	92:65	100:56	65:60
	significance	ns	ns	ns	ns
	(n) (N)	(22) (140)	(20) (72)	(1) (149)	(5) (149)
6. Female, 60+	Victim:Non-Victim	41:60	71:51	90:48	88:54
	significance	ns	ns	ns	ns
	(n) (N)	(13) (230)	(14) (92)	(5) (221)	(7) (225)
7. Male	Victim:Non-Victim	81:57	70:57	65:50	68:58
	significance	***	*	ns	ns
	(n) (N)	(89) (657)	(148) (384)	(85) (635)	(44) (689)
8. Female	Victim:Non-Victim	81:68	79:62	79:58	94:64
	significance	ns	**	*	**
	(n) (N)	(82) (774)	(115) (433)	(41) (788)	(40) (798)
9. All	Victim:Non-Victim	81:63	74:59	69:55	81:61
	significance	****	***	*	**
	(n) (N)	(171) (1432)	(262) (817)	(126) (1423)	(84) (1487)

n = n victimised; N = N non-victimised; ns = not significant; * = p<0.01; ** = p<0.001; *** = p<0.0001; **** = p<0.00001; all df = 1.

95

TABLE 5
Angry intercorrelations

	Anger about house-breaking	Anger about car crime	Anger about assault
Anger about car crime	.6009 (n = 971) sig .000	*	*
Anger about assault	.6154 (n = 1506) sig .000	.5944 (n = 960) sig .000	*
Anger about vandalism	.6243 (n = 1535) sig .000	.6051 (n = 963) sig .000	.7095 (n = 1498) sig .000

All correlations (Spearmans) positive, and all on unweighted data.

TABLE 6
Afraid intercorrelations

	Afraid about house-breaking	Afraid about car crime	Afraid about assault
Afraid about car crime	.3843 (n = 983) sig .000	*	*
Afraid about assault	.4393 (n = 1564) sig .000	.3008 (n = 987) sig .000	*
Afraid about vandalism	.4815 (n = 1535) sig .000	.3823 (n = 979) sig .000	.4874 (n = 1566) sig .000

All correlations (Spearmans) positive, and all on unweighted data.

Relevant correlations between the two are in Tables 5 and 6. Within the anger set, between 35% and 50% of the variance is shared. Within the afraid set, only between 9% and 24% of the variance is shared.

The anger set further correlates with the afraid set, although the shared variance is smaller. Anger and afraid within each set are higher (with a shared

The Fear of Crime

96

TABLE 7
Angry/Afraid intercorrelations

	Afraid about housebreaking	Afraid about car crime	Afraid about assault	Afraid about vandalism
Anger about vandalism	.4086	.1714	.2385	.2611
	(n=- 1559)	(n = 969)	(n = 1550)	(n = 1553)
	sig .000	sig .000	sig .000	sig .000
Anger about car crime	.2246	.3988	.1935	.2360
	(n = 983)	(n = 993)	(n = 987)	(n = 977)
	sig .000	sig .000	sig .000	sig .000
Anger about assault	.2898	.1707	.3879	.3288
	(n = 1508)	(n = 960)	(n = 1508)	(n = 1510)
	sig .000	sig .000	sig .000	sig .000
Anger about vandalism	.2873	.1025	.1884	.3817
	(n = 1537)	(n = 963)	(n = 1531)	(n = 1543)
	sig .000	sig .000	sig .000	sig .000

All correlations (Spearmans) positive, and all on unweighted data.

variance of between 15% and 17%), and the other intercorrelations only suggest a shared variance of between 1% and 11%. These are shown in Table 7.

For the purposes of further analysis, the four 'afraid' questions and the four 'angry' questions (each with a five point scale) were both composited into 17 point scales.[10] They intercorrelate at .5180 (n = 1092, p = .000) suggesting a shared variance of 27%. The 'afraid' scores bunch near the unafraid end of the 'afraid' spectrum, but the 'anger' scores bunch near the very angry end. The bottom five points of the scale contain 52% of the afraid scores but only 27% of the angry scores. Conversely, the top five points of the scale contain only 12% of the afraid scores, but 46% of the angry ones. This is shown in Figure 2, and in part confirms (at the ordinal as opposed to the mere nominal level) that anger exceeds fear.

The anger scale does not correlate with age or income, but when recoded as a nominal variable (around the median point of the scale, which was 14) showed women as significantly more likely to be angry (with points 14 to 20 defined as 'angry'), with 53% of women, but only 45% of men scoring this highly (p = 0.0067, 1df). Political persuasion was measured by a simple binary choice: 'If the government found that it had a surplus of cash available, what should it do? Should it do nothing? Cut taxes? Increase spending on public services?'[11] The angry were significantly more likely to say 'increase spending on public services' (54% said so, as opposed to only 42% of the angry wanting taxes cut, p = 0.0002, 1df).

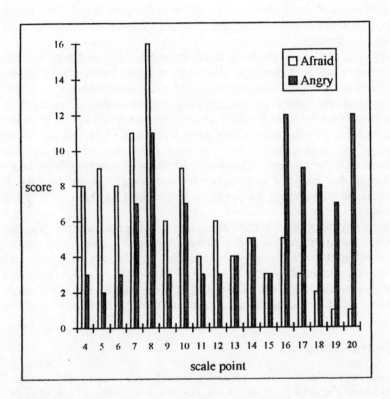

Figure 2. The 'Afraid' and 'Angry' scales compared

The afraid scale does not correlate with age or income either, but when recoded as a nominal variable (around the median point of its scale, which was 8) showed women as significantly more likely to be afraid (with points 8 to 20 defined as afraid), with 54% of women, but only 43% of men scoring this highly (p = 0.0007, 1df). The afraid were no more likely to say 'increase spending on public services' than 'cut taxes'.

CONCLUSION

As indicated earlier, we did not expect these results, and only included 'anger' about the threat of criminal victimisation as a possible general attitude because the term forced itself onto the research agenda in both individual interview and

degree of satisfaction with where they live, their rating of standard social problems, their health, their lifestyle, their leisure and media consumption activity, their sense of community, and so on) were designed to test 'fear' rather than 'angry' intercorrelations, and indeed, for some reason, do not correlate at all with the angry responses.

However, what is undeniable is that being angry about the prospect of criminal victimisation has been shown to be reported at higher levels than being afraid of it. Experiencing anger following actual criminal victimisation may seem naturally or common-sensically explicable (which may be why those researchers who have encountered it have typically chosen not to explain it). Nevertheless, we have no sense of what respondents mean when they claim that the 'thought of someone' victimising them in some or other way makes them 'angry' 'some of the time' or 'all of the time'. This may refer to anger stemming from the general perception that crime is seemingly ever-increasing, that the criminal justice system is too incompetent, the courts too lenient, or it may have entirely different correlates.

Yet, given the political and other importance of general and specific victimisation-reaction, further research concentrating on the nature and meaning of victimisation-anger is strongly recommended. Conducting such research in the manner recommended by Hale (1996; p. 132), and quoted earlier, perhaps much in the manner that the research reported here was carried out, might resolve the issue more swiftly than has been the case with research into the 'fear' of crime.[12]

ACKNOWLEDGEMENTS

The authors would like to acknowledge considerable assistance from Ken Pease in analysing the data presented here. Helpful comments on a first draft were provided by Wendy Hollway, Mike Hough, Tony Jefferson, Pat Mayhew, David Smith and Andromachi Tseloni.

NOTES

1 Specifically, as J. Ditton and J. Bannister, *Fear of Crime: Conceptual Development, Field Testing and Empirical Confirmation*, L210 25 2007.
2 The region was abolished as part of local government reform in April, 1996.
3 'Don't know' was treated as real data, and thus given a mid point on the scale from 'not' to 'a lot'.
4 The housebreaking questions ('burglary' in England and Wales) referred to 'someone breaking into your home'; the car crime questions, to 'someone stealing your car, van, motor cycle or other road vehicle'; the assault questions, to 'someone assaulting you'; and the vandalism questions, to 'someone vandalising your home'.
5 Percentages and absolute data given are for weighted data: significance tests were conducted on unweighted data.
6 Published victimisation data from both the major national crime surveys is actually based on

'screened' for victimisation using a set of common sense (rather than legally accurate) questions.

7 The one exception is in row 5 relating to assault. There is only one case here, and this is inadequate to support any assertion either way.

8 Which are in row 3, and relating to assault; and in row 6 and relating to housebreaking. Neither difference is significant.

9 Here, in row 6, female housebreaking victims are more likely to be afraid than angry; also in row 6, female vandalism victims are equally likely to be afraid as angry; and in row 1, male vandalism victims are equally likely to be afraid as angry.

10 Those with no household vehicle were excluded, with the resulting N being 1092 for both.

11 Only 22 (1%) said 'nothing' and these are excluded from analysis.

12 Such research might also test comparatively the relative strengths of questions on fear of crime when they are operationalised, respectively, as 'afraid', 'worried' or 'anxious'.

REFERENCES

Anderson, S. and Leitch, S. (1996). *Main Findings from the 1993 Scottish Crime Survey*, Central Research Unit; The Scottish Office.

DuBow, F., McCabe, E. and Kaplan, G. (1979). *Reactions to Crime: A Critical Review of the Literature*, NILECJ, US Govt. Printing Office; Washington, DC. (Quoted in Hale, 1996: 91).

Farrall, S., Bannister, J., Ditton, J. and Gilchrist, E. (1997). Measuring Crime and the 'Fear of Crime': Findings from a Methodological Study. *British Journal of Criminology*, 37 (4), 657–78.

Ferraro, K. and LaGrange, R. (1987). The Measurement of the Fear of Crime. *Sociological Inquiry*, 57 (1), 70–101.

Furstenberg, F. (1971). Public Reaction to Crime in the Streets. *The American Scholar*, 40 (Autumn), 601–10.

Gilchrist, E., Farrall, S., Bannister, J. and Ditton, J. (1998). Women and Men Talking about the 'Fear of Crime': Challenging the Accepted Stereotype. *British Journal of Criminology*, 38 (2), 283–98.

Hale, C. (1996). Fear of Crime: A Review of the Literature. *International Review of Victimology*, 4, 79–150.

Hough, M. (1995). *Anxiety about crime: Findings from the 1994 British Crime Survey*, Home Office Research Study 147, Home Office; London.

Kinsey, R. and Anderson, S. (1992). *Crime and the Quality of Life: Public Perceptions and Experiences of Crime in Scotland: Findings from the 1988 British Crime Survey*, Scottish Office Central Research Unit.

Lewis, D. and Salem, G. (1986). *Fear of Crime: Incivility and the Production of a Social Problem*. Transaction Books; New Brunswick.

Maguire, M. (1980). The impact of burglary upon victims. *British Journal of Criminology*, 20 (3), 261–275.

Mawby, R.I. and Walklate, S. (1997). The impact of burglary: a tale of two cities. *International Review of Victimology*, 4, 267–295.

Mayhew, P. (1985). The Effects of Crime: Victims, The Public and Fear. *Research on Victimisation*. Council of Europe, Collected Studies in Criminological Research, Vol. XXIII.

Mirrlees-Black, C., Mayhew, P. and Percy, A. (1996). *The British Crime Survey, England and Wales*. Home Office Statistical Bulletin, 19/96.

Ostrihanska, Z. and Wojcik, D. (1993). Burglaries as seen by the victims. *International Review of Victimology*, 2, 217–225.

Name Index